NEW MEDIA: A CRITICAL INTRODUCTION

'*New Media: a critical introduction* offers an excellent summary of emerging digital communications media. The book is written in a lively, accessible manner, yet it does not lower its standards of critical analysis. It provides an insightful examination of the diverse and growing realm of new media.' *John Pavlik, Center for New Media, Columbia University*

New Media: a critical introduction is a comprehensive introduction to the culture, technologies, history and theories of new media. Written especially for students, the authors consider the ways in which 'new media' really are new, assess the claims that a media and technological revolution is underway and formulate new ways for media studies to respond to new technologies.

Individual chapters introduce:

· Assessing the 'newness' of new media

· How to define the characteristics of new media

· Film, photographic realism and new forms of visual culture and entertainment

· Social and political uses of new media and new communications

· New media technologies, politics and globalisation

· Everyday life and new media

· Cyborgs, cybernetics and cyberculture

· Theories of interactivity

· The history of automata and artificial life

Illustrated with over fifty photographs, images and line drawings, key features of this textbook include:

· A user's guide

· A glossary of key terms and concepts

· Boxed case studies and examples

· Key terms defined in the margins with extensive cross-referencing

· Extensive bibliographies and web resources to help with further study

Martin Lister, Jon Dovey, Seth Giddings, Iain Grant and Kieran Kelly are all members of the School of Cultural Studies at the University of the West of England, Bristol.

NEW MEDIA: A CRITICAL INTRODUCTION

MARTIN LISTER / JON DOVEY / SETH GIDDINGS / IAIN GRANT / KIERAN KELLY

 Routledge
Taylor & Francis Group

LONDON AND NEW YORK

First published 2003
by Routledge
11 New Fetter Lane, London EC4P 4EE

Simultaneously published in the USA and Canada
by Routledge
29 West 35th Street, New York, NY 10001

Routledge is an imprint of the Taylor & Francis Group

Typeset in M Joanna by
M Rules
Printed and bound in Great Britain by St Edmundsbury Press, Bury St Edmunds, Suffolk

British Library Cataloguing in Publication Data
A catalogue record for this book is available from the British Library

Library of Congress Cataloging in Publication Data

New media: a critical introduction/Martin Lister . . . [et al.].
    p. cm.
  Includes bibliographical references and index.
  1. Mass media–Technological innovations. I. Lister, Martin, 1947–

P96.T42 N478 2002
302.23–dc21   2002029452

ISBN 0-415-22377-6 (hbk)
ISBN 0-415-22378-4 (pbk)

CONTENTS

ILLUSTRATIONS

CASE STUDIES

AUTHORS' BIOGRAPHIES

All of the authors are members of the **School of Cultural Studies at Bristol, University of the West of England**.

Martin Lister is Head of Cultural Studies and Professor of Visual Culture at UWE. He has written widely on photography, visual culture, and new media technologies. His publications include *The Photographic Image in Digital Culture* (Routledge, 1995), *Photography in the Age of Electronic Imaging* (Routledge, 1997). He produced the CD-Rom 'From Silver to Silicon: Photography, Culture and New Technologies' (1996).

Jon Dovey is a writer, lecturer and producer teaching in the School of Cultural Studies at UWE. He works in contemporary media theory and practice, and makes documentary and interactive media. Previous publications include *Freakshows: First Person Media And Factual TV* (2000) and *Fractal Dreams: New Media and Social Context* (1995).

Seth Giddings is a Senior Lecturer in Cultural Studies at UWE where he teaches theory and practice of digital media. His background is in media art and visual culture and he has written on popular film and animation. He is currently researching the relationship of new media technologies to popular culture – particularly video games and video game play.

Iain Grant is a Senior Lecturer in Cultural Studies at UWE. He researches the relations between the sciences, philosophy and culture.
He has published and lectured widely on issues of new technologies, postmodernism, the physical sciences, and philosophy. He has translated major works by Baudrillard and Lyotard. He is an editor of *Crash Cultures* (2002) and author of *On an Artificial Earth: The Philosophy of Nature After Schelling* (2003). Although responsible for Part 5, Iain Grant would like to akcnowledge the impetus given to the writing of this part of the book by the culture of enquiry established by all the contributors to this project.

Kieran Kelly is a Senior Lecturer in Cultural Studies at UWE where he teaches the theory and practice of digital media and IT. He started working in public sector computing over 20 years ago. His academic background lies in economic history and the two are combined in his work on the political economy of new media.

INTRODUCTION

THE BOOK'S PURPOSE

The purpose of this book is to offer students conceptual frameworks for thinking through a range of key issues which have arisen out of a period of intense speculation on the cultural implications of new media. It is first and foremost a book about the questions, the ideas and debates – the critical issues – that the emergence of new media technologies has given rise to. In this, we hope that it is a genuine contribution to the study of the new media and technologies. There is no such thing, however, as a wholly impartial, objective work that sets about cataloguing the debates, one after the other, without arguing for one thing rather than another, or judging some aspects of the problems to be important, and others not. The reader should therefore note in advance that it is a necessary component of this book, as of any other, that its authors judge what is important and what is not, and that they argue for some theoretical positions, and against others. We do not aim to summarise blandly the state of the art in new media and **technology**, but to present for the reader some of the contested issues that are rife within this emerging field. You will find in the book arguments for different positions. Where this is so, we are overt about it, and we let you the reader, know. Indeed, this is only to be expected, since the bodies of expertise this book uniquely brings to bear on its topic draw on our various disciplinary backgrounds in visual culture, media and cultural history, media theory, media production, philosophy and the history of the sciences, political economy and sociology. Finally, just as it is important to be aware of what differentiates the various arguments in this book, it is also crucial to note what all of our arguments share. This book's authors have in common a commitment to a synthetic approach to new media studies. We each individually hold that the field is so complex that it cannot be addressed other than by combining, or synthesising, knowledges. While this adds some complexity to the book as a whole, it all the more accurately embodies the contested field that is new media studies.

OUR APPROACH TO THE SUBJECT

Unlike some of the new media that we discuss in the following pages, this medium, the book, has clearly separated authors and readers. An author does not know her or his thousands of readers, yet an author must have some way of describing to themselves who they think their readers are likely to be. If they forget this then their publishers are likely to remind them, as they wish to sell the book; for them a successful identification of a body of readers is a market. In writing this book, how have we thought about our readership? We assume that the majority of our readers are students who have developed a special interest in the study of the new media forms that have appeared over the last fifteen years or so. We envisage them having some introductory knowledge of media studies or a related discipline.

Readers also want to know what to expect of their authors. This book has several, and we have something to say about this below. For the moment, however, we should recognise that the present occasion for a conjunction of authors and readers is the topic of this book: the new media. What, however, are they? We take them to be those methods and social practices of communication, representation, and expression that have developed using the digital, multimedia, **networked** computer and the ways that this machine is held to have transformed work in other media: from books to movies, from telephones to television. When did all this happen? What, in other words, is the period in which 'everything changed'? The process by which computerisation or 'digitisation' impacted upon the media of the twentieth century has moved on many fronts and at different speeds, so it is difficult to pinpoint a single date or decisive period for the emergence of new media. Even the key developments in computing, the core technology of this digitisation, which, over the long term, made this technically and conceptually possible, are many. However, we get some idea of the period that mainly concerns us by considering the emergence of the personal computer. We can point to the mid-1980s as a watershed, when the **PC** began to be equipped with **interactive** graphic **interfaces**; to possess enough memory to run the early versions of image manipulation software; and computer-mediated communications networks began to emerge. This was a moment when the ideas and concepts of earlier visionaries appeared to become real possibilities.

In turn, it is since that time, a period of less than 20 years, that speculation, prediction, theorisation and argument about the nature and potential of these new media began to proceed at a bewildering and breathless pace. A wide range of ideas, many of which challenged settled assumptions about media, culture and technology (and, indeed, nature) were generated and pulled along in the vortex of constant and rapid technological innovation. So too was a comparable quantity of 'hype' that accompanied the emergence of new media in the mid-1980s. This, of course, is still with us, but it has been met by some hard-headed reflection born of experience and enough time to recover some critical poise. New media have become a major focus of research and theory, an emerging field of media and cultural study which now possesses a complex body of thought and writing. Thinking about new media has become a critical and contested field of study.

Media studies, like any other field of study, thrives on problems. At the early stages in the study of any new phenomenon the very question of 'what the problems are' is part of the field of enquiry, the problems themselves are contested. What exactly is the problem? Which questions are worth bothering about? Which ideas are really significant? In this book, by bringing together a range of voices and disciplines, we have aimed to provide an initial map of the territory and its debates.

Such a project has its challenges. When we began to write this book we were conscious, above all, of the rapid pace of media-technological change that has characterised the end of the twentieth and the beginning of the twenty-first centuries. This became all the more apparent with the rise of what we might call 'upgrade culture': with the practice of upgrading, the computer itself becomes a technology in flux, rather than a finally achieved and stable piece of technology. Thus we were faced with the question of how to take a snapshot of a breaking wave. Constant technological and media change makes it absurd to tie a discussion of 'new media' to those particular media which are new at the time of writing. Rather, we set ourselves the task of investigating the more fundamental issues of what constitutes newness in media and what part technological change may play in that. Similarly, rather than taking notice only of those ideas that arise in the immediate context of discussions about 'cyberculture', we draw on a much wider range of historical and contemporary resources that offer to shed light on the present situation. So this book draws upon theories and frameworks – not only from media studies but also from art and cultural history, the study of popular culture, political economy, the sciences, and philosophy. It is our belief that this inclusiveness is the only way to begin to make sense of the cultural changes that new media are held to make. By taking this approach we try to get our heads above the tidal wave of media and technological change, to survey what lies in the distance, and not simply to concentrate on the froth on the crest of the wave. Even surfers chart a wave's history, trying to catch it at the optimal moment of its emergence; only a stupid surfer would ignore it! This is not a book, then, that contents itself with clutching at the latest software upgrade, gizmo, avant-garde experiment, or marketing ploy. Rather, what we hope distinguishes this book is that it focuses not just on these disparate things but also on what forms of understanding are being brought to bear on them, and what meanings are being invested in them.

It is in this way that this book is a critical introduction to new media and technology. However, being 'critical' does not mean adopting the view that 'there's nothing new under the sun'. The newness of new media is, in part, real, in that these media did not exist before now. But taking these changes into account does not mean abolishing all history because it (history) is full of similar moments of newness. By taking a critical and historical view of new media and technology we hope this book will not forsake newness for history, nor history for newness. Rather, it begins with a history of newness itself.

To make this point clear, consider how some so-called critical approaches often effectively deny that there has been any substantial change at all, either in the media or in the cultures of which they form part. Such critical accounts of new media frequently stress the continuity in economic interests, political imperatives, and cultural values that drive and shape the 'new' as much as the 'old' media. They seek to show that the dominant preoccupation with new media's difference, with the way that it outstrips and parts company with our old, passive, **analogue** media, is an ideological trick, a myth. They argue that new media can largely be revealed as the latest twist in capitalism's ruthless ingenuity for ripping us off with seductive **commodities** and the false promise of a better life. These are important voices, but computer and related digital technologies are at least candidates for inclusion in a list of cultural technologies (including the printing press and the book, photography, telephony, cinema and television) which, in however complex and indirect ways, have played a major part in social and cultural change. While it is true that, because of some of their uses and contents, none of these media can be simply celebrated as great and benign human achievements, neither can they be reduced to evil capitalist scams!

On the other hand, consider those critics who insist uncritically that everything has changed. Or those who read digital technologies as already having brought about a **utopia**, the like of which has never previously existed. Or again, there are those who simply refuse all critical comment, and insist that the old theoretical tools are simply redundant in the face of the enormity of the technological sea-change taking place. While it is clear that some change has indeed occurred, if it were true that these changes are as fundamental as all that, then we would find it impossible to put into words what is happening!

Pursuing our earlier metaphor, we could say that the critical critics are so deep underwater that they don't see the wave. Meanwhile, the uncritical utopians are so focused on the crest of the wave itself that they cannot see the ocean of which it is part. Opposing these positions does not really represent a genuine dispute. It is not 'business as usual', but nor has all business collapsed. Rather, in this book, we both stand back from the hype and investigate the nature of change. There is, it seems to us, no real alternative. We draw our readers' attention to two other features of this book.

THE BOOK'S HISTORICAL DIMENSION

It could seem that an introduction to thinking critically about new media, unlike one on, say, photography or film and cinema, would have little history to deal with. As we have already noted, we consider it a serious flaw not to engage with the histories of the technologies and media under discussion. New things do not have no history; rather, they make us search a little harder for their histories. Indeed, new things may bring out overlooked histories in order to answer the question of where they come from. Moreover, in the claims and ideas that currently surround new media, we can find many historical echoes. We need to consider that 'old' media technologies were themselves once new and held enormous significance for their contemporaries for that very reason. Attempts to come to terms with our own new machines and their products should prompt in us an awareness that we have been here before. Even printed books were once new. We can then ask, in what terms was this newness conceived, in what ways does it compare to our own, and what relation did it have to eventual outcomes? In responding to our contemporary 'new' we will learn something from other historical moments and times.

THE BOOK'S EMPHASIS ON WIDER QUESTIONS OF CULTURE AND TECHNOLOGY

In parts of the book we recognise how inextricable new media are from the technologies that have made them possible. This means that we needed to provide some bearings for thinking about the relationship of media and technology. This raises a larger topic and set of debates concerning the relationship between culture and technology; a matter that is precisely brought into focus in a term such as 'cyberculture'. It seems crucial that we have some ways of assessing the extent and intensity of the kind of changes that media technologies can bring about. If, as it seems, our contemporary culture is deeply immersed in changing technological forms, the important question is raised as to how far new media and communication technologies, indeed technologies in general, do actually determine the cultures that they exist within. Conversely we must also ask how cultural factors shape our use and experience of technological power. These are, as many commentators have noted recently and in the past, vexed and unsettled questions that new media put once again, firmly before us.

THE BOOK'S ORGANISATION

Rather than dedicating each chapter to a discrete or separate new media form (for example a chapter on the **Internet** or another on computer games) the five major parts of the book are based upon different kinds of discussion and ways of thinking about new media. In this way, each part foregrounds a different set of critical issues and arguments, alongside more detailed discussion of particular media or technological forms, as the occasion demands. Each part of the book considers new media through the prism of different kinds of questions and theories. The reader will find that many forms of new media are discussed in a number of places in the book, quite possibly in several locations across the five parts. ('Virtual reality', for example, is discussed in Part 1 as part of an analysis of the key or defining characteristics of new media, in Part 2 where changes in visual culture are explored, and in Part 5 where philosophical arguments about the relationship of the '**virtual**' to the 'real' are discussed.) To some extent, the different kinds of conceptual framework that are employed in each part of the book will reflect the kind of media studied. Part 3, for instance, presents studies of new media that use a political economy perspective and broadly sociological discussions of new media's role in the formation of **community** and identity. This part therefore has a good deal more to say about online media and communication networks, where these phenomena are thought to occur, than do other parts of the book.

HOW TO USE THE BOOK

As stated earlier, in considering our readership we have assumed a student reader who has some background in media studies or a related discipline and who now wishes to engage with the particular debates of new media studies. However, the very range of the issues which we introduce and consider in these pages means that much unfamiliar material will be met. To help the reader in this task we have adopted a number of strategies. We have tried to avoid the use of overly technical academic language wherever possible and we provide explanations of the concepts we use, both in the **text** as they arise or in the Glossary (see pp. 383–92). At appropriate points, arguments are illustrated with case studies. Where a particularly difficult set of ideas is met we provide a short summary for the reader, sufficient for them to follow the discussion in hand, and point them to further reading where the ideas can be studied in more depth. Alongside the main text a running series of margin notes are provided. These serve two main functions. They add detail to the main argument without disrupting its flow, and they provide important bibliographical references related to the point being discussed. All references are listed in extensive bibliographies at the end of each chapter.

This is a large book that covers a great deal of ground. It is likely that most readers will consult one part or another at different times rather than read it in a linear fashion from cover to cover. Given this, we briefly restate some points in more than one place in the book in order that the reader can engage with their chosen section without having to chase supporting material that is elsewhere in the book. Also, throughout the book we provide cross references which are designed to alert the reader to where there is more material on the topic in hand or where they can find another viewpoint on it.

THE BOOK'S PARTS

Part 1: New Media and New Technologies

In this part of the book some fundamental questions are asked about new media. Distinctions are made between the kinds of phenomena that are bundled up in the term 'new media' in order to make the field of study more manageable. Some key characteristics which have come to be seen as defining new media are mapped, discussed and exemplified and we ask how the 'newness' of new media is variously understood. In the latter sections, we discuss a number of ways in which new media have been given a history, and how, in that process, they are given significance. An important concept in the cultural study of media technology is introduced, 'the **technological imaginary**', and similarities between the ways that earlier twentieth-century 'new media' were received and current developments are discussed. Finally, in this part, we explore the roots of a contemporary debate about new media which centres upon the power of media to determine the nature of culture and society. We recognise the importance accorded to the work of Marshall McLuhan in much contemporary thinking about new media and revisit the terms in which Raymond Williams, and much academic media studies, contests this way of understanding new media.

Part 2: New Media and Visual Culture

In Part 2 we discuss the part played by media generally, and new media in particular, in visual culture. Throughout the twentieth century, visual culture has been dominated by one technological medium after another: photography, narrative film and cinema, broadcast television and video. Each has been credited with leading us to see the world in different ways. More widely, the very nature of vision has come to be understood as historically variable. Following a discussion of these arguments we ask how new visual media and imaging technologies are being seen as bringing about contemporary changes in visual culture. In order to explore this, we discuss recent thought about virtual reality and digital cinema. As a part of the discussion of virtual reality the cultural implications of the historical intersection of **simulation** technologies, developed within computer science in the 1960s, and the deeply embedded traditions of Western visual representation are considered. Central issues for theories of photography, film and cinema have been their **realism** and the nature of visual representation. Following on from the argument that, in virtual reality, representation is displaced by another practice, simulation, these issues are considered in the context of computer-generated animation, special effects and digital cinema.

Part 3: Networks Users and Economics

This section of the book puts developments in new media into their social context, with particular reference to claims about its impact on our changing sense of community and to the consideration of the political economies of new media. We explore the development of new media in its networked form – the Internet – and its domination by the World Wide Web, a particular use of networked new media. We explore the early uses of the information and communications technologies as shared communal spaces and examine the ways in which theorists have attempted to understand these new communications practices. As the software technology, the hardware and communications systems coalesced around digital media the Internet has become synonymous with the web. The short history of the net has included a major economic boom (and slump) in digital commerce, and it has even been credited as the source of a new economy. We touch upon the role of new media communication technologies in globalised forms of economic organisation as a determining factor upon their evolution. The particular characteristics of the digital media have stimulated changes in the law and in how people interact with each other. At the same time many of the hopes that new media had the potential to overcome many of the problems of minority domination of the means of communication have failed to be realised. The section therefore goes on to explore the ways in which the development of the Internet has been influenced by social, economic and political pressures and how these have tended to replicate existing power relationships. In this way we try to contextualise the problems of access and inequalities in use and availability that now characterise networked new media.

Part 4: New Media in Everyday Life

Claims for the revolutionary impact of new media technologies often assume profound transformations of everyday life, and the structures and relationships on which it is based: the sense of individual self or identity; consumption; the dynamics and politics of generation and gender in the family; connections between the local and global. Part 4 is concerned with the study of popular new media in everyday life. It looks at how the intersection of media technologies and networks with the spaces and relationships of the home has been theorised and explores what happens to the 'newness' of new media when it meets the well-established routines and relationships of households. We argue that a consideration of popular media culture is of critical importance in the understanding of new media. On the one hand, popular new media are inseparable from an established commercial media culture; on the other, theories of new media frequently draw on popular media texts (particularly science fiction) to advance and support their arguments. In order to explore this, we ask whether we can analyse new media as commodities like any other set of consumer goods, or whether we should view them as technologies which demand other conceptual frameworks. We ask for example whether we can think of these devices and networks as being used or consumed. Or, given the significance of the videogame in popular new media, whether a critical understanding of play (rather than use or consumption) might be more helpful. In Part 4 we also ask how new media are popularly understood and how new media might transform everyday life.

Part 5: Cyberculture: Technology, Nature and Culture

Pursuing questions asked in Part 1 of the book, Part 5 argues that the central dilemma facing any study of technology – media or otherwise – is how to understand the part played by a technology's sheer physical form and its influence on how a culture is lived and experienced. Here we consider arguments, some very old, that there may be a tighter relationship between technology and culture than is often admitted. We open the door onto perspectives that have recently made their appearance in a field adjacent to that of new media studies – the study of contemporary cyberculture. Given the self-acting and intelligent nature of new media, a key topic explored in this part of the book is the long history of efforts to build and to understand automata. As in other parts of the book, we are also concerned with historical precedents for current developments. Here we demonstrate that the sudden shift to digital technologies has equally important historical precedents, amongst which we discuss three: mechanics, steam, and **cybernetics**. The deep and structuring influence of each of these technologies on the cultures they existed within is discussed. The scientific, philosophical, and historical contexts in which these technocultural relationships occur are also examined. Finally, we compare ideas about these historical phenomena with current ideas about cyberculture, and seek to identify the most important and powerful of these arguments.

1 NEW MEDIA AND NEW TECHNOLOGIES

WHAT ARE NEW MEDIA?/CHARACTERISTICS OF NEW MEDIA/CHANGE AND
CONTINUITY/WHAT KIND OF HISTORY?/WHO WAS DISSATISFIED WITH OLD
MEDIA?/NEW MEDIA: DETERMINING OR DETERMINED?

1.1 WHAT ARE NEW MEDIA?

The question, 'What is new about "new media"?' is asked at many points in this book.
Here we ask a prior question: 'What are "new media"?' The question is put in the plural
because, even on the most cursory view, a whole range of different practices and processes
are subsumed by this blanket description.

Before looking at these differences, it is worth thinking a little more about the term
'new media' itself and the widespread currency it has gained over the last decade. We want
to note, in particular, the way that 'new media' is used as a collective singular noun as if
it referred to a more or less coherent entity. It is commonly used in this way, not only in
journalism and corporate marketing speak but within academic circles too. It is an
enormously general and hence vague term, yet its utterance suggests certainty, as if 'the
new media' already exist here and now as fully achieved material and social practices. Of
course this is not true. We use the term to mean different things. We also frequently use
it to conjure a future based upon the economic and educational promise of 'new media'
or the promise of new technologies for media forms to come. It is also very seductive in
its historical simplicity; there was the 'old media' and now there is the 'new'. We use it to
mark a break with history.

We might also ask why it has passed into everyday, as well as educational and
journalistic, language. Why it has captured our imaginations, and why it shows little sign
of becoming redundant even as we become more familiar with the media in question, as
they gain brief histories, and the rhetoric which surrounds them wears a little thin? Why
do even scholars and academics, famous for their careful use of language, subscribe to the
view that it is worth while to refer to a range of complex changes with the singular,
unifying term, 'new media'?

1.1.1 'The media' as an institution

First, we should remember that for some fifty years the word 'media', the plural of
'medium', has been used as a singular collective term, as in 'the media' (Williams 1976:
169). So, if we can speak of 'the media' surely we can speak of 'the new media' by simply
giving the solidity and familiarity of established media a prefix. Even here, however, it is
worth noting how, by doing this, we immediately imply a kind of social agency and
coherence to 'new media' that they do not yet possess.

'The media', in the established sense, usually refers to 'communication media' and the
institutions and organisations in which people work (the press, cinema, broadcasting,

publishing, and so on) and the cultural and material products of those institutions (the forms and **genres** of news, road movies, soap operas which take the material forms of newspapers, paperback books, films, tapes, discs) (Thompson 1995: 23–24). When systematically studied (whether by the media institutions themselves as part of their market research or by media academics inquiring critically into their social and cultural significance) we pay attention to more than the point of media production which takes place within these institutions. We also investigate the wider processes through which information and representations (the 'content') of 'the media' is distributed, received and consumed by its various audiences and is regulated and controlled by the state or the market. In this sense 'the media' is understood as a fully social institution, while 'new media', on the other hand, immediately suggests something far less settled, known and identified. At the very least, we face, on the one hand, a rapidly changing set of formal and technological experiments and, on the other, a complex set of interactions between new technological possibilities and established media forms. Despite this difference the singular term is applied unproblematically.

1.1.2 The intensity of change

The second sense in which 'new media' functions as a term is through its attempt to capture a sense that, quite rapidly from the late 1980s on, the world of media and communications began to look quite different and this difference was not restricted to any one sector or element of that world, although the actual timing of change may have been different from medium to medium. This was the case from printing, photography, through television, to telecommunications. Of course, such media have continually been in a state of technological, institutional and cultural change or development; they have never stood still. Yet, even within this state of constant flux, it seemed that the nature of change that was experienced warranted an absolute marking off from what went before. This experience of change is not, of course, confined only to the media in this period. Other, wider kinds of social and cultural change were being identified and described and had been, to varying degrees, from the 1960s onwards. We point to the following as indicative of such wider kinds of change with which new media are associated:

- *A shift from modernity to postmodernity*: a contested, but widely subscribed attempt to characterise deep and structural changes in societies and economies from the 1960s onwards, with correlative cultural changes. In terms of their aesthetics and economies new media are usually seen as a key marker of such change (see e.g. Harvey 1989).

- *Intensifying processes of globalisation*: a dissolving of national states and boundaries in terms of trade, corporate organisation, customs and cultures, identities and beliefs, in which new media have been seen as a contributory element (see e.g. Featherstone 1990).

- *A replacement, in the West, of an industrial age of manufacturing by a 'post-industrial' information age*: a shift in employment, skill, investment and profit, in the production of material goods to service and information 'industries' which many uses of new media are seen to epitomise (see e.g. Castells 2000).

- *A decentring of established and centralised geo-political orders*: the weakening of mechanisms of power and control from Western colonial centres, facilitated by the dispersed, boundary-transgressing, networks of new communication media.

New media are caught up with and seen as part of these other kinds of change (as both cause and effect), and the sense of 'new times' and 'new eras' which follow in their wake. In this sense, the emergence of 'new media' as some kind of epoch-making phenomena, is seen as part of a much larger landscape of social, technological and cultural change; in short, as part of a new **technoculture**.

1.1.3 The ideological connotations of the new

The third sense of the 'new' in new media as a reference to 'the most recent' also carries the ideological sense that new equals better and it carries with it a cluster of glamorous and exciting meanings. The 'new' is also 'the cutting edge', the 'avant-garde', the place for forward-thinking people to be (whether they be producers, consumers, or, indeed, media academics). These connotations of 'the new' are derived from a **modernist** belief in social progress as delivered by technology. Such long-standing beliefs (they existed throughout the twentieth century and have roots in the nineteenth and even before) are clearly being reinscribed in new media as we invest in them. New media appear, as they have before, with claims and hopes attached; they will deliver increased productivity, educational opportunity **(4.2.5)** and open up new creative and communicative horizons **(1.3, 1.5)**. Calling a range of developments 'new', which may or may not be new or even similar, is part of a powerful ideological movement and a narrative about progress in Western societies **(1.5)**. This narrative is subscribed to not only by the entrepreneurs, corporations who produce the media hardware and software in question, but also by whole sections of media commentators and journalists, artists, intellectuals, technologists and administrators, educationalists and cultural activists. This apparently innocent enthusiasm for the 'latest thing' is rarely if ever ideologically neutral. The celebration and incessant promotion of new media and **ICTs** in both state and corporate sectors cannot be dissociated from the globalising **neo-liberal** forms of production and distribution which have been characteristic of the past twenty years.

4.2.5 Edutainment edutainment edutainment
1.3 Change and continuity
1.5 Who was dissatisfied with old media?

1.1.4 Non-technical and inclusive

Finally, 'new media' gains currency as a term because of its useful inclusiveness. It avoids, at the expense of its generality and its ideological overtones, the reductions of some of its alternatives. It avoids the emphasis on purely technical and formal definition, as in **'digital'** or 'electronic' media; the stress on a single, ill-defined and contentious quality as in 'interactive media' (**Case study 1.3**), or the limitation to one set of machines and practices as in **'computer-mediated communication'** (CMC). So, while a person using 'new media' may have one kind of thing in mind (the Internet), others may mean something else (digital TV, new ways of imaging the body, a virtual environment or a game). All use the same term to refer to a range of phenomena. In doing so they each claim the status of 'medium' for the thing they have in mind and they all borrow the glamorous connotations of 'newness'. It is a term with broad cultural resonance rather than a narrow technicist or specialist application.

Cas study 1.3 'What is new about interactivity?'

There is then, some kind of sense as well as a powerful ideological charge in the singular use of the term. It is a term that offers to recognise some big changes, technological, ideological and experiential, which actually underpin a range of different phenomena. It is, however, very general and abstract.

We might, at this point, ask if we could readily identify some kind of fundamental change which underpins all new media – something more tangible or more scientific than the motives and contexts we have so far discussed. This is where the term 'digital media' is, for some, a preferable term as it draws attention to a specific means (and its implications) of the registration, storage, and distribution of information in the form of digital binary code. However, even here, although digital media is accurate as a formal description, it presupposes an absolute break (between **analogue** and digital) where we will see that none in fact exists. Many digital new media are reworked and expanded versions of 'old' analogue media (**1.2.1**).

1.1.5 Distinguishing between kinds of new media

The reasons for the adoption of the abstraction 'new media' such as we have briefly discussed above are important. We will have cause to revisit them in other sections of this part of the book (**1.3, 1.4, 1.5**) as we think further about the historical and ideological dimensions of thinking about 'newness' and 'media'. However, it is also very important to move beyond the abstraction, there is a need to regain and use the term in its plural sense. We do need to ask what the new media are in their variety and plurality. As we do this we can see that beneath the general sense of change we need to talk about a range of different kinds of change; a range that is not rooted in, or comprehensible as, solely technological developments. We also need to see that the changes in question are ones in which the ratios between the old and the new vary (**1.3**).

Below, as a first way of getting clearer about this, we provide a schema that breaks down the global term 'new media' into some more manageable constituent parts. Bearing in mind the question marks that we have already placed over the 'new', we take 'new media' to refer to the following:

- *New textual experiences*: new kinds of **genre, textual** form, entertainment, pleasure and patterns of media consumption (computer games, **hypertexts**, special effects cinema).

- *New ways of representing the world*: media which, in ways that are not always clearly defined, offer new representational possibilities and experiences (as in immersive virtual environments, screen-based interactive multimedia).

- *New relationships between subjects (users and consumers) and media technologies*: changes in the use and reception of image and communication media in everyday life and in the meanings that are invested in media technologies (**3.1–3.10 and 4.3**).

- *New experiences of the relationship between embodiment, identity and community:* shifts in the personal and social experience of time, space, and place (on both local and global scales) which have implications for the ways in which we experience ourselves and our place in the world.

- *New conceptions of the biological body's relationship to technological media:* challenges to received distinctions between the human and the artificial, nature and technology, body and (media as) technological prostheses, the real and the **virtual** (**5.1 and 5.4**).

- *New patterns of organisation and production:* wider realignments and integrations in media culture, industry, economy, access, ownership, control and regulation (**3.15–3.18**).

If we were to set out to investigate any one of the above novelties we would quickly find ourselves encountering a whole array of rapidly developing fields of technologically mediated production as the site for our research. These would include:

- **Computer-mediated communications: email**, chat rooms, **MUDs** and **MOOs**, **avatar**-based communication forums, voice image transmissions, the web, and mobile telephony.

- **New ways of distributing and consuming** media texts characterised by interactivity and hypertext formats – the World Wide Web, CD-ROM, DVD, and the various platforms for computer games.

- **Virtual reality**: from simulated environments to fully immersive representational spaces.

- **A whole range of transformations and dislocations of established media** (in, for example, photography, animation, television, film and cinema).

1.2 THE CHARACTERISTICS OF NEW MEDIA : SOME DEFINING CONCEPTS

In **1.1** we saw that that the apparently unifying term 'new media' actually refers to a wide range of changes in media production, distribution and use. These are more than technological changes, they are also textual, conventional and cultural. Bearing this in mind, we nevertheless have to recognise that since the mid-1980s at least, a number of *concepts* have come to the fore which offer to define the key characteristics of the field of new media as a whole. So, this section continues the definitional work of 1.1 above by considering how the difference of 'new media' has been conceived. The distinction between difference and novelty is important – having argued that new media are inevitably also old media we now move to thinking about what might be *different* about the particular combinations of old and new patterns that they entail. In other words, we will be looking at some of the key terms in discourses about new media. These are: **digitality, interactivity, hypertexuality, dispersal**, and **virtuality**.

By recognising these as key concepts we do not intend simply to endorse them but to explain their purchase for thinking about new media and to raise questions about them.

In recognising the prominence of these terms we are anxious to avoid falling into a trap, which we will call 'technological essentialism'. There is a difference between looking, on the one hand, at why and how usefully certain concepts and ideas have arisen in efforts to define and understand new media, and assuming that such concepts are real features or even satisfactory descriptions of the media in question, on the other.

Technological essentialism would amount to us saying 'Because a technology can do this the medium is indisputably like that . . .' Our approach here is different. We consider these concepts critically as ways of trying to pin down certain experienced characteristics of new media technologies and the directions in which they have been developed. An example from 'old' media will help show what we mean. We might think of a broadcast medium like television (or radio) as a centralised medium. This is not because the technology of television inevitably leads to centralisation – broadcasting out from a centre to a mass audience – but because it was developed and put to use in this direction. That is, television came to be organised in this way within a social structure which needed to communicate from centres of power to the periphery (the viewer/listener). Of course,

1.1   What are new media?

1.6   New media: determining or
determined?

5   CYBERCULTURE: TECHNOLOGY,
NATURE AND CULTURE

alternative uses of broadcast media exist as in 'ham' and CB radio, in local television initiatives in many parts of the world, or even the use of the television receiver as a light-emitting object in the video installations of the artist Nam June Paik. Recognising that a single media technology can be put to a multiplicity of uses, some becoming dominant and others marginal for reasons that have little or nothing to do with the nature of the technology itself, is one important way of understanding what a medium is (**1.6**; and see **5** for challenges to this view).

We might also add that any attempt at prescribing the singular essence and significance of new media (which is the way that some commentators use these concepts) is doomed from the outset by the extraordinary fluidity and promiscuity of form that characterises the field.

1.2.1 Digitality

New media are often referred to as 'digital media', or 'digital new media'. For most of us this is a shorthand for 'media that use computers'. We need first of all to think about why new media are described as digital in the first place – what does 'digital' actually mean in this context? In addressing this question we will have cause to define digital media against already existing forms of media as being analogue. This will bring us to a second question. What does the shift from analogue to digital signify for producers, audiences and theorists of new media?

In a digital media process all input data are converted into numbers. In terms of communication and representational media this 'data' usually takes the form of qualities such as light or sound or represented space which have already been coded into a 'cultural form' (actually 'analogues'), such as written text, graphs and diagrams, photographs, recorded moving images, etc. These are then processed and stored as numbers and can be output in that form from **online** sources, digital disks, or memory drives to be decoded and received as screen displays, or they can be output as 'hard copy'. This is in marked contrast to analogue media where all input data is converted into another physical object. 'Analogue' refers to the way that the input data (reflected light from a textured surface, the live sound of someone singing, the inscribed marks of someone's handwriting) and the coded media product (the grooves on a vinyl disc or the distribution of magnetic particles on a tape) stand in an analogous relation to one another.

Analogues
'Analogue' refers to processes in which one set of physical properties can be stored in another 'analogous' physical form. The latter is then subject to technological and cultural coding that allows the original properties to be, as it were, reconstituted for the audience. They use their skills at watching movies to 'see' the 'reality' through the analogies. *Analogos* was the Greek term which described an equality of ratio or proportion in mathematics, a transferable similarity that by linguistic extension comes to mean a comparable arrangement of parts, a similar ratio or pattern, available to a reader through a series of transcriptions. Each of these transcriptions involves the creation of a new object that is determined by the laws of physics and chemistry.

CASE STUDY 1.1:   Analogue and digital type

For example, consider how this book would have been produced by the traditional ('hot type') analogue print process which used discrete, movable pieces of metal type. Handwritten notes would have been transcribed by a typesetter who would have set the pages up using lead type to design the page. This type would then have been used with ink to make a physical imprint of the words onto a second artefact – the book proofs. After correction these would have been transcribed once more by the printer to make a second layout, which would again have been made into a photographic plate that the presses would have used to print the page. Between the notebook and the printed page there would have been several analogous stages before you could read the original notes. If, on the other hand, we write direct into word processing software every letter is immediately represented by a numerical value as an electronic response to touching a key on the keyboard rather than being a direct mechanical impression in paper caused by the weight and shape of a typewriter 'hammer' (see Hayles 1999: 26, 31). Layout, design and correction can all be carried out within a digital domain without recourse to the painstaking physical work of type manipulation.

Analogue media, mass production and broadcasting

The major media of the nineteenth and early twentieth centuries (prints, photographs, films and newspapers) were the products not only of analogue processes but also of technologies of mass production. For this reason, these traditional mass media took the form of industrially mass-produced physical artefacts which circulated the world as copies and commodities.

    With the development of broadcast media, the distribution and circulation of such media as physical objects began to diminish. In broadcast media the physical analogue properties of image and sound media are converted into further analogues. These are wave forms of differing lengths and intensities which are encoded as the variable voltage of transmission signals. In live broadcast media such as pre-video television or radio there was a direct conversion of events and scenes into such electronic analogues.

    This electronic conversion and transmission (broadcast) of media like film, which are physical analogues, suggests that digital media technologies do not represent a complete break with traditional analogue media. Rather, they can be seen as a continuation and extension of a principle or technique already in place; that is to say, the principle of conversion from physical artefact to signal. However, the scale and nature of this extension are so significant that we might well experience it not as a continuation but as a complete break. We now look at why this is so.

Digital

In a digital media process the physical properties of the input data, light and sound waves, are converted not into another object but into numbers; that is, into abstract symbols rather than analogous objects and physical surfaces. Hence, media processes are brought into the symbolic realm of mathematics rather than physics or chemistry. Once coded numerically, the input data in a digital media production can immediately be subject to the mathematical processes of addition, subtraction, multiplication and division through **algorithms** contained within software.

    It is often mistakenly assumed that 'digital' means the conversion of physical data into binary information. In fact, digital merely signifies the assignation of numerical values to

For a detailed discussion of the differences between analogue and digital processes see T. Binkley, 'Reconfiguring culture' in P. Hayward and T. Wollen, 'Future Visions: *new technologies of the screen*, London: BFI, 1993

See Walter Benjamin, 'The work of art in the age of mechanical reproduction' in H. Arendt (ed.) *Illuminations*, London: Fontana, 1973

See Brian Winston, *Media, Technology and Society: a history: from the Telegraph to the Internet*, London and New York: Routledge, 1998, pp. 243–275, for a history of broadcast networks

phenomena. The numerical values could be in the decimal (0–9) system; however, each component in the system would than have to recognise ten values or states (0–9). If, however, these numerical values are converted to binary numbers (0 and 1) then each component only has to recognise two states, on or off, current or no current, zero or one. Hence all input values are converted to binary numbers because it makes the design and use of the pulse recognition components that are the computer so much easier and cheaper.

This principle of converting all data into enormous strings of on/off pulses itself has a history. It is traced by some commentators from the late seventeenth-century philosopher Leibniz, through the nineteenth-century mathematician and inventor, Charles Babbage, to be formulated seminally by Alan Turing in the late 1930s (Mayer 1999: 4–21). The principle of binary digitality was long foreseen and sought out for a variety of different reasons. However, without the rapid developments in electronic engineering begun during the Second World War it would have remained a mathematical principle – an idea. Once the twin engineering goals of miniaturisation and data compression had combined with the principle of encoding data in a digital form massive amounts of data could be stored and manipulated.

In the last decades of the twentieth century the digital encoding of data moved out from the laboratories of scientific, military, and corporate establishments (during the mainframe years) to be applied to communications and entertainment media. As specialist software, accessible machines and memory-intensive hardware became available, first text and then sound, graphics and images became encodable. The process swiftly spread throughout the analogue domain, allowing the conversion of analogue media texts to digital bit streams.

See W.J. Mitchell, *The Reconfigured Eye*, Cambridge, Mass.: MIT Press, 1992, pp. 1–7, 18–19, and footnote on p. 231

The principle and practice of digitisation is important since it allows us to understand how the multiple operations involved in the production of media texts are released from existing only in the material realm of physics, chemistry and engineering and shift into a symbolic computational realm. The fundamental consequences of this shift are that:

- media texts are 'dematerialised' in the sense that they are separated from their physical form as photographic print, book, roll of film, etc.;

- data can be compressed into very small spaces;

- it can be accessed at very high speeds and in non-linear ways;

- it can be manipulated far more easily than analogue forms.

The scale of this quantitative shift in data storage, access and manipulation is such that it is experienced as a qualitative change in the production, form, reception and use of media.

Fixity and flux

Analogue media tend towards being fixed, where digital media tend towards a permanent state of flux. Analogue media exist as fixed physical objects in the world, their production being dependent upon transcriptions from one physical state to another. Digital media may exist as analogue hard copy, but when the content of an image or text is in digital form it is available as a mutable string of binary numbers stored in a computer's memory.

The essential creative process of editing is primarily associated with film and video production, but in some form it is a part of most media processes. Photographers edit contact strips, music producers edit 'tapes'; and of course written texts of all kinds are edited. We can use the process of editing to think further about the implications of 'digitality' for media.

To change or edit a piece of analogue media involves having to deal with the entire physical object. For instance, imagine we wanted to change the levels of red on a piece of film as an analogue process. This would involve having to 'strike' new prints from the negative in which the chemical relationship between the film stock and the developing fluid was changed. This would entail remaking the entire print. If the original and inadequate print is stored digitally every pixel in every frame has its own data address. This enables us to isolate only the precise shots and even the parts of the frame that need to be changed, and issue instructions to these addresses to intensify or tone down the level of red. The film as a digital document exists near to a state of permanent flux until the final distribution print is struck and it returns to the analogue world of cinematic exhibition. (This too is changing as films get played out from **servers** rather than projectors in both on-demand digital TV and movie theatres.)

Any part of a text can be given its own data address that renders it susceptible to interactive input and change via software. This state of permanent flux is further maintained if the text in question never has to exist as hard copy, if it is located only in computer memories and accessible via the Internet or the web. Texts of this kind exist in a permanent state of flux in that, freed from authorial and physical limitation, any net user can interact with them, turning them into new texts, altering their circulation and distribution, editing them and sending them, and so on. This fundamental condition of digitality is well summarised by Pierre Lévy:

> The established differences between author and reader, performer and spectator, creator and interpreter become blurred and give way to a reading writing continuum that extends from the designers of the technology and networks to the final recipient, each one contributing to the activity of the other – the disappearance of the signature.
>
> (Lévy 1997: 366)

Digital processes and the material world

So digitisation creates the conditions for inputting very high quantities of data, very fast access to that data and very high rates of change of that data. However, we would not want to argue that this represents a complete transcendence of the physical world, as much digital rhetoric does. The limits of physical science to miniaturise the silicon chip may have already been reached. Engineers cannot physically produce technology capable of miniaturising any further without working at the level of atomic measurement. The **bandwidth** for transmission of the digital media that futurologists foresee simply doesn't exist, it has to be physically dug into the earth. On a more day-to-day level the constant negotiations that any computer-based media producer has to make between memory and compression are also testament to the continuing interface with the physical world that has always been at the centre of media processing. For consumers worldwide, differences of wealth and poverty which underpin their highly differential access to other goods, services and technologies apply equally to digital media. The digital principle does not escape the demands of physics or the economic principles of scarcity.

CASE STUDY 1.2:   Email: the problem of the digital letter

The everyday example of **email** offers a useful case study in thinking about the significance of digitality.

The conventional letter has specific characteristics and histories – it requires physical production, it has to be written or typed, put into an envelope, licked, posted in a special box. It is then subject to the vast enterprise of the post office system in which each house is a physicalised data address.

In addition to these material properties the letter has an important history as a literary and cultural form. Until industrialisation interpersonal communication over distance by writing depended upon the physical transportation of the text by messenger, hand to hand. Public or private news took days or weeks to move from one part of a country, or empire, to another. This pace had an effect upon the status of the message: the arrival of a letter in pre-industrial society was an 'occasion', replete with significance. The commercial and military imperatives of industrialisation and imperialism demanded greater speed and accuracy in person-to-person communications, leading to developments in telegraphy, telephony and the modern postal service.

By contrast, we might characterise email in relation to the principles of digitality (i.e. speed, quantity, and flexibility).

The email process, though not instantaneous, is extremely fast compared to the physical transportation of a letter. So fast in fact that it might stand as one of the best examples of the kind of 'space–time compression' often referred to as typical of a **postmodern** communications environment. Distant locations are brought into the same communicative proximity as the office next door.

Additionally the email, because it exists only in digital not analogue form, is subject to multiple transformations and uses. Unlike the handwritten letter it can be multiply re-edited during composition, and the recipient can re-edit the original, interpolating comment and response. The email can be sent to individuals or groups, so the mail might be written in any number of registers on a private–public scale. Writing a mail to your co-workers will demand a different mode of address from writing a mail to your extended friends and family network. A one-to-one email will have a different tone from a group email – in composing we are constantly negotiating different positions on a private–public scale.

This flexibility is enhanced by the possibility of making attachments to the email. These might be anything from another text document to photos, moving image files or music. More or less whatever can be digitised can be attached. Here we see email exemplifying **convergence** of previously discrete media forms.

These qualities have led to a massive increase in the quantity of communications information processed via the PC. There is a net increase in communicative actions, a perceived increase in productivity for organisations, and arguably an increase in social and familial communicative traffic (amongst the privileged minority with domestic online access). At the level of administration and management this use of email represents an intensification of the paper-based form of the memo. However, this increase in traffic creates new problems of data storage and management; the sheer volume of email received by organisational workers creates 'information overload'.

These changes have a number of qualitative implications. For instance, whereas the postal letter has evolved a whole series of formal codes and conventions in modes of address (inscribed as core topics within British schools' National Curriculum) the new forms of digital text communication have evolved a whole set of far less formal conventions:

> Thoughts tend toward the experiential idea, the quip, the global perspective, the interdisciplinary thesis, the uninhibited, often emotional response. I Way [Internet] thought is modular, non-linear, malleable and co-operative. Many participants prefer internet writing to book writing as it is conversational, frank and communicative rather than precise and over written.
>
> (Kevin Kelly, editor, *Wired Magazine* in 'Guardian Online', 20 June 1994)

However, the responses prompted by the instantaneous availability of the reply button are not always so positive – hence the Internet-based practice of '**flaming**' – argumentative, hostile and insulting exchanges which can accelerate rapidly in a spiral of mutual recrimination. It is precisely the absence of the face-to-face exchange that leads to communication that can become dangerous. The carefully crafted diplomatically composed memo gives way to the collectively composed, often acrimonious, email debate.

With this kind of history in mind we can see how a consideration of even the banal case of email might give rise to a number of central critical questions:

1   Where does control over **authorship** lie when the email text can be multiply amended and forwarded?

2   What kind of authority should we accord the electronic letter? Why do we still insist on hard copy for contractual or legal purposes?

3   What are the possible consequences of an interpersonal communication system based increasingly not on face-to-face embodied interaction but on anonymous, instant, disembodied interaction?

In attempting to answer such questions we might have recourse to different kinds of analytic contexts. First of all an understanding of the cultural history and form of the letter itself. Secondly, an understanding of the **convergence** of discrete media forms through the process of digitisation. Thirdly, an attempt to assess those shifts through already existing analyses of culture – in this case theories of authorship and reading. Finally, the questions above would have to be answered with reference to the study of CMC in which the problem of the disappearance of face-to-face communication has been central.

1.2.2 Interactivity

As we have noted, digital media offer us a significant increase in our opportunity to manipulate and intervene in media. These multiple opportunities are often referred to as the **interactive** potential of new media.

Interactivity has become a broad term which carries a cluster of associated meanings. Most commentators agree that it is a concept that has to be further defined if it is to have any analytical purchase (see e.g. Jensen 1999, Shultz 2000, Huhtamo 2000, Aarseth 1997).

Case study 1.3   What is new about
interactivity?

For a more complete account of the social and cultural history of the term see **Case study 1.3**. For now it is sufficient for us to observe that this associative cluster of meanings operates at two levels, one ideological the other **instrumental**.

Some ideological dimensions of interactivity

> To declare a system interactive is to endorse it with a magic power.
>
> (Aarseth 1997: 48)

At the ideological level, interactivity is understood as one of the key 'value added' characteristics of new media. Where 'old' media offer passive consumption new media offer interactivity. The term stands for a more powerful sense of user engagement with media texts, a more independent relation to sources of knowledge, individualised media use, and greater user choice. These ideas about the value of 'interactivity' draw upon the popular discourse of neo-liberalism (**3.15**) which treats the user as, above all, a consumer. Neo-liberal societies aim to commodify all kinds of experience and offer more and more finely tuned degrees of choice to the consumer. People are seen as being able to make individualised lifestyle choices from a never-ending array of possibilities offered by the market. This ideological context then feeds into the way we think about the idea of interactivity in digital media. It is seen as a method for maximising consumer choice in relation to media texts.

3.15   Media studies and political
economy

BOX 1.1:   A whole new world

'Welcome to a whole new interactive world on digital satellite' offers the Sky Digital promotional literature for its 'Open' TV service. Sky is the UK digital TV service of News Corporation. When existing subscribers purchase the 'Open Keypad' (a standard QWERTY keyboard designed to interface with the set-top box) they gain access to a number of additional 'interactive' services. First, the ability to send and receive email through the digital TV network, using the TV screen as the display medium instead of the PC. Second, the chance to shop online through the 'Open' network: 'These stores are now open 24 hours a day 7 days a week.' The third service on offer is home banking; a fourth is an entertainment channel that offers a limited choice of games, plus listings and review information.

   This 'whole new interactive world' is a kind of 'stripped down' version of Internet access for domestic consumers troubled by the thought of PC-based access. This 'world' of email communications, shopping, banking, gaming and entertainment, is certainly a departure in the use of TV sets. It adds up, however, to an extremely restricted world. Here the idea of the value implicit in interactivity is being used to sell a service, indeed 'a world', which in fact offers extremely limited possibilities.

Instrumental (or functional) views of interactivity

We will be more concerned in this section with the second and instrumental level of meanings carried by the term 'interactive'. In this context, being interactive signifies the users' (the individual members of the new media 'audience') ability to directly intervene in and change the images and texts that they access. So the audience for new media becomes a 'user' rather than the 'viewer' of visual culture, film and TV or a 'reader' of literature. In interactive multimedia texts there is a sense in which it is necessary for the user actively to intervene as well as viewing or reading in order to produce meaning. This intervention actually subsumes other modes of engagement such as 'playing', 'experimenting', and 'exploring' under the idea of interaction. Hinting at the connection between instrumental definitions and ideological meanings, Allucquere Rosanne Stone suggests that the wide field of possibility suggested by the idea of interactivity has been 'electronically instantiated . . . in a form most suitable for commercial development – the user moves the cursor to the appropriate place and clicks the mouse, which causes something to happen' (Stone 1995: 8). We can break down this pragmatic account of interactivity further.

Hypertextual navigation

Here the user must use the computer apparatus and software to make reading choices in a database. (We are using the term 'database' in a general rather than specifically technical sense – a database is any collection of memory stored information, text, image, sound, etc.) In principle, this database could be anything from the entire World Wide Web to a particular learning package, an adventure game, or the hard drive on your own PC. The end results of such interactions will be that the user constructs for him or herself an individualised text made up from all the segments of text which they call up through their navigation process. The larger the database the greater the chance that each user will experience a unique text. **(1.2.3)**.

Immersive navigation

Peter Lunenfeld (1993) usefully distinguishes between two **paradigms** of interaction, which he calls the 'extractive' and the 'immersive'. Hypertextual navigation (above) is 'extractive'. However, when we move from seeking to gain access to data and information to navigating representations of space or simulated 3D worlds we move into 'immersive' interaction. In some sense both kinds of interaction rely upon the same technological fact – the existence of a very large database which the user is called upon to experience. At one level, a more or less realistically rendered 3D space like the game worlds of 'Tomb Raider' or 'Doom' is just as much a big database as Microsoft's 'Encarta' encyclopaedia. We might say that the navigation of immersive media environments is similar to hypertextual navigation, but with additional qualities **(1.2.5, 2.6)**. When interacting in immersive environments the user's goals and the representational qualities of the media text are different. Immersive interaction occurs on a spectrum from 3D worlds represented on single screens through to 3D spaces represented through the head-mounted displays of virtual reality technologies. Although the point-and-click interactivity of hypertextual navigation may well be encountered in such texts, immersive interaction will also include the potential to explore and navigate in visually represented screen spaces. Here the purpose of interaction is likely to be different from the extractive **paradigm**. Instead of a text-based experience aimed at finding and connecting bits of information, the goals of the immersed user will include the visual and sensory pleasures of spatial exploration.

Registrational interactivity

Registrational interactivity refers to the opportunities that new media texts afford their users to 'write back into' the text; that is to say, to add to the text by registering their own messages. The base line of this kind of interactivity is the simple activity of registration (i.e.

For full discussions of the problems of defining interactivity see Jens F. Jensen's 'Interactivity – tracking a new concept in media and communication studies', in Paul Mayer (ed.) *Computer Media and Communication*, Oxford: Oxford University Press, 1999, which offers a comprehensive review of theoretical approaches, and E. Downes and S. McMillan, 'Defining Interactivity', *New Media and Society* 2.2 (2000): 157–179 for a qualitative ethnographic account of the difficulties of applying theoretical definitions in practice

1.2.3 Hypertext

1.2.5 Virtuality
2.6 Immersive virtual reality

sending off details of contact information to a website, answering questions prompted in online transactions, or typing in a credit card number). However, it extends to any opportunity that the user has to input to a text. The original Internet **bulletin boards** and **newsgroups** were a good example – not interactive in the sense of face-to-face communication, yet clearly built up by successive inputs of users' comments. This 'input' or 'writing back' then becomes part of the text and may be made available to other users of the database. This mode of interactivity would therefore include the world-building activities of MUDs and MOOs in which participants created environments by writing. It would also include any media text which solicits users' views, feedback, or stories in any kind of recordable form.

Interactive communications

Case study 1.2   Email: the problem of the digital letter

As we have seen in the study of email (**Case study 1.2**), computer-mediated communications (CMC) appear to offer unprecedented opportunities for making connections between individuals, within organisations, and between individuals and organisations. Much of this connectivity will be of the registrational interactivity mode defined above where individuals add to, change, or synthesise the texts received from others. However, when email and chat sites are considered from the point of view of human communication, ideas about the degree of reciprocity between participants in an exchange are brought into play. So, from a Communication Studies point of view, degrees of interactivity are further broken-down on the basis of the kinds of communication that occur within CMC. Communicative behaviours are classified according to their similarity to, or difference from, face-to-face dialogue, which is frequently taken as the exemplary communicative situation which all forms of 'mediated' communication have to emulate. On this basis, the question and response pattern of a bulletin board, for instance, would be seen as less interactive than the free-flowing conversation of a chat site. This inflects the whole idea of interactivity by lending it a context of person-to-person connection.

Interactivity and new critical questions

There are a number of new critical questions that arise out of the gradual adoption of interactive forms of text.

PROBLEMS OF INTERPRETATION

With interactivity, traditional problems about how texts are interpreted by their readers (users) are multiplied. By the problem of interpretation we refer to the idea that the meaning of any given text is not securely encoded for all audiences to decode in the same way. This is based upon the recognition that the meanings of a text will vary according to the nature of its audiences and circumstances of reception. We all already have highly active interpretative relationships with the analogue texts we encounter. It is suggested that under conditions of interactivity this problem does not disappear but is exponentially multiplied.

The producer of an interactive text or navigable database never knows for certain which of the many versions of the text their reader will encounter. For critics this raises the essential question of how to evaluate or even conceptualise a 'text' that never reads the same way twice. For producers it raises essential problems of control and authorship. How do they make a text for a reader knowing that they have very many possible pathways through it?

PROBLEMS OF DEFINITION. WHAT IS THE INTERACTIVE TEXT?

Established methodologies for thinking about the way in which meaning is produced between readers and texts assume a stability of the text but a fluidity of interpretation. Under conditions of interactivity this traditional stability of the text also becomes fluid. Hence as critics we find ourselves having to reconceptualise the status of our own interpretations of the interactive text. What if the experience we had was different from that of the next user? What is the validity of any claim or observation that we might make about the text in these circumstances? We also find ourselves having to question the status of the text itself. How will it be able to achieve any kind of canonic status or a concensus as to its quality when readers will no longer share a common experience? Is my *War and Peace* the same as yours?

PROBLEMS FOR PRODUCERS

Producers find themselves having to negotiate similar problems about how much control to give the user and how much control to retain. How do you design an **interface** that offers navigational choice but at the same time delivers a coherent experience? These problems will of course vary from one text to another. For instance, a website with many embedded links to other sites will offer users many opportunities to take different pathways. The reader/user is quite likely to click onto another site whilst only halfway through your own. On the other hand, within an interactive learning package that runs off a discrete memory drive (i.e CD-Rom/DVD where there is a finite database) the user can be far more easily 'guided' in their navigation of pathways that the producers are able to pre-structure.

1.2.3 Hypertext

Histories

As we have seen, part of understanding the force of ideas and claims about computer media's 'interactivity' involves considering its ideological connotations. The same observation needs to be made about hypertext. The 'hype' in hypertext is also a key term used to point to the novelty of new media and their assumed difference from 'old' analogue media. Again, like interactivity, it is a term that has become widely used but rarely defined.

The prefix 'hyper' is derived from the Greek 'above, beyond, or outside'. Hence, hypertext has come to describe a text which provides a network of links to other texts that are 'outside, above and beyond' itself. Hypertext, both as a practice and an object of study, has a dual history.

One history ties the term into academic literary and representational theory. Here there has long been an interest in the way any particular literary work (or image) draws upon or refers out to the content of others, the process referred to as intertextuality. This places any text as comprehensible only within a web of association that is at once 'above, beyond or outside' the text itself. At another level, the conventional means of footnoting, indexing, and providing glossaries and bibliographies – in other words the navigational apparatus of the book – can be seen as antecedents of hypertexts, again guiding the reader beyond the immediate text to necessary contextualising information.

The other history is derived from the language of the computer development industry. Here, any verbal, visual or audio data that has, within itself, links to other data might be referred to as a hypertext. In this sense the strict term 'hypertext' frequently becomes confused with the idea and rhetoric of hypermedia (with its connotations of a kind of super medium which is 'above, beyond, or outside' all other media connecting them all together in a web of convergence).

Defining hypertexts

We may define a hypertext as a work which is made up from discrete units of material in which each one carries a number of pathways to other units. The work is a web of connection which the user explores using the navigational aids of the interface design. Each discrete 'node' in the web has a number of entrances and exits or links.

1.2.1 Digitality

As we have seen (**1.2.1**), in a digitally encoded text any part can be accessed as easily as any other so that we can say that every part of the text can be equidistant from the reader. In an analogue system like traditional video, arriving at a particular frame 10 minutes into a tape involves having to spool past every intervening frame. When this information is stored digitally this access can be more or less instantaneous (depending

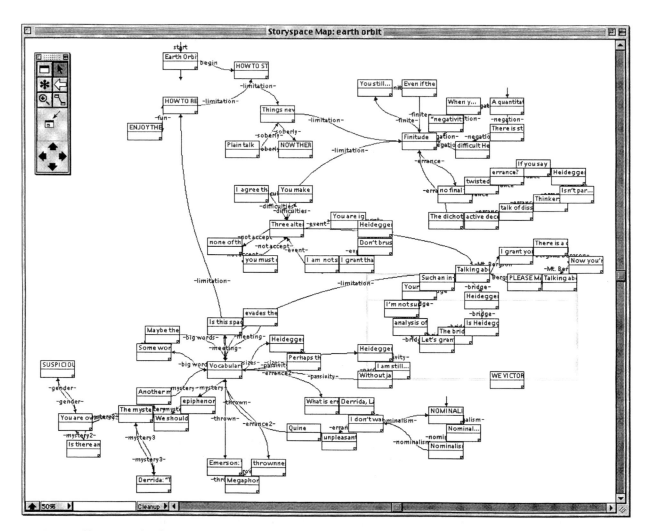

1.1 Diagram of hypertextual architectures – Storyspace Map: earth orbit, www.eastgate.com.

on the speed of the computer). Such technology offers the idea that any data location might have a number of instantly accessible links to other locations built into it. Equally the many interventions and manipulations which this facility enables create the qualities of interactivity (1.2.2).

1.2.2   Interactivity

Hypertext and a model of the mind

Vannevar Bush's 1945 essay 'As We May Think' is often seen as a seminal contribution to the idea of hypertext – Bush was motivated by the problem of information overload; the problem of the sheer volume of knowledge that specialists, even in the late 1940s, have to access and manipulate. Bush proposed that science and technology might be applied to the management of knowledge in such a way as to produce novel methods for its storage and retrieval. He conceptualised a machine, 'the Memex', in which data could be stored and retrieved by *association* rather than by the alphabetical and numerical systems of library indices. Bush argued that,

> The human mind operates by association. With one item in its grasp, it snaps instantly to the next that is suggested by the association of thoughts, in association with some intricate web of trails carried by the cells of the brain.
>
> (Bush in Mayer 1999: 33)

The data in the Memex would be individually coded according to the associative links that a user found meaningful to his or her own work,

> It [the Memex] affords an immediate step . . . to associative indexing, the basic idea of which is a provision whereby any item may be caused at will to select immediately and automatically another . . . The process of tying two items together is the important thing.
>
> (Bush in Mayer 1999: 34)

Bush's argument from 1945 carries within it many of the important ideas that have subsequently informed the technology and practice of hypertext. In particular his position rests upon the assertion that associative linkage of data is a more 'natural' model of information management than the conventional linear alphabetical methods of bibliography such as the Dewey library system. Associative linkage, argues Bush, replicates more accurately the way the mind works. The continuing appeal of hypertext as both information storage and creative methodology has been that it appears to offer a better model of consciousness than linear storage systems. We can observe this appeal continuing in speculation about the development of a global 'neural net' that follows on from Nelson's arguments below.

Hypertext as non-sequential writing

The microfiche technologies of the post-war period were unable to create Bush's vision. However, 20 years later, as digital computing began to be more widespread, his ideas were revived, most notably by Ted Nelson. His 1982 paper ' A New Home for the Mind' argues for the wholesale reorganisation of knowledge along hypertextual lines:

> This simple facility – call it the jump-link capability – leads immediately to all sorts of new text forms: for scholarship, for teaching, for fiction, for poetry . . . The link facility gives us much more than the attachment of mere odds and ends. It permits

fully non sequential writing. Writings have been sequential because pages have been sequential. What is the alternative? Why hypertext – non sequential writing.

(Nelson 1982, in Mayer 1999: 121)

However, Nelson does not stop at the idea of non-sequential writing, he also foresees, ten years before browser software made Internet navigation a non-specialist activity, a medium very close to contemporary website forms of the Internet. In this medium 'documents window and link freely to one another', 'every quotation maybe traced instantly', and 'minority interpretations and commentary may be found everywhere'. He envisages:

a hyperworld – a new realm of published text and graphics, all available instantly; a grand library that anybody can store anything in – and get a royalty for – with links, alternate visions, and backtrack available as options to anyone who wishes to publish them.

(Nelson 1982, in Mayer 1999: 124)

So, the postwar challenge of managing information overload, a model of the mind as a web of trails and associations, and a concept of non-linear writing then extended to a freely accessible 'grand library' of all kinds of media, finally lead us to the concept of hypermedia. Nelson's vision of the potential of hypertext opens out to encompass an emancipatory configuration of human knowledge based in accessibility and manipulation through associative links.

Hypermediacy

More recently the very specific application of hypertext as an information management principle has expanded to suggest all kinds of non-linear, networked paradigms. Here the term begins to overlap with the idea of hypermediacy. The ideological investment in the idea of hypertext spills over into use of the term 'hypermedia' to describe the effects of hypertextual methods of organisation on all mediated forms. More recently, Bolter and Grusin have used the concept of hypermediacy as a crucial term in their theory of new media:

the logic of hypermediacy acknowledges multiple acts of representation and makes them visible. Where immediacy suggests a unified visual space, contemporary hypermediacy offers a heterogeneous space, in which representation is conceived of not as a window on the world, but rather as 'windowed' itself – with windows that open on to other representations or other media. The logic of hypermediacy multiplies the signs of mediation and in this way tries to reproduce the rich sensorium of human experience.

(Bolter & Grusin 1999: 33–34)

Reproducing the 'rich sensorium of human experience' is the kind of claim that recalls Marshall McLuhan's assertion that media are to be understood as extensions of the human body **(1.6.2)**. It is a claim that as we have seen was present in the original formulations of ideas of hypertextuality – the assumptions about cognition in Vannevar Bush and Ted Nelson here become a principle in which hypermedia are valorised as somehow representing the ultimate augmentation of human consciousness.

1.6.2 Mapping Marshall McLuhan

Critical questions in hypertext

Much of the debate arising from the application of hypertext overlaps, or is contiguous with, discussions about the consequences of interactivity. However, the hypertext debate has been conducted with reference to literary theory where questions of interactivity tend to reference human computer interface studies and communication studies.

Clearly, considerations of interactivity and hypertext share a concern with the status and nature of the text itself. What happens when conventional ways of thinking about the text derived from literature or media studies are applied to texts that, allegedly, work in entirely new ways? If the existing structures of knowledge are built upon the book what happens when the book is replaced by the computer memory and hypertextual linking?

Since the Middle Ages human knowledge and culture has been written, recorded and in some sense produced by the form of the book (see, for example, Ong 2002; Chartier 1994). The printed word has established an entire taxonomy and classification system for the management and production of knowledge (e.g. contents, indices, reference systems, library systems, citation methods, etc.). It is argued that this literary apparatus of knowledge is defined around sequential reading and writing. When we write we order our material into a linear sequence in which one item leads into another within recognised rhetorical terms of, for example, argument, narrative or observation. Similarly the reader follows, by and large, the sequencing established by the author. Now, it is argued, hypertext offers the possibility of non-sequential reading and writing. There is no single order in which a text must be encountered.

Each 'node' of text carries within it variable numbers of links that take the reader to different successive nodes, and so on. Thus the reader is offered a 'non-linear' or, perhaps more accurately, a 'multilinear' experience. (Following a link is a linear process; however the variable number of links on offer in any given text produce high numbers of possible pathways.) Knowledge constructed as multilinear rather than monolinear, it is argued, threatens to overturn the organisation and management of knowledge as we have known it to date, since all existing knowledge systems are founded upon the principle of monolinearity.

Thus the very status of the text itself is challenged. The book which you hold in your hand is dissolved into a network of association – within the book itself numerous cross-linkages are made available which facilitate many different reading pathways; and the book itself becomes permeable to other texts. Its references and citations can be made instantly available, and other related arguments or converse viewpoints made available for instant comparison. In short, the integrity of the book and of book-based knowledge systems is superseded by network knowledge systems.

Hypertext scholarship

We can identify two trajectories in the first wave of hypertext scholarship that began to try and understand the significance of these developments.

The first was the return to previously marginal works in the history of literature which had themselves sought to challenge the linearity of text – these often experimental works are then constructed as 'protohypertexts'. So, for instance, works as diverse as the I Ching, Sterne's *Tristram Shandy*, Joyce's *Ulysses*, stories by Borges, Calvino, and Robert Coover and literary experiments with the material form of the book by Raymond Queneau and Marc Saporta are all cited as evidence that hypertextual modes of apprehension and composition have always existed as a limit point and challenge to 'conventional' literature. For students of other media we might begin to add the montage cinema of Vertov and Eisenstein, experiments with point of view in films like Kurosawa's *Rashomon* and time in a film like *Groundhog Day* (see, for example, Aarseth 1997: 41–54 and Murray 1997: 27–64). Equally, the montage of Dada, Surrealism and their echoes in the contemporary collage of screen-based visual culture might also be seen as 'hypermediated' in Bolter and Grusin's sense. Here then is another important point at which the history of culture is reformulated by the development of new media forms **(1.4)**.

Hypertext as the practice of literary theory

The second and, to date, dominant strand of hypertextual scholarship has been the identification and celebration of hypertext as the technological **embodiment** of a particular moment in literary criticism.

Here the theories of text proposed by Barthes, Foucault and Derrida are called upon as the most appropriate analytic frameworks within which to understand hypertextual form. In particular fragmentation, non-linearity, intertextuality and the 'death of the author' have all been cited as both literary theory *and* hypertext reality.

> hypertext has much in common with some major points of contemporary literary and semiological theory, particularly with Derrida's emphasis on de-centering and with Barthes' conception of the readerly versus the writerly text. In fact hypertext creates an almost embarrassingly literal embodiment of both concepts, one that in turn raises questions about them and their interesting combination of prescience and historical relations . . .
>
> (Landow 1992: 33)

This 'first wave' of hypertext scholarship can be seen as a response of American literary theorists to parallel but unrelated developments – the first being the translation and diffusion of European literary and cultural theory produced in the 1970s. The second was the adoption of the PC as a tool within the academic community. These developments both occurred in the early to mid-1980s, leading to Landow's 'embarrassingly literal embodiment' of theory in technology.

The criticism of Barthes, Derrida and Foucault, developed primarily through the 1970s, represented a sustained attack on conventional notions of the book. According to 'common-sense' notions of reading and understanding, the author, usually the great (male) artist, controlled the meaning of the books which he wrote. These 'great works' had an individual autonomy in the world, were the discrete products of the author's imagination. They were consumed by a reading public who were assumed to begin at the beginning and read until the end in order to understand the author's meaning. What subsequently became known as **'post-structural'** literary criticism, however, began to argue that these assumptions were wrong, that far from being discrete all texts have an 'intertextual' character, that all texts only make sense to us in relation to other texts, that we understand them as part of a web of textuality. Thus it was the reader as much as the author who created meaning out of the many possible ways of experiencing a text – ways that might include non-linear understandings as well as skipping, reading the end first, navigating the text through indices and footnotes. Moreover, the integrity of the 'whole text' came under fire through a new focus on the tiny components that go to make up the work; each fragment, it was argued, had its own representative framework.

These apparent homologies between hypertextual form and post-structuralist literary theory are indeed seductive. However, later critics have sounded a note of caution around the methodological relevance in 'reading off' a set of conclusions drawn from one object of study (the book) to a set of problems posed by another (the computer-mediated hypertext). A second wave of hypertext scholarship has been characterised by a critique of

1.4   What kind of history?

The primary literature and debates arising are by now extensive, and have become one of the most important points of contact between European critical theory and American **cyberculture** studies. This section offers a brief introductory overview of the key questions. For further study see, for example, Jay David Bolter, *Writing Space: The Computer, Hypertext and the History of Writing*, New York: Erlbaum, 1991; George Landow and Paul Delaney (eds) *Hypermedia and Literary Studies*, Cambridge, Mass.: MIT, 1991; George Landow, *Hypertext: The Convergence of Contemporary Literary Theory and Technology*, Baltimore and London: Johns Hopkins University Press, 1992 (especially pp. 1–34); George Landow (ed.) *Hyper/Text/Theory*, Baltimore and London: Johns Hopkins University Press, 1994; Mark Poster, *The Mode of Information*, Cambridge: Polity Press, 1990, pp. 99–128.

the 'hypertext equals post-structuralism on the computer screen' position and by calls for new hybrid methodologies that recognise the *differences* between a computer system and a book (see, for example, Aarseth 1997: 83–85).

One of the first and most commonly experienced criticisms of the positions outlined above comes from readers' response to literary hypertexts. Our experience of reading hypertext works is often far from the liberating, empowering experience we might expect from the above. On the contrary we often find ourselves positioned in particular pathways, unable to see beyond the next link, revisiting the same nodes over and over in loops – in short, having to work extremely hard to make any sense whatsoever of the text. This is particularly the case where hypertext is the basis for cultural production like stories, poems or films where our attachment to existing narrative forms of textual organisation is fierce. In fact, the book is already a perfect random access system: we can read from anywhere, find out the ending before we arrive at it, and we are free to navigate the book in ways that hypertext often denies us. Experience of hypertext stories often sends readers hurrying back to the comfort of the book.

> For Roland Barthes, tmesis is the unconstrained skipping and skimming of passages, a fragmentation of the linear text expression that is totally beyond the author's control. Hypertext reading is in fact quite the opposite: as the reader explores the labyrinth, she cannot afford to tread lightly through the text but must scrutinize the links and venues in order to avoid meeting the same text fragments over and over again.
>
> (Aarseth 1997: 78)

The second, and perhaps more significant, criticism of the post-structuralist approach to hypertext lies in its construction of the relationship between reader and text in which the system itself, the software and processing units of the computer, is left out. Existing methods for conceptualising the relationship between texts and readers assume a model of signification in which the reader–text interface becomes the site of interpretation, cognition and meaning production. However, under hypertextual conditions we are forced to ask Aarseth's question: 'Where does the user action stop and system action begin?' (Aarseth 1997: 39). The enormous complexity of hypertextual systems now available has the effect of making it impossible to predict what text will be produced by the user–machine interaction – in these conditions the system itself becomes a determining agent in the outcomes of the text–reader meeting. Here we move into the region of what Aarseth has described as 'cybertextuality', in which the machine, the text(s) and the reader/user are all equally implicated in the production of meaning. The point about **cybernetic** systems is that they possess an autonomy beyond human agency: cybernetic feedback systems reorder the texts on offer – in this case, for instance, through the logic of the search engine rather than the narrative structure – and reimpose themselves upon the pattern of material phenomena and textuality.

Bush and Nelson clearly conceived of hypertext as a form which would naturally find its home in information retrieval as an aid to the production of knowledge. However, as we have seen, the major studies of hypertext have considered that it raises important aesthetic questions rather than addressing Bush's aim of improving information retrieval. Here, with the addition of rapid search engines, multiple **windows** and the ability to track 'path histories', the application of hypertext is more successful. It is possible to argue that this has to do with the difference between data and knowledge – information stored as data is inert until the user begins to impose pattern upon it through navigation. We create

See Eastgate Systems website (**www.eastgate.com**) for literary hypertexts

For further accounts of the development of an approach to hypertext that goes beyond the post-structuralist paradigm, see especially Aarseth (1997), but also Michael Joyce, *Of Two Minds: hypertext pedagogy and poetics*, Ann Arbor: University of Michigan Press, 1995; Stuart Moulthrop, 'Toward a Rhetoric of Informating Texts', in *Hypertext 1992 Proceedings*, New York, Association for Computing Machinery, 1992, 171–179; M. Rieser & A. Zapp (eds) *New Screen Media: cinema/art/narrative*, London: British Film Institute, 2002.

knowledge through the ability of the mind to synthesise data. Hypertext does indeed appear to offer dynamic methods for data retrieval that support this synthetic activity of consciousness.

It is clear that we are in the process of understanding, through theory and practice, the implications of hypertextual organisation for texts and readers. However, it is equally clear that the principle of hypertextuality is key to understanding new media.

1.2.4 Dispersal

Continuing our attempt to suggest key differences that distinguish 'new media' from existing forms of mass media this section will explore the idea that what confronts us is a dispersed media system. In order to understand new media we will have to develop a framework that recognises the way in which both the production and distribution of new media have become decentralised, highly individuated and woven ever more closely into the fabric of everyday life.

This dispersal is the product of shifts in our relationships with both the consumption and production of media texts.

Consumption

Through the period 1980–2000 our consumption of media texts has been marked by a shift from a limited number of standardised texts to a very large number of highly differentiated texts. The media audience has fragmented and differentiated as the number of media texts available to us has proliferated. From an era of a limited number of network TV stations, no VCRs or DVD players, very limited use of computers as communication devices and no mobile media at all we find ourselves confronted by an unprecedented penetration of media texts into everyday life. 'National' newspapers are produced as geographically specific editions, network and terrestrial TV stations are surrounded by independent satellite and cable channels, the networked PC in the home offers a vast array of communication and media consumption opportunities, mobile telephony and **ubiquitous computing** offer a future in which there are no 'media free' zones in everyday life.

> In sum, the new media determine a segmented, differentiated audience that, although massive in terms of numbers, is no longer a mass audience in terms of simultaneity and uniformity of the message it receives. The new media are no longer mass media in the traditional sense of sending a limited number of messages to a homogeneous mass audience. Because of the multiplicity of messages and sources, the audience itself becomes more selective. The targeted audience tends to choose its messages, so deepening its segmentation, enhancing the individual relationship between sender and receiver.
>
> (Sabbah 1985: 219; quoted in Castells 1996: 339)

Traditional mass media were the products of the communicative needs of the first half of the twentieth century in the industrialised world. As such they had certain characteristics. They were centralised, content was produced in highly capitalised industrial locations like newspaper printworks or Hollywood film studios. In broadcast media, press and cinema, distribution was tied to production, studios owned cinema chains, newspapers owned fleets of distribution vans, the BBC owned its own transmission stations and masts. Consumption is here characterised by uniformity: cinema audiences all over the world see the same movie, all readers read the same text in a national newspaper, we all hear the same radio programme. Twentieth-century mass media can be characterised by standardisation of content, distribution and production process. These tendencies toward centralisation and standardisation in turn reflect and create the possibility for control and regulation of media systems, for professionalisation of communicative and creative processes, and for very clear distinctions between consumers and producers.

A useful way to conceptualise the difference between centralised and dispersed media distribution systems might be to think about the differences between radio and television broadcast networks and computer networks. The technology at the heart of the original radio and TV broadcast systems is radio wave transmission; here transmission suites require high investment in capital, plant, buildings, masts, etc. Airwave transmission is supplemented by systems of coaxial cable transmission, again where massive investments throughout the twentieth century have established a global network of cable systems. The technology of transmission has the idea of 'one to many' at its core – one input signal can be relayed to many points of consumption. The radio transmitter works on a centralised model.

The computer **server** is the technology at the heart of the dispersed systems of new media. A server, by contrast to a transmission mast, is a multiple input/output device, capable of receiving large amounts of data as input as well as making equally large quantities available for downloading to PC. The server is a networked device. It has many input connections and many output connections, and exists as a node in a web rather than as the centre of a circle.

A radio transmitter capable of handling broadcast radio and TV signals is an expensive capital investment way beyond the reach of most enterprises or individuals. The server, on the other hand, is cheap, being commonplace in medium or large enterprises of all kinds. Access to server space is commonly domestically available as part of online subscription packages.

However, this simple opposition between the centralised and the dispersed prompts as many questions as it answers. Most interestingly, this points up how there is no radical and complete break between 'old' and 'new' media. **Networked** media distribution could not exist without the technological spine provided by existing media routes of transmission, from telephone networks to radio transmission and satellite communications. 'Old' media systems of distribution are not about to disappear – they are essential to new media. However, new media, multimedia, and CMC networks have, as it were, been able to reconfigure themselves around this core to facilitate new kinds of distribution that are not necessarily centrally controlled and directed but are subject to a far higher degree of audience differentiation and discrimination. Many different users can access many different kinds of media at many different times around the globe using network-based distribution. Consumers and users are increasingly able to customise their own media use to design highly individualised menus that serve very particular and specific needs.

See also Jeanette Steemers, 'Broadcasting is dead, long live digital choice', *Convergence* 3.1 (1997) and J. Cornford and K. Robins, 'New media', in J. Stokes and A. Reading (eds) *The Media in Britain*, London: Macmillan, 1999

This market segmentation and fragmentation should not be confused with a general democratisation of media – as Steemers, Robins and Castells have argued, the multiplication of possible media choices has been accompanied by an intensification of merger activities amongst media corporations: 'we are not living in a global village, but in customised cottages globally produced and locally distributed' (Castells 1996: 341).

Production

This sense of the increasing flexibility and informality of our interaction with media texts of all kinds is equally present in the field of media production. Here, too, we have seen the development of production technologies and processes that begin to challenge the centralised methods of industrial organisation that had previously characterised mass media production sectors. These changes can be perceived to be operating both within the professional audio-visual industries as well as within the domestic and everyday spheres.

The media industries themselves are having to face the fact that the conjunction of computer-based communications and existing broadcast technologies is creating whole new fluid areas of media production. The traditional boundaries and definitions between different media processes are breaking down as craft skills of media production become more generally dispersed throughout the population as a whole in the form of IT skills.

> Lightweight technology has taken programme making out of the studios into the streets. Content, once created, can be reworked for dozens of different outlets. You can edit a Hollywood movie from a loft in Soho. You can watch a friend's wedding in Australia as it happens. All this means that the way people work has changed. A new breed of independent television producer appeared in the 1980s, to be followed in the 1990s by a wave of digital content producers. New sectors, like computer games, are meeting consumer demands for interactive entertainment inside and outside the home. Above all, the arrival of the Internet and the rapid take-up of computers at home and at work have created thousands of jobs with titles nobody had heard of in the twentieth century.
>
> (Laughton *et al.* 2001: 9)

While existing media corporations position themselves to take advantage of their role within the so-called '**knowledge economy**',

> At the same time there has been a rapid growth in the numbers of start ups and mergers of companies involved specifically in digital content creation. These start ups are characterised by decentralised informal structures and extremely flexible working patterns.
>
> (Laughton *et al.* 2001: 267)

The number of sites for the production of media content is expanding – production is dispersing itself more thoroughly into the general economy as it becomes the 'knowledge economy'.

This dispersal of production can also be observed from the perspective of the everyday worlds of work and domesticity. Consider the 'proximity' of media production processes to a citizen over the historical period of the late twentieth century. In 1970 in the UK, for instance, the nineteenth-century media processes of print and photography would probably have been the only kind of media production processes that were commonly used or discussed in everyday life as part of publicising civic, commercial, cultural and political activity. Apart from this, broadcasting and publishing systems were mostly very distant from the lives of ordinary people. However, by the end of the century print production was easier than ever through desktop publishing, editorial and design technologies all of which are available in domestic software packages. Photographic production through manipulation, and distribution through compression, has opened out the possibilities for the domestic photographer. Television has moved much closer to the viewer in the sense that very many of us have now seen our own image in domestic camcorder footage, 'For all the limitations of this self production of images, it actually modified the one way flow of images and reintegrated life experience and the screen' (Castells 1996: 338).

This process of media production diffusing itself within everyday life is at its most striking in the production of the 'home page'. The home page might stand as the most clear example of how the distinction between producer and consumer has broken down – anyone with an online account can now potentially publish, with little or no reference to the kinds of market constraints or regulatory controls that characterised previous twentieth-century forms of mass media (4.2.6).

The integration of media process into everyday life is not confined to the domestic sphere – as work has increasingly moved towards service rather than production economies all kinds of non-media workers find themselves called upon to be familiar with various kinds of media production processes from web design to Powerpoint presentation and computer-mediated communication software. Both at home and at work media production processes are far closer to the rhythms of everyday life. Whilst we certainly would not wish to overemphasise the degree of this proximity by echoing claims of cyber pioneers for the total collapse of the distinction between consumption and production it is certainly the case that the distance between the elite process of media production and everyday life is smaller now than at any time in the age of mass media.

Consumption meets production

Across a range of media we have seen the development of a market for 'prosumer' technologies; that is, technologies that are aimed at neither the professional nor the (amateur) consumer market but both – technologies that enable the user to be both consumer and producer. This is true in two senses – the purchaser of a £2,000 digital video camera is clearly a consumer (of the camera), and may use it to record home movies, the traditional domain of the hobbyist consumer. However, they may equally use it to record material of a broadcast quality for a Reality TV show, or to produce an activist anti-capitalist video that could have global distribution or pornographic material that could equally go into its own micro circuit of distribution. This is new. Until the 1990s the technological separation between what was acceptable for public distribution and what was 'only' suitable for domestic exhibition was rigid. The breakdown of the professional/amateur category is a matter ultimately of cost. To acquire 'broadcast standard' cameras and editing equipment would still cost around £50,000 for a standard Betacam and Avid set up – however, we can now produce 'broadcast acceptable' equipment costing a tenth of that figure.

We can see the impacts of these developments most clearly in the music industry. Digital technologies have made possible a dispersal and diffusion of music production that has fundamentally changed the nature of the popular music market. The apparatus of analogue music production, orchestral studios, 20-foot sound desks and 2-inch rolls of tape can all now be collapsed into a sampling keyboard, a couple of effects units, and a computer. The bedroom studio is clearly one of the myths of 'making it' in the 1990s; however, it is not without material foundation. The popular success of dance music in all its myriad global forms is in part the consequence of digital technologies making music production more accessible to a wider range of producers than at any time previously. (Of course the industry of promotion and manufacture is still necessary and the ultimate control of the record industry majors, although threatened, remains by and large undiminished.)

4.2.6   Home pages: everyday identity in global networks

'It is implied that such technology is poised to invade the human interior blurring distinctions between hardware, software, and user. On such evidence it is possible to postulate that what will characterise such media is the convergence of the means of production and consumption on the user. Media which we are familiar with as passive will become active, and the domestic means of consumption will also become the professional means of production" (Simon Biggs, 'Media art and its virtual future', London Video Access Catalogue, LVA 1991)

The PC itself is in many ways the ultimate figure of media 'prosumer' technology. It is a technology of distribution, of consumption, as well as a technology of production. We use it to look at and listen to other people's media products, as well as to produce our own, from ripping CD compilations to editing videotape, mixing music or publishing websites. This overlap between consumption and production is producing a new zone of media exhibition that is neither 'professionalised' mainstream nor amateur hobbyist. The net becomes a space in which critical and satirical journalism flourishes (e.g. The Drudge Report in the US or Tehelka.com in India), in which fans get a chance to participate in the realm of media celebrity, and independent film-makers begin to organise new alternative distribution networks.

In the media industries the craft bases and apprenticeship systems that maintained quality and protected jobs have broken down more or less completely, so that the question of how anyone becomes 'qualified' to be a media producer is more a matter of creating a track record and portfolio for yourself than following any pre-established routes. This crisis is also reflected in media education. Here the debate ranges from a new vocationalism aimed at producing graduates skilled in networking and the production of intellectual and creative properties and those who conversely argue that, in the light of the new developments outlined above, media studies should be seen as a central component of a new humanities, in which media interpretation and production are a core skillset for all kinds of professional employment.

New media are dispersed in comparison to mass media – dispersed at the level of consumption where we have seen a multiplication, segmentation and resultant individuation of media use; dispersed at the level of production where we have witnessed the multiplication of the sites for production of media texts and a higher diffusion within the economy as a whole than was previously the case. Finally, new media can be seen as dispersed rather than mass for the way in which consumers can now more easily extend their participation in media from active interpretation to actual production.

1.2.5 Virtuality

In a little over ten years the term 'virtual reality' has become part of everyday language. The more abstract concept 'virtuality' or 'the virtual' is the topic of many academic texts about contemporary media and culture. Any attempt to survey the field of developments associated with these terms is made difficult because they are applied to several different forms of media and image technologies simultaneously, and beyond these to the very character of everyday life in technologically advanced societies. We meet the 'virtual' in discussions of the Internet and the World Wide Web; immersive, 3D, and spectacular image technologies; screen-based multimedia (virtual **desktops** and 'windows') and in the transformation and convergence of older media as in digital cinema, video, and computer animation. Alongside these uses, the 'virtual' is frequently cited as a feature of postmodern cultures in which, it is argued, so many aspects of everyday experience are technologically simulated. Older certainties about 'reality' have become problematic, and questions arise about the kind of identity or sense of self that individuals who live in such cultures may have. Many discussions make reference to all of these factors. They move from one form of virtual reality and virtual state to another, eclectically gathering evidence to make a general case or argument about the state of media culture, postmodern identity, art, entertainment, and visual culture. In some ways, the convergence of digital image technologies both with older kinds of analogue media and with computer-mediated telecommunications networks makes this situation inevitable. The discussion of one leads to another. However, for the purposes of analysis and clarity, we make some distinctions between kinds of virtual reality at the outset of this section.

1.2.6 Which virtual reality?

In the now extensive body of literature about VR there are two major but intertwined reference points: the immersive, interactive experiences provided by new forms of image and simulation technology, and the metaphorical 'places' and 'spaces' created by or within communications networks. Hence, while they are often discussed as if they were the same thing, the term 'virtual reality' is used as a label for two kinds of technologically facilitated experience and a number of new media genres. First, it is used to describe the experience of **immersion** in an environment constructed with computer graphics and digital video with which the 'user' has some degree of interaction. Its popular icon is the headset-wearing, crouching and contorted figure perceiving a computer-generated 'world' (in **cyberspace**), while their body, augmented by helmets carrying stereoscopic LCD screens, a device that monitors the direction of their gaze, and wired gloves or body suits providing tactile and positioning feedback, remains in physical space.

A second meaning is the space where participants in online communication feel themselves to be. This is a space famously described as 'where you are when you're talking on the telephone' (Rucker *et al.* 1993: 78). Or, more carefully, as a space which 'comes into being when you are on the phone: not exactly where you happen to be sitting, nor where the other person is, but somewhere in between' (Mirzoeff 1999: 91). **(See 3.3, 5.4.)**

Also described as virtual realities are the non-immersive and screen-based 3D worlds explored by computer game players, and the images that are perceived by a technician or pilot when their physical bodies are in one place while they act remotely on an object or event using data and imagery produced by cameras, sensors, and robot vision.

Further to these uses of VR, we increasingly find the term being used retrospectively. We have already noted the case of the telephone, but also the experience of watching film and television, reading books and texts, or contemplating photographs and paintings are being retrospectively described as virtual realities (see Morse 1998; Heim 1993: 110; Laurel in Coyle 1993: 150; Mirzoeff 1999: 92–99). These uses of the term can be understood in two ways: either as a case of the emergence of new phenomena casting older ones in a new light (Chesher 1997: 91) or that, once it is looked for, experience of the 'virtual' is found to have a long history (Mirzoeff 1999: 91).

1.2.7 Cyberspace

There is a clear difference between these two kinds of VR: one is a site-specific enclosure in technology and the other a way of imagining the invisible space of communication networks. Immersive VR is predominantly an image environment, in which the aural and tactile senses are also engaged. The VR of online networks (as in the worlds of MUDs and MOOs – see **Case study 4.5**) is the product of text. (The places and persons in these kinds of virtual worlds are described in written language much as they have been traditionally in literature. In fact certain genres of literature predominate.) However, in many accounts of VR these differences are seldom paid much attention and, instead, they are interwoven or collapsed into one another, each filling out the dimensions of the other. On closer inspection, immersive VR tends to provide the ground for discussing:

Related to this interest in virtual reality, a more general quality or mode of existence, 'virtuality', has seen revived interest. The concept has a long history in philosophy and theology (see Pierre Levy, *Becoming Virtual: Reality in the Digital Age*, New York: Plenum Press, 1998). See also 5.4.2.

5.4.2 Cybernetics and the virtual

(But see Heim [1996: 65–77], who discusses the 'profound' difference between this kind of 'HMD' [head-mounted display] VR and 'CAVE' VR in which the body is unencumbered by a headset and can move in a 'surround screen' projection.)

3.3 Networks and identity
5.4 Theories of cyberculture

For a view which challenges the idea that the Internet is a space, or should be thought of as a space at all, see Chesher (1997: 91)

The experience of acting remotely via robotics on a simulation can more accurately be described as telepresence. While telepresence is often subsumed as a kind of VR, see Ken Goldberg, 'Virtual reality in the age of telepresence', *Convergence* 4.1 (1998) for a fuller discussion of the difference.

The way in which media history is more generally recast in the light of present preoccupations is discussed in **1.4**

1.4 What kind of history?

Case study 4.5 MUD ethnography

- visual, tactile and aural experiences in a situation where the senses and the consciousness (the human sensorium) are felt to be in one place (the virtual environment or world) while the corporeal body of the user is in another, the physical and material world;

- the capacity of contemporary technology to simulate reality on the one hand and to generate fantasy on the other.

On the other hand, in discussion of the virtual spaces produced by communication networks, other factors are emphasised:

- the opportunities for the user to adopt markers of identity (personality, gender, status, physical attributes) that differ from their identities as constituted in the physical and everyday social world;

- the possibility of forming new kinds of association and community which are not dependent upon spatial location and which can transcend geographical, social, and political boundaries and divisions.

Why then are these two kinds of VR so frequently thought about as different aspects or instantiations of the same phenomena? Why is an observation about one used to reinforce a point made about the other?

A future scenario
A common denominator between these two kinds of VR, and the ideas and discussions which they give rise to, are the puzzling relationships of these new technologies to our experiences and conceptions of space, **embodiment** (literally: of having and being conscious of having bodies) and identity. The generic concept which subsumes both kinds of VR is 'cyberspace'. It is cyberspace that they are both seen to produce, and it is the notion of inhabiting such a space that raises questions about embodiment, as 'body' seems to become detached from the 'identity' that a person might assume. However, it is especially the promise of a future fusion of the two kinds of VR – the relative sensory plenitude of immersive VR and the connectivity of online communication – that lies behind the habit of discussing the two kinds of VR in the same frame. This is because, in such a scenario, full sensory immersion would be combined with extreme bodily remoteness.

The middle term, the ground for anticipating such a fusion of the two VRs, is the digital simulation of 'high resolution images of the human body in cyberspace'. While it is clear that these are 'years away', cybertheorists argue that they will 'arrive' (see Stone 1994: 85).

The empirical grounds for venturing such a claim are seen in the form of virtual actors or synthespians (computer simulations of actors) that now appear in cinema, TV, and computer games, and, less convincingly, experiments in 'inhabited television' (http://www.i3net.org). The grounds for doubting the claim are partly technological. The computing power and the telecommunications bandwidth which would be necessary to produce and transmit simulations of human beings and their environments, let alone the programming that would enable them to interact with one another in real time, is difficult to conceive. Yet, further questions arise. Where does the desire for such developments lie? And, what goals or purposes might attract the financial investment necessary for such technological developments? (See **1.5**.) In speculating about or anticipating this fusion, its desirability and its purposes, we also have to take into account the **technological imaginary** (**1.5.2**) which so powerfully shapes thinking about new media of all kinds. Currently, it is difficult to underestimate the part played by science fiction in providing us with ideas and images with which to think about the abstractions and immaterial processes of cyberspace. For Stone (1994: 84), 'when the first "virtual reality" environments come on-line' they will be realisations of William Gibson's famous 'consensual hallucination' in his novel *Neuromancer*.

Hence, several factors can be found to explain how discussion of current 'quasi' forms of VR are so readily collapsed into one another and force the prospect of a full-blown VR 'to come' onto the speculative edge of current cyberculture agendas. To sum up, these are:

- already existing and operational, but relatively new forms of image and communications media;

- an already present cultural familiarity with 'virtual' image forms;

- the apparently non-physical space of online communicative interaction;

- ongoing developments in computer animation and digital cinema;

- the scenarios of cyber-science fiction.

1.2.8 Conclusion

The characteristics which we have discussed above should be seen as part of a dynamic matrix of qualities that we argue is what makes new media different. Not *all* of these qualities will be present in *all* examples of new media – they will be present in differing degrees and in different mixes. This dynamic matrix will inflect and modify all our mediated experiences as new media become increasingly available over time. However, these qualities are not *wholly* functions of technology – they are all imbricated into the organisation of culture, work and leisure with all the economic and social determinations that involves. To speak of new media as dispersed, for instance, is not just to speak of the difference between server technology and broadcast transmitters but also to talk about the deregulation of media markets. To talk about the concept of the virtual is not just to speak of head-mounted display systems but also to have to take into account the ways in which experiences of self and of identity are increasingly mediated in a 'virtual' space. This discussion of the 'characteristics' of new media has merely established the grounds upon which we might now begin substantially to address the questions that they raise.

1.3 CHANGE AND CONTINUITY

In this section and sections **1.4** and **1.5** we consider new media's relation to the past, to 'older' media and history.

1.3.1 Introduction

Media theorists, and other commentators, tend to be polarised over the degree of new media's newness. While the various camps seldom engage in debate with each other, the

1.5 Who was dissatisfied with old media?

1.5.2 The technological imaginary William Gibson, in *Neuromancer* (1986: 52), describes cyberspace as 'a consensual hallucination experienced daily by billions of legitimate operators in every nation . . . a graphic representation of data abstracted from the banks of every computer in every human system. Unthinkable complexity. Lines of light ranged in the nonspace of the mind, clusters and constellations of data. Like city lights receding.' This has become the standard science fictional basis for imagining cyberspace as an architectural (cartesian) space, in which 'a man may be seen, and perhaps touched as a woman and vice versa – or as anything else. There is talk of renting pré-packaged body forms complete with voice and touch . . . multiple personality as commodity fetish!' (Stone 1994: 85)

1.4 What kind of history?
1.5 Who was dissatisfied with old media?

1.5.3   The discursive construction
of new media

argument is between those who see a media revolution taking place and those who claim that, on the contrary, behind the hype we largely have 'business as usual'. To some extent this argument hinges upon the disciplinary frameworks and **discourses (1.5.3)** within which proponents of either side of the argument work. What premises do they proceed from? What questions do they ask? What methods do they apply? What ideas do they bring to their investigations and thinking?

In this section we simply recognise that while the view is widely held that new media are 'revolutionary' – that they are profoundly or radically new in kind – throughout the growing literature on new media there are also frequent recognitions that *any attempt to understand new media requires a historical perspective.* Many reasons for taking this view will be met throughout the book as part of its detailed case studies and arguments. In this section we look at the general case for the importance of history in the study of new media.

1.3.2 Measuring 'newness'

The most obvious question that needs to be asked is: 'How do we know that something is *new* or *in what way it is new* if we have not carefully compared it with what already exists or has gone before?' We cannot know with any certainty and detail *how new* or *how large* changes are without giving our thinking a historical dimension. We need to establish from what previous states things have changed. Even if, as Brian Winston observes, the concept of a 'revolution' is implicitly historical, how can one know 'that a situation has changed – has revolved – without knowing its previous state or position?' (Winston 1998: 2). In another context, Kevin Robins (1996: 152) remarks that, 'Whatever might be "new" about digital technologies, there is something old in the imaginary signification of "image revolution".' Revolutions then, when they take place, are historically relative and the idea itself has a history. It is quite possible to take the view that these questions are superfluous and only divert us from the main business. This certainly seems to be the case for many new media enthusiasts who are (somewhat arrogantly, we may suggest) secure in their conviction that the new *is new* and how it got to be that way will be of a lot less interest than what comes next!

However, if asked, this basic question can help us guard against missing at least three possibilities:

1   Something may *appear* to be new, in the sense that it looks or feels unfamiliar or because it is aggressively presented as new, but on closer inspection such newness may be revealed as only superficial. It may be that something is new only in the sense that it turns out to be a new version or configuration of something that, substantially, already exists, rather than being a completely new category or kind of thing. Alternatively, how can we know that a medium is new, rather than a hybrid of two or more older media or an old one in a new context which, in some ways, transforms it?

4   NEW MEDIA IN EVERYDAY LIFE

2   Conversely, as the newness of new media becomes familiar in everyday use or consumption (**see 4**) we may lose our curiosity and vigilance, ceasing to ask questions about exactly what they do and how they are being used to change our worlds in subtle as well as dramatic ways.

3   A final possibility that this simple question can uncover is that on close inspection and reflection, initial estimates of novelty can turn out not to be as they seem. We find that some kinds and degrees of novelty exist but not in the ways that they were initially thought to. The history of what is meant by the new media buzzword 'interactivity' is

a prime example of the way a much-lauded quality of new media has been repeatedly qualified and revised through critical examination.

(See **Case study 1.3**.)

Case study 1.3 What is new about interactivity?

The overall point is that the 'critical' in the critical study of new media means not taking things for granted. Little is assumed about the object of study that is then illuminated by asking questions and attempting to answer questions about it. An important way of doing this – of approaching something critically – is to ask what its history is or, in other words, how it came to be as it is.

Lastly, in this review of reasons to be historical in our approach to new media, we need to recall how extensive and heterogeneous the range of changes, developments, and innovations are that get subsumed under the term 'new media'. This is so much the case that without some attempts to break the term or category down into more manageable parts we risk such a level of abstraction and generalisation in our discussions that they will never take us very far in the effort to understand one or another of these changes (see **1.1**). A better approach is to look for the different *ratios of the old and the new* across the field of new media. One way of doing this is, precisely, historical. It is to survey the field of new media in terms of the degree to which any particular development is genuinely and radically new or is better understood as simply an element of change in the nature of an already established medium.

1.1 What are new media?

Old media in new times?

For instance, it can be argued that 'digital television' is not a new medium but is best understood as a change in the form of delivering the contents of the TV medium, which has a history of some fifty years or more. This would be a case of what Mackay and O'Sullivan describe as an 'old' medium 'in new times' as distinct from a 'new medium' (1999: 4–5). On the other hand, immersive virtual reality or interactive multimedia look to be, at least at first sight, mediums of a radically and profoundly new kind. This, however, still leaves us with the problem of defining what is truly new about them.

Before we accept this 'new/old' axis as a principle for distinguishing between kinds of new media, we have to recognise immediately that the terms can, to some extent, be reversed. For instance, it can be argued that the some of the envisaged versions or outcomes of transmitting TV digitally will have quite profound effects upon its programming and modes of audience reception such that the medium of TV will be significantly changed (**Case study 1.7**). It could also be claimed that the increased size and digitally enhanced resolution and quality of the traditionally low-definition TV image effectively transforms the medium. Whether we would want to go as far as saying that it will be a new medium still seems unlikely, if not impossible. On the other hand, the apparently unprecedented experiences offered by the technologies of immersive VR or online, interactive, multimedia can be shown to have histories and antecedents, both of a technological and a cultural kind, upon which they draw and depend (**1.2, 1.3**). Whether, in these cases, however, we would want to go as far as saying that therefore VR is adequately defined by tracing and describing its many practical and ideological antecedents is another matter.

Case study 1.7 The technological imaginary and the shaping of new media

1.2 The characteristics of new media: some defining concepts
1.3 Change and continuity

The idea of 'remediation'

A third possibility is that put forward by Jay Bolter and Richard Grusin (1999) who, following an insight of Marshall McLuhan, effectively tie new media to old media as a structural condition of all media. They propose and argue at some length that the 'new' in new media is the manner in which the digital technologies that they employ 'refashion older media', and then these older media 'refashion themselves to answer to the challenges of new media' (p. 15). It seems to us that there is an unassailable truth in this formulation. This is that new media are not born in a vacuum and, as media, would have no resources to draw upon if they were not in touch and negotiating with the long traditions of process, purpose, and signification that older media of communication, representation, and expression possess. Yet, having said this, many questions about the nature and extent of the transformations taking place remain.

CASE STUDY1.3: 'What is new about interactivity?'

During the 1990s 'interactivity' became a key buzzword in the world of new media. The promise and quality of interactivity has been conceived in a number of ways.

The creative management of information

This concept of interactivity has roots in the ideas of those early computer visionaries such as Vannevar Bush and Alan Kay (Bush [1945] and Kay and Goldberg, both in Mayer 1999). It is a vision of interactive computer databases liberating and extending our intellects. Such concepts, conceived in the years after the Second World War, were in part responses to the perceived threat of information overload in the modern world. Searchable databases that facilitated a convergence of existing print and visual media and the information they contained were seen as a new way for the individual to access, organise, and think with information.

Interactivity as consumer choice technologically embodied

1.2   The characteristics of new media: some defining concepts

We saw in our discussion of the concept in **1.2** how it has been central to the marketing of personal computers by linking it to contemporary ideas about consumer choice. Being interactive means that we are no longer the passive consumers of identical ranges of mass-produced goods, whether intellectual or material. Interactivity is promoted as a quality of computers that offers us active choices and personalised commodities, whether of knowledge, news, entertainment, banking, shopping and other services.

The death of the author

More recent cybertheorists have understood interactivity as placing authorship in the hands of the 'reader' or consumer (Landow 1992). Here, the idea is that interactive media are a technological realisation of a theory, first worked out mainly in relation to literature, known as 'post-structuralism'. We had, it was suggested, witnessed the 'death of the author', the central, fixed and god-like voice of the author behind the text (see, for example, Landow 1992). Interactivity meant that users of new media would be able to navigate their way across uncharted seas of potential knowledge, making their own sense of a body of material, each user following new pathways through the matrix of data each time they set out on their journeys of discovery.

A related idea is that the key property of interactivity is a major shift in the traditional relationship between the production and reception of media. This resides in the power that computers give the reader/user to 'write back' into a text. Information, whether in the form of text, image, or sound, is received within software applications that allow the receiver to change – delete, add, reconfigure – what they receive. It has not been lost on many thinkers that this practice, while enabled by electronic digital technology, resembles the medieval practice of annotating and adding extensive marginalia to manuscripts and books so that they became palimpsests. These are surfaces upon which generations of additions and commentaries are overwritten on texts, one on the other. Whilst this is true it has only a limited sense. There is after all a tremendous difference between the operation of the Internet and the highly selective access of the privileged class of medieval monks to sacred texts.

More recently, in the face of exaggerated claims for the almost magical powers of interactivity and on the basis of practice-based critical reflection, more critical estimations have been made. As the artist Sarah Roberts has put it:

> the illusion that goes along with [interactivity] is of a kind of democracy, . . . that the artist is sharing the power of choice with the viewer, when actually the artist has planned every option that can happen . . . it's a great deal more complex than if you [the user] hadn't had a sort of choice, but it's all planned.

(Penny 1995: 64)

These concepts of interactivity are less descriptions of particular technical, textual, or experiential properties and more claims or propositions rooted in the inspired founding visions, imaginative marketing strategies, and the sophisticated analogies of academic theorists about new, real or imagined, possibilities of human empowerment. However, whatever merits these ideas have, whether visionary or opportunistic, they have been subjected to methodical enquiry from within a number of disciplines which we need to attend to if we are to get beyond these broad characterisations of interactivity.

Human–computer interaction: intervention and control

A technical idea of interactivity has taken shape most strongly within the discipline of human–computer interaction (HCI). This is a scientific and industrial field which studies and attempts to improve the interface between computers and users.

An 'interactive mode' of computer use was first posited during the years of mainframe computers when large amounts of data were fed into the machine to be processed. At first, once the data was entered, the machine was left to get on with the processing (batch processing.) Gradually however, as the machines became more sophisticated, it became possible to intervene into the process whilst it was still running through the use of dialogue boxes or menus. This was known as operating the computer in an 'interactive' mode (Jensen 1999: 168). This ability to intervene in the computing process and see the results of your intervention in real time was essentially a *control* function. It was a one-way command communication from the operator to the machine. This is a very different idea of interaction from the popularised senses of hypertextual freedom described above (Huhtamo 2000).

This idea of *interaction as control* continued to develop through the discipline of HCI and was led by the ideas of technologists like Licklider and Engelbart (Licklider and Taylor 1999; Engelbart 1999). If the kind of symbiosis between operator and machine that they envisaged was to take place then this interactive mode had to be extended and made available outside of the small groups who understood the specialised programming languages. To this end, during the early 1970s, researchers at the Xerox Palo Alto Research Center developed the GUI, the graphical user interface, which would work within the simultaneously developed standard format for the PC: keyboard, processor, screen and mouse. In what has become one of the famous moments in the history of computers, Xerox failed to exploit their remarkable breakthroughs. Later, Apple were able to use the GUI to launch their range of PCs in the early 1980s: first the Apple Lisa, then in 1984 the celebrated Apple Mac. These GUI systems were then widely imitated by Microsoft.

Communication studies and the 'face-to-face' paradigm

However, this idea of interaction as control, as interface manipulation, is somewhat at odds with the idea of interactivity as a mutually reciprocal communication process, whether between user and machine/database or between user and user. Here we encounter an understanding of the term derived from sociology and communications studies. This tradition has attempted to describe and analyse interactivity and computers in relation to interactivity in face-to-face human communication. In this research interaction is identified as a core human behaviour, the foundation of culture and community. For communications theorists interaction is a quality present in varying degrees as a quality of communication. So a question and answer pattern of communication is somewhat 'less' interactive than an open-ended dialogue (see, for example, Shultz 2000; Jensen 1999). Similarly the modes of interactivity described in **1.2** would here be classified on a scale of least to most interactive, with the various kinds of CMC 'most' interactive and the navigational choices 'least' interactive.

Various commentators (for example, Stone 1995: 10; Aarseth 1997: 49) quote Andy Lippman's definition of interactivity generated at MIT in the 1980s as an 'ideal'. For Lippman interactivity was 'mutual and simultaneous activity on the part of both participants, usually working toward some goal, but not necessarily'. This state needed to be achieved through a number of conditions:

> mutual interruptibility
> limited look ahead *(so that none of the partners in the interaction can foresee the future shape of the interaction)*
> no default *(there is no pre programmed route to follow)*
> the impression of an infinite database *(from the participants' point of view)*.
>
> (Stone 1995: 10–11)

This sounds like a pretty good description of conversation, but a very poor description of using a point-and-click interface to 'interact' with a computer.

The study of artifical intelligence

There seem to us to be some real problems with the application of communications theories based in speech to technologically mediated communications. Unresolved, these problems lead to impossible expectations of computers, expectations that open up a gap between what we experience in computer-based interaction and what we might desire. Often this gap gets filled by predictions drawn from yet another methodological field – that of **artificial intelligence** (AI). The argument usually goes something like this. Ideal human–computer interaction would approach as close as possible to face-to-face communication; however, computers obviously can't do that yet since they are (still) unable to pass as human for any length of time. Futuristic scenarios (scientific and science fictional) propose that this difficulty will be resolved as chips get cheaper and computing enters into its ubiquitous phase (see **ubiquitous computing**). In the meantime we have to make do with various degrees along the way to 'true' (i.e. conversational) interaction. In this construction interactivity is always a failure awaiting rescue by the next development on an ever-shifting technological event horizon.

1.2   The characteristics of new media: some defining concepts

Media studies

Understandings of interactivity not only draw on HCI, communications studies, and AI research but often call up debates around the nature of media audiences and their interpretations of meanings that are generated within media studies. Influential strands within media studies teach that audiences are 'active' and make multiple and variable interpretative acts in response to media texts:

> the meaning of the text must be thought of in terms of which set of discourses it encounters in any particular set of circumstances, and how this encounter may restructure both the meaning of the text and the discourses which it meets.

(Morley 1980: 18)

This reading of audience behaviour is sometimes referred to as an 'interactive' activity. As readers we already, it is argued, have 'interactive' relationships with (traditional analogue) texts. This position is then extended to argue that not only do we have complex *interpretative* relationships with texts but *active material relationships* with texts; we write marginalia, stop and rewind the videotape, dub music from CD to tape, physically cut and paste images and text from print media into new arrangements and juxtapositions. In this reading, interactivity comes to be understood as, again, a kind of technological correlative for theories of textuality already established and an extension of material practices that we already have. So, for instance, even though we might not all share the same experience of a website we may construct a version of 'the text' through our talk and discussion about the site; similarly it is argued we will not all share the same experience of watching a soap opera. Indeed, over a period of weeks we will almost certainly not see the same 'text' as other family members or friends, but we can construct a common 'text' through our responses and talk about the programme. The text and the meanings which it produces already only exist in the spaces of our varied interpretations and responses.

In other words there is a perspective on interactivity, based in literary and media studies, that argues that nothing much has changed *in principle*. We are just offered more opportunities for more complex relationships with texts but these relationships are essentially the same (Aarseth 1997: 2). However, we would argue that the distinction between interaction and interpretation is even more important now than previously. This is because the problems which face us in understanding the processes of mediation are multiplied by new media: the acts of multiple interpretation of traditional media are not made irrelevant by digital and technological forms of interactivity but are actually made more numerous and complex by them. The more text choices available to the reader the greater the possible interpretative responses. The very necessity of intervention in the text, of manipulation of the text's forms of interaction, requires a more acute understanding of the act of interpretation.

Grassroots democratic exchange

Beyond the particular ways of understanding interactivity that flow from the four methodologies we have discussed, there lies another, more diffuse yet extremely powerful, discourse about interactivity that is so pervasive as to have become taken for granted. Within this usage 'interactive' equals automatically better – better than passive, and better than just 'active' by virtue of some implied reciprocity. This diffuse sense of the virtue of interactivity also has a social and cultural history, dating from the late 1960s and early 1970s. In this history, democratising challenges to established power systems were led by constant calls for dialogue and increased lateral, rather than vertical and hierarchical, communications as a way of supporting social progress. This ideological attack on one-way information flows in favour of lateral or interactive social communications lay behind much of the radical alternative rhetorics of the period. A community arts and media group active in London through the 1970s and 1980s, under the name of 'Interaction', is characteristic of the period in its analysis:

> The problems of a pluralist urban society (and an over populated one dependent on machines as well) are very complex. Answers, if there are any, lie in the ability to relate, to inform, to listen – in short the abilities of creative people.
>
> (Berman 1973: 17)

The abilities to 'relate' and to 'listen' are the skills of face-to-face dialogue and social interaction recast as a progressive force. This valorisation of social dialogue was 'in the air' in the early 1970s. It informed a radical critique of mainstream media which took root not only in the burgeoning of alternative and community media practices of the period but also in early ideas about computer networking. As was pointed out by Resource One, a community computing facility based in the Bay area of San Francisco:

> Both the quantity and content of available information is set by centralised institutions – the press, TV, radio, news services, think tanks, government agencies, schools and universities – which are controlled by the same interests which control the rest of the economy. By keeping information flowing from the top down, they keep us isolated from each other. Computer technology has thus far been used . . . mainly by the government and those it represents to store and quickly retrieve vast amounts of information about huge numbers of people. . . . It is this pattern that convinces us that control over the flow of information is so crucial.
>
> (*Resource One Newsletter*, 2 April 1974, p. 8)

1.5.5 The return of the Frankfurt School critique in the popularisation of new media

This support for 'democratic media' is a kind of popular and latter-day mobilisation of ideas derived from the **Frankfurt School**, with its criticisms of the role of mass media in the production of a docile population seduced by the pleasures of consumption and celebrity (**1.5.5**). In this reading 'interactive' media are constructed as a potential improvement on passive media in that they appear to hold out the opportunity for social and political communications to function in a more open and democratic fashion which more closely approaches the *ideal* conditions of the **public sphere**.

We are now in a position to see that the idea of interactivity, as one of the primary 'new' qualities of new media, comes to us as an automatic asset with a rich history. Yet, as we have also seen, it is a term that carries the weight of a number of different, and contradictory, histories. It may be possible to argue that it is precisely this lack of definition which makes it such a suitable site for our investment in the idea of 'the new'.

1.4 WHAT KIND OF HISTORY?

> 'I Love Lucy' and 'Dallas', FORTRAN and fax, computer networks, comsats, and mobile telephones. The transformations in our psyches triggered by the electronic media thus far may have been preparation for bigger things to come.
>
> (Rheingold 1991: 387)

In **1.3** we posed a number of basic questions that need to be asked if critical studies of new media are to proceed without being based upon too many assumptions about what we are dealing with. We strongly suggested that asking these questions requires us to take an interest in the available histories of older media. There is, however, another important reason why the student of new media may need to pay attention to history. This is because, from their very inception, new media have been provided with histories, some of which are misleading.

From the outset, the importance of new media, and the kind of futures they would deliver, has frequently been conceived as part of a historical unfolding of long-glimpsed possibilities. As the quote above suggests, such accounts imply that history may only have been a preparation for the media technologies and products of our time. In other words, a historical imagination came into play at the moment we began to strive to get the measure of new media technologies. These historical perspectives are often strongly marked by paradoxically old-fashioned ideas about history as a progressive process. Such ideas rapidly became popular and influential. There is little exaggeration in saying that, subsequently, a good deal of research and argument in the early years of 'new media studies' has been concerned with criticising these 'histories' and outlining alternative ways of understanding media change.

While this book is not the place to study theories of history in any depth, a body of historical issues now attaches itself to the study of new media. Some examples, and an idea of the critical issues they raise, are therefore necessary. In this section we first consider what are known as **teleological** accounts of new media (**1.4.1**). The meaning of this term will become clearer through the following discussion of some examples but, broadly, it refers to the idea that new media are a direct culmination of historical processes. By taking another example from recent work on the history of new media we seek to show that there can be no single, linear historical narrative that would add to our understanding of all that 'new media' embraces. We are clearly faced with a large number of intersecting histories. These are unlikely to fall into a pattern of tributaries all feeding regularly and incrementally into a main stream – as we might picture the root system of a tree feeding its main trunk. We would be hard put to think, let alone prove, that all of the developments, contexts, agents and forces that are involved in these histories had anything like a shared goal or purpose. We then outline the approaches of some theorists of new media who, rejecting the idea that new media can simply be understood as the utopian end point of progressive historical development, seek alternative ways of thinking about the differences and the complex connections between old and new media. In doing this we will consider how Michel Foucault's influential 'genealogical' theory of history has found a place in studies of new media (**1.4.1**).

Lastly, we consider a view derived from modernist aesthetics, which argues that for a medium to be genuinely new its unique essence has to be discovered in order for it to break itself free from the past and older media (**1.4.2**). In questioning this idea we introduce a number of examples in which new media are seen to recall the past, rather than break with it (**1.4.3**).

1.4.1 Teleological accounts of new media

From cave paintings to mobile phones
A popular and influential history of virtual reality takes us to the Upper Palaeolithic cave paintings of Lascaux, where 30,000 years ago, 'primitive but effective cyberspaces may have been instrumental in setting us on the road to computerized world building in the

1.3 Change and continuity

1.4.1 Teleological accounts of new media

1.4.2 New media and the modernist concept of progress

1.4.3 The return of the Middle Ages and other media archaeologies

first place' (Rheingold 1991: 379). Rheingold breathlessly takes his reader on a journey which has its destination in immersive virtual environments. En route we visit the origins of Dionysian drama in ancient Greece, the initiation rites of the Hopi, Navajo, and Pueblo tribes 'in the oldest continuously inhabited human settlements in North America', the virtual worlds of TV soap operas like I Love Lucy and Dallas, arriving at last to meet the interactive computing pioneers of Silicon Valley, major US universities and Japanese corporations. In Rheingold's sweeping historical scheme, the cave painting appears to hold the seeds of the fax machine, the computer network, the communications satellite and the mobile phone (Rheingold 1991: 387)!

Few examples of this way of understanding how we came to have a new medium are as mind-boggling in their Olympian sweep as Rheingold's. But, as we shall see, other theorists and commentators, often with more limited ambitions, share with him the project to understand new media as the culmination or present stage of development of all human media over time. When this is done, new media are placed at the end of a chronological list that begins with oral communication, writing, printing, drawing and painting, and then stretches and weaves its way through the image and communication media of the nineteenth and twentieth centuries, photography, film, TV, video and semaphore, telegraphy, telephony and radio. In such historical schemas there is often an underlying assumption or implication – which may or may not be openly stated – that new media represent a stage of development that was already present as a potential in other, earlier, media forms. A further example will help us see how such views are constructed and the problems associated with them.

From photography to telematics: extracting some sense from teleologies

Peter Weibel, a theorist of art and technology, former director of Ars Electronica and now director of ZKM, offers an eight-stage historical model of the progressive development of technologies of image production and transmission which, having photography as its first stage, spans 160 years (1996: 338–339).

Weibel notes that in 1839 the invention of photography meant that image making was freed for the first time from a dependence upon the hand (this is Stage 1). Images were then further unfixed from their locations in space by electronic scanning and telegraphy (Stage 2). In these developments Weibel sees 'the birth of new visual worlds and telematic culture' (1996: 338).

Then, in Stages 3–5, these developments were 'followed by' film which further transformed the image from something that occupied space to one that existed in time. Next, the discovery of the electron, the invention of the cathode ray tube, and magnetic recording brought about the possibility of a combination of film, radio, and television – and video was born. At this stage, Weibel observes, 'the basic conditions for electronic image production and transfer were established' (1996: 338).

In Stage 6, transistors, integrated circuits and silicon chips enter the scene. All previous developments are now revolutionised as the sum of the historical possibilities of machine-aided image generation are at last united in the multimedia, interactive computer. This newly interactive machine, and the convergence of all other technological media within it, then join with telecommunications networks and there is a further liberation as 'matterless signs' spread like waves in global space (Stage 7). A new era (first glimpsed at Stage 2) now dawns: that of post-industrial, telematic civilisation.

So, Stage 7, Weibel's penultimate stage, is that of interactive telematic culture, more or less where we may be now at the beginning of the new millennium. His final Stage 8 tips us into the future, a stage 'until now banished to the domain of science fiction' but 'already beginning to become a reality' (1996: 339). This is the sphere of advanced sensory technologies in which he sees the brain as directly linked to 'the digital realm' (ibid.).

Wiebel clearly sees this history as progressive, one in which 'Over the last 150 years the mediatisation and mechanisation of the image, from the camera to the computer have advanced greatly' (1996: 338). There is a direction, then, advancing toward the present and continuing into the future, which is revealed by the changing character of our media over time.

As we look back over Wiebel's eight stages we see that the 'advances' all concern the increasing dematerialisation of images and visual signs, their separation from the material vehicle which carries them. The final, culminating stage in this dynamic is then glimpsed: neurological engineering which is about to usher in a direct interfacing of the brain with the world – a world where no media, material or immaterial, exist. We have the end of media or, as his title states, *The World as Interface*.

What kind of history is being told here?

- Each of Weibel's stages points to real technological developments in image media production and transmission. These technologies and inventions did happen, did and do exist.

- Moving out from the facts, he then offers brief assessments of what these developments have meant for human communication and visual culture. In these assessments, the insights of other media theorists show through.

- Overall, Weibel organises his observations chronologically; the stages follow each other in time, each one appearing to be born out of the previous one.

- There is an ultimate point of origin – photography. The birth of this image technology is placed as a founding moment out of which the whole process unfolds.

- He finds a logic or a plot for his unfolding story – his sequential narrative of progress. This is the story of the increasing automation of production and increasing separation of signs (and images) from any physical vehicle that carries them.

This story is not without sense. But it is important to see that it is, in actuality, an argument. It is an organisation and integration of facts and ways of thinking about those facts. Facts? Photography and then telecommunications were invented. Hard to contest. Ways of thinking about the significance of those facts? Photography and telecommunications converged to mean that reality (real, material, physically tangible space) disappeared. A dramatic pronouncement that, at the very least, we may want to debate.

By selectively giving each fact a particular kind of significance (there are many others that he could have found), Weibel is making a case. Although it is more focused than the example we took from Rheingold's 'history' of VR, it is basically similar in that an argument is made in the form of a historical narrative. Within Weibel's 'history' he foregrounds and makes us think about some very important factors. Good, perceptive and well-researched stories have always done this.

However, at the same time, there are some big problems with Weibel's account if we take it as a credible historical account without asking further questions about its implications. This is because he does not tell us why and how the apparent unfolding of events takes place. What drives this march of media from machine-aided production of material images (photography) to the simulation of 'artificial and natural worlds', and even the coming simulation of the 'brain itself'? What, in this pattern of seamless evolution, has he detected? How was the bloom of interactive 'telematic civilisation' always contained in the seed of photography?

Historical narratives of the kind that Rheingold and Weibel tell are forms of teleological argument. These are arguments in which the nature of the past is explained as a preparation for the present. The present is understood as being prefigured in the past and is the culmination of it. Such arguments seek to explain how things are in terms of their 'ends' (their outcomes or the purposes, aims and intentions that we feel they embody) rather than in prior causes. There have been many versions of such teleological historical explanation, beginning with those that saw the world as the outcome of God's design, through various kinds of secular versions of grand design, of cosmic forces, the unfolding of a world soul, through to dialectical explanation in which the present state of things is traceable to a long historical interplay of opposites and contradictions which inevitably move on toward a resolution. Related, if slightly less deterministically teleological, versions of historical explanation think in terms of history as a process of problem solving. Often a kind of relay race of great geniuses, in which each one takes up the questions left by their predecessors and, in each case, it is implied that the project is somehow communicated across and carried on over centuries of time as the final answer is sought.

Such attempts to find a (teleo)logic in history were strong in the nineteenth century, particularly in Western Europe and North America. Here, a dominant sense of optimism and faith in the progress of industry and science encouraged the view that history (as the growth, evolution and maturing of human societies) was drawing to a close.

Operating over very different timescales, both Rheingold and Weibel continue to tell stories about the rise of new media by adopting a kind of historical perspective which is as old as the hills. There is something of a paradox in the way in which new media have rapidly been provided with histories of a rather naive and uncritical (we are tempted to say old-fashioned) kind.

While we have stressed the importance of historical knowledge and research to understanding the contemporary field of new media, it does not, in our view, readily include these kinds of **teleology** which can be highly misleading in their grand sweep and the way in which they place new media, far too simply, as the end point of a long process of historical development.

Seeing the limits of new media teleologies

We now look at a third and recent contribution to the history of new media. This is a historical overview, in which Paul Mayer identifies the 'seminal ideas and technical developments' that lead to the development of computer media and communication. He traces the key concepts which lead from an abstract system of logic, through the development of calculating machines, to the computer as a 'medium' which can 'extend new possibilities for expressions, communication, and interaction in everyday life' (Mayer 1999: 321).

The important point for our present discussion is that as Mayer's thorough historical outline of 'pivotal conceptual insights' proceeds, we can also see how other histories that are quite distinct from that of the conceptual and technical development of computing itself are entwined with the one he traces. At various points in his history, doors are opened through which we glimpse other factors. These factors do not contribute directly to the development of computer media, but they indicate how quite other spheres of activity, taking place for other reasons, have played an essential but contingent part in the history of new media. We will take two examples.

In the first section of his history Mayer traces the long history of conceptual and practical leaps which led to the building of the first mainframe computers in the 1940s. He begins his history with the project of the late seventeenth-century philosopher, Leibniz, to formulate a way of reasoning logically by matching concepts with numbers, and his efforts to devise a 'universal logic machine' (Mayer 1999: 4). He then points to a whole range of other philosophical, mathematical, mechanical, and electronic achievements occurring in the 300-year period between the 1660s and the 1940s. The history leads us to the ideas and practical experiments in hypermedia carried out by Vannevar Bush and Ted Nelson (**1.2.3**) in the mid-twentieth century. It is a history which focuses on that part of technological development that involves envisioning: the capacity to think and imagine possibilities from given resources.

1.2.3 Hypertext

Clearly, many of these achievements, especially the earlier ones, were not directed at developing the computer as a medium as we would understand it. Such a use of the computer was not part of the eighteenth- and nineteenth-century frame of reference: it was not a conceivable or imaginable project. As Mayer points out, Leibniz had the intellectual and philosophical ambitions of his period (the late seventeenth and early eighteenth centuries) as one of the 'thinkers who advanced comprehensive philosophical systems during the Age of Reason' with its interest in devising logical scientific systems of thought which had universal validity (Mayer 1999: 4). Neither were our modern ideas about the interpersonal communications and visual-representational possibilities of the computer in view during the nineteenth-century phase of the Industrial Revolution. At this time the interest in computing was rooted in the need for calculation, 'in navigation, engineering, astronomy, physics' as the demands of these activities threatened to overwhelm the human capacity to calculate. (This last factor is an interesting reversal of the need that Vannevar Bush saw some 100 years later, in the 1950s, for a machine and a system that would augment the human capacity to cope with an overload of data and information [**1.2.3**].)

1.2.3 Hypertext

Hence, as we follow Mayer's historical account of key figures and ideas in the history of computing, we also see how the conceptual development of the modern computer as medium took place for quite other reasons. At the very least these include the projects of eighteenth-century philosophers, nineteenth-century industrialisation, trade and colonisation, and an early twentieth-century need to manage statistics for the governance and control of complex societies. As Mayer identifies, it is only in the 1930s when, alongside Turing's concept of 'the universal machine' which would automatically process any kind of symbol and not just numbers, the moment arrives in which, 'the right combination of concepts, technology and political will colluded to launch the construction of machines recognisable today as computers in the modern sense' (1999: 9). In short, while Mayer traces a set of chronological connections between 'pivotal concepts' in the history of computing, we are also led to see:

1   That the preconditions were being established for something that was not yet conceived or foreseen: the computer as a medium.

2   That even the conceptual history of computing, formally presented as a sequence of ideas and experiments, implies that other histories impact upon that development.

To sum up, we are led to see that a major factor in the development of computer media is the eventual impact of one set of technologies and practices – those of computing numbers – on other sets: these being social and personal practices of communication and aural, textual and visual forms of representation. In short, a set of technological and conceptual developments which were undertaken for one set of reasons (and even these, as we have seen, were not stable and sustained, as the philosophical gave way to the industrial and the commercial, and then the informational) have eventually come to transform a range of image and communication media. It is also apparent that this happened in ways that were completely unlooked for. New image and communications media were not anticipated by the thinkers, researchers, technologists and the wider societies to which they belonged, during the period between the eighteenth and the mid-twentieth century in which digital computing develops (Mayer 1999).

If this first example begins to show how teleological accounts obscure and distort the real historical contingency of computer media, our second example returns us to the greater historical complexity of what are now called new media. Mayer's focus is on the computer as a medium itself: the symbol-manipulating, networked machine through which we communicate with others, play games, explore databases and produce texts. Returning to our initial breakdown of the range of phenomena that new media refers to (**1.1**), we must remind ourselves that this is not all that new media has come to stand for. Computer-mediated communication, Mayer's specific interest, is only one key element within a broader media landscape that includes convergences, hybridisations, transformations, and displacements within and between all forms of older media. These media, such as print, telecommunications, photography, film, television and radio, have, of course, their own, and in some cases long, histories. In the last decades of the twentieth century these histories of older media become precisely the kinds of factors that began to impact upon the development of computer media, just as the demands of navigators or astronomers for more efficient means of calculating did in the nineteenth.

This is a vital point as Mayer's historical sketch of the conceptual development of the computer ends, with Alan Kay and Adele Goldberg's 1977 prototype for an early personal computer named the 'Dynabook'. He observes that the 'Dynabook' was conceived by its designers as 'a metamedium, or a technology with the broadest capabilities to simulate and expand the functionality and power of other forms of mediated expression' (Mayer 1999: 20). Kay and Goldberg themselves make the point somewhat more directly when they write that 'the computer, viewed as a medium itself, can be all other media'. In the late 1970s, Kay and Goldberg's vision of the media that the Dynabook would 'metamediate' was restricted to text, painting and drawing, animation and music. (Subsequently, of course, with increased memory capacity and software developments, the 'other media' forms which the computer 'can be' would include photography, film, video and TV.)

On the face of it, this seems simple enough. What Kay and Goldberg are saying is that the computer as a 'medium' is able to simulate other media. However, both they and Mayer, in his history, seem to assume that this is unproblematic. As Mayer puts it, one of the great things about the Dynabook as a prototype computer medium, is that it is an 'inspiring realisation of Leibniz's generality of symbolic representation' (1999: 21) due to its ability to reduce all signs and languages – textual, visual, aural – to a binary code (**1.2.1**). It does a great deal more besides, of course: it 'expand[s] upon the functionality and power of other forms of mediated expression' (1999: 20). However, this convergence and interaction of many previously separate media actually makes the picture far more complicated. We have to remind ourselves that this range of 'old' media, that the

1.1   What are new media?

1.2.1   Digitality

computer carries and simulates, have in turn their own histories. Ones which parallel, and in some cases are far older than that of the computer.

The media which the computer 'simulates and expands' are also the result of conceptual and technical, as well as cultural and economic, histories which have shaped them in certain ways. In an expanded version of Mayer's history, space would need to be made for the ways in which these traditional media forms contributed to thinking about the Dynabook concept itself. For, if we are to understand the complex forms of new media it is not enough to think only in terms of what the computer might have offered to do for 'other forms of mediated expression' but also to ask how these other media forms shaped the kind of 'metamediating' that Goldberg and Kay envisaged. The universal symbol-manipulating capacity of the computer could not, itself, determine the forms and aesthetics of the computer medium. This is because the very media that the computer (as medium) incorporates (or metamediates) are not neutral elements: they are social and signifying practices. We would want to know, for instance, what the outcomes of other histories – the conventions of drawing, the genres of animation, the trust in photographic realism, the narrative forms of text and video, and the languages of typography and graphic design, etc. – brought to this new metamedium. These are, in fact, the very issues which have come to exercise practitioners and theorists of new media, and which the various parts of this book discuss.

Foucault and genealogies of new media

A widely read theorist of new media, Mark Poster, has suggested:

> The question of the new requires a historical problematic, a temporal and spatial framework in which there are risks of setting up the new as a culmination, telos or fulfillment of the old, as the onset of utopia or **dystopia**. The conceptual problem is to enable a historical differentiation of old and new without initialising a totalising narrative. Foucault's proposal of a genealogy, taken over from Nietzsche, offers the most satisfactory resolution.
>
> (Poster 1999: 12)

In this way, Poster sums up the problems we have been discussing. How do we envisage the relationship of new and old media over time, sequentially, and in space (what kind of co-existence or relationship with each other and where?) without assuming that new media bring old media to some kind of concluding state for good or bad? How do we differentiate between them without such sweeping, universalising schemas as we met above? Foucault's concept of genealogy is his answer.

Jay Bolter and Richard Grusin, whom we have met briefly above (see **1.2.3**, **1.4.1**), introduce their book on new media, entitled *Remediation*, with an explicit acknowledgement of their debt to Foucault's method:

1.2.3 Hypertext
1.4.1 Teleological accounts of new media

> The two logics of remediation have a long history, for their interplay defines a genealogy that dates back at least to the Renaissance and the invention of linear perspective. Note 1: Our notion of genealogy is indebted to Foucault's, for we too are looking for historical affiliations or resonances, and not of origins. Foucault . . . characterised genealogy as 'an examination of descent', which 'permits the discovery, under the unique aspect of a trait or a concept of the myriad events through which – thanks to which, against which – they were formed'.
>
> (Bolter and Grusin 1999: 21)

How does an idea or a practice, which for Bolter and Grusin is the concept and practice of remediation (the way that one medium absorbs and transforms another), reach us (descend)? What multiple factors have played a part in shaping that process?

We should note that Poster is particularly keen to avoid thinking of history as a process with a 'culmination' and end point. Bolter and Grusin, like Foucault, are not interested in the origins of things. They are not interesting in where things began or where they finished. They are interested in 'affiliations' (the attachments and connections between things) and 'resonances' (the sympathetic vibrations between things). They want to know about the 'through' and 'against' of things. Instead of images of linear sequences and chains of events we need to think in terms of webs, clusters, boundaries, territories, and overlapping spheres as our images of historical process.

Theorists of new media seeking alternative ways of thinking about the differences and the complex connections between old and new media have drawn upon the influential 'genealogical' theory of history, as argued and put into practice in a number of major

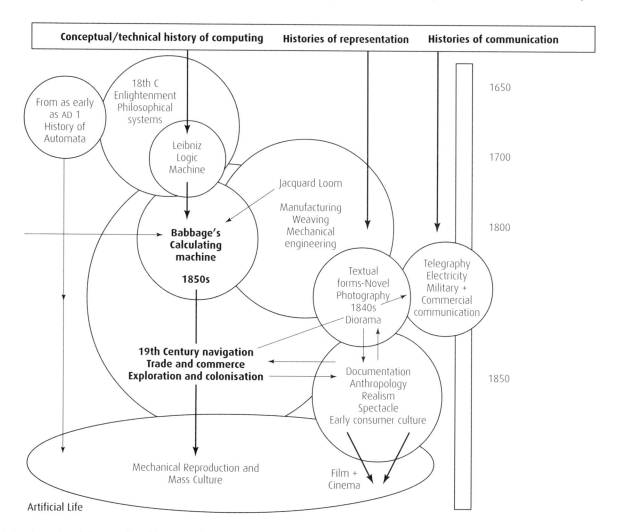

1.2 A simple model of the complex of histories 'through' and 'against' which new media emerge.

works of cultural history by the philosopher-historian Michel Foucault. It is a historical method which offers the possibility of thinking through new media's relationship to the past while avoiding some of the problems we have met above. In doing this, theorists of new media are following in the footsteps of other historians of photography, film, cinema and visual culture such as John Tagg (1998), Jonathan Crary (1993) and Geoffrey Batchen (1997) who have used what has become known as a 'Foucauldian' perspective.

1.4.2 New media and the modernist concept of progress

the full aesthetic potential of this medium will be realised only when computer artists come to the instrument from art rather than computer science. . . . Today the kind of simulation envisioned . . . requires a $10 million Cray-1 supercomputer, the most powerful computer in the world . . . [T]he manufacturers of the Cray-1 believe that by the early 1990s computers with three-fourths of its power will sell for approximately $20,000 less than the cost of a portapak and editing system today . . . [F]inally accessible to autonomous individuals, the full aesthetic potential of computer simulation will be revealed, and the future of cinematic languages . . . will be rescued from the tyranny of perceptual imperialists and placed in the hands of artists and amateurs.

(Youngblood 1999: 48)

In the name of 'progress' our official culture is striving to force the new media to do the work of the old.

(McLuhan and Fiore 1967a: 81)

In order to conceive a properly genealogical account of new media histories we need not only to take account of the particular teleologies of technohistory above but also the deeply embedded experience of **modernism** within aesthetics.

Commentators on new media, like Gene Youngblood, frequently refer to a future point in time when their promise will be realised. Thought about new media is replete with a sense of a deferred future. We are repeatedly encouraged to await the further development of the technologies which they utilise. At times this takes the simple form of the 'when we have the computing power' type of argument. Here, the present state of technological (under)development is said to constrain what is possible and explains the gap between the potential and actual performance.

Related to views of this kind, there are some which embody a particular kind of theory about historical change. It is not technological underdevelopment *per se* that is blamed for the failure of a new medium to deliver its promise; rather, the culprit is seen to be ingrained cultural resistance. Here, the proposal is that in their early phases new media are bound to be used and understood according to older, existing practices and ideas, and that it is largely such ideological and cultural factors that limit the potential of new media. (See also **1.6.**) The central premiss here is that each medium has its own kind of essence; that is, some unique and defining characteristic or characteristics which will, given time and exploration, be clearly revealed. As they are revealed the medium comes into its own. This kind of argument adds ideas about the nature of media and culture to the simpler argument about technological underdevelopment.

Such a view has quite a long history itself, as will be seen in the example from the pioneering writer on 'expanded' cinema, Gene Youngblood, quoted at the beginning of

1.6 New media: determining or determined?

this section. Writing in 1984, in an essay on the then emerging possibilities of digital video and cinema (in Druckery 1999), he looks forward to the 1990s when he foresees affordable computers coming to possess the kind of power that, at his time of writing, was only to be found in the $10 million Cray-1 mainframe supercomputer. Then, in a clear example of the modernist argument that we have outlined, he adds that we must also look forward to the time when the 'full aesthetic potential of the computer simulation will be revealed', as it is rescued from 'the tyranny of perceptual imperialists' (in Druckery, 1999: 48). Such imperialists being, we can assume, those scientists, artists and producers who impose their old habits of vision and perception upon the new media (see **2.6.3**).

2.6.3   Spheres collide: from imitation to simulation – VR's operational history

In a more recent example, Steve Holzmann (1997: 15) also takes the view that most existing uses of new media fail to 'exploit those special qualities that are unique to digital worlds'. Again, this is because he sees them as having as yet failed to break free of the limits of 'existing paradigms' or historical forms and habits. He, too, looks forward to a time when new media transcend the stage when they are used to fulfil old purposes and when digital media's 'unique qualities' come to 'define entirely new languages of expression'.

As Bolter and Grusin have argued (1999: 49–50), Holzmann (and Youngblood before him in our other example) represents the modernist viewpoint. They believe that for a medium to be significantly new it has to make a radical break with the past.

A major source of such ideas is to be found in one of the seminal texts of artistic modernism: the 1961 essay 'Modernist Painting' by art critic and theorist Clement Greenberg. Although the new, digital media are commonly understood as belonging to a *post*-modern period, in which the cultural projects of modernism are thought to have been superseded, Greenbergian ideas have continued to have a considerable pull on thinking about new media. Clearly, the point of connection is between the sense that new media are at the cutting edge of culture, that there is an opening up of new horizons and a need for experimentation, and the ideology of the earlier twentieth-century artistic avant-garde movements in painting, photography, sculpture, film and video.

We meet these modernist ideas whenever we hear talk of the need for new media to break clear of old habits and attitudes, the gravity field of history and its old thought patterns and practices. It is also present when we hear talk about the essential characteristics of new media; when the talk is of the distinctive *essence* of 'digitality' as against the 'photographic', the 'filmic' or the 'televisual' (**1.2**).

1.2   The characteristics of new media: some defining concepts

Greenberg himself did not think that modern art media should or could break with the past in any simple sense. But he did think they should engage in a process of clarifying and refining their nature by not attempting to do what was not proper to them. This process of refinement included ditching old historical functions that a medium might have served in the past. Painting was the medium that interested him in particular, and his efforts were part of his search to identify the importance of the painting in an age of mechanical reproduction – the age of the then relatively 'new' media of photography and film. He argued that painting should rid itself of its old illustrative or narrative functions to concentrate on its formal patterning of colour and surface. Photography was better suited to illustrative work and showed how it was not, after all, appropriate to painting. Painting could now realise its true nature.

Greenberg also made his arguments in the mid twentieth-century context of a critique of the alienating effects of capitalism on cultural experience. He shared with other critics the view that the heightened experiences that art had traditionally provided were being eroded and displaced by a levelling down to mere 'entertainment' and popular kitsch (see

1.5.5). He argued that the arts could save their higher purpose from this fate 'by demonstrating that the kind of experience they provided was valuable in its own right and not obtained from any other kind of activity' (Greenberg 1961, in Harrison & Wood 1992: 755). He urged that this could be done by each art determining, 'through the operations peculiar to itself, the effects peculiar and exclusive to itself' (ibid.). By these means each art would exhibit and make explicit 'that which was unique and irreducible' to it (ibid.). The task of artists, then, was to search for the fundamental essence of their medium, stripping away all extraneous factors and borrowings from other media. It is often thought that this task now falls to new media artists and forward-looking experimental producers.

However, the manner in which a new medium necessarily adopts, in its early years, the conventions and 'languages' of established media is well known. There is the case of the early photographers known as the Pictorialists, who strove to emulate the aesthetic qualities of painting, seeing these as the standards against which photography as a medium had to be judged. In Youngblood's terms they would be examples of 'perceptual imperialists' who acted as a brake on the exploration of the radical representational possibilities afforded by photography as a new medium. Similarly, it is well known that early cinema adopted the conventions of the theatre and vaudeville, and that television looked for its forms to theatre, vaudeville, the format of the newspaper, and cinema itself.

As we have seen, Bolter and Grusin's theory of 'remediation' (1999) deploys a Foucauldian historical perspective to argue against the 'comfortable modernist rhetoric' of authentic media 'essences' and 'breaks with the past' that we have discussed here. They follow McLuhan's insight that 'the content of a medium is always another medium' (1999: 45). They propose that the history of media is a complex process in which all media, including new media, depend upon older media and are in a constant dialectic with them (1999: 50). Digital media are in the process of representing older media in a whole range of ways, some more direct and 'transparent' than others. At the same time, older media are refashioning themselves by absorbing, repurposing, and incorporating digital technologies (see **2.8**).

Such a process is also implied in the view held by Raymond Williams, whose theory of media change we discuss fully later (**1.6.3**). Williams argues that there is nothing inherent in the nature of a media technology that is responsible for the way a society uses it. It does not, and cannot, have an 'essence' that would inevitably create 'effects peculiar and exclusive to itself'. In a closely argued theory of the manner in which television developed, he observes that some 20 years passed before, 'new kinds of programme were being made for television and there were important advances in the productive use of the medium, including . . . some kinds of original work' (Williams 1974: 30). Productive uses of a new medium and original work in them are not precluded, therefore, by recognising their long-term interplay with older media.

We need, then, to ask a number of questions of the modernist and avant-garde calls for new media to define itself as radically novel. Do media proceed by a process of ruptures or decisive breaks with the past? Can a medium transcend its historical contexts to deliver an 'entirely new language'? Do, indeed, media have irreducible and unique essences (which is not quite the same as having distinguishing characteristics which encourage or constrain the kind of thing we do with them)? These seem to be especially important questions to ask of new digital media which, in large part, rely upon hybrids, convergences and transformations of older media (**2**).

1.5.5 The return of the Frankfurt School Critique in the popularisation of new media

2.8 Digital cinema

1.6.3 Williams and the social shaping of technology

2 NEW MEDIA AND VISUAL CULTURE

1.4.3 The return of the Middle Ages and other media archaeologies

This section looks at yet another historicising approach to new media studies; here, however, insights from our encounters with new media are drawn upon to rethink existing media histories. Such revisions imply a view of history that is far from teleological, or a basis in the belief in inevitable 'progress'. Unlike the previous examples we turn here to a kind of historical thinking that neither looks at new media as the fulfilment of the recent past nor does it assume a future time in which new media will inevitably transcend the old. Rather, it is suggested that certain uses and aesthetic forms of new media significantly recall residual or suppressed intellectual and representational practices of relatively, and in some cases extremely, remote historical periods. In the context of his own argument against 'sequential narratives' of change in image culture, Kevin Robins observes that:

> It is notable that much of the most interesting discussion of images now concerns not digital futures but, actually, what seemed until recently to be antique and forgotten media (the panorama, the camera obscura, the stereoscope): from our post-photographic vantage point these have suddenly acquired new meanings, and their re-evaluation now seems crucial to understanding the significance of digital culture.
>
> (Robins 1996: 165)

The ludic: cinema and games

A major example of this renewed interest in 'antique' media is in the early cinema of circa 1900–1920 and its prehistory in mechanical **spectacles** such as the panorama. Its source is in the way the structures, aesthetics and pleasures of computer games are being seen to represent a revival of qualities found in that earlier medium. It is argued that this 'cinema of attractions' was overtaken and suppressed by what became the dominant form of narrative cinema, exemplified by classical Hollywood in the 1930s–1950s. Now, at the beginning of the 21st century, changes in media production and in the pleasures sought in media consumption, exemplified in the form of the computer game and its crossovers with special effects 'blockbuster' cinema, indicate a return of the possibilities present in early cinema. These ideas and the research that supports them are discussed in more detail later (**2.8**). What is significant in the context of this section is the way that noticing things about new media has led some of its theorists to find remarkable historical parallels which cannot be contained within a methodology of technological progress.

2.8   Digital cinema

Rhetoric and spatialised memory

Benjamin Woolley, writing about Nicholas Negroponte's concept of 'spatial data management', exemplified in computer media's metaphorical **desktops**, and simulated 3D working environments, draws a parallel with the memorising strategies of ancient preliterate, oral cultures. He sees the icons and spaces of the computer screen recalling the 'mnemonic' traditions of classical and medieval Europe. Mnemonics is the art of using imaginary spaces or 'memory palaces' (spatial arrangements, buildings, objects, or painted representations of them) as aids to remembering long stories and complex arguments (Woolley 1992: 138–149). Similarly, with a focus on computer games, Nickianne Moody (1995) traces a related set of connections between the forms and aesthetics of role play games, interactive computer games and the allegorical narratives of the Middle Ages.

Edutainment and the eighteenth-century Enlightenment

Barbara Maria Stafford observes that with the increasingly widespread use of interactive computer graphics and educational software packages (**4.2.5**) we are returning to a kind of 'oral-visual culture' which was at the centre of European education and scientific experiment in the early eighteenth century (1994: xxv). Stafford argues that during the later eighteenth century, and across the nineteenth, written texts and mass literacy came to be the only respectable and trustworthy media of knowledge and education. Practical and the visual modes of enquiry, experiment, demonstration and learning fell into disrepute as seductive and unreliable. Now, with computer animation and modelling, virtual reality, and even email (as a form of discussion), Stafford sees the emergence of a 'new vision and visionary art-science', a form of visual education similar to that which arose in the early eighteenth century, 'on the boundaries between art and technology, game and experiment, image and speech' (ibid.). However, she argues, in order for our culture to guide itself through this 'electronic upheaval' (ibid.) we will need 'to go backward in order to go forward', in order to 'unearth a past material world that had once occupied the centre of a communications network but was then steadily pushed to the periphery' (ibid.: 3).

Stafford's case is more than a formal comparison between two periods when the oral, visual and practical dominate over the literary and textual. She also argues that the use of images and practical experiments, objects and apparatuses, that characterised early **Enlightenment** education coincided with the birth of middle-class leisure and early forms of consumer culture (1994: xxi). Stafford also suggests that our late twentieth- and early twenty-first-century anxieties about 'dumbing down' and 'edutainment' are echoed in eighteenth-century concerns to distinguish authentic forms of learning and scientific demonstration from quackery and charlatanism. Her argument, overall, is that the graphic materials of eighteenth-century education and scientific experiment were the 'ancestors of today's home- and place-based software and interactive technology' (ibid.: xxiii).

In each of these cases, history is not seen simply as a matter of linear chronology or unilinear progress in which the present is understood mainly as the superior development of the immediate past; rather, short-circuits and loops in historical time are conceived. Indeed, it chimes with the postmodern view that history (certainly social and cultural history) as a continuous process of progressive development has ceased. Instead, the past has become a vast reservoir of styles and possibilities that are permanently available for reconstruction and revival. The most cursory glance at contemporary architecture, interior design and fashion will show this process of retroactive culture recycling in action.

We can also make sense of this relation between chronologically remote times and the present through the idea that a culture contains dominant, residual, and emergent elements (Williams 1977: 121–127). Using these concepts, Williams argues that elements in a culture that were once dominant may become residual but do not necessarily disappear. They become unimportant and peripheral to a culture's major concerns but are still available as resources which can be used to challenge and resist dominant cultural practices and values at another time. We might note, in this connection, how cyber-fiction and fantasy repeatedly dresses up its visions of the future in medieval imagery. The future is imagined in terms of the past. As Moody puts it:

4.2.5 Edutainment edutainment edutainment

> Much fantasy fiction shares a clearly defined quasi-medieval diegesis. One that fits snugly into Umberto Eco's categorisation of the 'new middle ages' . . . For Eco it would be entirely logical that the 'high tech' personal computer is used to play dark and labyrinthine games with a medieval diegesis.
>
> (Moody 1995: 61)

For Robins, the significance of these renewed interests in the past, driven by current reflections on new media, is that they allow us to think in non-teleological ways about the past and to recognise what 'modern culture has repressed and disavowed' (1996: 161) in its overriding and often exclusive or blind concern for technological rationalism. The discovery of the kind of historical precedents for new media which our examples stand for, may, in his terms, be opportunities for grasping that new media are not best thought of as the narrow pinnacle of technological progress. Rather, they are evidence of a more complex and richer co-existence of cultural practices that the diverse possibilities of new media throw into fresh relief.

1.4.4 A sense of *déjà vu*

The **utopian**, as well as **dystopian**, terms in which new media have been received have caused several media historians to record a sense of *déjà vu*, the feeling that we have been here before. In particular, the quite remarkable utopian claims made for earlier new media technologies such as photography and cinema have been used to contextualise the widespread technophilia of the contemporary moment (e.g. Dovey 1995: 111). So, the history in question this time is not that of the material forerunners of new image and communication media themselves but of the terms in which societies responded to and
1.5   Who was dissatisfied with old media?
discussed earlier 'media revolutions'. This is discussed more fully later (**1.5**).

Two kinds of historical enquiry are relevant here. The first is to be found in the existing body of media history, such as: literacy (Ong 1982), the printing press (Eisenstein 1979), the book (Chartier 1994), photography (Tagg 1998), film and television (Williams 1974). These long-standing topics of historical research provide us with detailed empirical knowledge of what we broadly refer to as earlier 'media revolutions'. They also represent sustained efforts to grasp the various patterns of determination, and the surprising outcomes of the introductions, over the long term, of new media into particular societies, cultures and economies. While it is not possible to transfer our understanding of the 'coming of the book' or of 'the birth of photography' directly and wholesale to a study of the cultural impact of the computer, because the wider social context in which each occurs is different (**1.5**), such studies provide us with indispensable methods and frameworks to guide us in working out how new technologies become media, and with what outcomes.

Second, a more recent development has been historical and ethnographic research into our imaginative investment in new technologies, the manner in which we respond to their appearance in our lives, and the ways in which the members of a culture repurpose and subvert media in everyday use (regardless of the purposes which their inventors and developers saw for them). This is also discussed more fully in (**1.5**), where we deal with
1.5.2   The technological imaginary
the concept of the 'technological imaginary'(1.5.2).

1.4.5 Conclusion

Paradoxically, then, it is precisely our sense of the 'new' in new media which makes history so important – in the way that something so current, rapidly changing and running toward the future also calls us back to the past. This analytic position somewhat challenges the idea that new media are 'postmodern' media; that is, media that arise from, and then contribute to, a set of socio-cultural developments which are thought to mark a significant break with history, with the 'modern' industrial period and its forerunner in the eighteenth-century age of Enlightenment. We have seen that thinking in terms of a simple separation of the present and the recent past (the postmodern) from the 'modern' period may obscure as much as it reveals about new media. We have argued instead for a history that allows for the continuation of certain media traditions through 'remediation', as well as the revisiting and revival of suppressed or disregarded historical moments in order to understand contemporary developments. Our review of (new) media histories is based in the need to distinguish between what may be new about our contemporary media and what they share with other media, and between what they *can* do and what is ideological in our reception of new media. In order to be able to disregard what Langdon Winner has called 'mythinformation' we have argued that history has never been so important for the student of media.

1.5 WHO WAS DISSATISFIED WITH OLD MEDIA?

> We live in this very weird time in history where we're passive recipients of a very immature, noninteractive broadcast medium. Mission number one is to kill TV.
>
> (Jaron Lanier, quoted in Boddy 1994: 116)

> Photographers will be freed from our perpetual restraint, that of having . . . to record the reality of things, . . . freed at last from being the mere recorders of reality, our creativity will be given free rein.
>
> (Laye, quoted in Robins 1991: 56)

1.5.1 The question

The question that forms the title of this section is asked in order to raise a critical issue – what is the problem to which new communications media are the solution? In thinking about such a question we will find ourselves considering the discursive frameworks that establish the conditions of possibility for new media. This in turn will allow us to look at some of the ways in which previously 'new' media have been considered in order to understand the discursive formations present in our contemporary moment of novelty.

In the rumours and early literature about the coming of multimedia and virtual reality, and as soon as new media forms themselves began to appear, they were celebrated as overcoming, or at least as having the promise to overcome, the negative limits and even the oppressive features of established and culturally dominant analogue media. As the above statements about television and photography imply, in the reception of new media there was, and still is, an implication that we *needed* them in order to overcome the limits of the old.

On this basis it could seem reasonable to ask whether media were in such bad odour in pre-digital days, that a mass of criticisms formed a body of pressure such that something better was sought. Or, alternatively, we might ask if ideas about the superiority of new media are merely retrospective projections or *post-hoc* rationalisations of change; simply a case of being able to say that what we have is better than what went before.

However, these questions are too reductive to arrive at an understanding of how our perceptions and experiences of new media are framed. In order to arrive at a better explanation, this section considers how the development and reception of new media have been shaped by two sets of ideas. First, the socio-psychological workings of the 'technological imaginary'; second, earlier twentieth-century traditions of media critique aimed at the 'mass' broadcast media and their perceived social effects. We will be interested in these traditions to the extent that they are picked up and used in the evaluation of new media.

1.5.2 The technological imaginary

The phrase the 'technological imaginary', as it is used in critical thought about cinema in the first place (De Lauretis et al. 1980) and now new media technologies, has roots in psychoanalytic theory. It has migrated from that location to be more generally used in the study of culture and technology. In some versions it has been recast in more sociological language and is met as a 'popular' or 'collective' imagination about technologies (Flichy 2000). Here, tendencies that may have been originally posited (in psychoanalytical theory) as belonging to individuals are also observed to be present at the level of social groups and collectivities. However, some of the specific charge that the word has in psychoanalytic theory needs to be retained to see its usefulness. The French adjective *imaginaire* became a noun, a name for a substantive order of experience, *the imaginaire*, alongside two others – the 'real' and the 'symbolic' in the psychoanalytic theories of Jacques Lacan. After Lacan, *imaginaire* or the English 'imaginary' does not refer, as it does in everyday use, to a kind of poetic mental faculty or the activity of fantasising (Ragland-Sullivan 1992: 173–176). Rather, in psychoanalytic theory, it refers to a realm of images, representations, ideas and intuitions of fulfilment, of wholeness and completeness that human beings, in their fragmented and incomplete selves, desire to become. These are images of an 'other' – an other self, another race, gender, or significant other person, another state of being. Technologies are then cast in the role of such an 'other'. When applied to technology, or media technologies in particular, the concept of a technological imaginary draws attention to the way that (frequently gendered) dissatisfactions with social reality and desires for a better society are projected onto technologies as capable of delivering a potential realm of completeness.

This can seem a very abstract notion. **Case studies** show how, in different ways, new media are catalysts or vehicles for the expression of ideas about human existence and social life. We can begin to do this by reminding ourselves of some typical responses to the advent of new media and by considering the recurring sense of optimism and anxiety that each wave of new media calls up.

As a new medium becomes socially available it is necessarily placed in relation to a culture's older media forms and the way that these are already valued and understood. This is seen in expressions of a sense of anxiety at the loss of the forms that are displaced. Well-known examples of this include the purist fears about the impact of photography on painting in the 1840s, and of television and then video on cinema in the 1970s. More recently, regret has been expressed about the impact of digital imaging on photography

(Ritchen 1990) and graphics software on drawing and design as they moved from the traditional craft spaces of the darkroom and the drawing board to the computer screen. In terms of communication media this sense of loss is usually expressed in social, rather than aesthetic or craft terms. For instance, during the last quarter of the nineteenth century it was feared that the telephone would invade the domestic privacy of the family or that it would break through important settled social hierarchies, allowing the lower classes to speak (inappropriately) to their 'betters' in ways that were not permitted in traditional face-to-face encounters (Marvin 1988). (See **Case study 1.5**.) A more recent example is the anxiety that email eradicates the time for reflection and considered response to messages that was a feature of traditional terrestrial mail (See **Case study 1.2**).

Conversely, during the period in which the cultural reception of a new medium is being worked out, it is *also* favourably positioned in relation to existing media. The euphoric celebration of a new medium and the often feverish speculation about its potential is achieved, at least in part, by its favourable contrast with older forms. In their attempts to persuade us to invest in the technology advertisers often use older media as an 'other' against which the 'new' is given an identity as good, as socially and aesthetically progressive. This kind of comparison draws upon more than the hopes that a culture has for its new media, it also involves its existing feelings about the old (Robins 1996).

Traditional chemical photography has played such a role in recent celebrations of digital imaging (see Lister 1995; Robins 1995), as has television in the talking-up of interactive media. Before the emergence and application of digital technologies, TV, for instance, was widely perceived as a 'bad object' and this ascription has been important as a foil to celebrations of interactive media's superiority over broadcast television (Boddy 1994; see also **Case study 1.5**). Television is associated with passivity, encapsulated in the image of the TV viewer as an inert 'couch potato' subject to its 'effects', while the interactive media 'user' (already a name which connotes a more active relation to media than does 'viewer') conjures up an image of someone occupying an ergonomically designed, hi-tech swivel chair, alert and skilled as they 'navigate' and make active choices via their screen-based interface. Artists, novelists, and technologists entice us with the prospect of creating and living in virtual worlds of our own making rather than being anonymous and passive members of the 'mass' audience of popular television. As a broadcast medium, TV is seen as an agent for the transmission of centralised (read authoritarian or incontestable) messages to mass audiences. This is then readily compared to the new possibilities of the one-to-one, two-way, decentralised transmissions of the internet or the new possibilities for narrowcasting and interactive TV. Similar kinds of contrast have been made between non-linear, hot-linked, hypertext and the traditional form of the book which, in this new comparison, becomes 'the big book' (like this one), a fixed, dogmatic text which is the prescriptive voice of authority.

So, a part of understanding the conditions in which new media are received and evaluated involves (1) seeing what values a culture has already invested in old media, and this may involve considering whose values these were, and (2) understanding how the concrete objects (books, TV sets, computers) and the products (novels, soap operas, games) of particular media come to have good or bad cultural connotations in the first place (see **Case studies 1.5, 1.6**). In order to do this we first consider how apparent the technological imaginary is in the ways we talk and write about media.

Case study 1.4   New media as arenas for discussing old problems

ase study 1.2   Email: the problem of the digital letter

Case study 1.5   The technological imaginary and the culture reception of new media

Case study 1.5   New media as arenas for discussing old problems

Case study 1.6   The technological imaginary and the culture reception of new media

1.5.3 The discursive construction of new media

> It is essential to realise that a theory does not find its object sitting waiting for it in the world: theories constitute their own objects in the process of their evolution. 'Water' is not the same theoretical object in chemistry as it is in hydraulics – an observation which in no way denies that chemists and engineers alike drink, and shower in, the same substance.
>
> (Burgin 1982: 9)

Victor Burgin offers this example of the way that the nature of a common object of concern – water – will be differently understood according to the specific set of concepts which are used to study it. A key argument of post-structuralist theory is that language does not merely describe a pre-given reality (words are matched to things) but that reality is only known through language (the words or concepts we possess lead us to perceive and conceive the world in their terms). Language, in this sense, can be thought of as operating as microscopes, telescopes and cameras do – they produce certain kinds of images of the world; they construct ways of seeing and understanding. Elaborated systems of language (conversations, theories, arguments, descriptions) which are built up or evolved as part of particular social projects (expressing emotion, writing legal contracts, analysing social behaviour, etc.) are called discourses. Discourses, like the words and concepts they employ, can then be said to construct their objects. It is in this sense that we now turn to the discursive construction of new media as it feeds (frames, provides the resources for) the technological imagination.

1.3 Change and continuity
1.4 What kind of history?

In sections **1.3** and **1.4** we considered some ways in which histories of media form part of our contemporary responses to new media. On meeting the many claims and predictions made for new media, media historians have expressed a sense of déjà vu – of having 'seen this' or 'been here' before (Gunning 1991). This is more than a matter of history repeating itself. This would amount to saying that the emergence and development of each new medium occurs and proceeds technologically and socio-economically in the same way, and that the same patterns of response are evident in the members of the culture who receive, use and consume it. There are, indeed, some marked similarities of this kind, but it would be too simple to leave the matter there. To do this would simply hasten us to the 'business as usual' conclusion which we have rejected as conservative and inadequate (**1.1** and **1.3**). More importantly, it would be wrong. For, even if there are patterns that recur in the technological emergence and development of new media technologies, we have to recognise that they occur in widely different historical and social contexts. Furthermore, the technologies in question have different capacities and characteristics.

1.1 What are new media?

1.3 Change and continuity

For example, similarities are frequently pointed out between the emergence of film technology and the search for cinematic form at the end of the nineteenth century and that of multimedia and VR at the end of the twentieth century. However, film and cinema entered a world of handmade images and early kinds of still photographic image (at that time, a difficult craft), of venue-based, mechanically produced theatrical spectacles in which the 'movement' and special effects on offer were experienced as absolutely novel and would seem primitive by today's standards. There was no broadcasting, and even the telephone was a novel apparatus. And, of course, much wider factors could be pointed to: the state of development of mass industrial production and consumer culture, of general education, etc. The world into which our new media have emerged is very different; it has

For compelling, but very different accounts of common patterns of media development see Winston (1998) and Bolter & Grusin (1999). Where Winston offers a thesis on the material history of media development and Bolter & Grusin a thesis on the aesthetics of media development, neither deal with the discursive framework of the technological imaginary which seems to us particularly potent in the contemporary situation

seen a hundred years of increasingly pervasive and sophisticated technological visual culture (Darley 1991).

It is a world in which images, still and moving, in print and on screens, are layered so thick, are so intertextual, that a sense of what is real has become problematic, buried under the thick sediment of its visual representations. New media technologies which emerge into this context enter an enormously complex moving image culture of developed genres, signifying conventions, audiences with highly developed and 'knowing' pleasures and ways of 'reading' images, and a major industry and entertainment economy which is very different from, even if it has antecedents in, that of the late nineteenth century.

What then gives rise to the sense of *déjà vu* mentioned above? It is likely that it does not concern the actual historical repetition of technologies or mediums themselves – rather, it is a matter of the repetition of deeply ingrained ways in which we think, talk, and write about new image and communication technologies. In short, their discursive construction. Whatever the actual and detailed paths taken by a new media technology in its particular historical context of complex determinations (the telephone, the radio, TV, etc.) it is a striking matter of record that the responses of contemporaries (professionals in their journals, journalists, academic and other commentators) are cast in uncannily similar terms (Marvin 1988; Spigel 1992; Boddy 1994).

In noticing these things, the experience of loss with the displacement of the old, the simultaneous judgement of the old as limited, and a sense of repetition in how media and technological change is talked and written about, we are ready to consider some more detailed examples of the 'technological imaginary' at work.

For a clear example see Lev Manovich (2000) 'What is digital cinema' in P. Lunenfeld (ed.) *The Digital Dialectic: essays on new media*, Cambridge, Mass.: MIT Press, 2000. Manovich points out that while close parallels can be found between the late nineteenth-century development of a cinematic language and late twentieth-century developments in the manipulation of music video and CD-ROM games, there is also a difference. In the late nineteenth century early cinema was 'developing toward the still open horizon of many possibilities' (Manovich 2000: 187), while the development of commercial multimedia is precisely driven by the goal of achieving cinematic realism. Realism, only one of the many possibilities explored in the era of early film, is now the goal which computer hardware and storage formats like DVD strive to make possible

Spigel (1992) reports a feeling of historiographic *déjà vu*. The point she notes, however, 'is not to argue that history repeats itself, but rather that the discursive conventions for thinking about communication strategies are very much the same . . . our culture still speaks about new communication technologies in remarkably similar ways (p. 182)'

CASE STUDY 1.4: The technological imaginary and the 'new media order'

Key text: Kevin Robins, 'A touch of the unknown', in K. Robins (1996) *Into the Image*, Routledge, London and New York.

> Entering cyberspace is the closest we can come to returning to the Wild West . . . the wilderness never lasts long – you had better enjoy it before it disappears.
>
> (Taylor and Saarinen 1994: 10)

As we have seen, a broad definition of the 'technological imaginary' refers us to the way that new technologies are taken up within a culture and are hooked into, or have projected onto them, its wider social and psychological desires and fears. Kevin Robins has applied the ideas of the psychoanalyst Wilfred Bion and other philosophers and political theorists to argue this case. He has returned to this theme in a number of essays dealing with new media and cyberculture, especially VR and new image and vision technologies (Robins 1996). In these essays he seeks to show how the dominant way in which we are asked to understand new media is exclusively driven by utopian, rationalist and transcendental impulses to escape the difficulties of social reality, and that these have deep roots in Western capitalist societies:

The new image and information culture is now associated with a renewed confidence in technological solutions to the problems of human culture and existence. The new technologies have revitalised the utopian aspirations in the modern techno-rationalist project. The progressivist and utopian spirit is articulated through ordinary, spontaneous and commonsensical accounts of what is happening: through the culture, there is a sense of almost limitless possibilities inherent in the "cyber-revolution". *Indeed, such is the dominant technological imaginary, that it is almost impossible to discuss the new techno-culture in any other way.*

(Robins 1996: 13; emphasis added)

He argues that behind the transcendental rhetorics of late twentieth and early twenty-first century techno-culture is an old human project to contain and master the ever present threat of **chaos** and disorder.

What is psychically compelling about the technologies I am considering here . . . is their capacity to provide a certain security and protection against the frightful world and against the fear that inhabits our bodies. They provide the means to distance and detach ourselves from what is fear provoking in the world and in ourselves.

(Robins 1996: 12)

For Robins, the technological imaginary of the 'new media order' is but the latest instance of a long history of similar 'psychic investments we make in technological forms'. He sees the modern (nineteenth and early twentieth-century) 'social imaginary' as having always been expansionist and utopian, leading us to seek out new frontiers, the other side of which lie better worlds. As real places and frontiers become exhausted, the cyberspaces and places of virtual life promised by new media become the new utopias which we reach for across a new technological frontier (1996: 16). Now, assessments of the value of computer-mediated communication, online communities, and the new virtual selves that await us in cyberspace can be understood as elements of a 'distinctive social vision' born of the contemporary technological imaginary (1996: 24).

Robins argues that this desire for better, less problematic (cyber) spaces is driven by a deep fear of disorder, of the unknown and meaninglessness. In a manner that is reminiscent of McLuhan, Robins sees the modern world 'surveyed by absolute vision', as a world which could be ordered, controlled, surveilled and manipulated from an omnipotent distance. This has been, and continues to be, 'massively facilitated by the development of a succession of new technological means' (1996: 20). Co-existing with this desire for technologically empowered control, the technological imagination leads us to dream of the pleasure of shifting our existence to 'an alternative environment, one that has been cleansed of the real world's undesirable qualities' by entering 'into the image'. This is now achieved through the IMAX screen and lies behind our fascination with the prospect of immersive VR; formerly it was sought in the form of Hayles tours, panoramas, and early cinema (1996: 22). (See **2.8**.)

2.8 Digital cinema

CASE STUDY 1.5: New media as arenas for discussing old problems

Key text: Carolyn Marvin (1988) *When Old Technologies Were New: Thinking About Electric Communication in the Nineteenth Century*, Oxford University Press, New York and Oxford.

> Discussions of electrical and other forms of communication in the late nineteenth century begin from specific cultural and class assumptions about what communication ought to be like among particular groups of people. These assumptions informed the beliefs of nineteenth-century observers about what these new media were supposed to do . . .
>
> (Marvin 1988: 6)

If Robins's understanding of the contemporary technological imaginary of the 'new media order' stresses its utopian character, Carolyn Marvin, in her research into the early history of electric communications technologies, sees them as 'arenas for negotiating issues crucial to the conduct of social life'. She argues that beneath their more obvious functional meanings (the ways in which new media offer greater speed, capacity, and better performance) a whole range of 'social meanings can elaborate themselves' (Marvin 1988: 4). She describes the varied, surprising and furious experiments that were undertaken to see how the new technologies might extend existing social and cultural practices. In its early years, the telephone was used to relay orchestral concerts to the homes of the wealthy and privileged, it was informally co-opted by groups of lonely musicians in order to 'jam' together over the telephone lines, and telephone operators used their vantage point to gossip and spread private information within small communities. As such things happened, questions were raised about who, in society, has the power to define the use of technologies, who should use them and to what ends, what are their implications for settled patterns of social life, what needs to be defended, and whose interests should be furthered?

For Carolyn Marvin, 'the introduction of new media is a special historical occasion when patterns anchored in older media that have provided the stable currency of social exchange are re-examined, challenged, and defended' (Marvin 1988: 4). While an orthodox way of studying new communication technologies, like the telephone, involves examining how the new machine or instrument may introduce new practices and contribute to the building of new social relationships, Marvin sees new media as 'providing new platforms on which old groups confront one other'. The appearance of a new medium becomes a kind of occasion for a 'drama', whereby the existing groups and hierarchies within a society attempt to assimilate the new technology into their familiar worlds, rituals and habits. On the one hand, a society works to use the new technology to fulfil old and existing social functions, while at the same time it projects onto the technology its fears about its own stability and already existing social tensions.

Marvin shows how a technological imaginary is at work long before a new communications technology settles into a stable form. The new groups of 'experts' and professionals who formed around new media technologies, with their particular visions and imaginaries (such as Negroponte or the French HDTV researchers discussed in **Case study 1.6**), are only one group in a wider society that seeks to experiment with and imagine the possibilities of the new medium in order to 'reduce and simplify a world of expanding cultural variety to something more familiar and less threatening' (1988: 5).

Case study 1.7 The technological imaginary and the shaping of new media

CASE STUDY 1.6   The technological imaginary and the cultural reception of new media

Television and the gendering of a 'bad' object

Key text: William Boddy (1994) 'Archaeologies of electronic vision and the gendered spectator', *Screen 35.2* (Summer): 105–122.

> the . . . exploration of the history of technology is more than technical . . . technology can reveal the dream world of society as much as its pragmatic realisation.
>
> (Gunning, quoted in Boddy 1994: 105)

1.2   The characteristics of new media: some defining concepts

William Boddy has adopted Marvin's approach to examine how, earlier in the twentieth century, a technological imaginary shaped our perceptions of radio and television in ways which now inform our ideas about the value of new digital media.

Radio and, later, television were media technologies that had to be 'filled' with content after they were designed (Williams 1974: 25). With its beginnings in the transmission of 'one-to-one' secret messages for military and trading purposes, radio started its civil life in the 'attic' as a hobby or an enthusiast's activity. In the 1920s radio receivers of various kinds of complexity were self-assembled by men and boys from parts and kits. Isolated from the rest of the family by their headphones, these male enthusiasts 'fished' the airwaves. 'The radio enthusiasts . . . envisioned radio as an active sport . . . in which the participant gained a sense of mastery – increased masculinity – by adjusting the dials and "reeling" in the distant signals' (Spigel 1991: 27). This was a gendered activity, being almost exclusively pursued by men. During this period radio was also hailed for its potential social good. A medium to weld a nation together in solidarity, and to build community where none existed or where it was threatened by racist tensions (the parallels with the internet are strong).

From the mid-1920s, in the US and Europe, sound broadcasting was transformed by investment in the production of 'user friendly' domestic receivers in order to open up the growing markets for consumer durables in the family home – the box camera, washing machine, the gas range, and the vacuum cleaner. There was a determined attempt on the part of broadcasters and hardware manufacturers to shift the popular perception of the radio away from an untidy mass of wires, valves and acid-filled batteries used in intense isolation by men in their attics. Instead it was marketed as a piece of furniture suitable for siting in the living room and audible through camouflaged speakers. Radio came to be perceived as background atmosphere, a cosmetic domestic addition to furniture and wallpaper, for the distracted housewife (Boddy 1994: 114). As a 1923 trade journal advised the retailers who were to sell the new sets, 'don't talk circuits. Don't talk in electrical terms . . . You must convince everyone . . . that radio will fit into the well appointed home' (Boddy 1994: 112).

The reaction of the male radio enthusiast was predictable (and foreshadows that of the **hacker**-ish internet users' response to the mid-1990s emergence of the commercialised, animated banner-ad commodification of the 'information wants to be free' internet). Radio amateurs bemoaned the loss of an engrossing hobby and the thrilling business of 'conquering time and space', while wrestling ingeniously with the technology (Boddy 1994: 113).

Instead, with the 'distracted housewife' as the ideal audience, radio came to be seen as 'passive listening', a matter of 'mere' enjoyment. A commercialised, trivial regime of 'programmes' aimed at an 'average woman listener [who] is neither cosmopolitan nor sophisticated. Nor does she have much imagination' (Boddy 1994: 114). Fears grew that radio would isolate and lead to the stagnation of family life. After its heroic 'attic days' radio was judged to have become a pacifying, emasculating and feminising activity.

CASE STUDY 1.7: The technological imaginary and the shaping of new media

Key text: Patrice Flichy (1999) 'The construction of new digital media', *New Media and Society* 1.1: 33–39.

> communication technologies, in particular, like network technologies, are often the source of an abundant production by the collective imagination . . . in which innovations are celebrated by the media even before being launched.
>
> (Flichy 1999: 33)

Patrice Flichy proposes that the technological imaginary plays a role in the very creation of a new medium. It is a factor that interplays with actual technological developments, planning, and the lifestyles and modes of work into which the technology is designed to fit. It is an element which owes more to certain ideologies and desires that circulate within a culture than to hard-headed calculations and credible expectations of how a medium is likely to be used (Flichy, 1999: 34). Flichy uses recent debates over the future of digital television as one of his examples (see also Winston 1996). In the 1990s three different views on how digitisation should be applied to the medium of television competed. These were:

- HDTV (high-definition digital television)
- Personalised, interactive television (push media)
- Multi-channel cable and satellite television

HDTV involved the use of digitisation to give television a high-resolution image. This was, initially, a primarily European concept and Flichy traces it to a French habit of thinking of television 'cinematographically'; that is, rather than thinking of television in terms of its flow of images, to be preoccupied instead with the quality of the framed image 'on the screen'.

The second conception, that championed by Nicolas Negroponte, the 'digital guru' from MIT, envisions the future of TV as a 'gigantic virtual video library' delivering personalised contents to its interacting users. This concept of TV as breaking free of linear, centralised programming and scheduling, and emphasising 'user choice', is related to a sort of interactive 'essence' of digital technology (**1.2**).

The third option, to use increased digital bandwidth to multiply the number of TV channels, is technologically and economically driven in the sense that it builds upon previous corporate investments in cable and satellite transmission. This option, which in many ways is to 'provide more of the same', now appears to be the direction actually being taken by the early operators of digital television.

However, which (if any) of these visions for future TV is ultimately realised is not the point at hand. The point is that such visions are driven by cultural values upon which a technological

1.2 The characteristics of new media: some defining concepts

imaginary is based and not on technological necessities: it is possible that the technology could deliver any or all of the options.

The debate and practical competition over how to employ digital technology in relation to the existing medium of television are based upon three kinds of technological imaginary: the desire to elevate television to the status of cinema by providing it with the detail and beauty of the film image; a conviction that television should be radically transformed in line with the new principles of digital culture; and, finally, the profit-driven ambition to use the technology to provide more of the same while creating more televisual 'niche' markets.

1.5.4 Conclusion

The examples above argue that the processes that determine the kind of media we actually get are neither solely economic nor solely technological, but that all orders of decision in the development process occur within a discursive framework powerfully shaped by the technological imaginary. The evidence for the existence of such a framework can be tracked back through the introduction of numerous technologies and goods throughout the modern period. Its precise formation will in part depend upon the ways of thinking about and using existing or related technologies. The power of desire that this imaginary represents can hardly be overestimated – the entire **dotcom** investment boom and crash of the late 1990s could, for instance, be seen as an object lesson in the disastrous operation of the technological imaginary.

Case study 1.3   What is new about
interactivity?

1.5.5 The return of the Frankfurt School critique in the popularisation of new media

We now return to a broader consideration of the points raised in **Case study 1.3** concerning the allegedly 'democratic' potential of interactivity. Here, however, we point out how a tradition of criticism of mass media finds itself reappropriated as another discursive framework that shapes our ideas about what new media are or could be.

This tradition of media critique expressed profound dissatisfaction with the uses and the cultural and political implications of broadcast media throughout the early and mid-twentieth-century. Such critics of the effects of twentieth century mass media did not normally think that there was a technological solution to the problems they identified. They did not suggest that new and different media technologies would overcome the social and cultural problems they associated with the media they were familiar with. To the extent that they could conceive of change in their situation they saw hope lying in social action, whether through political revolution or a conservative defence of threatened values. In another tradition it was more imaginative and democratic uses of existing media that were seen as the answer. Nevertheless, the critique of mass media has become, in the hands of new media enthusiasts, a set of terms against which new media are celebrated. The positions and theories represented by these media critics have been frequently rehearsed and continue to be influential in some areas of media studies and theory. Because of this they need not be dealt with at great length here as many accessible and adequate accounts already exist (Strinati 1995; Stevenson 1995; Lury 1992).

The 'culture industry', the end of democratic participation and critical distance

From the 1920s until the present day the mass media (especially the popular press and the broadcast media of radio and television) have been the object of sustained criticism from intellectuals, artists, educationalists, feminists and left-wing activists. It is a (contentious) aspect of this critique, which sees mass culture as disempowering, homogenising, and impositional in nature, that is of relevance in this context. Strinati sums up such a view:

> [there] is a specific conception of the audience of mass culture, the mass or the public which consumes mass produced cultural products. The audience is conceived of as a mass of passive consumers . . . supine before the false pleasures of mass consumption . . . The picture is of a mass which almost without thinking, without reflecting, abandoning all critical hope, buys into mass culture and mass consumption. Due to the emergence of mass society and mass culture it lacks the intellectual and moral resources to do otherwise. It cannot think of, or in terms of, alternatives.
>
> (Strinati 1995: 12)

Such a conception and evaluation of the 'mass' and its culture was argued by intellectuals who were steeped in the values of a literary culture. Alan Meek has described well a dominant kind of relationship which such intellectuals and artists had to the mass media in the early and mid-twentieth century:

> The modern Western intellectual appeared as a figure within the public sphere whose technological media was print and whose institutions where defined by the nation state. The ideals of democratic participation and critical literacy which the intellectual espoused have often been seen to be undermined by the emerging apparatus of electronic media, 'mass culture', or the entertainment industry.
>
> (Meek 2000: 88)

Mass society critics feared four things:

- The debasement and displacement of an authentic organic folk culture;

- The erosion of high cultural traditions, those of art and literature;

- Loss of the ability of these cultural traditions (as the classical 'public sphere') to comment critically on society's values;

- The indoctrination and manipulation of the 'masses' by either totalitarian politics or market forces.

The context within which these fears were articulated was the rise of mass, urban society. Nineteenth- and early twentieth-century industrialisation and urbanisation in Western Europe and America had weakened or destroyed organic, closely knit, agrarian communities. The sense of identity, community membership and oral, face-to-face communication fostered and mediated by institutions like the extended family, the village, and the Church were seen to be replaced by a collection of atomised individuals in the new industrial cities and workplaces. At the same time the production of culture itself became subject to the processes of industrialisation and the marketplace. The evolving Hollywood mode of film production, popular 'pulp' fiction, and popular music were particular objects of criticism. Seen as generic and formulaic, catering to the lowest common denominators of taste, they were assembly line models of cultural production. Radio, and later television, were viewed as centralised impositions from above. Either as a means of trivialising the content of communication, or as a means of political indoctrination, they were seen as threats to democracy and the informed critical participation of the masses in cultural and social life. How, feared the intellectuals, given the burgeoning of mass electronic media, could people take a part in a democratic system of government in which all citizens are active, through their elected representatives, in the decisions a society makes?

With the erosion of folk wisdom and morality, and the trivialisation, commercialisation and centralisation of culture and communications, how could citizens be informed about issues and able, through their educated ability, to think independently and form views on social and political issues? Critical participation demanded an ability and energy to take issue with how things are, to ask questions about the nature or order of things, and a capacity to envision and conceive of better states as a guide to action. In the eyes of theorists such as those of the Frankfurt School, such ideals were terminally threatened by the mass media and mass culture.

Further, such developments took place in the context of twin evils. First, the twin realities of Fascism and Stalinism which demonstrated the power of mass media harnessed to totalitarianism. Second, the tyranny of market forces to generate false needs and desires within the populations of capitalist societies where active citizens were being transformed into 'mere' consumers.

This 'mass society theory', and its related critiques of the mass media, has been much debated, challenged and qualified within media sociology, **ethnography,** and in the light of postmodern media theory in recent years (see, for example, our discussion of audience interaction with mass media texts in **Case study 1.3**). Despite the existence of more nuanced accounts of the mass media which offer a more complex view of their social significance, it has now become clear that some of the main proponents of the twenty-first century's new communications media are actually celebrating their potential to restore society to a state where the damage perceived to be wrought by mass media will be undone. In some versions there is an active looking back to a pre-mass culture golden age of authentic exchange and community. We can especially note the following:

Case study 1.3   What is new about interactivity?

3.8   Networks as public spheres
3.9   The net as postmodern public sphere
3.10   Critique of the net as public sphere

- The recovery of community and a sphere of public debate (see **3.8–3.10**). In this formulation the Internet is seen as providing a vibrant counter public sphere. In addition, shared online spaces allegedly provide a sense of 'cyber community' against the alienations of contemporary life.

- The removal of information and communication from central authority, control and censorship.

  The 'fourth estate' function of mass media is seen here to be revived as alternative sources of news and information circulate freely through online publishing.

- The creative exploration of new forms of identity and relationship within virtual communities.

  Online communication is here seen as productive not of 'passive' supine subjects but of an active process of identity construction and exchange.

These arguments all in some way echo and answer ways in which conventional mass media have been problematised by intellectuals and critics.

The Brechtian avant-garde and lost opportunities

These 'answers' to a widespread pessimism about mass media can be seen in the light of another tradition in which the emancipatory power of radio, cinema, and television (also the mass press) lay in the way that they promised to involve the workers of industrial society in creative production, self-education and political expression. A major representative of this view is the socialist playwright Bertolt Brecht. Brecht castigated the form that radio was taking in the 1930s as he saw its potentials being limited to 'prettifying public life' and to 'bringing back cosiness to the home and making family life bearable'. His alternative, however, was not the male hobby, as described by Boddy above (**Case study 1.6**), but a radical practice of exchange and networking. It is interesting to listen to his vision of radio conceived as a 'vast network' in 1932:

> radio is one-sided when it should be two. It is purely an apparatus for distribution, for mere sharing out. So here is a positive suggestion: change this apparatus over from distribution to communication. The radio would be the finest possible communication apparatus in public life, a vast network of pipes. That is to say, it would be if it knew how to receive as well as submit, how to let the listener speak as well as hear, how to bring him into a relationship instead of isolating him.
>
> (Brecht 1936, in Hanhardt 1986: 53)

Brecht's cultural politics have lain behind radical movements in photographic, television and video production from the 1930s to the 1980s. In a final or latest resurgence they now inform politicised ideas about the uses of new media. Here it is argued that new media can be used as essentially two-way channels of communication that lie outside of official control. Combined with mobile telephony and digital video anti-capitalist demonstrators are now able to webcast near live information from their actions, beating news crews to the action and the transmission.

Finally, it is necessary to mention the influential ideas of a peripheral member of the Frankfurt School, Walter Benjamin. He took issue, in some of his writing, with the cultural pessimism of his colleagues. In 'The Work of Art in the Age of Mechanical Reproduction', and 'The Author As Producer', he argues that photography, film, and the modern newspaper, as media of mass reproduction, have revolutionary potential. Benjamin roots his argument in noticing some of the distinctive characteristics of these media, and the implications that he draws from them can be heard to echo today in the more sanguine estimations of the potential of new (digital) media. However, Benjamin sees that whether or not this potential will be realised is finally a matter of politics and not technology.

1.5.6 Conclusion

Sections **1.5.4** and **1.5.5** serve to illustrate how the debates about new media, what it is, what it might be, what we would like it to be, continue to rehearse many positions that have already been established within media studies and critical theory. Though the debates above are largely framed in terms of the amazing novelty of the possibilities that are opening up, they in fact revisit ground already well trodden. The disavowal of the history

Case study 1.6 The technological imaginary and the cultural reception of new media

of new media thus appears as an ideological sleight of hand that recruits us to their essential value but fails to help us understand what is happening around us.

1.6 NEW MEDIA: DETERMINING OR DETERMINED?

Many sections of Parts 3 and 4 owe much to the kind of approach which stresses human agency, power, control, and the social shaping of technology which can be broadly associated with Raymond Williams's influence on cultural and media studies. Part 5 explores other non-humanist approaches to the question of technology, including that of McLuhan and the causes of cultural change.

In previous sections of Part 1 of this book we have been looking at what kinds of histories, definitions and discourses shape the way we think about new media. We begin this final section by turning to examine two apparently competing paradigms, or two distinct approaches to the study of media, both of which underlie different parts of what will follow in this volume.

At the centre of each of these paradigms is a very different understanding of the power media and technology have to determine culture and society. The long-standing question of *whether or not a media technology has the power to transform a culture* has been given a very high profile with the development of new media. It will repay the good deal of attention that we give it here and in Part 5. In this section we will investigate this issue and the debates that surround it by turning back to the writings of two key but very different theorists of media: Marshall McLuhan and Raymond Williams. It is their views and arguments about the issue, filtered through very different routes, that now echo in the debate between those who see new media as revolutionary or as 'business as usual' that we pointed to in (1.1).

Although both authors more or less ceased writing at the point where the PC was about to 'take off' their analysis of the relationships between technology, culture and media continues to resonate in contemporary thought. As media theorists, both were interested in new media. It is precisely McLuhan's interest to identify and 'probe' what he saw as big cultural shifts brought about by change in media technologies. Williams, too, speaks of 'new media' and is interested in the conditions of their emergence and their subsequent use and control. While McLuhan was wholly concerned with identifying the major cultural effects that he saw new technological forms (in history and in his present) bringing about, Williams sought to show that there is nothing in a particular technology which guarantees the cultural or social outcomes it will have (Williams 1983: 130). McLuhan's arguments are at the core of claims that 'new media change everything'. If, as McLuhan argued, media determine consciousness then clearly we are living through times of profound change. On the other hand, albeit in a somewhat reduced way, the 'business as usual' camp is deeply indebted to Williams for the way in which they argue that media can only take effect through already present social processes and structures and will therefore reproduce existing patterns of use and basically sustain existing power relations.

1.6.1 The status of McLuhan and Williams

In the mainstream of media studies and much cultural studies the part played by the technological element that any medium has is always strongly qualified. Any idea that a medium can be reduced to a technology, or that the technological element which is admitted to be a part of any media process should be central to its study, is strongly resisted. The grounds for this view are to be found in a number of seminal essays by Raymond Williams (1974: 9–31; 1977: 158–164; 1983: 128–153), which, at least in part, responded critically to the 'potent observations' (Hall 1975: 81) of the Canadian literary and media theorist Marshall McLuhan. Williams's arguments against McLuhan subsequently became touchstones for media studies' rejection of any kind of **technological determinism.**

Yet, and here we meet one of the main sources of the present clash of discourses around the significance of new media, McLuhan's ideas have undergone a renaissance – literally a rebirth or rediscovery – in the hands of contemporary commentators, both popular and academic, on new media. The **McLuhanite** insistence on the need for new non-linear ('mosaic' is his term) ways of thinking about new media, which escape the intellectual protocols, procedures and habits of a linear print culture, has been taken up as something of a war cry against the academic media analyst. The charge that the neo-McLuhan cybertheorists make about media studies is made at this fundamental, epistemological level; that they simply fail to realise that its viewpoints (something, in fact, that McLuhan would claim we can no longer have) and methodologies have been hopelessly outstripped by events. As an early critic of McLuhan realised, to disagree with McLuhanite thinking is likely to be seen as the product of 'an outmoded insistence on the logical, ABCD minded, causality mad, one-thing-at-a-time method that the electronic age and its prophet have rendered obsolete' (Duffy 1969: 31).

Both Williams and McLuhan carried out their influential work in the 1960s and 1970s. Williams was one of the founding figures of British media and cultural studies. His rich, if at times abstract, historical and sociological formulations about cultural production and society provided some of the master templates for what has become mainstream media studies. Countless detailed studies of all kinds of media are guided and informed by his careful and penetrating outlines for a theory of media as a form of cultural production. His work is so deeply assimilated within the media studies discipline that he is seldom explicitly cited; he has become an invisible presence. Wherever we consider, in this book, new media as subject to control and direction by human institutions, skill, creativity and intention, we are building upon such a Williamsite emphasis.

On the other hand, McLuhan, the provoking, contentious figure who gained almost pop status in the 1960s, was discredited for his untenable pronouncements and was swatted away like an irritating fly by the critiques of Williams and others (see Miller 1971). However, as Williams foresaw (1974: 128), McLuhan has found highly influential followers. Many of his ideas have been taken up and developed by a whole range of theorists with an interest in new media: Baudrillard, Virilio, Poster, Kroker, De Kerckhove. The work of McLuhan and his followers has great appeal for those who see new media as bringing about radical cultural change or have some special interest in celebrating its potential. For the electronic counterculture he is an oppositional figure and for corporate business a source of propaganda – his aphorisms, 'the global village' and 'the medium is the message', 'function as globally recognised jingles' for multinational trade in digital commodities (Genosko, 1999). The magazine *Wired* has adopted him as its 'patron saint' (*Wired*, January 1996).

Williams's insights, embedded in a grounded and systematic theory, have been a major, shaping contribution to the constitution of an academic discipline. McLuhan's elliptical, unsystematic, contradictory and playful insights have fired the thought, the distinctive stance, and the methodological strategies of diverse but influential theorists of new media. We might say that Williams's thought is structured into media studies while, with respect to this discipline, McLuhan and those who have developed his ideas stalk its margins, sniping and provoking in ways that ensure they are frequently, if sometimes begrudgingly, referenced. Even cautious media academics allow McLuhan a little nowadays. He is seen as a theoretically unsubtle and inconsistent thinker who provokes others to think (Silverstone 1999: 21). It matters if he is wrong. One or another of his insights is often the jumping-off point for a contemporary study.

Eventually the intellectual distance between Williams and McLuhan was great, but this was not always so. In a review of McLuhan's *Gutenberg Galaxy*, published in 1962, Williams writes of his preoccupation with the book (Stearn 1967: 188). He considers it to be 'a wholly indispensable work'. It was a work that stayed in his mind for months after he first read it and to which he returned frequently; but he was already uneasy about McLuhan's singling out of the medium of print as the single causal factor in social change (Stearn 1967: 190). However, by 1974 his estimation of McLuhan's importance had deteriorated markedly. He saw McLuhan's projection of totalising images of society – its 'retribalisation', the electronic age, 'the global village' – projected from his 'unhistorical and asocial' study of media as 'ludicrous' (Stearn 1967: 128)

McLuhan's major publications appeared in the 1960s, some two decades before the effective emergence of the PC as a technology for communications and media production. It is a shift from a 500-year-old print culture to one of 'electric' media, by which he mainly means radio and television, that McLuhan considers. He only knew computers in the form of the mainframe computers of his day, yet they formed part of his bigger concept of the 'electric environment', and he was sharp enough to see the practice of time-sharing on these machines as the early signs of their social availability. By the 1990s, for some, McLuhan's ideas, when applied to developments in new media, had come to seem not only potent but extraordinarily prescient as well. It is quite easy to imagine a student at work in some future time, who, failing to take note of McLuhan's dates, is convinced that he is a 1990s writer on cyberculture, a contemporary of Jean Baudrillard or William Gibson. While this may owe something to the way that his ideas have been taken up in the postmodern context of the last two decades of the twentieth century by writers such as Baudrillard, Virilio, De Kerckhove, Kroker, Kelly, and Toffler, this hardly undermines the challenging and deliberately perverse originality of his thought.

The debate between the Williams and McLuhan positions, and Williams's apparent victory in this debate, left media studies with a legacy. It has had the effect of putting paid to any 'good-sense' cultural or media theorist raising the spectre of the technological determinism associated with the thought of McLuhan. It has also had the effect of foreclosing aspects of the way in which cultural and media studies deals with technology by implicitly arguing that technology on its own is incapable of producing change, the view being that whatever is going on around us in terms of rapid technological change there are rational and manipulative interests at work driving the technology in particular directions and it is to these that we should primarily direct our attention. Such is the dismissal of the role of technology in cultural change that, should we wish to confront this situation, we are inevitably faced with our views being reduced to apparent absurdity: '*What!?* Are you suggesting that machines *can* and *do* act, cause things to happen *on their own?* – that a *machine caused* space flight, rather than the superpowers' ideological struggle for achievement?'

However, there are good reasons to believe that technology cannot be adequately analysed only within the **humanist** frame Williams bequeathed cultural and media theorists. Arguments about what causes technological change may not be so straightforward as culturalist accusations of political or theoretical naivety seem to suggest. In this section, therefore, we review Williams's and McLuhan's arguments about media and technology. We then examine the limits of the humanist account of technology that Williams so influentially offered and ask whether he was correct in his dismissal of McLuhan as a crude technological determinist. Finally, we explore other important non-humanist accounts of technology that are frequently excluded from the contemporary study of media technologies. The latter are then more fully elaborated in **Part 5**.

BOX 1.2:   Humanism

'**Humanism**' is a term applied to a long and recurring tendency in Western thought. It appears to have its origins in the fifteenth- and sixteenth-century Italian Renaissance where a number of scholars (Bruno, Erasmus, Valla, and Pico della Mirandola) worked to recover elements of classical learning and natural science lost in the 'dark ages' of the medieval Christian world. Their emphasis on explaining the world through the human capacity for rational thought rather than a reliance on Christian theology fostered the '[b]elief that individual human beings are the fundamental source of all value and have the ability to understand – and perhaps even to control – the natural world by careful application of their own rational faculties' (*Oxford Companion to Philosophy*). This impetus was added to and modified many times in following centuries. Of note is the seventeenth-century Cartesian idea of the human subject, 'I think, therefore I am. I have intentions, purposes, goals, therefore I am the sole source and free agent of my actions' (Sarup 1988: 84). There is a specifically 'Marxist humanism' in the sense that it is believed that self-aware, thinking and acting individuals will build a rational socialist society. For our purposes here it is important to stress that a humanist theory tends only to recognise human individuals as having agency (and power and responsibility) over the social forms and the technologies they create and, even, through rational science, the power to control and shape nature.

1.6.2 Mapping Marshall McLuhan

Many of McLuhan's more important ideas arise within a kind of narrative of redemption. There is little doubt that much of McLuhan's appeal to new media and cyber enthusiasts lies in the way that he sees the arrival of an 'electronic culture' as a rescue or recovery from the fragmenting effects of 400 years of print culture. McLuhan has, indeed, provided a range of ideological resources for the technological imaginary of the new millennium.

Here, we outline McLuhan's grand schema of four cultures, determined by their media forms, as it is the context in which some important ideas arise. Ideas which are, arguably, far more important and useful than his quasi-historical and extremely sweeping narrative. We then concentrate on three key ideas. First, 'remediation', a concept that is currently much in vogue and finds its roots in McLuhan's view that 'the content of any medium is always another medium' (1968: 15–16). Second, his idea that media and technologies are extensions of the human body and its senses. Third, his famous (or notorious) view that 'the medium is the message'. This section is the basis for a further discussion, in **1.6.4**, of three 'theses' to be found in McLuhan's work: his extension thesis, his environmental thesis, and his anti-content thesis.

1.6.4 The many virtues of Saint McLuhan

A narrative of redemption

McLuhan's view of media as technological extensions of the body is his basis for conceiving of four media cultures which are brought about by shifts from oral to written communication, from script to print, and from print to electronic media. These four cultures are: (1) a primitive culture of oral communication, (2) a literate culture using the phonetic alphabet and handwritten script which co-existed with the oral, (3) the age of mass-produced, mechanical printing (*The Gutenberg Galaxy*), and (4) the culture of 'electric media': radio, television, and computers.

'PRIMITIVE' ORAL/AURAL CULTURE

In pre-literate 'primitive' cultures there was a greater dominance of the sense of hearing than in literate cultures when, following the invention of the phonetic alphabet (a visual encoding of speech), the ratio of the eye and the ear was in a better state of equilibrium. Pre-literate people lived in an environment totally dominated by the sense of hearing. Oral and aural communication were central. Speaking and hearing speech was the 'ear-man's' main form of communication (while also, no doubt, staying alert to the sound of a breaking twig !). McLuhan is not enthusiastic about this kind of culture. For him it was not a state of 'noble savagery' (Duffy 1969: 26).

> Primitive man lived in a much more tyrannical cosmic machine than Western literate man has ever invented. The world of the ear is more embracing and inclusive than that of the eye can ever be. The ear is hypersensitive. The eye is cool and detached. The ear turns man over to universal panic while the eye, extended by literacy and mechanical time, leaves some gaps and some islands free from the unremitting acoustic pressure and reverberation.
>
> (McLuhan 1968: 168)

THE CULTURE OF LITERACY

McLuhan says that he is not interested in making judgements but only in identifying the configurations of different societies (1968: 94). However, as is implied in the above passage, for McLuhan the second culture, the culture of literacy, was an improvement on pre-literate, oral culture. For here, via the alphabet and writing, as extensions of the eye, and, in its later stages, the clock, 'the visual and uniform fragmentation of time became possible' (1968: 159). This released 'man' from the panic of 'primitive' conditions while maintaining a balance between the aural and the visual. In the literate, scribal culture of the Middle Ages McLuhan sees a situation where oral traditions co-existed alongside writing: manuscripts were individually produced and annotated by hand as if in a continual dialogue, writers and readers were hardly separable, words were read aloud to 'audiences', and the mass reproduction of uniform texts by printing presses had not led to a narrowing dominance and authority of sight over hearing and speaking. Writing augmented this culture in specialised ways without wholly alienating its members from humankind's original, participatory, audio-tactile universe (Theal 1971: 81).

PRINT CULTURE

For McLuhan, the real villain of the piece is print culture – the Gutenberg Galaxy with its 'typographic man', where the sensory alienation which was avoided in literate culture occurs. Here we meet the now familiar story of how the mass reproduction of writing by the printing press, the development of perspectival images, the emerging scientific methods of observation and measurement, and the seeking of linear chains of cause and effect came to dominate modern, rationalist print culture. In this process its members lost their tactile and auditory relation with the world, their rich sensory lives were fragmented and impoverished as the visual sense dominated. In McLuhan's terms this is a culture in which the 'stepping up of the visual component in experience . . . filled the field of attention' (1962: 17). The culture was hypnotised by vision (mainly through its extensions as typography and print) and the 'interplay of all the senses in haptic harmony' dies. Fixed points of view and measured, separating distances come to structure the human subject's relation to the world. With this 'instressed concern with one sense only, the mechanical principle of abstraction and repetition emerges', which means 'the spelling out of one thing at a time, one sense at a time, one mental or physical operation at a time' (1962: 18). If the primitive pre-literate culture was tyrannised by the ear, Gutenberg culture is hypnotised by its eye.

ELECTRONIC CULTURE

The fourth culture, electronic culture, is 'paradise regained' (Duffy 1969). Developing from the invention of telegraphy to television and the computer, this culture promises to short-circuit that of mechanical print and we regain the conditions of an oral culture in acoustic space. We return to a state of sensory grace; to a culture marked by qualities of simultaneity, indivisibility and sensory plenitude. The haptic or tactile senses again come into play, and McLuhan strives hard to show how television is a tactile medium.

The terms in which McLuhan described this electric age as a new kind of primitivism, with tribal-like participation in the 'global village', resonates with certain strands of new age media culture. McLuhan's all-at-onceness or simultaneity, the involvement of everyone with everyone, electronic media's supposedly connecting and unifying characteristics, are easy to recognise in (indeed, in some cases have led to) many of the terms now used to characterise new media – connectivity, convergence, the network society, wired culture, and interaction.

McLuhan's ideas about television received very short shrift from British cultural and media studies, even its formative period (see Hall 1975).

Remediation (see also 1.1.4 and 1.3)

First, and most uncontentiously because it was an idea that McLuhan and Williams shared, is the idea that all new media 'remediate' the content of previous media. This notion, as developed by McLuhan in the 1960s, has become a key idea, extensively worked out in a recent book on new media. In *Remediation: Understanding New Media* (1999), Jay David Bolter and Richard Grusin briefly revisit the clash between Williams and McLuhan as they set out their own approach to the study of new media. They define a medium as 'that which remediates'. That is, a new medium 'appropriates the techniques, forms, and social significance of other media and attempts to rival or refashion them in the name of the real' (ibid.: 65). The inventors, users, and economic backers of a new medium present it as able to represent the world in more realistic and authentic ways than previous media forms, and in the process what is real and authentic is redefined (ibid.). This idea owes something to McLuhan, for whom 'the "content" of any medium is always another medium' (1968: 15–16).

1.1.4   Non-technical and inclusive

1.3   Change and continuity

See Williams (1974) on music hall and parlour games in broadcasting

Bolter and Grusin have something interesting to say about Williams and McLuhan which bears directly upon our attempt to get beyond the polarised debates about new media. They agree with Williams's criticism that McLuhan is a technological determinist who single-mindedly took the view that media technologies act directly to change a society and a culture, but they argue that it is possible to put McLuhan's 'determinism' aside in order to appreciate 'his analysis of the remediating power of various media'. Bolter and Grusin encourage us to see value in the way that McLuhan 'notices intricate correspondences involving media and cultural artefacts' (1999: 76), and they urge us to recognise that his view of media as 'extensions of the human sensorium' has been highly influential, prefiguring the concept of the **cyborg** in late twentieth-century thought on media and cyberculture or technoculture. It is precisely this ground, and the question of the relationship between human agency and technology in the age of cybernetic culture, which the neo-McLuhanites attempt to map.

Extending the sensorium

McLuhan reminds us of the technological dimension of media. He does so by refusing any distinction between a medium and a technology. For him, there is no issue. It is not accidental that he makes his basic case for a medium being 'any extension of ourselves' (1968: 15) by using as key examples the electric light (ibid.) and the wheel (ibid.: 52) –

respectively a system and an artefact which we would ordinarily think of as technologies rather than media. Basically, this is no more than the commonplace idea that a 'tool' (a name for a simple technology) is a bodily extension: a hammer is an extension of the arm or a screwdriver is an extension of the hand and wrist.

In *The Medium is the Massage* (1967) McLuhan drives this point home. We again meet the wheel as 'an extension of the foot', while the book is 'an extension of the eye', clothing is an extension of the skin, and electric circuitry is an 'extension of the central nervous system'. In other places he speaks of money (1968: 142) or gunpowder (ibid.: 21) as a medium. In each case, then, an artefact is seen as extending a part of the body, a limb or the nervous system. And, as far as McLuhan is concerned, these are 'media'.

McLuhan conflates technologies and mediums in this way because he views both as part of a larger class of things; as extensions of the human senses: sight, hearing, touch, and smell. Wheels for instance, especially when driven by automotive power, radically changed the experience of travel and speed, the body's relationship to its physical environment, and to time and space. The difference between the view we have of the world when slowly walking, open on all sides to a multisensory environment, or when glimpsed as rapid and continuous change through the hermetically sealed and framing window of a high-speed train, is a change in sensory experience which did and continues to have cultural significance. (See, for instance, Schivelbusch 1977.) It is this broadening of the concept of a medium to all kinds of technologies that enabled McLuhan to make one of his central claims: that the 'medium is the message'. In understanding media, it matters not, he would claim, why we are taking a train journey, or where we are going on the train. These are irrelevant side issues which only divert us from noticing the train's real cultural significance. Its real significance (the message of the medium itself) is the way it changes our perception of the world.

McLuhan also asserts (he doesn't 'argue') that such extensions of our bodies, placed in the context of the body's whole range of senses (the sensorium), change the 'natural' relationships between the sensing parts of the body, and affect 'the whole psychic and social complex' (1968: 11). In short, he is claiming that such technological extensions of our bodies affect both our minds and our societies. In *The Gutenberg Galaxy* (1962: 24) he expresses the idea of technological extension more carefully when he says, 'Sense ratios change when any one sense or bodily or mental function is externalised in technological form.' So, for McLuhan, the importance of a medium (seen as a bodily extension) is not just a matter of a limb or anatomical system being physically extended (as in the hammer as 'tool' sense). It is also a matter of altering the 'ratio' between the range of human senses (sight, hearing, touch, smell) and this has implications for our 'mental functions' (having ideas, perceptions, emotions, experiences, etc.).

Media, then, change the relationship of the human body and its sensorium to its environment. Media generally alter the human being's sensory relationship to the world, and the specific characteristics of any one medium change that relationship in different ways. This is McLuhan's broad and uncontestable premiss upon which he spins all manner of theses – some far more acceptable than others. It is not hard to see how such a premiss or idea has become important at a time of new media technologies and emergent new media forms.

The medium is the message

As we saw above, in what has been widely condemned as an insupportable overstatement, McLuhan concludes from his idea of media as extensions of man that 'understanding

There is also an important reversal of this idea as with industrial mechanisation we come to think of the human body as a mere extension of the machine. An idea powerfully represented by Charlie Chaplin in *Modern Times* and theorised by Marx and Benjamin amongst others (see also 1.6.4)

media' has nothing to do with attending to their content. In fact he maintains that understanding is blocked by any preoccupation with media content and the specific intentions of media producers. He views the 'conventional response to all media, namely that it is how they are used that counts', as 'the numb stance of the technological idiot. For the "content" of a medium is like the juicy piece of meat carried by the burglar to distract the watchdog of the mind' (1968: 26).

McLuhan will have no truck with questions of intention whether on the part of producers or consumers of media. In a seldom referred to but telling passage in *Understanding Media* (1968: 62) he makes it clear that 'It is the peculiar bias of those who operate the media for the owners that they be concerned about program content.' The owners themselves 'are more concerned about the media as such'. They know that the power of media 'has little to do with "content".' He implies that the owner's preoccupation with the formula 'what the public wants' is a thin disguise for their knowing lack of interest in specific contents and their strong sense of where the media's power lies.

Hence his deliberately provocative slogan 'The medium is the message'. This is where his use of the electric light as a 'medium' pays off. It becomes the exemplary case of a 'medium without a message' (1968: 15). McLuhan asserts that neither the (apparent and irrelevant) messages that it carries (the words and meanings of an illuminated sign) nor its uses (illuminating baseball matches or operating theatres) are what is important about electric light as a medium. Rather, like electricity itself, its real message is the way that it extends and speeds up forms of 'human association and action', whatever they are (1968: 16). What is important about electric light for McLuhan is the way that it ended any strict distinction between night and day, indoors and outdoors and how it then changed the meanings (remediated) of already existing technologies and the kinds of human organisation built around them: cars can travel and sports events can take place at night, factories can operate efficiently around the clock, and buildings no longer require windows (1968: 62). For McLuhan, the real '"message" of any medium or technology is the change of scale or pace or pattern that it introduces into human affairs' (1968: 16). Driving his point home, and again moving from technology to communication media, he writes:

> The message of the electric light is like the message of electric power in industry. Totally radical, pervasive, and decentralised. For the electric light and power are separate from their uses, yet they eliminate time and space factors in human association exactly as do radio, telegraph, telephone and TV, creating involvement in depth.
>
> (McLuhan 1968: 17)

Also, like the effects of the electric light on the automobile, McLuhan claims that the content of any medium is another medium which it picks up and works over (the medium is the message).

McLuhan's absolute insistence on the irrelevance of content to understanding media needs to be seen as a strategy. He adopts it in order to focus his readers upon:

1   the power of media technologies to structure social arrangements and relationships, and

2   the mediating aesthetic properties of a media technology. They mediate our relations to one another and to the world (electronic broadcasting as against one-to-one oral

communication or point-to-point telegraphic communication for instance). Aesthetically, because they claim our senses in different ways, the multidirectional simultaneity of sound as against the exclusively focused attention of a 'line' of sight, the fixed, segmenting linearity of printed language, the high resolution of film or the low resolution of TV, etc.

We should now be in a better position to see what McLuhan offers us in our efforts to 'understand new media', and why his work has been seen to be newly important in the context of new media technologies:

It is McLuhan's view that these mediating factors are qualities of the media technologies themselves, rather than outcomes of the way they are used, which is criticised by Williams and many in media studies

- McLuhan stresses the physicality of technology, its power to structure or restructure how human beings pursue their activities, and the manner in which extensive technological systems form an environment in which human beings live and act. Conventional wisdom says that technology is nothing until it is given cultural meaning, and that it is what we do with technologies rather than what they do to us that is important and has a bearing on social and cultural change. However, McLuhan's project is to force us to reconsider this conventional wisdom by recognising that technology also has an agency and effects that cannot be reduced to its social uses.

- In his conception of media as technological extensions of the body and its senses, as 'outerings' of what the body itself once enclosed, he anticipates the networked, converging, cybernetic media technologies of the late twentieth/early twenty-first centuries. He also distinguishes them from earlier technologies as being more environmental. In his words, 'With the arrival of electric technology, man extended, or set outside himself, a live model of the central nervous system itself' (1968: 53). This is qualitatively different from previous kinds of sensory extension where 'our extended senses, tools, and technologies' had been 'closed systems incapable of interplay or collective awareness'. However, 'Now, in the electric age, the very instantaneous nature of co-existence among our technological instruments has created a crisis quite new in human history' (1962: 5). McLuhan's sweeping hyperbolic style is much in evidence in that last statement. However, the evolution of networked communication systems and present anticipations of a fully functioning, global neural net is here prefigured in McLuhan's observations of broadcast culture in the 1960s.

- McLuhan's ideas have been seen as the starting point for explanation and understanding of the widely predicted conditions in which cybernetic systems have increasingly determining effects upon our lives. At a point in human history where for significant numbers of people 'couplings' with machines are increasingly frequent and intimate, where our subjectivity is challenged by this new interweaving of technology into our everyday lives, he forces us to reconsider the centrality of human agency in our dealings with machines and to entertain a less one-sided view.

1.6.3 Williams and the social shaping of technology

We noted at the outset of this section that media studies has by and large come to ignore or reject the views of Marshall McLuhan in favour of Raymond Williams's analysis of similar terrain. In this section we draw out the major differences in their approaches to the question of technology's relation to culture and society.

Human agency versus technological determination

Williams clearly has McLuhan's concept of the 'extensions of man' in mind when writes that 'A technology, when it has been *achieved*, can be seen as a general human property, *an extension of a general human capacity*' (1974: 129; our italics). McLuhan is seldom interested in why a technology is 'achieved', but this is a question that is important for Williams. For him 'all technologies have been developed and improved to help with known human practices or with foreseen and desired practices' (ibid.). So, for Williams, technologies involve precisely what McLuhan dismisses. First, they cannot be separated from questions of 'practice' (which are questions about how they are used and about their content). Second, they arise from human intention and agency. Such intentions arise within social groups to meet some desire or interest that they have, and these interests are historically and culturally specific.

McLuhan holds that new technologies radically change the physical and mental functions of a generalised 'mankind'. Williams argues that new technologies take forward existing practices that particular social groups already see as important or necessary. McLuhan's ideas about why new technologies emerge are psychological and biological. Humans react to stress in their environment by 'numbing' the part of the body under stress. They then produce a medium or a technology (what is now frequently called a prosthesis) which extends and externalises the 'stressed out' sense or bodily function. Williams's argument for the development of new technologies is sociological. It arises from the development and reconfiguration of a culture's existing technological resources in order to pursue socially conceived ends.

McLuhan insists that the importance of a medium is not a particular use but the structural way that it changes the 'pace and scale' of human affairs. For Williams, it is the power that specific social groups have that is important in determining the 'pace and scale' of the intended technological development – indeed, whether or not any particular technology is developed (see Winston 1998). Williams's emphasis called for an examination of (1) the reasons for which technologies are developed, (2) the complex of social, cultural, and economic factors which shape them, and (3) the ways that technologies are mobilised for certain ends (rather than the properties of the achieved technologies themselves). This is the direction which the mainstream of media studies came to take.

The plural possibilities and uses of a technology

Where, for the most part, McLuhan sees only one broad and structuring set of effects as flowing from a technology, Williams recognises plural outcomes or possibilities. Because he focuses on the issue of intention, he recognises that whatever the original intention to develop a technology might be, subsequently other social groups, with different interests or needs, adapt, modify or subvert the uses to which any particular technology is put. Where, for McLuhan, the social adoption of a media technology has determinate outcomes, for Williams this is not guaranteed. It is a matter of competition and struggle between social groups. For Williams, the route between need, invention, development, and final use or 'effect' is not straightforward. He also points out that technologies have uses and effects which were unforeseen by their conceivers and developers. (A point with which McLuhan would agree.) Overall, Williams's critique of McLuhan adds up to the premise that there is nothing in a particular technology which guarantees or causes its mode of use, and hence its social effects. By viewing media the way he does, he arrives at the opposite conclusion to McLuhan: what a culture is like does not directly follow from the nature of its media.

Concepts of technology

We have noted how broadly, following a basic (nineteenth-century) anthropological concept of 'man' as a tool user, McLuhan defines a technology and how he subsumes media within this definition without further discussion. Williams does not. First, he distinguishes between various stages or elements in a fully achieved technology. The outcome of this process is subject to already existing social forces, needs and power relations.

In line with the 'social shaping of technology' school of thought (Mackenzie and Wajcman 1999), Williams is not content to understand technologies only as artefacts. In fact the term 'technology' makes no reference to artefacts at all, being a compound of the two Greek roots *techne*, meaning art, craft or skill, and *logos*, meaning word or knowledge (Mackenzie and Wajcman 1999: 26). In short, technology in its original form means something like 'knowledge about skilful practices' and makes no reference at all to the products of such knowledge as tools and machines. So, for Williams, the knowledges and acquired skills necessary to use a tool or machine are an integral part of any full concept of what a technology is. McLuhan is largely silent on this, his attention being fully centred upon the ways in which technologies 'cause' different kinds of sensory experience and knowledge ordering procedures.

CASE STUDY 1.8   The social nature of a media technology

Williams takes the technology of writing, which was so important in McLuhan's scheme of things, as an example (Williams 1981: 108). He differentiates between:

· **Technical inventions and techniques** upon which a technology depends, the alphabet, appropriate tools or machines for making marks, and suitable surfaces for accurately retaining marks;

· **The substantive technology** which, in terms of writing, is a distribution technology (it distributes language) and this requires a means or form – scrolls of papyrus, portable manuscripts, mass-produced printed books, letters, or e-mails and other kinds of electronic text;

· **The technology in social use.** This includes (a) the specialised practice of writing which was initially restricted to 'official' minorities and then opened up, through education, to larger sections of society. But always, each time this happened, it was on the basis of some kind of argued need (the needs of merchants, of industrial workers, etc.), and (b) the social part of the distribution of the technologically reproduced language (reading) which again was only extended in response to perceived social needs (efficient distribution of information, participation in democratic processes, constituting a market of individuals with the ability to consume 'literature', etc.).

As Williams points out, at the time of his writing in 1981, after some thousands of years of writing and 500 years of mass reproduction in print, only 40 per cent of the world's population were able to read and hence had access to written texts. In this way, Williams argues that having noted the strictly technical and formal aspects of a technology we are still crucially short of a full grasp of what is involved. For these basic techniques and forms to be effective as a technology within a society, we also have to add the ability to read and to be constituted as part of a readership or market by publishers. Simply put, writing cannot be understood as a communications technology unless there are readers. The ability to read, and the control of, access to, and arrangements for learning to read, are part of the distributive function of the technology of writing. In this sense, Williams argues, a full description of a technology, both its development and its uses, is *always* social as well as technical and it is not simply a matter of the 'social' following the technological as a matter of 'effects'. Clearly this is an argument that can be extended to new media as policy debates about the growing existence of a 'digital divide' illustrate. The extent to which the technology can have transformative 'effects' is more or less in relation to other pre-existing patterns of wealth and power.

The concept of a medium

While McLuhan uses the term 'medium' unproblematically and is quite happy to see it as a kind of technology, Williams finds the term problematic and he shares with some other theorists (Maynard: 1997) an uneasiness about conflating 'media' and 'technology'. It is often implicit for Williams that a medium is a particular use of a technology; a harnessing of a technology to an intention or purpose to communicate or express.

CASE STUDY 1.9   When is a technology a medium?

Here we might take the much-considered case of photography. Clearly there is a photographic technology; one in which optical and mechanical systems direct light onto chemically treated surfaces which then become marked in relation to the way that configurations of light fall on that surface. This, however, is not a medium. The manufacture of silicon chips, which is a technical process upon which the manufacture of computers now depends, uses this photographic technology. It is used to etch the circuits on the microscopic chips. This is a technological process – a technology at work. However, another use of the photographic technology is to make pictures – to depict persons or events in the world. This may also be a technology at work. However, when it is said that these pictures or images provide us with information, represent an idea, express a view, or in some way invite us to exercise our imaginations in respect to the contents and forms of the image, then we may say that photography is being used as a medium. Or, more accurately, the technology of photography is being used as a medium of communication, expression, representation or imaginative projection. On this line of argument, a medium is something that we do with a technology. Clearly, what we do needs to be of an order that the technology can facilitate or support but it does not necessarily arise from the technology itself. Having an intention for a technology is not synonymous with the technology *per se*. A technology becomes a medium through many complex social transformations and transitions; it is, in Williams's reading, profoundly the product of culture and not a given consequence of technology.

Williams is also wary about the theoretical implications that the term 'medium' has come to carry. First, he criticises and virtually dismisses it as always being a misleading **reification** of a social process. Second, he sees that it is also a term that is used to recognise the part that materials play in a practice or process of production, as in artistic processes where the very nature of paint, ink, or a certain kind of camera will play a part in shaping the nature of an artistic product (1977: 159).

Medium as a reification of a social process

When he thinks about the sense in which a medium is a reification, McLuhan can be seen as very much in the centre of Williams's line of fire. Williams uses the following seventeenth-century statement about the nature of vision to demonstrate what he sees to be the major difficulty, still present in contemporary thought, with the concept of a 'medium': 'to the sight three things are required, the Object, the Organ and the Medium' (1977: 158).

The problem, he argues, is that such a formulation contains an inherent duality. A 'medium' is given the status of an autonomous object (or the process of mediation is given the status of a process that is separate from what it deals with) which stands between and connects two other separate entities: that which is mediated (an object) and that which receives the results of the mediating process (the eye). With language as his example, Williams points out that when this concept of a medium is being used, 'Words are seen as objects, things, which men [sic] take up and arrange into particular forms to express or communicate information which, before this work in the "medium" they already possess' (1977: 159).

Williams argued against this position – for him the process of mediation is itself constitutive of reality; it contributes to the making of our realities. Communication and interaction are what we do as a species. The 'medium' is not a pre-given set of formal characteristics whose effects can be read off – it is a process that itself constitutes that experience or that reality. So for Williams to argue that 'the medium is the message' is to mistake and to reify an essentially social process taking place between human agents and their interests as if it were a technological object outside of human agency. As a theoretical conception which structures thought it necessarily leaves us with sets of binary terms: the self and the world, subject and object, language and reality, ideology and truth, the conscious and unconscious, the economic base and the cultural superstructure, etc. (see **5.1.8** for some problems with binary terms).

5.1.8   A problem with binary definitions

Medium as material

One way of avoiding this problem is to narrow the definition of a medium. This is the other direction which Williams's thought on the subject takes. He recognises that a 'medium' can also be understood as 'the specific material with which a particular kind of artist worked', and 'to understand this "medium" was obviously a condition of professional skill and practice' (Williams 1977: 159). The problem here, writes Williams, is that even this down to earth sense of a medium is often extended until it stands in for the whole of a *practice*, which he famously defines as 'work on a material for a specific purpose within certain necessary social conditions' (1977: 160). Once again we see that Williams wants to stress that a medium is only part of a wider practice, a material that is worked upon to achieve human purposes pursued in determining social contexts; a means to an end.

1.6.4 The many virtues of Saint McLuhan

Introduction

1.6.2   Mapping Marshall McLuhan
Following our 'mapping' of McLuhan's ideas in **1.6.2**, we will now move on to a discussion of three core theses that emerge from those ideas. These are:

1 the extension thesis: technology is an 'extension of man' (1964);

2 the environmental thesis: 'the new media are not bridges between man and nature: they are nature' (1969: 14);

3 the anti-content thesis: 'Societies have always been shaped more by the nature of the media by which men communicate than by the content of the communication' (1964: 1).

If Williams, as we noted in **1.6.1**, has become, as it were, the 'deep structure' of cultural and media studies' address to technology, McLuhan's theses spring up, barely disguised, whenever a new medium arises and draws attention to the question of technology. It is important to note, then, that while the debate between Williams and McLuhan centres around the 'old medium' of TV, that debate continues to frame contemporary cultural discussions of technology in general, and of cyberculture in particular.

Since his 1967 review of *Understanding Media*, for instance, McLuhan has been one of the constant references in the work of Jean Baudrillard. One of Baudrillard's most famous theses, concerning 'The Implosion of Meaning in the Media' (in Baudrillard 1997), is precisely concerned to analyse further McLuhan's anti-content thesis. Similarly, Baudrillard's critics (see, for example, Kellner 1989; Gane 1991; Genosko 1999) have consistently drawn attention to his debt to, and criticisms of, McLuhan: if he rejects McLuhan's optimistic neo-tribal future, Baudrillard extends the idea that 'the medium is the message' further than McLuhan ever did. Moreover, as Istvan Csisery-Ronay (in McCaffery 1992: 162) has noted, it is precisely his concern with systems over meaning in his analyses of media that makes him a 'philosopher of **cyberpunk** and a practitioner of cybercriticism'.

Again, Arthur Kroker's analysis of technology and postmodernity places McLuhan's extension thesis at the centre of that discussion, quoting from *Counterblast* (1969: 42) McLuhan's assertion that the rise of electronic technologies makes the technological environment one composed from 'the externalisation of the human nervous system' (Kroker 1992: 64). Finally, the extension thesis recurs wherever cyborgs, 'couplings of organisms and machines' (Haraway 1991: 150), are concerned (and, as we shall see below, the longest-lived theory of technology in general is precisely the extension thesis). These examples are far from exhaustive. Indeed, while some theorists make partial use of McLuhan's work, others (de Kerckhove 1997; Genosko 1998; Levinson 1999) maintain simply that McLuhan is the theorist of cyberculture. We are not asking, however, whether Williams or McLuhan provides the more accurate or 'correct' theory. Rather, what we want to show is that this 'old media' debate continues to provide essential co-ordinates on the map of new media and cybercultural studies. As we show in **1.1**, we have been here before: debates about 'new media' have been around for a long time!

We shall examine each of McLuhan's three theses in turn.

The extension thesis

The 'extensions of man', although widely recognised as McLuhan's coinage, expresses the functional differences in human capabilities introduced by the (then) new media. It was not, however, a new idea. In fact, it stretches back to Aristotle in the fifth century BC. By tracing the long history of this thesis, however, we will see that it is clearly based in the nature of the human body. We will look at four versions of this thesis: Aristotle, Marx, Ernst Kapp, and Henri Bergson.

1.6.1 The status of McLuhan and Williams

Donald MacKenzie and Judy Wajcman's influential collection, *The Social Shaping of Technology* ([1985] 1999), for example, while it does not use Williams overtly, mounts a clearly Williamsite challenge to the question of technological determinism

1.1 What are new media?

ARISTOTLE

In two works on practical philosophy – the *Eudemian Ethics* and the *Politics* – Aristotle discusses the idea that tools are extensions of soul and body. Thus, in the former work he writes:

> For the body is the soul's natural tool, while the slave is as it were a part and detachable tool of the master, the tool being a sort of inanimate slave.
>
> (*Eudemian Ethics*, book VII, 1241b; in Barnes, 1994: 1968)

And he repeats the point in the *Politics*:

> Now instruments are of various sorts; some are living, others lifeless; in the rudder, the pilot of the ship [the *kybernetes*] has a lifeless, in the look-out man, a living instrument; for in arts [*techne*], the servant is a kind of instrument.
>
> (*Politics* book I, 1253b; in Everson 1996: 15)

5.3 Biological technologies: the history of automata

We can see a certain prefiguration of cybernetics in these passages (see **5.3**), if not of cyborgs: detachable tools, inanimate slaves, living and lifeless instruments. The core of the idea is, however, that instruments extend the functions of the labouring body.

MARX

This idea receives a further twist in Marx, where he proposes that technology is a human means of self-extension. Where Aristotle sees instruments as lifeless servants, and servants as living instruments, Marx, in *Grundrisse*, although continuing to root the thesis in the human body, is simultaneously concerned to distance the technological world from the natural realm:

> Nature builds no machines, no locomotives, railways, electric telegraphs, self-acting mules, etc. These are the products of human industry; natural material transformed into organs of the human will over nature . . . They are organs of the human brain, created by the human hand.
>
> (Marx [1857] 1993: 706)

While *part of nature*, the technological extension of human industry creates non-natural organs that in turn extend the human brain's dominion over nature. Political economist that he was, however, Marx would also note the cost of these benefits, in so far as they also transform the relation between the labouring individual and the method of working. When using hand tools, Marx writes, the labouring individual retains an independent capacity to labour; on the other hand, when it is a question of larger machines and systems of machinery (such as are found in factories; ibid.: 702), then

> The worker's activity . . . is determined and regulated on all sides by the movement of machinery, and not the opposite . . . The science which compels the inanimate limbs of the machinery, by their construction, to act purposively, as an automaton . . . acts upon [the worker] through the machine as an alien power, as the power of the machine itself.
>
> (ibid.: 693)

By extending the natural body, then, that body becomes transformed by its own extensions. If the question of who is in control of the machine is unambiguous in

Aristotle, it becomes highly complex in Marx, and the socially structuring force forming the labouring body in industrial capitalism.

KAPP

A mere twenty years after Marx's *Grundrisse*, Ernst Kapp wrote *Outlines of a Philosophy of Technology* (1877), in which the phrase 'philosophy of technology' was coined for the first time. In it Kapp wrote, apparently presciently, of a 'universal telegraphics' that would transform (i.e., shrink) time and (manipulate) space. Kapp argues that telegraphics is an extension of the nervous system, just as railways extend the circulatory system. So, like Aristotle and Marx, he viewed technology as a form of 'organ projection'. Thus:

> [s]ince the organ whose utility and power is to be increased is the controlling factor, the appropriate form of a tool can be derived only from that organ. A wealth of intellectual creations thus springs from hand, arm and teeth. The bent finger becomes a hook, the hollow of the hand a bowl; in the sword, spear, oar, shovel, rake, plough and spade, one observes the sundry positions of arm, hand, and fingers.
>
> (Kapp 1877: 44–45; cited in Mitcham 1994: 23–24)

As can be seen from this passage, Kapp is more concerned to demonstrate that the forms of tools recapitulate those of human organs. He thus echoes a well-known principle of nineteenth-century biology, but draws no more lessons from this other than to 'naturalise' the production of technological artefacts.

BERGSON

At the turn of the twentieth century we find the same idea in Henri Bergson's *Creative Evolution* ([1911]1920), where the philosopher notes that technology 'reacts on the nature of the being that constructs it', much as Marx indicates, in so far as it 'confers on him . . . a richer organisation, being an artificial organ by which the natural organism is extended' ([1911] 1920: 148).

In Bergson ([1911] 1920: 148) as in Marx, the extension is thus extended itself, as this later passage makes clear:

> If our organs are natural instruments, our instruments must then be artificial organs. The workman's tool is the continuation of his arm, the tool-equipment of humanity is therefore a continuation of its body. Nature, in endowing each of us with an essentially tool-making intelligence, prepared for us in this way a certain expansion. But machines which run on oil or coal . . . have actually imparted to our organism an extension so vast, have endowed it with a power so mighty, so out of proportion with the size and strength of that organism, that surely none of all this was foreseen in the structural plan of our species.
>
> ([1932] 1935: 267–268)

Bergson was no techno-enthusiast; on the contrary, he astutely criticised a technologically dominated way of thinking as mere 'cinematographic thought' ([1911] 1920: 287ff), and delivered thereby one of the first critical analyses of the technology and effects of cinema

Here extension has run *full circle*: the extensions, although grounded in the human body, extend themselves in such a way as to *alter* that body. While nature endowed that body, say Marx and Bergson, with a tool-making capacity with which to extend itself, that capacity has grown in scale so much that it must act on its *own* plans, having outstripped nature.

The basis of the extension thesis becomes clear: it is rooted in the nature of the human body. In all the accounts of this thesis we have examined, technology is rooted in the natural capacities or forms of that body. In some, particularly Marx and Bergson, it *feeds back* on that body and alters it, *and thereby alters its environment*. Thus we arrive at the second of McLuhan's theses: the environmental thesis.

The environmental thesis

> [T]he new media are not bridges between man and nature: they are nature.
>
> (McLuhan 1969: 14)

Whereas Marx and Bergson make explicit their claims concerning the difference between hand-tools and large-scale machines or systems of machinery, Aristotle and Kapp do not: all technology simply *extends* the body. However, the key question that Marx and Bergson pose concerns the *scale* of technological extension, or what sociologist Jacques Ellul called 'the self-augmentation of technology' ([1954] 1964: 85ff.). This thesis entails two main things:

- firstly, that above a certain threshold of *quantitative* change (the number of technologies a society uses) there arises a *qualitative* change in the structure and functioning of that society;

- secondly, that technology, at that point, becomes *autonomous*, determining its own future and that of the society it shapes.

5.2.4 Determinisms

We can see a very different account of technological determinism arising here than that Williams ascribed to McLuhan. We shall return to this account when we revisit the issue of determinism in **5.2.4**. We can immediately note, however, that the qualitative change Ellul describes evokes a relationship between what Bergson describes as the *scale* of a given technology once it has left the category of the hand-tool, and that of technology's environmental impact: we hold a hammer, but we work *in* a printing press. In this sense alone, technology clearly changes society, not only in the environmental scale of its impact but in the changes to the working relationships between human and machine this entails.

When McLuhan considers the technological environment, however, he means something quite different from the obvious, physical bulk of a factory. This means, in turn, that McLuhan does not make any qualitative distinction between tools and systems of machinery. His sense of the technological environment remains physical, but in a far more subliminal, hard-to-perceive way. When writing about the electronic media, McLuhan coins the phrase 'the hidden environment' (1969: 20–21) to describe the effects of their presence:

> Media of all kinds exert no effect on ordinary perception. They merely serve human ends (like chairs!) . . . Media effects are new environments as imperceptible as water to a fish, subliminal for the most part.
>
> (McLuhan 1969: 22)

In other words, McLuhan's idea of media effects is not of the tabloid type: Rambo machine-guns a Vietcong village, therefore an impressionable but disaffected teenager runs amok in suburbia. Rather, they subtly alter everything, so that now all human actions take place in a technologically saturated environment that has become the natural world, never rising above the threshold of perception.

An excellent illustration of what McLuhan is getting at here can be found in Paul Verhoeven's *Robocop* (1984). After Murphy (Peter Weller), a cop in soon-to-be New Detroit, is gunned down, his dying body is taken to hospital where he is 'prepped' for various cybernetic implants: titanium-cased arms and legs, capable of exerting enormous pressures, their muscular power amplified by servo-motors; a microchip memory, and so on. The last implant we witness being fitted is his visual grid, which the viewer sees being bolted down over his face plate. The grid itself becomes increasingly visible as it is screwed into place, but disappears again once fully fitted. Robocop has utterly absorbed this visual filter, no longer seeing it, but actually seeing *through* it.

Just as Kapp sought to naturalise the forms of tools and technologies, so McLuhan points to the naturalisation of effects: if we want to understand the scale of the impact of technological change on culture, we must dig deeper than the content of the media and look at the technological effects of the media themselves. This, then, brings us to the third of Saint McLuhan's many virtues: the elevation of the media above the message. Before we move on, however, note the difference between the technological environments Marx, Bergson and Ellul describe, and that which McLuhan describes: the first is a process that necessarily gets out of hand, spiralling beyond human control; the second is like the screen fitted to Robocop's ocular implants – you notice it on its way in, but not once it *becomes* the preconscious experiential filter.

THE ANTI-CONTENT THESIS: 'THE MEDIUM IS THE MASSAGE'

The above phrase is the real title of McLuhan's often misquoted but most famous work (1967). The 'massage' brings out the *tactile, sensory* effects of the media, as discussed above. At the beginning of that book, a very hypertextual collage of image and text, he writes,

> Societies have always been shaped more by the nature of the media by which men communicate than by the content of the communication.
>
> (McLuhan 1967: 1)

In other words, McLuhan is arguing that it is not the content of the media that matters at all: whatever the narrative, representational strategy or the ideological mystifications taking place in media narratives, they are decidedly unimportant next to the constant sensory assault stemming from radio and television. As he puts it in an interview, the 'massage' of his 1964 work is created by

> the shaping, the twisting, the bending of the whole human environment by technology . . . a violent process, like all new technologies, often revolting, as well as revolutionary.
>
> (McLuhan, in Stearn 1968: 331)

In contrast to this 'violent massage', to pay attention to the content of a medium or a text deludes the viewer, reader or listener into a sense of mastery over these wayward machines. McLuhan delivers his scornful verdict on those (academics) who practise this: 'Content analysis divorces them from reality' (in Stearn 1968: 329). In this view, media effects do not so much provoke violence in viewers as exert violence on them. The human sensorium is under assault from the very media into which it extended itself.

McLuhan's critical element is often left out. He is not arguing, as do Adorno and Horkheimer (1996), for example, that popular media are formally repetitive and therefore a cultural evil, but that, materially, their effects constitute a violent alteration of the sensory environment humans inhabit

If we take all three theses together, the same set of concerns emerges: the body is *physically* extended by the media; *the senses and the environment they sense* undergo a 'revolution' (Stearn 1968: 331) with every new piece of media technology. McLuhan's analyses are based on the body, the senses, and the technological environment. What unites all three is what we might call their *physicalist* emphasis – precisely what humanism in cultural and media studies has been unable to address! We will continue our discussion of the **physicalism** of new media and cybercultural studies in Part 5.

5.2.2 Causalities

In **5.2.2** we will have one further occasion to return to the McLuhan–Williams problematic, in the context of a thorough examination of what is entailed by the idea of technological determinism. Since any determinism relies on a conception of causality (to say 'X is determined by Y', is to argue that X causes Y), and since there are many accounts of causality, we have yet to establish what notion of causality Williams ascribes to McLuhan and what notion of causality McLuhan is working with.

1.6.5 Conclusion: the extent of the 'extensions of man'

At the root of the McLuhan/Williams debate lies the question of whether it is a machine's users that are in control of what they are using, or whether the machine in some sense determines its uses. In the first case, a more or less free human agency governs all historical processes, so that any event that takes place can be traced back to the actions of groups and individuals holding a certain view of things. Thus *how* we use technology is the only question we need ask of it, creating a gulf between the technology itself and its uses: it is as if technology simply does not exist until it is used. We tend, therefore, not to ask what a technology is, but what purposes it serves. That a technology is used in a particular way (the bomb to kill, television to reproduce the ideological status quo) is an accident of the views held by the controlling group. Therefore the point of studying the uses of a technology is not to study the technology but to analyse and contest the governing ideology that determines its uses. On this view, every technology is a tool.

While such a view works well for individual technologies (especially for isolated communications technologies – consider the displacement of the military ARPANET system into the Internet), it works less well if we consider the extent to which technology becomes environmental. In other words, there are *quantitative* changes in the scale of the work that can be accomplished in the shift from the tool to the machine, but as a consequence there are also fundamental *qualitative* shifts that alter the relation of human and machine. Rather than being reducible to tools for human purposes, when technology becomes environmental it can no longer be localised, isolated from the networks it forms the material basis of. This is the point from which McLuhan begins. Moreover, 'the medium is the massage' indicates the *physical* basis of the effects of technology: it is less concerned with a specific or isolated medium in the classical media studies sense (television, radio, film, etc.) than with the sense in which technology becomes the medium we inhabit. Thus, 'the new media are not bridges between man and nature: they are nature' (McLuhan 1969: 14). Accordingly, we need pay less attention to the content of a medium than its physical effects (hence 'massage' rather than *message*). These are effects principally on the body, since, beginning from the same tool-based conception of technology as does Williams, McLuhan famously views technology as 'extensions' of human capacities and senses. Technology therefore *becomes* a physical medium that alters the physical capacities of the human body. What therefore has traditionally within media studies been disparaged as technological determinism turns out merely to be taking the physical constitution and effects of a technologically saturated civilisation or culture seriously.

We have thus returned to the point from which section **1.6.4** began: the view that technology is an 'extension' of human capacities, senses, labour, and so on, a view that has such a long history in how human cultures have conceived their technologies. If, however, we seem *merely* to have come full circle, we need to re-examine what we have found out along the way. Thus we see that this definition of technology poses increasingly complex questions as technology itself becomes more complex. It is worth reiterating the points at which technology has become more complex:

1.6.4   The many virtues of Saint McLuhan

1   Materially: the relation between biological and technological things (between humans and machines) gives rise to several questions. Have our interactions with technology become so all-pervasive as to produce *hybrids* of biological and technological components, thus unsettling the distinction between the natural and the artificial, or do they result in large-scale actor-networks that resist reduction either to biological or technological bases?

2   Causally: if biology is becoming increasingly inseparable from technology (as for example in the case of the Human Genome Project), what sort of causality is involved in technology producing effects? If in a *determinist* sense, then how? Does technology now, or will it, possess or acquire agency? If so, of what kind?

3   We have seen that conceiving of technology in this way constitutes a critique of humanism, which imagines the agent as separable, isolable from his/her/its physical, causal environment. If we do not thus imagine the agent, then in what sense is technology reducible to an 'extension of man', and at what point does it begin to become 'self-extending'?

4   We therefore see that studying the question of technology in culture entails opening questions regarding what culture is, and whether it is isolable from its physical environment and the forces therein, as Williams insists it is.

For example, cloning, xenotransplantation, increasingly technological reproductive therapies, genetic engineering, artificial organs, genomics in general and the human genome in particular: the biosciences or biotechnologies seem to produce precisely such hybrids, but the possibilities go further. Cyberneticist Kevin Warwick, for example, recently conducted a year-long experiment using subcutaneously implanted microchips in his own body. Do such technologies extend or alter biological bodies?

If we answer (4) in the negative, then we see how the question of technology opens onto the question of the physical basis of culture. It also therefore opens onto scientific and, in the strictest sense, *metaphysical* issues. One such metaphysical issue, which has enormous consequences in the sciences, is causality. We have seen that some forms of determinism (of the sort that Williams accused McLuhan of holding) presuppose a *linear* causality (of the sort that McLuhan argues so strenuously against). For Williams, it is essential to pose the problem of technological effects on culture in this manner if what he called 'cultural science' is to be separable from *physical* science. A second such problem concerns *realism* and **nominalism**. Generally speaking, nominalists argue that general terms such as 'technology' constitute nothing more than collective names to designate the totality of actually existing technological artefacts. This view is called *nominalism* because it believes that general terms such as 'technology' are nothing but *names* for collections of specific individuals. When nominalists talk about technology itself (or when they spot others talking in this way), then they say this amounts to nothing other than talk about empty names. Some nominalists suggest that such terms therefore be eradicated, voided of all but numerical or grammatical sense; others accept this lack of reference to the real world as an inescapable condition of human knowledge, since it is linguistically mediated, and the reference of a term is merely a structural artefact. Realists, by contrast, argue that 'technology' as such has characteristics not necessarily instantiated in all or even in some individual and actual artefacts. Many things are technological: not only mechanical, steam, electrical or digital machines, but also social structures or 'soft technologies' as Jacques Ellul calls them (Ellul [1954] 1964). Moreover, the realist may include in the concept of technology things that do not have any actual instantiation, but that remain real in some other form or function (a good example here is Babbage's Difference Engine, which was not fully constructed until 1991: prior to that date, did such technology really exist?). The crucial difference, however, is that realists need not view language either as simply naming things, or as a screen that either frames or obscures the stuff and matter of things and forces: physics.

Both these issues come clearly into focus when we consider history in general, and the history of technology in particular. Before moving on to a discussion of these topics, which pick up from sections **1.4.** and **1.5.**, we must also note the consequences of another aspect of the extension thesis as regards technology: that is, that as technology becomes simultaneously less massive and more environmental, deterministic consequences become correspondingly more likely. This is something McLuhan missed, but that Lyotard picks clearly up on. This position, known as 'soft determinism' (determinist consequences resulting from indeterminate causes; see **5.2.4**), recognises the difference in outcome of introducing a new tool into an agrarian culture, a new power source into an industrial culture, or a new programme into a digital culture. Such considerations give rise to the view that technological determinism is not a historical constant (as hard determinists, if they exist anywhere, would argue), but is historically specific to a degree of technological complexity in a given cultural frame. Moreover, it poses the question of *what* it is that is thus extended: is it the human sensorium, will, muscles, or bodies, as Aristotle, McLuhan and Marx say, or is it technology itself, as Ellul and Lyotard argue? If the latter, is there any such place as 'nature' or 'culture' that remains exempt from the actions of technology, or do we require, as Latour demands, a new constitution for the actor-networks, neither reducibly human nor machinic, but instead, bio-socio-technical?

What then are the consequences of taking the physical effects of technology seriously? Firstly, as we shall see in **Part 5**, it entails that we can no longer separate physical from cultural processes, or matter from meaning. We can thus see how in attempting to answer the question 'what is technological determinism?' we are led to pose questions that carry us necessarily from the sphere of culture to those of technology and, finally, nature.

BIBLIOGRAPHY

Aarseth, Espen Cybertext - Experiments in Ergodic Literature, Baltimore, Md., Johns Hopkins University Press: 1997.

Barbrook, Richard and Cameron, Andy Californian Ideology, http://www.hrc.wmin.ac.uk/

Barnes, Jonathan The Complete Works of Aristotle, vol. 2, Princeton, N.J.: Princeton University Press, 1994.

Barthes, Roland S/Z, trans. Richard Miller. London: Cape, 1975.

Batchen, Geoffrey Burning with Desire, Cambridge, Mass. and London: MIT Press, 1997.

Baudrillard, Jean Simulacra and Simulations, trans. Sheila Faria Glaser. Ann Arbor: University of Michigan Press, 1997.

Benjamin, Walter 'The work of art in the age of mechanical reproduction', in Illuminations, ed. H. Arendt. Glasgow: Fontana, 1977.

Bergson, Henri, Creative Evolution, trans. Arthur Mitchell. London: Macmillan, [1911] 1920.

Berman, Ed The Fun Art Bus - An InterAction Project, London: Methuen, 1973.

Boddy, William. 'Archaeologies of electronic vision and the gendered spectator', *Screen* 35.2 (1994): 105–122.

Bolter, Jay David *Writing Space: the computer, hypertext and the history of writing*, New York: Lawrence Erlbaum Associates, 1991.

Bolter, J. and Grusin, R. *Remediation: understanding new media*, Cambridge, Mass. and London: MIT Press, 1999.

Brecht, Bertolt 'The radio as an apparatus of communication', in *Video Culture*, ed. J. Hanhardt. New York: Visual Studies Workshop, 1986.

Burgin, Victor *Thinking Photography*, London: Macmillan Press, 1982.

Bush, Vannevar. 'As we may think' [*Atlantic Monthly*, 1945], in P. Mayer, *Computer Media and Communication: a reader*, Oxford: Oxford University Press, 1999.

Castells, M. *The Rise of the Network Society*, Oxford: Blackwell, 1996.

Castells, M. *The Rise of the Network Society*, Oxford: Blackwell, 2000.

Chartier, R. *The Order of Books*, Cambridge: Polity Press, 1994.

Chesher, C. 'The ontology of digital domains', in D. Holmes (ed.) *Virtual Politics*, London, Thousand Oaks (Calif.), New Delhi: Sage, 1997.

Coyle, Rebecca 'The genesis of virtual reality', in *Future Visions: new technologies of the screen*, eds Philip Hayward and Tana Woollen. London: BFI, 1993.

Crary, Jonathan *Techniques of the Observer: on vision and modernity in the nineteenth century*, Cambridge, Mass., and London: MIT Press, 1993.

Darley, A. 'Big screen, little screen: the archeology of technology', *Digital Dialogues. Ten 8* 2.2 (1991): 78–87.

Darley, Andrew *Visual Digital Culture: surface play and spectacle in new media genres*, London and New York: Routledge, 2000.

Davies, Char 'Osmose: Notes in being in immersive virtual space', in *Digital Creativity* 9.2 (1998): 65–74.

De Kerckhove, Derrick. *The Skin of Culture*, Toronto: Somerville House, 1997.

De Lauretis, T., Woodward K., Huyssen A. *The Technological Imagination: theories and fictions*, Madison, Wisconsin: Coda Press, 1980.

Derrida, Jacques *Of Grammatology*, Baltimore, Md.: Johns Hopkins University Press, 1976.

Dery, Mark *Culture Jamming: hacking, slashing, and sniping in the empire of signs*, Westfield: Open Media, 1993.

Dovey, J. ed. *Fractal Dreams*, London: Lawrence and Wishart, 1995.

Druckery, T. ed. *Ars Electronica Facing the Future*, Cambridge, Mass. and London: MIT Press, 1999.

Duffy, Dennis Marshall *McLuhan*, Toronto: McClelland and Stuart Ltd, 1969.

Eastgate Systems. http://www.eastgate.com Hypertext Fiction.

Eisenstein, E. *The Printing Press as an Agent of Change*, Cambridge: Cambridge University Press, 1979.

Ellul, Jacques, *The Technological Society*, New York: Vintage, [1954] 1964.

Engelbart, Douglas 'A conceptual framework for the augmentation of man's intellect', in *Computer Media and Communication*, ed. Paul Mayer. Oxford: Oxford University Press, 1999.

Enzenberger, Hans Magnus 'Constituents of a theory of mass media', in *Dreamers of the Absolute*, London: Radius, 1988.

Everson, Stephen, ed. *Aristotle, The Politics and The Constitution of Athens*, Cambridge: Cambridge University Press, 1996.

Featherstone, M. ed. *Global Culture*, London, Thousand Oaks (Calif.), New Delhi: Sage, 1990.

Flichy, P. 'The construction of new digital media', *New Media and Society* 1.1 (1999): 33–38.

Foucault, Michel *The Archaeology of Knowledge*, London: Tavistock, 1972.

Foucault, Michel 'What is an author', in *Modern Criticism and Theory*, ed. David Lodge. London: Longman, 1998.

Gane, Mike *Baudrillard: critical and fatal theory*, London: Routledge, 1991.

Genosko, Gary *McLuhan and Baudrillard: the masters of implosion*, London: Routledge, 1998.

Gibson, W. *Neuromancer*, London: Grafton, 1986.

Gonzalez, J. 'Envisioning cyborg bodies: notes from current research', in *The Cyborg Handbook*, ed. C. Hables Gray. New York and London: Routledge, 1995.

Graham, Beryl 'Playing with yourself' in *Fractal Dreams*, ed. J. Dovey. London: Lawrence and Wishart, 1996.

Greenberg, Clement 'Modernist painting' [1961] in *Modern Art and Modernism: a critical anthology*, eds Francis Frascina and Charles Harrisson. London: Harper Row, 1982.

Gunning, Tom 'Heard over the phone: the lonely villa and the De Lorde tradition of the terrors of technology', *Screen* 32.2 (1991): 184–196.

Hall, S. *Television as a Medium and its Relation to Culture*, Occasional Paper No. 34. Birmingham: The Centre for Contemporary Cultural Studies, 1975.

Hanhardt, J. G. *Video Culture*, Rochester, N.Y.: Visual Studies Workshop Press, 1986.

Haraway, Donna *Simians, Cyborgs and Women*, London: Free Association, 1991.

Harrison, C. and Wood, P. *Art in Theory: 1990–1990*, Oxford and Cambridge, Mass.: Blackwell, 1992.

Harvey, D. *The Condition of Postmodernity*, Oxford: Blackwell, 1989.

Hayles, N. Katherine 'Virtual bodies and flickering signifiers', in *How We Became Post-Human*, ed. N. Katherine Hayles. Chicago and London: University of Chicago Press, 1999.

Hebdige, Dick *Hiding in the Light: on images and things*, London and New York: Comedia and Routledge, 1988.

Heim, Michael 'The erotic ontology of cyberspace', in *Cyberspace: the first steps*, ed. Michael Benedikt. Cambridge, Mass.: MIT Press, 1991.

Heim, Michael *The Metaphysics of Virtual Reality*, New York and Oxford: Oxford University Press, 1993.

Holmes, David ed. *Virtual Politics*, London, Thousand Oaks (Calif.), New Delhi: Sage, 1997.

Holzmann, Steve *Digital Mosaics: the aesthetics of cyberspace*, New York: Simon and Shuster, 1997.

Huhtamo, Erkki 'From cybernation to interaction: a contribution to an archeology of interactivity', in *The Digital Dialectic*, ed. P. Lunenfeld. Cambridge, Mass.: MIT Press, 2000.

Jensen, Jens F. 'Interactivity – tracking a new concept in media and communication studies', in *Computer Media and Communication*, ed. Paul Mayer. Oxford: Oxford University Press, 1999.

Joyce, Michael *Of Two Minds: hypertext pedagogy and poetics*, Ann Arbor: University of Michigan, 1995.

Kapp, Ernst. *Grundlinien einer Philosophie des Technik. Zur Entstehungsgeschichte der Kultur ans neuen Gesichtspunkten* [Outlines of a Philosophy of Technology: new perspectives on the evolution of culture], Braunschweig: Westermann, 1877.

Kay, Alan and Goldberg, Adele 'Personal dynamic media', *Computer*, 10 March 1977.

Kay, Alan and Goldberg, Adele 'A new home for the mind', in *Computer Media and Communication*, ed. P. Mayer. Oxford: Oxford University Press, 1999.

Kellner, Douglas. *Jean Baudrillard: from Marxism to postmodernism and beyond*, Cambridge: Polity Press, 1989.

Kroker, Arthur. *The Possessed Individual*, New York: Macmillan, 1992.

Landow, George *Hypertext: the convergence of contemporary literary theory and technology*, Baltimore, Md.: John Hopkins University Press, 1992.

Landow, George ed. *Hyper/Text/Theory*, Baltimore, Md.: Johns Hopkins University Press, 1994.

Landow, George and Delaney, Pauls eds. *Hypermedia and Literary Studies*, Cambridge, Mass.: MIT Press, 1991.

Laughton, R. *et al. Skills for Tomorrow's Media – Report of Skillset/DCMS Audio Visual Industries Training Group*, London: Skillset, 2001. http://www.skillset.org.

Levinson, Paul *Digital McLuhan*, London: Routledge, 1999.

Lévy, Pierre 'The aesthetics of cyberspace', in *Electronic Culture*, ed. T. Druckery. New York: Aperture, 1997.

Licklider, J.C.R. 'Man computer symbiosis' in *Computer Media and Communication*, ed. Paul Mayer. Oxford: Oxford University Press, 1999.

Licklider, J.C.R. and Taylor, R.W. 'The computer as communication device', in *Computer Media and Communication*, ed. Paul Mayer. Oxford: Oxford University Press, 1999.

Lister, M. 'Introductory essay', in *The Photographic Image in Digital Culture*, London and New York: Routledge, 1995.

Lunenfeld, Peter 'Digital dialectics: a hybrid theory of computer media', *Afterimage* 21.4 (1993):

Lury, Celia 'Popular culture and the mass media', in *Social and Cultural Forms of Modernity*, eds Bocock and Thompson, Cambridge: Polity Press and the Open University, 1992.

Mackay, H. and O'Sullivan, T. eds *The Media Reader: continuity and transformation*, London, Thousand Oaks (Calif.), New Delhi: Sage, 1999.

MacKenzie, Donald and Wajcman, Judy *The Social Shaping of Technology*, Buckingham and Philadelphia: Open University Press, 1999.

Manovich, Lev 'What is digital cinema', in *The Digital Dialectic: essays on new media*, ed. P. Lunenfeld, Cambridge, Mass.: MIT Press, 2000.

Martin, Jay. 'Scopic regimes of modernity', in *Vision and Visuality*, ed. Hal Foster. Seattle: Bay Press, 1988.

Marvin, C. *When Old Technologies Were New*, New York and Oxford: Oxford University Press, 1988.

Mayer, Paul. *Computer Media and Communication: a reader*, Oxford: Oxford University Press, 1999.

Maynard, Patrick. *The Engine of Visualisation*, Ithaca, N.Y.:Cornell University Press, 1997.

Marx, Karl *Grundrisse*, trans. Martin Nicolaus. Harmondsworth: Penguin, [1857] 1993.

McCaffrey, Larry ed. *Storming the Reality Studio: a casebook of cyberpunk and postmodernism*, Durham, N.C.: Duke University Press, 1992.

McLuhan, Marshall *The Gutenberg Galaxy: the making of typographic man*, Toronto: University of Toronto Press, 1962.

McLuhan, Marshall *Understanding Media: the extensions of man*, Toronto: McGraw Hill, 1964.

McLuhan, M. *Understanding Media*, London: Sphere, 1968.

McLuhan, Marshall *Connterblast*, London: Rapp and Whiting, 1969.

McLuhan, M. and Carpenter, E. 'Acoustic space', in *Explorations in Communications*, eds M. McLuhan and E. Carpenter. Boston: Beacon Press, 1965.

McLuhan, Marshall and Fiore, Quentin *The Medium is the Massage: an inventory of effects*, New York, London, Toronto: Bantam Books, 1967a.

McLuhan, Marshall and Fiore, Quentin *War and Peace in the Global Village*, New York, London, Toronto: Bantam Books, 1967.

Meek, Allen 'Exile and the electronic frontier', *New Media and Society* 2.1 (2000): 85–104.

Miller, J. *McLuhan*, London: Fontana, 1971.

Mirzoeff, N. *An Introduction to Visual Culture*, London and New York: Routledge, 1991.

Mitcham, Carl *Thinking Through Technology*, Chicago: University of Chicago Press, 1994.

Moody, Nickianne 'Interacting with the divine comedy', in *Fractal Dreams: new media in social context*, ed. Jon Dovey. London: Lawrence and Wishart, 1995.

Morley, David *The Nationwide Audience*, London: British Film Institute, 1980.

Morse, Margaret *Virtualities: television, media art, and cyberculture*, Bloomington: Indiana University Press, 1998.

Moser, Mary Anne and McAllen, Douglas *Immersed in Technology: art and virtual environments*, Cambridge, Mass. and London: MIT Press, 1996.

Moulthrop, Stuart 'Toward a rhetoric of informating texts in hypertext', *Proceedings of the Association for Computing Machinery*, New York, 1992.

Murray, Janet *Hamlet on the Holodeck - The Future of Narrative in Cyberspace*, Cambridge, Mass. and London: MIT Press, 1997.

Neale, Steve *Cinema and Technology: Image, Sound, Colour*, London: BFI, 1985.

Nelson, Ted 'A file structure for the complex, the changing, and the indeterminate', *Proceedings of the 20th Annual National Conference for Computing Machines*, New York, 1965.

Nelson, Ted 'A new home for the mind' [1982], in *Computer Mediated Communications*, ed. P. Mayer. Oxford: Oxford University Press, 1999.

Ong, W. *Orality and Literacy*, London and New York: Routledge, 2002.

Penny, Simon 'The Darwin machine: artifical life and interactive art', *New Formations, TechnoScience* 29.64 (1966): 59–68.

Poster, Mark *The Mode of Information*, London: Polity Press, 1990.

Poster, Mark 'Underdetermination', *New Media and Society* 1.1 (1999): 12–17.

Ragland-Sullivan, Ellie 'The imaginary', in *Feminism and Psychoanalysis: a critical dictionary*, ed. E. Wright. Oxford: Basil Blackwell, 1992.

Rheingold, Howard *Virtual Worlds*, London: Secker and Warburg, 1991.

Rieser, M. and Zapp, A. eds *Interactivity and Narrative*, London: British Film Institite, 2001.

Ritchen, Fred *In Our Own Image: the coming revolution in photography*, New York: Aperture, 1990.

Robins, K. 'Into the image', in *PhotoVideo: photography in the age of the computer*, ed. P. Wombell. London: River Orams Press, 1991.

Robins, K. 'Will images move us still?', in *The Photographic Image in Digital Culture*, ed. M. Lister. London and New York: Routledge, 1995.

Robins, Kevin *Into the Image: Culture and Politics in the Field Of Vision*, London and New York: Routledge, 1996.

Sabbah, Françoise 'The new media', in *High Technology Space and Society*, ed. Manuel Castells. Beverly Hills, Calif.: Sage, 1985.

Sarup, M. *Post-structuralism and Postmodernism* Hemel Hempstead: Harvester Wheatsheaf, 1988.

Schivelbusch, Wolfgang. *The Railway Journey: the industrialisation of time and space in the 19th century*, Berkeley and Los Angeles: University of California Press, 1977.

Shutz, Tanjev 'Mass media and the concept of interactivity: an exploratory study of online forums and reader email', *Media, Culture and Society* 22.2 (2000): 205–221.

Silverstone, Roger. *Why Study the Media*, London, Thousand Oaks (Calif.) and New Delhi: Sage, 1999.

Spiegel, Lynn *Make Room for TV: television and the family ideal in postwar America*, Chicago: University of Chicago Press, 1992.

Stafford, Barbara Maria *Artful Science: enlightenment entertainment and the eclipse of visual education*, Cambridge, Mass. and London: MIT Press, 1994.

Stearn, G.E. *McLuhan: hot and cool*, Toronto: Signet Books, 1968.

Stevenson, Nick *Understanding Media Cultures: social theory and mass communication*, London: Sage, 1995.

Stone, Roseanne Allucquere 'Will the real body please stand up', in *Cyberspace: First steps*, ed. Michael Benedikt. Cambridge, Mass. and London: MIT Press, 1994.

Stone, Rosanne Allucquere *The War of Desire and Technology at the Close of the Mechanical Age*, Cambridge, Mass.: MIT Press, 1995.

Strinati, Dominic 'Mass culture and popular culture and The Frankfurt School and the culture industry', in *An Introduction to Theories of Popular Culture*, London and New York: Routledge, 1995.

Tagg, J. *The Burden of Representation*, London: Macmillan, 1998.

Taylor, M.C. and Saarinen, E. *Imagologies: media philosophy*, London and New York: Routledge, 1994.

Theal, Donald *The Medium is the RearView Mirror*, Montreal and London: McGill-Queens University Press, 1995.

Thompson, J.B. *The Media and Modernity: a social theory of the media*, Cambridge: Polity Press, 1971.

Weibel, Peter 'The world as interface', in *Electronic Culture*, ed. Timothy Druckery. New York: Aperture, 1996.

Williams, R. *Television, Technology and Cultural Form*, London: Fontana, 1974.

Williams, R. *Culture*, London: HarperCollins, 1981.

Williams, R. *Towards 2000*, Harmondsworth: Penguin, 1983.

Williams, Raymond *The Long Revolution*, London: Penguin. 1961.

Williams, Raymond *Keywords: a vocabulary of culture and society*, Glasgow: Fontana, 1976.

Williams, Raymond *Marxism and Literature*, Oxford: Oxford University Press, 1977.

Williams, Raymond 'Means of production', in *Culture*, London: Fontana, 1986.

Winston, B. *Media, Technology and Society: a history from the telegraph to the internet*, London and New York: Routledge, 1998.

Winston, Brian 'The case of HDTV: light, camera, inaction: Hollywood and Technology', in *Technologies of Seeing: photography, cinematography and television*, London: BFI, 1996.

Youngblood, Gene 'A medium matures: video and the cinematic enterprise' in *Ars Electronica Facing the Future*, ed. T. Druckery. Cambridge, Mass. and London: MIT Press, 1999.

2 NEW MEDIA AND VISUAL CULTURE

NEW TECHNOLOGIES AND THE ISSUES FOR VISUAL CULTURE/VISUAL
CULTURE/VISUALITY/COULD THERE BE A DISTINCT DIGITAL VISUAL CULTURE/NEW
IMAGE TECHNOLOGIES/IMMERSIVE VIRTUAL REALITY/VR AS A MEDIUM OF
ART/DIGITAL CINEMA

2.1 NEW TECHNOLOGIES AND THE ISSUES FOR VISUAL CULTURE

In our discussion (1.2) of two of the characteristic features of new media, digitality and virtuality, we stressed their implications for the social practice of media – what did they mean for the ways in which media products are produced, distributed and received? These social aspects are further discussed in **Part 3**. In this part of the book we will be centrally concerned with how such technologies may be contributing to changes taking place in visual culture. We ask a specific question which has social implications: how do new media technologies contribute to change in the qualities of images produced in our already highly technologised visual culture – a culture dominated throughout the twentieth century by the visual media of chemical photography, narrative film and cinema, broadcast television and video? How might these changes contribute to the long history of the life and culture of images? We also consider the argument that the nature of vision, understood as a cultural practice rather than a biological function, and the relationship that viewers have to images, is changing. Is it possible to argue that new 'ways of seeing' are emerging alongside the image-making and envisioning capacities of new media?

1.2 The characteristics of new media: some defining concepts

3 NETWORKS USERS AND ECONOMICS

In Part 2 we open up these questions by examining three main claims:

- First, that image-making, vision, and the image itself are undergoing radical shifts in their nature as they become increasingly autonomous and machinic and, some argue, acquire a life of their own.

- Second, that a new aesthetic is emerging in which depth, narrative and meaning are being replaced with the pleasures of sensuous experience and spectacular effects.

- Third, that recent developments in image technology may be revealing that the images produced by mechanical media – particularly photography and film – merely represent a historical phase in visual culture, which is now being displaced by current developments and the experience of being immersed within images.

We discuss these issues for visual culture by looking, in some detail, at two developments:

- the building of immersive virtual environments and the concept of virtual reality (VR);

- the introduction of digital techniques into film production and cinema exhibition.

A dialectic can be defined as the meeting of elements or processes (in our case, traditional forms of visual representation and new technological possibilities), the contradictions and tensions which arise, and then the possible outcomes or resolutions of those contradictions

Although one of these developments (immersive VR) is a relatively rare phenomenon and a largely experimental practice, while digital cinema is an increasingly familiar and popular form, they are related in a number of ways. Further, in concentrating on these two topics we are able to consider in more detail the dialectic between established traditions in vision and representation and new technological possibilities. However, before we do this it will be useful to remind ourselves of what the concept of a 'visual culture' holds and the role that media technologies, new or old, play in it.

2.2 VISUAL CULTURE

The term 'visual culture' invites us to take account of the specific roles that visual images, and visual experience more generally, play within a particular society or community, rather than considering only the content of images or their **referentiality.**

By 'referentiality' we mean to the manner in which images refer to things in the world outside them (and the very idea that they do) – how, in other terms, an image depicts or re-presents an object or event existing in the physical world (including, of course, the manner in which such depictions may be combined by the image-maker to represent an imagined event)

The study of visual culture also draws attention to the cultural, economic, technical and political institutions within which visual things are produced and circulated. To sum up, the study of visual culture includes paying attention to:

1   the signifying systems, the 'languages', skills and techniques that a culture employs in producing the visual, and its members' ability to read, decode or otherwise make sense of these signs;

2   the uses and values accorded to vision in a particular culture – consider how, in the West, to see something clearly is often thought to be a guarantee of the truth of a situation, while in traditional Islamic cultures, and at periods in Christian cultures, images and visions are seen to be seductive and unreliable illusions which mask the truth;

3   the power that the ability to see (in a way that is historically and culturally particular) confers upon the seer over the seen; this has been particularly noted in connection with the exercise of power by one social class, ethnic group, or gender over others;

4   the manner in which technologies (a telescope or microscope), media (a camera or a DVD player), and ideas or ideologies (that alert us to look for certain things rather than others) extend, amplify or selectively restrict the realm of the visual.

2.7   VR as a medium of art: a quantum leap forward?

Some examples will be useful. First, by attending to the particular 'signifying systems, the "languages", skills and techniques' employed in producing images, we are led to see that the meaning or interest that a historically specific set of images has depends upon the kind of skills and expectations possessed by the viewer (their 'visual literacy'). Consider, for example, the use of mathematical techniques such as perspective and proportion (as discussed in **2.7**) in the kind of painting that was new in fifteenth-century Italy. On the one hand, the development and use of such techniques could be said to reflect that period's new faith in human powers and capacities, and the challenge to mystical, religious or god-centred explanations of things. This tells us a great deal about the intellectual history of the period, and, in turn, it helps explain the production of such works. However, it does not explain their consumption. While some highly informed viewers and patrons of such art may well have understood, and therefore appreciated, the artists' use of such mathematical techniques in themselves, this does not adequately explain their broader legibility and interest to their contemporary viewers. A second argument, therefore, concerning the legibility of these new mathematised images is that their construction reflected a more widely distributed social skill, amongst significant groups of fifteenth-century Italians, in judging proportions and volumes. This was a skill that was especially used in trading circles – a literacy in judging volumes and proportion that stemmed from the measuring of goods for sale and consumption in barrels, flasks and bales, and would therefore be familiar to anyone buying or selling grain, for example (Baxandall 1972: 86–94).

Second, the study of visual culture concerns itself with the distribution of powers of seeing. While clearly not a biological difference, nor even an absolute cultural difference, John Berger (1972) and Laura Mulvey (1973) after him, advanced arguments in the 1970s concerning the gendered distribution of vision: men look, women are looked at. Such conventional practices are reinforced through cinema and advertising, for example, and spill over into general cultural attitudes and debates concerning pornography, 'objectification' and the 'male gaze'. But such imbalances of power centred upon vision are by no means confined to the use of media. They are also found in the arrangements and institutions of everyday life. Michel Foucault's famous account of Jeremy Bentham's panoptic (wide – or all seeing) prison designs of the eighteenth century, for instance, led him to see them as apparatuses of surveillance and to conclude that 'visibility is a trap' (Foucault 1977: 200). In such prisons the inmates were always conscious that they could be seen by a centrally positioned guard *whom they could not see*; indeed, whom they could not always be sure was occupying their central surveillance point. However, the uneven distribution of the power of vision that was designed into this building conferred control upon the seer over the seen.

We might also consider the legal status that is accorded to certain types of image. Being 'caught in the act' by other persons, at the site of a crime, differs greatly from being caught on film or video, as the episode of Rodney King's assault by the LAPD makes abundantly clear (Nichols: 1994). As this case demonstrated, between the actual event on site and seeing it remotely, there is room for a whole world of plausible denial based on the technical capacities of image manipulation technologies. While the popular saying urges us to accept that 'the camera does not lie', we now have to deal with seeing the image of a deceased Richard Nixon seamlessly interact with Tom Hanks on film, Steve McQueen coming back from the dead to advertise cars, and digital image-processing extending the image-making possibilities of photography beyond the recording of an event to its very construction (Mitchell 1992: 23–57).

Finally, we can consider the role played by instruments of visualisation. Scientific visualisation, for example, depends on codes of visual literacy that are highly specialist and restrictive and yet embody considerable power and authority. How do you read an X-ray? Medicine now relies increasingly on a number of technical visual regimes (apart from the X-ray): CAT scans, PET scans, heart and respiration monitors, and so on. The employment of such techniques emphasises the distance between patient and agent in medical transactions (Kember 1995). Recently, given the advent of the human genome, scientific visual artefacts have acquired ever greater status as arbiters, not only of health but also of what is 'normal' in human forms, as they become new devices for locating genetic deviancy. The complex imaging techniques involved in such practices lend the scientific image an extraordinary currency and authority. Meanwhile, in training, education and public relations exercises, computer-generated diagrams and 'presentations' are increasingly used to lend weight and convey (but also to reduce and simplify) what it is 'essential' to see or know.

Clearly then, the study of visual culture is a broader field of enquiry than traditional art

For a discussion of Foucault's theory of panopticism see N. Mirzoeff, *An Introduction to Visual Culture*, London and New York: Routledge, 1999, pp. 50–51

history, as it does not confine itself to the special range of images, historical and contemporary, that are produced and placed by a society as 'Art'. The proponents of this field of study find the conditions which led to the intellectual project to study a wider visual culture than the history of art in the mid-nineteenth-century. For it was from that time on that the mechanical production and reproduction of images and visual entertainments filled the Western world with images, visually symbolic objects, spectacles and sights on a wholly new scale. Alongside the use of photography (still and moving) we also have to take account of the advent of electricity and image projection, illustrated newspapers and magazines, advertising, design and packaging, increased leisure time, the growth of commodity consumption and display, public museums, artificial lighting, and the construction of new urban spaces and vistas. In such a world the unique and handmade images of art and craft were sucked into a 'frenzy of the visual'.

The images produced by the traditional technologies of painting and other autographic processes (drawing, manual and mechanical printing) of artists could no longer stand alone as discrete objects of attention for a minority of educated people. For the majority of people in Western industrialised countries, ideas and information came to be mediated through this fabricated, sensory environment of images, displays and sights. In such an environment any one medium or mode of visual representation no longer stood alone, feeding only on its own traditions. In such a situation, 'The meanings and effects of any single image are always adjacent to this overloaded and plural sensory environment and to the observer who inhabited it' (Crary 1993: 23).

Scenes of such visual overload, at least partly based in some of our everday realities, are frequently presented in films such as *Bladerunner* (Ridley Scott, 1982). They are there equally a part of the experience of our cityscapes filled with revolving supersite hoardings, video walls, screens, neon, and traffic signs. In such environments, we must all of necessity become editors, jump-cutting from one piece of visual input to another, and becoming incapable of action if we step back to gaze upon the bewildering whole. In this sense, visual culture becomes a term to describe a modern social world in which the whole history of images is stored, reproduced and re-presented, while new image commodities are rapidly and continuously produced, circulated and consumed via sophisticated visual technologies. They mediate our experience and condition our ideas, relationships, and social lives at every turn.

However, the study of visual culture is similar to the history of art in at least one important respect. This is that it recognises that the effort to understand visual phenomena and artefacts requires special procedures and conceptual frameworks. We do not make, receive, or otherwise experience visual images, nor perceive the physical world, in the same ways as we experience writing or speech or that we read and listen. The visual has a different kind of power, and it engages our senses in different ways, than does the written word. Put simply, the visual has another 'language'.

With an explosion of imaging and visualising technologies in the early twentieth century (the industrialisation and penetration of photography and film into many areas of social life), the coming of TV and video, and another at the end of the century (digitisation, satellite imaging, new forms of medical imaging, multi-media, virtual reality, etc.), it has been suggested that visual culture is not just a part of everyday life but 'is everyday life' (Mirzoeff 1998: 3).

If we take this suggestion seriously, we encounter the question as to whether visual culture may no longer be just one aspect of culture but is, instead, the dominant or overwhelming form that culture now takes. If we consider the history sketched above,

These are the developments discussed in a celebrated essay by Walter Benjamin, 'The work of art in the age of mechanical reproduction' [1935] 1970

It has been argued that this new **visuality** of culture calls for its own, new, field of study concerned with all kinds of visual information and its meanings, pleasures, and consumption, including the study of all visual technologies, from 'oil painting to the internet' (Mirzoeff 1998: 3)

which is seen to lead to this state (a history of image media and technologies coming to increasingly pervade culture and everyday life, from the mid-nineteenth century onwards), we are returned to the wider question about what causal relationship technology has to cultural change, visual or otherwise (**Part 5**) – a question that lies at the heart of current debates about new media.

2.3 VISUALITY

The study of visual culture includes, then, more than the study of images, however widely that category is cast; it also studies their meanings, pleasures, and our modes of consumption. Such consumption (literally 'taking into oneself'), and finding meaning and pleasure in that act, is precisely the act of seeing, the operation of vision. Within visual cultural studies, the term 'visuality' stands for the way that vision and the various modes of attention that we commonly identify – seeing, looking, gazing, spectating and observing – are historically variable. It reminds us that 'vision is an active, interpretative process strongly governed by communities and institutions, rather than an innocent openness to natural stimuli' (Wood 1996: 68). So, while the human eye, as an organ, may have changed little if at all, over millennia, there is evidence that the complex psychological and intellectual processes involved in experiencing the world through the sense of sight do change. We may say that the biologically healthy eye as a mere organ is 'innocent' and 'open' to natural stimuli, but the eye as one element in the complex process of visual perception, and all of the tasks given it, is far from innocently open. The capacity to see is educated and disciplined, habituated and interested, and primed to be alert or dormant in one way or another; ways that are specific to culture and history. Broadly speaking, there are different 'ways of seeing' (Berger 1972) at different historical times and within different cultures that are shaped by the ideas, interests, social institutions and technologies of an era or culture. From this perspective it is argued that the study of visual culture cannot be confined to the study of images, but should also take account of the centrality of the active practice of vision in everyday experience. As Irit Rogoff puts it:

> In the arena of visual culture the scrap of an image connects with a sequence of film and with the corner of a billboard or the window display of a shop we have passed by, to produce a new narrative formed out of both our experienced journey and our unconscious. Images do not stay within discrete disciplinary fields such as 'documentary film' or 'Renaissance painting', since neither the eye nor the psyche operates along or recognises such divisions.
>
> (Rogoff 1998: 16)

It is not hard to see that the flow and complex relations between kinds of images which Rogoff points to is likely to be accelerated and thickened in an image-biased world of networked and converging new media. Further, her examples of how the active, connecting, narrativising, remembering, and sometimes unconscious, 'cultural' eye all refer to material or fixed images (a film, a billboard, a window display). How much farther might the subversion of academic categories and divisions between kinds of image (a documentary, a renaissance painting) be carried within the contemporary environment and networked flows of digital images? To what extent, indeed, is digital culture the domain of the image in general; a predominantly visual culture?

Some theorists of visual culture are worried by the repetitive nature of this history. They worry that the study of contemporary visual culture is being 'subsumed under often unsubstantiated and metaphysical claims about contemporary cultural developments, operating under the banner of "postmodern", "simulation", and even more recently, "prosthetic" culture'. While, at the same time, these current preoccupations look like a recycling, 'one time too many', of an older history; a history of the explosion of images, spectacles, displays and 'phantasmagoria' brought about by the new image technologies, entertainments, and consumer markets of the nineteenth century and the early twentieth (Evans and Hall 1990: 5)

2.4 COULD THERE BE A DISTINCT DIGITAL VISUAL CULTURE?

In considering the entry of new media technologies into contemporary visual culture we now need to ask, 'To what extent can dramatic contemporary change in the kinds of visual images we meet and the power we have to see, be accounted for in terms of new technologies?' For example: has the possibility of being immersed in a three-dimensional visual environment, in a VR game or a 3D Imax feature, sprung from nowhere? Was it simply born of an unexpected technological event that has cut us loose from the kind of relationship we have historically had with images? Finally, is our consumption of new visual media and use of vision technologies a clear case of a 'new way of seeing' emerging?

Ways of seeing

Before we examine some responses to these questions, we should note two things at the outset. First, that there can be little ground for arguing that we are likely to find anything like a *distinct* digital visual culture or a related, autonomous way of seeing that simply replaces, once and for all, the complex, historically sedimented visual cultures that already exist. Second, media technologies are not monolithic and can have multiple uses or outcomes. We will take each point in turn.

In complex societies (and especially to the extent that societies are subject to hybrid and globalising processes) different visual cultures, different sets of aesthetic values, and different ways of seeing co-exist alongside one another. One visual culture does not supplant another altogether; rather, different technologies of image production, transmission and distribution co-exist alongside each other and engage our attention in different ways (going to the movies as against watching the television). Despite some thought-provoking attempts to argue that there are dominant 'ways of seeing' within a culture, the ensuing debate and research aroused by these arguments point strongly to the fact that there are no unitary ways of seeing within a culture, or that a newly emergent kind simply replaces or wholly dominates over historical ones. (See **Case study 2.1**.)

CASE STUDY 2.1   Ways of seeing

A good example of one such proposal, its challenge and subsequent qualification can be found in the area of film studies (Linda Williams 1995).

We are here taking the film theoretical concept, a 'viewing position', as a specialised version of a specific 'visuality' or 'way of seeing'

In the 1970s, the film theorist Laura Mulvey influentially pronounced that the era of classical Hollywood movies had produced a specific kind of visuality (Mulvey 1973). The nature of these Hollywood movies was such as to lead viewers to look as voyeuristic, fetishistic, men. Mulvey saw this as a kind of vision or 'looking' generated both by the form of the movie and by an ideology of masculinity, which allowed the male viewer to feel in control of the female. In wider terms she saw this as an extension of a historically dominant form of visuality – a way of looking associated with white, middle-class males who looked to survey and give order and coherence to the world in which they were socially dominant and desired to control. A look which desired to see everything in its proper place!

However, as Linda Williams points out, a combination of the very brilliance with which Mulvey constructed her analysis and an uncomfortable sense that it was too totalising or absolute encouraged further thought. While saving Mulvey's insight (and that of others such as Metz and Baudry) into the way a film and other kinds of image offer their audiences a position and an identity from which to look at the world they depict, the idea that there is one such position, even for one film, has been convincingly shown to be untenable. The situation is far more complex. A whole range of spectators with different social, sexual, or ethnic identities do not see the film as if their eyes were innocently 'open' to its (crafted) stimuli. There are indeed 'visualities' in play, but they are not of one dominant kind. As Williams puts it, 'The singular, unitary spectator . . . has gradually been challenged by diverse viewing positions. Whereas 1970s and 1980s film theory tended to posit . . . a unitary way of seeing, contemporary discussions of spectatorship emphasise the plurality and paradoxes of many different *historically distinct* viewing positions' (1995: 3; our emphasis).

So, while 'viewing positions' (a film theory concept with close affinities to 'visuality') still needs to be thought of as historically distinct and historically changing, it is a mistake to look for single, unitary forms of visuality as if they are the only, or inevitable, outcomes of a certain media technology, form or genre. In fact the problem for the study of changing visualities, such as we may consider is taking place with the advent of new media, is now different. It is similar to that which faced film theory once the idea of a unitary, ideology prone spectator was successfully challenged: 'The issue that now faces the once influential sub-field of spectatorship within cinema – *and indeed all visual-studies* – is whether it is still possible to maintain a theoretical grasp of the relations between moving images and viewers without succumbing to an anything-goes pluralism' (Williams 1995: 4).

We will now turn our attention to the technology itself. The key point here is that while we may be able to identify some distinguishing characteristics of a specific image technology (1.2), which have implications for how we use it, such technologies are not monolithic. We might note Lev Manovich's remark about the usefulness of the term 'website': 'We can't go on simply using technical terms such as "a website" to refer to works radically different from each other in intention and form' (http://jupiter.ucsd.edu/~culture/main.html). Manovich is not just making a point about language; he is recognising that even in a relatively short period of time the WWW has developed a range of genres and is being used for a range of purposes that now require us to recognise that its contents are not adequately described simply as 'websites'.

1.2 The characteristics of new media: some defining concepts

CASE STUDY 2.2   A previous new technology

Again, it is useful to look back at a precursor 'new medium' in order to examine the relationship between technological change and changes in ways of seeing. If we take the example of photography, a new technology in 1839, with a subsequent history of some 160 years, it is now easy to see that no single or unitary practice is based upon it. It has many uses of very diverse, even opposite, kinds. Consider the difference between fashion and surveillance photography, or its results in the hands of a surrealist artist or a documentary maker. While a single, or at least similar, technology may be employed in each case, thinking in technological terms alone will blind us to the enormous range of differences in use and form that the technology is capable of (Tagg 1988: 4; Sontag 1977). Neither can we think about the meaning that photography has for us without taking into account the institutions which are involved in its production and circulation: magazines, newspapers and their picture editors, advertising agencies and their creative directors, camera manufacturers and their eye for new markets, for example. Such institutions involved in the production of photography then interact with other social and cultural institutions. Evans and Hall (1990) provide an example:

> One cannot understand . . . for example, the practices of the amateur snapshot photographer, nor account for the severely restricted 'style' of the images he or she typically produces, without also considering how this practice intersects with the camera and film manufacturing industry, with the developing and processing companies, with the relationships in modern societies between work and leisure, with definitions and idealisations and activities of family life, and, not least, with localised and historically specific gendered conceptions of identity, beliefs, and the skills of the photographer.
>
> (Evans and Hall 1990: 3)

Having looked at these two key points, the co-existence of a multiplicity of viewing positions and visualities, and the multiple uses of a media technology, how might we begin to see new image technologies as a part of a similarly complex visual culture? First, what precisely are the new developments in image technologies and, second, how is their significance being assessed?

2.5 NEW IMAGE TECHNOLOGIES

We are all now more or less familiar, through report or first-hand experience, with the following:

- computer-aided design and the **simulation** of objects and events that do not actually exist;

- software techniques such as 'ray tracing' and 'texture mapping' which digitally generate the visual forms and surfaces of invented objects 'as if' they conformed to the physical laws of optics;

- the production, animation and seamless fusion of still and moving photo-realistic images;

- the equipping of robot machines with the ability to see;

- the hybrid collection of technologies that produce the illusion of inhabiting and moving within virtual places;

- the technologies of telepresence that allow the body to act, through vision and touch, on remote objects;

- new forms of medical and scientific imaging (such as magnetic resonance imaging) that allow the interior spaces of the human body to be non-invasively seen and imaged;

- synoptic images of the earth and space in which a range of data gathered by satellites is translated into photographic form.

The roots of these imaging technologies lie mainly in military funded research, undertaken in the 1960s and 1970s, into flight simulators, the display of computer 'output' (the results of digital computation otherwise existing as electronic pulses within the machine) in a graphic, rather than a numeric, form, and beyond that, a visionary concept of 'an ultimate display', a three-dimensional, interactive, tactile, interface with the computer. (See Ivan Sutherland in **2.6.3.**)

By the beginning of the 1990s, this laboratory-based research, funded largely by the military, had moved into the sphere of media and entertainment. Computer graphics were established as an important part of the computer industry (worth an estimated $11 billion a year in the US alone and growing at an annual rate of 15 to 29 per cent (Woolley 1992: 13)). They had also become a new medium, a potential successor even, to television and print. It was the money earned in this industry that was then used to develop and launch the first virtual reality systems as cultural products, with their subsequent impact on our visual experience and our ideas about it.

It is these developments which involve computers and digital techniques deeply in processes of seeing, and their employment, with dramatic effect, in the production of images, that lead some commentators to argue that we are witnessing the emergence of new forms of visuality and a transformation in visual culture. An influential and sophisticated version of such a view is offered in a much-quoted passage from the theorist of visual culture, Jonathan Crary:

> The formalisation and diffusion of computer-generated imagery heralds the ubiquitous implantation of fabricated visual 'spaces' radically different from the mimetic capacities of film, photography, and television. These latter three, at least until the mid-1970s, were generally forms of analogue media that still corresponded to the optical wavelengths of the spectrum and to a point of view, static or mobile, located in real space.
>
> (Crary 1993: 1)

Crary suggests that as new 'visual spaces' are opened up, vision is relocated to 'a plane severed from a human observer', and that this means that 'Most of the historically important functions of the human eye are being supplanted by practices in which visual images no longer have any reference to the position of an observer in a "real", optically perceived world' (Crary 1993: 2). For Crary, then, the various forms of technologically augmented or machinic vision that we listed above are taken as evidence that a radically different form of visual culture is emerging. He judges that it will amount to a transformation as profound as that which 'separates medieval imagery from Renaissance perspective' (Crary 1993: 1) (see **Case study 2.1.**)

The key point is that we are looking at the prospect of a visual culture within which images are increasingly synthetic, independent of objects outside of them as their referents (see **referentiality**) or direct causes, being constructed digitally from the ground up, by machines, the data they store and the **algorithms** that guide their operations.

Clearly, this is a situation that can be overstated, as Crary can be seen to do. That is, unless we note his warning (one that recalls Linda Williams' arguments in **Case study 2.1**) that 'other older and more familiar ways of "seeing" will persist and co-exist . . . alongside these new forms'. If we are to begin to understand these developments as more than technological operations we have to ask, as Crary does, a number of questions:

Darley (1991: 85) points to a noticeable movement of expertise and key personnel from industrial-military research to computer graphics research, and the computer games, entertainment and media industries from the 1970s on. For instance, 'The research and development team at Lucasfilm [a leader in the field of special effects and computer animations] were noted for the amount of expertise they imported from such places as NASDA, IBM, and the Jet Propulsion Laboratory. It would appear that in no way were they exceptional in this regard.'

- [W]hat are the elements of continuity that link contemporary imaging with older organisations of the visual?

- [W]hat forms or modes are being left behind?

- What kind of break are we witnessing?

(Crary 1993: 2)

Such questions are necessary for four reasons. First, because we still meet and consume new media images largely in relation to more established forms of media and the ideas we have about them. This emergent culture of synthetic and autonomous images jostles alongside an already wide range of modes, genres and expectations of several kinds of lens-based media, including:

- the fictional world of the cinema (taking place 'on' the screen);

- the apparently first-hand and immediate reports on a wider world of events given by television;

- the compelling testimony to fact in documentary film and photo-journalism;

- the sheer fabricated seductions of advertising photography.

Second, while some of the new image technologies in our list (p. 104), are an increasingly familiar part of contemporary visual culture, others are not. Many kinds of images produced wholly or in part by new media technologies, or forms of vision which are mediated by sophisticated new image technologies, are only to be found, at least for now and the foreseeable future, in very specialist situations: from the supersonic fighter pilot to the well-resourced astronomer or medic. Computer vision (telepresence, medical imaging, scientific simulation, the perception of virtual spaces and objects) is not most people's 'bread and butter' experience.

Third, another class of 'new media' images, digitised photographs or digital images having a photo-realistic appearance, are only very infrequently passed off as analogue documents of reality in our daily newspapers. More often, they inhabit the realms of self-conscious graphic display, media art, and fantasy genres. Their producers will clearly know that such images are not analogue. Whether such knowledge is available to consumers will partly depend upon the context or the vehicle of consumption. We may assume that a photo-realistic image in a computer game is digitally generated, while another, printed in a newspaper, we may take to be analogue. Our sense, then, of whether an image is digital or analogue is partly dependent upon the kind of platform on which it is deployed – that is, whether this is newsprint or a website.

Fourth, even when new image technologies are used to produce images that may look different to traditional images, that may engage attention differently and offer new kinds of pleasures to their viewers (we might think of immersive virtual environments or digital special effects in cinema, both of which we discuss in more detail in **2.6–2.8**), we are surely not pitched wholesale into a new culture (visual or otherwise). We do not personally or collectively undergo a change in the ways we see the world that is on a level with the changes that historians describe as happening in the 'Renaissance' or in the 'age of mechanical reproduction'. Moreover, when we dig behind such labels for past change, we find that the changes in question were extremely complex, uneven, and worked out over the long term.

The kind of break or rupture with history and tradition that Crary proposes has, then, to be understood as provocative: it cannot be empirically grounded. Empirical evidence for such changes can only be amassed over long periods of time and, therefore, at second hand. They necessarily remain open to strong interpretation. That a fundamental change took place in the Renaissance can indeed be supported with reference to changes in how images where made, why they were made, and by attempting to establish how their significance was understood by their contemporaries. Yet, at the same time, other evidence points to the continuance of older ways of making and understanding images. Changes that began to occur in fifteenth-century image making played themselves out, in more than one way, over a further 300 years. Similarly, when Walter Benjamin explores what he sees as the 'mode of perception' and visual reproduction brought about by the technologies and social uses of photography and film in the early twentieth century, he is explicit that it has taken more than half a century for the changes that he discerns to reach a stage where it is possible to even 'indicate' the form they have taken (Benjamin 1970: 220).

We have seen that a visual culture, a culture's production and consumption of images, together with the way it organises and understands the power of vision, always involves the coexistence of several kinds of images and ways of seeing. The media technologies that are available to a culture play a part in this production and organisation of the visual, but, again, in more than one way. From the middle of the nineteenth century to the beginning of the twenty-first a series of new visual media have played an important part in an exponential proliferation of image production, the pervasion of culture by images, and the technological augmentation of vision. In one sense, our current new image media can be seen to be part of an intensification and acceleration of this 200-year process. Yet, at the same time, some key differences between the analogue lens-based technologies of the nineteenth and twentieth centuries (film, photography, and television with their mimetic capacities), and the new, digital, synthetic, and simulating technologies beg new questions.

2.6 IMMERSIVE VIRTUAL REALITY

In **1.2** we distinguished one kind of virtual reality (VR), the **immersion** in, and interaction with, an environment constructed with computer graphics and digital video, from other situations and experiences that are referred to as virtual: the virtual 'spaces' and 'communities' of cyberspace. This section is best read in conjunction with that earlier discussion (**1.2**). Immersive VR has widespread, if often experimental, practical applications in many spheres, and it holds intense interest for a wide range of theorists in many disciplines, from politics to geography.

For examples of the range of theorists who discuss virtual reality see a social and political theorist (Holmes 1997), a cultural geographer (Hillis 1996), the artist and art theorist (Ascott http://www.artmuseum.net/w2vr/timeline/Ascott.html) and the philosopher (Levy 1998), and for a further philosophical account of the 'virtual' see **Part 5** of this book.

We will be concerned here with the critical issues that VR poses for visual culture as we have defined it in the previous section (**2.1–2.3**)

2.6.1 Is VR a new 'visual' medium?

While we will refer here to 'immersive VR' as a new medium we do so cautiously, as a kind of shorthand. It may be more accurate to see VR as a prime example of a technology

1.2 The characteristics of new media: some defining concepts

The building of immersive virtual realities (VR) is now the object of diverse experimentation and development in industry, medicine, education, architecture, entertainment, art and other areas (see UK virtual reality Forum, 'The Case Study Matrix', http://www.vrforum.org.uk/CaseStudies/matrix.htm).

5 CYBERCULTURE: TECHNOLOGY, NATURE AND CULTURE

2.1 New technologies and the issues for visual culture
2.2 Visual culture
2.3 Visuality

Even VR's status as a single technology is suspect. As Hillis (1996: 70) asks, does anything set VR apart from 'TV and telephony from which [it] is partly cobbled, imagined and extended?'

This, however, is not to imply that a medium, so defined, is neutral. Whether or not we want to go so far as Marshall McLuhan in proclaiming that the 'medium is the message', a medium is never separable from the information or content it carries; it contributes to, shapes, allows or disallows meaning

1.2   The characteristics of new media: some defining concepts

(or collection of technologies) which is a stage where development and investment are taking place for a variety of speculative reasons.

However, whether the technology merits the status of a visual 'medium', in the widely accepted social sense, is open to question. An important way to understand a medium is as a set of social, institutional and aesthetic (as well as technological) arrangements for carrying and distributing information, ideas, texts, and images.

Immersive VR has no firmly settled institutional pattern of distribution, exhibition or use and for this reason it is difficult to describe as a medium in a fully social sense. A medium is more than the technology it depends upon; it is also a practice. It is a kind of skilled work on raw materials (whether they be words, photographic materials or digitised analogue media) which uses conventions, structures and sign systems to make sense, to convey ideas and construct experiences. The jury must still be out on whether or not VR will ever achieve the status of a medium in this sense. Whether, in other words, it will become a form of social communication and representation in the manner of radio, cinema or television. We have already briefly discussed Stone's conviction that immersive or simulational VR will fuse with online forms at a future time to become a medium of a new and dramatic kind (1.2). However, the important point here is that neither visionary speculation nor sheer technological potential is itself a sufficient guarantee that a medium, in the ways that we have defined above, will actually be the outcome of a technology.

The social development of technologies as media

This takes us directly onto the terrain researched in considerable historical detail (with a primary interest in communications media) by Brian Winston (1999). On the basis of his research, Winston formulates and tests a number of stages through which potential communications technologies or 'media' ('From the Telegraph to the Internet' is the subtitle of his book) will pass. In a simplified form they are these:

1   There must be a basis in a society's general scientific competence so that a certain kind of technology is feasible. This is the ground for a technology's possibility.

2   Next, there is the stage of 'ideation' when an idea or concept of how that available scientific competence may be given a technological application is envisaged – typically not by one inspired individual but by several in their supporting contexts and in a number of locations. This may lead to the building of prototypes, but these, as only modelled potentialities, are not yet widely recognised or confirmed as useful social technologies by the social groups with the will to invest in them or the power to realise them.

3   Then there is the stage of a technology's 'invention'. Invention, on this view, is clearly not an original idea, an unprecedented inspiration, or an occasion for shouting 'Eureka!' This is when a technology can be said to exist properly as it moves beyond an idea, and the prototype stage, as a clear necessity or use is seen and it finds social acceptance.

There is no smooth passage between these stages. Winston's research demonstrates that there is no guarantee that a technology will successfully pass through each of these stages to full social realisation and use. Prototypes do not proceed to be inventions unless a social purpose or need is evident. Further, even those which do can then be 'suppressed'. History is replete with technologies that could have been, for which prototypes existed but social need or commercial interest did not. There are also cases of technologies being invented twice, the telegraph being a case in point. The 'invention' a second time around succeeded because it was received into a social moment where there was a perceived need for it. The earlier invention was possible but redundant – to coin a phrase, 'ahead of its time' (Winston 1999: 5).

The development of VR has a complex and contingent genealogy of the kind that we outline in (**1.3**). From the 1950s onwards, several spheres of 'blue-sky' research in universities linked to programmes of military-industrial research into flight simulators and trainers, and related economic and cultural activity overlap one another. It is only latterly, in the late 1980s, that VR begins to constitute something like a media industry as well as an intense focus of cultural interest. With regard to the virtual space of the internet we have to remember that it was 'Designed by a confluence of communities which appear to have little in common – such as Cold War defence departments, the counter-cultural computer programming engineer community, and university research throughout the world – the Internet's infrastructure was designed to withstand nuclear attack' (Hulsbus 1997). Immersive VR's history dates from circa 1989 (the SIGGRAPH conference of that year), with foundational experiments being traced to Ivan Sutherland's experiments in the 1960s (see Coyle 1993: 152; Woolley 1992: 41; also **2.6.3**).

1.3   Change and continuity

The social availability of VR

Using Winston's terms, we might say that, currently, the hybrid technologies of immersive VR appear to be teetering between repeatedly reinvented prototype and invention. VR occasionally flickers into life (often for no more than an hour or two) at prestigious art or media festivals and trade shows. Each such event or 'exhibition' is unique and of short duration. The construction of 'state of the art' virtual spaces and environments is intensive in its use of technology and hence, outside of the military–industrial sphere, such realisations are restricted to a few fleeting occasions, usually requiring expensive travel and maintenance in real time and space for those who wish to participate. Ironically, the viewer or user has to be in a precise (and expensive) institution or place in the real world if they wish to be in 'virtual' reality.

CASE STUDY 2.3   VR, art and technology

Douglas MacLeod, director of 'The Art and Virtual Environments Project' held in 1994 at the Banff Centre for Arts, Canada, explains that it took two years of intensive and groundbreaking work for artists and technologists to bring a range of VR projects to completion. Reflecting on the practical dimensions of the project, MacLeod writes, 'It was like staging nine different operas in two years while at the same time trying to invent the idea of opera.' Judging that this huge effort had only provided 'a suggestion of what this medium could be', he then worries that the works will never be shown again; 'Some are simply too complex to remount. In other cases, the team of artists and programmers that produced the piece has dispersed, taking with them the detailed knowledge of the assembly and installation of a particular work' (Moser and MacLeod 1996: xii; also see Morse 1998: 200).

In terms of spatial or geographical distribution, it is very likely that VR is rarer than handmade pictures were in the era before photography and mass reproduction. A popular work on VR (Rheingold 1991) reads like a personal world tour of university research departments and the R&D divisions of major multinational entertainment and communications corporations: the University of North Carolina; Kansai Science City, Kyoto; NASA, Massachusetts; MIT; Tsukuba Japan; the US Marine Corps research facility in Honolulu; an inventor's house in Santa Monica; companies in California's Silicon Valley; a computer science laboratory in Grenoble, France (Rheingold 1991: 18–19). Such places are hardly public or even semi-public venues for the consumption of a new medium.

Few can travel to expensive installations and exclusive institutions; so how is VR experienced as a medium in the social sense? The most ubiquitous form of VR is the stripped-down version seen in 'shoot-em-up' arcades. While this genre of VR may be of social and cultural significance it barely matches the promise of VR's advocates, whom we shall meet shortly. Outside of commercial arcades and theme parks, university or corporate research departments, immersive VR is hardly accessible to most of us.

We can contrast this situation with the increasing ubiquity of the personal computer. It is possible to say that the PC is used for 'entertainment, interpersonal communication, self-expression, and access to information of many kinds', and therefore 'Computers are being used as media' (Mayer 1999: xiii). It is also clear that such uses are developing distinct genres (hypertext, edutainment, games), institutional frameworks (service providers, user groups, training in software use) and patterns of consumption (browsing, surfing, gaming, participation in online communities, newsgroups). As we have seen, at this time it is difficult to say the same for immersive VR. The importance of VR as a proto-technology must lie elsewhere. This, we will argue, is an implied challenge to settled historical practices of image making and receiving, and to the technological conditions which augment our visual and related aural and tactile experiences. However, for the same reasons that immersive VR is not a generally available experience, the basis or evidence for such claims needs careful inspection.

2.6.2 The importance of that which hardly exists

2.5   New image technologies

Let us remind ourselves of Crary's view that we met in section **2.5**. Crary sees a 'vast array of computer graphics techniques' bringing about an 'implantation of fabricated visual "spaces" radically different from the mimetic capacities of film, photography, and television'. It is this that he sees as bringing about a transformation in visual culture that is 'probably more profound than the break that separates medieval imagery from Renaissance perspective'. This break with tradition is 'relocating vision to a plane severed from a human observer' and is supplanting 'most of the historically important functions of the human eye' (Crary 1993: 1–2). Yet another commentator considers that in VR we are witnessing a 'quantum leap into the technological construction of vision' (Hayles 1999: 38).

These are heady claims that call us to investigate several ideas. They face us with the need to understand what the 'fabricated spaces' are that Crary sees as so different from the mimetic (or imitative) character of photography. If we trace the early history of VR technology we find, in a practical and intrumental context, a strange shift taking place in the relationship of images and other sensory experience to external or pre-existing reality. This has been conceptualised as a shift from the practice of 'imitation' (or 'mimesis') to that of 'simulation'. This is discussed in **2.6.3**.

2.6.3   Spheres collide: from imitation to simulation – VR's operational history

We should also think hard about the metaphors that are energetically employed to capture the nature and significance of immersive VR. Many of these are used by the artists

2.1 *The Daily Telegraph* front page: 'Dawn of another World'.

and producers who experiment with the technology with the aim of developing it as a medium of art and cultural expression, and the theorists who reflect upon and debate the outcomes. How do they understand the 'profound' transformation of visual culture and 'quantum leaps' in the nature of vision? In doing this we will find that there is a wide, possibly unbridgeable gap between the metaphors that are used to grasp the significance of VR and reports of its actuality. These are discussed in **2.6.4** and **2.6.5**.

2.6.4   VR: the actuality and the hyperbole
2.6.5   VR: trimming the metaphors

A third issue that will repay attention is Crary's yardstick for measuring the profundity of the change brought about by the new 'fabricated visual "spaces"': Renaissance perspective. The importance given to pictorial perspective in many discussions of immersive VR is summed up in a frequently used phrase: VR is like 'stepping through Alberti's window' or entering 'into the image' (Robins 1996). This is a metaphor for the experience of immersion, but pictorial perspective is also a technology (especially in the sense of 'know-how' (see **1.6.3**)) that, together with the 'point of view' that it constructs, has been more or less central to a Western tradition of image making. It has structured many of the possible relationships viewers can have to images for several centuries. Key to the cultural forms of the image that utilise perspective are the frame and the surface, the edge between real world and virtual world, and the presence of images as artefacts within

1.6.3   Williams and the social shaping of technology

2.7   VR as a medium of art: A
quantum leap forward?

the world. What is involved in breaking with these conditions that we have associated with images for so long? What is involved in this 'quantum leap into the technological construction of vision'? This is investigated in **2.7**.

2.6.3 Spheres collide: from imitation to simulation – VR's operational history

VR as the ultimate computer interface

A continuing source of interest in VR is its use as an ultimate kind of human–computer interface; the means by which a human interacts with the machine. It offers to provide an interface that removes all signs of a mediating apparatus between the user and computer-generated or stored image, information or content.

See Bolter and Grusin (1999: 161–167) for a brief discussion of VR in these terms or as 'the end of mediation'

It is seen as promising to dispense with the residual forms of the computer screen, keyboard, and mouse (hang-overs from television, typewriters and mechanical controls). As the 1960s pioneer of graphic and immersive computer interfaces Ivan Sutherland put it, we should 'break the glass and go inside the machine' (quoted in Hillis 1996), or, in the words of the more recent developer of VR systems, Jaron Lanier: in VR 'the technology goes away' because 'we are inside it' (quoted in Penny 1995: 237).

From the end of the Second World War, the US government began serious funding of research aimed at improving flight simulation and the computation of ballistic tables, the calculation of the trajectory of shells and missiles necessary to accurate targeting. The great cost of modern military aircraft, and the enormous demand for ballistic calculation, fuelled the development of electronic/digital computation. This was not the first time that the demand for calculation threatened to outstrip the human capacity to produce them fast enough and then drove the development of computers. See Mayer (1999: 506) on Babbage's Difference Engine (a version of which was completed in 1854), a mechanical computer which was partly a response to the demands for maritime navigation in the nineteenth century. Woolley (1992: 49) reports that in the 1940s the 60-second trajectory of a single missile would take 20 hours to work out by hand. One of the first electronic mainframe computers, the ENIAC (1944) took 30 seconds. For more on the military origins of cybernetics, and therefore contemporary computing, see **Part 5**

Ivan Sutherland was a key figure in the operational and conceptual history of VR, and a pioneer of computer graphics and simulation technologies, who worked within military funded research programmes. In this context, Sutherland tackled the question of what symbolic form a computer's output might take or, as we would now put it, what would be the form of the human–computer interface? Given that a computer's internal activity is a vast and continuous stream of electrical impulses, Sutherland asked how the results of this invisible activity might be 'output' or externalised. What form – language or sign system – should be used to display the results of computation? Sutherland demonstrated that these impulses could be translated into an electron beam that was visible on a visual display unit – a screen. The origin of contemporary computer graphic interfaces, such as those used by the Apple Mac or Microsoft Windows, is first seen in his now famous prototype 'Sketchpad'.

Sutherland also envisaged the possibility of going beyond graphic display to make the results of computation tangible. He conceived that if a computer reduced and processed any kind of information as a series of impulses, given the appropriate algorithms and programming, the physical movement of the human body – and even material resistance to that movement – could also be encoded as information which the computer could process.

From imitation to simulation

Sutherland's inspiration was the joystick of a Link Flight Trainer in which 'the feel' of a mocked-up aircraft's parts, moving as if against wind and air pressure, was mechanically fed back to the trainee pilot. In working upon the development of flight simulators, Sutherland drew upon several breakthroughs in technology and mathematics (see Woolley 1992: 42–48). Sutherland's work showed how human actions could become computable information that was then passed back to the human subject, via servo mechanisms and sensors, to then inform or control their further actions. This took a graphic and tactile form in a cybernetic 'feedback loop' between computer and human being **(see Part 5)**.

5   CYBERCULTURE: TECHNOLOGY, NATURE AND CULTURE

Where Sutherland's inspiration makes empirical references to a real aeroplane by a functionally quite unnecessary copying of its wings and tailplane, after Sutherland the flight simulator eventually becomes an enclosed environment, a 'black box', with no external, morphological reference to aeroplanes at all. Yet once such a 'black box' is entered the sensory conditions experienced in real flight can be more fully generated to include, for instance, the programmed vicissitudes of the weather, or engine failure, acting upon the virtual aircraft. Such simulators, without any external mimetic reference to real planes, can then simulate planes that have not yet been built or flights that have not yet been taken. Let alone there being no imitation of wings or tailfins as in the Link Trainer, there are no particular planes to imitate. Here we meet the distinction between imitation and simulation: the notion that in simulation (as against imitation or **mimesis**) the model now, in some senses, precedes the reality – a reversal of the expectation that 'models' are built (imitate) pre-existing realities. (See Woolley 1992: 42–44 for a more detailed discussion.)

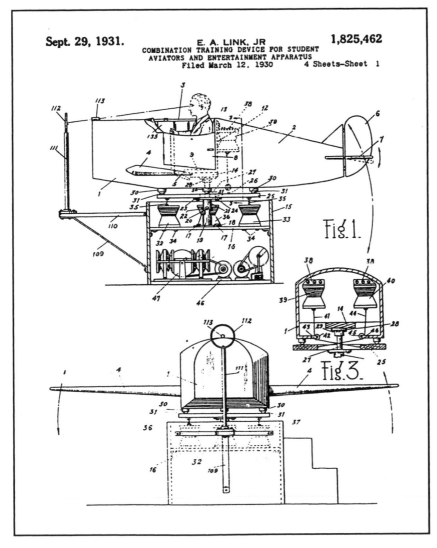

2.2 A Link Jnr Combination Training device.

'A head-mounted three dimensional display'

In a 1968 scientific paper of this name, Sutherland reported on an apparatus that would, in effect, *generalise* the flight simulator. Here, Sutherland made a conceptual move similar to that made by Alan Turing when he conceived of the computer as a 'universal' machine. Sutherland built an apparatus that included a rudimentary head-mounted display. The HMD's basic purpose was to 'present the user with a perspective image which changes as he moves' (Sutherland 1968: 757). The space that the wearer of the helmet 'saw', and which shifted as they moved their head, was generated mathematically. It was structured by a three-dimensional **Cartesian grid** with its three spatial co-ordinates imaged stereoscopically on the binocular TV screens held close before their eyes.

For Sutherland, this apparatus had no specific purpose such as flight simulation. It was a visual and tactile interface with a computer, an alternative to the early punch cards, or to a keyboard, light pen and screen. Instead of human–computer interfaces being holes punched in paper tape or two-dimensional manipulable graphics displayed on a VDU, this interface was, however rudimentary, spatial, visual, tactile and kinaesthetic. A prototype of the kind of interface described at the start of this section.

How can we connect this short instrumental and technological history with ideas about change in visual culture: the sphere on which these developments will later impact in the form of VR? Two important elements in the history of Western visual culture make an appearance in our brief account of Sutherland's work. We have already met the concept of imitation or mimesis, which is now challenged by that of simulation. Now we also meet a conception of space which is historically and culturally specific to Western art and science – in the form of a Cartesian grid which appeared to the wearer of Sutherland's head-mounted display.

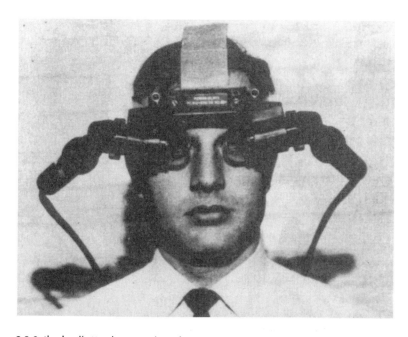

2.3 Sutherland's Head Mounted Display.

Mimesis

Mimesis, the studied and skilful copying of the appearance of nature, lying at the centre of a traditional theory of visual representation dating back to ancient Greece, seems to have given way to another activity – simulation. This is the way in which a reality effect – an image drawing upon the culturally accepted ways in which reality is understood to be faithfully represented – is produced without copying any particular pre-existing thing.

Despite its subsequent theorising (see Baudrillard 1988: 166–185), this is a distinction that can be hard to grasp. For present purposes we will be content with the following recognition: what distinguishes simulation from imitation is that an artefact *that is a simulation* (rather than a copy) can be experienced as if it were real, even when no corresponding thing exists outside of the simulation itself. We are, after all, now familiar with such simulated reality effects from watching the seamless insertion of computer animations and special effects in contemporary blockbuster movies and television adverts.

However, one increasingly sophisticated practice of 'mimesis' in the history of Western art did have a 'simulational' character in rendering as if real or natural the artificial and the unnatural – as in **trompe-l'oeil** painting (see Kubovy 1988: 65-86)

Cartesian space

Sutherland's prototype VR helmet made visible to its wearer a 'Cartesian grid', a schema or conception of space defined by the co-ordinates of height, width, and depth, a cubic, gridded, measurable space: the classical, mathematical representation of three-dimensional space. A conception of space that after some 400 years of habit and assimilation within Western science and culture, and wherever its techniques and knowledges have been imposed or adopted, is for most work-a-day purposes how we experience and negotiate space as part of our visual culture. We are obliged, when we think of imaging and visualising (and this clearly includes computer scientists) to recognise the Cartesian grid. Such a conception of space is anticipated by the employment of pictorial perspective in the Western pictorial tradition, which emerged in the painting of the fifteenth century, was built into the lenses of photographic and movie cameras in the nineteenth and twentieth centuries, and is currently the space produced by digital image software programs. (For a fuller discussion of this see **2.3**.)

For a discussion of the scopic regime of Cartesian perspectivalism in Western representation see Jay (1988)

2.3 Visuality

2.6.4 VR: the actuality and the hyperbole

Virtual reality's metaphors and 'as ifs'

Immersive virtual reality (and the more generic 'cyberspace') are largely thought about with the aid of metaphors, drawn from the social and cultural world that we are familiar with, and existing media forms.

Immersive VR is frequently talked about in terms of entering into images, being swallowed by television (Dery 1993: 6), walking into the computer (Morse 1998: 181), passing through the cinema screen, etc. (As we shall see in **2.7.1**, such metaphors owe a great deal to one founding idea – that of 'stepping through Alberti's window'.)

2.7.1 What is Alberti's window?

Another set of metaphors seek to give content to the 'non-space' of the founding metaphor of networked VR – 'where you are when you are on the telephone'. These tend to conjure up familiar and comforting visions of lost communities regained: the village pump, the town square, the ancient meeting place or agora, or a neighbourhood in a digital city (Robins 1996: 96–102). Such metaphors have become key ways in which VR and cyberspace are conceived as objects of study within circles of academic and critical thought. However, they are also used to promote and market VR in various forms, and are thus 'just barely removed from the commercial hype' (Hillis: 1996).

Metaphors help us to see things in terms of what we are already familiar with; that is,

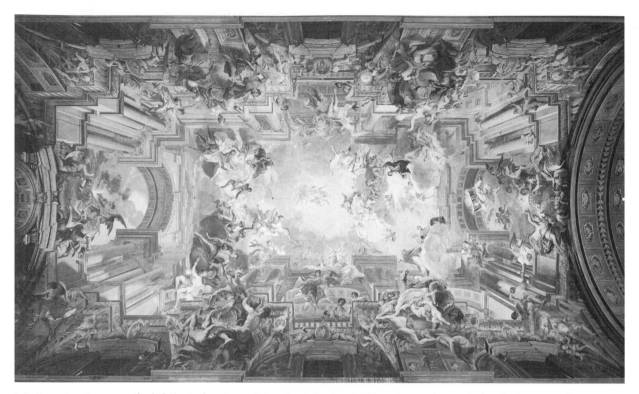

2.4a Fresco in a Baroque cathedral: Fra Andrea Pozzo, St Ignatius Being Received into Heaven (1691–4). Church of Sant Ignazio, Rome. Courtesy of Scala.

1.5.3   The discursive construction of new media

they enable us to map the familiar onto the unfamiliar. Metaphors are also dangerous. They can be overextended, we can push them too far and they flip from being useful to obscuring our view of what interests us. When this happens the metaphor forecloses our enquiry prematurely. The metaphor stands between us and the event, object or situation that we want to understand. Most dangerous of all, the metaphors we use become part of our discourse; they become the very terms that we use to define what we wish to analyse. (See on discourse **1.5.3**.) As a result of the way that metaphors eventually part company with any sustained attempts at understanding, a yawning gap has opened up between the actuality of VR and the discourses which surround it. This is a situation which demands that we look closely and critically at the metaphorical terms employed and seek an alternative account of VR.

The launch of VR

The yawning gap opened up with the earliest appearances of immersive VR technology. Benjamin Woolley's acute and entertaining account of the launch of early VR systems at the SIGGRAPH (Special Interest Group, Graphics of the American Association of Computing Machinery) conferences of 1989 and 1990 tracks this process (Woolley 1992: 11–38). At this early stage the metaphors were truly grandiose, as VR was immediately likened to dreams, childhood imagination, and to parallel universes where the laws of (Newtonian) physics did not apply.

2.4b Quod Libet, Edward Collier (1701). Victoria and Albert Museum, London.

Woolley contrasts his experience of these early VR systems with the euphoric terms in which they were described by the computer graphics pioneers who presented them. On trying out VPL's demonstration of 'RB2', Woolley recalls: 'I . . . experienced a crudely rendered primary coloured series of badly co-ordinated images.' Simultaneously, Jaron Lanier, the head of VPL Research, the company that built the system that so disappointed Woolley, described VR as 'an experience when you are dreaming of all possibilities being there, that anything can happen, and it is just an open world where your mind is the only limitation' (Woolley 1992: 14). Another panellist, an academic from University of Washington's Human Interface Technology Laboratory, suggested that 'virtual reality' was 'about much more than reality'. VR was not merely a way of simulating the real world (with its physics and constraints) but a way of building worlds in which the constraints of reality could be thrown away. Virtual reality was a subjective reality that existed only in the 'eye of the beholder'. For Lanier, this aspect of VR was comparable with the (supposed) freedom of dreams or the lost freedom of childhood imagination: 'The thing that I think is so exciting about virtual reality is that it gives us this freedom again. It gives us this sense of being able to be who we are without limitation' (Wolley 1992: 14).

As Woolley points out, the gap between what he actually experienced and these euphoric metaphors could not be accounted for by the crude state of the technology's development at the time. 'Lanier's rhetoric was not about the future, it was about the present. This technological liberation was already underway' (1992: 16).

It can be argued that the difference in Lanier's and Woolley's estimations of VR's power or effectiveness in 1989 is still typical of contemporary thought about VR. It entails a collapse of past, present and future; in short:

See Robins (1996: 89–90, 94–95) on infantilist tendencies and VR

- what actually exists (immersive and interactive VR technologies and their crude products);

- rapid and visible development (especially as now seen in the application of digital simulation technologies in film);

- their future promise (vividly imagined in cyber-fiction and cinematic representations of future virtual worlds);

- the rediscovery of historical 'virtual' cultural forms such as the phantasmagoria.

The 'phantasmagoria' was a nineteenth-century form of visual entertainment in which slides were back-projected onto a translucent screen facing an audience. It was accompanied by artificial lighting effects and dramatic sound to produce, usually, effects that were intended to suggest the supernatural (see Neale 1985: 25). However, the term has also been used (see Buck-Morss 1992) to describe the way that 'a narcotic was made out of reality' in the introduction of new forms of spectacular and sensuous experience in the nineteenth century (urban vistas, displays of goods in the new department stores, elaborate domestic interiors of nineteenth-century consumer culture)

Overall, we have a situation where the past, the present and the potential or future are, at the very least, difficult to disentangle.

An unbridgeable gap

Even as its technical resources have developed, this contrast between the visually impoverished or trivial sensory experience of 'being in' VR, on the one hand, and a sense of its profound cultural implications, on the other, has become a constant theme in critical discussions about immersive virtual reality. VR seems to be both crude or trite (in its form and content) *and* something profound and new in the history of visual culture. There continues to be an immense gap between the way that the general significance of VR is expressed and the way that it is extrapolated from a relatively small number of privileged and inaccessible examples.

For example, in 1998, some nine years after Lanier's euphoric description, we find a philosopher of 'virtuality', Pierre Lévy, judging that

> virtual reality systems enable us to experiment with the dynamic integration of different perceptual modalities. We are practically able to relive someone else's *complete* sensory experience.
>
> (Lévy 1998: 38; our emphasis)

In short, in VR it is *as* if an 'I' were experiencing the world as someone else. Leaving aside the question of how we can even begin to know that what we perceive and feel in VR is a *reliving* of someone else's '*complete*' sensory experience, this continues to fly in the face of any actual experience of virtual reality systems. In any but the most fanciful accounts of first-hand experience of 'being in virtual reality' their crude approximation to anything like 'complete sensory experience' is always noted.

Throughout the 1990s this point was made again and again. In a discussion of the difficulties facing interactive media in achieving the kind of content-rich absorption traditionally associated with narrative cinema, Andy Cameron (1995: x) observes that the demands made on computing power, merely in order to construct the bare bones of an interactive VR environment, are such that, 'VR to date has barely been able to dress the set, let alone cry "action", or murmur "once upon a time".' Jeremy Walsh (1995: 113–119) judges that VR, in its popular forms, is a 'sterile technological form' animated only by a kind of cyber-sexuality of leather fetishism, pornography and violence. In the work of more experimental VR artists, folkloric new age themes, nature myths and childlike dramas predominate.

See Char Davies (1998) for her own account of her work 'Osmose', and Brenda Laurel and Rachel Strickland's account of their work 'Placeholder' (in Moser and MacLeod 1996) as examples of such themes

Jon Dovey (1996: xi–xii) recalls his experience of navigating a virtual environment which simulated deep space. He found as he grasped the stars that appeared to rush toward him ('No mean feat when your hand is encased in a medieval gauntlet') that they were actually 'digital' packets of Marlboro cigarettes. Nicola Green (1997: 57–78), in her analysis of the immersive VR game 'Dactyl Nightmare', concludes that the identities acted out by participants in VR turn out to have a great deal to do with the real world in the sense that they borrow from familiar media stereotypes to be found in television drama and advertising.

2.6.5 VR: trimming the metaphors

Can we think about VR in ways that bridge this stubborn gap between such experiences and the hyperbole that invests them with great historical significance? In other words, can we find less metaphoric ways of understanding VR? As a concept, virtual reality has been contested since its inception in the late 1980s. Many developers and practitioners, as well as academic critics, have felt uneasy about its connotations. By paying attention to these critics we can begin to arrive at a way of thinking about VR as a practice utilising quite particular technologies (often with problematic outcomes in terms of the visual and sensory experiences produced). This will help us pursue our interest in VR as a medium. However, at the same time, we will see that misleading metaphors continue to figure in these critical accounts.

VR is an overextended term

Michael Heim, a philosopher, and author of *The Metaphysics of Virtual Reality*, who in much of what he writes has a euphoric view of VR, has nevertheless pointed out that the term 'virtual reality' is open to a kind of over-extension that threatens to make it meaningless:

> On first hearing the term virtual reality, many people respond immediately: 'Oh, sure, I live there all the time.' By this they mean that their world is largely a human construct. Earth itself has become an artifice, a product of natural and human forces combined. Nature itself . . . no longer escapes human influence . . . But once we extend the term virtual reality to cover everything artificial, we lose the force of the phrase. When a word means everything, it means nothing.
>
> (Heim 1993: 112)

Heim warns us of a confusion. A confusion between a way of characterising our contemporary 'postmodern' world and a specific technological and cultural project to develop a new medium (VR).

VR is not the same as the virtualisation of culture

The heart of Heim's complaint is that it is hard to think about VR as a 'medium' that produces a 'virtual' sense of reality if we fail to distinguish it from thinking about something else; that is, the way that technologies of all kinds have deeply penetrated and refashioned nature and culture – to such an extent, some argue, that we should no longer think of them as separate realms. The experience produced by immersive VR technologies may be a vivid symbol for certain ways of understanding postmodern techno-culture, but this is another matter. From the point of view of VR as a technology, or as a proto-medium, it is not a symptom of a world which has lost touch with reality, it is simply a material technology that is used to produce situations that have some of the qualities of reality. David Holmes, a sociologist, makes a similar point. For him it is an especially potent example of wider kinds of technological and cultural change:

> Of the myriad technological and cultural transformations taking place today, one has emerged to provide perhaps the most tangible opportunity for understanding the political and ethical dilemma of contemporary society. The arrival of virtual reality and virtual communities, both as metaphors for broader cultural processes and as the material contexts which are beginning to enframe the human body and human communication . . .
>
> (Holmes 1997: 1)

So, not only is VR conceived of largely in terms of metaphors it is also used as a metaphor in itself. A metaphor for the condition of the contemporary world: 'Oh, sure, I live there (or like that) all the time.' But, as Holmes also suggests, VR is also a material context which 'enframes' (is the context in which we have come to understand) the human body and human communication. That is, it is a specific set of technological and cultural arrangements that we encounter and use in physical and social space – much like any media. A VR installation and the machines that power it may not be as cumbersome and grossly physical as a 1940s Hollywood film set, or a television news studio, but they are material. Media are real and material things. It is only on this material basis that VR is able to produce illusions (however imperfect) of being virtually present with other objects in electronically constructed spaces, or, for that matter, of feeling that we are 'with' others in the 'spaces' created by online communication.

See Bolter and Grusin (1999) on this point

The point is that both ways of thinking about VR are important: as a metaphor for a contemporary condition and as a material and technological context for bodies and ways of seeing. However, the fervour with which the first way of thinking has been pursued – the metaphoric value of VR itself – has tended to divert us from thinking about the latter: what VR actually is in the material world. In fact, it seems likely that we will not get far in understanding VR as a new medium (if it is, how it is, why it is, and with what implications) simply by noticing how it nicely represents the way that the world at large is increasingly artificial. This, at least, is one meaning we can take from Heim's warning. This physical aspect of VR is explored further in **5.4**.

5.4   Theories of cyberculture

VR is not complete sensory experience

A second kind of impatience with metaphorical overload comes from Brenda Laurel, researcher, interface designer and VR artist, who argues that 'virtual reality' is an oxymoron, or a contradiction in terms:

> Most of us in the [VR] business dislike it a lot. The word 'virtual' is okay because in fact we're creating environments or realities that don't necessarily have concrete physical components to them. But the use of the word 'reality' in the singular belies a certain cultural bias that most of us are not very comfortable with.
>
> (Laurel, quoted in Coyle 1993: 162n)

We should stop to consider this statement. One of Laurel's arguments, that 'virtual' and 'real' cannot be joined together as a sensible name for something, only has bite if we agree that what is 'virtual' cannot by definition be 'real'. This obviously depends upon accepting a popular conception of the virtual as 'not real'. (See **5.4.2** for an account of why the virtual and the real should not simply be opposed.) More importantly, given the material, technological production of virtual environments that we have discussed above, what could she mean when she descibes VR as 'environments or realities that don't necessarily

5.4.2   Cybernetics and the virtual

have concrete physical components to them'. This may not be metaphorical but neither does it make sense. The experience of VR, however, facilitated by invisible electronic or digital processes, is, of course, physical. It involves receptive, sensing, human bodies and technologically generated, physical channels of information.

Laurel suggests an alternative to virtual reality: 'telepresence'. She defines this as 'a medium that allows you to take your body with you into some other environment'. Immediately, Laurel checks herself because she feels that this attempt at redefinition is still 'kind of metaphorical'. She then offers a further definition of VR: 'What it really means is that you get to take some *subset of your senses* with you into another environment' (our emphasis). This, we should immediately note, is a far cry from Lévy's opinion that VR is a reliving of someone else's 'complete sensory experience'. And, despite Laurel's odd (and in our opinion, mistaken) view that virtual environments are non-physical, her attempt to guard against metaphorical inflation in her definition helps close the gap between actuality and metaphor.

VR technologies construct 'environments' not 'realities'

Like Laurel, Mary Anne Moser, writer on contemporary art and co-editor of *Immersed in Technology* (1996), also prefers 'environment' to 'reality'. She is unhappy with the latter term because of the sensationalist 'ballyhoo' that was immediately attached to it, and warns that VR should not be seen as differing fundamentally from all other technologies. She urges (1996: xvii–xviii) that virtual reality technology needs to be viewed as part of a continuum of technological developments. In an attempt to focus attention on VR's social, cultural, ethical and political implications, rather than the sensationalist 'allure' of the new technology itself, she and her colleagues (at the Art and Virtual Environments Project, Banff, Canada) abandoned the term 'virtual reality' for the less sensational 'virtual environments'. An *environment*, understood as the surrounding conditions in which people (or other organisms) live and act, is something that can be built and arranged. It is more manageable than 'reality': a term with many meanings which always begs further definition and context.

VR is part of a series of historical technological developments

Moser's view (1996) that VR needs to be understood as part of a 'continuum of technological developments' refutes the absolute novelty of VR. Geoffrey Batchen (1998: 276) asks us to recall the stereoscope, 'an early nineteenth-century technology of seeing that would appear to parallel closely the VR experience that so many commentators want to call "revolutionary" and "altogether new"'.

He quotes a contemporary response to the stereoscope's image and the sense of disembodiment that it created: '[I] leave my outward frame in the arm-chair at my table, while in spirit I am looking down upon Jerusalem from the Mount of Olives' (Holmes 1859, quoted in Batchen 1998: 275–6). The three-dimensionalisation of photography which the stereoscope achieved (in photography's early days) is only one way in which, at the beginning of the nineteenth century, a number of boundaries between what was real and what was represented began to blur: 'the very dissolution which some want to claim is peculiar to a newly emergent and postmodern VR' (276).

VR involves the technological management of the senses

Finally, the sociologist David Holmes (1997: 1) adds something to Laurel's recognition that in VR only a subset of our senses are engaged. He suggests we think of immersive VR

See also margin note on 'phantasmagoria' (p. 118)

See also Erkki Huhtamo, 'Armchair traveller on the ford of Jordan: the home, the stereoscope and the virtual voyager', *Mediamatic* **6.2/3**, (n.d.): 13-23, and 'Encapsulated bodies in motion: simulators and the quest for total immersion', in Simon Penny (ed.) *Critical Issues in Electronic Media*, New York: SUNY Press, 1995

1.6.2   Mapping Marshall McLuhan
1.6.4   The many virtues of Saint
McLuhan

as 'the technological management of the body's senses'. In some ways this echoes the McLuhanite definition of media technologies as extensions of the body or the senses (**1.6.2, 1.6.4**), but it also adds a sense of agency. Management is more than extension. It involves direction and control for some identified purpose. Hence, in VR, and again like any other medium, the viewer or user is in some part subject to the designs of the producer. It follows from Holmes's definition that we must ask 'If VR is a world of dreams, then whose dreams are they?'

VR disturbs the body's relationship to its senses and mental activity

Simon Penny, VR artist and critic, puts some detail on Laurel's reminder that only a subset of the senses is involved in VR: 'The VR condition is . . . the limited case of a simulated, interactive, stereoscopic, visual (and occasionally auditory) environment, in which the body is represented only visually' (1994: 243). For this reason, Penny suggests, VR involves a 'dislocation and dissociation' of the human body. However, in pursuing this observation, metaphor creeps back into Penny's account: in immersive VR, 'it is as if we have two partial bodies – a corporeal body that wears the apparatus' and 'an incomplete electronic "body image"'. As he pursues this metaphor, the 'as if' of having two partial bodies in VR, matters go wrong:

> One does not take one's body into VR: one leaves it at the door. VR reinforces Cartesian duality by replacing the body with a body image, a creation of the mind (for all 'objects' in VR are a product of the mind). As such, it is a clear continuation of the rationalist dream of disembodied mind, part of a long Western tradition of the denial of the body. Augustine is the patron saint of cyberpunks.
>
> (Penny 1995: 243)

A compelling image, no doubt, and yet another instance of VR being placed within long traditions of Western thought and feeling. Yet we should note two things. First, Penny has been led to think of the act of entering virtual or cyberspace as like walking through a door, of passing physically across extended space, as we do when we move from one room to another. By definition, this is something that bodies do. If the body stays (is left) at the door then what moves through it? A somehow disembodied mind? (No wonder that Descartes is so frequently invoked to explain VR.) It is surely better to revert to the conception of VR as 'the technological management of the body's senses', and Penny is on safer ground when he suggests that in VR the body is provided with an incomplete image of itself (the image of a gloved hand hovering in advance of the body's movement, the kinaesthetic sense of walking on a treadmill, etc.). Second, Penny compounds the idea that a disembodied mind or consciousness enters VR without 'its' body, by then suggesting that 'all "objects" in VR are a product of the mind'. Surely the objects in VR are also the products of computers processing masses of data and analogue image inputs?

Summary: another take on VR

Where does this critical review of the thoughts and comments of practitioners and theorists of VR leave us? Some of the qualifications we have discussed (and there could be others) are steps toward refusing the seductions of the runaway metaphors that surround VR. However, as we have seen, some of these very attempts to pin down the experience of VR carry yet more overextended and confusing metaphors in their train. Let us sum up what we have learnt. As we do we can now also return to Crary's phrase with which we started and look again at his suggestion that virtual environments are 'implantation[s] of fabricated visual "spaces"'.

When we 'use' VR, some of our senses (principally vision, but also hearing and to some extent touch) are technologically managed within an artificial or constructed environment; in Crary's terms, 'fabricated "visual spaces"'.

- While we can be easily led to think of VR as a powerful symbol of a new cybercultural condition (and possibly be seduced by the existential glamour of the idea) we always meet it within material circumstances. These may be research laboratories, hospitals, amusement arcades, art installations in galleries, or high-end PCs in our homes. The visual spaces fabricated by VR are implanted within the material reality of such institutions and places. They are not in a parallel universe of some kind.

- This technological management of the senses has elements of continuity with a history of other media-technological developments and their cultural meanings. However radically different immersive VR may seem to be from other image media, it has precedents; it has a history.

- The experience we have in a virtual environment has disturbing consequences for our sense of embodiment as it dislocates or dissociates our senses, and the mental activity they give rise to, from our bodies. This does not mean, however, that we lose or 'escape' our bodies in VR.

- This sense of disembodiment has led theorists of VR to see it as a technology that compounds a problematic way of thinking of the body and the mind as separate and separable entities, derived from the influential seventeenth-century philosopher Descartes.

2.6.6 VR as a discursive object

We have argued that, at best, VR has to be seen as a proto-medium but that this is itself of particular interest when thinking about new media. In **1.5.3**, through a series of case studies, we introduced the notion of (new) media and technologies as discursive objects. We need, briefly, to take this idea up again in considering VR. We saw that the emergence of new technologies and media focus the attention of different groups within a society (through its press, journals, professional bodies, its communications media, and as an everyday topic of conversation) on issues and preoccupations that it already has. VR is a striking case of this and may help us understand the gap between its actuality or social availability and its perceived significance. We saw earlier in this section how VR is socially inaccessible on the one hand and impermanent on the other. Despite this, throughout the 1990s little can have exercised the minds of technologists, artists, academics and journalists so much as these technologies of virtual space. It now seems to be the case that VR is something that is reported upon rather than seen; the 'presence' of which is talked up and its significance elaborated through intense speculation rather than first-hand experience. And it is now also the case that it is not so much the widespread social use of VR environments that is important, but the way that VR seems to call up questions about the nature of 'reality' and the relationship of the physical or organic human body to 'experience'. It is also still largely the case that knowledge of VR is highly dependent upon

1.5.3 The discursive construction of new media

its representation in other media: cinema, TV, novels, and comics, rather than frequent first-hand experience (Hayward 1993; Holmes 1997).

For each of these reasons, the apparatuses which produce the phenomena of 'virtual reality' are, for most people, 'discursive objects' in this sense rather than concrete operational technologies which are frequently met in the everyday world, like telephones, TVs, VCRs or PCs (which, of course, also have significant discursive presence as well, as the case studies in **1.5.3** reveal).

1.5.3 The discursive construction
of new media

The historian of visual culture, Jonathan Crary, whose theories we have been discussing, provides a detailed account of an image technology which can be seen as an antecedent to the VR apparatus: the camera obscura of the eighteenth century (1993: 25–66). Today, we mainly think of the camera obscura as a forerunner to the photographic camera, a kind of camera without film, which was used by painters and draughtsmen as an aid to constructing images in perspective; an instrumental technology. Crary disagrees; he argues that we only think of the camera obscura predominantly in these terms due to the fact that it is mainly art historians who have paid attention to it. He argues that throughout the eighteenth century the main use of the camera obscura was not the making of visual images. More frequently, it was an object which was possessed by people in order to stimulate philosophical reflection and speculation on the nature of perception and knowledge, the external world, the eye and the brain (Crary 1993: 29). It was a practical model and a point of conversation and discourse, used in the effort to understand the processes of perception and our experience of the visual world more generally.

With the difference that the camera obscura can be thought of as a discursive object, because of how it was used, and that the VR apparatus is one because it is seldom available for use, it looks as if both apparatuses serve similar functions, some two and a half centuries apart, in the way that they promote intense abstract speculation about vision, embodiment and the nature of experience.

2.6.7 VR's cultural resources

Any medium utilises (and may transform and recombine) the signifying resources (codes, conventions, languages) of other existing and established media. This is evident in VR in a number of ways. In some genres of VR, photographic verisimilitude is the goal and the standard of realism against which its often stretched resources are judged (Cameron 1995: x; Penny 1995). In other versions which stress that the potential of VR is not to simulate photorealism or material reality with its 'physics' but to construct fantasy worlds, or when it is used by artists who explore other sensory states and situations, a range of ideas, themes, and conventions are drawn from the history of art.

See Char Davies's 'Osmose' (1998)
and the examples discussed by
Morse (1998: 186) for discussions
of VR in traditional artistic terms

In the context of popular entertainment there is a direct reliance on cinematic content and the key convention derived from the coincidence of the camera and the spectators' viewpoint in mainstream cinema – the cinematic 'point of view' now adopted, and entered into in VR jargon as POV. Morse has pointed out that the 'fly throughs' of contemporary TV graphics and advertisements (the twisting and tumbling logos and images which appear to emerge from behind the TV viewer to zoom into the TV screen and recede into its infinite space) share much with VR producers' use of 'flight' to move 'users' around virtual space. The connections between early twentieth-century theme parks, white-knuckle rides and VR has also been researched (Darley 2000: 43–47). VR, then, is deeply concerned with the 'remediation' of other media forms, as Bolter and Grusin argue (1999: 161–167).

2.6.1 Is VR a new 'visual'
medium?

2.7 VR AS A MEDIUM OF ART: A QUANTUM LEAP FORWARD?

We saw in **2.6.1** that VR has been described as a medium which breaks with a long Western tradition of visual representation stretching back to at least the beginnings of the European Renaissance in the fifteenth century. We met it described as a 'quantum leap into the technological construction of vision' (Hayles 1999: 38). Essentially this is because the technologies employed by VR are literally 'worn' by the viewer as extensions of their visual and tactile senses, and the experience that results is that of entering 'into the image' (see Robins 1996). This experience is captured in the widespread use of the phrase that is, arguably, the main metaphor for immersive VR: when a user dons the head-mounted display of a VR apparatus they are thought to 'step through Alberti's window'. The reference here is to Leon Battista Alberti, a fifteenth-century Italian art theorist, who formulated a practical method of perspectival depiction in which he conceived of the framed surface of a picture as a window through which a view of the world was seen. This puts contemporary thought about VR in touch with a long history of perspectival image making in Western culture.

However remote and ancient the reference to Alberti and painting may appear to be in the context of 'new media', it is not at all at odds with making other connections between VR and the more 'modern' technological media of photography, film and television. We find clear Albertian echoes in, for instance, Mark Dery's *Culture Jamming: hacking, slashing, and sniping in the empire of signs* (1993), where he suggests that 'in virtual reality, the television swallows the viewer

2.5 Mantegna's 'window': detail from Andrea Montegna, St Christopher's Body Being Dragged Away after His Beheading (1451–5), Ovetari Chapel, Eremitani Church, Padua

headfirst'. In *Virtualities: television, media art, and cyberculture* (1998), Margaret Morse draws extensively upon an (unacknowledged) Albertian framework when she likens VR to 'passing through the movie screen to enter the fictional world of the "film"'. Or, she suggests, entering a virtual environment is like 'being able to walk through one's TV or computer, through the vanishing point or vortex and into a three-dimensional field of symbols' (Morse 1998: 181). Morse thinks of the TV screen as a thin membrane between an immaterial world of symbols – a 'pocket of virtuality' – and the material world from which we view it. She also suggests that virtual environments which use perspectival frameworks 'may even be considered the last gasp of Renaissance space' and the VR user is a spectator whose 'station point is inside the projection of an image, transformed from a monocular and stationary point of view into mobile agency in three-dimensional space' (Morse 1998: 182). In short, references to the Western pictorial tradition underpin much of our thinking about the new medium of VR.

In this section will pursue this conception of VR to see what it holds. This will mean looking at the implications of the proposition that in VR images are no longer artefacts that we *look at* but environments that we *inhabit*. Imagine that instead of watching a movie you were in it, 'wearing', as it were, one of the characters. Such is the proposition of VR.

Such references can be found in Morse (1998), Mirzeoff (1998), Heim (1993), Bolter and Grusin (1999), Marchessault (1996), Nunes (1997), Hillis (1996)

Della Pittura, first published 1435–6: a key, founding text on pictorial perspective. See Alberti (1966)

See William Gibson's concept of the 'sim-stim' in his novel *Neuromancer* (1986)

This formulation of perspective in the fifteenth century was partly a recovery and systematisation of a less systematic and consistent form of pictorial perspective evident in the 'classical world' some 1,500 years before

There have been a number of moments in the history of Western art when perspectival space and representation have been challenged or subverted. Clear examples are (1) the Baroque in the seventeenth century, where images are expressively distorted and the space of a picture is shot through with inconsistencies, (2) the exploration of multiple perspectives, and a deliberate play between surface and illusion, the visual and the tactile, in Cubism during the first two decades of the twentieth century, and (3) the rigorous denial of any illusion of three-dimensional depth in favour of the material, painted surface (an exploration of the 'plane' rather than the 'window') in much mid- and late twentieth-century 'abstract' art. However, these styles and experiments are exceptions which prove the rule in that they self-consciously attempt to depart from the dominant perspectival tradition. See Jay (1988) for a discussion of this tradition

Michael Kubovy (1986: 140, fig 8.8, calls this pictorial space 'virtual space'

2.7.1 What is Alberti's window?

Although a number of practical achievements in perspective representation precede Alberti's work he is recognised as systematically formulating the principles of pictorial perspective and making explicit a practical method. With many subsequent embellishments and modifications, and the major break from figurative representation in the modernist art of the twentieth-century, this system of perspectival construction underlies the Western tradition of pictorial representation throughout the last five centuries. Alberti's method can be broken down into the following ideas and stages:

1   He conceived of vision as a *pyramid of rays with their apex at the eye* and their destinations at points on the surface of an object of sight or representation.

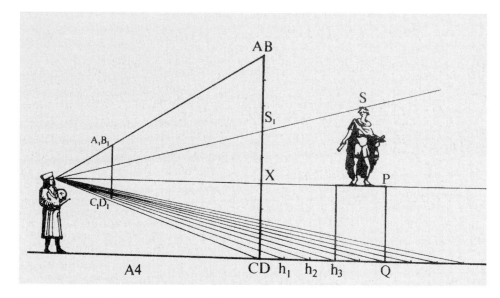

2.6 Diagram of Alberti's system: Beinecke Library.

2   He then showed how a drawing or painting could be thought of as a *plane* intersecting this pyramid.

3   He conceived of this intersecting plane as the surface of the painting (the picture plane) — *a material surface*.

4   He also thought of this plane as a *window*. 'First of all about where I draw. I inscribe a quadrangle of right angles, as large as I wish, which is considered to be an open window through which I see what I wish to paint' (Alberti 1966: 56; first published 1435–6).

5   The part of the pyramid 'behind' this plane is *pictorial space*; the world of the picture itself. Importantly, the persons and objects which are depicted as occupying the picture space are seen from the precise point of view of the 'eye' where the rays of sight converged.

6 Alberti's system gives this eye *a location in the real world* (from which the represented world is viewed) and places it at a precise distance from the picture plane and at the height of an average person.

7 The overall achievement of this system is to give the impression that the represented world and the pictorial space behind the picture plane is *continuous with the viewer's position in real space*.

In the detail of Mantegna's painting (Figure 2.5) the point where the real space of the spectator meets (and becomes) the picture space is drawn attention to by placing (depicting) an arm as if it were located at the very edge existing between the spectator's and the painting's worlds – it is suggested that it occupies both. This frequently adopted convention is evidence of the awareness, on the part of many fifteenth-century painters, of the implications of the new method they are using. The use of perspective connects the depicted world with that of the spectator.

2.7.2 The camera lens and the industrialisation of perspective

Before we consider the shift from these depicted spaces to those of VR and 'cyberspace', set apart by centuries, it is important to say a little more about photography and film. We observed that 'stepping through Alberti's window' is a phrase that is applied to the screen images of TV, film and computers as well as its original reference to painting. The degree of continuity between the kinds of image produced by perspectival painting, photography, movie film, cinema, and TV and computer graphics, is matter of some debate. It is quite possible, and in most cases far more important, to highlight the very real differences between the images that are produced by these media, rather than to stress their continuities and similarities. Histories of image making have been written on either basis, but any good historical account needs to pay attention to the complex interplay between the two. However, in the present context (the claims that VR involves a change of such magnitude that it represents a break in visual culture as important as the Renaissance) it has to be the similarities between all older-image media that VR dramatically leaves behind that concern us here. Typically, claims about new media do force us to deal with some very stark contrasts.

Any particular image or genre of photography may or may not be strongly perspectival. In fact, in many photographs there is a distinct flattening effect and lack of perspectival depth cues. In other photographs they are strongly evident. The same is true of cinematic and TV images (see **2.4**). The camera obscura, a filmless camera or room ('camera' means room in Italian), was, amongst other things, the photographic camera's forerunner and 'the very instrument for the mechanical production of monocular perspective'. Photography itself became the 'means by which it [a perspectival image] could be mechanically and chemically fixed, printed, marked and inscribed' (Neale 1985: 20). Camera lenses are designed and engineered to produce perspectival vision, and were intended to do so from the very invention of photography. One of photography's pioneers, Nicephore Niepce, explicitly stated his aims as being to discover an 'agent' that would durably imprint the images of perspectival representation. This would no longer be a system of drawing (à la Alberti), but a machine – the photographic camera.

With the rapid spread of photography in the first decades after its invention it was possible to conclude that as 'Strong as the mathematical convention of perspective had

2.4 Could there be a distinct digital visual culture?

2.7 Masaccio 'Trinita' 1425, Santa Maria Novella, Florence, Italy. A classic case of the kind of image that was produced by Alberti's method, which actually predates the publication of his treatise by about 10 years. This is Masaccio's painting of the 'Trinity', circa 1425. It seems clear that Masaccio had a firm practical grasp of the system that Alberti was to make explicit later. The view that this painting offers implies that it is being 'seen' by a virtual spectator whose eyeline coincides with the top of the painted sarcophagus. If the picture is treated as an 'elevation' (a frontal plan of a building or structure) it can be used to make a 'section' through the depicted or virtual space from the front edge of the sarcophagus to the deepest recess of the niche which holds the figures. Courtesy of Scala.

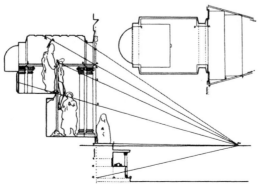

2.8 Diagram of depicted space in the 'Trinita'.

become in picture making before the pervasion of photography, that event definitely clamped it on our vision and our beliefs' (Ivins 1964: 108, cited in Neale 1985). In short, the photographic camera industrialised perspective and naturalised the Cartesian conception of space which is anticipated by perspective.

Some 50 years later, movie film, utilising the photographic lenses in which perspective is mechanically encoded, complicates the picture in many ways. In film the 'centred eye' of Albertian perspective is still at work, but it is multiplied and mobile as we look:

- from our cinema seats – in the dark – as spectators of the projection screen;

- with the camera – in its movement – sometimes as if it was with us in our seats (as in certain kinds of long shot) but more often looking from some place within the 190 degree space depicted by the film itself;

- with a depicted character (usually a main protagonist) within the fictional world of the film narrative (as in the subjective shot-reverse shot).

Having established something of the character of perspectival representation, and noted its continuing embodiment in modern technological media, we are now in a position to address a number of problems that VR brings to this long tradition of image production and the modes of spectatorship associated with it. We can do this by considering three key elements of this visual culture and other related narrative and performative practices. These are:

- perspective as a symbolic form;

- the framing of images;

- images as material surfaces.

2.7.3 Perspective as symbolic form

The term 'perspective as symbolic form' is borrowed from the art historian Erwin Panofsky, whose famous essay of this title was written in 1924. Panofsky's premiss is that perspective is more than a geometry or a mathematics of pictorial space. Debates about the status of perspective have been complex and long running. Does it match, in some especially truthful way, the conditions of human vision (the regular diminution of objects with distance, the convergence of railway lines, for instance)? Are the principles of pictorial perspective consistent with the laws of optics; the physics of vision? Or is pictorial perspective a set of cultural conventions for depicting space that have become dominant but which, in principle, exist alongside several others – the Western medieval, the Japanese, the Australian native peoples, for example (this is largely Panofsky's argument)? Is it, in short, a theory and a method of image making which has a privileged relation to the optics of human perception or is it a set of expressive and representational symbols: is it best understood in terms of natural science or semiotics (cultural science)? Is perspective 'real' or 'symbolic'? Our best guess is that it is, in part, both. However, Panofsky's contribution to the debate is to emphasise and show, through detailed exposition, how perspective works as a symbolic form. He shows how, from its very inception, artists like Masaccio in Italy and Van Eyck in the Netherlands grasped perspective as not only a way of constructing pictorial space or modelling the processes

Published in English in 1991, Erwin Panofsky, *Perspective as Symbolic Form*, New York: Zone Books, 1997.

of vision but also as a means of giving expressive significance to their images and of expressing ideas in visual form.

Panofsky begins by noting the expressive or communicative problem which perspective presented to artists. The problem arose from the manner in which perspective worked to construct a unified space, one which begged to be lit coherently and coloured naturalistically rather than according to a logic of symbolic significance. When using the new perspective, the size and prominence of depicted objects was determined by their position in space rather than their conventional, widely understood symbolic importance. In this way, perspective caused considerable representational problems for artists who adopted it as they emerged from a medieval tradition; artists who were skilled at arranging icons and symbols laden with meaning on flat surfaces and for whom space, depth, and volume were treated differently in different parts of the picture.

It is likely that perspective also presented problems for contemporary viewers of paintings. The problem for painters was how to mark out what was significant in an image when matters such as size, scale, and appearance were determined by a degree of perspectival naturalism not symbolic importance. For spectators, the other side of the problem was how to discern what was significant and what was not? Panofsky's demonstration of how painters began to tackle these issues is extremely detailed and complex. Here, we can return to the work of Masaccio to see perspective 'in action' as symbolic form. It is clear from Figure 2.9 that Masaccio uses perspective to project and integrate pictorial space into the architectural space in which he worked. He constructs the space of pictures that are placed upon opposite sides of the central altar as if their pictorial space continues or extends behind the altar. But he uses perspective to achieve more than this. He uses the depth axis of perspective to solve a narrative problem: how to depict the unfolding of an act over time, in a single, static scene.

In 'The Baptism of the Neophytes' we see one neophyte in the process of undressing, another waits, naked and shivering, and a third receives baptism. These three images can also be read as three moments in a continuous process. We can read this as an image of three men doing different things or as stages of one man's actions. Elsewhere in the 1420s such narrative conventions take place 'simultaneously' on the picture plane but in different spaces. Telling stories by painting a sequence of separate moments, rather like a series of frames in an animation or the panels in a comic book, was a common practice in the fifteenth century. Normally, however, each moment would be separately framed or placed on a separate part of the picture plane. In Masaccio's work, they become embodied and embedded in depicted space, and a sense of anticipation as well as physical experience is expressed.

This expressive use of perspective is even stronger in the section on the other side of the altar: 'St Peter Raises the

As has been noted, such a use of iconic images organised and marked according to significance is now to be seen in screen-based multimedia (Woolley 1992)

2.9 Masaccio: Overview of fresco cycle in the Brancacci Chapel, Santa Maria del Carmine, 1421–7.

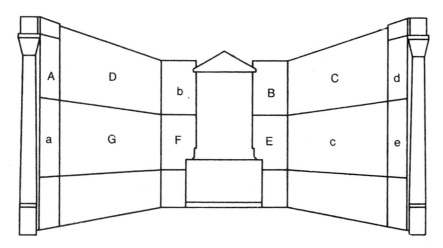

2.10 Diagram of fresco sections in Fig. 2.9.

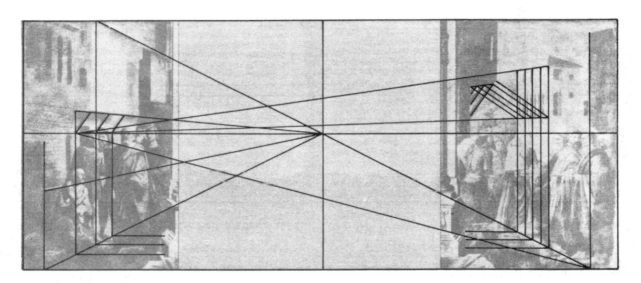

2.11 Diagram of perspective construction of Brancacci Chapel frescoes – vanishing points.

Cripples with his Own Shadow'. Here, the perspective which integrates pictorial and architectural space also enables Masaccio to represent St Peter as walking past three beggars, and as he does the cripples are cured and rise up. They appear to be cured in the time that he passes by: the cripple furthest back in space, whom Peter has passed, now stands upright while the man he is about to draw level with is still unable to stand but will (so the narrative promises) imminently be cured. More than this, Peter looks ahead, out of the picture space and above the head of the spectator, whose viewpoint, also constructed by the image, is beneath the saint. He appears to walk, curing the sick as he passes, and with a powerful implication that he is about to enter into (our) real space. Are we, therefore, next in line?

We might even think of perspective as a kind of 'software'. The knowledge and technique once held in the painter's 'head' is now not only replicated in the optical lenses of mechanical cameras, it is replicated in the form of the algorithms and programming which guide digital virtual cameras in 3D software applications

2.12 Fresco section: 'St Peter raises the cripples with his own shadow'.   2.13 Fresco section: The Baptism of the Neophytes.

This question is given some edge by claims that VR promises a form of 'post-symbolic' communication. On this view, immersive VR is 'post-symbolic' because we experience its worlds as we do those of real life, where we interact directly through our bodies and bodily actions with objects and spaces. It is a claim that also draws upon the distinction between simulation and representation: where a simulation (rather than a copy) can be experienced as if it were real, even when no corresponding thing or situation exists outside of the simulation itself (see **2.2.3**). In this sense, immersive VR, as a simulation, does not refer, copy, imitate, signify or symbolise in the same way that analogue media may do, in order to represent this or that particular thing existing 'out there' in the world. However, this cannot mean that in VR we no

Virtual reality and pictorial perspective

At this point in our analysis we might think of pictorial perspective as a technology, a technology for constructing the space in an image. But, as we have seen here, it can also be used to give expressive force and add meaning to what is represented. We have seen how the pictorial space that perspective constructs is used to extend material, architectural space. It also reaches out, as it were, to position the embodied viewer in real space, in relation to what is depicted or represented. In one case, that of St Peter raising the cripples, the pictorial space effectively 'envelops' the spectator as it is implied, visually, that the saint's temporal progress through space continues toward the spectator.

Given that the immersive nature of VR is described as 'stepping through Alberti's window' it can appear in principle to be a stage further on, a progressive development of the achievements of perspective. In the perspectival images, there was only a connection or alignment of real and contructed space, however powerful in some cases; now, in VR (the metaphor proposes), one becomes the other – they become synonymous. However, given this radical reconfiguration of the relationship between spectator and image that takes place in VR (the idea that the spectator is now inside the image) the question arises: how can VR function as a symbolic form? In other words, how do the technologies of VR operate as the technology of perspective has: *as more than a technology* for constructing pictorial space *but also as a means of giving form and expression to ideas?*

For artists and experimental producers of virtual environments a practical barrier stands in the way of finding solutions to this question. At present, at least, the intense and expensive work entailed in constructing VR, together with their short duration, means, amongst other things, that it is difficult to accrue experience, from one experiment to another, of solutions to problems and to develop conventions. As Margaret Morse points out:

> Virtual environments are produced like packages that are designed without knowing what they might hold on the inside. In a field where the lore of veterans is nonexistent and where conventions are invented ad hoc as one goes along, even the artists . . . could not be sure what to expect once the machine or 'environment' . . . was finished.
>
> (Morse 1998: 200)

This is not the only practical problem, for if the massive computing power needed to run a VR work can only be achieved for brief periods (in work that Morse is considering – only two hours) and the work subsequently exists only as memory (the users and the computers, and as video documentation) how will we ever arrive at answers (Morse 1998)? However, there may be a still larger problem. This is that the act of 'stepping through' a window or 'into an image' makes no sense. VR may indeed lead to a new kind of relationship between spectators and images, but it is a very problematic relationship which raises some difficult questions for the use of VR as a medium. It is to this question that we now turn.

2.7.4 The condition of Alberti's window after VR

It is instructive to see what happens if we take the diagram or schema that locates Alberti's window (and therefore the image) in relation to a spectator (Figure 2.6) and then reconfigure in terms of VR. Figure 2.14 takes the key elements of Alberti's method – the viewing station of the spectator (A), the picture plane (B), and the image or pictorial space (C) – and uses them to conceptualise what occurs in a 'virtual reality' or 'environment'. By looking at the three points A, B and C we can observe the following.

First, a question arises. What remains at point A – the position traditionally occupied by a spectator of an image? The viewer's (now user's or immersant's) body remains there. But it is a body that cannot *see* the world it occupies. Its field of vision is wholly filled by the electronic stimulus provided by the small, binocular LCD screens held close to the user's eyes. They are rendered blind to the world that they stand in and therefore they are also unable to establish their relationship to the virtual world that they see. In terms of the sociality or social rituals of spectating (sharing the act and occasion of looking with others, especially important in the way we consume cinema and television, and once important in the way that paintings and prints were used as a basis of discussion and conversation) we should also recognise that the immersant is sealed off from others. At point A there can be other viewers, who are not immersed in the virtual environment but are an audience for the VR event. What they see is the immersant's body moving to the logic of a space that they, in turn, cannot see.

longer deal with representational elements (visual languages, sign systems or symbols) at all. The digitally processed and reconfigured data that are fed to the VR user via helmets carrying stereoscopic LCD screens and wired gloves or body suits providing tactile and positioning feedback, are normally built from analogue, photographic or video images of objects, persons and places. It would otherwise be meaningless. Its immersive, stereographic, and interactive simulation, or production, of a world that is virtually real, harnesses images and symbols that we would otherwise understand as representations. This is a proposition that is echoed in the notion that VR may be the 'ultimate' display or interface with a computer by doing away with the screen, the mouse and keyboard, etc. (see **2.6.3**)

The fact that only one or two people can normally enter a virtual environment is a problem for the exhibition of VR. One solution is for a 'secondary' set of spectators to watch the immersant's 'exploration' of a virtual world, while also seeing a projected video version of the immersant's visual experience on a screen

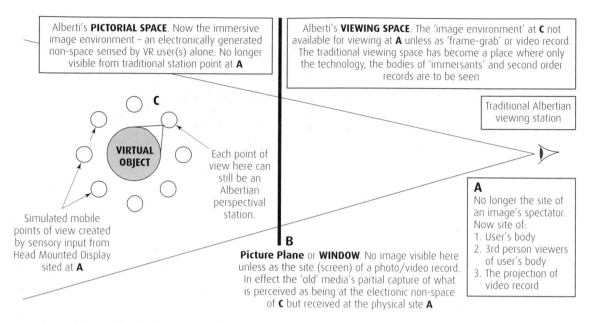

Alberti's **PICTORIAL SPACE**. Now the immersive image environment – an electronically generated non-space sensed by VR user(s) alone. No longer visible from traditional station point at **A**

Alberti's **VIEWING SPACE**. The 'image environment' at **C** not available for viewing at **A** unless as 'frame-grab' or video record. The traditional viewing space has become a place where only the technology, the bodies of 'immersants' and second order records are to be seen

Traditional Albertian viewing station

C

VIRTUAL OBJECT

Each point of view here can still be an Albertian perspectival station.

A
No longer the site of an image's spectator. Now site of:
1. User's body
2. 3rd person viewers of user's body
3. The projection of video record

Simulated mobile points of view created by sensory input from Head Mounted Display sited at **A**

B
Picture Plane or **WINDOW**. No image visible here unless as the site (screen) of a photo/video record. In effect the 'old' media's partial capture of what is perceived as being at the electronic non-space of **C** but received at the physical site **A**

2.14 The condition of Alberti's Window after VR.

The overcoming of the solitary or private nature of VR experience lies in the development of 'avatars' (a Hindu word for the visible form of a deity). Here representations of the self and others exist in cyberspace. Presently, they take extremely crude forms and their future development may lie in the same realm as we discussed in section **1.2.7**: the digital simulation of high resolution images of the human body in cyberspace

We can recall that Ivan Sutherland's prototype, his head mounted 'ultimate' display, provided its user with a Cartesian spatial grid of space (see **2.6.3**), From imitation to simulation) as does the VR world 'Osmose' built by the artist Char Davies (Davies 1998)

2.6.5   VR: trimming the metaphors

Point B is the site of the old picture plane or window, the material surface or substrate of an image. Nothing is left here. Rather than being 'stepped through' it is more accurate to say that it has dissolved or, more accurately still, that the extreme proximity of the binocular LCD screens that carry the image to the eyes of the spectator is such that no edge can be detected and no consciousness of the surface of the image be maintained. However, this picture plane or surface may be resurrected for the 'secondary' audience in the form of a return to 'old' media, video or photographs, which partially capture and put into public space what is individually experienced in the virtual environment.

Point C (this could only be an imagined, notional point inside Albertian 'picture space') is now an electronically generated environment: the virtual world itself. In many examples of virtual environments, perspectival images (of cartesian space) survive here, at least in the immersant's perception. They are mobile and dependent upon the immersant's point of view in a way that is reminiscent of perspectival lines of sight in cinema. This perceived reality or simulation is being generated and managed by technological extensions and data inputs to the human sensorium which is taking place at point A, the place where the spectator's body remains, its sensorium split in two. As we saw in **2.6.5** you only get to take some of your senses with you into VR. At point C there is nobody, partial or otherwise.

From this comparative analysis of spectatorship as it is structured by (a) the technique of perspective and (b) the technology of VR (which amounts to an inspection of the sense contained in the metaphor, 'stepping through Alberti's window'), we can conclude the following: no stepping through has occurred but two other things have – the spectator has lost sight of the frame and the surface of the image, and they cannot gauge their relationship to it, perceptually, imaginatively, or physically.

2.7.5 Frames and surfaces

Our analysis of the shift from perspectival image making to immersive VR, summed up in the phrase 'stepping through Alberti's window', has allowed us to discuss VR in terms of the pictorial conventions which have been central to most forms of image making in the West since the fifteenth century. We have also seen that these conventions work to bring about a certain relationship between spectator and image; a relationship which has served many purposes as well as being the source of several pleasures. The next problem we address is that as VR surrounds the user's (or the old spectator's) vision, 'the frame of earlier visual technologies, from landscape painting to TV, recedes from view and with it a degree of awareness of our separation from the machine' (Hillis 1996: 84).

Frames

The physical picture frame begins to appear in the fifteenth century. Frames are coeval with perspective (with the conception of the window), but also appear for social reasons concerning the ownership and uses of pictures. Pictures began to shift from being literally a part of walls to become smaller portable, often domestic, objects. Framed images or pictures, with their material substrates, are clearly in the same physical world as the viewer. They are both part of the everyday material world and conventionally separated off, by their frames, as being a special kind of object or event in the world. They are spaces of representation and surfaces which invite imaginative projection. Frames, of course, are not confined to paintings and photographs; we might also note the proscenium arch of the theatre, the edges between the cinema screen and the darkness which surrounds it, the physical limits of the TV screen. Indeed, the covers, title and end pages of a novel perform a similar framing function; within them imagined worlds are represented, outside of them the real world extends.

There are also temporal frames: the occasions for telling stories in the communities of oral cultures, the serialised narration of drama on radio, the allotted 'bedtime' story within contemporary family units. We can even think of carnivals and festivals as occasions which are a combination of spatial and temporal frames as, on certain dates and within certain neighbourhoods, identities and behaviours are performed that are discontinuous with those we occupy in the real world.

In all of these cases, the frame functions to distinguish the fictional, possible, rehearsed, imagined, or desired (and the virtual) from everyday physical and social reality. It is largely this framing which marks out spaces in which the unthinkable, the terrifying or the transgressive can be explored from a position of 'relative safety'.

Watching transgressive acts form a position of 'relative safety' is clearly a major element in the experience provided by cinema. See Morse (1998: 19)

Surfaces

Images also have surfaces (we usually only notice this about windows when they have smudges on them). The oscillation between *seeing the surface* or *looking through it* has been crucial to our experience of visual media. Image-makers of all kinds know that the play and tension between erasing the picture surface and stressing it as a sight of sensual pleasure and reflection is a main site of our fascination with images.

Again, this is not only true of the 'old' medium of painting, even if this is a paradigm case. Consider the acknowledged tension in movies – between (1) the onward drive of a narrative sequence in which each image or shot has to be subsumed to the logic of the narrative, and (2) the iconic image which film can also give us, as in the lustrous images

See Bolter and Grusin (1999: 20-52), for whom seeing the surface or looking through it are elements in their concepts of 'immediacy' and 'hypermediacy' as the twin poles of attention given to media images

of the modern 35mm print or the now lost technique of black and white cinematography of classical Hollywood — the tellingly named 'silver screen'. In the first case, the image passes relatively unnoticed as we are caught up in the temporal unfolding or **diegesis** of the character's psychologies and actions. In the second, the narrative is punctured or arrested by the single image held before us on the screen — for as long as the director may dare.

A virtual environment or installation also has a spatial and temporal frame of sorts: it is obvious, although seldom mentioned in VR discourses, that you have to be present in an institution, at the appropriate time, to experience VR. (See **2.6.1** for a further discussion of how rare and inaccessible such events are.) But it is a form which, at the level of consumption, attempts to deny it even more radically than some kinds of cinema, a medium which has attracted criticism as a form that hides its own means of production (**2.4**). The 'blinded' body, the split sensorium, and the absence of a social form of exhibition or performance are all major difficulties facing VR which arise from this absence of framing.

2.6.1 Is VR a new 'visual' medium?

2.4 Could there be a distinct digital visual culture?

Conclusion

This discussion has left us with more questions than it has provided answers. How does a culture in which frames, of the many kinds listed above, are crucial to its forms of expression, narration and representation, use a medium which has none? How can we deal with the prospect of a medium which seeks to collapse the boundaries between its representations (or its simulations) and the material world in which the representing and simulating is taking place?

To put this another way, in the history of Western visual representation, the aesthetic forms that we have been discussing — perspective, as a way of positioning viewers of images and as expressive form, the framing of images, and their material surfaces — have been used to refer meaningfully to the material and social world. At the same time, they have provided spaces or opportunities within that world for reflecting on it and thinking beyond its immediate limits. That has been one function of art and also of many forms of popular culture (the latter usually being turned into the former at some point in their history). If we think of media production as a cultural practice we could say it is, at its best, a way of commenting on and possibly criticising, celebrating or envisioning alternatives to the world we live in. How can we do this 'in' VR? What part does the difference between representation and simulation play in thinking about this? What is the difference between a representation with its frame, referring to a reality outside of itself, and a VR simulation with no apparent frame which seeks to generate an apparently real world which may, or may not, refer to anything outside of itself? Just how unresolved, just how problematic, immersive VR is, when we attempt to think of it as a medium, should now be clear.

The relationship between immersive VR's imperfect simulations that stand as realities in themselves and the history of media representations which refer to the world in especially realistic ways is a complex and hardly explored area. However, as the technologies that underpin VR are also being put actively to work in the production of popular film and cinema, we now need to shift our attention to what has come to be known as digital cinema.

2.8 DIGITAL CINEMA

[Virtual reality] is frequently seen as part of a teleology of the cinema — a progressive technological fulfilment of the cinema's illusionistic power.

(Lister 1995: 15)

Popular ideas about, and expectations for, the potential of VR are inseparable from the cinema as aesthetic form. Whilst the ubiquity and simultaneity of broadcast television, or the communication 'spaces' of the telephone or Internet are in many ways more significant to the development of VR technologies and applications, it is the clarity and seduction of cinema's visual imagery and the 'immersion' of its viewers against which emerging (and potential) VR experiences are measured. As we will see, cinema is a key factor in VR's 'remediations'.

Conversely, cinema has developed and disseminated images, ideas and dreams of VR and the virtual, particularly in recent science fiction films. Moreover, the design of certain VR systems draws heavily on cinematic imagery, forms, and conventions.

In this section we will consider the popularisation of **CGI** (computer-generated imagery), and its use in special effects and computer animation. These forms will be considered as, on the one hand, materially and historically situated technologies and media, and on the other as informing a technological imaginary in which the impact of digital technology on cinema is presented as either symptomatic of, or a causal factor in, the 'virtualisation' of the modern world.

There is great excitement about the future possibilities of immersive or interactive entertainment, but also fear that digital technologies are leading film into a descending spiral of spectacular superficiality. Such fears are evident in both popular film criticism and academic, **postmodernist** discourses. The latter extend the argument to Western culture as a whole, now characterised by a waning of 'meaning', becoming (and the metaphors are telling) simulated and flattened, screen-like.

2.8.1 Virtual VR

To the distinction between immersive and metaphorical VR (**2.6**) we could here add one more, what Ellen Strain calls 'virtual VR' (Strain 1999: 10). On one level this is simply the representation of speculative forms of VR and cyberspace in science fiction films such as *Lawnmower Man* (1992), *Strange Days* (1995) and *Johnny Mnemonic* (1995). On another level Strain refers to the phenomenon of fictional and speculative images of VR becoming blurred with actual existing forms and uses of VR technologies. Given the point made in **2.6**, that VR is in fact a rather exclusive experience and not a mass medium, it is not surprising that films have projected fantasies of digital worlds that have generated a misleading sense of the current state, or putative soon-to-be-realised future, of VR.

What is perhaps more surprising is that both VR researchers and cultural theorists have drawn so heavily on popular science fiction literature and film as if they were technological fact.

Philip Hayward lists the subcultural and popular cultural points of reference of the early VR enthusiasts: to science fiction he adds New Age mysticism, psychedelia and rock culture. This promotion of the possibilities of VR through popular cultural discourses not only shapes public expectations but may even affect VR research itself:

> These discourses are significant because they have shaped both consumer desire and the perceptions and agenda of the medium's developers. In a particularly ironic twist . . . they have created a **simulacrum** of the medium in advance (against which its products will be compared).

> (Hayward 1993: 182 [bold added])

Margin notes

See special issues of *Screen* 40.2 (Summer 1998), and *Convergence* **5.2** (1999)

The terms 'virtual' and 'virtualisation' are, in this section, used in the rather imprecise sense prevalent in much academic and popular film criticism. See **1.2.5, 1.2.6, 2.6, 5.4.2** for more considered discussion of 'the virtual

1.2.5 Virtuality
1.2.6 Which virtual reality?
2.6   Immersive virtual reality?
5.4.2 Cybernetics and the virtual

2.6   Immersive virtual reality

This, however, is not always naive; there are instances where this is a particular strategy: reading (science) fictions as one would read any other document or source of data. See David Thomas, 'The technophiliac body: on technicity in William Gibson's cyborg culture', in David Bell & Barbara M. Kennedy (eds) *The Cybercultures Reader* London: Routledge, 2000, pp. 175–189. Thomas there reads William Gibson's fictional worlds as straight sociological data, from which informative results are gathered (see **5.1**)

Key text: Philip Hayward, 'Situating cyberspace: the popularisation of virtual reality', in Philip Hayward and Tana Wollen (eds) *Future Visions: new technologies of the screen*, London: BFI, pp. 180–204

See Part 4 for further discussion of the relationships between popular culture and the development of computer media

4 NEW MEDIA IN EVERYDAY LIFE

It should be pointed out that, although VR raises fascinating questions, we could address the emergence of 'digital cinema' in different terms. For example, at another level, but one with profound implications for dominant forms of production and consumption, is the convergence at the corporate level of Hollywood studios and consumer electronic multinationals. By owning the studio's back catalogue of films, Sony etc. have the 'software' that can determine which new 'hardware' formats (from Betamax versus VHS to laser disk and DVD) will prevail in the domestic market for film viewing.

On the other hand, some predict that the potential impact of digital technology on the production and distribution of films is at least as significant as on narrative and aesthetics. Following the success of *The Blair Witch Project*, at the time of writing a number of successful feature films have been shot on handheld digital cameras. The director Mike Figgis (who himself made the innovative film *Timecode* [2000] with digital cameras) predicts that digital satellite transmission of feature films to cinemas (or any building with a digital projector) removes the need for expensive copies of films, with the power of the established distributors often blamed for restricting the progress of less conventional films. (See www.dogme95.dk)

For an example of moving image-making for online distribution, see http://www.plugincinema.com/

Ellis points out that forms not generally seen as 'realist', such as horror and comedy, are made coherent by these conventions (Ellis 1982: 6–9)

See MacCabe (1974). For an introduction to theories of realism in film, see Lapsley and Westlake (1988: 156–180)

In this section we will argue that whilst notions of virtual reality offer an imaginative framing of technological and aesthetic change in cinema in particular and visual culture in general, they can also detract from other important factors in the shaping and transformations of cinema as an entertainment medium today. If the introduction of digital technology to film production is seen as paradigmatic of the virtualisation of culture, then any charting of the intricate relationships between media, new technology, aesthetics, cultural/entertainment institutions and economies may be foreclosed.

2.8.2 Virtual realism

Film theory and media studies are centrally concerned with the relationship between popular representations and the real world. The term **'realism'** is therefore a useful one in this context, not least because it highlights the argument that any representation, however technologically advanced, is a cultural construction and not the 'real' itself. That is to say, a critical notion of realism foregrounds not the 'capture' of the real but its articulation or constitution in representations.

Realisms in cinema

[T]here is no realism, but there are realisms.

(Ellis 1982: 8)

John Ellis identifies a number of realist conventions in cinema and television. They include:

• common-sense notions and expectations, such as correct historical details in costume drama, or racial stereotypes in war films;

• adequate explanations of apparently confusing events, establishing logical relationships between cause and effect in events;

• coherent psychological motivations for characters.

Some of these are contradictory, they often co-exist within the same film or television programme. We could add others: the assumption of truth in documentaries, or the social realism of politically motivated film-makers such as Ken Loach.

Film theory has extensively explored the ideological workings of realisms in cinema. Debates in the French journal *Cahiers du Cinema* and the British journal *Screen*, in the late 1960s and 1970s, though diverse and at times antagonistic, shared the premiss that dominant cinematic realist codes construct a fundamentally conservative view of reality. In establishing a coherent 'real world' within the film, this critique argues, Hollywood films deny the contradictions of a reality characterised by class conflict, gender inequalities and hidden power structures. Realist codes ensure that conflicting points of view and power relationships within the film's fictional world are always resolved or reconciled. A world riven by contradiction is always, by the end of the last reel, whole, coherent – if the ending is not always entirely happy, it does at least provide narrative 'closure' (McCabe 1974). These debates argue, then, that Hollywood film production and reception do not present the real world; quite the opposite, they mask or mediate the real world and real social relations. Different realisms are not mere aesthetic choices, but each correlate with a particular ideology of what constitutes the 'real world' in the first place.

There are a number of ways in which these debates relate to our discussion of digital cinema. They represent a sustained and influential enquiry into the relationships between representations and the real. They raise questions of the meanings of popular visual culture in terms of ideology, and of audience. However, it is significant that of the various realisms discussed so far most do not rely for their effects on the photographic image as an index of reality, or even on visual communication at all. Some would apply equally well to radio as to television and cinema. Similarly, whilst the technological apparatus of cinema and television is sometimes discussed in these debates, it is rarely identified as a key factor in the construction of the ideological effects of these realisms. The following quotes give an indication of a significant shift in the critical consideration of realism when applied to recent technological change in cinema:

> The drive behind much of the technical development in cinema since 1950 has been towards both a greater or heightened sense of 'realism' and a bigger, more breathtaking realization of spectacle. Both of these impetuses have been realized through the development of larger, clearer, more enveloping images; louder, more multi-layered, more accurately directional sound; and more subtle, 'truer-to-life' colour. The intention of all technical systems developed since the beginning of the 1950s has been towards reducing the spectators' sense of their 'real' world, and replacing it with a fully believable artificial one.
>
> (Allen 1998: 127)

> [S]ince the early days of cinema, innovations in audiovisual technologies have aimed to provide a series of new, notionally improved experiences for audiences . . . Their improvements have always resulted in a more vivid capture of the real: greater clarity, firmer focus, richer hues.
>
> (Hayward and Wollen 1993: 2)

It is clear then that the visual image and its technologies are central to these comments.

It is also clear that the concepts of realism used to address CGI in recent film are quite distinct from those usually associated with critical film theory. What we see here is an uncomfortable but widespread conflation of three distinct notions of realism: photographic or cinematographic verisimilitude, the spectacular or illusionistic, and the 'immediate' grasping of reality in which the medium itself seems to flicker out of the picture. Thus the more visually 'realistic' (or in Bolter and Grusin's terms 'immediate') a film or special effects sequence is, the more artificial or illusionistic it is. So, as Bolter and Grusin, discussing special effects-driven films like *Jurassic Park* and *Lost World*, point out:

> We go to such films in large part to experience the oscillations between immediacy and hypermediacy produced by the special effects . . . the amazement or wonder requires an awareness of the medium. If the medium really disappeared, as is the apparent goal of the logic of transparency, the viewer would not be amazed because she would not know of the medium's presence.
>
> (Bolter and Grusin 1999: 157)

Interestingly, it is not only recent developments in cinematic technology that are addressed here. The contemporary concerns of the writers revisit aspects of the history of cinema (technological change, the spectators' relationship with cinema as media technologies), aspects that had not been generally seen as important until now

To suggest how CGI in popular film might be critically examined as spectacular imagery and technological advance, we will define four key terms: verisimilitude, photo-realism, simulation/**hyperrealism**, and spectacular realism.

VERISIMILITUDE

As we have seen, discussions of the application of digital imaging to cinema generally centre around the realism of the image, or verisimilitude. Verisimilitude, as a type of representation, is the imitation of the visual appearance of the world, people and objects, as it appears to the human eye. Special effects and computer animation are measured by their proximity to an 'unmediated' view of the real world. Verisimilitude is by and large taken for granted in conventional cinematography, but in computer-generated imagery it becomes an object of interest to both producers and spectators. In the computer-animated feature *Toy Story* (1995), for example, the toy soldiers are lovingly rendered complete with the imperfections and tags of excess plastic characteristic of cheap moulded toys. This detail is offered to the audience as visually pleasurable – a knowing reference to the minutiae of childhood experience, and an invitation to acknowledge the animators' wit and attention to detail.

PHOTO-REALISM

> In cases where a real-life equivalent is clearly impossible, such as the morphing effects in *Terminator 2*, the pictorial quality of the effect must be sophisticated and 'photo-realistic' enough to persuade the audience that if, for example, a tiled floor transformed into a human figure in real life, it would look exactly like its screen depiction does.
>
> (Allen 1998: 127)

Here we see verisimilitude again, but with an important difference. These CGI sequences are not so much capturing external reality as simulating another medium: in Bolter and Grusin's terms, 'remediation' – the visual replication of photography and cinematography. Indeed photo-realism is measured more by its figuration of these other media than by any capture of the look of the real itself.

The quote from Allen (1998) demonstrates that this distinction is not always a clear one. Confusion and slippages between the 'real' and 'representation as realist' characterises much recent criticism of the digital moving image. A number of important issues relate to this confusion. The term photo-realistic implies a representation that has not been produced by photographic techniques, but looks as though it has. What does 'photo-realistic' mean when applied to an event or effect that couldn't be photographed? Some special effects construct real world events which are difficult or expensive to film conventionally (explosions, ships sinking, etc.), whilst others, as in the *Terminator 2* sequence or in *The Matrix*, depict events that could never be photographed and hence have no referent against which their effectiveness can be measured. Thus photography here functions not as some kind of mechanically neutral verisimilitude but as a mode of representation that creates a 'reality effect'; that is to say, the onscreen event is accepted because it conforms to prevailing or emergent realist notions of screen spectacle and fantasy, not the 'real world'. Thus, as Lev Manovich argues, again in relation to *Terminator 2*:

> For what is faked, of course, is not reality but photographic reality, reality as seen by the camera lens. In other words, what digital simulation has (almost) achieved is not realism, but only photorealism ... It is only this film-based image which digital

technology has learned to simulate. And the reason we think that this technology has succeeded in faking reality is that cinema, over the course of the last hundred years, has taught us to accept its particular representational form as reality.

(Manovich 1996)

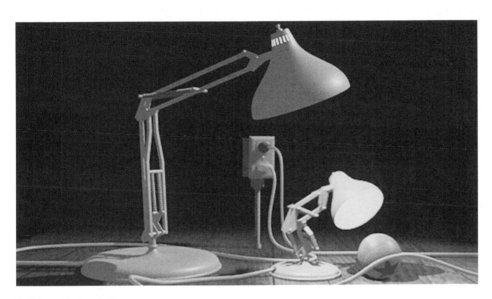

2.15 Luxor Junior, © Pixar.

HYPERREALISM

The use of terms such as 'simulation', 'virtual reality' and 'hyperrealism' in the criticism of popular new media is often confused and imprecise. With science fiction associations, hyperreality is used by postmodernist thinkers Jean Baudrillard and Umberto Eco, though with different implications. Both take the theme park Disneyland as an example. For Eco Disneyland is the ultimate example of what he sees as an emergent postmodernist culture characterised by the 'fake' (others include waxwork museums and animatronic displays), whereas for Baudrillard our enjoyment of the theme park's emphasis on its own spectacular 'hyperreality' serves to distract us from the fact that the real world as a whole is now hyperreal: there is no real left to 'fake'. For Baudrillard hyperreality is synonymous with simulation (Eco 1986; Baudrillard 1983).

The term 'hyperrealism' however, is ostensibly quite different. It is used to identify a distinct and dominant aesthetic in popular animation, developed by the Walt Disney Corporation in their animated feature films, beginning with Snow White in 1937. Disney's hyperrealist aesthetic is pertinent to the study of digital cinema.

Disney animation presents its characters and environments as broadly conforming to the physics of the real world. For example, Felix the Cat or even the early Mickey Mouse were never constrained by gravity or immutability as Snow White or Pocahontas are. They were characterised by what Eisenstein called 'plasmaticness', the quality of early cartoon characters and environments to stretch, squash and transform themselves (Leyda 1988). Hyperrealism also covers the Disney studio's application of realist conventions of narrative,

This distinction between 'simulation' and 'imitation' or representation is discussed further in **2.6.3** and **5.3.1** (see also Glossary)

2.6.3 Spheres collide: from imitation to simulation – VR's operational history
5.3.1 Automata: the basics

However, given the important role of Disney in the development of popular spectacular culture in general (theme parks as well as movies), and in the pioneering of new cinematic technologies (from sound and colour in cartoons, the Multiplane camera in Snow White, through to the CGI innovations of Tron and the corporation's collaborations with the computer animation studio Pixar in the 1990s), it could be argued that the concept of hyperreality and the animation aesthetics of hyperrealism are closely connected

2.16a The Skeleton Dance

2.16b Flowers and Trees

2.16c Snow White and the
Seven Dwarfs
© Disney Enterprises, Inc.

logical causality and character motivations – breaking with the largely non-realist and anarchic dynamics of the cartoon form. Here, then, hyperrealism is a measure not so much of the proximity of the representation to its referent but of the remediation of the codes (and attendant ideologies) of live action cinema.

However, hyperrealism in the context of animation, as its 'hyper-' prefix suggests, is not wholly constrained by live action conventions. Disney hyperrealist animation never fully remediated the live action film – it always exceeded verisimilitude. This is evident in the graphic conventions of caricature in character design, as well as in the exaggeration of the forces of the physical world. The verisimilitude of these films always operates in tension with the graphic limitations and possibilities of drawn animation, the vestiges of plasmaticness in conventions of 'squash and stretch', metamorphosis, as well as the often fantastic subject matter (talking animals, magic, fairy tales and monsters).

Thus 'hyperrealism' can conflate the 'remediation' of live action film within animation (and photo-realism in CGI) with a rather indistinct notion of contemporary culture as increasingly virtual. These two senses come together in a more concrete way in recent computer-animated films, notably the collaborations between the Pixar Studio and Disney on feature films such as *Toy Story* (1995) and *A Bug's Life* (1998), or in Dreamworks' *Antz* (1998) and *Shrek* (2001).

Materialism

Materialism is a critical approach to studying culture. Materialist approaches are particularly pertinent for understanding developments in digital cinema because they foreground the reality or materiality of cinema and its technologies within the contexts of economic, ideological and historical change. The term establishes an opposition with 'idealist' film criticism. From a materialist perspective, any particular realism is determined not by any technological or aesthetic teleology but by competing and historically contingent aesthetic conventions, technical developments and economic and social forces. The Hollywood film industry often presents an idealist view of cinematic technological progress to ever-greater realism and immersion for its audiences. What is perhaps more surprising, as we will see, is that this idealism, reanimated by the novelty and excitement of digital technologies, has re-emerged within critical studies of digital cinema.

Jean-Louis Comolli's essay 'Machines of the Visible' (1980) develops such a materialist approach. Though written before the advent of digital technology, Comolli's argument – that the history of technological change and realist forms is fundamentally discontinuous, not a linear path to mimetic perfection – is entirely relevant to current developments in film technology and aesthetics. For Comolli, this discontinuous history of cinema is not merely the product of competing technologies, studios and institutions, but of cinema as a 'social machine' – a form through which the dominant social configuration (class relationships within capitalism) attempts to represent itself. From this perspective verisimilitude is seen to be ideological, a set of realist codes, not the product of inevitable technological and aesthetic evolution. 'Realism' in general, and verisimilitude in particular, cannot be understood

without considering determinations that are not exclusively technical but economic and ideological: determinations which go beyond the simple realm of the cinematic . . . which shatter the fiction of an autonomous history of the cinema (of its 'styles and techniques'). Which effect the complex articulation of this field and this history with other fields, other histories.

(Comolli 1980: 127)

See Wells (1998: 25–26)

Materialist approaches implicitly or explicitly oppose themselves to 'idealist' film criticism. The French critic André Bazin (1918–1958) is the key figure here. For Bazin, 'cinematic technology and style move toward a "total and complete representation of reality"' (Manovich 1997: 6). He sees cinema as the culmination of art's mimetic function, evidence of which can be seen in ancient cultures (see **1.4.1** for discussion of teleological accounts of technological change). Cinematic realism, moreover, should also 'approximate the perceptual and cognitive dynamics of natural vision' (ibid.). Hence Bazin's particular interest in techniques of photography generating depth of field, within which 'the viewer can freely explore the space of film image' (ibid.). See Bazin (1967). For a reassessment of Bazin's work, see Matthews (n.d.)

1.4.1 Teleological accounts of new media

Jean Louis Comolli's (1980) essay is directly brought to bear on debates around new media in Timothy Druckrey (ed.) *Electronic Culture: Technology and Visual Representation*, New York: Aperture, 1996. See also Lev Manovich's application of Comolli's ideas to digital cinema (Manovich 1996)

We will look at three examples, the first from Comolli, the second relating to the historical development of animation, and the third a more recent example of the technology of cinematic realism.

PANCHROMATIC FILM STOCK

From an idealist position the introduction, around 1925, of panchromatic film stock (black-and-white film which renders the colour spectrum into shades of grey more sensitively than previously) would be evidence of cinema's inevitable progress towards greater verisimilitude. However, Comolli argues that this 'progress' is as ideological as it is technical. A key determinant for the adoption of panchromatic stock lay outside cinema. It was a response to developments in the realist aesthetics of another popular medium: photography. 'The hard, contrasty image of the early cinema no longer satisfied the codes of photographic realism developed and sharpened by the spread of photography.' Significantly, this technical development entailed the decline of a previously accepted standard of visual realism: depth of field. Thus codes of shade, range and colour overthrow perspective and depth as the dominant 'reality effects' (Comolli 1980: 131).

ANIMATION

For Bazin cinematic realism was predicated on the photographic image and the assumption that it 'captures' the real world in a way that no other medium can. The privileged status of photography as a medium of verisimilitude accounts for much of the confusion around CGI. We have touched on this already in our definition of 'photo-realism'. The often-stated aim of CGI is to replicate the live action cinematographic image convincingly. Yet the hyperrealism of early animated feature films and shorts in the 1930s was introduced for reasons that were economic as much as aesthetic. Techniques such as the line test were established to industrialise this relatively expensive mode of production, allowing divisions and hierarchies of labour and restricting the independence of individual animators.

In an analysis of the introduction of cel techniques to Hollywood cartoons such as those by Warner Brothers, Kristin Thompson explores the complex relationships between changes in technique, relations between different cinematic forms (live action and animation) and dominant ideologies in the Hollywood system. As in Disney's feature films, the cel animation techniques in cartoons served to industrialise cartoon production, but also offered new techniques of experimentation with, and disruption of, visual realist codes. The aesthetics of the cartoon and its position within Hollywood was the result of a struggle between two opposing forces:

> We have seen how cartoons use some devices which are potentially very disruptive (for example, mixtures of perspective systems, anti-naturalistic speed cues). As we might expect within the classical Hollywood system, however, narrative and comic motivations smooth over these disruptions . . . The fact that cel animation lends itself so readily to disruptive formal strategies suggests one reason why the conservative Hollywood ideology of cartoons developed as it did . . . Since disruption unmotivated by narrative is unwelcome in the classical system, Hollywood needed to tame the technology. Trivialisation provided the means.
>
> (Thompson 1980: 119)

The line test or pencil test is a method by which an animated sequence is roughly sketched out on sheets of paper to establish timing, continuity and control over characters' movement, before the cels are painted. See Wells (1998: 21–28) for a materialist study of Disney hyperrealism.

Cel animation is the use of layers of transparent sheets (cels), each painted with elements of the image which are to move independently. For example, a figure's torso might be painted on one cel, each leg on separate layers of cels. This removes the need for a separate drawing for each frame of animation

Disney's hyperrealist aesthetic has also been interpreted as motivated by moral and ideological concerns. See Forgacs (1992), Giroux (1995), Giddings (1999/2000)

IMAX

The attraction of IMAX cinema lies primarily in its technology of spectacle. The 70 mm IMAX film is projected onto a 60-foot high screen, immersing the audience's field of vision with high-resolution images. Yet the technology that delivers this visually immersive experience at the same time rules out other well-established realist codes. Due to the practical difficulties of close framing, IMAX films tend not to use the shot–reverse shot conventions for depicting dialogue central to audience identification with character-driven narrative (Allen 1998: 115). IMAX films have to draw on alternative realist codes, for example natural history documentary or the 'hyperrealism' of computer animation.

We will now ask how these contradictory discourses of realism help us to understand the impact of digital media on popular cinema.

Spectacular realism?

We will introduce the term 'spectacular realism' to denote, on the one hand, the aesthetics (and address to the audience) of popular film containing significant elements of CGI and computer animation, and, on the other, criticism and debate around these films.

This term serves to foreground three important factors:

1 the paradoxical nature of the presentation of the spectacular or illusionistic as 'realist', implying the capture of external reality (or perhaps the construction or simulation of a new one);

2 the identification by a number of critics of significant continuities with earlier spectacular forms – not only in cinema, or even twentieth-century popular culture more generally, but even further back – to the nineteenth or even the seventeenth century;

3 the critical concern with the visual image over other aspects of cinema.

In addressing the latter point – the dominance of the visual – it should be noted that the term 'spectacle' has two main connotations here. In everyday usage it refers to the visual seductions of cinema (special effects, stunts, song-and-dance routines, and so on) that apparently oppose, temporarily halt, or distract the spectator's attention from narrative and character development. The other connotation of spectacle is drawn from Guy Debord's book *The Society of the Spectacle*. Debord, a leading figure in the radical art/political group the Situationist International in the 1950s and 1960s, has been influential on both cyberculture and postmodernist thought. In a series of epigrammatic paragraphs *The Society of the Spectacle* asserts that post-war capitalism has reinforced its control over the masses through the transformation of culture as a whole into a commodity. Thus the spectacle is not so much a set of particular cultural or media events and images, but characterises the entire social world today as an illusion, a separation from, or masking of, real life:

> The spectacle is the moment when the commodity has attained the *total occupation* of social life. Not only is the relation to the commodity visible but it is all one sees: the world one sees is its world.

> (Debord 1983: 42)

Debord's spectacle is profoundly, though negatively, influential on Baudrillard's notion of simulation

This suspicion of the illusory potential of visual (especially photographic) images is evident in film theory. Because the photographic image, it is argued, captures the surface appearance of things, rather than underlying (and invisible) economic and social relationships, it is always, by its very nature, ideological. For example, in a lengthy footnote Comolli relates photographic realism in Hollywood (and bourgeois society as a whole) to gold, or money. Its illusions are those of commodity fetishism:

> [that] the photo is the money of the 'real' (of 'life') assures its convenient circulation and appropriation. Thereby, the photo is unanimously consecrated as general equivalent for, standard of, all 'realism': the cinematic image could not, without losing its 'power' (the power of its 'credibility'), not align itself with the photographic norms.
>
> (Comolli 1980: 142)

But if these images are realism as illusion and artifice what do they tell us, if anything, of our 'real world' today? If we are sceptical about the ability of these, or any, images to speak the truth in any straightforward way, what might these images mean, what might they tell us (if anything) about our world (and their place within it)?

2.8.3 Special effects and hyperreality

The Mask (1994) is a good example of a film the form and popularity of which were predicated on its advanced use of computer-generated special effects. Special effects in films have often been regarded as at best distractions from, and at worst, deleterious to, the creative or artistic in cinema:

> The Mask underscores the shrinking importance of conventional story-telling in special-effects-minded movies, which are happy to overshadow quaint ideas about plot and character with flashy up-to-the-minute gimmickry.
>
> (Janet Maslin, New York Times, quoted in Klein 1998: 217)

Evident in genres preferred by the young – science fiction, horror, fantasy, action films – special effects-driven films are commonly seen as illusory, juvenile and superficial, diametrically opposed to more respectable aspects of popular film such as character psychology, subtleties of plot and mise-en-scène. They are often associated more with the technology, rather than the 'art' of cinema.

Claims that blockbuster films are symptomatic of, or are bringing about, the 'dumbing-down' of culture are a familiar feature of popular film criticism. These fears find a resonance in certain theoretical discourses on the relationships between digital and/or electronic technologies, popular culture and culture as a whole. In an essay in Screen, Michele Pierson identifies a fusion, in the work of critics such as Sobchack and Landon, of established pessimistic attitudes to spectacle in cinema with more recent 'cyberculture' discourses. Thus, it is argued,

> the popularization and pervasiveness of electronic technology has profoundly altered our spatial and temporal sense of the world. [Sobchack and Landon] agree that the hyperreal space of electronic simulation – whether it be the space of computer-generated special effects, video games, or virtual reality – is characterized by a new depthlessness.
>
> (Pierson 1999: 167)

We can identify, then, a set of overlapping discourses, all characterised by an idealist approach, some mourning the loss of 'earlier' realist aesthetics as 'meaningful', some celebrating developments in the technologies of verisimilitude. These discourses can be broken down as follows:

1 The forms and aesthetics of CGI are the latest in an evolutionary process of ever-increasing verisimilitude in visual culture. For example, regarding the dinosaurs in *Jurassic Park* as the technical perfection of the pioneering stop motion special effects of Willis O'Brien and Ray Harryhausen in films like *The Lost World* (1925) and *One Million Years BC* (1966).

2 A pessimistic version of 1, characterised by a suspicion of special effects and image manipulation as illusory, superficial and vulgar. The spectacular is posited as in binary opposition to the 'true' creative qualities of film as a medium. Here, the significance of digital effects lies not in any sense of virtuality *per se* but rather in their popular appeal (perceived as taking over 'traditional' cinema) and the technical virtuosity they bring.

3 A cyberculture perspective, from which this digitally generated verisimilitude marks a new, distinct phase in Western culture. 'Simulation' and the 'hyperreal' are key terms here; the computer modelling of '3D', 'photo-realistic' environments and characters is seen as ontologically distinct from photographic representation.

4 An inversion of this cyberculture perspective, in which cinematic technology is symptomatic of technological change more generally, but which sees this change as one of a slide into digital illusion and depthlessness rather than the creation of new 'realities'.

Key text: Andrew Darley, *Visual Digital Culture: surface play and spectacle in new media genres,* London: Routledge, 2000

Position 4 is evident in a number of postmodernist accounts of developments in media. For example, Andrew Darley (2000) places computer-generated special effects as an important cultural form within an emergent 'digital visual culture', alongside video games, pop videos, digital imaging in advertising and computer animation. Drawing on the ideas of postmodernist theorists Jean Baudrillard and Fredric Jameson, he argues that these visual digital forms

lack the symbolic depth and representational complexity of earlier forms, appearing by contrast to operate within a drastically reduced field of meaning. They are direct and one-dimensional, about little, other than their ability to commandeer the sight and the senses. Popular forms of diversion and amusement, these new technological entertainments are, perhaps, the clearest manifestation of the advance of the culture of the 'depthless image' . . .

(Darley 2000: 76)

In this account, mass culture is not yet entirely dominated by this 'neo-spectacle', but it occupies 'a significant aesthetic space . . . within mainstream visual culture', a space that is 'largely given over to surface play and the production of imagery that lacks traditional depth cues. Imagery that at the aesthetic level at least is only as deep as its quotations, star images and dazzling or thrilling effects' (Darley 2000: 124).

Though he establishes important precedents for, or continuities with, contemporary spectacular visual culture (early cinema, Hales's Tours, amusement parks, for example), this 'depthlessness' is new, the product of technological developments. Darley argues that there is a qualitative difference from earlier, pre-digital effects: 'it is the digital element that is introducing an important new register of illusionist spectacle into such films' (Darley 2000: 107).

Critique of the depthless model: inverted idealism?

This reading of changes in realist aesthetics, as bound up in the loss of the 'real' itself, curiously invokes nostalgia for the dominant realist codes ('traditional depth cues') once the object of film theory's critique. If any given 'realism' assumes and articulates its own particular model of the 'real world' then it is not surprising that in postmodernist theories the 'hyperrealism' of computer graphics has been interpreted as not presenting a more analogous image of the real world, but rather as heralding its disappearance.

In the contemporary critique of 'meaningless', 'depthless' digital popular culture, there is the implication, never fully spelt out, that it is exactly the characteristics of the classic realist text criticised by film theory (character psychology depth, narrative coherence, and so on) that embody the 'meaning' now lost in postmodernist digital culture. Classical realist narrative and photography, whilst perhaps not telling the truth, had 'meaning' and depth. With this lament for lost idealism comes, not surprisingly, a kind of media/technological determinism. This depthless culture is engendered by a closed circuit of the techniques and technologies themselves, 'the specific – and now extensive – ways in which digital image making is both enabling and stimulating this aesthetic preoccupation with signifiers and their formal arrangement' (Darley 2000: 124).

A number of questions are raised for a materialist study of digital cinema:

- How new is neo-spectacle? Whilst digital technologies clearly generate a great deal of interest and facilitate new, spectacular images, even new ways of making films, it isn't clear exactly what the distinction is between the 'second-order' realism of digitally produced special effects and, for example, the stop motion animation of Ray Harryhausen's famous skeleton army in *Jason and the Argonauts* (1963). Or, for that matter, the distinction between pre-digital and digital animation, neither of which rely on the photographic capture of external reality.

- Concomitantly, we could ask again the question posed throughout this book: in what ways are digital media themselves new? According to Baudrillard, for example, hyperrealism has already arrived with television and other electronic media.

- What about the films themselves: are spectacular images necessarily meaningless? Action sequences and effects in films, along with song-and-dance numbers and the presentation for visual pleasure of women's bodies, are distinct from narrative – but is meaning only to be found in narrative and character?

- If films such as *Jurassic Park* and *Terminator 2* are evidence of an emergent postmodernist condition, do they escape the historical, economic and ideological contexts of earlier technological change in Hollywood?

These last two points raise questions of audience – are the people who enjoy the spectacular realism of CGI merely dupes; seduced and exhilarated?

We should note that there have been a number of films hoping to emulate the successes of *Terminator 2*, *Jurassic Park* and *The Mask* through reliance on special effects, which instead became expensive flops, whilst films characterised by realist codes other than the spectacular, such as *The Full Monty* (1997), proved extremely popular. Neo-spectacle, it appears, is not immune from the mundane operations of the entertainment market

2.8.4 Thoroughly (post)modern Méliès, or the return of the repressed in digital cinema

[D]igital media returns to us the repressed of cinema.

(Manovich 1999: 192)

2.17 The Praxinoscope: pre-cinematic apparatus.

Critical studies of digital cinema often establish histories: either an implicit history of technological evolution towards verisimilitude or immersion, or, more interestingly, a discontinuous history in which early cinematic (and pre-cinematic) technologies return at the end of the twentieth century.

See also 1.4 What kind of history?

Early cinema to digital culture

What happened with the invention of cinema? It was not sufficient that it be technically feasible, it was not sufficient that a camera, a projector, a strip of images be technically ready. Moreover, they were already there, more or less ready, more or less invented, a long time before the formal invention of the cinema, 50 years before Edison and the Lumière brothers. It was necessary that something else be constituted, that something else be formed: the cinema machine, which is not essentially the camera, the film, the apparatuses, the techniques.

(Comolli 1980: 121–122)

As we have seen, this 'cinema machine' is the product of social and economic forces, drawing from the diverse range of photographic and other technologies for the presentation of moving images. Recent research into the early years of cinema has explored this 'cinema machine' as the reining in of early cinema's many competing technologies and modes of presentation and representation, undermining any notion that the emergence of the feature film was somehow inevitable, evolutionary (Gunning 1990a: 61).

Parallels are drawn between this 'radical heterogeneity' and the multifarious, yet interlinked, digital technologies today – technologies which operate across the boundaries between entertainment, art, science, governments and the military – seeming to offer an analogous cultural, historical and technological moment. A moment of flux in which future directions are up for grabs. Of course, unlike cinema, digital technologies emerge into a world already familiar with a century's development of mass media. We have already seen how VR and CGI are being shaped discursively and actually by the codes and institutions of dominant entertainment media. On the other hand, this revisiting of cinema's 'prehistory' also highlights alternative cinematic forms that appeared to have fallen victim to the dominance of the feature film, but continued, marginalised, repressed or channelled into other media (and may now themselves be poised to take over). Animation is one such form, special effects are another, as we shall see.

Lev Manovich argues that with the advent of digital media we are seeing not so much the end of cinema as the end of cinema's privileged status as recorder of reality and the dominance of the fiction film (he calls this the 'super-genre', after the film theorist Christian Metz). At the end of the twentieth century, he argues, this super-genre is revealed as an 'isolated accident', a diversion from which cinema has now returned (Manovich 1999). The return of repressed alternatives to the super-genre displaces cinematic realism to being just the 'default option', one among many others.

This is one of Andrew Darley's key arguments – that digital visual culture, though 'new' in important ways, is at the same time continuous with a 'tradition' of spectacular entertainment that runs throughout the twentieth century (from vaudeville and 'trick' films at the turn of the century, through theme park rides, musicals to music video, CGI, IMAX, motion simulators, etc.), but with its origins much earlier in the magic lantern shows, phantasmagoria and dioramas of the eighteenth and nineteenth centuries. Some cultural theorists reach further back, to the seventeenth century, seeing the intricacy and illusionism of baroque art and architecture as prefiguring the forms and aesthetics of digital entertainment (Cubitt 1999; Klein 1998; Ndalianis 1999).

Despite their diversity all these forms share, it is argued, an invitation to their audiences to engage with the visual or kinaesthetic stimulation of these spectacles, and to be fascinated by their technical ingenuity, by entertainment technology itself as spectacle. The classic realist codes (character motivation and psychological depth, logical causality and narrative complexity), if present at all, function merely as devices to link together these dynamic sequences.

Key text: Tom Gunning (1990a) 'The Cinema of Attractions: early film, its spectator and the avant-garde', in Thomas Elsaesser (ed.) *Early Cinema: space, frame, narrative*, London: BFI London

'Cinema of attractions'

The film historian and theorist Tom Gunning has established the year 1906 as pivotal to the establishment of narrative cinema. Before then narrative, where it had existed, was used very differently, primarily as a pretext for sequences of tricks, effects or 'attractions'. The films of George Méliès are paradigmatic here. Méliès' career began in fairground magic and illusionism, and his innovations in cinema continued this non-realist mode. His studio, Méliès said, 'was the coming together of a gigantic photographic studio and a theatrical stage' (Méliès 1897, in Comolli 1980: 130). The actualities films (records of trains entering stations, people disembarking from boats, etc.) of the Lumière brothers,

2.18 Ladislav Starewicz, 'The Cameraman's Revenge', 1911.

2.19 *Antz*, 1998.

though today more commonly regarded as pioneering a documentary – rather than spectacular – realism, are included by Gunning in this 'cinema of attractions'. Ian Christie points out that the first presentations of the Lumière projector began with a still image, which then 'magically' started to move. Similarly, films could be projected at varying speeds or even backwards (Christie 1994: 10). It was as much the spectacle of the cinematic technology and images in motion as the scenes and events depicted that drew the attention of audiences. This is evident in the fact that publicity for the films more often used the names of the projection machines, rather than the titles of the films. Films would often be presented as one item on a vaudeville bill, one attraction within the discontinuous sequence of sketches, songs and acts (Gunning 1990a).

> Theatrical display dominates over narrative absorption, emphasizing the direct stimulation of shock or surprise at the expense of unfolding a story or creating a diegetic universe. The cinema of attractions expends little energy creating characters with psychological motivations or individual personality . . . its energy moves outward towards an acknowledged spectator rather than inward towards the character-based situations essential to classical narrative.
>
> (Gunning 1990a: 59)

Thus, the 'realism' of the photographic capture of movement was not originally allied to the 'realism' of the classical realist text.

This 'cinema of attractions' does not disappear after 1907, but continues in other media and cultural forms. Animation, for example, has remained a cinema of theatrical display and technical virtuosity. Thompson implies that cartoons, whilst marginalised and trivialised, were not repressed so much as positioned in a dialectical relationship with classical live action films. The anti-realist and disruptive potential of animated attractions, though tamed, sustain a sense of wonder in Hollywood films; 'they brought the mystery of movie technology to the fore, impressing people with the "magic" of cinema. Animation made cinema a perpetual novelty' (Thompson 1980: 111).

Animation, in both its popular and avant-garde contexts, has very often explored its own status as a form not predicated on the photographic analogue, revelling in the artificial, the fantastic, the illusionistic, or indeed its own apparatus

The cinema of attractions was by no means entirely removed from the feature film. It persists as spectacle within narrative, whether sweeping landscape, show-stopping *femme fatale* or breathtaking stunts, emerging more forcefully in genres such as the musical (Gunning 1990a: 57)

CASE STUDY 2.4 The digital cinema of attractions

2.20 *Cyberworld 3D*. 2000 Imax Ltd.

The film *Cyberworld 3D* (2000) is an encyclopaedia of the contemporary cinema of attractions: made for IMAX, and in 3D, it immerses the spectator in visual excess and visceral kinaesthesia, and revels in the spectacular presentation of its own virtuosity. Images reach out from the vast screen as if to pull the polarised glasses from the face of the spectator, and recede back into a fantastically deep focus in which the eye is wrenched from impossible perspectives and pushed up against gleaming surfaces, animated characters, or, in one sequence, the gleefully rendered squalor of peeling paint and refuse.

It is a film made up of other films, linked by a VR conceit: a gallery of animated short films through which the spectator is guided by a computer-generated 'host' – a cross between Lara Croft and the avatar in the AOL advertisements (see **3.16**). The films within films range from a special episode of *The Simpsons*, to extended advertisements for the skills and services of software houses and animation studios. Overall it is a commercialised vaudeville: a digital phantasmagoria of baroque fantasy, of generic promiscuity: science fiction, music video, fantasy, horror, whimsy, Victoriana, monsters, and chases.

3.16 The social form of new media

But what does it mean to identify these aesthetic and technical connections across the history of cinema? Critics like Bolter, Grusin and Darley have identified important areas of continuity and rupture within the technological development of visual culture, rejecting any utopian 'newness'. However, their histories are largely chronological or associative:

questions of determination, beyond the immediate circumstances and characteristics of the media in question, are largely absent. We see, then, a critically productive set of analogies and continuities between the 'old' and the 'new' in cinema, but crucial questions of history and change remain. Without the explicit development of a materialist analysis of technological and cultural change we are left with either 'remediation' as an idealist logic of media themselves, or a postmodernist 'end of history' in which earlier cultural forms are reanimated, zombie-like, to dazzle, excite or terrify their audience into some Baudrillardian ecstasy of communication.

2.8.5 Audiences and effects

What then are the implications of the fact that 'depthless' digital cinema has a history as well as a future? Does the shift to centre-stage of the cinema of attractions and animation reinforce or undermine discourses of postmodernist depthlessness? What does the 'acknowledged spectator' make of it all? Gunning's research highlights the active role the audience of the cinema of attractions plays in making sense of these spectacles, as well as the moral anxieties these attractions (and their audiences) provoked:

> The Russell Sage Survey [commissioned by a middle-class reform group in the 1910s] of popular entertainments found vaudeville 'depends upon an artificial rather than a natural human and developing interest, these acts having no necessary and as a rule, no actual connection' . . . A night at the variety theatre was like a ride on a streetcar or an active day in a crowded city . . . stimulating an unhealthy nervousness.
>
> (Gunning 1990a: 60)

Whatever these attractions mean, their significance does not lie solely in the 'artificial acts' themselves, but in their effect on the audience. This is not the ideal, non-specific and disembodied audience of 1970s film theory. This audience is addressed physically as much as intellectually, the 'nervous', embodied spectators experiencing kinaesthetic 'rides'.

If the dialectical relationship between dominant fictional film and the cinema of attractions is comparable with contemporary developments in digital visual culture, then the assumption within VR discourses of a disembodied experience – the rediscovery of the Cartesian divide, could be seen as analogous to the ideal audience of film in both popular and theoretical accounts (see Strain 1999). CGI, as the popular and vulgar repressed of VR, assumes like its spectacular forebears, a nervous, sensual audience – we see the return of the body

Terry Lovell has questioned 1970s film theory precisely because of its assumption of naive audiences 'petrified' in their subject-positions. Lovell argued that audiences 'are . . . much more aware than conventionalist critics suppose, or than they themselves can articulate, of the rules which govern this type of representation' (Lovell 1980: 80). Notions of a depthless 'neo-spectacle', like earlier film theory, also assume popular cinematic forms to be dangerous (though perhaps distracting and superficial rather than ideological). Audiences may recognise the illusions, but there is no meaning beyond a play with expectations.

So, if the audiences for digital spectacular realism (or popular film in general for that matter) are not deluded or tricked, we could ask whether the notion of depthlessness is adequate to the analysis of popular understanding of, and pleasure in, special effects. Indeed a knowledge and appreciation of special effects as effects is a necessary part of the pleasure of spectatorship. The familiar notion of 'suspending disbelief' is not enough: the spectator is never completely immersed in or 'fooled' by the spectacle, and it is important that they are not – spectacular special effects are there to be noticed. There is then a play between the audience's willing acceptance of illusory events and images and their pleasure in recognising the sophistication of the artifice (see Darley 2000: 105). Here we are back with the notion of spectacular realism as simultaneously immediate and hypermediate. Without a sense of the immediate, the effects would lose their thrilling plausibility and 'reality effect', but the pleasure is equally in the implicit recognition of their hypermediacy – as technical wizardry or as an example of cutting-edge technology.

Michele Pierson has argued that this pleasurable awareness of cinematic artifice is key to the popular reception of special effects-driven blockbusters. Her analysis is historically located and sensitive to distinct categories of special effects. The late 1980s and early 1990s, then, were a 'golden age' for these films, films in which the main selling point and attraction was their innovative and spectacular use of computer-generated special effects. This period includes *The Abyss* (1989), *The Mask* (1994), *Terminator 2: Judgement Day* (1991). The release and theatrical presentations of these blockbusters were cultural events in their own right, centring on the presentation of digital spectacle as entertainment.

Michele Pierson, 'CGI effects in Hollywood science-fiction cinema 1989–95: the wonder years', *Screen* 40.2 (1999): 158–176

For Pierson the CGIs in these particular science fiction films both represent futuristic technology and present themselves as cutting-edge technology. The special effects in and of themselves marked 'the emergence of a popular, techno-futurist aesthetic that foregrounds the synthetic properties of electronic imagery' (Pierson 1999: 158). Science fiction special effects (or indeed, any 'cinema of attractions') could then be seen as a particular kind of realism: though they may *represent* the fantastical and the speculative, they *present* actual cinematic technological developments.

In this context the terms 'presentation' and 'representation', as used by Gunning and Pierson, are roughly equivalent to Bolter and Grusin's 'hypermediacy' and 'immediacy'

CASE STUDY 2.5 What is Bullet Time?

Audiences for CGI special-effects-driven films are also addressed through supplementary books, magazines and films, detailing 'The Making of . . .' the effects and spectacle, profiling key figures in the industry, offering explanations of how the effects were achieved, etc. In recent years, VHS and DVD releases of some such films have included documentaries on the making of the effects.

If in *The Matrix*, as in other special-effects-led films, the pleasures of viewing lie in the tension between immediacy and hypermediacy, then *What is Bullet Time?* (a short documentary included on *The Matrix* VHS and DVD [1999]) is positively orgiastic. It explains how the effects were achieved, and presents the stages of the construction of the illusion: from wireframe computer simulations of the positioning of cameras and actors, to actors suspended from wires against green screens bounded by a sweeping arc of still cameras, and so on through digital compositing and layering of backgrounds and the effects of bullets in flight.

The 'timeslice' technique (now much replicated, and parodied) is a striking example of parallels between the technologies of early and late cinema. A sweeping arc of cameras surround an actor suspended by wires, and simultaneously shoot a single frame. A movie camera at each end of the arc records motion up to and after the 'snapshots'. By editing all the single frames together the director can then generate the illusion of the freezing of movement and action – a frozen image around which the 'camera' appears to roam. The comparison with Eadweard Muybridge's experiments with sequences of still cameras to capture movement in the 1880s and 1890s is striking (see Coe 1992).

What is Bullet Time? carefully explains that to all intents and purposes the bullet time and timeslice sequences in *The Matrix* are animation. Indeed animation is needed 'inbetween' the extra frames to manipulate the timespan of slow motion scenes without losing clarity. We could add that the physical abilities of the film's protagonists are informed by animation's hyperrealist codes (the film was originally proposed as an animated film) fused with other spectacular forms, such as Hollywood action films and Hong Kong martial arts cinema.

Pierson's study highlights the importance of not treating special effects as a homogeneous set of spectacular images, or indeed a teleological trajectory towards either simulation or verisimilitude. Special effects aesthetics and meanings are discontinuous and historically contingent. Each category of effects entails a specific relationship with the film's narrative on the one hand, and with its audience on the other. Indeed, we could begin to categorise the functions of distinct types of digital effects in films:

- Most Hollywood feature film production now features digital effects, but they are not always presented as such to the audience. Here, digital imaging is used to generate backdrops or climatic conditions that prove difficult or expensive to film conventionally.

- Some effects are designed not to simulate ostensibly normal events (or at least events not characterised by the supernatural or alien). An example here would be James Cameron's *Titanic* (1997). Effects were used to depict a real historical event, but still aimed to inspire awe in the technological spectacle.

- Special effects may play with other registers of filmic realism. For example, in *Forrest Gump* (1994), the protagonist is depicted meeting historical figures such as John Lennon and John F. Kennedy. The effects place Tom Hanks's character 'within' news footage of these figures. Here the technological trickery impacts on the documentary status of film.

- In *Who Framed Roger Rabbit* (1988) and *The Mask* (1994) the effects mark the irruption of other media (animation) as disruptive force. In fact the computer animation disrupts the form of these films, just as the animated characters disrupt the fictional worlds of the films.

We have seen that audiences respond to spectacular cinema as shared cultural event and as object of specialist 'fan' knowledges and practices. Steve Neale, in an essay on John Carpenter's remake of *The Thing* (1982), analyses the complex relays of signification between the 'acknowledged spectator' and the film text itself. Drawing on work by Philip Brophy, Neale bases his argument on a specific line in the film. The line is uttered at the end of a scene characterised by a series of particularly gruesome and spectacular metamorphoses in which the 'thing' itself (an alien which assumes the appearance of its victims) eventually transforms into a spider-like creature, legs sprouting from a 'body' formed from the severed head of one of its human victims: 'As it "walks" out the door, a crew member says the line of the film: "You've got to be fucking kidding!"'(Brophy, quoted in Neale 1990: 160). As Neale summarises Brophy's argument, this line exists as an event within the diegesis of the film, but it is also an 'institutional' event,

> a remark addressed to the spectator by the film, and by the cinematic apparatus, about the nature of its special effects. The scene, in its macabre excess, pushes the audience's acceptance of spectacular events within the codes of the science fiction–horror film beyond conventional limits, a transgression negotiated and accepted because of the film's ironic and reflexive acknowledgement of the transgression. Not only is the film 'violently self-conscious', but 'It is a sign also of an awareness on the part of the spectator (an awareness often marked at this point by laughter): the spectator knows that the Thing is a fiction, a collocation of special effects; and the spectator knows that the film knows too. Despite this awareness, the special effects have had an effect. The spectator has been, like the fictional character, astonished and horrified'.
>
> (Neale 1990: 161–162)

2.21 Phantasmagoria to Resident Evil:
body horror before and after cinema.

2.22 Magic Lantern.

Here, then, special effects are not 'meaningless', rather they often develop a complex relationship with the audience's expectations and pleasures.

Could this merely mean that the spectator has a sophisticated relationship with a meaningless text? Judith Williamson shares Lovell's assertion of the more epistemologically 'active' nature of popular audiences, as well as arguing that popular films themselves are neither meaningless nor exhaustively ideological. As popular products they must find resonances, however contradictory, with collectively felt sentiments:

> Popular films always address – however indirectly – wishes, fears and anxieties current in society at any given moment . . . Anyone interested in the fantasies and fears of our culture should pay close attention to successful films, for their success means precisely that they have touched on the fantasies and fears of a great many people.
>
> (Williamson 1993: 27)

As we have seen, Pierson argues that part of the pleasure of science fiction special effects of this period is that they not only represent the future, but are the future, or, at least, the most up-to-date technological developments. For her, 'techno-futurism' is progressive in that it encourages its audiences to imagine and speculate about possible futures. So popular spectacular genres are not necessarily empty of meaning; indeed the opposite could be argued. As Judith Williamson points out: 'Through use of genre conventions an apparently run-of-the-mill horror movie may speak eloquently about sexuality and the body, or a "second-rate" thriller articulate widespread fears about knowledge and secrecy' (Williamson 1993: 29).

The persistence of particular images and spectacles from pre-cinema to the contemporary cinema of attractions has been noted. We do not have the space to suggest why such images and figures resonate in popular culture, but refer the reader to some excellent work done in this field in recent years, particularly in terms of gender in popular genres. See for example Kuhn (1990), Creed (1993) on science fiction and horror, and Tasker (1993) on action films. Clover (1992) is an exemplary discussion of slasher films and their audiences

CASE STUDY 2.6 Computer animation

If, as has been argued, cinema's presentation of its own technological (yet 'magical') attractions was channelled into animation, digital cinema welcomes this marginalised form back to the centre of moving image culture. Assumptions that computer animation will achieve full photo-realism (generating characters and environments indistinguishable from those filmed conventionally) are only one factor. The materialist analysis of competing codes of verisimilitude is instructive here. For example, the *Toy Story* films made by Pixar (also a software developer) and Disney are characterised by a play between spectacular realism (sophisticated rendering of depth, lighting, texture, and so on) and cartoon-derived codes of character design, action, humour and movement. Indeed, it becomes evident that computer animation in *Toy Story* brings together Disney with the Disney hyperrealist aesthetics that have often been placed as the yardstick of digital spectacular realisms.

However, the specific material limitations and characteristics of computer animation help to determine the modes of spectacular realism developed. On the one hand there are technical and economic obstacles to the digital rendering of complex textures and shapes. Toys, and the insects of *A Bug's Life* and *Antz*, because of their stylised shapes and generally smooth surfaces, suit the medium perfectly; organic, complex structures like human bodies and hair, or atmospheric effects do not. Hence the human characters in *Toy Story* ironically appear as cartoon-like, less 'realistic' than the toys themselves. Of course, toys also perfectly suit the industrial strategies and structures,

For histories of computer animation, see Allen (1998), Binkley (1993), Darley (1991), Manovich (1996)

Evidently, developments in the technologies and aesthetics of computer animation may allow more diverse imagery. However, there is no evidence as yet that this will be a smooth 'evolution' toward photo-realism. At the time of writing, the Disney/Pixar feature *Monsters Inc.* is about to be released: as with all such films, the technical virtuosity and innovations are an important part of the publicity. Particular

the tried and tested language of children's moving image culture that established Disney as a global media conglomeration, generating new child-oriented characters for merchandising, licensing of images, new theme park attractions.

The drive to full verisimilitude in computer animation is only one possible trajectory of digital spectacular realism. Animation has never been entirely separated off from the 'super-genre' of the fictional feature film; most notably it has maintained its presence through the techniques of the production of special effects. Animation has provided a means of imaging that which cannot be conventionally photographed (for example, dinosaurs, from McCay to Harryhausen to Spielberg), and also functions, as we have said, as spectacular realism, simultaneously figuring magic, dreams and illusion in films, and fulfilling Hollywood's ideological need for a tamed presentation of technological 'magic' and illusion. What is new about contemporary developments in spectacular film is the increasingly sophisticated integration of animation and live action. This integration is not adequately described by the term 'remediation'; this is not so much the re-presenting of one medium by another as the emergence of a new hybrid cinema (Klein 1998).

Klein argues that *The Mask*, for example, not only makes direct references to the imagery of 1940s cartoons (in particular Tex Avery's *Red Hot Riding Hood* [1943]), but also draws closely on the form of this mode of animation: the extremely rapid editing and precision of timing developed in the chase cartoon. This type of cartoon timing is now widely used in conventional action scenes as well as in digital special effects. 'Today, essentially everyone working in special effects is expected to understand techniques from the chase cartoon. Knowing cartoon cycles and extremes helps the artist time an action sequence or splice in midaction: the offbeat aside, the wink to the audience' (Klein 1998: 210). We have already noted that the innovative special effects of *The Matrix* mark a fusion of live action cinematography and frame-by-frame manipulation that cannot easily be described as either live action or animation.

We could therefore invert Manovich's argument – that the live action feature film is only the default option in a wide spectrum of moving image forms – and argue that animation is the default option of cinema and moving images. Most computerised moving images are constructed by graphic manipulation rather than cinematographic recording, by default animation as 'frame by frame manipulation'. So, if we look beyond the theatrical film and to moving image culture at large, new animated forms predominate, developing through the material possibilities and restrictions of digital technologies and networks.

attention is being paid to the sophistication of the rendering of the monsters' fur. The recent Dreamworks computer animated feature *Shrek* similarly revelled in its generation of fire, smoke and light

Norman M. Klein, 'Hybrid cinema: the mask, masques and Tex Avery', in Kevin S. Sandler (ed.) *Reading the Rabbit: explorations in Warner Bros. animation*, New Brunswick, N.J.: Rutgers University Press: 209–220, 1998

Not least the World Wide Web, now animated by GIFs, Shockwave and Flash

BIBLIOGRAPHY

Alberti, L.B. *On Painting*, New Haven, Conn.: Yale University Press, 1966.

Allen, Michael 'From Bwana Devil to Batman Forever: technology in contemporary Hollywood cinema' in *Contemporary Hollywood Cinema*, eds Steve Neale and Murray Smith, London: Routledge, 1998.

Ascott, R. http://www.artmuseum.net/w2vr/timeline/Ascott.html

Balio, Tino 'A major presence in all of the world's important markets. The globalization of Hollywood in the 1990s' in *Contemporary Hollywood Cinema*,. eds Steve Neale and Murray Smith. London: Routledge, 1998.

Batchen, G. 'Spectres of cyberspace', in *The Visual Culture Reader*, ed. N. Mirzeoff. London and New York: Routledge, 1998.

Baudrillard, Jean *Simulations*, New York: Semiotext(e), 1983.

Baudrillard, J. 'Simulacra and simulations' in *Jean Baudrillard: Selected Writings*, ed. Mark Poster. Cambridge: Polity Press, 1988.

Baxandall, M. *Painting and Experience in Fifteenth Century Italy: A Primer in the Social History of Pictorial Style*, Oxford: Clarendon Press, 1972.

Bazin, Andre *What is Cinema?*, Berkeley: University of California Press, 1967.

Benjamin, W. 'The work of art in the age of mechanical reproduction' [1935], in *Illuminations* ed. H. Arnedt. Revised edn, Glasgow: Fontana. 1970.

Berger, J. *Ways of Seeing*, London: Penguin, Oxford and Cambridge, Mass.: Blackwell, 1972.

Binkley, Timothy 'Refiguring culture', *Future in Visions:. new technologies of the screen*, London: BFI, 1993, pp. 90–122.

Bolter, Jay David and Grusin, Richard *Remediation: understanding new media*, Cambridge, Mass. and London: MIT, 1999.

Brooker, Peter and Brooker, Will *Postmodern After-Images: a reader in film, television and video*, London: Arnold, 1997.

Buck-Morss, Susan 'Aesthetics and Anasthetics: Walter Benjamin's Artwork essay reconsidered', *October* 62, MIT Press (1992): 23.

Buckland, Warren 'A close encounter with Raiders of the Lost Ark: notes on narrative aspects of the New Hollywood blockbuster', in *Contemporary Hollywood Cinema*, eds Steve Neale and Murray Smith. London: Routledge, 1998.

Buckland, Warren 'Between science fact and science fiction: Spielberg's digital dinosaurs, possible worlds, and the new aesthetic realism', *Screen* 40.2 Summer (1999): 177–192.

Bukatman, Scott. 'There's always tomorrowland: Disney and the hypercinematic experience', *October* 57, Summer (1991): 55–70.

Cameron, A. 'Dissimulations', in *Mute, Digital Art Critique*, no. 1 (Spring), 1995.

Cartmell, Deborah *Trash Aesthetics: popular culture and its audiences*, London: Pluto, 1997.

Cholodenko, Alan 'Who Framed Roger Rabbit, or the framing of animation', in *The Illusion of Life: essays on animation*, ed. Alan Cholodenko. Sydney: Power Publications, 1991, pp. 209–242.

Christie, Ian *The Last Machine – early cinema and the birth of the modern world*, London: BFI, 1994.

Clover, Carol J. *Men, Women and Chainsaws: gender in the modern horror film*, London: BFI, 1992.

Coe, Brian *Muybridge and the Chronophotographers*, London: Museum of the Moving Image, 1992.

Comolli, Jean-Louis 'Machines of the visible', in *The Cinematic Apparatus*, eds Teresa de Lauretis and Stephen Heath. London: Macmillan, 1980, pp. 121–142.

Cotton, Bob & Oliver, Richard *Understanding Hypermedia from Multimedia to Virtual Reality*. Oxford: Phaidon, 1993.

Cotton, Bob *The Cyberspace Lexicon: an illustrated dictionary of terms from multimedia to virtual reality*, Oxford: Phaidon, 1994.

Coyle, R. 'The genesis of virtual reality', in *Future Visions: new technologies of the screen*, eds P. Hayward and T. Wollen, London: BFI, 1993.

Crary, J. *Techniques of the Observer: on vision and modernity in the nineteenth century*, Cambridge, Mass. and London: MIT, 1993.

Creed, Barbara *The Monstrous Feminine – film, feminism, psychoanalysis*, London: Routledge, 1993.

Cubitt, Sean 'Introduction: Le réel, c'est l'impossible: the sublime time of the special effects', *Screen* 40.2 Summer (1999): 123–130.

Cubitt, Sean 'Introduction: the technological relation', *Screen* 29.2 (1988): 2–7.

Darley, A. 'Big screen, little screen: the archeology of technology', *Digital Dialogues. Ten-8* 2.2. (1991): 78–87.

Darley, A. *Visual Digital Culture: surface play and spectacle in new media genres*, London and New York: Routledge, 2000.

Davies, C. 'Osmose: notes in being in immersive virtual space', *Digital Creativity* 9.2 (1998): 65–74.

Debord, Guy *The Society of the Spectacle*, Detroit: Black and Red, 1983.

De Lauretis, Teresa and Heath, Stephen eds *The Cinematic Apparatus*, London: Macmillan, 1980.

Dery, M. *Culture Jamming: hacking, slashing, and sniping in the empire of signs*, Westfield: Open Media, 1993.

Dovey, J. ed. *Fractal Dreams: new media in social context*, London: Lawrence and Wishart, 1996.

Eco, Umberto *Faith in Fakes: travels in hyperreality*, London: Minerva, 1986.

Ellis, John *Visible Fictions*, London: Routledge, 1982.

Elsaesser, Thomas *Early Cinema: space, frame, narrative*, London: BFI, 1990.

Evans, Jessica and Hall, Stuart 'Cultures of the visual: rhetorics of the image', in *Visual Culture: the reader*, London: Sage, 1990.

Featherstone, Mike and Burrows, Roger *Cyberspace, Cyberbodies, Cyberpunk: cultures of technological embodiment*, London: Sage, 1995.

Flanagan, Mary 'Digital stars are here to stay', *Convergence: the journal of research into new media technologies*, 5.2 Summer (1999): 16–21.

Forgacs, David 'Disney animation and the business of childhood', *Screen* 53 Winter (1992): 361–374.

Gibson, William *Neuromancer*, London: Grafton, 1986.

Foucault, M. *Discipline and Punish: the birth of the prison*, Harmondsworth: Penguin, 1977.

Giddings, Seth 'The circle of life: nature and representation in Disney's The Lion King', *Third Text* 49 Winter (1999/2000): 83–92.

Giroux, Henry A. 'Animating youth: the Disnification of children's culture', 1995. http://www.gseis.ucla.edu/courses/ed253a/Giroux/Giroux2.html.

Gunning, Tom 'An aesthetics of astonishment: early film and the (in)credulous spectator', *Art and Text* 34 Spring (1989): 31.

Gunning, Tom 'The cinema of attractions: early film, its spectator and the avant-garde', in *Early Cinema: space, frame, narrative*, ed. Thomas Elsaesser. London: BFI, 1990a.

Gunning, Tom. '"Primitive" cinema: a frame-up? Or the trick's on us', in *Early Cinema: space, frame, narrative*, ed. Thomas Elsaesser. London: BFI, 1990b.

Hall, Stuart 'The work of representation', in *Cultural Representations and Signifying Practices*, ed. Stuart Hall. London: Sage, 1997.

Harvey, Silvia 'What is cinema? The sensuous, the abstract and the political', in *Cinema: the beginnings and the future*, ed. Christopher Williams. London: University of Westminster Press, 1996.

Hayles, N.K. *How We Became Posthuman: virtual bodies in cybernetics, literature, and informatics*, Chicago and London: University of Chicago Press, 1999.

Hayward, Philip *Culture, Technology and Creativity in the late Twentieth Century*, London: John Libbey, 1990.

Hayward, Philip 'Situating cyberspace: the popularisation of virtual reality', in *FutureVisions: new technologies of the screen*, eds Philip Hayward and Tana Wollen. London: BFI, 1993, pp. 180–204.

Hayward, Philip and Wollen, Tana eds *Future Visions: new technologies of the screen*, London: BFI, 1993.

Heim, M. *The Metaphysics of Virtual Reality*, New York, Oxford: Oxford University Press, 1993.

Hillis, K. 'A geography for the eye: the technologies of virtual reality', in *Cultures of the Internet*, ed. R. Shields. London, Thousand Oaks (Calif.), New Delhi: Sage, 1996.

Holmes, D. *Virtual Politics*, London, Thousand Oaks (Calif.), New Delhi: Sage, 1997.

Hulsbus, M. 'Virtual bodies, chaotic practices: theorising cyberspace', *Convergence* 3.2, 1997.

Jameson, Fredric *Postmodernism, or the Cultural Logic of Late Capitalism*, London: Verso, 1991.

Jay, M. 'Scopic regimes of modernity', in *Vision and Visuality*, ed. Hal Foster. Seattle: Bay Press, 1988.

Kember, Sarah 'Medicine's new vision, in *The Photographic Image in Digital Culture*, ed. Martin Lister. London and New York: Routledge, 1995.

Kipris, Laura 'Film and changing technologies', in *The Oxford Guide to Film Studies*, eds John Hill and Pamela Church. Oxford: Oxford University Press, 1998, pp. 595–604.

Klein, Norman M. 'Hybrid cinema: The Mask, Masques and Tex Avery', in *Reading the Rabbit: explorations in Warner Bros. animation*, ed. Kevin S. Sandler. New Brunswick, N.J.: Rutgers University Press, 1998, pp. 209–220.

Kline, Steven *Out of the Garden: toys and children's culture in the age of TV marketing*, London: Verso, 1994.

Kubovy, M. *The Psychology of Perspective and Renaissance Art*, Cambridge, New York, New Rochelle, Melbourne, Sydney: Cambridge University Press, 1988.

Kuhn, Annette ed. *Alien Zone – cultural theory and contemporary science fiction cinema*, London: Verso, 1990.

Langer, Mark 'The Disney–Fleischer dilemma: product differentiation and technological innovation', *Screen* 53 Winter (1992): 343–360.

Lapsley, Robert and Westlake, Michael *Film Theory: an introduction*, Manchester: Manchester University Press, 1988.

Levy, P. *Becoming Virtual: reality in the digital age*, New York and London: Plenum Trade, 1998.

Leyda, Jay ed. *Eisenstein on Disney*, London: Methuen, 1988.

Lister, M. ed. *The Photographic Image in Digital Culture*, London and New York: Routledge, 1995.

Lister, M. and Wells, L. 'Cultural studies as an approach to analysing the visual', in *The Handbook of Visual Analysis*, eds van Leewun and Jewitt. London: Sage, 2000.

Lovell, Terry *Pictures of Reality: aesthetics, politics and pleasure*, London: BFI, 1980.

Lunenfeld, Peter *The Digital Dialectic: new essays on new media*, Cambridge, Mass.: MIT, 1999.

MacCabe, Colin 'Realism and the cinema: notes on some Brechtian theses', *Screen* 15.2 Summer (1974): 7–27.

MacCabe, Colin. 'Theory and film: principles of realism and pleasure', in *Theoretical Essays: film, linguistics, literature*, Manchester: Manchester University Press, 1985, pp. 58–81.

Manovich, Lev. http://jupiter.ucsd.edu/~culture/main.html

Manovich, Lev. 'Cinema and digital media', in *Perspectives of Media Art*, eds Jeffrey Shaw and Hans Peter Schwarz. Cantz Verlag Ostfildern, Germany, 1996 (http://www.manovich.net/).

Manovich, Lev. 'Reality effects in computer animation', in *A Reader in Animation Studies*, ed. Jayne Pilling. London: John Libbey, 1997, pp. 5–15.

Manovich, Lev. 'What is digital cinema?', in *The Digital Dialectic: new essays on new media*, ed. Peter Lunenfeld. Cambridge, Mass.: MIT, 1999.

Manovich, Lev. 'Database as symbolic form', *Convergence* 5.2 (1999): 172–192.

Marchessault, J. 'Spectatorship in cyberspace: the global embrace', *Theory Rules*, eds J. Berland *et al.* Toronto: YYZ Books, 1996.

Matthews, Peter 'Andre Bazin: divining the real', http://www.bfi.org.uk/sightandsound/archive/innovators/bazin.html [n.d.]

Mayer, P. *Computer Media and Communication: a reader*, Oxford: Oxford University Press, 1999.

Mirzoeff, Nicolas ed. *The Visual Culture Reader*, London and New York: Routledge, 1998.

Mitchell, William J. 'The reconfigured eye: visual truth', in *Photographic Era*, Cambridge, Mass.: London: MIT, 1992.

Morse, M. *Virtualities: television, media art, and cyberculture*, Bloomington, Ind.: Indiana University Press, 1998.

Moser, M.A. and MacLeod, D. *Immersed in Technology: art and virtual environments*, Cambridge, Mass. and London: MIT Press, 1996.

Mulvey, L. 'Visual pleasure and narrative cinema', *Screen* 16.3 (1973): 6–18.

Murray, Janet H. *Hamlet on the Holodeck: the future of narrative in cyberspace*, Cambridge, Mass.: MIT Press, 1997.

Ndalianis, Angela 'Architectures of vision: neo-baroque optical regimes and contemporary entertainment media', Media in Transition conference at MIT on 8 October 1999. http://media-in-transition.mit.edu/articles/ndalianis.html

Neale, S. *Cinema and Technology: images, sound, colour*, London: Macmillan, 1985.

Neale, Steve 'You've got to be fucking kidding! Knowledge, belief and judgement in science fiction' in *Alien Zone – cultural theory and contemporary science fiction cinema*, ed. Annette Kuhn. London: Verso, 1990, pp. 160–168.

Neale, Steve 'Widescreen composition in the age of television', in *Contemporary Hollywood Cinema*, eds Steve Neale Murray Smith. London: Routledge, 1998.

Neale, Steve and Smith, Murray *Contemporary Hollywood Cinema*, London: Routledge, 1998.

Nichols, Bill 'The work of culture in the age of cybernetic systems', *Screen* 29.1 (1988): 22–46.

Nichols, B. *Blurred Boundaries*, Bloomington and Indianapolis: Indiana University Press, 1994, pp. 17–42.

Nunes, M. 'What space is cyberspace: the Internet and Virtual Reality' in *Virtual Politics*, ed. D. Holmes. London, Thousand (Calif.), New Delhi: Sage, 1997.

Penny, S. *Critical Issues in Electronic Media*, New York: State University of New York Press, 1995.

Penny, S. 'Virtual reality as the end of the Enlightenment project', in *Culture on the Brink*, eds G. Bender and T. Drucken. San Francisco: Bay Press, 1994.

Panofsky, E. *Perspective as Symbolic Form*, New York: Zone Books, 1997.

Pierson, Michele 'CGI effects in Hollywood science-fiction cinema 1989–95: the wonder years', *Screen* 40.2 Summer (1999): 158–176.

Pilling, Jayne ed. *A Reader in Animation Studies*, London: John Libbey, 1997.

Rheingold, H. *Virtual Reality*, London: Secker and Warburg, 1991.

Robins, K. *Into the Image: culture and politics in the field of vision*, London and New York: Routledge, 1996.

Rogoff, I. 'Studying visual culture', in *The Visual Culture Reader*, ed. Nicolas Mirzeoff. London and New York: Routledge, 1998.

Silverman, Kaja *The Subject of Semiotics*, Oxford: Oxford University Press, 1983.

Sontag, S. *On Photography*, London: Penguin, 1977.

Spielmann, Yvonne 'Expanding film into digital media', *Screen* 40.2 Summer (1999): 131–145.

Strain, Ellen 'Virtual VR', *Convergence: the journal of research into new media technologies* 5.2 Summer (1999): 10–15.

Sutherland, I. 'A head-mounted three dimensional display', *Joint Computer Conference, AFIPS Conference Proceedings* 33 (1968): 757–764.

Tagg, J. *The Burden of Representation*, London: Macmillan, 1988.

Tasker, Yvonne *Spectacular Bodies: gender, genre and the action cinema*, London: Routledge, 1993.

Thompson, Kristin 'Implications of the Cel animation technique', in *The Cinematic Apparatus*, eds Teresa de Lauretis and Stephen Heath. London: Macmillan, 1980.

Virilio, Paul 'Cataract surgery: cinema in the year 2000', in *Alien Zone: cultural theory and contemporary science fiction cinema*, ed. Annette Kuhn. London: Verso, 1990.

Walsh, J. 'Virtual reality: almost here, almost there, nowhere yet', *Convergence* 1.1, 1995.

Wasko, Janet *Hollywood in the Information Age*, Cambridge: Polity Press, 1994.

Wells, Paul *Understanding Animation*, London: Routledge, 1998.

Willemen, Paul 'On realism in the cinema', *Screen Reader* 1: *cinema/ideology/politics*, London: SEFT, 1971, pp. 47–54.

Williams, Christopher ed. *Cinema: the beginnings of the future*, London: University of Westminster Press, 1996.

Williams, L. *Viewing Positions*, New Brunswick, N.J.: Rutgers University Press, 1995.

Williamson, Judith *Deadline at Dawn: film criticism 1980–1990*, London: Marion Boyars, 1993.

Winston, B. *Media, Technology and Society: a history from the telegraph to the Internet*, London and New York: Routledge, 1999.

Wollen, Peter 'Cinema and technology: a historical overview', in *The Cinematic Apparatus*, eds Teresa de Lauretis and Stephen Heath. New York: St Martins Press, 1980.

Wood, Christopher 'Questionnaire on visual culture', *October* 77 Summer, 1996.

Woolley, B. *Virtual Worlds: a journey in hype and hyperreality*, Oxford: Blackwell, 1992.

3 NETWORKS USERS AND ECONOMICS

INTRODUCTION/NETWORKS: COMMUNITIES, AUDIENCES, USERS/WHAT IS THE
INTERNET?/NETWORKS AND IDENTITY/LEARNING TO LIVE IN THE
INTERFACE/NETWORKS AND COMMUNITIES/VISIONARY COMMUNITIES/DEFINING
COMMUNITY ONLINE/NETWORKS AS PUBLIC SPHERES/THE NET AS POSTMODERN
PUBLIC SPHERE/CRITIQUE OF THE NET AS PUBLIC SPHERE/POST-WEB
INTERNET/REMEDIATION AND ECONOMICS/TOWARDS THEORISING WEB
USERS/RAYMOND WILLIAMS FIXES BASE AND SUPERSTRUCTURE/MEDIA STUDIES AND
POLITICAL ECONOMY/SOCIAL FORM OF NEW MEDIA/NEW MEDIA AND POST-
INDUSTRIAL ECONOMIES/DEVELOPMENT OF THE NEW ECONOMY/INVENTIONS AND
DEVELOPMENTS/GLOBALISATION AND TELECOMMUNICATIONS/DIGITAL
DIVIDE/UNEVEN GLOBALISATION/INVESTMENT IN THE NEW MEDIA/INTELLECTUAL
PROPERTY RIGHTS/INFORMATION AS COMMODITY/FRAGMENTATION AND
CONVERGENCE/CONCLUSION

3.0 INTRODUCTION

1.6   New media: determining or determined?

Our discussion of the McLuhan/Williams debate in **1.6** indicates that new media and their networked forms must be considered to be as much products of social circumstances as of technology. We have to see technology and its development as a dynamic process in which the dominant culture, in our period represented by ideas of **neo-liberalism**, influences emergent technologies and cultures. We also have to explore the ways in which networked communications construct a media culture of their own.

Therefore, we ask, what are the uses that the means of communication, in this case new media, are put to and how is their potential realised? Not only that, but how do possible uses interact with issues of power and control that are central to networks and consequent upon issues of ownership and investment associated with them? We are concerned with the characteristics of networks and how they have consequently been considered to have an important (some say revolutionary) impact, both on the ways in which we live our lives and on the economic organisation of society. In this section we survey the development of the Internet as a communications medium. We then explore, using the tools of political economy, how the potential for the development of interactive new media has been influenced by the introduction of commercial interests.

3.1 NETWORKS: COMMUNITIES, AUDIENCES AND USERS

The rapid spread of networked communication through PCs and servers has attracted enormous popular excitement, critical attention and commercial interest. In truth, the growth of the Internet since the invention of World Wide Web software ranks as a truly remarkable cultural achievement. The quantity of human labour and ingenuity that has gone into building net-based communication systems in a very short space of time is unprecedented. It is impossible to contemplate the mass of data that has been written into web-based software without experiencing a vertiginous sense of cultural endeavour. Clearly the growth of the Internet has been the site for major investments of the 'technological imaginary' (**1.5.2**); successive waves of visionary speculation have accompanied its growth from a very limited enthusiasts' network to its current status as a popular and widely distributed form of media and communications.

1.5.2 The technological imaginary

In this section we will be looking at the uses of the Internet and some of the dominant ways in which media and communication scholars have sought to conceptualise these developments. The critical history of the Internet has thrown up its own discipline, the study of computer-mediated communication (CMC). The study of CMC has primarily developed as a socio-linguistic discipline based in communications theory and sociology. Whilst there is some overlap with media studies in a common concern for understanding forms of technologically mediated communication it is by no means clear how 'the Internet' is a medium in the same way as TV, film or photography are distinct media (**1.4**). This section will also argue that cultural studies, with its central concerns for the relationship between text, identity and culture, has an important role to play in synthesising some of the methodological difficulties that have arisen in trying to understand the impact of networked communications.

1.4 What kind of history?

3.2 WHAT IS THE INTERNET?

The Internet simply describes the collection of networks that link computers and servers together. An official definition was made by the Federal Networking Council in the US:

> The Federal Networking Council agrees that the following language reflects our definition of the term 'Internet'. 'Internet' refers to the global information system that (i) is logically linked together by a globally unique address space based in the Internet Protocol (IP) or its subsequent extensions/follow-ons; (ii) is able to support communications using the Transmission Control Protocol/Internet Protocol (TCP/IP) suite or its subsequent extensions/follow-ons, and/or other IP-compatible protocols; and (iii) provides, uses or makes accessible, either publicly or privately, high level services layered on the communications and related infrastructure described herein.

See the Internet Society site for definitions and technical development www.isoc.org/Internet-history)

This primarily technical definition argues for an Internet defined by the ways in which computers are able to send and receive data, through the globally agreed protocols that permit computers to link together. The important aspect of such a definition is how minimal it is – the Internet is here simply a means for computers to communicate in order to provide (undefined) 'high level services'. The definition is intended to facilitate flow and exchange of data. Built into such a definition is the concept of 'open architecture' – there is no attempt here to prescribe how or where such data flows. Previous 'mass media' (e.g. newspapers, film or TV) were designed as systems to send messages from a centre to a periphery; here is a system designed from the outset to provide for the circulation of information. This 'open architecture' model was envisioned as early as 1962 by the visionary J.C.R. Licklider who wrote a series of memos at MIT describing his 'Galactic Network' concept. Licklider became the first head of computer research for the Defence Advanced Research Projects Agency (DARPA) in the US, and it was this Pentagon-funded agency that eventually developed the protocols referred to above in order to allow computers to form networks that could send small packets of data to one another. The Internet Society records the astonishing growth of computer-based communications from a system based round four hosts/servers in 1969 to 19,540,000 hosts in 1997 (www.isoc.org/Internet-history). These hosts support an enormous variety of networks, all of which have developed from the initial scientific and defence-oriented networks of the original Internet.

In truth, this variety of networks would suggest that we might more accurately refer to Internets, rather than the Internet. It is a measure of the methodological difficulty presented to existing disciplines that we lump together the enormous variety of network-based, computer-mediated communication under the singular term of 'the Internet'. We can develop our understanding by thinking more concretely about some of the activities that we do using the Internet. For example:

- Use of email and email list services; one to one and one to group text-based message distribution.

- participation in **Usenet** and news groups; topic-based comment and discussion sites. Someone 'posts' a message, the next person reproduces and comments, and so it goes on as a developing conversation. The historic 'soul' of the Internet, where much of the research and ideas into CMC have been generated.

- **Bulletin Board Systems**: mini Usenet sites, as above, often linked by more specific and particular interests or geographical locale.

- Chat rooms, or 'Internet relay links' (IRLs) in which live synchronous text-based conversations are constructed by participants.

- MUDS (multi-user domains), in which many users create a text-based imaginary environment, increasingly replaced by 'object-oriented' environments (MOOs) and visually represented 3D spaces inhabited by avatars.

- Websites combining the text, image, sound, animation, moving image and graphics of previous media into newly convergent and limited interactive forms.

Using the World Wide Web is just one of a range of activities that we do with Internet networks, though clearly since its creation in 1993 it has become the dominant face of the Internet. This shift toward homogeneity (the Internet = WWW) has created some disciplinary problems for the study of networked media, since the construction of CMC as a socio-linguistic discipline has been almost exclusively on the basis of pre-web forms of Internet use.

3.3 NETWORKS AND IDENTITY

4   NEW MEDIA IN EVERYDAY LIFE

Some of the key issues of identity and the mass media 'subject' are also dealt with in **Part 4** of this volume in so far as they impact upon our day-to-day experiences of new media technologies. Here we want to look at the issue of identity as far as it relates to our sense of community and group belonging. The experience of 'group identity' is a major part of individual subjectivity, as well as a major object of study for researchers in CMC.

The issue of identity in CMC is raised in a number of ways. At the primary level of our own experience we know that different forms of computer-based communication will inflect how we present ourselves and therefore how we experience ourselves. Our email 'identity' is different to our letter-writing self. In the chat room, MUD, or bulletin board we will often take on a nickname or handle that allows us to participate in the carnival-like masquerade of online identity play. Wearing the mask of a 'handle' in communication without physical or verbal cues appears to produce a deliberately flirtatious and provocative 'wavelength'. We can experiment with other parts of ourselves, take risks or express aspects of self that we find impossible to live out in day-to-day 'meatspace'. As Bolter & Grusin observe: 'MUDs and chatrooms serve almost no other cultural function than the remediation of the self' (Bolter & Grusin 2000: 285).

These experiences of CMC have been conceptualised in various ways that share a common post-structuralist history. Within this theoretical framework, identity is seen as anything but essential or fixed; on the contrary, identity is understood as a fluid process in which 'self' and environment are constantly interacting. This idea rests upon the proposition that identity is constructed through discourse. (Or, conversely, since identity cannot be expressed as anything but discourse it must therefore exist as discourse.) Similarly arguments have long been advanced in sociology that social reality is created through discursive activity. The way we talk about (and represent) our experiences in some way creates the possibility for the conditions of those experiences.

See, for example, P.L. Berger and T. Luckmann, *The Social Construction of Reality*, New York: Anchor Books, 1967

Much of the critical enthusiasm for new online forms of communication stems from its construction as in some way the technological embodiment of post-structuralist theory. Here is a text-based form of communication that actually builds worlds (e.g. MUDS); a form of speech that actually leads the speaker to become other than themselves, to transform, to be formed by the acts of speaking (e.g. chat lines):

Internet discourse constitutes the subject as the subject fashions him or herself.

(Poster 1997: 222)

The central question that emerges from this position is 'Who are we when we are online?' It is argued by, for instance, Allucquere Rosanne Stone (1995: 18–20) that in previous ages identity was in part guaranteed through embodiment, the body and identity being coterminous. The king guaranteed his signature by a seal carried on his finger; the signature is a token of physical presence. Increasingly, however, using a McLuhanite argument based in the idea of technology as human extension, we have used technology to communicate our selves over distance. Through the telegraph, the telephone, mass media and now online communications we have learnt that the self does not subsist only as an embodied presence but also as a networked presence. It is these shifts in the status and experience of identity that are at the heart of Stone's understanding of what she calls the virtual age:

By the virtual age I don't mean the hype of virtual reality technology, which is certainly interesting enough in its own ways. Rather, I refer to the gradual change that has come over the relationship between sense of self and body, and the relationship between individual and group, during a particular span of time. I characterise this relationship as virtual because the accustomed grounding of social interaction in the physical facticity of human bodies is changing.

(Stone 1995: 17)

The retreat from 'physical facticity' in our experience of identity is key to understanding the debates that constitute the study of CMC. The fact that online communication is 'cues filtered out' interaction with no physical codes to locate gender, race or class is the basis for arguing that the Internet facilitates the development of different experiences of identity and different experiences of group belonging.

In *Life on the Screen*, Sherry Turkle (1996a) also explores at length the possibilities that online communications offer for identity reconstruction work. Both Stone and Turkle in different ways also make connections between these new experiments with individual identity and our sense of group or community identity. Turkle argues for instance:

> The networked computer serves as an "evocative object" for thinking about community. Additionally, people playing in the MUDs struggle toward a new, still tentative, discourse about the nature of community that is populated both by people and by programs that are social actors. In this, life in the MUD may serve as a harbinger of what is to come in the social spaces that we still contrast with the virtual by calling them 'real'.
>
> (Turkle 1996b: 357)

3.4 LEARNING TO LIVE IN THE INTERFACE

At this point, we want to introduce two competing critical paradigms that will inform the way this section of the book unfolds. The first is the idea that in some way these identity experiments in cyberspace represent a retreat from, or an alternative to, social reality. This view could be seen as consistent with the idea that the spread of 'the virtual' (as identity, as media, as reality) is a radical epistemic break with all that we have known. This is the paradigm that underpins a good deal of the first wave of critical writing about online communications, a technophiliac appreciation of the possibilities for alternative realities that CMC might bring about.

For a review of these positions see Baym (1998: 35–39). For a consistent critique of techno-utopian positions see Robins (1996)

The second paradigm, and the one to which this section will incline, understands cyberspace not as a separate or distinct 'realm' but as part of our already existing social reality. In this view, online experiences are determined by social reality, by material resources, by gender, sexuality and race. In short, by precisely those 'embodied' presences and social structures including the political and economic, from which Stone argues we are retreating.

What becomes increasingly clear is that we are in need of an epistemological framework that enables us to speak about the complex interplay between our experiences of the 'virtual' and the 'real', since in fact there is a constant process of interaction between them. Baym (Baym 1998: 63) describes a similar position:

> The research I have reviewed and the model I have proposed suggest that online groups are often woven into the fabric of off-line life rather than set in opposition to it. The evidence includes the pervasiveness of off-line contexts in online interaction and the movement of online relationships off line.

This interplay between on/offline can be observed in two well-known case studies.

The first is the case of the cross-dressing psychiatrist cited by Stone (1995). Here 'Julie Graham', a self-declared disabled and disfigured woman, set herself up as an online therapist, offering feminist support and counselling to other women within what the participants experienced as a clearly marked feminist framework. However, after nearly two years 'Julie Graham' was revealed as the 'handle' of male therapist Sanford Lewin who had begun posing as Julie as a pleasurable experiment, but then felt increasingly compelled to continue his 'deception'. In the process informal therapeutic relationships were formed

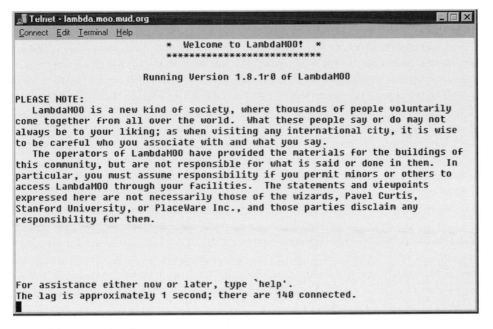

```
Telnet - lambda.moo.mud.org                              _ □ ×
Connect  Edit  Terminal  Help

                  *   Welcome to LambdaMOO!   *
                  *****************************

              Running Version 1.8.1r0 of LambdaMOO

PLEASE NOTE:
  LambdaMOO is a new kind of society, where thousands of people voluntarily
come together from all over the world.  What these people say or do may not
always be to your liking; as when visiting any international city, it is wise
to be careful who you associate with and what you say.
  The operators of LambdaMOO have provided the materials for the buildings of
this community, but are not responsible for what is said or done in them.  In
particular, you must assume responsibility if you permit minors or others to
access LambdaMOO through your facilities.  The statements and viewpoints
expressed here are not necessarily those of the wizards, Pavel Curtis,
Stanford University, or PlaceWare Inc., and those parties disclaim any
responsibility for them.




For assistance either now or later, type `help'.
The lag is approximately 1 second; there are 140 connected.
```

3.1 Lambdamoo text interface.

which were of great significance to the real lives of the participants. When the gender of the therapist was revealed there was enormous distress and real world fallout for 'client' and therapist. Here, then, online interactions and behaviours fed back into the 'real' (offline) world.

In the second case, of the online rapist Mr Bungle, again there is real distress caused by online interaction. However, more interestingly we also see attempts to import 'real world' conventions of community and legality into cyberspace. In My Tiny Life, Julian Dibbell (1999) gives an account of events at LamdaMoo, a shared online world, when a character called Mr Bungle used a sub-program called a 'voodoo doll' to rob other participants of agency and have them enact fantasies of rape and violent sexual humiliation. This led to widespread disgust and debate amongst the Moo community in which rules and conventions, such as there were, evolved organically through interaction. It had become a self-governing community and/or communicative space in which the 'wizards' who had created it had abandoned authority. The group members were therefore forced into having to try to construct a whole new set of laws and sanctions that would accommodate the possibility of a Mr Bungle. This involved arguments about democratic, authoritarian and libertarian solutions to the 'governance' of the shared communication. Here, then, we can see the 'real world' structures of civic governance imported to cyberspace. Dibbell claims that online interaction is real, it has agency in the world and in our lives; this realisation suggests doubts about 'the tidy division of the world into the symbolic and the real':

> For I have come to hear in them an announcement of the final stages of our decade long passage into the information age, a paradigm shift that the classic liberal firewall between word and deed (itself a product of an earlier shift known as the

Enlightenment) is not likely to survive intact. After all anyone familiar with the workings of the new era's definitive technology, the computer, knows that it operates on a principle impracticably difficult to distinguish from the pre-Enlightenment principle of the magic word: the words that you type into it are a kind of speech that doesn't so much communicate as make things happen, directly and ineluctably – like pulling a trigger.

(Dibbell 1999)

A similar blurring of boundaries between word and deed can be discerned in the burgeoning relationships formed online. These interactions are not 'virtual' in the sense of 'immaterial'. On the contrary, Andrea Baker (1998) has shown from a study of eighteen couples who first met online that these relationships are every bit as actual as those formed IRL (in real life). Six of her sample couples were married, with a further four either engaged or cohabiting. The couples in her sample met in a variety of locations, the majority not in chat spaces designed for pick-ups or sex but in topic-based conversations of mutual interest. Couples were initially attracted both by the usual kinds of cues ('good sense of humour', 'having something in common') and also by medium-specific qualities such as 'response time' and 'style of writing'. This suggests that there are medium-specific qualities to the communication.

The interaction formed in the supposedly 'virtual' environment has profoundly 'real world' consequences for those concerned. These are real human fleshy relationships formed in the space between the 'actual' and the 'virtual' – suggesting perhaps again that this may be a false dichotomy, that our engagements with CMC are every bit as embodied and embedded in social reality as our engagement with any other media. The problematic dichotomy only arises when identity and social reality are assumed to be entirely material as opposed to discursive, and when 'cyberspace' is assumed to be entirely discursive rather than material.

This dichotomy can also be seen at work in the very idea of online communications as a new space. The metaphor of space appears to suggest not only an entirely new realm, like 'outer space', but also a realm equally open to all, just waiting to be created and colonised.

However, discussing the way that the 'cyberspace' of communications networks or of virtual environments could also alert us to the way that many types of space and time already co-exist (the different proximities brought about by the train, the car, air travel, the telephone, etc.), Pierre Lévy feels able to state that,

The contemporary multiplication of spaces makes us nomads again . . . we leap from network to network . . . spaces metamorphose and bifurcate beneath our feet, forcing us to undergo a process of heterogenesis.

(Lévy 1998: 31)

In his preparatory discussion of the space of the train etc., Lévy is quite clear that such spaces are not valid for (because they are not experienced by) those whose environments are not structured, historically or geographically, by railways. However, immediately he turns to think about the new virtual spaces of communication networks he seems to be convinced that these apply to a generalised 'we' or 'us'. In cyberspace, apparently we all leap from virtual place to place, change our shape, split and transform ourselves, wander like nomads.

Such sweeping generalisations empty the politics out of discussions of cyberspace by implying that somehow cyberspace sidesteps the economics of scarcity; or, conversely, they smuggle into the discussion a sense that it is distinguished by being more democratic and provides universal individual mobility and freedom, which as we shall see in **3.21**, is hardly the case.

3.21 The digital divide

A better conception of the multiplicity of spaces and times to be found in the world is provided by Doreen Massey, a cultural geographer who is also interested in the collapse or compression of time and space that is brought about partly by new media and communication networks. It is worth quoting at length:

> Imagine for a moment that you are on a satellite, further out and beyond all actual satellites: you can see 'planet earth' from a distance and, rarely for someone with only peaceful intentions, you are equipped with the kind of technology which allows you to see the colours of people's eyes and the numbers on their number plates. You can see all the movement and tune in to all the communication that is going on. Furthest out there are the satellites, then aeroplanes, the long haul between London and Tokyo, and the hop from San Salvador to Guatemala city. Some of this is people moving, some of it is physical trade, some is media broadcasting. There are faxes, e-mail, film distribution networks, financial flows and transactions. Look in closer and there are ships and trains, steam trains slogging laboriously up hills somewhere in Asia. Look in closer still and there are lorries and cars and buses, on down further, somewhere in sub-Sahara Africa, there's a woman on foot who still spends hours a day collecting water.
>
> (Massey 1991: 234)

Massey is demonstrating that the experience and effects of 'time–space compression' are not evenly distributed. She sees that there are important changes in the contemporary experience of time and space that are facilitated by faster and more intense flows and interconnections of communications and transportation. She also sees the new spaces that these forces create as co-existing with older kinds. New media space occupies the same world as that of steam trains in Asia and travel by foot in the sub-Sahara. The 'multiplication of space' does not 'make us all nomads'. Rather, what Massey sees is that

> Different social groups have distinct relationships to this . . . differentiated mobility: some people are more in charge of it than others; some initiate flows and movement, others don't; some are more on the receiving end of it than others; some are effectively imprisoned by it.
>
> (Massey 1991: 234)

For Massey we are all subject to the effects of networks, but not in the same way. Some people may, in Lévy's words, 'leap from network to network', while others have the power to determine who gets to leap, and yet others become imprisoned by the leaping that happens around them.

We should be alerted to the fact that cyberspace is produced, expensively, in the material world through the ownership and control of data and data storage space, the use of satellites, and access to expensive fibre-optic cabling dug into streets. It cannot be accessed without the prior technologies of electricity and telephone, even before ownership or access to a modern PC and up-to-date Internet software is even envisaged.

3.23   Investment in new media:
intention and use

As we discuss in **3.23**, the sheer scale of the investment also requires the mobilisation of chunks of capital that are only available to large corporations. If we return from the cultural geographer's view of the uneven effects of time–space compression to terms closer to the study of cyberspace we might adopt Margaret Morse's image of the 'dark side' of cyberspace:

> Since electronic networks involve a choice about who will be connected and who won't, a network consists of holes as well as its links and nodes. There is a negative or shadow cyberspace that is material and devoid of technological resources that those who seek to understand electronic culture must take into account. Relations to cyberspace as a nightmare and/or utopia are understandably related to one's position in this economy and the mode of access to it . . .

> (Morse 1998: 188)

This grasp of uneven access to cyberspace, or the digital divide as it is called elsewhere (**3.21**) has been largely absent from early studies of online interaction. Here the seductive idea of 'community' has been key, offering, like previous electronic media, a resolution to the alienations of everyday life.

3.5 NETWORKS AND COMMUNITIES

As we have seen, the Internet provided the means for people to communicate not just individually and one to one but as part of a group, to participate in group communication exchanges in which their mode of address was semi-public rather than private (as in one to one). This section will look at some of the critical responses occasioned by the formation of such groups. These responses have in the main centred round the idea of 'community'.

See, for example, Steven G. Jones
(ed.) *Cybersociety* 2.0, Thousand
Oaks, Calif.: Sage, 1998; Steven G.
Jones (ed.) *Cybersociety*, Thousand
Oaks, Calif.: Sage, 1994; David
Holmes (ed.) *Virtual Politics*,
London: Sage, 1997

Popular understandings of group identities in CMC have ranged from the idea of the online community as an antidote to the social fragmentation of contemporary life, envisaged as a particularly American edenic moment as the online 'frontier homestead' (Rheingold 1994), to an idea of online groups as the heart of a newly revived public sphere (Kellner 1998; Poster 1997). Academic inquiry has focused on attempting to define the new kinds of belonging brought about by online communities.

Sociology itself has made questions of community and group identification a central part of its endeavour without, however, agreeing on what 'a community' actually is (Jones 1997: 3). The study of CMC has developed out of the intersection of sociology and communication studies – hence the assumption that questions of community should be a starting point for many discussions of online culture.

In part, this assumption derives from the metaphors of online communications as a space; the 'digital superhighway' is constructed as an infrastructural development of the same significance as highways and roads (**3.17**):

3.17   New media and post-
industrial economies

> Computer mediated communications, it seems, will do by way of electronic pathways what cement roads were unable to do, namely connect us rather than atomize us, put us at the controls of a 'vehicle' and yet not detach us from the rest of the world.

> (Jones 1994: 10)

Given that our everyday and 'common-sense' understandings of community have at least in part been determined by spatial relationships and a sense of belonging to a place, then the metaphor extends into thinking about belonging with one another in particular 'spaces' in the non-place of cyberspace. The discipline of the study of CMC itself has developed around the questions that such an assumption throws up – how do we define community? Can communities be separate from physical location? What kinds of discursive or behavioural strategies define communities? What value or significance might such communities have to the polity at large? What social policy frameworks might be necessary both to take advantage of the potential for online communities and to limit the 'digital divide' that they create?

3.6 VISIONARY COMMUNITIES

Some of the questions above arise out of the over-inflated and visionary claims made on behalf of computer-mediated communication. Jones (1994: 26) summarises the claims that CMC will

1   Create opportunities for education and learning.

2   Create new opportunities for participatory democracy.

3   Establish countercultures on an unprecedented scale.

4   Ensnarl already difficult legal matters concerning privacy, copyright and ethics.

5   Restructure man/machine interaction.

As Jones himself notes, this is a familiar enough litany of technophiliac enthusiasms. However, it fails to convey the more diffuse sense of expectation that developed round the idea of computer-mediated communities within some of the user groups of the 1980s. The Bulletin Board System known as 'The Well', for instance, was widely cited (Smith 1992; Rheingold 1994; Hafner 1997) as an example of the potential for utopian online communal interaction. This system, built by individuals based in the San Francisco region, seemed to embody the libertarian aspirations of the early 1970s for a less alienated and more communal way of life:

> There's always another mind out there. It's like having a corner bar complete with old buddies and delightful newcomers and new tools waiting to take home and fresh graffiti and letters, except instead of putting on my coat, shutting down the computer and walking down to the corner, I just invoke my telecom programme and there they are. It's a place.
>
> (Rheingold 1995: 62)

Rheingold's description of his cyber community recalls the fictional locales of soap operas – in which the audience are witness to simulated community. Here, however, there is active participation. Rheingold's account of the parenting conference on 'The Well' provides compelling evidence for the emotional utility of this form of communication for its participants. He offers the 'case study' of Jay Allison, who posted messages describing his baby daughter's surgery, and describes how,

> Sitting in front of our computers with our hearts racing and tears in our eyes, in Tokyo and Sacramento and Austin, we read about Lillie's croup, her tracheotomy, the days and nights in Massachusetts General Hospital . . .
>
> (Quoted in Rheingold 1995: 61)

At one level this sounds exactly like a description of watching a reality style documentary set in a children's hospital – yet there is a difference since the communication here is two way. The reader/audience is able to reply with similar experiences, support, to offer direct interaction that supports the 'working through' of the trauma. Allison himself later wrote of his experience of discussing his daughter's illness online:

> Any difficulty is harder to bear in isolation. There is nothing to measure against, to lean against. Typing out my journal entries into the computer and over the phone lines, I found fellowship and comfort in this unlikely medium.
>
> (quoted in Rheingold 1995: 62)

At the level of emotional affect, there are material consequences for online communication here, just as there are for those people who do their dating and mating online. However, even John Perry Barlow, a scion of the online community and the author of a declaration of independence for cyberspace, has pointed out there are many differences between such communications and belonging to a community. There is a lack of diversity of age, ethnicity and social class. The communication is disembodied, manufactured, inorganic. The group has no common bonds of shared adversity. Barlow's apparent (and well-publicised) recantation of his former cyber enthusiasm might be viewed as an inevitable part of the process in which a new medium finds its own communication bandwidth. Initial claims are tempered by experience as users; in this case, learning to integrate the satisfactions of online with those of embodied interactions. However, this process has not been just driven by users' experience – it also takes place within a context in which the 'open frontiers' of cyberspace have become increasingly colonised by commercial interests. To sustain themselves these interests have to be as interested in promoting consumption as in promoting community.

John Perry Barlow, 'A Declaration of the Independence of Cyberspace' (www.eff.org/pub/Censorships/ Internet_censorship_bills/barlow_ 0296declaration). 'Cyberhood vs. Neighbourhood', *UTNE Reader*, March-April 1995, pp. 53-56)

3.7 DEFINING COMMUNITY ONLINE

The circulation of visionary claims about online communities in popular culture was accompanied by scholarly attempts to define what might constitute an 'online community'. These attempts emanated primarily from the study of **computer-mediated communications**. This project was in part determined by its intellectual history in sociology, which has made community and group belonging a central object of study – in particular a sociological tradition derived from Durkheim in which group identity is identified through shared values and norms. In turn, this idea overlaps with an idea of community based in ties of family, work and economic relations that may often be associated or represented through physical location. In thinking about the meaning of new forms of online communication scholars have used this analytic triad of common relationships, shared values and shared spaces through which to begin to define online community. This sociological trajectory meets politics at the point at which we begin to think about how our sense of group belonging is either empowering or disempowering, how new communities might presage new formations of power and how new (online) communities might reconstitute the public sphere of political and cultural debate.

Many of these attempts proceed from the assumption that community can be identified through its own internal discursive practices. If it is assumed that discourse shapes social reality then particular discursive practices shared by a group may be said to construct a social reality, and that reality, it can be argued, would constitute a community. Since any online community exists as just text (unless the participants choose to meet 'IRL' [in real life]) we can see that there is an apparent 'fit' between 'discourse is social reality' and 'text as virtual social reality'.

Within this model it is therefore possible to argue that one indicator of community might be common discursive practices represented in textual norms and behaviours. The simplest forms here are the numerous abbreviations (LOL, BTW, etc.) and emoticons (:-) (= smile) developed as specialised language to communicate in conditions of bandwidth scarcity (i.e. online) – these conventions have now of course been massively popularised through mobile phone text-messaging. McLaughlin *et al.* (1995) argued that the evolution of codified forms of acceptable communicative behaviours in Usenet groups similarly begins to constitute a group identifiable through communication patterns. They identified, for instance, that Usenet users would be criticised for 'incorrect novice use of technology', 'bandwidth waste', or violation of existing networking or news group conventions. Similarly the creation of language norms and pragmatic communication tactics had also led to the generation of ethical codes (identifiable through their violation) and a shared awareness of appropriate language.

In her study of the rec.arts.tv.soaps Usenet group, Baym (1998) argues that more substantive shared bonds develop online. These bonds emerge out of the work of creating a functional communicative space and involve:

- users habitually communicating with one another in recognised and repeated patterns;

- the generation of 'group-specific meanings' ('insider' knowledge);

- the generation of group-specific identities (participants became known in a special or different way only in the group);

- forming a wide variety of relationships, that existed both on and offline;

- generating normative communicative behaviours that make interaction work as smoothly as possible.

Baym emphasises, however, that these communicative qualities of the online group are not isolated from material context but are situated within a matrix made up by:

- time structure of the communication (is it synchronous like a chat room or asynchronous like a Usenet posting system?);

- the design of the software system itself, the capabilities of the readers or browsers we use;

- the 'group's purpose' – what group members want from their interactions, what kind of work users want the group to do for them;

- what kind of people want to use the group ('participant characteristics'); especially significant here are computer literacies, sociability and gender.

Baym finally side-steps some of the questions around whether or not these interactions constitute community, and if so what implications for the polity at large this might have, in her carefully measured conclusion:

The social and cultural forces I've examined here often emerge into stable patterns within a group. It is these stable patterns of social meanings, manifested through a group's ongoing discourse that enable participants to imagine themselves part of a community.

(Baym 1998: 62)

Another way to think about understanding and defining online communities is through a paradigm based on space rather than discursive practice. Quentin Jones (1997), for instance, has argued that virtual community has to mean more than just 'a series of messages' and that virtual communities create 'virtual settlements'. Jones argues that virtual settlements are characterised by 'a minimum level of interactivity', in which the term is understood not as an effect of the technology but as a characteristic of human conversation (from Rafaeli 1988) that crucially relies upon the contextualisation of the conversation by what has gone before. So Jones's minimum is for there to be two-way exchange that takes into account what has already been said. He goes on to argue for online settlement to be defined in terms of:

- 'a variety of communicators'; there should be a group involved.

- a common space; the interactive group should be able to identify a common space for its activities, a site or address to which all group members have access and where they can find contact with other community members – so this might be a conference site, a website with associated discussion group or an **IRC** dedicated to a common topic.

- 'a minimum level of sustained membership'; there has to be some continuity of users to make the transition from 'just messages' to 'place'. Jones observes that the level this membership needs to achieve is currently difficult to establish.

Group interaction facilitated by computer-mediated communication has clearly opened up a series of new debates about the relationship between communication practices, polity and identity. It should be noted, however, that all of the above is predicated upon interactive and primarily text-based communication systems such as Usenet or email groups. The more recent domination of the Internet by the far lower levels of interactive participation offered by the World Wide Web might argue that the peak moment for the consideration of the significance of 'online community' has already passed. Certainly the interactive estate agents, travel agents and other buying opportunities have reduced much of it to a simple retail interaction. Despite this, the idea of 'cyberspace' as an alternative space with its own social norms and community behaviours continues to have some purchase within popular ideas about new media.

3.8 NETWORKS AS PUBLIC SPHERES

The idea of participation in online groups as a utopian communal project overlaps with a more sharply defined set of discussions that see networked CMC as constituting a new **public sphere**. The essentially participatory and interactive elements of the pre-web Internet clearly suggest attractive homologies with Habermas's description of the idealised public sphere (Habermas 1989). Newsgroups, bulletin boards and email groups all have the facilitation of group communications as their technological *raison d'être*. Many of them were devoted to discussion of 'affairs of the day' and culture of all kinds (including culture that Habermas would certainly consign to the outer limits of the public sphere!). The pre-web Internet was essentially about dialogue, a fundamental basis for democratic political systems and culture – hence some of the excited political pronouncements associated with the Internet from the 1970s (see **Box 3.1**, p. 193). The participatory nature of the pre-web Internet also answered some of Habermas's critique of mass media – namely, that the mass media had played a key role in the dissolution of a healthy public sphere by replacing a discourse of critical reason with entertainment and spectacle (Habermas 1989: 170–172). Here, in the Internet, was a communication system that demanded not channel-flicking passivity but active engagement and dialogue.

Box 3.1   The rosy future

This diffuse theoretical understanding of the net as new public communication space hardens round two positions. The first is that the Internet, through democratising the means of media production, revives the participatory nature of the idealised public sphere. It encourages us to take part in debate and offers us the chance to 'talk back' to the media, creating dialogue instead of passivity. The second 'public sphere' position extends from this specific function of extending access to media to the construction of the net as a new public sphere capable of representing new subjectivities (**3.9**).

3.9   The net as postmodern public sphere

The first position – the extension of access to media – relates to the idea of the function of media as the fourth estate in post-**Enlightenment** political structures. In this formulation the actions of the state are held responsible to the public sphere which is represented by the press – it becomes the job of the press to scrutinise the operations of power. The development of interactive news services is held to offer a revivification of the public sphere role of the press – again with the emphasis on communication and interaction rather than passive consumption. Here the culture-consuming public is constructed as being in a more active dialogic relationship with journalists; the news agenda, it is argued, could be more directly shaped in dialogue with 'the public' (Shutz 2000). Unfortunately, Shultz also shows how the journalists in his study paid scant attention to reader online forums, rarely if ever responding to concerns raised in reader-led chatrooms. Therefore, although newspaper readers felt able to 'participate' in some way in their newspaper of choice they finished up being no more represented than in pre-online publication.

On the other hand, it can be argued that the scope of the 'fourth estate' is exponentially expanded by the rapid development of web journalism and by the associated possibilities for the rapid publication online of news documents that normally would not find their way into the public domain. The online publication of a document like the Starr Report (into President Clinton's business and sexual affairs), or the court judgment in high profile trials such as the Louise Woodward case, does indeed suggest a shift in the 'mediation' of news content. Here the raw documentation is made available, unmediated, unadorned and unreported, for those of us with an online connection. (And one might add the time and inclination to plough through them – journalism may mediate but it also summarises!) In addition, the volume of comment, interpretation, response and generalised 'talking back' around the news agenda is increased by the Internet. Some of the culture of the pre-web Internet has been maintained and consolidated by alternative news sites like the Drudge report (www.drudge.com). Drudge is one of a small number of sites that have managed to build an audience for alternative news and opinion big enough to register on the cultural event horizon of conventional print and broadcast news media. This combination of immediate news data and an extended range of opinion has gone some way toward broadening our experience of the news agenda in ways that its critics have often called for:

The range of possibilities has widened: we are no longer certain of what is reported in the news, and we are much more likely to allow alternative explanations. And perhaps the widening of the range of possibilities leads to a destabilisation of the present. It is not so much that we do not believe what we read, see, and hear in the news as it is that we are inclined to believe that there is more than what we read, see, and hear.

(Jones 2000: 177)

The 'fourth estate' function of news media in the public sphere can then be seen to have developed considerably through computer-mediated communication. Existing patterns of 'newsroom culture' have not been replaced, and most news is still manufactured and distributed by major multinational corporations; however, the 'range of possibility' is wider with a new margin for critique and comment.

3.9 THE NET AS POSTMODERN PUBLIC SPHERE

The age of the public sphere as face to face talk is clearly over; the question of democracy must henceforth take into account new forms of electronically mediated discourse.

(Poster 1997: 220)

The Internet appears to do the trick of giving the concept of the public sphere a new lease of life by reformulating it in a way that answers some of the major defects that critics have pointed out since its original formulation by Habermas (1989). These are well summarised by Garnham (1992) – the public sphere described by Habermas was far from democratic or even public. It was public only in the sense that a British public school is public (i.e. exclusive to all but white bourgeois males). Predicated on exclusion it could only ever be the basis for a partial version of democracy that would inevitably exclude other genders, sexualities, ethnicities and classes. Moreover the Habermas version of the public sphere, and particularly his account of the role of the mass media, is resolutely serious; pleasure and desire are denied space in a culture determined by 'critical reasoning'. The whole idea of universal enlightenment values ('We hold these truths to be self-evident . . .') is undermined by postmodern critics who, after Foucault, perceive in them new structures of power and authority. In its place the postmodern critical theorist argues for specificity and particularity:

For a number of post modern theorists – Foucault, Rorty, Lyotard, Laclau and Mouffe etc. – macropolitics that goes after big institutions like the state or capital is to be replaced by micropolitics, with specific intellectuals intervening in spheres like the university, the prison, the hospital or for the rights of specific oppressed groups like sexual or ethnic minorities.

(Kellner 1998: 3)

As a 'public' communicative space the Internet does indeed appear to offer highly specific and limited engagements – whatever your politics, whatever your fetish, a corresponding website and 'sense of community' can be found online. The Internet as postmodern communication space has almost become a 'given' of cyberculture studies. There are no grand narratives here, rather micro fragments are encountered through an aleatory **hypertext** reading; 'critical reasoning' is replaced by opinion and subjective comment.

Kellner argues that the pluralism of the Internet as mediated communication offers uniquely new opportunities for dissident marginal and critical points of view to circulate:

Democracy involves democratic participation and debate as well as voting. In the Big Media Age, most people were kept out of democratic discussion and were rendered by broadcast technologies passive consumers of infotainment. Access to media was controlled by big corporations and a limited range of voices and views were allowed to circulate. In the Internet age, everyone with access to a computer, modem, and Internet service can participate in discussion and debate, empowering large numbers of individuals and groups kept out of the democratic dialogue during the Big Media Age.

(Kellner 1998: 6)

Kellner goes on to cite the Zapatistas and anti-capitalist movements' use of Internet communications as examples of how the new media offer new spaces and mechanisms for radical political organisation. However, such specific engagements and campaigns, though certainly based in enlightenment meta-narratives of humanism (e.g. freedom, equality, dignity), appear online as a series of fragmented, single-issue information clusters. Nowhere is there any necessary or prescribed causal or dialectical linkage between them, only the hyperlinkage of network media.

For Mark Poster (1997) the postmodern public sphere is based on the idea that it is a mediated and mediating space, not a technology. The space of communications flows is a space in which our subjectivities cannot remain fixed but both engage and are engaged by the network. This is a space characterised most of all by a post-structuralist critique of Habermas that questioned the autonomous rational subject at the heart of his idealised public sphere.

Poster is quite specific about which parts of the Internet might build such a new public sphere; his 'margin of novelty', the genuinely new, are virtual communities, MOOs and the (as yet purely fantasy) 'synthesis of virtual reality technology with the Internet'.

Internet technology imposes . . . a dematerialization of communication and, in many of its aspects, a transformation of the subject position of the individual who engages with it.

(Poster 1997: 215)

Poster's new public sphere is predicated on this alleged new fluidity of subject position that online communication calls into play:

the salient characteristic of Internet community is the diminution in prevailing hierarchies of race, class, age, status and especially gender.

(Poster 1997: 224)

Given that Habermas's account of the public sphere has been fatally undermined by criticism based on its exclusions, this new communicative forum in which the signifiers of 'otherness' no longer operate is assumed to be automatically emancipatory and democratic. However, as Poster himself makes clear, we can only call this a public sphere by redefining its original formulation:

> In a sense, they [MOOs] serve the function of a Habermasian public sphere, however reconfigured, without intentionally or even actually being one. They are places not of validity-claims or the actuality of critical reason, but of the inscription of new assemblages of self-constitution.
>
> (Poster 1997: 224)

3.10 CRITIQUE OF THE NET AS PUBLIC SPHERE

However, a number of important reservations have been expressed since these positions were advanced. First are the methodological and theoretical objections to the 'transcendent transformation of the subject' position developed by Poster. These rest upon the question of how far public communication, and our understandings of our place within it, is determined entirely by electronic mediated communications and how far it still relies on different kinds of face-to-face communication. If we accept that our subjectivities are in some major and significant way formed through discursive interrelationships with mediated texts then clearly Poster's argument above is convincing. If, on the other hand, we view the media text's role in experience of self as occupying only a limited 'bandwidth' of our everyday lives then the Internet, like film, radio or women's magazines, can hardly be said to be changing the entire public sphere since mediated communications are only part of our experience of public space rather than the whole of it.

There are also numerous political and practical contexts that the positions outlined above fail to address. A public sphere must by definition be characterised by maximum access. Despite the assumptions of universality that underlie much writing about the Internet, access to cyberspace remains a scarce resource, determined by economic and social power. Differential (i.e. non universal) access is objectively a feature of the Internet. The Internet will never work like pre-deregulated television where we all shared more or less the same kind of technology, could access the same channels and all experience the same TV texts. Universal access is in this case built out of the technology by the logic of upgrade culture – that is to say there will always be better software and faster computer architecture creating uneven access conditions. The economics of the entire computer production industry is based upon an accelerating principle of 'faster and smaller'. This induces in many users a kind of technological anxiety produced by the knowledge that your capability is always lagging behind what is possible. This can be illustrated by, for instance, the current differential availability of broadband and narrowband technologies, or the problems of web designers who have to design alternatives into their sites to cope with differently abled machines. The idea that we will all, globally or even just in terms of the rich countries of world, at some point be equally technologically able is based on some notion that this 'upgrade culture' will at some point stop and we will all be able to 'catch up'. A **cyberpunk** future seems more likely, in which the 'digital divide' between the technology rich and the technology poor is only bridged by adaptation and recycling, on the one hand, and a range of social entrepreneurship initiatives on the other.

Poster also makes the 'diminution' of class, race and gender hierarchy central to his cybersubject public sphere. However, there is a good deal of empirical research which unfortunately draws our attention to the fact that 'meatspace' is never left behind. In an excellent review of the field, Danet (1998) quotes research by Lori Kendall (1996)

See, for instance, Infoxchange, a Melbourne-based social entrepreneurship company which recycles used PCs from the corporate sector to disadvantaged groups, as well as offering training and consultancy to voluntary and state sector civic initiatives (http://www.infoxchange.net.au)

expressing considerable pessimism about the possibility of change; in the MUD she studied, whatever gender people chose for their characters, they often were pressed to reveal their RL gender (Kendall 1996: 217). Moreover when attempting to role play the opposite gender, players often resort to gender stereotypes, thereby, perhaps, actually reinforcing conventional gender thinking rather than destabilizing it (Kendall 1996: McRae 1996: 249).

(Danet 1998: 149)

Nor is cyberspace necessarily a safe space for online masquerade; on the contrary, especially because of post-web pornography and paedophile moral panics, the Internet is often seen by consumers as a potentially open channel for frightening materials to enter the home:

Women have to add computers as a new way of receiving threats. The teen hackers are often called the revolutionaries of cybersociety. Nonetheless, the revolutionary purpose often is not clear. The goal appears to be unimpeded access to information, but it is not clear for what cause. The hackers' work often appears to be electronic trespassing for the sake of trespassing, or the capturing or destroying of electronic files as a personal skills challenge, rather than from a principled effort to keep cyberspace as a free space.

(Kramarae 1998: 124)

The ever-present reality of flaming or obscene conversations in chat rooms, added to the justifiable fear of viral contamination through file exchange and download, make the Internet anything but a safe space for many users. In addition, empirical work with net users shows that the experience of being online is subject to material context in just the same way as access to broadcast TV. That is to say that politics of the family are likely to actually inflect users' experiences, especially those of young people:

The digital landscape, then, rather than being a circumscribed free space 'for children' as compensation for the lack of freedom in public spaces, is also subject to practices of surveillance and discipline. Access to and occupation of the much celebrated disembodied cyberspace in which age, gender, religion and geography are insignificant, therefore, can only in many cases be accessed by young people through a process of complex negotiation based on age, sex, family income, perceived maturity and culture.

(Facer et al. 2000: 25)

In this analysis the Internet is hardly the seamless techno-utopian public sphere imagined by Kellner and Poster. On the contrary, it emerges as a public communications space as thoroughly uneven. Moreover the experience of being there, online, is thoroughly entwined with the embodied and material conditions of our social and everyday lives.

3.11 THE POST-WEB INTERNET

Most academic writing in the socio-linguistic tradition about the Internet is based on a pre-World Wide Web model – that is to say, the Internet systems that had been growing for more than twenty years by the time Tim Berners Lee proposed his net-based hypertext language for the exchange of scientific data. By 1993 the first graphical 'front end' was being designed for documents produced in HyperText Markup Language; the software was intended to make a graphical interface for the navigation of hyperlinked documents. Previously everything online was only text, with **ASCII** being the format within which most documents circulated. Experienced net users also became used to dealing with the Unix languages that ran servers. Graphical navigation combined with the first browser software to create the World Wide Web – the network that by far the majority of users would now recognise as 'the Internet'. The growth in numbers of websites in less than ten years is one of the most remarkable aspects of the contemporary communications landscape. (See **3.22**.)

3.22   Uneven globalisation

It is hard to emphasise how much these developments have altered the character of network-based communications. Fundamentally, the text-based Internet required writing (sending) and reading (interpretation) for the user to function. The web requires 'clicking', selecting from graphic menus, reading, and further selecting. Any writing required is more often than not the submission of personal details, 'registrational' interaction (Jensen J. 1999: 163), rather than the active conversational writing of bulletin board systems or newsgroup participation. Of course, with the increase in numbers of online subscribers and the explosion of commercial online use, the popularity of chat rooms in particular has increased, especially those that are associated with well-used sites. There is very little evidence that would allow us to measure the kinds of interactivity that the web facilitates, especially since the commercial data on web use is based on 'page impressions' or downloads, precisely in fact a measure of 'reading' not writing. Our contention is that the web has made the Internet a fundamentally less interactive space and that this shift in the character of the Internet necessitates a shift in analytic methodology that is more in line with ways of thinking about active audiences seeking participatory spaces in mediated culture rather than transformative new patterns of human communication and subjectivity.

3.12 REMEDIATION AND ECONOMICS

One of the reasons the web has become so popular so fast is because it allowed the mass of text-based screen data and operating codes to be repackaged in the familiar layout of the magazine page. It allowed the new and difficult technocratic space of the Internet to appear in a far more familiar user-friendly guise: the point-and-click magazine. This development fits perfectly into the argument that Bolter and Grusin make in *Remediations*, that all 'new media' refashion existing media in order to find a mass audience:

> the World Wide Web could now refashion a much larger class of earlier media. In addition to the letter and the scientific report, it could now remediate the magazine, the newspaper and graphic advertising.
>
> (Bolter and Grusin 2000: 198)

The last point is especially significant. The point-and-click magazine naturally facilitated the inclusion of advertising, and within a short time many websites, especially portals and search engines (the most publicly open spaces online), were floating screen-based advertising hoardings, busy with pop-ups, pull-downs and all manner of banners advertising services to users. This boom in online advertising in turn played its part in the speculation around the **dotcom** industries in the period 1998–2000, in which advertising revenue was by and large the only revenue stream that web producers could rely on. (Subscriptions and retail also offered revenue opportunities but were for a variety of reasons not considered as reliable as advertising.) Again it is possible to see in these developments the outcome of the interaction of the forces of ownership, investment and ideology referred to on pp. 186–216. The pre-web Internet has been reshaped through the search for profitability and competitive advantage, both of which have marginalised its earlier role as a publicly funded information exchange resource.

From this vantage point it is hard to believe that even in the mid-1990s arguments raged online about whether or not the Internet should carry any advertising content! A number of commentators (Roszak 1986; Kapoor 1993; Dovey 1996) have expressed their dismay at these developments, although they had been predicted. Bettig made a convincing argument that the open and public spaces of cyberspace were being commodified and enclosed:

> The end result of both concentrated control of the new communications environment and the infiltration of advertising is the narrowing of diversity of information and culture output along with the magnification of those voices that stay within the boundaries of hegemonic discourses.
>
> (Bettig 1997: 157)

Previous notions of online 'community' have been reformulated as a method for creating a market for your site and its associate products, especially after the publication of *Net Gain: Expanding Markets Through Virtual Communities* (Hagel and Armstrong 1997). The book argued that virtual communities created a sense of belonging and brand identification that advertisers would be unable to resist. Significantly, it tried to conflate the identification that users felt with a text-based site like 'The Well', the authors' main model, with the post-text Internet of the web (Senft 2000: 188).

Previously enthusiastic theorists of the Internet have found these developments distressing in interesting and significant ways. Steven Jones, one of the leading academics within CMC worldwide, wrote:

> until recently, I had found the Web less than interesting. It is not the interactive medium that I had believed the Internet would provide us with; e-mail and Usenet were much more like the media that I hoped could bring about social change in ways I envisioned.
>
> (Jones 2000: 171)

To be fair Jones goes on to describe how his understanding of web-based journalism has revised his view of the web; however, this is still nothing like the interactive communications space envisaged in the study of CMC. Writing in the same collection, one of the foremost theorists of hypertext, Stuart Moulthrop, describes his own distress at the form the web has taken and urges his readers to recognise that

> as a community of scholars we – especially those of us trained from the 1960s through the 1980s – belong to a communications regime that differs fundamentally from what may be emerging on the Internet . . . perhaps a print based academic can say nothing useful about the Web. Maybe we should consign its strange productions to the cultural Oort cloud along with pop songs, TV shows, comic books, professional sports, and other *excremental spectacles*.
>
> (Moulthrop 2000: 263; our emphasis)

Moulthrop here fails to recognise that the 'Oort cloud' of popular culture is precisely the domain of cultural studies. Here is a discipline with a rich tradition of methods for understanding the relationships that we make with popular culture texts, from soaps, to comics or computer games. This tradition has developed a variety of theorised, often reflexive, empirical research methods for attempting to understand the significance of our interpretations and enjoyments of cultural artefacts. The structuration and commodification of the Internet through the World Wide Web makes it a field now perhaps more amenable to some of those methods. Cultural studies pitches its tent in the field of Moulthrop's 'excrement'.

Moulthrop's comment on the World Wide Web is interesting too for the way in which it reflects a wider sense that the web is an unreliable and intermittent communicative space, both in the sense of its technical performance ('Error 404') but also for the dubious quality of many of its products. The web, it is perceived, is the haunt of neo-nazis and sex fiends:

> a vast repository of porn and drivel. This lament is typically followed by the observation that home pages tend to feature photos of pets or Beanie Babies, that more people use the Web to fawn over celebrities and document UFO sightings than, say, to grapple with the constitutional implications of a recent Supreme Court decision.
>
> (Dean 2000: 67)

For some academics and critics alike it as if the post-web Internet has suddenly been colonised by the vast mass of unruly, pleasurable and expressive forms of popular culture. Like the classical public sphere the text-based net was a 'restricted zone', both technologically and as a class-specific activity that grew out the sober civic worlds of university and government technocracies. Moreover, just as Habermas argues that mass media have undermined or transformed the classical public sphere, the web as a popular medium is seen to transform and threaten the new interactive public sphere of the text-based Internet.

3.13 TOWARDS THEORISING WEB USERS

4   NEW MEDIA IN EVERYDAY LIFE

Elsewhere (**Part 4**) we draw attention to some specific research projects based in ethnographic study of web use. Here we wish simply to locate these emerging methods within audience theory research. Rafaeli (1988) has argued that user relationships with interactive media should be understood in terms of the existing 'uses and gratifications' theory of audience behaviour. In this model media audiences are seen not as passive consumers but as subjects with specific social requirements or needs – for information, entertainment, for models of identity and communication, for consumer data. This approach was originally developed around studies of mass communication in the 1970s; however, it does have particular new relevance for thinking about the very specifically need-oriented tasks that are the dynamic of our engagements with the web. We go there looking for something far more specific than the materials we seek in television; sitting on the couch with a remote control and operating a computer so as to surf are very different kinds of activities measured in terms of goals.

However uses and gratifications work within a scientist mass communications paradigm and within Cultural Studies at least has been subsumed into the history of empirically based active audience theories in which audience behaviours and discourses are actively brought into the same frame as ideology. So a consideration of the 'active audience' will be in part be generated by an attempt to understand the relationships between hegemonic or resistant readings of particular texts by particular audiences (Tulloch 2000; Dickinson et al. 1998: 194–309). In particular the work in audience theory based between Silverstone's insistence on our experience of media as part of the fabric of everyday life and Fiske's understanding of the multiple interpretative strategies deployed by different audiences might both offer useful ways for beginning to think about what it is that we do when we use the web. Web use is usually individual, so it would appear reasonable to look to theorisations that stressed the individual subject. However, this use is often in very particular domestic and work contexts which also determine interpretation (Facer et al. 2000).

Moreover, the web has implicated itself at every level of culture, every cultural institution, every artist and TV programme has its own site. A mass of website material exists in a symbiotic relationship with other media. On the one hand this seamless lattice of mediation can be seen as the extension of mass mediation into more and more of our time, more and more of our space. On the other, it also brings within our reach the possibility of becoming producers in our own right. Every message to a bulletin board or conversation in a chat room, every home page and downloaded **MP3** home music compilation facilitates the individual communicating in a pseudo-public mode of address. What is clear is that a great deal of web use facilitates a feeling of participation in media space. Senft (2000) offers an analysis of web use around the Diana, O.J. Simpson and Louise Woodward sites. She suggests this model of a participatory (rather than interactive) media zone on the basis that the Woodward sites had become not a 'court of public opinion' but a 'cult of public opinion'. Moreover, the Woodward sites were literally enmeshed in a network of links featuring O.J. Simpson and Diana. Users are here able to participate in the space of media representation. The conversations, interactions and arguments about TV that active audience researchers have studied are here enacted in numerous interactive chat rooms linked to the primary information-based parts of the site. For instance, in the UK in 2000 Channel 4's biggest hit programme was the reality show *Big Brother*. Demand for access to the chat rooms to talk to the recently evicted member of the household far outstripped the ability of the servers to keep track. 'Overflow rooms' were filled with viewers eager to discuss the latest episode with one another. Significantly the climactic moment of the entire UK series occurred in the daytime and was therefore seen first by viewers to the programme's live web cams in a moment already spoken of as a breakthrough for UK web use. This desire to 'be part of it', to continue the moment of the text through its constant reiteration and circulation, might also appear to have something in common with a tradition of work around fan cultures (Barker 1989; Jenkins 1992; Tulloch and Alvarado 1983). Certainly the web is the space to go to find any aspect of fan culture it is possible to imagine; the sites are out there. However, much of this audience 'work' in relation to websites, based on broadcast media agendas, functions under the sign of celebrity (Senft 2000: 195). The websites devoted to our favourite celebrities somehow bring us closer to them.

It would at this stage be ill-advised to argue for a single methodology for thinking about web users, given that multiplicity and process are defining characteristics. However, it is clear already that the web has irredeemably built itself into mass culture and vice versa. It must therefore follow that web uses and users have some relation to the audience subjectivities constructed in existing theories of mass culture (see 4.3.3).

4.3.3 The subject of (new) media

The argument that emerges from the above moves slowly away from the individual networked subject toward an understanding of how that subject functions as part of the bigger multinational media landscape. Within this landscape our individual experiences of networked communication are subject not only to the particular material circumstances of our identities (age, race, gender, class and place) but also to determining and limiting factors that emerge from wider forces. For instance, the interactive, communicative public sphere potentialities of networked communications have, it is argued, been weakened by their emergence as mass media through integration with existing economic patterns.

We have outlined a significant part of the economic and legal pressures on the development of new media, particularly in its networked formation. However, if we are to remain true to the opening comments of this section it is not enough to describe only the experiences of users of networked communications. We have also to survey the economic and legal characteristics of the development of new media in order to think about how the complex interplay between determining pressures and individual consumption actually shapes the 'character' of these media. This is not to extract consumption and use of networked media from their context; rather, it is to recognise that the experiences, uses, and more importantly the potential for new communicative spaces are not purely abstract, they do not exist only in the idealised space of the 'technological imaginary'. The possibilities of new media are embodied, material and *produced through* the dynamic exchange between determining/limiting forces and our own experience of using them. Our experiences of self, of group identity, of our spaces of 'cultural belonging' emerge through our interaction with the mediated communications produced through the social processes which we will now explore.

3.14 RAYMOND WILLIAMS FIXES BASE AND SUPERSTRUCTURE

Because we are concerned with economic development, cultural uses and their interaction we draw on a theory of base and superstructure, particularly as developed by Raymond Williams. For Williams this was not simply a case of the economic base of society defining the kinds of cultural and social formations that might exist – rather the notion of the relationship between base and superstructure is an interactive one and primarily about determination. The relationship is one by which each aspect both enables and limits the other. In other words, the development of communicative and information technologies is both about possible technical uses and about the social and economic circumstances within which they develop. It is, as Garnham has argued, about the way in which production takes place and is associated with particular social practices (Garnham, 1997). To put it simply: where a free and open system of communicative networks (the Internet) has developed within an economic system based on property and profits (capitalism) one has to come to an accommodation with the other.

It is certainly true that commercial pressures have significantly influenced the development of new media; this was not an inevitable outcome of the technology but rather a product of the relationship between a variety of factors that we explore in this section. Williams saw that the appropriation of new means of communication for a range of democratic uses was a possibility, whereas, as we discuss in section **3.17**, the dominance of neo-liberalism in the economic sphere has severely limited the growth of these potential uses. All in all, we want to avoid any sense of inevitability, either that the technology leads to particular outcomes or that the use of new media as a broadcast technology inevitably supersedes its communicative capability.

One of the central problems in studying media is the question of control and the sheer

See 'Base and superstructure in Marxist cultural theory' in Williams (1980) for this discussion

'Much of the advanced technology is being developed within firmly capitalist social relations, and investment, though variably, is directed within a perspective of capitalist reproduction, in immediate and in more general terms' (Williams 1980: 59)

3.17 New media and post-industrial economies

See 'Means of communication as means of production' (Williams 1980: 62)

scale of the capital investment required to develop communications technology. In view of the fact that a server can be set up in a bedroom for a thousand pounds, use free software and a few pounds a month for an Internet connection why is it that far from increasing communications potential, as many have thought possible, the Internet has become increasingly dominated by commercial interests? Why is it not actually meeting the hopes and aspirations of many of its early users? We can explain this in terms not only of cash and costs but also within the dynamics of a capitalist economic system. More than that we also need to be aware of the political and social pressures that not only constrain the development of technology (and other ways of thinking about that are offered in **Part 5**) but also the ways in which their use is directed and determined. Some of that work is also done in **Part 4**, particularly in the domestic domain. In this section we want to concentrate on the ways in which commercial, social, legal and political factors impinge on the communicative potential of the new technologies, as well as their uses. For this reason we refer to the work done under the rubric of political economy – in the US as the Political Economy of Communications, and in the UK as a part of Media Studies and particularly as developed by Nicholas Garnham amongst others.

However, it is not enough to deal simply in abstract categories. Williams himself continually differentiates between abstraction and the actual experience of culture. Rather, it is important to survey the dynamics of the processes underway and to consider them in relationship to the theoretical approaches being utilised. This is particularly important when using the work of Williams who, although within sight of the oncoming tide of market dominance, frequently writes hopefully of the potential of new technologies to connect to the long *alternative* traditions of communication as opposed to the *amplificatory* and *durative*.

Williams argued that these last two – the amplificatory and the durative – due to their dependence on capital investment, were much less easily made available outside of the control of the state and industry. It is for this reason that we continue by surveying the uses of the new technologies and networks and the debate about their use and potential to overcome the limitations of one-way broadcasting. This has most commonly been discussed within the terms of the debate set by Habermas and his identification of a public sphere within which debate and discussion could take place (Habermas 1989). In fact what we find is that much empirical research indicates that although there is a growth in access to the Internet it is severely limited in terms of hardware, in terms of appropriate skills and in terms of literacy. It is also limited in the sense of an ability to create media content as much as to read it and in the usability and relevance of the content that is made available. Much of the discussion about the use of networks and access to them assumes that it is universal and that their use is free and autonomously determined (see **3.8**). There is much to be argued with in these assumptions, and within this part of the book we consider both the actual uses and cultures that exist within networks and the relationships that construct those cultures and networks.

It is also true that new media, in its networked form, has been closely identified with processes of globalisation and there are fundamental disagreements about the nature of this relationship. Many working in the tradition of political economy would claim that it is an extension of the 'universalist' tendencies present in capitalism from its early origins (Meiksins Wood 1998). More importantly, particularly in relation to the arguments about the compression of time and space (Giddens 1990), we must consider the ways in which the global and local are interlinked and whether this is particular to the Internet. In fact we find that the interaction is a common one and part of a widespread practice in commerce

5   CYBERCULTURE: TECHNOLOGY, NATURE AND CULTURE

4   NEW MEDIA IN EVERYDAY LIFE

Williams identifies three forms of communication technology. The amplificatory, that allows the spread of speech over distance; the durative, that allows its storage; and the alternative which is made up of the use of signs – that is, methods alternative to the use of speech to convey meaning (e.g. writing, graphics etc.) (Williams 1980: 55–57)

3.8   Networks as public spheres

that depends on fairly conventional practices of investment and control of intellectual property.

In the rest of this section we will be dealing with some of the most important claims for the social impact of new media, particularly in relation to their new networked formation. This can be found at its most robust in the work of Manuel Castells who goes so far as to state, 'The internet is the fabric of our lives' (2000: 1). For those of us who are regular users, and that is about 400 million people, it is certainly an important place of work, entertainment, or source of useful information.

The opening line in *The Internet Galaxy*, Manuel Castells's book of reflections on the internet, business and society. At the heart of Castells's position lies a belief that the impact of the Internet is as great as that of electricity distribution or the development of the modern corporation

However, such a claim raises more questions than it answers; in what way are our lives infiltrated by a net-based experience and in what way is that experience influenced by the social, political and economic shaping of the technologies involved? It is also true that within this discussion we must be careful to hold onto the central idea of Williams that 'culture is material'; that is, that culture is not simply an influence on the way that we live our lives, but also that it is our lives (**1.6.3**).

1.6.3 Williams and the social shaping of technology

3.15 MEDIA STUDIES AND POLITICAL ECONOMY

Although there is a long tradition of paying attention to the variety of contexts within which cultural production takes place, political economy differs from much of media studies in that it places the focus of research on the circumstances of production. First, it asks the question to what extent is the production of culture a practice of *material* production? This is not to say that media studies has not been concerned with the circumstances of the production of texts as well as with their content (**1.5.5, 1.6**). In the 1980s and 1990s there was, however, a turn to a greater concern with the text, to audience interpretation and the reception of media texts. Work by Ien Ang on how the audience of the glossy American series *Dallas* related to the programme and David Morley's work on viewers' relationships with the UK current affairs programme *Nationwide* are good early examples of this approach (Ang 1985; Morley 1980). Earlier work, for example the Glasgow Media Group's study of news media, was much more concerned with the ways in which the content maintained and replicated existing relationships of ownership and power in society. The move away from the use of political economy intensified, with theorists such as McRobbie and Radway using studies of female experience to argue that economics did not necessarily determine cultural experience (see Tulloch 2000). Recently, some theorists have argued for a need to move back towards the study of the contexts of production of media texts, but without losing the insight generated by more recent work (Curran 2000: 9–11).

See 'Culture is ordinary' in N. McKenzie (ed.) *Conviction*, London: Monthly Review Press, 1959, pp. 74–92

1.5.5 The return of the Frankfurt School critique in the popularisation of new media

1.6 New media: determining or determined?

McChesney *et al.* (1998) state the theoretical basis of political economy of communication as follows:

> The scholarly study of the political economy of communication entails two main dimensions. First, it addresses the nature of the relationship of media and communications systems to the broader structure of society. In other words, it examines how media (and communication) systems and content reinforce, challenge, or influence existing class and social relations. Second . . . looks specifically at how ownership support mechanisms (e.g. advertising), and government policies influence media behavior and content. This line of inquiry emphasizes structural factors and the labor process in the production, distribution and consumption of communication.
>
> (McChesney *et al.* 1998: 3)

Our understanding of political economy in this context is very broad, but central to what follows is a materialist grasp of the circumstances of new media production and consumption. This means we are concerned with ownership, the economics of production and consumption, competition and the role of the state, law and regulation in determining both how we experience new media and how they in turn shape our world. In other words, the central questions in this section echo those encountered elsewhere in this volume; namely, how far do our existing methods and analyses continue to be useful for understanding new media and how far do we need to reinvent them for networked media, a newly emergent object of study? We have attempted in what follows to outline some of what have become 'orthodox' ideas about the economic significance of new media, while at the same time providing enough critical analysis to open up the debate.

If we apply this tradition of political economy to new media, we might develop a number of central areas of research:

- What are the patterns of ownership of new media?

- How do regulation and the policies of state and supra-state organisations influence the 'social form' of new media?

- What are the conditions of access to new media? How much does this access cost? What is its social distribution?

Because the very forms of new media that are made available for use depend on the interaction of these forces with the activities and interests of users we also consider the early practices in the use of new media and information and communications technologies (ICT) and the potential for new types of media activities and interactions. As Graham Murdock has argued, in this way we can move towards an understanding of cultural practices and the conditions in which they take place: situations that include the dynamic process of political and economic development (Murdock 1997).

Production in a capitalist society is primarily, but not exclusively, organised around the production of goods and services (i.e. commodities) for profit. In media production, capitalism therefore leads to the creation of cultural commodities such as books, television programmes, music CDs, websites, CD-ROMs, and so on. With these types of commodity, the ways in which profitable distribution can be achieved can be quite complex. For instance, in commercial television this happens primarily through securing audiences so that advertising space can be sold. Indeed, Dallas Smythe has argued that it is the audience viewing figures or 'ratings' that are actually for sale (Smythe, 1981). It also increasingly takes place for the purposes of programme or programme format sales. In the US, the major studios have long been directly involved in programme production for sale to an international array of customers. In all of these cases, there is the production of a commodity that has real monetary value in the marketplace. The production of culture also requires the development of studios, the purchase of kit and the utilisation of the labour of real people. Into this process of cultural production also enter less tangible factors of taste, aesthetics, audience desire, novelty, and so on, which are difficult to predict but nonetheless are important arbiters of commercial success. In all these ways, and no less in the case of new media, there is an actual process of production underway. The problem is to explain how cultural commodities are both part of the economic base of society but also function symbolically or ideologically as cultural artefacts and texts. For example, regulations claiming to ensure taste and decency in television exist in the US and the UK

Vincent Mosco provides an extremely useful overview of the political economy of the cultural industries in his book *The Political Economy of Communications: rethinking and renewal*, London: Sage, 1996 and are increasingly being sought for new media as well. Breaching social mores might increase profitability in one area but cause considerable difficulty in terms of public opprobrium. Political economy tells us that there is a balance to be discovered between how the power relationships in society, corporate and state, interact with social attitudes and audience taste to determine what is possible in a particular media arena.

We can see these forces in play in advertisements aired in early 2001 on UK commercial television. The international giant, AOL (America Online), a long-term provider of Internet services, was offering a 50-hour free Internet connection as an introductory offer to its subscription services. The format consisted of a balding father who wanted to assist his children with the Internet. AOL, in the guise of a young female 'avatar', offered a 'safe' and helpful environment for surfing the web. The adverts offer a service to even the most inexperienced computer user who 'knows' that he has to get online. They play on fears about unsuitable websites and concern for educational opportunity. They also are clearly aimed at men and offer a 'bright young thing' to help. Behind all the advertisers' connotation lies a simple message: the Internet revolution is underway and you had better not be left behind. Underneath lies the desire of AOL to secure additional customers for its subscription-based services, the only model of commercial development of the web that has so far generated any substantial profits.

3.16 THE SOCIAL FORM OF NEW MEDIA

In this way we can see that new media are as much the product of social, political and economic forces as they are of technological endeavour. Media not only influence the way in which we see and experience our world but are products of the world in which we live.

1.1.2   The intensity of change

As we discussed earlier (**1.1.2**) our contemporary experience of intense change is not only associated with new media but also with other wider kinds of social, economic and political experience. It is also true that the very intensity of change is something we associate with the capitalist economic system. This process of 'social shaping' (**1.6.3**)

1.6.3   Williams and the social shaping of technology

leaves a medium with a *social form*, an identity, which influences the way it is used and its impact on the world; it is never quite shaken off. So it is that in a modern economy the development and use of media are deeply imprinted by the circumstances of their creation. Williams pointed out in theoretical terms (1989: 120) how the 'social significance' of a technical invention only came about once it had been selected for investment and

See Brian Winston, *Media Technology and Society: a history from the telegraph to the internet*, London: Routledge, 1998, for more on the operation of these forces on technological development

production, 'processes which are of a general social and economic kind, within existing social and economic relations, and in a specific social order . . .' (1989: 120).

To understand this process better we will look at three examples, starting with the personal computer, the machine that plays such an extremely important role in the growth of new media (**see 4.2.4**).

4.2.4   Home computers: new media ethnography

See 4.2.3 for a discussion of the social form of the PC as a domestic commodity

The IBM PC originated in the company's research labs in the 1980s because of the pressure on its traditional business from the new desktop computers. To get the new machines onto the market as rapidly as possible they were assembled from readily available components. They were, therefore, always going to be easy to replicate. The operating system, Microsoft's Disk Operating System (MS-DOS), used on the new PCs was also sold as PC-DOS. It was widely available and easily distributed on cheap floppy disks. Overall the very origins of the IBM PC made it very difficult to protect it from copying, since almost everything that made it work was already widely available. The fact that it was assembled from all sorts of bits and pieces also meant that it was impossible to use patent law to protect the design of the hardware. The IBM PC may have been clunky and inelegant but anyone could make one, and they did. To make matters worse (for IBM), because of a commercial miscalculation Microsoft were left with the rights to the operating system, which was where the new monopoly in software was eventually to flower.

The importance of social form is also exemplified by the failure of the Apple computer to dominate the market for PCs. The Apple PC, developed by Steve Jobs and put on the market in 1978, utilised an extremely elegant and innovative iconic interface. However, the machine and the operating system were only available from Apple Corporation, and software could only be developed with the co-operation of the company. This meant that it was impossible to copy without infringing some aspects of the patents owned by them. The novelty and sophistication of the relationship between the operating system and the hardware made it easy to protect using the law. Attracted by the business opportunities in the PC industry newcomers recognised the ease with which it was possible to build a machine that would do the same things as the IBM PC. Microsoft, unlike Apple, unconcerned with building hardware, was happy to sell their rather clunky operating system to anyone who wanted one. Consequently the cheaper, if less sophisticated, generic forms of the IBM PC rapidly became the dominant form of the personal computer.

In our third example, the origins of the World Wide Web, we can see how the idea of social form applies not only to hardware and commercial objects but also to forms of knowledge. The web depends on a widely readable computer code, **HTML** (HyperText Markup Language), first published in 1990. It was developed in the scientific academic world to transfer images and text within the international user community associated with CERN (Organisation Européenne pour la Recherche Nucléaire).

Since that community was using a variety of types of software, many with their own ways of handling text and images, the challenge was to develop a code that would work equally well on all of them. Rather than try to develop yet another set of international standards for files, the new code simply told a wide range of computer systems what to do with the files they were receiving. To make the new code even easier to use web browsers were developed at the university-based National Centre for Supercomputer Applications (NCSA). The code was made publicly available and is still the basis of both Netscape and Internet Explorer. Once web browsers became items of commercial interest, extra gimmicks and capabilities gave a business advantage and meant that there was good reason for private companies to keep some code developments to themselves. In consequence, business organisations were now creating new standards that only their own products could interpret. Commercial investment building on academic research has thus given the web browser a new social form. In other words, the form and distribution and capabilities of a web browser are as much a product of the ownership of the code as of technical potential. Moreover the fact that this code was first developed in the public sector, as part of an attempt to promote co-operation and exchange, has a legacy within the social form of the web browser despite its subsequent development within a market framework.

We have seen in these examples that the form of a medium is a product not only of what is technically possible, but also of the material and economic circumstances of its creation. These circumstances may be commercial or intellectual, or a mixture of these and other factors, but they leave the medium with a social form that cannot be ignored. The outcome of these three vital developments is hardly determined any more by the technology that they contain than by the social circumstance of their development. But the 'social form' which they take, along with other developments, and investment in communications combine to give us the Internet.

We can see that new media, how they are represented, how they are sold and the

See Robert X. Cringely, *Accidental Empires: how the boys of Silicon Valley make their millions, battle foreign competition and still can't get a date,* London; Penguin 1996, for a well-informed and entertaining description of the ups and downs of the invention of the Personal Computer

3.2 The history of the web browser in the Internet Explorer Browser. Courtesy of Microsoft.

commercial interests underlying them, are the complex outcomes of the interaction between our existing culture, business interests, and major investments in telecommunications. All are underpinned by the availability of computing power in an average home that far exceeds that which put a man on the moon in 1969. But on its own this is not enough to explain the particular form that information and communications technologies have taken. We now turn therefore to one of most prominent ways of understanding the relationship between new media and the organisation of the world we live in: theories of globalisation.

3.17 NEW MEDIA AND POST-INDUSTRIAL ECONOMIES

3.3 Networks and identity

New media can, as discussed in **3.3**, carry a sense of being the technological correlative of postmodern thought. Speed, flexibility, digitality, hypertextuality have all been posited as characteristic both of new media and of postmodernity. If this is the case, can political economy explain these apparently radically innovative technological and social forms? It could be argued that postmodernism, with its emphasis on fluidity, the immediate, and the constant re-referencing of texts, sits uneasily alongside the more materialist approach of political economy. However, it is equally true that to attempt to develop a critical method for thinking about cyberculture without recourse to its material history is to operate entirely from within its own discourse. To allow history to be dematerialised or production to masquerade as entirely virtualised is to lose an important critical perspective. Therefore, we must now turn to some economic history in order to offer a broad context within which to understand the relationships between networked communication and economic development.

Economic production

Distinctively different, but not wholly new, forms of economic production were established in the last quarter of the twentieth century. These have been variously described as 'late capitalism' (Jameson 1991), 'post-fordism' (Coriat 1990), or earlier formulations such as 'post-industrialism' (Touraine 1969; Bell 1976), and by Castells as 'the network society'. Castells summarises the shift:

> In the industrial mode of development, the main source of productivity lies in the introduction of new energy sources, and the ability to decentralise the use of energy throughout the production and circulation process. In the new, informational mode of development the source of productivity lies in the technology of knowledge generation, information processing, and symbol communication.
>
> (Castells 1996: 17)

This idea of the 'information economy' is by now also a cultural commonplace, disseminated by technophiliac enthusiasts, industrialists and governments alike.

BOX 3.1:   The rosy future

Here are three quotations that show very different understandings of the political meaning and economic potential of new media:

> Community memory is convivial and participatory. A CM system is an actively open 'free' information system, enabling direct communications among its users, with no centralised editing of or control over the information exchanged. Such a system represents the precise antitheses to the dominant uses both of electronic communications media which broadcast centrally determined messages to mass passive audiences, and of cybernetic technology, which involves centralised processing of and control over data drawn from or furnished to direct and indirect users. The payoff is efficient, unmediated (or rather self mediated) interaction, eliminating roles and problems that develop when one party has control over what information passes between two or many others. This freedom is complemented by the way the system democratises information – power, for no group of its users has more access to its main information than the least user has.
>
> (Michael Rossman, 'What is community memory?',
> mimeo, 1979; Roszak [1984: 140])

> We are on the verge of a revolution that is just as profound as the change in the economy that came with the industrial revolution. Soon electronic networks will allow people to transcend the barriers of time and distance and take advantage of global markets and business opportunities not even imaginable today, opening up a new world of economic possibility and progress.
>
> Vice President Albert Gore, Jr, in President William J. Clinton
> and Vice-President Albert Gore, Jr, *A Framework*
> *For Global Electronic Commerce*, Washington, D.C.

Our world is changing, and communications are central to this change. Digital media have revolutionised the information society. Multi-channel television will soon be available to all. More and more people can gain access to the Internet, through personal computers, televisions, mobile phones, and now even games consoles. The choice of services available is greater than ever before. High-speed telephone lines give households access to a whole new range of communications services and experiences. Using their TV sets people are able to email, shop from home, and devise their own personal viewing schedules. The communications revolution has arrived.

Foreword to *A New Future for Communications*
UK Government White Paper (Policy Proposal)
DTI/DCMS, December 2000 [www.dti.gov.uk]

Success for enterprises or economies in this economic structure is determined, according to Castells, through competition in their abilities to generate knowledge, process information and communicate symbols. In other words through all the activities which in their broadest definition the 'new media' are assumed to pursue. In this understanding then the new media are constructed as central to the operations of the new economic structures. These new economic structures are further identified by a number of characteristics:

- *Globalisation*. The autonomy of local or national economies has, it is argued, been subsumed within a single global economy brought about by the increased reach of international business organisations, the ability of financial markets to operate simultaneously worldwide and the increasing global standardisation of products and services.

- *Networked forms of organisation*. By this we mean structures and businesses which depend not only on centres of production, studios, offices and factories but also on their ability to correlate organisation across a wide number of centres. Centralised locations of business organisation and linear operational hierarchies are replaced by dispersed semi-autonomous units of production: they become multiply connected nodes.

- *Flexibility and fluidity*, defining new characteristics of the way in which capital flows. It is argued that competitive success is now determined by the ability of business organisations to move capital around to find the best rates of return, from the operation of particular financial markets to shifting production capacity to favourable locations in terms of cheap labour or state subsidy for inward investment.

- *The aggressive development of new markets*, both in terms of looking to 'commodify' goods or services previously outside pure market relations and in terms of looking for new opportunities in locations – particularly the least-developed nations and former Soviet countries previously closed or unattractive to private enterprise.

- *Deregulation*: areas of society that had previously been widely assumed, in Europe at least, to be only possible on a non-profit basis were opened up to business. Education, health and other aspects of social provision are increasingly offered to business to operate on a profit basis.

In the US the school system had increasingly become a sphere for investment opportunity. An important example was the provision of necessary equipment to cash-strapped public schools in exchange for running Channel One, an 'educational' television network that carried advertisements aimed at children right into the classroom (McChesney et al. 1998: 135–149). Although an example based on old media, it illustrates the blurring of boundaries between content, advertising, provision and the public and private sectors that is associated with the economy of new media (**4.4.1**).

4.4.1 New media's 'other'

Overall these changes in the ways in which capitalism operates work primarily at the level of intensity rather than any significant change in the underlying principles. They make it easier for investors to operate in parts of the economy (or the globe) from which they were previously excluded. However, such changes cannot be simply dismissed as 'more of the same' (Garnham 1997).

3.18 THE DEVELOPMENT OF THE NEW ECONOMY

Strong claims have been made for the apparently obvious association of information processing technologies with new economic structures (see Castells 1996, or the UK Government White Paper quotation in **Box 3.1**). To understand more about this relationship we have to go back to the roots of the economic change, of increased flexibility, mobility of finance, and free markets described by theories of globalisation.

Box 3.1 The rosy future

During the 1970s Western capitalism experienced a crisis. Increases in unemployment, the closure of production plants and the slashing of public expenditure and welfare budgets all ensued. It is with this crisis that accounts of the post-industrial economy begin. Variations of **Keynesian** economic models had been adopted within social democratic frameworks in the West during the post-war years as a way of managing and stabilising the capitalist industrial economies. Keynesianism, which had involved the government increasing public investment at times of low private investment, had been intended to smooth over the booms and slumps associated with the great depression of the 1930s and earlier periods of economic difficulty. However, during the 1970s low economic growth rates combined with high inflation in ways that began to demonstrate the limits of the Keynesian economic model. In particular growth prompted by government spending came to be perceived as a significant cause of inflation, which itself then undermined the value of savings and purchasing power. This underlying problem was exacerbated and elevated to crisis by sudden sharp increases in the price of oil.

The response of owners of investment capital to the limits of growth that this crisis seemed to represent was to devise three new strategies. First was to seek to reduce the costs of production and to cultivate new markets. This was followed by the generation of a demand for the release of resources controlled by the state (e.g. energy, telecommunications, transport) into the marketplace. The third strategy was to produce an intensified search for cheaper sites of production as well as new markets across national borders. These developments were represented politically by the rise of a newly militant right-wing politics, based on economic **monetarism**, represented most clearly in the West by the Reagan–Thatcher axis of the 1980s.

This first strategy led to large-scale programmes of deregulation as part of what we might now call the ideology of **neo-liberalism**; that is to say, the belief that the commodity market is the best way of distributing resources, and to that end as many goods and services must be available for trading, and at as many sites and in as many markets as possible. Hence markets that had been 'regulated', managed or protected by state

Monetarism was also known as 'Thatcherism' after Margaret Thatcher, UK Premier from 1979 to 1990. The policy involved the state divesting itself of publicly owned enterprises such as gas, electricity and telecommunications. This was allied with a reduction in public sector investment and tax cuts that primarily benefited the wealthy. In addition, there was a considerable reduction in the power of organised labour achieved partly by the imposition of legal fetters on the right to strike. Overall, it involved a further significant shift in the uneven distribution of wealth across society. Justified by 'trickle down', it was argued that the concentration of wealth in fewer hands would overcome poverty as it was reinvested in new firms and jobs. Because of its impact on public services it was characterised in a term first used by the American economist J.K. Galbraith as 'private wealth, public squalor'. It represented a repudiation of social responsibility for every member of society. See J.K. Galbraith, *The Affluent Society*, London: Hamilton, 1958

legislation, were thrown open to competition, leading to large-scale transfers of capital from state to private sectors and to increases in profitability. Equally, production processes such as steel or coal that had been 'regulated' (i.e. protected through subsidy) were thrown open to an allegedly free market.

The second of these strategies led to what we now recognise as the phenomenon of globalisation – the rate of annual increase in investment from abroad in individual economies soared from 4 per cent from 1981–1985 to 24 per cent in the period 1986–1990 (Castells 1996: 84). One of the outcomes of this process was an economy largely freed from the constraints of national borders and local time. It was argued that this was something different, 'an economy with the capacity to work as a unit in real time on a planetary scale' (Castells 1996: 92).

From this discussion the new global economy could be seen as not only the cause of huge developments in information and communications technologies but also as the result of the demand generated for them. Add to that the perception that older industries were no longer profitable investment vehicles and the grounds have been laid for a growth in new, seemingly very profitable, fields with unlimited room for growth. It is now, therefore, time to unite them in two new questions. Where do the technologies of new media appear in this sketch of recent economic history? Where can they be said to have agency in this sequence and where can they be said to have been affected by it?

3.19 TECHNOLOGICAL AGENCY, ECONOMICS AND POLITICS: INVENTIONS AND DEVELOPMENTS

The history of the development of new media technologies and their positioning in relation to dominant economic systems is one of their move from being peripheral by-products to actors on centre-stage. This narrative can be traced over a thirty-year period; its plot is driven by the communications problems posed by a global economy.

Many of the key breakthroughs that made the '**information revolution**' possible were made during the 1970s. The microprocessor or silicon chip was invented by Ted Hoff in 1971 whilst designing a hand-held calculator for the Japanese market (Castells 1996: 51). The first PC was the Altair hobbyist kit marketed in 1975, and Apple introduced the first complete PC in 1977. The windowed interface design with which we are now familiar as standard computer 'front end' was first developed by Xerox during the early 1970s as part of a research project into the 'paperless office', which took as its goal the creation of computers that were usable 'by human beings' rather than specialist technicians. The Xerox team came up with WIMPS ('windows', 'icons', 'mouse', 'pull-down menus'). Significantly, Xerox, the big photocopier corporation, could see no potential value in this system and it was not until Steve Jobs of Apple came across WIMPS and imitated it for the Apple that it became a standard design. Similarly this had the effect of challenging IBM to produce their own PCs, which were soon running on operating systems sold to them by Bill Gates at the fledgling Microsoft, again founded in the late 1970s (**3.16**). The Internet was first established by the US Defense Agency's Advanced Research Project in 1969. It gained widespread diffusion through academic and scientific communities after 1974 as a result of the writing of the TCP/IP protocol systems by Cerf and Kahn, which allow data to be easily exchanged across different networks and negotiate blockages in them.

These technological breakthroughs, developed during the 1970s, had at best a tenuous relationship with the leading trends in global economics. They were occurring whilst

3.16 The social form of new media

global capitalism found itself in crisis, but they provided no immediate solution. Indeed, on more than one occasion, as we have seen in the case of Xerox, the corporate state could not quite see the point of this growing emphasis on the personal computer, on interactivity and connectivity (**1.2.2**). The culture that led to these developments was formed through a collision between the remnants of the counter-culture idealism of the late 1960s and technological communities supported by corporate-state initiatives and mainly centred on the defence industries.

1.2.2   Interactivity

This early development took place within a culture that was often at odds with the idea that business and commercial development was necessarily the (or even a possible) route for progress. In contrast, the Internet, as a functioning information exchange system, was built by enthusiasts and a quantity of free labour unprecedented in human history. The Apple II was unveiled in 1977, not at an international trade fair but at the Menlo Park Home Brew Computer Club, which was a loose grouping of enthusiasts based in southern California. Overall, the first wave of hi-tech culture was driven by what Barbrook & Cameron (1998) call 'the hi-tech gift economy'. Within this culture the idea of 'shareware' (i.e. freely distributed software) emerged as a fundamental ethos, as did the notion that 'information wants to be free'. In other words, those qualities of new media that we identified above as central (i.e. digitality, hypertextuality, interactivity, and dispersal) were formulated in a culture that was in many ways oppositional to the mainstream corporate culture of the 1970s. It was these attitudes which also influenced many of the early uses discussed later in this section.

Stewart Brand, an early propagandiser for the free computing, is credited with the first use of the phrase 'information wants to be free' at a **hacker** conference in 1984. Reported in *Whole Earth Review* 49 (May 1985)

3.20 TECHNOLOGICAL AGENCY, ECONOMICS AND POLITICS: GLOBALISATION AND TELECOMMUNICATIONS

However, this picture of home brew clubs and the accidental convergence of PC and networks began to shift as a result of the economic trend toward globalisation and neo-liberalism described in **3.19**. Global economic interests and the emergent social form of information and communication technologies began to converge and mutually shape one another. First, the globalised economy requires a different order of communication technologies to a national economy. Globalisation requires transnational instantaneous communication technologies that facilitate a massively extended sphere of operations. The head office of a large enterprise operating within one national territory during the 1970s could have run on the basis of paper-based communications, memos, postal services, phone calls and the occasional telex. By the end of the 1980s such an enterprise, if it survived at all, would in all likelihood have opened branches in other countries to support its globalised marketing, and would need at the very least a constant stream of fax communications and improved telecommunications of every kind. It would increasingly rely upon telephone lines and network-based communication systems, including commercial satellites, which had begun to be deployed in the early 1970s.

3.19   Technological agency, economies and politics: inventions and developments

In addition to the drive to seek new markets outside national boundaries, enterprises also began to export their manufacturing bases to other countries, especially those of the Pacific Rim, in an effort to find cheaper production based on lower wages, lower taxes and fewer social obligations: hence the widespread relocation of smokestack industries from the rich Northern Hemisphere countries to the poorer countries of the South and East. This development required increased use of subcontractors and their plants, and increased global information flow to manage such mobility. To this picture was added a new factor when in the 1990s the deregulation of international financial markets combined with the

In 1997, sixty-five companies signed an agreement under the aegis of the World Trade Organisation to transfer all state-owned telecommunications enterprises into private hands. The process had started in the UK with British Telecom in 1984 and in the US through the break up of telecom corporation AT&T in 1984. Deregulation of telecoms generally refers to the removal of public service obligations from telecommunications companies. The role of bodies such as the Federal Communications Commission in the USA is now primarily in the preservation of a number of providers and to maintain competition in a system prone to the development of monopoly. Privatisation was a way of divesting the state of ownership of industries and transferring considerable resources into the private sector at a low cost to it. The acceptability of both approaches depends on an acceptance by society as a whole that the market is the most efficient method for the allocation of resources (Baran 1998)

Box 3.1   The rosy future

deregulation of telecommunications to generate an important new opportunity for investment in ICTs (Baran 1998).

The development of a global economy required the deregulation of international financial markets, characterised in the UK as the Stock Exchange Big Bang of 1988. An international deregulated financial market was more easily achievable because of computer networking and the increasing capacity of such networks to handle complex data. The result was a large inflow of capital into the telecom industries and the loosening of laws governing cross-media ownership (e.g. of newspapers and television broadcasters) that had previously been designed to maintain a certain diversity of view in public debate. The recognition that networked communications held the key to the success of newly globalised systems of production together with the deregulation of telecommunications combined to produce very high levels of investment and attendant euphoria around the emergent digital media industries.

The economic changes that determined the development of networked communications were accompanied by political arguments for the importance of the information economy as the saviour of capitalism (**Box 3.1**). The widespread exaggeration of the efficacy of digital communications that characterised the early 1990s (see Dovey 1996: xi–xvi) had been prefigured during the previous decade by politicians and futurologists keen to embrace the technological implications of the new global economies of neo-liberalism. It is during the mid-1980s that we begin to see the rhetoric surrounding the emergence of computer communications shift from a kind of pan-educational enthusiasm for civic revival to a rhetoric of economic regeneration.

As we have illustrated in **Box 3.1**, many early predictors of the information economy foresaw utopian humanist possibilities in the technology. However, as Roszak has pointed out (1986: 23–30) by the middle of the 1980s hi-tech had been identified by politicians of the new radical right, such as Newt Gingrich in America, as the economic engine of change. The aim of this enthusiasm for hi-tech was, argues Roszak, 'to design a flashy, updated style of conservatism that borrows heavily upon the futurologists to create a sense of forward looking confidence' (Roszak 1986: 24).

The idea of the information economy was being promoted as a political future at the same time as the economic conditions (of neo-liberalism) that would bring it about were being established. The idea of the information economy was promoted incessantly as the alternative to the dirty, worn-out, politically intransigent industrial economy. With remarkable prescience, Roszak poses the question as early as 1986:

> can the latest generation of micro and mini computers be merchandised on a larger scale as mass communication items? Can the general public be persuaded to see information as a necessity of modern life in the same way it has come to see the refrigerator, the automobile, the television as necessities? The computer makers are wagering billions that it can. Their gamble has paid handsomely and lost disastrously with each turn of the business cycle. Yet it is primarily from their advertising and merchandising efforts that information has come to acquire a cultlike following in society.
>
> (Roszak 1986: 30)

In the first half of the 1990s we see these two strands, economic determinations and the discourse of marketing, combine to produce the all-pervasive idea of 'the information economy'. This dynamic historical interaction between technology, economics and politics has been described as 'the old society's attempt to retool itself by using the power of technology to serve the technology of power' (Castells 1996: 52). It has been argued by Garnham that the use of terms such as 'knowledge' or 'information' economy are in this sense ideological; that is, that they are used to fix critics of these processes as old fashioned and unprepared to modernise (Garnham 2000). More importantly, the central claim that we all live in an 'information age' is also open to question on the basis of the actual spread of the technologies and access to them and the nature of the content of new media. We now therefore turn to an examination of the digital divide between the haves and the have-nots.

3.21 THE DIGITAL DIVIDE

Not only is access to online resources globally uneven, as is discussed in **3.4** and **3.19**, it has also been shown that the digital divide mirrors income inequality in Western countries. It is therefore not possible to talk about simple, universal, levels of involvement with, and experience of, new media. The raw data about the distribution of servers and PCs tells as much about internal difference within nation-states as it does about the division between countries.

In 1999 the US Department of Commerce reported that urban households with incomes of $75,000 and higher were more than twenty times more likely to have access to the Internet than rural households at the lowest income levels, and more than nine times as likely to have a computer at home. Whites are more likely to have access to the Internet from home than Blacks or Hispanics have from any location. Black and Hispanic households are approximately one-third as likely to have home Internet access as households of Asian/Pacific Islander descent, and roughly two-fifths as likely as White households.

In other words, across the richest country in the world access to new media is hugely differentiated. The report also indicated that there was little or no difference on an ethnic basis; the ethnic disparities in access referred to above simply mirror economic inequalities. The report also found that, in the US at least, the divide was actually getting worse, because as more families in upper-income groups acquired computers and Internet connections there was a much lower rate of increase amongst those with less cash to spare.

Novack and Hoffman also argue that differential access to online resources is a function of income. However, they also discovered more specific instances of 'unevenness' in their study; for example, African Americans were more likely to have access at work and black students had less likelihood of having a computer and Internet connection at home. Although they do not offer reasons for these differences they are clearly important in considering the ways in which the places from which we access online affect what we can do when we go there.

When it comes to the question of gender there is a similar picture of differentiated access on the basis of income - except for one peculiarity in that for groups between the ages of 17 and 47 women are actually more likely to be Internet users than men. A possible explanation is that women are increasingly concentrated in clerical jobs that provide computer access at work.

But the question of access to digital information is not restricted to questions of hardware and telecommunications links. There is also a problem in what is actually provided over the net and what uses can be made of it. The emphasis on the dotcom explosion was on the provision of services and purchasing opportunities, the important factor being the extraction of surplus cash by variations of a retail market. By contrast, for low-income families net use concentrated on improving educational opportunities for

3.4   Learning to live in the interface

3.19   Technological agency, economics and politics: inventions and developments

The full report, 'Falling through the Net', can be found at http://www.ntia.doc.gov/ntiahome/fttn99/

Thomas P. Novak and Donna L. Hoffman, 'Bridging the digital divide: the impact of race on computer access and internet use', Project 2000, Vanderbilt University, 2 February, 1998. See http://www2000.ogsm.vanderbilt.edu/papers/race/science.html 22 January 2002

Up-to-date figures on US computer use and Internet access can be obtained from http://www.ntia.doc.gov/ntiahome/fttn00/chartscontents.html

On-Line Content for Low Income and Underserved Americans: http://www.childrenspartnership.org/pub/low_income/index.html

Pierre Bourdieu identifies the non-economic forces such as family background, social class, varying investments in, and commitments to, education, different resources, etc. which influence academic success as 'cultural capital': a form of non-financial advantage. Pierre Bourdieu, 'The forms of capital', in John Richardson (ed.) *Handbook of Theory and Research for the Sociology of Education*, New York: Greenwood Press, 1986, pp. 241–258

children. At its heart the question of content, the purpose of content and what it might be used for is also differentiated according to income and even to other uses, such as to keep in touch with dispersed families. Unfortunately the costs in simply gaining access to such opportunities in the first place remain prohibitive for many.

Interviews with those on low incomes in the US indicated that their desire to use the Internet is informed by a wish to overcome just those factors that impeded their access to it. People want access to job listings, community services, housing, and so on. The coincidence of low incomes and recent immigration status and widespread problems with literacy also adds another dimension to people's information requirements, raising questions of the level of content, as well as opportunities to overcome poor education. In other words, the much-lauded capabilities of the Internet, the ability to connect communities and to provide access to social resources are unavailable to precisely those people who would benefit most. This is not an insuperable problem, but the ideology of neo-liberalism, so closely associated with the digital revolution, is inimical to those without the cultural capital or economic wherewithal to get past the first hurdle of affordable access.

The response of government, both in the UK and in the US, has been to see computer use as primarily about the acquisition of computer skills. Once these skills are acquired employment should follow and then income will resolve any other questions about access. Of course this might be the case for those who are excluded from the labour market for the sole reason of poor employability. The problem remains that those who are excluded for other non-employment related reasons (e.g. language, caring responsibilities, lack of 'cultural capital') remain cut off from an increasingly important part of our society. Even if the technological convergence of the telephone and the television enables 'universal' access the question of inclusive content and non-commercial viability remains in place.

The report of the Children's Partnership made nineteen recommendations to overcome these problems, and some of them, such as availability of public information in appropriate languages, are well within the capabilities of many government departments. However, it is the delivery of skills, the creation of practically useful community based resources, and ongoing research and development that are difficult to supply in a commercial environment.

See http://www.childrenspartnership.org/pub/low_income/index.html

See 'Broadcasting is dead. Long live digital choice', Jeanette Steemers in *Convergence* 3.1 (1997): 51–71, for a review of regulation in regard to digital television

In other words, the digital divide reproduces other kinds of inequalities in the society at large and has become a key site for debates about social inclusion. However, the outcome of these debates will be determined by precisely the kind of complex interactions between ownership, regulation, technology and ideology previously referred to. In particular the resolution of the 'digital divide' will depend upon whether any notion of public service media can be maintained in the face of a context dominated by neo-liberalism's antipathy toward regulation and state intervention.

3.22 UNEVEN GLOBALISATION

3.19 Technological agency, economics and politics: inventions and developments

Section **3.19** follows what has become a more or less conventional account, based in a broad political economy perspective, of the relationship between new media and its economic context. What follows is an attempt to both challenge and develop this account by looking in more detail at particular cases and specific examples.

One of the implications of the account above is that the internationalisation of the world economy could only have happened with high-speed digital communications. These concurrent developments need to be examined carefully to disentangle those elements that are genuinely novel from those that are simply the intensification of existing tendencies. For example, capitalism has always been associated with international trade and that trade has always been associated with social upheaval. The earliest capitalist epoch, that of mercantilism, generated the largest migration in human history when some 11 million slaves were transported from Africa to the Americas, a cultural impact that has probably never been equalled.

The period of modern industrial development since the mid-eighteenth century introduced the most rapid and unrelenting social change (Hobsbawm 1987). Once the demise of peasant and artisanal production was complete the speed of development of new technologies, from steam to petrol to fission, was only equalled by their spread across the face of the world. However, there are still major inconsistencies in access to even the basics of existence, as is indicated by the term 'least-developed countries' that now describes the Third World. The promise of even industrial capitalism, enjoyed so deeply by some, is still to reach many.

This inconsistency is a part of the industrial character of our world and can be seen in its very origins. The Industrial Revolution uprooted traditional small-scale communities, set large-scale migrations of workers in process, destroyed traditional craft skills and ways of life, introduced new patterns of work and rhythms of daily life, reconstituted the nature of the family unit and, above all, brought all kinds of production, including cultural production, face to face with the demands of the marketplace. Populations increased rapidly and were concentrated in new urban industrial centres – traditional institutions of communication and education (church, word of mouth, broadsheets, basic literacy) were outstripped by newer mass media. The scale of the changes begs the question of whether we can really compare the digital revolution with the almighty upheaval of the relatively recent past.

To see globalisation as purely a product of a technological push into digital media is to run the danger of succumbing to a form of technological determinism (**5.1.1**). As was discussed at **1.6**, a more complex view offers technology as a cultural construct as well as an influence on culture and human development. For instance, it has been argued that the increased global interconnections facilitated by ICTs offer great potential progress for social change (Featherstone 1990). That this view of the interconnectedness of globalisation and the advent of ICTs should gain widespread support is hardly surprising if we consider the major changes in international relations that have taken place at the same time as the growth of the digital technologies. The 'new era' of global geo-politics is contemporaneous with the development of networked communications media.

With the fall of the Berlin Wall and the collapse of the Soviet bloc at the end of the 1980s, the supporters of US-style, market-based capitalism went so far as to declare its final victory. Certainly increased deregulation, privatisation and the ending of protectionism under the aegis of the World Trade Organisation (WTO) have meant that the increased dominance of the market has been widely felt. Changes in technology have also played a role in fostering these destabilising feelings of change. When the security cameras in Swiss banks are watched by guards stationed in North Africa, the world can also appear compressed in time and space. However, since none of the North African nations where the guards were stationed had more than one Internet host per 10,000 people in 1999 it was also likely that their monitors were the guards' only connection with the new technology (ILO 2000; World Bank 1999). We must therefore be prepared to look very closely, not just at the claims made by the proponents of these views but also at the actual

5.1.1 Technology as real and material: media studies' blindspot?

1.6 New media: determining or determined?

Hobsbawm (1987) brings together the history of economic and political change consequent upon the development of industrial production in the UK in the period 1750–1960. Although published some years ago it is still a vibrant study of the relationship between industry, politics and international economy

In his book *The End of History and the Last Man* (Harmondsworth: Penguin, 1993), Francis Fukuyama put forward the idea that the collapse of the Berlin Wall and the end of the Soviet Union implied the final victory of Western democratic capitalism. There was to be no more significant social or political change

3.3 McDonald's Soviet-style: Multimedialibrary.com.

business structures and social organisations associated with the global. We will start with one of the best-known examples of an international business that has been frequently used as an example of the globalisation of culture.

McDonald's is an important symbol of the internationalisation of a particular aspect of American culture and business practices. McDonald's presence in Moscow was widely seen as the ultimate symbol of a return to market-style capitalism in Eastern Europe. Standard recipes, low-skilled interchangeable staff and an internationally recognised image characterise the globalised economy (Ritzer 2000). A closer look shows that because they are a franchise operation they also depend on infrastructure and other resources in the areas where they operate. Local tastes – a beefburger is unwelcome in Hindu India, a baconburger cannot be sold in Muslim countries – demand alterations to the recipes. McDonald's must operate as much on a local basis as it does on an international one if people are to consume the burgers and relish. Let's take this a little further.

In the commercial world, franchising is normally a form of marketing or distribution in which one party, the franchiser, allows another, the franchisee, to exploit a trade name, trademark process or other resource in return for a fee. The franchiser carries out the activities that benefit from economies of scale, such as the marketing of the product, nationally or globally, while local operations, not enjoying economies of scale, are undertaken by franchisees (Cave 1995). It is the symbolic exchanges that take place on an international scale, the information on how to make the burger, its presentation; staffing and image are adapted, consistent with the international image, to local circumstances, while actual production, delivery and consumption take place within local cultural modes in real places. In other words the international brand image of McDonald's is the commodity on sale as well as the locally produced burger. The truly global aspect of the organisation is its image.

In Russia, the pre-eminence that Coca-Cola enjoyed in the years after the collapse of the Soviet Union has been shaken by the collapse of the local economy. Poverty, combined with a resurgent nationalism, has pushed people back to the cheaper locally produced drink, *kvass*. It is the combination of elements of cultural nationalism and the lower costs of the unpromoted, unfranchised product that enabled this resurgence. It is unlikely that either of the factors outlined above would have been enough on their own to knock back Coca-Cola (*Christian Science Monitor*, 15 October 1997).

We can see that the globalisation of the economy also has an important local dimension. It is also true that it is not a simple, inexorable, one-way process. There are important adjustments to be made in the light of local cultures, of economic shifts and of local habits. If this is the case in the best-known examples of globalisation, McDonald's and Coca-Cola, might it not also be true of networked communications? We can apply some of the ideas generated in these examples to our consideration of ICTs. What, for example, are the differences between the international image and the local reality of access to ICTs? What, as we discuss later, is the impact of the development of a web or Internet culture on the development of new media?

These non-media examples demonstrate that, as McChesney *et al.* (1998) have argued, much of what has been called globalisation is rather another version of neo-liberalism (i.e. the opening up of markets to international investment). This local/global relationship is also extremely important in the media industry. Local companies owned by global media businesses such as Bertelsmann, Sony, etc., frequently source local products to fit with particular musical styles and tastes.

It has also been argued that the possibility of a genuinely global economy is limited by the inability of capitalism to provide the required material resources (Amin 1997). In other words, that far from delivering social and economic development the very spread of digital media is handicapped by the capitalist economic system within which it came into existence. The disparity between the claims for world dominance of the Internet and its actual spread around the world needs to be kept in mind if we are to develop a more sophisticated and open model of globalisation. Similarly, while corporations and world bodies such as the World Trade Organisation are increasingly important, individual states have considerable power to develop or inhibit the growth of new systems of communications. For example, the reluctance of the Chinese government to allow free access to the Internet is an inhibitory factor just as the enthusiasm of the US government plays a role in its growth.

Globalisation, in the preceding account of the development of the post-industrial information economy, has become its own 'meta-narrative', implying an unrealistic degree of homogenisation and inevitability. Well-known global processes such as McDonald's or Coca-Cola already have regional difference built into their global reach; there is no reason to suppose ICT use should be any different. On the contrary, we would argue that it is even more likely to be characterised by regional variation because of the limited potential for interactive engagement with new media in its networked form and the elements of **'prosumerism'** that they offer.

In addition, unequal patterns of access are likely to be the dominant shaping factor of the global character of ICT use. Dan Schiller has gone further and argued that, if anything, the Internet is likely to exacerbate existing social inequalities. Certainly, access to networked communication is not a global enveloping phenomenon. Internet hosts and

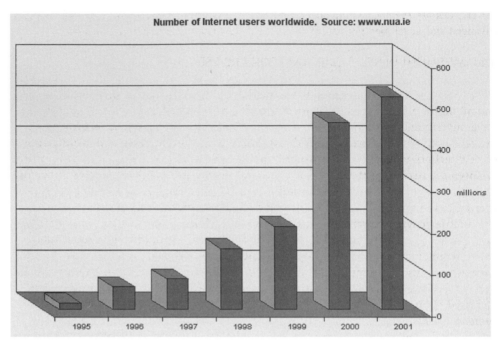

3.4 Growth of Internet users: Nua.com.

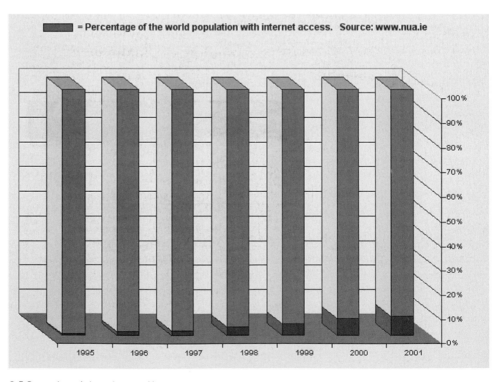

3.5 Percentage Internet users: Nua.com.

servers, despite their rapid spread (**1.2.4**), are still overwhelmingly concentrated in the advanced and developed nations. We will return to these questions of access again.

3.23 INVESTMENT IN NEW MEDIA: INTENTION AND USE

Williams (1974: ch. 1) argues for a model of thinking about the outcomes of communication technologies that are shaped by, on one the hand, what he refers to as social investment, and, on the other, by 'community needs' (**1.6.3**). Social investment includes both state and private capital investment in the development and manufacture of new technologies, for reasons of both profit and social value. For example, e-mail has been the reason for the sale of many computers because it has also allowed people to keep in touch at home as well as in business. 'Community need' includes both the market, in the sense of a collection of potential purchasers with the ability to pay, and also a more generalised sense of what communicative needs different kinds of societies and cultures might have. So, for instance, the communication needs of a feudal village are different from the communication needs of an early twentieth-century house dweller, not just in terms of the kinds of information in use but also in terms of methods of delivery. The village can survive with one-to-one communications; the increased complexity of the urban setting requires systems that can deal with a mass audience.

One of the factors determining the use of technologies of communication will be the kinds of investments made in equipment, and personnel, who makes them and what they

1.2.4 Dispersal

Dan Schiller, *Digital Capitalism: Networking The Global Market System*, Cambridge, Mass.: MIT 1999

1.6.3 Williams and the social shaping of technology

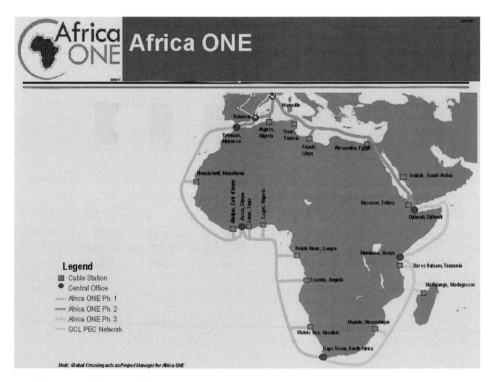

3.6 Africa One: Africa ONE Ltd.

expect in return. There is no guarantee, however, that the investment will necessarily be in forms of communication that are most appropriate for the majority of people. Because the ownership of investment funds tends to be in the hands of commercial organisations the modernisation of communications infrastructure only takes place on the basis of potential profitability. Take, for example, the installation of the Africa One undersea fibre-optic communications cable. Not one single African nation was involved in its development and its operational structures will be oriented to those who can pay for access. Contracts have yet to be negotiated, but a return on the $1.9 billion investment may be difficult to achieve unless oriented to business users. Many states that might wish to use it for education and information may not only find it too expensive but also simply unavailable to them. (McChesney et al. 1998: 79; hyperlink: http://www.kagan.com/archive/reuters/2000/06/05/2000060523bbd.html). There can be no doubt that the project has been led by investment opportunity rather than community demand. At the same time, it will undoubtedly provide much-needed communications facilities, but their actual availability is clearly not being pursued primarily for the public good. The consequences of the uneven access that will flow from such an investment are not always possible to predict.

See the Internet History Timeline at http://www.isoc.org/guest/zakon/Internet/History/HIT.html

The uses to which media technologies are put, including attempts to mobilise them for practices resistant to their commercial ethos, will also have an impact upon the social form they come to assume. Throughout the period in which economic imperatives were positioning new media of communications as central to the global economy (the 1980s) a worldwide community of users and developers was growing whose direct material communicative aims had far more in common with pleasure and entertainment, such as music, dating and photography, than with competitive advantage, profitability and commercial use.

It has been argued that the big Internet service providers in the US, Prodigy and CompuServe, completely misinterpreted the demands that users would begin to make of the Internet in the 1980s (Stone 1995). They assumed they would be able to market information on a broadcast model such as booking services, weather forecasts, news services, etc. However, it transpired that the subscribers who formed their early users were more interested in connectivity, in chat, bulletin boards and email – in new collaborative or intimate communication experiences.

3.3 Networks and identity

These uses of ICTs had not been predicted by commercial investors, nor had the fact that they opened up a communicative realm of participation (**3.3**) that took users into direct conflict with the owners of commodified artefacts. So, for instance, the producers of *Star Trek* fan sites, or online 'slash' movies in which well-known characters are re-edited into subversively sexualised parodies of themselves, posed direct problems to the owners of the rights in *Star Trek*. The 'consumer as producer', together with the ease of reproduction offered by digital technologies, has created a fundamental challenge to existing laws of intellectual property ownership. Ownership of copyright, regulation and the law had already been determined in relation to older media forms and practices. The exploitation of intellectual property rights is an extremely important source of income for traditional media producers. We now to turn to this area of the law and its impact on new media.

3.24 INTELLECTUAL PROPERTY RIGHTS, DETERMINED AND DETERMINING

One of the great promises of digital media is the ease with which material can be copied again and again without any degradation in quality. However, scarcity of copies, and access to them, has been one of the ways in which the owners of cultural objects have ensured that they received an income. For example, cinemas, as the only place one can easily see a film on a large screen, also meant that they were convenient places to charge for its use. To explain this requires a short diversion. Since political economy holds that the organising principal of a capitalist economy is the production of commodities (i.e. objects which are both useful and exchangeable) it is important to know if this is true for cultural products such as music, art, web pages and so on. When an object is made it usually has a certain usefulness and a price in the market. In the case of a personal computer, for example, this is easy to understand, how much it is worth, the cost of the expertise, metals, plastics, distribution and labour that went into it, along with what it will do, word-processing, image manipulation, make an Internet connection, and so on. When it comes to a cultural commodity, for example say a web page, what exactly is its value? In the past this question has created some difficulties for the discussion of broadcast media. How was the price established and how do you characterise the process by which it was turned into income? For some such as Dallas Smythe, the process in terrestrial commercial television involved turning the audience into a commodity, which was then sold to advertisers. This model of selling audiences to advertisers has been widely used on the web but has proved to be a commercial failure. The question of how to disseminate material that people want and obtain a payment for its use lies at the heart of the current developments of new media by business.

The essential characteristic of the capitalist economy is the way that it uses systems of property, particularly the ownership of commodities. The right to ownership demands the acceptance of all parties that it is 'common sense' and also supported by the courts where necessary. In this way television broadcasters, for example, are able to disseminate their material as widely as possible without fear of copying and re-broadcasting on a commercial basis. The acceptance that it is impossible without legal retribution means that it is rarely attempted. However, social practice imposes limits on the extent to which copying can be prevented and although home copying is an everyday occurrence and is, strictly speaking, an infringement of the law, its prosecution would be unacceptable to most people.

This is just the beginning of the story since the wholesale reproduction of material, particularly in analogue forms, also had problems with degradation of the image, increasingly poor sound, and so on. In contrast digital material is much more easily copied, altered and integrated. This potential for infinite reproduction was explored in law in 1999 and 2000 around the Napster organisation and the way its software facilitated the free distribution of music files between Internet users. (See **Case study 3.1** for further discussion of this important case.)

Case study 3.1 Napster: from community to commerce

A different kind of attempt to determine property rights in new media had previously been explored in a landmark case between Microsoft and Apple corporations over issues of 'look and feel'.

'Look and feel' primarily related to the way in which graphical user interfaces developed by Microsoft out of its relationship with Apple brought about infringement of copyright in the digital age. The case was mainly concerned with the integration of known and unprotectable elements (e.g. icons, simple images and screen layouts) which when brought together constituted an overall similarity to an existing interface. Although the case was settled out of court, with Microsoft preserving its right to use a graphical user interface originated by Apple (who incidentally had obtained the idea from Rank Xerox), it established a set of tests for the identification of a property right in a screen representation.

The importance of the 'look and feel' case was that it took notice of the ease of replicability enshrined in digital media. Most importantly, it was the first signal that the new media was not to be left to its own devices in this important aspect of commercial use just as television and film had been brought under firm regulatory control.

Digital reproduction has again become a major problem with the continued development of the web. The control of distribution has always been a major concern for the owners of cultural commodities. When such commodities could only be distributed by printed page, the pressing of vinyl or by controlled access to the cinema, the difficulty of high capital requirements for the equipment or venue prevented much effective piracy.

However, the development of the law in relation to trading in commodities came second to the problems of the protection of ideas that form the property of corporations.

The selling of home copying equipment has given rise to a new problem: how to prevent the consumer infringing the copyright of the owner. This difficulty first arose with the development of home taping and in the US gave rise to specific legislation that allowed recording in digital or analogue media for personal non-commercial use. The response was to make home taping legal, and to ensure that businesses that made their profits from selling domestic recording equipment gave some of their income to those that depended on the enforcement of copyright (i.e. the software or content producers). The way in which the law developed cannot be seen as purely the result of right or justice but also the way in which a balance of influence and power was exerted on the US legislative process. It is no accident that the owners of copyright, such as major music companies and film and television businesses, reside mainly in the US and recording equipment is primarily an import. There is no similar law in the UK. Now with the advantages of digital reproduction the infringement of copyright presented itself in a new and potentially virulent form.

The Internet, allied with digital reproduction, has generated a new problem for the owners of copyright because the ability to record is allied with the ability to distribute. However, at the same time the availability of powerful computing capabilities in the home has stimulated the development of new preventative measures in the form of cryptography, or secret codes. Cryptography works by encoding the data involved in reproducing a media text and requiring the user to have another piece of data, a 'key', that will allow the user's computer to make sense of the information sent by the provider. The speed of modern methods of computer encoding means that a new 'lock' and 'key' can be made and sold every time the text is sent. The incorporation of these measures into US law is a reflection of an important new direction in the distribution of cultural commodities. The intention is undoubtedly to control the use of commodities on a pay per use basis. The new law, at least in the USA, will make it illegal to try to circumvent the techniques used for the encryption of the material. In other words, a piece of music sold to you over the web may only be decrypted with the key supplied. Any attempt to decode it would be against the law, as would be the distribution of a machine with such a capability. The control over intellectual property is not only a commercial question, it also influences the development of cultural practices, of reuses and revisits to material; it even deters spoofing. The great potential for the cheap and easy distribution of our cultural heritage and shared cultural life is actively limited by these legal pressures. This is one way in which the potential of new media is greatly foreshortened.

The new US legislation may well bring about the ultimate commodification of cultural objects. By integrating technological capability with powerful systems for encrypting and then decrypting in the home, it will enable 'pay per use'. Each use of the cultural

Gaines's (1991) work makes it clear that the priority remained the prevention of theft between capitalist organisations rather than by consumers

Audio Home Recording Act of 1992, Pub. L. No. 102–563, 106 Stat. 4237 amending title 17 of the United States Code by adding a new chapter 10, enacted 28 October 1992

Digital Millennium Act: http://lcweb.loc.gov/copyright/legislation/hr2281.pdf

commodity has to be paid for. No longer have you necessarily purchased book, magazine, film or the new media variation; what you have purchased is the single use of that item. This is not necessarily a new phenomenon; the temporary nature of the newspaper is known to us all, as is the one-off visit to the cinema, the single viewing of a television programme, or the rental of a video. What is different here is that the technology exists to make it possible to view, store and reuse cultural commodities, and makes it cheap to reproduce them infinitely. Instead of which powerful technology is to be developed to inhibit all of these potentials. Cultural production may now come to be organised around impeding the very gains that new technology was assumed to provide. It is also true that the establishment of corporate control is not to be assumed to be an easy matter, and the development of a new media industry has not been without its problems. A particular problem has been how to secure an income stream in the absence of control over distribution, an expectation by users that the web is free, and in the face of the high costs involved in establishing a new business dependent on scarce skills and powerful computers.

In view of the accessibility of the web it is also necessary to consider other non-technical aspects of media distribution. One of the promises of new media is ease of access and distribution, but this is to ignore the control over resources enjoyed by large media corporations. In the US to make a Hollywood-style film will cost a minimum of $50 million, even domestic UK production of a costume drama will cost in the region of £400,000 per hour (see *Broadcast Magazine* and www.imdb.com/business). A large part of that money is spent on locations, special effects, rehearsal time, famous name actors, costumes and make-up, as well as distribution and advertising. The question has to be asked: how many people are prepared to settle for the home-made video of someone in Alaska, even if it is sent free over the net? In other words, each consumer of a cultural commodity as they sit and view or listen can interact with the product of very large inputs of finance and resources. New media will allow the distribution of huge amounts of material, but the filtering role, the exercise of taste and judgement, may still have to be paid for. One of the reasons that corporations can charge for access to their commodities is that they control the resources required to produce particular kinds of content. Put simply, control of distribution is the way in which corporations achieve a return on the investment in resources used to select and create media content. Until media corporations can solve the problems of distribution and the consequence of security of income streams the spread and utilisation of new media may be somewhat inhibited. In this way we can see how new media has entered into a world of law, economic organisation and regulation that has been developing since the eighteenth century and will upset many practices and accepted interests.

CASE STUDY 3.1   Napster: from community to commerce

In July 2000 the Recording Industry Association of America (RIAA) attempted to have Napster Inc. closed down. Napster used software to facilitate the sharing of music files between personal computers across the net. The RIAA argued that the copyright in music belonging to record companies was being infringed and that Napster was responsible. The initial injunction was quashed on the grounds that similar software was widely available across the Internet and that it was a simple technical question. This court case and others like it will be one of the factors determining the character of new media, just as was the case with old media. Just because something is technically possible does not mean that it can be freely implemented.

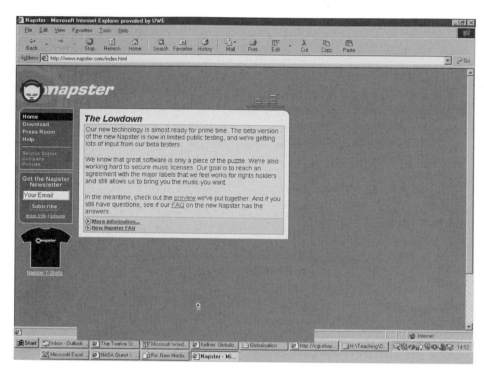

3.7 Napster seeks a legal way to make money offering licensed music.

One of the great claims for the Internet has been that it would enable people to share digital media with great ease. It may be the case that this is technically possible since one of the great advantages of digital media is its ease of duplication. However, in a system within which property rights and network protocols play such an important role the question of ownership of cultural commodities in digital formats was always certain to become significant. Once the Internet provided an alternative to the extremely expensive distribution systems of old, primarily capital investment in presses, cinema chains and so on, the law had to adapt to new circumstances.

The importance of adaptability in commercial law is demonstrated clearly in the Napster case. Its response was to identify its distribution of **MP3** files over the Internet as just another form of home recording. The core of the case revolved around legal detail about the difference between copying sound and copying file information. To concentrate on the detail, however, would be to ignore the underlying principle, which is that the law is as important a determinant of the form of new media as is the technology.

It is in the laws covering commerce that much of the content and the relationship between the users of cultural commodities and their producers will be decided; that is, who can buy, own and distribute material.

An important twist occurred when the German-owned Bertelsmann Corporation announced that rather than support the case against Napster it had negotiated an agreement with the company to work on subscription models of distribution. This shows, in a particularly acute way, how the technical capabilities of the technology, for free and easy distribution of infinitely copyable music, can be subordinated to corporate interests.

See Gaines (1991) for more on the relationship between media, meaning and the law

3.25 INFORMATION AS COMMODITY

By the middle of the 1990s, the idea of information as the commodity of the post-industrial economy had become firmly established. The centrality of computing and of networked communication had become clear. However, during the final years of the century there was an increased awareness that new media, particularly information (rather than entertainment) had a specific economic identity and value of its own. This expressed itself in two related ways and represents another point at which we start to bring ICTs and the global economy back together in our analysis.

First, massive amounts of capital have been invested in hi-tech industries themselves, especially communications networks and the associated computers. Here we see the technology that had previously played only a propaganda role in the ideas of neo-liberalism become the object of real investment in the new liberated market economy. Investment funds, unable to find a profitable home in more traditional industries, were sucked into the seemingly undeniable promise of hi-tech stocks which found their own market on the NASDAQ (National Association of Securities Dealers Automated Quotation).

Second, the speculative market in hi-tech stocks on the NASDAQ was at least in part fuelled by the second aspect of the intensification of the economic character of new media. By the end of the century, the idea of the 'information society' as representing the dissemination of humanist educational value, an arguable conception as Garnham has pointed out, had all but withered in the face of a neo-liberal reconstruction of the idea of cyberspace itself. The innovative informational spaces, interactive, information-rich and largely free, opened up by new media, and discussed in greater detail above, were transformed from open fields of human potential to marketplaces pure and simple.

Here we come to another clear point of intersection between economic determination and media form. We would argue that the website, as a form, has changed in quality over the past two years as a direct result of economic context. The owners of investment capital placed in NASDAQ-listed companies also saw cyberspace as a marketing and consumption opportunity. Despite the difficulties of actually trading over the net innumerable businesses were set up in order either to sell directly – web-based mail order – or to sell site users to advertisers and hence create profit through advertising revenue. The website was redefined on a broadcast economic model in which 'page impressions' became the measure of 'eyeballs' delivered to advertisers and therefore the determinant of the rate at which ads on a site can be charged. Interactivity is here limited to the expressions of willingness and ability to purchase (**3.3**).

However, the dotcom businesses proved to be another example of one of finance capital's oldest experiences, the speculative boom. Common to many periods, from the eighteenth-century South Sea Bubble to tulipomania, through railways to the Wall Street crash, each spectacular explosion of speculative investment has risen like a rocket and come down again like the stick.

Through 1999 and early 2000 the rush to invest in dotcoms reached a frenzy, with investment funds offering returns of more than 100 per cent in less than a year. However, this promise was based on little more than enthusiasm and technophilic passion – very few direct consumer service providers were able to demonstrate that their sites could actually maintain secure income streams. Continuing security and cryptography problems disadvantaged the Internet as a site of consumption. Dotcom entrepreneurs chose to overlook the fact that many consumers actually enjoy the physical as opposed to virtual aspect of shopping. When it became clear that the new dotcom businesses could not

The NASDAQ was formed to provide a home for the dealing in shares of companies too small for the New York Stock Exchange. It went live on 8 February 1971. It later became a home for fledgling computer companies and many of them have kept their listing on the computer-based system. In 1994, it overtook the NYSE in volumes of shares dealt. See http://www.nasdaq.com/about/timeline.stm and for a more critical view http://slate.msn.com/Assessment/00-04-21/Assessment.asp

3.3 Networks and identity

Peter Fearon, *The Origins and Nature of the Great Slump 1929–1932*, Macmillan, London, 1979

See www.nasdaq.com for the data and John Cassidy's *dot.con: The Greatest Story Ever Sold*, London: Allen Lane, 2002 for the details

deliver the promised rates of investment share prices began to fall. Between the end of 1999 and mid-2000, NASDAQ shares fell by 40 per cent, proving that the new information economy was subordinate to at least some of the laws of capitalist economics.

Our experience of new media is likely to be directly affected in conditions of such high market volatility, not only by the disappearance of favourite sites or other services but also by the way in which the structuring of the website as a commodity within a capitalist regime will determine something of its character. For instance, there are a wide variety of travel sites on the web, offering advice to travellers and the possibility for them to plan their own journeys directly and outside of the markets of the big tour operators. Many of these sites are simply a marketing operation of existing destinations, electronic brochures that offer the benefit of direct contact with service providers at a distance. However, there are also sites such as lastminute.com, one of the best known of UK dotcom businesses, offering cheap travel deals. Lastminute lost £15.3 million in the last quarter of 2000 – they then announced a joint venture with the oldest travel operator in the world, Thomas Cook. The potential for 'new' patterns of travel consumption (i.e. more individualised, less pre-packaged) here takes a blow as the newest operator in the sector makes alliance with the oldest in order to survive economically. Our experiences and choices are directly subject to financial and market conditions.

The consequence of this discussion is that we cannot simply deduce the shape of new media from their technological capability – their economic context, investment strategies and methods of return will profoundly affect our experience and use of networked media.

3.26 FRAGMENTATION AND CONVERGENCE

The dispersal of media production and distribution offers the user an unprecedented range of choice. Compared to even ten years ago there is now an enormous range of media inputs to the home: from services delivered via cable and satellite, to the terrestrial broadcast of both radio and TV, and in portable media such as DVD or computer games. Every consumer, it is argued, will be able to create his or her own customised and individual media consumption pattern. We will be assisted in this task by smart set-top boxes, such as the hard-disk-based intelligent recording system marketed under the name TiVO, that remembers our viewing choices, anticipates and digitises them. On the web, it may be offered by sophisticated bookmarking and search engine facilities that offer us individualised web surfing pathways. In this way, it is argued, the individual consumer can become another producer in the sea of multiple media outputs, creating media in the shape of online journals, digital films, or personal home pages.

See Gates (1996) for a not surprisingly very strong version of this argument

However, an analysis based in political economy has shown that beneath the surface new media structures of ownership and investment build on all the existing patterns of 'old media'. Although we might appear to inhabit newly built, custom-designed and individual media environments it turns out that they are all owned by the same small number of financial interests.

Case study 3.2 Time-Warner and aol: the world's biggest merger (so far)

Cornford and Robins (1999) have shown how the major Internet service providers' search for exclusive content has led them into alliances with already existing producers of media content (**Case study 3.2**). They argue that the UK market for subscription-based content is dominated by six corporations: AOL, CompuServe, Microsoft, News International, Virgin and British Telecom (Stokes and Reading 1999: 119–120). Similarly, the costs of producing and updating a financially viable website or CD-ROM are of a scale comparable to existing media, the same 'high costs of the first copy' still apply as does the cost of marketing. Cornford and Robins show that a CD-ROM will cost around £500,000 to produce and will have to sell 50–60,000 units to recover the initial costs. They also quote from *The Economist* that it costs over $3m per year to maintain a high profile commercial website. In other words, the level of capitalisation required to sustain production in the fields of new media is just as high as it was for the existing media. Hence the fact that the emergent dominant players in the field of new media are either extensions of existing media concerns or are in alliance with existing content providers.

CASE STUDY 3.2 Time-Warner and aol: the world's biggest merger (so far)

In January 2001, the Federal Communications Commission (FCC) put their seal of approval on the marriage of Time-Warner and AOL (TWOL) – convergence had arrived. This new business organisation brought together the media content provider, rooted in cinema and print, with the Internet Service Provider. The Holy Grail of the digital entertainment revolution. The £130 billion value of this new company represented the ownership of newspapers, magazines, cinema, video distribution, television networks, programme makers, and cable companies allied to the subscription model of interactive connection. You can log on to the TWOL connection, download the cinema details at the TWOL megaplex, and go to watch a TWOL-produced film. You might have seen the trailer on the TWOL Cinema channel, provided over your TWOL Digital Cable, and you have ordered the tickets for collection via the interactive link. Of course, you might just have driven there and paid cash for your ticket. There is no inevitability that you will be embroiled in the web of TWOL, and if you are, so what?

Far from the intense freedom of the digital world, the corporate economy increases concentration, and the one claimed benefit of competition – diversity of provision – disappears and is replaced by homogeneous products from a narrow range of suppliers. In the absence of competition, the responsibility for the preservation of access to the culture of society has to be guaranteed by the state, in this case the FCC in the US and The European Commission. The state organisations were concerned that the new organisation would, through its ownership of cables, prevent other providers offering alternative services. They were also concerned that the 25 million subscribers to AOL would be so locked into particular software for music and video that no one else would be able to distribute their material. The Disney Corporation used just this comparison in its attempts to scupper the deal before the FCC hearings. In the end, TWOL demonstrated their commitment to open access to the 12.6 million households connected to cable by signing a deal with an independent by the name of Imius.

In all of the to-ing and fro-ing, the role of the state as regulator of communications media had undergone an important change. The FCC had no interest in the regulation of the content to be provided within the new arrangements. The strictures about bad language, sex and violence that apply to TV and other media played no role in the discussion. That argument had been settled with the demise of the Communications Decency Bill in 1999. The net is free. Instead, the state and its agencies had reverted to the role of holding the ring for the competing commercial bodies involved in commercial production. The regulatory bodies do have real powers to control the structure of the media industry. For example, music lovers have their favourite bands provided by just five organisations: Time-Warner, EMI, Sony, Bertelsmann and Universal. The European Commission, when it refused to approve the merger of Time-Warner and EMI, prevented 90 per cent of the music industry ending up as the property of just four companies. Permission was refused despite the claims of the companies that their inability to dominate the Internet would preserve competition.

See **Case Study** 3.1, which shows that Bertelsmann is already actively interested in music distribution over the net

The dominance of the market in cultural commodities that will be enjoyed by TWOL and its merged successor will not allow it to escape from the particularities of cultural production. The difficulties in predicting aesthetic choices, the expense of prototyping and the need to create and maintain markets will all remain.

One of the buzzwords of the new media explosion has been 'convergence' – the idea that at some point the digital delivery of media would all come together. Television, online video delivery, Internet communications and telecommunications combined in one mobile phone-type delivery. In reality, the form of convergence has taken place first in the commercial organisations integral to the creation of cultural commodities.

Why does it matter if Time-Warner-AOL dominate the market in new media? They will still have to deliver material that people will buy, the services will have to be effective, and with the de facto implementation of standards then access is made easier. It is at this point that the moral questions, the concerns about democracy, power and ownership have to be aired. In a utopian moment common to the advent of new technologies, the early days of the Internet promised the return to public spaces. Regulation of the airwaves and the maintenance of the cultural mores by the state agency have been replaced by the straightforward conception that what the market provides and the consumer chooses is sufficient regulation. Why regulate the messages of the media if the biggest message, the market is king, is best expressed by putting it into practice?

The only basis, therefore, for the regulation of the merger of AOL and TW is its overall impact on the general health of the economic system, as interpreted by the proponents of the free market. Ironically, the tendency of the free market is to foster monopoly, particularly where there are, as in the media industry, considerable advantages in concentrated ownership.

Sources: HYPERLINK http://www.redherring.com
www.ft.com

CASE STUDY 3.3   Microsoft, and how to dominate the net from behind

It is hard to believe that the guru of the personal computer entirely failed to appreciate the impact of the Internet. As late as 1997 there were only four Internet connections inside the Redmond headquarters of Bill Gates's corporation. In just three years Microsoft's web browser, Internet Explorer, had become the preferred gateway to the net. The competition, and earlier example, the Netscape browser had become the property of AOL, itself part of the largest newly merged corporation in the world, Time-Warner-AOL. When the US State intervened in 1999 it opened a window on the working practices of the world's dominant software provider of operating systems. With echoes of the cases against Bell, IBM and the industrial magnates of the early years of American capitalism, the US Department of Justice accused the company of using its position to dominate the Internet in a way that would prevent further development of the industry. The State Attorneys who joined the action had no moral problem with the dominance of part of life by corporate commercial interest, indeed why should they? Rather, the fear was that if Microsoft could dominate the Internet by commercial muscle alone then further development of the actual capabilities of computer software could be felt unnecessary and abandoned. Indeed, there is some evidence that Microsoft has actually given up original development (if it ever did it anyway), as evidenced by its acquisition of forty-two different companies in the 12 months to January 2000.

The consequence of Microsoft's dominance of the PC market and its extension into the Internet is that the medium is dominated by the technology of the 1960s, the personal computer itself being an outcome of an earlier period of dynamic economic and social turmoil in the USA. The mouse, the operating system, and applications, all had to be maintained in order to preserve the Microsoft empire, even though the new systems of applets, networked software and distributed resources all point to the need for a second computer revolution. It is the fear of just such a revolution of the type that overthrew IBM that now motivates Bill Gates.

The irony is that there may be something to be said for the preservation of the Microsoft monopoly. It provides a de facto world standard for the interchange of computer files. In June 2000, a Federal Court accepted the arguments of the Department of Justice that the Microsoft Corporation should be broken into two. The order, if carried out, would separate the operating systems from the applications, the integration of which has given Microsoft its dominance of the market. Microsoft's response to the Department of Justice has been twofold: first, to carry on regardless; second to point out that to throw away the corporation's supremacy in the PC industry would be to lose a major chunk of American corporate dominance.

The countervailing pressure is an important one. Just as with Time-Warner-AOL the real concern is that Microsoft, although huge, might be smaller than a sector that could develop if other corporations were allowed to enter the industry. It is in this arena that the US government is prepared to intervene.

Overall, the case of Microsoft and the web browser raises an important issue. Precisely because dominance of the operating systems industry confers a great advantage, production takes place with great economies of scale. Each piece of software will make its costs back across huge markets, thus reducing costs per use. The creation of de facto software standards also makes it much easier to handle data, but Microsoft is one corporation dominated by a small group of people whose interests may not be those of the rest of society. On the other hand, the bundling of Internet Explorer with Windows, motivated by competition with Netscape, created problems of its own. David J. Farber summarised the problem in two parts in his evidence to the *US* v. *Microsoft* case:

> (b) combining applications with an operating system into a single product available only with all functions combined imposes technical inefficiencies for OEMs, other software developers and retail end users, including redundancy, performance degradation of unused software and increased risks of 'bugs'; and
>
> (c) any function provided by an operating system (as distinct from higher level files) that does not satisfy the criteria of simplicity, general applicability and accessibility reduces the efficiency of the operating system environment and applications that use it . . .
>
> Auletta (2001)

In other words the developments made by Microsoft to their software may, if directed towards the preservation of their monopoly, make the software less dependable and more difficult to use.

3.27 CONCLUSION

In this part of the book we have tried to offer an understanding of new media based in its existence as the production of human intention and structural limitations. In other words we have tried to explain that one of the ways of understanding new media, and particularly its networked form, is by considering it as the product of social relations as much as of technological capability. We have also argued that whilst it is possible to identify the major economic narratives that have shaped new media we should be as cautious of an economic as of a technological determinism. To use one of Gibson's cyberpunk epithets, 'The street finds uses for technologies.' We have argued that attention to the history of the Internet, of networks and the way in which they are constructed by commercial interests as much as use, is a particular advantage in understanding them. We also offer the opinion that there is no reason necessarily to abandon long-established methods of understanding media and its use. In fact, we would go further and say that any close-grained understanding of how we experience online communications will be informed by the kind of specific ethnographies of audience use already undertaken within cultural studies. This is partly because of the ways in which new media have penetrated into our lives to become a constitutive part of popular culture. However, in order to understand the continuing operation of boundaries of possibility within the pluralism of online communications we will have continuing recourse to political economy.

BIBLIOGRAPHY

Amin, Samir *Capitalism in the Age of Globalization*, London and Atlantic Highlands, N.J.: Zed Books, 1997

Ang, Ien *Watching Dallas*, London: Methuen, 1985.

Auletta, Ken *World War 3.0: Microsoft and its Enemies*, New York: Profile Books, 2001.

Baker, Andrea 'Cyberspace couples finding romance online then meeting for the first time in real life', *CMC Magazine*, 1 July 1998. http://www.december.com/cmc/mag/1998.

Baran, Nicholas 'Privatisation of telecommunications', in *Capitalism and the Information Age: the political economy of the global communication revolution*, eds Robert McChesney, Ellen Meiksin Wood and John Bellamy Foster. New York: Monthly Review Press, 1998.

Barbrook, R. and Cameron, A. 'The hi-tech gift economy'. www.hrc.wmin.ac.uk.

Barker, Martin *The Video Nasties: freedom and censorship in the media*, London: Pluto, 1984.

Baym, Nancy 'The emergence of online community', in *Cybersociety 2.0*, ed. Steven G. Jobes. Thousand Oaks, Calif.: Sage, 1998.

Bell, Daniel *The Coming of Post Industrial Society*, New York: Basic Books, 1976.

Bettig, R. 'The enclosure of cyberspace', *Critical Studies in Mass Communication* 14 (1997): 138–157.

BFI Industry Tracking Survey, London: BFI, 1999.

Bolter, J. and Grusin, R. *Remediation*, Cambridge, Mass.: MIT, 2000.

Castells, Manuel *The Rise of the Network Society*. Oxford: Blackwell, 1996.

Castells, Manuel *The Internet Galaxy*. Oxford: Oxford University Press, 2000.

Cave, Martin. 'Franchise auctions in network infrastructure industries', in *Report to the OECD Conference on Competition and Regulation in Network Infrastructure Industries*, Budapest, 9–12 May 1995. http://www.oecd.org/daf/clp/non-member_activities/BDPT206.HTM.

Christian Science Monitor. Wednesday, 15 October 1997.

Coriat, Benjamin *L'Atelier et le Robot*, ed. Christian Bourgois, 1990.

Cornford, James and Robins, Kevin. 'New media', in *The Media in Britain*, eds Jane Stokes and Anna Reading. London: Palgrave, 1999.

Cringely, Robert X. *Triumph of the Nerds*, Harmondsworth: Penguin, 1996.

Curran, J. *Media Organisations in Society*, London: Arnold, 2000.

Danet, Brenda 'Text as mask: gender, play and performance on the internet', in *Cybersociety 2.0*, ed. Steven G. Jones. Thousand Oaks, Calif.: Sage, 1998.

Davis, Jim, Hirschl, Thomas and Stack, Michael *Cutting Edge Technology, Information, Capitalism and Social Revolution*, London: Verso, 1997.

Dean, Jodi. 'Webs of conspiracy', in *The World Wide Web and Contemporary Cultural Theory*, ed. A. Herman and T. Swiss. London: Routledge, 2000.

Department for Culture Media and Sport. *The Report of the Creative Industries Task Force Inquiry into Television Exports*, London: 2000. http://www.culture.gov.uk/pdf/dcmstv.pdf.

Dibbell, Julian: *Independent On Sunday: Extract from My Tiny Life: crime and passion in a virtual world*, 24 January 1999: 14–24 (Published by Fourth Estate, London, 1999.)

Dickinson, R., Linne, O. and Harindrinath, R. eds. *Approaches to Audiences*, London: Arnold, 1998.

Dovey, Jon ed. *Fractal Dreams*, London: Lawrence and Wishart, 1996.

Electronic Freedom Foundation. http://www.eff.org/pub/Censorship/Exon_bill/.

Facer, K.L., Furlong, V.J., Sutherland, R.J. and Furlong, R. 'Home is where the hardware is: young people, the domestic environment and access to new technologies', in *Children, Technology and Culture*, eds I. Hutchby and J. Moran Ellis. London: Routledge/Falmer, 2000.

Farber, David J. http://www.usdoj.gov/atr/cases/f2000/2059.htm

Featherstone, M. ed. *Global Culture: nationalism, globalization and modernity*, London: Sage, 1990.

Financial Times. http://www.ft.com.

Gaines, Jane M. *Contested Cultures: the image, the voice and the law*, Chapel Hill: University of North Carolina Press, 1991.

Garnham, Nicholas. *Capitalism and Communication: Global Culture and the Economics of Information*, ed. F. Inglis. London: Sage, 1990.

Garnham, Nicholas. 'The media and the public sphere', in *Habermas and the Public Sphere*, ed. Craig Calhoun. London: MIT, 1992.

Garnham, Nicholas 'Political economy and the practices of cultural studies', in *Cultural Studies in Question*, eds Marjorie Ferguson and Peter Golding. London: Sage, 1997.

Garnham, Nicholas 'Information society as theory or ideology: a critical perspective on technology, education and employment in the information age' ICS 3.2 Summer (2000): Feature article. http://www.infosoc.co.uk/00110/feature.htm

Gates, Bill. *The Road Ahead*, London: Penguin, 1996.

Giddens, A. *The Consequences of Modernity*, Cambridge: Polity Press, 1990.

Goodwin, Pete *Television Under The Tories: broadcasting policy, 1979–1997*, London: BFI, 1998.

Habermas, Jürgen. *The Structural Transformation of the Public Sphere*, Cambridge: Polity Press, 1989.

Hafner, K 'The epic saga of the Well', *Wired*, May 1997.

Hagel, John and Armstrong, Arthur G. *Net Gain*, Watertown, Mass.: Harvard Business School Press, 1997.

Hobsbawm, E.J. *Industry and Empire*, London: Pelican, 1987.

ILO. *Globalizing Europe. Decent Work in the Information Economy*, Geneva: International Labour Organisation, 2000.

Jameson, Fredric *Post Modernism or the Cultural Logic of Late Capitalism*, London: Verso, 1991.

Jenkins, H. *Textual Poachers: television fans and participatory culture*, London: Routledge, 1992.

Jensen, Jens F. 'Interactivity – tracking a new concept in media and communication studies', in *Computer Media and Communication*, ed. Paul Mayer. Oxford: Oxford University Press, 1999.

Jones, Quentin. 'Virtual communities, virtual settlements and cyber-archeology: a theoretical outline': www.ascusc.org/jcmc/vol3/issue3/jones.html

Jones, Steven, G. ed. *Cybersociety*, Thousand Oaks, Calif.: 1994.

Jones, Steven, G. ed. *Cybersociety*, Thousand Oaks, Calif.: 1998.

Jones, Steven G. 'The bias of the web', in *The World Wide Web and Contemporary Cultural Theory*, eds A. Herman and T. Swiss. London: Routledge, 2000.

Kapoor, Mitch 'Where is the digital highway really heading?', *Wired*, August 1993.

Kellner, Douglas 'Techno-politics, new technologies, and the new public spheres', in *Illuminations*, January 2001. http://www.uta/edu/huma/illuminations/kell32.htm

Kendall, Lori 'MUDder? I Hardly Know 'er! Adventures of a feminist MUDder' in *Wired Women: gender and new realities in cyberspace*, eds L. Cherny and E.R Weise. Washington, D.C.: Seal Press, 1996, pp. 207–223.

Kramarae, Cheris 'Feminist fictions of future technology', in *Cybersociety 2.0*, ed. Steven G. Jones. Thousand Oaks, Calif.: Sage, 1998.

McChesney, Robert W., Wood, Ellen Meiksins, Foster, John Bellamy eds *Capitalism and the Information Age: the political economy of the global communication revolution*, New York: Monthly Review Press, 1998.

McLaughlin, Margaret L., Osborne, Kerry K. and Smith, Christine, B. 'Standards of conduct on Usenet' in *Cybersociety*, ed. Steven G. Jobes. Thousand Oaks, Calif.: Sage, 1995.

McRae, S. 'Coming apart at the seams: sex text and the virtual body', in *Wired Women: gender and new realities in cyberspace*, eds L. Cherny and E.R. Weise. Washington, D.C.: Seal Press, 1996, pp. 242–264.

Massey, Doreen 'A global sense of place', in *Studying Culture – an introductory reader*, eds Gray, A. and McGuigan, J.. London: Arnold, 1993.

Mayer, Paul *Computer Media and Communication*, Oxford: Oxford University Press, 1999.

Meiskins, E. Wood 'Modernity, postmodernity or capitalism', in *Capitalism and the Information Age*, R. McChesney et al. New York: Monthly Review Press, 1998.

Morley, David *The Nationwide Audience*, London: BFI, 1980.

Moulthrop, Stuart 'Error 404 doubting the web' in *The World Wide Web and Contemporary Cultural Theory* eds A. Herman and T. Swiss. London: Routledge, 2000.

Murdock, Graham 'Base notes: the conditions of cultural practice', in *Cultural Studies in Question*, eds Marjorie Ferguson and Peter Golding. London: Sage, 1997.

Poster, Mark 'Cyberdemocracy: the internet and the public sphere' in *Virtual Politics*, ed. David Holmes. Thousand Oaks, Calif.: Sage, 1997.

President William J. Clinton and Vice-President Albert Gore, Jr. *A Framework For Global Electronic Commerce*, Washington, D.C., 1994.

Rafaeli, S. 'Interactivity from media to communication', in *Annual Review of Communication Research Vol. 16 Advancing Communication Science*, eds R. Hawkins J. Wiemann and S. Pirgree (1988): 110–34.

Rheingold, H. *The Virtual Community – homesteading on the virtual frontier*, London: Secker and Warburg, 1993.

Rheingold, H, *Cyberhood vs Neighbourhood*, UTNE Reader, March–April 1995.

Ritzer, Martin *The McDonaldization of Society*. New York: Sage, 2000.

Robins, Kevin. 'Cyberspace and the world we live', in *Fractal Dreams*, ed. J Dovey. London: Lawrence and Wishart, 1996.

Roszak, Theodore. *The Cult of Information*, Cambridge: Lutterworth Press, 1986.

Schiller, Herb *Culture Inc.: The Corporate Take-over of Cultural Expression*, New York, Oxford University Press, 1989.

Senft, Theresa 'Baud girls and cargo cults', in *The World Wide Web and Contemporary Cultural Theory*, eds A. Herman and T. Swiss. London: Routledge, 2000.

Shultz, Tanjev 'Mass media and the concept of interactivity: an exploratory study of online forums and reader email', *Media, Culture and Society* 22 (2000): 205–221.

Smith, M. 'Voices from the Well', 1992. http://netscan.sscnet.ucla.edu/csoc/papers.

Smythe, Dallas *Dependency Road, Communications, Capitalism Consciousness and Canada*, Norwood: Ablex Publishing, 1981.

Stokes, J. and Reading, A. (eds), *The Media in Britain: current dabates and developments*, London: Palgrave, 1999.

Stone, Allucquere Rosanne *The War of Desire and Technology at the Close of the Mechanical Age*, Boston, Mass.: MIT Press, 1995.

Touraine, Alain *La Société Post Industrielle*, Paris: Denoel, 1969.

Tulloch, J. *Watching Television Audiences: cultural theory and methods*, London: Arnold, 2000.

Tulloch, J. and Alvarado, M. *Doctor Who: the unfolding text*, Basingstoke: Palgrave, 1983.

Turkle, Sherry *Life on the Screen*, London: Weidenfeld and Nicolson, 1996a.

Turkle, Sherry 'Constructions and reconstructions of the self in virtual reality', in *Electronic Culture: Technology and Visual Representation Aperture*, ed. T. Druckery. Aperture: New York, 1996b.

US Department of Justice. hyperlink http://www.usdoj.gov/atr/cases/ms_index.htm

Williams, Raymond *Television, Technology and Cultural Forms*, London: Fontana, 1974.

Williams, Raymond *Problems in Materialism and Culture*, London: Verso, 1980.

Williams, Raymond *The Politics of Modernism*, London: Verso, 1989.

World Bank Data See Table 5.11 'The Information Age'.
http://www.worldbank.org/data/wdi2000/pdfs/tab5_11.pdf

4 NEW MEDIA IN EVERYDAY LIFE

EVERYDAY LIFE IN CYBERSPACE/DOMESTIC SHAPING OF NEW MEDIA/NEW MEDIA,
IDENTITY AND THE EVERYDAY/GAMEPLAY

4.1 EVERYDAY LIFE IN CYBERSPACE

4.1.1 Cyberspace in everyday life: the material and the virtual

At first glance the terms 'everyday life' and 'cyberspace' seem distinct, even irreconcilable concepts. The former implies the mundane and quotidian, the routine and ordinary – all the features of daily existence from which the latter, in both its fictional and actual forms, promises to liberate us. Cyberspace, then, is disembodied and exhilarating – promising the new: new worlds, new frontiers, new identities. Virtual reality has been seen as a new world in direct opposition to the old world of everyday life, of individuals socially and geographically located, a world in which social problems and urban decay are finally

See 1.2.5 Virtuality, 1.2.7 Cyberspace, 3.5 Networks and communities

overwhelming. In its stead we can find a new kind of life and society online, a democratic public sphere unencumbered by the stultifying routines and alienating hierarchies of the real world.

Discussions of virtuality frequently juxtapose the everyday and ordinary with the revolutionary and unsettling. The abstract realm of cyberspace in cyberpunk fiction is accessed from decaying, grimy, hyper-material streets and houses. A recent BBC television programme on predictions for the future of computers presented two visions: one a simulated city of a million people in a videogame, the other of the miniaturisation of digital technology to the point at which computers become like confetti, scattered and near invisible, saturating the world. Though very different on one level, each presents an everyday environment inseparable from, and coextensive with, digital technology – a dream of virtual reality or a material world in which we breathe in technology with the air.

New media are embedded in everyday life and its domestic and urban environments with CCTV, spectacular advertising and new forms of

4.1 The Sims: everyday life as cyberspace. © 2002 Electronic Arts Inc. All rights reserved.

mobile communication all permeating the mundane activities of banking, shopping, entertainment. Blinking LEDs, synthesised tunes and slowly panning cameras are the visual and audible indication of the intangible and tangled network of cables, signals and fibre optics that connect and mediate buildings and people, institutions and homes, towns and continents, bodies and machines. Our awareness of them flickers between excitement (or anxiety) at the news of new devices and networks, and familiarity as some become part of the fabric of daily life and fall below the horizon of the new and exciting.

4.1.2 Why everyday life?

For accounts of everyday life in the study of media and media technologies, see Silverstone (1994) and Mackay (1997). See also Highmore (2001)

The concept of everyday life is central to the study of culture and media, but is often absent from accounts of new media technologies. By everyday life we mean the family relationships, routines, cultural practices and spaces through which people make sense of the world. On the one hand, then, everyday life is the site in which the popular meanings and uses of new media are negotiated and played out. On the other hand, nearly all of the discussions of new media, to a greater or lesser degree, make claims that they transform, or will soon transform (or transcend), day-to-day life, its spatio-temporal limits, its restrictions and power structures. The nature of this transformation is contentious: for some observers new media offer new creativities and possibilities, for others they reinforce and extend existing social constraints and power relationships.

Everyday life is important as:

- the market for which companies develop consumer hardware and software;

- the site of practices and relationships in which sense is made of new media;

- the focal point of an interlocking set of convergences of consumer, media, educational and entertainment technologies and markets;

- the social conditions which are, to a greater or lesser degree, transformed by the use and consumption of new media;

- the absent or underplayed term in utopian visions of new knowledges and shifting identities in cyberspace – as alienation and routine to the connectivity and creativity emerging in Internet communication media;

- the site of consumption of mediated popular culture, not least the images and dramas from comics, television and video that constitute a commercial technological imaginary.

Emphasising everyday life in the study of media technologies and their uses foregrounds the following key issues:

- Media technologies and forms do not spring from a vacuum, they are the products of already existing social and economic structures and forces.

- It follows that the meanings and uses of new media are not fixed in advance by inventors and producers, but negotiated or struggled over by a number of agents, including governments, educationalists, retailers and consumers.

- However innovative, new media technologies have to find their place within more stable and established social structures (e.g. the family) and environments often already characterised by existing media.

• Practices of consumption are of crucial significance; that is, the day to day, local, choices, relationships and politics of individuals, families and other groups are integral not only to the commercial success of new media but also to the ways in which new media are used, to what they mean.

4.1.3 Why cyberspace?

Cyberspace is a rather loose buzzword, but it is persistent. We are using it here in its broadest sense, the sense we have of a space behind the monitor screen, or the network 'in' which we communicate with distant others or from which we receive images, information and services, as opposed to the material space of homes, libraries, streets from which we 'enter' these spaces.

'We inhabit cyberspace when we feel ourselves moving through the interface into a relatively independent world with its own dimensions and rules. The more we habituate ourselves to an interface, the more we live in cyberspace' (Michael Heim, quoted in Bromberg 1996: 144–145). For Heim, cyberspace offers us new dimensions to live in, autonomous from the time and space of already existing life. However, as numerous advertisements for cable television and Internet services depicting awestruck consumers being sucked into their television or computer screens show, dreams of stepping into the interface – of a literally unmediated experience of information and communication – are as evident in consumerist discourses as in cyberculture. In section **2.6** we looked in detail at the persistent notion of stepping through the screens or windows of visual media, a concept that characterises much comment on virtual reality. Here this vision is presented on the domestic scale, with consumers, like Alice, reaching through glass into other realms, the time and space of their living rooms dissolving.

2.6 Immersive virtual reality

In their ethnographic study of Internet use in Trinidad, Daniel Miller and Don Slater question these assumptions of the virtual and the everyday or material as distinct realms. They argue that the Internet *cannot* be explained as cyberspace, as 'a kind of placeless place' (Miller and Slater 2000: 4). Indeed we can only make sense of it as it is encountered in concrete places and through specific practices. For the individuals, families and groups studied, Internet media such as email and websites are experienced not as virtual but as 'concrete and mundane enactments of belonging'. Just as new media in this case were not experienced as places apart from 'real life', so too the changes brought about through the interaction of new media and Trinidadian culture, whilst significant, were not experienced as revolutionary transformation but as continuous, with already

4.2 Telewest brochure. Courtesy of Telewest.

For thorough discussions of virtual
reality technologies and the
concept of 'the virtual', see 1.2.5
Virtuality, 2.6 Immersive VR and
5.4.2 Cybernetics and the virtual

existing social structures and senses of identity. Indeed the authors argue that new media quickly cease to represent exciting new futures and are incorporated into the fabric of everyday experience.

This is not to argue that there is nothing new or revolutionary in the mediations of the Internet and everyday life (or that the widespread sense of 'space' within new media is false). Rather, it is to suggest that any progressive understanding of the possibilities of new media in everyday life is only possible by rejecting a notion of 'a self-enclosed cyberian apartness' (Miller and Slater 2000: 5). We could instead think of a productive tension between the places and practices of new media: 'these spaces are important as part of everyday life, not apart from it' (Miller and Slater 2000: 7).

5   CYBERCULTURE: TECHNOLOGY,
NATURE AND CULTURE

However, before we throw the overheated term 'cyberspace' out, we should be sure there isn't a baby in the bath water. Many of the issues around new media and everyday life examined in this section of the book can be addressed through a critical reading of 'cyberspace'. The prefix 'cyber-', referring to the science of cybernetics, is significant (as will be argued in **Part 5**) for the analysis of the consumption of new media as media *technologies*. The emphasis of the term 'cyberspace' on the spatial characteristics, metaphors and imagery in new media resonates throughout the diverse theoretical approaches to new media consumption and use, as well as the language of everyday Internet use, in which web browsers invite us to be navigators or explorers. The term originated in popular culture, coined by William Gibson in his science fiction novel *Neuromancer*. The influence of popular culture, in particular the science fiction genre cyberpunk, runs like a seam throughout theoretical accounts of new media.

This part of the book, then, will address how all these 'spaces' and networks: the home, the Internet, the simulated spaces of videogames, the 'virtual space' of networked communication, intersect in our day-to-day experiences and relationships with new media.

4.1.4 Key questions

This part of the book will raise a number of questions about the relationships between new media, popular culture and everyday life:

- What do new media mean in everyday practices: are they instrumental technologies or tools to be used, media to be consumed or toys to play with?

- In what ways are new media absorbed into the space, time and dynamics of everyday life? How are they understood?

- Do new media transform everyday life?

- Profound claims are made for the transformation of the self, identity, subjectivity in new media spaces – who might a mediated or technologised subject be when he or she is at home?

- What happens to dreams of cyberspace when computers and networks are marketed, commodified and popularised as consumer goods and media?

- To what extent has the popular reception and theoretical study of new media been shaped by the texts and practices of commercial popular culture?

- How do we address these questions? How do we make sense of audiences of interactive media? How do we conduct ethnography of digital media?

4.2 THE DOMESTIC SHAPING OF NEW MEDIA

4.2.1 Telecommuting from the smart house

The 'smart home' gives householders control over their home environment. On the way home from the airport you call up a program on your laptop and, via a modem and mobile phone, you can switch on lights, disable your security alarm, draw the curtains, set a CD to play as you arrive, select the level of heating in different rooms, and even run a bath so that it is ready when you get in (Sykes 1998).

    The 'smart home' is only the latest manifestation of a long-established tradition of imagining an everyday existence transformed by new technologies. Today the Internet and mobile telephony extends earlier dreams of computer-controlled central heating, in turn derived from the wall-sized televisions and personal helicopters of the 1950s techno-consumerist optimism. Today's smart house reflects contemporary excitement around Internet connectivity, predictions of animate or 'intelligent' domestic appliances, and fears of crime and personal safety. Nicholas Negroponte, the MIT futurologist and *Wired* columnist, predicts a future in which computers vanish from view, but permeate the very matter of domestic life:

> computers as we know them will . . . disappear into things that are first and foremost something else: smart nails, self-cleaning shirts, driverless cars, therapeutic Barbie dolls, intelligent doorknobs . . . computers will be a sweeping yet invisible part of our everyday lives: we'll live in them, wear them, even eat them.

> (Negroponte 1998)

The point here is not whether such predictions will come true, but what they tell us about our attitudes to technology in general, and new media in particular, in everyday life. The smart home is also commercial speculation – the particular version mentioned above is a prototype developed by the energy utility, Scottish Power, and is calculated to exploit the commercial possibilities of both UK energy market deregulation and US e-commerce (the article was written before the 'dotcom bubble' of the late 1990s burst (**3.25**)). Thus these predictions are not mere fantasies: they may be designed to generate a general excitement rather than widely available products, but they are shaped by producers' commercial strategies and in turn shape consumer expectations and attitudes. In its always yet-to-be-realised perfection, the smart house is just one factor among many shaping the uses and meanings of domestic technology.

    Critiques of technological determinism frequently refer to the domestic consumption of technologies as a zone where the uses and meanings assumed by any particular device's producers are adapted, appropriated and fought over (MacKenzie & Wajcman 1999; Silverstone and Hirsch 1992). In these terms the smart house represents not a perfect blueprint for future living but a commercial technological imaginary of domestic control, comfort and security. It also becomes clear that whatever changes such technological developments make to the everyday life of their individual consumers, these are not blueprints for fundamental social change. A common set of assumptions underlies the smart home, its precursors since the 1950s, and to some extent 'ubiquitous computing'. These assumptions are that technology and media developments in everyday life will be primarily aimed at and experienced in the home. This home, beyond its steady progress towards full cybernetic status, will remain largely unchanged in social, economic and

Key texts: Donald and MacKenzie, Judy Wajcman (eds) *The Social Shaping of Technology: how the refrigerator got its hum,* Buckingham: Open University Press, 1999; Roger Silverstone and Eric Hirsch *Consuming Technologies – media and information in domestic spaces,* London, Routledge, 1992, pp. 67–81

See also 3.16 The social form of new media

This is sometimes referred to as ubiquitous computing

3.25 Information as commodity

See 3.17 New media and post-industrial economies and 3.18 The development of the new economy

See for example: http://www.orange.co.uk/ orangeathome/intro.html and http://www.smart-house.net/index.shtml

Negroponte (1995) and
www.media.mit.edu/people/
nicholas/ See also Fidler (1997:
168–175) for a remarkable example
of a media theorist's fantasies of
techno-bourgeois private life

The post-web Internet

cultural terms. Technological change will not transform family relationships, the relationship of the family to its broader social context, and it certainly will not threaten the home as a privileged site for the consumption of commercial goods and services. For example, many of Negroponte's predictions for new media in everyday life, from possible future services such as intelligent digital 'butlers' selecting and filtering Internet information according to the individual's interests and taste, to a 'newspaper' version of the same concept: 'The Daily Me', are predicated on a well-established ideal of the individual consumer.

These visions of a digital consumerism, with at least some sensitivity to existing ways of life and daily routines, appear more grounded than those premissed on the notion of cyberspace as a distinct and autonomous realm, but are in fact closely linked. Both approaches, for example, assume an ideal of the empowered individual. Each underplays the material role of economic relations in their new media world – cyberspace, because it leaves all such mundane matters behind, and digital consumerism because consumer capitalism itself has become a 'second nature', a perfect market eco-system (Kelly 1995; Dyson 1997). Both positions are also linked in the pages of *Wired* and that magazine's faith that the contradictions and iniquities of the modern world are being overcome through the virtuous alliance of free market economics and digital technology.

We are, for reasons of focus,
primarily studying everyday life as
located in the home, though
evidently the impact of new
media on working environments
and practices is equally important.
The development of public access
to the Internet through cybercafés
and libraries *does* represent an
alternative to domestic new media
consumption

BOX 4.1:   Telecommuters and digital artisans

The notion of 'telecommuting' is an example of a new home-based practices that can be seen either as an extension of the entrenchment of the domestication and privatisation of new media technologies and their use, or as offering new individual and social freedoms. Facilitated by information and communication technologies and networks, telecommuting means working exclusively or predominantly from home whilst connected to the office or clients via a PC and modem.

Not only can we work from home, it is claimed, we can do new kinds of work. PCs allow individuals to perform the roles of whole chains of production – through desktop publishing software for example. Specialised expertise and centralised sites of production disperse to networked nodes of domestic activity. Any distinction between media production and creative consumption becomes harder to identify in interactive media engagement, and new kinds of media products such as MP3 and shareware.

This merging of office and home, work and leisure, public and private is sometimes seen as part of a broader shift away from clear distinctions between cultural consumption and production facilitated by developments in digital technology: 'New ICTs such as the Internet (or the camcorder) challenge the authority of the producer, democratise production capability, and empower consumers' (Mackay 1997: 292). Thus it is not only consumer technology manufacturers and *Wired* columnists who celebrate this apparent shift. It is also evident in (more or less) oppositional cultural politics. The do-it-yourself approach of post-punk media culture, for example, has found on the Internet new possibilities for its cottage industries of small record labels, fanzine production, independent film-making, art practice, etc.

In an essay which begins with a critique of *Wired* digital neo-liberalism, Richard Barbrook celebrates an Internet DIY cultural economy, driven by 'digital artisans':

As the history of the Net demonstrates, hacking, piracy, shareware and open architecture systems all helped to overcome the limitations of both state and commercial interests . . . one of the major attractions of the Net for its users is that it is not tightly controlled by any major public or private bureaucracy. Already, a minority of the population can use the Net to inform, educate and play together outside both the state and the market . . . Most current Net users don't simply download other people's products. They also want to express themselves through their own websites or within online conferences. Unlike traditional media, the Net is not just a spectacle for passive consumption but also a participatory activity.

(Barbrook 1997)

However, other critics of consumer capitalism see the effects of digital media quite differently. For Kevin Robins and Frank Webster the dispersed production of telecommuting and new forms of digital media participation do not overcome the limits of state and commerce, but reinforce and extend them. As digital technology spreads out from the workplace, they argue, the 'electronic home' can be seen as embedded in 'the increasing technological mediation of everyday life'. Information technology for Robins and Webster is neither progressive nor neutral. Far from being open to appropriation by ordinary people these technologies are shaped by the corporate and bureaucratic systems that develop them, and, in turn, through their dissemination they colonise everyday life:

The category of 'everyday life' . . . can help us to see the pervasive and intrusive nature of the 'information revolution'. For it points to the ways in which the rhythm, texture, and experience of social life – the very segmentation of time and space – are being transformed and informed by capital. And, furthermore, it allows us to see how relations of power penetrate and infuse the social body.

(Robins and Webster 1988)

We may wish to question the glum conclusions drawn by Robins and Webster, but their analysis is invaluable. We would argue that any attempt to understand the place of, and possibilities for, new media within everyday life requires consideration of the fundamental connections between 'smart houses', cable television, and so on, at the local level, and social, economic and technological change at the global level. Not least, new media devices marketed for home consumption, and the images and messages they carry, are the product of, and rationale for, convergences of entertainment and information/ communications corporations.

See 3.25 Information as commodity

4.2.2 Selling the black box

1.5.3 The discursive construction of new media

3.16 The social form of new media

By popular new media we mean those technologies such as PCs, video games, certain Internet media – technologies commercially available and relatively accessible – as opposed to, for example, the more exclusive experience of immersive VR. The division between old and new popular media is a fluid one. Manufacturers, retailers and advertisers will draw on the atmosphere of innovation and excitement that attends technological change in promoting a new product, yet may simultaneously emphasise the ways in which it will enhance established domestic life and existing media consumption practices. See Miles *et al.* (1992) and Boddy (1999)

However, in a consumer economy, with its drive for constant upgrades, no black box is likely to remain closed for long. Even the relatively long-established media technology of television is undergoing transformation, from cable and satellite to digital television and computer-based personal video recorders

However we theorise the 'newness' and promise of new media, we cannot escape the fact that in many of their popular forms they are profoundly enmeshed in existing economic and cultural contexts. The innovations of DVD, for example, have (at the time of writing at least) been mainly limited to facilitating a convergence of existing 'old' and 'new' media: video viewing, home PCs, video game consoles and hi-fi systems. Whilst more exciting uses may well develop for the medium, it is clear that the innovations of DVD are those of the market: to encourage consumers to invest in new domestic entertainment systems and to begin new collections of 'software' (whether feature films or video games). Whatever else they may be, popular new media are commodities.

Just as new technologies do not spring fully formed from the research lab, their uses and effects pre-programmed, so too we should avoid assuming that commodities (whether technological or not) are similarly imposed on consumers, their meanings fully determined by their manufacturers. Designing and marketing a new consumer technology is an anxious process. Any particular new device may well find that the functions and uses it offers are not those desired by consumers. Moreover, these artefacts may be technological, but as commodities their meanings are not limited to the instrumental: 'technologies, far from being merely technical, are at once material and symbolic' (Bingham *et al.* 1999: 656). They enter environments full of existing media technologies, some of which they replace; others they complement or compete with. Of course, they may well be commercially unsuccessful.

Consumer electronics producers refer to 'black boxes', a particular configuration of entertainment and/or information technologies packaged as a single, commercially successful product. The term is developed critically in theories of the sociology of technology. Cynthia Cockburn, drawing on the work in this field of John Law and Bruno Latour, points out that no technological artefact (whether destined for domestic consumption or not) is ever a coherent, discrete device, but always a more or less arbitrary (and temporary) closure on a diverse field of uses, technologies and meanings. This closure is effected by a network of agents (in the case of popular new media this network might include producers, consumers, retailers, software publishers, legal and governmental agencies):

> To build a 'black box', whether this is a theory or a machine, it is necessary to enrol others so that they believe it, take it up, spread it. The control of the builder is therefore seldom absolute. The new allies shape the idea or the artefact to their own will – they do not so much transmit as translate it.

> (Cockburn 1992: 34)

BOX 4.2:   The black X-Box

4.3 X-box. Courtesy of Microsoft.

At the time of writing Microsoft is preparing to enter the domestic video game console market. The initial success of their machine (in this case literally a black box) will depend as much on the nuances of its marketing strategy as on the console's technical specifications and the quality of its games. Microsoft's target audience is 'serious' gamers, the 18–24-year-old age group that now dominates the video game market. Learning from Sony's tremendously successful marketing strategies for its Playstation console in the 1990s, Microsoft is battling against its staid image. The cosmetic design of the console, then, is very important, and is being modelled on hi-fi components: 'People are really into the design, and they've said they weren't expecting something as cool or as sleek from Microsoft, and that they thought it captured the enthusiasm and excitement behind gaming' (Edge 2001: 71). One strategy for convincing sceptical consumers of Microsoft's commitment to serious gameplayinging is to not allow the X-Box to be used as a DVD player for films (distinguishing it from other new video game consoles such as the Playstation 2). Thus the drive toward producing a multifunctional consumer entertainment system, and a potential selling point, is balanced against the need to match the device's symbolic status to the attitudes and preferences of the target audience.

So, it is not only the choice of particular technical features included in any new black box device that determines its commercial success; its symbolic status is also crucial. William Boddy argues that advertisers, retailers and producers construct elaborate, but instrumental, fantasies around new media. 'Every electronic media product launch or network debut carries with it an implicit fantasy scenario of its domestic consumption, a polemical ontology of its medium, and an ideological rationale for its social function' (Boddy 1999).

The development of the X-Box demonstrates that the creation of a marketable symbolic status of any new product is by no means an exact science. It is an appeal to an unpredictable market, with no guarantees of success. This market is the domestic consumer. We will now address the role that consumers might play in the shaping of popular new media technologies.

4.2.3 Consuming new media

In the study of media and culture in modern everyday life, the concept of consumption is key. As we will see, it is a contested term: seen variously as the primary cultural practice in a passive, greedy consumer society, or as a potentially rich and creative way of making sense of individual identity in a complex world. Within the diverse debates around new media the concept of consumption may be configured differently, ignored or substituted by terms with different connotations. We will now set out the key discursive positions on the everyday consumption of media technologies. This grouping of discourses is far from definitive, and each brackets together some quite divergent positions, but they do give an indication of the debates and issues.

CYBERCULTURE

Key texts referred to in this part of the book include: Poster (1995a), Stone (1995), Haraway (1990), Hayles (1999). See 5.4 Theories of cyberculture

This term brackets together a relatively diverse range of theoretical approaches to new cultural technologies. They share a premiss that technology, especially computer technology, is instrumental in profound transformations in contemporary culture and beyond – from the individual's sense of self to new, intimate relationships between the human and the technological. The cybercultural tone is by and large optimistic about this change, and can fall into utopian assumptions about the emancipatory possibilities of digital media such as virtual reality and certain Internet media.

The term 'consumption' itself is rarely used in this context, indeed its absence tells us something of cyberculture's constitution of digital media. In popular celebrations of the 'newness' of new media, consumption is browsing, surfing, using, 'viewsing', not consuming. Digital media and virtual culture are generally to transcend, or render obsolete, mundane questions of commercial interests or already existing practices of media use. Either new relationships with technology – from immersion in cyberspace to the various notions of the cyborg – are so intimate that any sense of 'consuming' technology as a distinct set of devices and media becomes impossible, or 'consumption' as a mode of engaging in culture belongs to the bad 'old' pre-digital media. These electronic media are centralised and authoritarian whereas new information and communication media are interactive and decentralised. The pioneer of personal computing, Ted Nelson, talking about the potential of computer media, hoped that: 'Libertarian ideals of accessibility and excitement might unseat the video narcosis that now sits on our own land like a fog' (Nelson 1982, quoted in Mayer 1999: 128).

Cyberculture discourses may well be informed by progressive politics, however; indeed, cyberspace is seen as a realm in which social divisions based on bodily and material attributes and positions (age, gender, class, race, etc.) can be transcended (**4.3**).

4.3 New media, identity and the everyday

'BUSINESS AS (OR EVEN WORSE THAN) USUAL'

Here the role of economic production in determining the meanings and uses of new technology in everyday life is emphasised. Drawing on a Marxist model of consumption as operating in the sphere of the cultural superstructure, determined and shaped by the economic base of capitalist production, consumer goods and mass media serve primarily to sustain and reproduce the existing economic and social order.

This approach holds that the development, dissemination and consumption of media technologies is instrumental in the commodification and reification of everyday life. Culture is made subservient to the interests of bureaucratic control and capitalist accumulation. Thus this 'left pessimist' position might be superficially similar to cyberculture in its analysis of 'old' broadcast media as hierarchical, stultifying, and serving commercial and state interests. The difference is of course that the pessimists do not see new media as any escape from this controlling logic; there is a fundamental continuity between the dynamics of digital technologies and the electronic and industrial technologies of the nineteenth and twentieth centuries.

If anything, new media are seen as even *worse* than earlier media. On the one hand, the technologies of computer media are seen as lending themselves to the production of spectacular but empty images and narratives – addictive immersion that makes the TV viewing couch potato seem lively – and on the other to new forms of political and commercial surveillance and domination of the time and space of everyday life. For Julian Stallabrass, the new medium of the video or computer game, far from offering new interactive possibilities, instead presents 'an ideal image of the market system'. Computer games' meanings are locked into their code, and consumption only realises their repressive potential:

> In their structure and content, computer games are a capitalist, deeply conservative form of culture, and their political content is prescribed by the options open to democracy under modern capitalism, from games with liberal pretensions to those with quasi-fascist overtones. All of them offer virtual consumption of empty forms in an ideal market.
>
> (Stallabrass 1993: 104)

Computer games master the consumer or player, rather than vice versa, and ultimately 'there is a shadowy ambition behind the concept of the virtual world – to have everyone safely confined in their homes, hooked up to sensory feedback devices in an enclosing, interactive environment which will be a far more powerful tool of social control than television' (Stallabrass 1993: 104).

From this 'business as usual' perspective certain connections between the progressive cyberculture position (see p. 228) and a neo-liberal celebration of digital media become evident. Without an analysis of the persistence of social and economic power in, and through, the everyday consumption of new technologies, any analysis of a new media age would be a delusional and utopian projection of future possibilities into the here and now, eliding or ignoring current power relationships and struggles.

POPULISTS AND POSTMODERNISTS

Most postmodernist theories of the meanings of new media technologies subscribe to the view that it is now consumption and leisure rather than production and work that determine the texture and experiences of everyday life. Consumer culture is now the dominant, if not the only, cultural sphere. Again there are widely divergent versions of this mediated world. Jean Baudrillard, for example, presents a vision of a postmodern society in which the consumption of goods, images, and fashions has become so all-encompassing that not only the economic base, but any sense of an external or determining reality, disappears. In this hyperreal world there is no point of reference

See for example, Kevin Robins, 'Cyberspace and the world we live in', in Dovey (1996), and Robins and Webster (1999). Sometimes referred to as a 'left pessimist' approach, in reference to an earlier critique of culture and cultural technology – that of the Frankfurt School in the 1920s and 1930s (Adorno 1991)

See 1.5.5 The return of the Frankfurt School critique in the popularisation of new media

See 3.16 The social form of new media
3.17 New media and the post-industrial economies
3.25 Information as commodity

See Fiske (1992), McRobbie (1986), Willis (1990)

beyond the commodity, beyond signifying and symbolic practices – any sense of technologies as material or instrumental is lost.

On the other hand, some theorists celebrate the pleasures and freedoms of consumption, of individuals and groups actively constructing their identities through their choices in media and consumer culture. 'Rather than being a passive, secondary, determined activity, consumption . . . is seen increasingly as an activity with its own practices, tempo, significance and determination' (1997: Mackay 3–4).

There is some overlap with cyberculture theory here; indeed, cyberculture is very much rooted in postmodernist ideas. Baudrillard's hyperreal and simulated media world of pure consumption often strikes a chord with those attempting to theorise the apparently non-material, disembodied and textual characteristics of virtual reality, hypertext and the Internet. However, whereas for cyberculture it is specifically the digital age which promises creative mediated pleasure, for postmodernists it is the media/consumer society as a whole.

CULTURAL AND MEDIA STUDIES

Key text: Hugh Mackay, *Consumption and Everyday Life: culture, media and identities,* London: 1997. See also Dewdney and Boyd (1995), duGay *et al.* (1997), Silverstone and Hirsch (1992), Howard (1998)

These discursive categories are not mutually exclusive, and any particular approach to the analysis of new media may entail one or more of them. The academic discipline most thoroughly concerned with theorising everyday cultural consumption is cultural and media studies. Itself characterised by a wide range of conceptual and methodological approaches, it includes its own versions of both postmodernist and left-pessimist discourses, and, when cultural and media technologies are explicitly addressed, the influence of cyberculture becomes evident. However, to generalise, analyses of technology and consumption in cultural and media studies tend to be based on certain premises.

Firstly, digital or computer media technologies tend not to be seen as fundamentally distinct from 'old' electronic media, or even, in some studies, other domestic technologies such as microwaves or freezers. Secondly, there is a general (though not universal) reluctance to privilege either consumption or production. That is to say, the meanings and uses of consumer goods and mediated images are not fixed in their production or in the act of consumption; rather, they are the always contingent product of the relationship between the constraint or 'encoding' of meaning through production and marketing, and the creative activities through which individuals and groups make sense of or 'decode' these meanings.

The divisions between cultural studies and postmodernist positions can be hard to maintain. Whilst downplaying the significance of production, notions of active consumption are not necessarily without an analysis of power. Paul Willis, for example, doesn't see consumption of commodities and popular media as transcending the class system of capitalist production; rather, he is celebrating working-class culture in the face of bourgeois arts funding and privilege. Indeed he argues that working-class youth should be given access to the production of the media images they appropriate (Willis 1990).

Alternatively, the feminist analysis of cultural consumption is critical of arguments that economic structures (and the social formations of class they entail) are all-determining. Addressing the gendered structures of consumption highlights different constellations of power and resistance in the face of commodified (and technologised) everyday life. Feminist debates have also pointed out that the marginalisation of the study of media consumption is related to issues of gender, in which domestic consumption generally and communications media like television in particular have been commonly ascribed to the feminine.

Returning to the study of the technologies of media, then, we can see that a focus on consumption tends to militate against conceptions of technological determinism; it foregrounds the conflicting nature of meaning generation – between production and consumption. Producers' attempts to build in meanings, and articulate them through promotion and advertising, can never result in anything more than 'preferred readings' of their products. They may wish us to see the Betamax video format or laser discs as the future of home entertainment, but they cannot make them mean that. Early **home computers** in the 1980s were often sold as information technologies, but were widely consumed as games machines (**4.4**). All commodities and media, then, are 'texts', 'encoded' products which may be 'decoded' in their consumption to reveal a quite different message (Mackay 1997: 10). So, 'the effects of a technology ... are not determined by its production, its physical form or its capability. Rather than being built into the technology, these depend on how they are consumed' (Mackay 1997: 263).

Issues and questions

We would argue that the study of the consumption of new media in everyday life needs to draw on, and challenge, each of these theoretical categories. Though many of the examples and case studies cited in this part of the book come from cultural and media studies, the study of technology in everyday life raises important questions for this discipline. As we have seen already, the meanings and uses of popular new media such as the web or video games are by no means fixed.

The distinction (or lack of distinction) between 'media' and 'technology' underlies these shifting meanings. The sense of excitement (or anxiety) generated by the introduction of a new media technology (such as the domestic PC) is inseparable from the understanding that this new device or network is technological: it can be used to do things and make changes. Of course its uses, and even its survival as a consumer technology, are not predetermined, and its meanings will be constructed as much around its symbolic status as its actual uses and effects.

The challenge here is to recognise this dynamic of encoding and decoding without losing sight of the unique characteristics and possibilities for popular new media as both media and technologies. To assert that a PC, for example, is a 'text' is a useful metaphor for exploring its multiple meanings in contemporary culture, but it begs certain questions:

- How do we account for the instrumental nature of the PC and its uses in the home (spreadsheets, word processing, etc.)? After all, it is a machine which can be used to do and make things. Are the practices of computer-related media – programming, information processing, communication, games playing, adequately accounted for with these literary metaphors?

- If hardware is a 'text' do we need to distinguish it from software as text? If we accept that a games console, for example, is textual, then surely the game played on it must be seen as a different kind of text?

Media technologies, however 'open', do facilitate or invite certain uses, precisely by their status as machines and tools. The binary of constraint and creativity does not seem fully adequate here. Many commentators discuss the ways in which information and communication technologies facilitate new relationships between people in their local domestic circumstances and global networks (Moores, 1993b; Silverstone and Hirsch

See Cockburn and Furst Dilic (1994), Gray (1992), Green and Adam (2001), McNamee (1998) and Terry (1997)

4.4 Gameplay

1992). Marilyn Strathern sees domestic information and communication technologies not so much as textual but as 'enabling'. In terms which seem to assign some agency to these technologies themselves, she suggests that '[t]hey appear to amplify people's experiences, options, choices. But at the same time they also amplify people's experiences, options and choices in relation to themselves. These media for communication compel people to communicate with them' (Strathern 1992: xi).

BOX 4.3:   The mobile phone: new media as gadgets

Over the past few years the status of the mobile telephone has shifted from that of a rather exclusive communication device to that of ubiquitous status symbol. It has been 'decoded' by a generation of teenagers, who have at once bought into the producers' logic (coveting particular brands for example) and generated new communication practices such as text messaging. Texting, as a function, is built into particular models of mobile phones, but the ways in which it has been adopted and the kinds of message sent represent a genuinely new communication medium in everyday life. The technical limitations of the keypad have proved to be not so much a constraint on texting's potential as facilitating a new vernacular shorthand of everyday communication. The commercial strategy of selling new ringtones and display graphics demonstrates a commercial consumerist strategy of selling us new commodities we never knew we needed, but at the same time seems inseparable from other new media practices such as the customising and personalising of computer desktops or online services (**Case study 4.1**).

> Jean Baudrillard, 'The gadget and the ludic', in *The Revenge of the Crystal* (1990). 'Ludic' means playful. The concept of 'play' as a mode of media consumption is an important one, and will be discussed further in **4.4**

> 4.4   Gameplay

Jean Baudrillard, taking an earlier mobile personal communication device, the Dictaphone, as an example, highlights the uneasy status of the technological in a consumer culture:

> whisper your decisions, dictate your instructions, and proclaim your victories to it . . . Nothing could be more useful, and nothing more useless: when the technical process is given over to a magical type of mental practice or a fashionable social practice, then the technical object itself becomes a gadget.
>
> (Baudrillard 1990: 77)

If popular media technologies are only ever symbolic and 'textual' and never practical or instrumental, then they may well be these gadgets of Baudrillard's. For Baudrillard tools and machines in contemporary consumer culture lose their instrumental functions, their practical uses, their use value. They instead operate as signs, fashion, toys or games. Digital personal organisers, text messaging on mobile phones, mobile phones themselves, may be sold as useful tools – but all seem to invite us to play. After all, who felt the need to 'text', to change a PC desktop's wallpaper or nurture a Tamagotchi virtual pet until a consumer device suggested we might?

Baudrillard's assertions, on the one hand, illustrate the logical conclusion of the argument that popular technologies are 'textual' and, in themselves, have no causal or instrumental function in everyday use: we are only ever *playing* at doing things, at performing useful tasks. On the other, his definition of a gadget as a 'ludic' device, a technological artefact with which we play, is an important one, though not perhaps in the way Baudrillard sees it. It asks us to consider what the significance of playful technology might be. The mobile phone user's weaving of spoken and written communication through the spare moments of the day may not be 'instrumental', but neither is it reducible to 'fashionable practice', or to the decoding of Nokia's marketing strategies.

As we will see, the distinction between the consumption of technologies as instrumental use and as play is not always easily drawn.

CASE STUDY 4.1   The 'open' PC

The personal computer (and the home computer, or 'micro' before it) introduced the new worlds of computer technology and communication into the home. Despite the 'black box' intentions of PC manufacturers and retailers, the machine (or perhaps more accurately, grouping of computer-based information, communication and entertainment technologies) has been widely seen as a uniquely multifunctional 'open device' (Mackay 1997: 270–271), 'chameleonlike' in its applications and possibilities (Turkle 1984). This 'openness' meant that it was not clear, despite the excitement that attended their production and sale, quite what the owners of home computers would actually do with them. It is not surprising then that, as research by Haddon and Skinner shows, 'producers and consumers constantly searched for and tried to construct the "usefulness" of this mass market product after it had been developed and launched' (cited in Haddon 1992: 84).

This multifunctionality reminds us of this new medium's status as computer technology. Ambiguity around its use can be traced back to its origins in the hacker culture of students at MIT and Stanford from the late 1950s. This culture has been seen as a struggle against the rigid rituals of number-crunching mainframes in university research and business applications, by the hackers' celebration of experimentation and the free sharing of computer codes and information. The hackers' development of real-time, interactive information processing led to the first commercially available domestic computers in the 1970s (Levy 1994). At first the hackers' 'do it yourself' ethic meant that the consumer had to build the machine themselves from a kit, and even when they became available as completed products home computers retained their hobbyist image and market. To use a home computer in the late 1970s and early 1980s the owner had to learn programming. Indeed, if nothing else the purpose and pleasure of home computers lay in learning to program, exploring the machine and its system, not, initially at least, consuming commercially produced software and services.

These early users of home computers would seem closer to the hobbyist enthusiasts of early radio than Ted Nelson's dream of Computer Lib activists espousing 'libertarian ideals of accessibility and excitement' (cited in Mayer 1999: 128). However, as Leslie Haddon pointed out in his research into the discourses of home computing in Britain in the early 1980s, the spare room tinkering with these new devices could not be separated from a sense of excitement about this machine as evidence of an unfolding information revolution. Through the exploration of these enigmatic machines, some users felt a sense of participation in the larger technological forces of a changing modern world (Haddon 1988b). As Klaus Bruhn Jensen puts it, 'The personal computer . . . offers both a symbol and a touchstone of the information society' (Jensen 1999: 192).

The migration of the Apple or IBM compatible personal computer from office to home in the late 1980s served to establish dominant platforms over the multitude of home computer formats, and signalled the end of the hobbyist era. If the home computer fostered a new media cottage industry of hardware and software manufacturers, then the PC marked the beginning of the commercial development of this technology as a mass medium. The marketing of PCs through the existing media

Haddon (1992) and Jensen (1999). For a different account of the significance of the PC, see 3.16 The social form of new media

See Levy (1984) for an entertaining account of this important aspect of new media history. It should be noted that the term 'hacker' did not originally mean the destructive figure constructed by the popular press in the 1980s. See 4.4.1 for further discussion of the term 'hacking'

4.4.1   New media's 'other'

See Case study 1.6 The technological imaginary and the cultural reception of new media

of advertising and promotion added further levels of complexity to the polysemic machine. Jensen sees in the advertising of PCs in the 1980s a contradictory discourse of individual empowerment through technology and images of social revolution. He points to Apple's television advertisement inspired by Orwell's *Nineteen Eighty-Four*, and to the print advertisement, in a *Newsweek* special election issue in 1984 under the headline 'One Person, One Computer'. Thus the PC fits into an established pattern of individualised domestic consumption, but, Jensen argues, the desires and anxieties surrounding PCs in the information revolution may still threaten to disrupt this consumerist norm (Jensen 1999).

It would be a mistake to regard the various meanings and uses of the chameleonlike PC as of equal weight. Its 'openness' is always limited by powerful discourses. Since computing became a 'family' rather than a hobbyist activity, both producers and consumers have struggled over a key distinction in the proper use of the home computer and PC. This distinction was (and still is) between education and entertainment. From the early 1980s government and educational discourses (and those of computer manufacturers wishing to establish respectability for their products) of domestic computing as information technology have clashed with both software producers targeting a lucrative market for computer games, and willing consumers. Today, games are a significant entertainment medium in their own right and account for most PC use in the home (though family PCs are usually bought for educational purposes, children in 80 per cent of British households with a PC use it for playing games – *Motorola* 2000). Videogame consoles are

See 4.2.5 Edutainment Edutainment Edutainment, and 4.4 Gameplay

themselves dedicated personal computers and cannot be separated from the development, dissemination and meanings of the domestic PC. The distinction between instrumental PC and the electronic toy is a fluid, and often fraught, one. Thus from a notion of an open-ended artefact, we could instead focus on two main currents of usage. 'The home computer provides an instance where we have to be sensitive to the interrelationship of different technological forms, specifically of computing and interactive games. These were to provide the micro with a dual heritage and identity' (Haddon 1992: 91).

Whether toy or tool, the domestic computer has invited excitement and contemplation that mark it out as distinct from the average consumer electronic device. It has been seen as a device within which we could see or create artificial 'microworlds' (Sudnow 1983). On a prosaic level this may mean individual customisation of the computer: changing desktop 'wallpaper', adding distinctive screensavers or sounds. On a more profound level it has suggested some fundamental shifts in our relationship with technology. In particular it invites comparisons with the human brain and has inspired popular ideas of artificial intelligence. Sherry Turkle evokes both these aspects in her study of the culture of programming. When programming, the computer is a 'projection of part of the self, a mirror of the mind' (Turkle 1984: 15). She quotes an interview with a school-child: 'you put a little piece of your mind into the computer's mind and now you can see it' (Turkle 1984: 145).

The association of the computer and the self can also be an anxious one. See Andrew Ross (1991) on the popular association of AIDS and computer viruses, Turkle (1984: 14) on parents' fears about their children's intimate relationships with electronic toys, or Pryor's (1991) critique of the notion of 'disembodiment' in the association of computer and brain

3.3 Networks and identity

When you create a programmed world, you work in it, you experiment in it, you live in it. The computer's chameleonlike quality, the fact that when you program it, it becomes your creature, makes it an ideal medium for the construction of a wide variety of private worlds and through them, for self-exploration. Computers are more than screens onto which personality is projected. They have already become a part of how a new generation is growing up. For adults and for children who play computer games, who use the computer for manipulating words, information, visual images, and especially for those who learn to program, computers enter into the development of personality, of identity, and even of sexuality.

(Turkle 1984: 6)

It is not only information and images that this technology allows us to experiment with and manipulate, she argues, but also the user's personality, identity and sexuality (Turkle 1984: 15). This experimentation offers us, the artist Sally Pryor asserts, a way of 'thinking of oneself as a computer' (Pryor 1991: 585).

At the time of writing the domestic PC is embroiled in a struggle over developments in the media technology market. The arrival and popularisation of the World Wide Web has introduced a new set of meanings and predictions, not least of the 'death' of the PC itself, its functions replaced by dumb terminals on networks. Alternatively, new convergences of domestic media technologies – such as digital television systems offering email and interactive service, and DVD-playing, networked videogame consoles – could displace the PC as the privileged symbol of the information revolution in the home.

4.2.6 Home pages: everyday identity in global networks
4.3 New media, identity and the everyday

4.2.4 Home computers: new media ethnography

To understand the consumption of technologies in households, we have to understand the practices of everyday life there – how new technologies are implicated in household routines and activities.

(Mackay 1997: 277)

Hugh Mackay, *Consumption and Everyday Life: culture, media and identities*, London: Open University Press/Sage, 1997

To this end, Hugh Mackay (1997: 278) identifies four key areas of enquiry:

- the significance of consumption of ICTs for domestic lives and relationships;

- how ICTs are implicated in shifting individual and family identities;

- the relationship between household members' public and private worlds;

- how technology (as well as the household) is transformed in processes of domestication and incorporation.

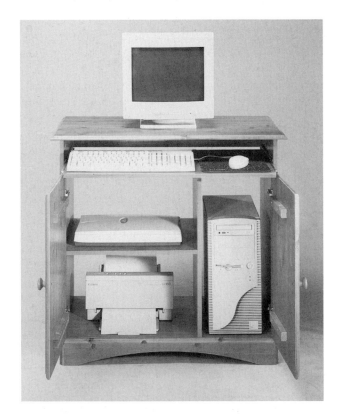

4.4 Argos computer cabinet.

BOX 4.4:   The 'insertion' of a new media technology into family life

Key text: Shaun Moores, 'Satellite TV as cultural sign: consumption, embedding and articulation', *Media, Culture and Society* 15 (1993a): 621–639

In a study of the 'domestication' of satellite television Shaun Moores addresses these issues of the 'embedding' of media technology in everyday life. Concerned with the ways in which media audiences understand media technologies, he questions assumptions that consumption is a passive activity. He is careful to argue, however, that production itself needs to be taken into account. There is always, he argues, a degree of closure of possible meanings and uses of media technologies at the point of their manufacture and promotion.

Further, it should not be assumed that any particular household is a static environment into which media technologies are inserted. Often the purchase of new media technologies coincides with 'the redrawing of domestic boundaries and relationships' (Moores 1993a: 627). For example, as we will see, growing children may make new demands for educational and entertainment hardware. Also, households have their own dynamics and politics, not least along the lines of gender and generation. Such power relationships intersect and interact with producers' expectations of the uses and meaning of new media products: 'Social divisions of gender or generation produce differential dispositions towards a technology like satellite TV' (Moores 1993b: 633).

See Case study 1.5 The technological imaginary and the cultural reception of new media:

Though some media technologies are often quickly 'stitched into the fabric' of everyday life, this apparent seamlessness does not mean they cease to have any effects on household dynamics. They continue to articulate points of argument and differences in taste and identity in the home. Television, perhaps the medium most thoroughly integrated into the time and space of the domestic environment, can still be the focus of conflicts (Moores cites David Morley's study of the micropolitics of the television remote control or 'zapper').

Moores's research tracks how changes in television technology and broadcasting are shaped by, and exacerbate, divisions within households. For example, there is a marked distinction between ideas of the 'modern' and the 'traditional' evident in the households studied, a distinction commonly following gender lines. In one family the 'hobbyist' father bought into satellite television as much because of his interest in the modernity of technology or gadgets as in the programmes and channels available. His wife was ambivalent about the new medium, her hobby of collecting antique furniture demonstrating her investment in notions of 'traditional' culture.

This research involved detailed questionnaires to 855 school children in Wales and the South West of England about their ICT use outside school, and case studies of sixteen families from different social backgrounds, focusing on children's 'techno-popular culture' and its implications for education. See Facer *et al.* (2001a: 91–108) and (2001b: 13–27)

The lines of conflict may be as much generational as gendered. In another household the teenage son shared his mother's interest in 1960s pop music, but clashed with his father over the former's extensive interest in, and purchase of, consumer media technology. This had the direct result of the father taking up antique furniture renovation as a hobby, thus asserting his investment in tradition and heritage in the face of his son's technological 'modernity'. Here, then, the consumption of media technologies is both shaped by and shapes existing family dynamics.

The Screen Play research project recently drew attention to issues of access to new media, firstly by recognising that many children do not have a PC in their home, and secondly by pointing out that constraints on access to, and use of, ICTs exist even in those households which did have computers.

As we argued at the start of this section (**4.1**), the popular conception of cyberspace as a separate, virtual realm into which we can insert ourselves, leaving our normal existence behind, does not stand up to scrutiny:

the computer in the home environment cannot be seen merely as a gateway to cyberspace, like the wardrobe providing access to Narnia, but rather that the materiality of this technology, as a shared and expensive family resource, is central to shaping the ways in which young people are able to access new technologies in the home.

(Facer *et al.* 2001b: 25)

Not only does the medium or interface stubbornly remain, but even the physical location of the user and hardware has significant effects on the ways in which computers and networks are accessed. The families studied in the Screen Play research tended not to place PCs in the main communal spaces of the house – for example in the living room alongside the television – but rather in spare or 'dead' space: landings, spare bedrooms, under stairs, lofts:

Mrs H Well because it's the other side of the house at the back so you don't have to hear it. So if you were in here watching television and we've got company then they're out the way.

Q   Why did it go in the spare room? What was the reason? What was the thinking?

Mr D   Because it was a spare room.

Mrs D   Because its nobody's room in there and just let everybody else use it. It's a sort of spare room cum office.

Steven, 13   It's not as private as your bedroom.

(Facer *et al.* 2001b: 18)

It is clear that the existing layout and use of space in the house has a reciprocal relationship with the uses of the new technologies. Computers were occasionally placed in children's bedrooms, though this was never the ideal 'one child one computer' image of the furniture catalogues.

As Sara McNamee observes in her study of the domestic gender politics of video gameplaying, the location within the home of a computer or games console can lead to unequal use. This inequality is frequently structured around gender. She notes that girls say they like playing video games as much as boys, but often play less. This is in part due to the fact that although consoles are often shared within the family, especially between siblings, they are usually kept in the boys' rooms, and hence, girls' access is controlled by their brothers: 'the machine becomes a symbolic focus around which gender relations are negotiated and expressed in domestic space' (McNamee 1998: 197).

Ironically, the same 'open' nature of computers that appears to free them from established media constraints can also entail complex negotiations around access. In households that can only afford one machine (i.e. most: 14 out of the 16 Screen Play case studies), new systems of 'time-sharing' have to be developed to allow different family members to perform different uses, 'managed around the temporal organisation . . . of the family':

Mum   . . . Steven normally gets in first you see, so he would always get the opportunity of going to the computer first. So we said 'that's not fair'. So Mondays and Thursdays Helen has first choice. She can decide whether she wants to go on the computer or watch television and on the other . . . I mean it tends to be just the Tuesday and Wednesday because Friday you're quite often not here or doing other things. – But we try and stick to only two hours on the computer each in any one day. – Generally speaking that's probably about enough. In terms of playing games. If they want to then go on and do some homework, then that's fine.

(Facer *et al.* 2001b: 19).

4.5 An 'instrumental fantasy' of techno-childhood; the bedroom arranged around the individual PC.

This organisation is also partly determined by discourses of computer use that originate outside the home, in particular the conflict between the domestic computer as an educational resource and as a leisure/entertainment device (see **4.2.5**).

4.2.5   Edutainment edutainment
edutainment

This conflict is evident even at the level of the arrangement of the 'space' of the computer itself. In many families, for example, one person (often, but not always, an adult) takes responsibility for the set-up of file-management systems, installing short-cuts, de-installing software and freeing up memory for authorised or 'preferred' practices, perhaps removing games from the hard drive.

Thus the different levels of knowledge and authority within the family in relation to the computer ensure a different relationship to its use. Facer *et al.* (2001b) draw on Michel de Certeau's concept of 'tactics' to analyse the various methods by which the 'less powerful' in this context attempt to use the computer in their own ways. For example, by disguising games playing as homework or the grasping of an opportunity to use the computer in the competitive game of access:

Helen, 10   And I was having a go at that and I couldn't get past this particular bit and I called Steven . . .

Steven, 13   I did it in 30 seconds.

Helen   He did it in 30 seconds.

Q   Right. So if Steven shows you something . . .

Steven   He normally does it.

Q   He normally does it and then you carry on.

Helen   And then I carry on. Or he normally does it. He pushes me off and he goes the rest of the game. He does that a lot of the time.

(Facer *et al.* 2001b: 20)

Alternatively, the tactical 'occupation of the digital landscape', though 'only ever temporary and transient' (Facer *et al.* 2001b: 20) can also be effected through changing the computer's desktop and settings, adjusting screen savers, etc. Thus, the features that can in some circumstances be seen as making the computer 'personal' are here tactics within a struggle for ownership of a communal 'space'.

The open, multifunctional nature of domestic computer technology can be seen, then, as a site of conflict or self-assertion. Family members may try to establish their own 'black boxes', however partial and temporary: 'This poaching of the computer space, a temporal appropriation of technology . . . can also be seen as a negotiation to fix the meaning and, subsequently, function of a technology which has the potential for multiple purposes' (Facer *et al.* 2001b: 21).

The networked home

So far we have been discussing the negotiation of access and construction of meaning of stand-alone PCs. We will now address questions of domestic access to the Internet. Everyday constraints of time, space, access and resources on online activity can be even more restrictive than for stand-alone computers. One factor commonly cited by parents interviewed by Screen Play for monitoring and restricting their children's access to the Internet is the cost of telephone calls for Internet access in the UK. Another is anxiety about the Internet as potentially dangerous, threatening intrusion of pornography or even – through chat rooms – paedophiles, into children's lives. There is an irony here: many parents bought computers for their children because of the perception of the increasing dangers of them playing outside. Now the Internet seems to bring a dangerous outside world directly into the hitherto safe private realm. These anxieties had led some of the parents either to not go online in the first place, or strictly to control access through passwords or adult supervision:

As the permeable boundaries of domestic space are made apparent in the introduction of the Internet (and television before it) into the home, the space of the networked home computer becomes a site of surveillance in which children's activities are monitored in not dissimilar ways to those employed in the space outside the front door.

(Facer *et al.* 2001b: 23)

So, even where everyday consumption or use of digital networks is possible, it is constrained by socio-economic factors, established household politics and relationships of gender and age, by material constraints of space and time and by anxieties about the relationships between everyday space and cyberspace.

4.2.5 Edutainment edutainment edutainment

As we have seen, the purchase and use of home computers and new media in the home has often been for broadly educational reasons. Both optimistic cyberculture discourses and more cautious analyses of the effects of computers on everyday life share the view that

However, emphasising new media's materiality, the embodied nature of their use, and their continuities with existing media and consumer products does not mean that all is 'business as usual'. In the rest of 4.2, and in 4.3, we will examine claims that new media are transforming everyday life and forging new connections between the domestic and everyday, and the global and historic digital technologies cannot be understood only at the local, domestic level but through their linking of individual use and global forces and relationships. So, if we take a concern with 'knowledge': on a local level the computer may invite comparisons with the human brain, whilst on the 'global' level a broader sense of information or networks is invoked to explain current economic and social transformation.

See Nixon (1998)

However, the conflicting discourses of micros as educational or games machines was also discussed. These conflicts continue today within commercial and governmental discourses around computer media in education. The dividing lines between ICTs and computer entertainment media – or between educational software and games – are anxiously drawn.

The line between these types of software is not so much blurred as constantly renegotiated and re-established. Helen Nixon's study of Australian parent-consumer magazines on domestic software shows how a publishing genre has been established largely on its promises to help parents differentiate between the educational and entertainment. The kinds of educational software reviewed by these magazines represent a commercial strategy to reconcile this historic conflict in children's computing, a strategy sometimes referred to as 'edutainment', the use of entertainment, toys and games as a medium for learning.

See 4.4 Gameplay

The dual connotations of the term 'edutainment' illustrate the contradictory discourses around new media and education. On the one hand it is a derogatory term, a trivialising, 'dumbing down' or commercialisation of knowledge and learning. This fusion of popular media forms and learning is identified with other media offering hybrids of knowledge and information with commercial and/or fictional forms: the 'advertorial', 'infotainment' and 'docusoap'. On the other hand edutainment has now been adopted, without irony, by the educational software industry itself. However it is used, 'edutainment' alludes to a broad belief that boundaries are dissolving between education and the consumption of commercial media. This phenomenon is not limited to new media, but it is the digital multimedia forms of CD-ROM encyclopaedias and learning games (and new technologies such as interactive whiteboards) that seem to be of central significance.

See 3.25 Information as commodity

The promotion of educational software for domestic PCs, and the ambitions of governments' policies, together attempt to reconstitute the home and time spent at home, as no longer separate from school, but connected and interrelated. This is more than a simple technologising of traditional homework however: edutainment software is promoted by both manufacturers and governments' educational policies as central to an emerging 'knowledge economy' in which divisions between work and play, home and school are to be less and less important. These media technologies and texts are intended to transform young people's domestic leisure activities into 'more productive' and stimulating learning.

Seymour Papert is a mathematician and early pioneer of AI, as well as of computers in education. In the early 1960s he set up the Artificial Intelligence Lab at MIT with Marvin Minsky.
www.media.mit.edu/~papert/

Case study 4.1   The 'open' PC

Before we look at the implications for this insertion of the home into the knowledge economy, it should be noted that these recent applications of ICTs to education are predated by earlier visions of computers as uniquely new and progressive tools for education. The key figure here is Seymour Papert. The Logo programming language developed by Papert in the 1970s is predicated on the notion of the computer as a 'thinking machine' (**Case study 4.1**), encouraging philosophical enquiry into the nature of intelligence and the human brain. Logo allows children to give sequences of instructions to 'turtles' (either a small robot with a pen, or a cursor on a monitor) to try to get these objects to move and draw simple pictures. This often involves complex mathematical problem-solving, but, Papert argues, without the child realising that is what they are doing. Papert sees programming not as training for work in computing industries but as a way of modelling or playing with maths and physics. Logo encourages children, in a process of 'active and self-directed' learning, to develop a 'sense of mastery over a piece of the most modern and powerful technology and establish an intimate contact with some of the deepest ideas from science, from mathematics, and from the art of intellectual model-building' (Papert 1980: 5). Before edutainment, then, computing practices were seen as inherently playful and creative.

See 3.17 New media and Post-industrial Economies, 3.18 The development of the new economy

The knowledge economy at home

In this earlier discourse of computers and education, computers are seen both as machines and as metaphors for 'thinking about thinking'. For Papert, computers 'enhance thinking and change patterns of access to knowledge' (Papert 1980: 3–4). Contemporary discourses and policies around the use of ICTs in education have a different understanding of the nature and uses of knowledge. As examined in **Part 3**, there are a number of 'third stage' models of historical and cultural change in which knowledge and/or information usually play a crucial, if not a determining role. Knowledge and information, it is often claimed, are the currency or capital of current global economic change. Hence, attempts by government, business or other agencies to engage with the information revolution see education as a primary tool. As the UK government's Central Office of Information puts it:

3 NETWORKS USERS AND ECONOMICS

> Education and the information age will support and reinforce each other. The information age will transform education, at all levels and for all ages. Education in turn will equip people with the necessary skills to profit from the information age.
>
> (Central Office of Information 1998: 7)

In these arguments, knowledge is not only central to economic development, it becomes both raw material and commodity. Potter talks of 'replacing capital' with what he terms 'knowledge stock'. Thus multinational and highly successful corporations such as Microsoft, Intel, Disney, 'are all characterised by their IPR [intellectual property rights], and knowledge-content. Their value bears no relation whatsoever to their net worth or capital stock' (Potter 1999).

This economistic concept of knowledge is evident in educational discourses too, according to David Hakken who calls it the 'banking' concept of learning. 'Under this conception, "knowledge" is a discrete, bounded, measurable, inert, uniform commodity' (Hakken 1999: 180–181). Its primary function is to extract economic value in expanding production. The banking concept is nothing new, but Hakken argues that it has undergone a significant change in recent years in relation to notions of a knowledge society and economy in 'cyberspace'. Here knowledge, whilst still a commodity, gains new super powers: 'Contained within the normal notion of "cyberspace as knowledge society", however, is the implication that cyberians do knowledge not just differently, they do it better – as if cybernauts have leapt a quantum from "normal" to "super-knowledge"' (Hakken 1999: 181–182).

There seems to be a hierarchy of knowledge in this revolution: science and technology are valued for their instrumental and economic potential. In a talk published in the UK government's online magazine *10 Downing Street*, David Potter asserts that: 'The drivers of economic change are science and technology and the political-philosophic [*sic*]. Philosophies can come around in cycles but science and the knowledge it brings are irreversible' (Potter 1999)

See also Jean-François Lyotard, *The Post-Modern Condition: a report on knowledge*, Manchester: Manchester University Press, 1984. Lyotard analyses the transformations in knowledge through the technologies of the post-industrial. He, too, identifies 'the neo-liberal marketisation of education in terms of the systemic, self-regulatory nature of global capitalism. Education then loses its Enlightenment ideals of, precisely, enlightenment, and instead we see "the mercantilisation of knowledge and education" . . . a kind of education under capitalism which merely socially reproduces students to fulfil the technical demands of the system' (Peters 1999)

Instrumental progressivism

Robins and Webster argue that even Papert's apparently progressive ideas are ultimately instrumental. Indeed it is their utopianism itself which betrays them. In seeing computers (and maths and physics) as neutral and untouched by the structures of educational authority, it is assumed relations of power will simply 'dissolve away'. Yet any model of education and socialisation which does not address broader relations of power and knowledge will unwittingly become complicit with them. They call this 'instrumental progressivism', 'the emergence of a new strategic philosophy of education/training, one that was dedicated to producing an adaptable, flexible, integrated, self-controlling workforce for the embryonic regime of neo-Fordism' (Robins and Webster 1999: 175).

Recent developments have added popular entertainment to this strategic philosophy. In a commercially driven version of Papert's notion that computers are in themselves progressive, ultimately schools will have to become fun houses: mathematical equations turned into computer animation, and 'Every primary school will be its own Hollywood' (Brown 1999: 2). The apparently innocuous games and puzzles of edutainment software, then, could be seen as an ever more complete penetration of disciplinary power into everyday life. Instrumental computer use is extended from formal education into the home, and from work into leisure. But also in its modes of consumption and popular imagery, edutainment represents an aesthetisation of instrumentalism, reflecting perhaps that the marked convergence of media, entertainment, communications and information technology at the level of corporate ownership only reinforces this sense.

The study of edutainment software itself, and its consumption in the home or school, however, whilst not denying the very real significance of these instrumental forces, may indicate a more productive assessment of play and learning with new media. The term 'edutainment', as we have noted, is itself an uncomfortable fusion and its inherent contradictions and tensions are not easily resolved.

See also Sefton-Green and Parker (2000). Their research project, Edit-Play, worked with schoolchildren and assessed the potential in commercial edutainment software for editing moving images, thus engaging with computer technology and engaging creatively with their own popular culture

Crystal Rainforest 2000, Sheraton Software Ltd and Simon Hosler 1998

CASE STUDY 4.2   Crystal Rainforest

An ecological drama unfolds in a multimedia story as the reader or player clicks on hot spots and navigational symbols. The king of an alien rain forest tribe is shot by a poisoned dart, fired by an agent of a logging company. While the king is in hospital, the player is directed to guide a small robot through a pyramid using simple strings of commands. The game reveals its secrets and stories through a collage of graphics, animated sequences, puzzles and photographs. The knowledge thus mediated is similarly eclectic – despite appearances this is not primarily a narrative about the environment; rather, the anthropological, ecological elements are laced with eco-friendly science fiction/fantasy. The game operates on two levels: the pleasures of the narrative, graphics and puzzles lure the player in, and frame the real pedagogical project – through playing with the robots the player learns Logo. There is a hierarchy of discourses here: the mathematical discourse of programming (and, inadvertently perhaps, popular fantasy genres) over the geographical or socio-political.

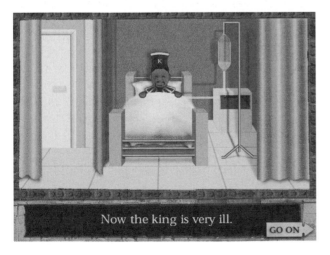

4.6 The Crystal Rainforest. Images from Crystal Rainforest 2000 reproduced by kind permission of Sherston Software Limited.

Facer *et al.* (2001a: 91–108)

CASE STUDY 4.3   Visual Basic Sucks!

The Screen Play researchers argue that the dominant discursive construction of young computer users as 'future workers' in the knowledge economy leaves little space for them to articulate their pleasure in using computers in non-authorised ways – primarily, though not exclusively, gameplaying. The following exchange, in which parents discussing their agenda for encouraging computer use at home are interrupted by their 'earwigging' teenage son, captures something of the ways in which these broader discourses and policies (and their contradictions) are struggled over in everyday family relationships:

> *Dad*   But we did get stuff for the kids to use on it.
> *Mum*   We got some educational software for the kids, at that point we were determined they weren't going to play games. [*Laughter*] I would like Steven to get involved in other things. I've tried a few times to interest him in various things and it's the games, definitely, that dominate his computer usage.
> *Q*   Right. And so that's a ...
> *Mum*   Steven, what's the problem?
> *Steven*   I'm just saying that I'm going to bed now. And games rule!
> *Steven*   Visual Basic sucks!
>
> (Facer *et al.* 2001a: 103)

Steven's outburst, like the immediate pleasures of computer gameplaying he refers to, disrupt the discourses of future rewards for 'educational' computer use.

3.3 Networks and identity
3.5 Networks and communities

4.2.6 Home pages: everyday identity in global networks

In studies of the culture of media technology, claims that new information and communications media are implicated in significant social and cultural change are generally premissed on the identification of shifting relationships between:

- the local and the global;

- the private and the public;

- consumption and production;

- constraint and creativity in consumption;

- and the impact of all of these on the sense of self or identity held by individuals and communities.

Of course, the various theoretical discourses of new media constitute these relationships very differently, and draw very different conclusions.

What is new about networks?
In the cyberculture corner, Allucquere Rosanne Stone asks 'what is new about networking?' and gives two possible answers. The first is 'nothing', communicating via a

computer network is little different from using the telephone. The second possible answer is 'everything': networks could be seen as more like public theatre than 'old' media, as new arenas for social experience and dramatic communication, 'for qualitative interaction, dialogue and conversation' (Stone 1995: 16). If this second answer is true (and Stone suspects it is), she argues that this has profound implications for our sense of our selves as bodies in space, our sense of 'presence'.

However, these claims appear to echo the concerns of the critical study of 'old' media and everyday life. Both 'old' media (e.g. television and radio) and 'new' digital media (e.g. Internet media such as chat rooms and MUDs) offer everyday local access to what Moores (1993a) calls 'global image spaces', promising significant transformations of the everyday understanding of collective identities such as community and nationality. From this perspective, the consumption of both new *and* old media is thoroughly bound up in the construction, or performance, of identity.

In an example from Moores' (1993a) research, an adolescent's consumption of media technologies (hi-fi, satellite television) is understood as an active process of identity construction. His choices of consumer technology marked his autonomy from his parents, as well as asserting his sense of his own modernity and technical competence. Stone on the other hand, makes a clear distinction between old and new. The distinction rests on the networked structure of new media use. Thus the 'one-to-one' telephone conversations and 'one-to-many' model of broadcast media are superseded by 'many-to-many' communications facilitated by Internet media. One important difference between these two examples is that the satellite television consumer's identity is primarily constructed through his *choice* of consumer technology: the mere fact of ownership of these media devices is symbolic of his interests and sense of self. The arguments that digital media and networks are quite distinct from 'old' electronic media tend to be premised on the assertion that it is through the *use* of, or *communication* through, new media that the individual may construct their identity. We return to the notion of cyberspace in everyday life: online arenas in which we feel our sense of presence to be transformed.

To explore these issues we will look at an example of 'cyberspace' as an everyday medium. We will take as a case study research into the amateur production of World Wide Web 'home pages'. This research draws productively on both the conceptual approaches outlined above.

This distinction between electronic and digital media is not always valid however. Moores (1993a) discusses the investment of some satellite television viewers in a sense of their 'Europeanness' through the consumption of continental television output

See Chandler (2000a)

Home pages and identity 'under construction'

The Web is one of the most widely accessed Internet media and can be seen as both continuous with, and offering distinct new possibilities for, established relationships between public and private space, public and private selves. The personal home page is an example of the web encouraging not only 'consumption' (online shopping, access to information and entertainment) but also a relatively accessible, and distinctly new, form of media 'production'. Designing and publishing a personal website is relatively easy and inexpensive, and allows the designer to address a worldwide audience beyond the scope of any earlier DIY media production.

Daniel Chandler has studied individual websites and interviewed their designers. He links their production with other forms of personal documentation, communication or samizdat publishing (diaries, newsletters, 'round robin' letters, fanzines), but points out that where home pages differ is precisely their potential for a global audience. The spare room or bedroom shift in their relationship with the outside world, becoming permeable: 'a home in the real world is, among other things, a way of keeping the world out . . . An

The term 'home page' itself highlights the relays between public and private space. Even in large-scale commercial websites this reassuringly domestic terminology offers the lost browser a return to a familiar page

online home, on the other hand, is a little hole you drill in the wall of your real home to let the world in' (John Seabrook, quoted in Chandler 1998).

Chandler's main interest, however, is in the ways in which individuals present, or construct, their identities on websites. Borrowing a metaphor from the conventions of web page design, Chandler argues that just as personal web pages are often labelled as 'under construction', so too are the identities of their designers. He describes the aesthetics and construction methods of home page design as 'bricolage'. This term originates in anthropology, denoting the improvised use by pre-industrial peoples of everyday materials and objects to hand in the symbolic practices of art and rituals. The term has been adopted by cultural studies to describe the appropriation and manipulation – even subversion – of the meanings of commodities by youth subcultures:

> the extraordinary symbolic creativity of the multitude of ways in which young people use, humanize, decorate and invest with meanings their common and immediate life spaces and social practices – personal styles, and choice of clothes; selective and active use of music, TV, magazines; decoration of bedrooms.

See also Hebdige (1979: 103–106)

(Willis 1990: 2)

BOX 4.5:   Girls, boys, and the construction of identity on the web

Susanna Stern also makes the connection between the content and aesthetics of young people's public presentation and self-expression through web page production and the bricolage of the bedroom wall. Through her research into the home pages of adolescent girls, she argues that the construction and presentation of identity is mapped onto 'real world' gendered practices and spaces. Thus, Stern's research does not find 'fluid' identities as such, rather a more complex picture of self-presentation and construction of image: 'in this study, girls' home pages were ultimately regarded as texts that reflect in some way the selves girls think they are, the selves they wish to become, and most likely, the selves they wish others to see' (Stern 1999: 24).

There are distinct approaches to self-representation in the sites studied, which Stern summarises as 'spirited', 'sombre' and 'self-conscious' sites. Each of these develops new ways of making private practices of identity construction public, from light-hearted listings of likes and dislikes to the presentation of very personal, often painful, reflections or poetry, modes of writing previously confined to diaries and journals. Stern takes this further: the bedroom as a 'safe' if restricted social space for girls is transformed through the use of Internet media into a space for self-expression which is more public, but still safe:

Individual web page production does not always assume a global, anonymous audience. Some may be produced specifically to be viewed by friends and family to interact with, or establish, broader online communities. Chris Abbott argues that the use of the web by young people to disseminate poetry, autobiography, polemics is qualitatively different to non-digital media, because 'publishing on the Web creates communities of readers and writers in ways that are very difficult to do in print – especially for this age group' (Abbott 1998: 85)

> It seems likely that for some girls, the web presents the 'safe company' they need to 'speak their experience' and 'say what is true'. It also seems to grant some girls the freedom to 'develop their sense of possibility and to experience themselves as active agents in their own lives.

(Stern 1999: 38)

Russ Tobin has studied his son's involvement with an online 'community' of fellow fans of the role-playing game Warhammer. The boy's understanding of identity in such a community is congruent with aspects of cyberculture discourse – he sees the Web as a communicative space in which age, appearance, race, class or gender are irrelevant. It does appear that this is a community structured along the meritocratic lines of technical and artistic skill in web page design, in which a teenage boy can be an authoritative figure. Even the firmly gendered pastime of fantasy wargames, which we might assume would reinforce a dominant masculine identity, undergoes surprising transformations when extended through a networked 'community' and web media production. Tobin observes that his son's online life 'provides him with a male performative identity, but also, simultaneously, with a way to pursue less macho interests, including art, corresponding and even interpersonal intimacy' (Tobin 1998: 145).

The research discussed here identifies a tension between social constraints and creative possibilities in individual Internet media production, particularly in relation to the presentation or construction of identity. What these studies do not make clear is exactly what is meant by identity. On the one hand it seems to mean little more than the day-to-day choices about what we wear to present ourselves to the world, on the other a sense of identity 'under construction' implies more fundamental changes in our senses of self, closer to the claims of cyberculture. The next section will address issues of new media and identity.

4.3 NEW MEDIA, IDENTITY AND THE EVERYDAY

Our interaction with the world around us is increasingly mediated by computer technology, and that, bit by digital bit, we are being 'Borged', as devotees of *Star Trek: The Next Generation* would have it — transformed into cyborgian hybrids of technology and biology through our ever-more-frequent interaction with machines, or with one another through technological interfaces.

(Dery 1994: 6)

One of the most far-reaching claims made for new media is that, through individual or collective engagement with online networks and VR, fundamental changes are manifested in those individuals' or groups' senses of self or identity. However, the importance, scale and quality of such transformations vary within the distinct discourses studying new media. This section will outline these discursive positions and suggest how a critical understanding of everyday life and popular media might inform them.

See Poster (1995a)

Theories of the radical effects of VR technologies or Internet media (and the two are often conflated) on individual identity are often premised on the simple fact that, in using these particular new media, conventional markers of identity become irrelevant because users cannot see each other:

In bulletin boards like The Well, people connect with strangers without much of the social baggage that divides and alienates. Without visual cues about gender, age, ethnicity, and social status, conversations open up in directions that otherwise might be avoided. Participants in these virtual communities often express themselves with little inhibition and dialogues flourish and develop quickly.

(Poster 1995a: 90)

There is a second broad conceptual approach to the status of human identity within cyberculture. Drawing on cybernetics, it is argued that digital networks in particular (but other cybernetic systems too) raise profound questions about humanist assumptions of the absolute distinction between the human and the technological. See Hayles (1999). This approach is touched on in Part 4, but see 5.4 Theories of cyberculture for a thorough discussion of the significance of cybernetics for the study of new media and technologies

3.3 Networks and identity
3.4 Learning to live in the interface
3.5 Networks and communities
3.6 Visionary communities
3.7 Defining community online
3.8 Networks as public spheres
3.9 The net as postmodern public sphere
3.10 Critique of the net as public sphere

3 NETWORKS USERS AND ECONOMICS

The everyday world is sometimes factored in to these prophesies, albeit usually as a realm about to undergo radical transformation. Poster, for example, speculates that virtual reality technologies will become available through the home computer, and '[i]f such experiences become commonplace, just as viewing television is today, then surely reality will have been multiplied' (Poster 1995a: 94)

From this, some make the bolder claim that in online communication in 'cyberspace' or virtual reality, not only can we not be seen, but in some way our bodies are left behind; it is 'incorporeal interaction', through which 'users can float free of biological and sociocultural determinants' (Dery 1994: 3). Thus not only can we present ourselves as a different gender, race or species, we are also being 'disembodied'.

The following discussion should be seen as closely linked with, and complementary to, sections **3.3** through to **3.10**. In **Part 3** we cover theories of identity and networks in relation to the constitution of communities. Evidently community and individual identity are inseparable; we separate them here in order to address the different overall concerns of **Part 3** and this part of the book. Thus here we are concerned more with the local, domestic uses of new media, whilst **Part 3** looks to the broader — though interrelated — public, political and economic spheres.

4.3.1 Identity workshops

Sherry Turkle has extended her research on early personal computer use to studies of the Internet, in particular MUDs and other 'virtual worlds'. She is still concerned with the individual's sense of self in new media use, but here it is not the computer as 'second self' so much as the computer network as communication medium that is challenging users' senses of identity. Instead of computer programming's potential as a therapeutic 'working through' of personal concerns, we see instead an 'identity workshop'. Instead of the use of the stand-alone computer reflecting aspects of personality, we now see a refraction of identity through role-play and interaction with other users: 'The self is not only decentered but multiplied without limit. There is an unparalleled opportunity to play with one's identity and to "try out" new ones' (Turkle 1996a: 356).

Does then the everyday engagement with Internet media escape established patterns of embodied, situated, media use? What is the relationship, if any, between virtual identity play and the negotiations and constructions of identity in 'old' media consumption? On what notions of historical, technological or cultural change are these incorporeal virtual identities based? Is, as Allucquere Rosanne Stone argues, the relationship between the material nature of the body — the 'physical envelope' — and the identity it once seemed coterminous with 'embedded in much larger shifts in cultural beliefs and practices [including] repeated transgressions of the traditional concept of the body's physical envelope and of the locus of human agency' (Stone 1995: 16)? For Stone, these larger shifts are symptomatic of nothing less than the end of the 'mechanical age', and the beginning of the 'virtual age' (Stone 1995: 17).

Theories of the virtual age promise the transformation of the everyday, or they take us into realms far distant from the everyday. There is a tendency for them to define themselves in opposition to the embodied and material: identity versus corporeality (and all the body's historical and cultural 'baggage'), the virtual versus the real, play versus consumption, utopia versus the mundane politics and contractions of the real world, cyberspace or VR versus commercial and material communications and information media.

To question the 'virtual age' thesis is not to argue that identities are not being constructed or transformed, or to deny that our increasingly intimate relationships with machines and networks challenge long-held conceptual oppositions between the local and global, public and private, or consumption and production. Indeed media technologies can be seen as implicated in a shifting sense of identity in numerous ways, including the following:

- through changes in mass media: we have seen, for example, how developments in television broadcasting can facilitate the presentation or performance of identity;

- through consumption as an active practice of bricolage, constructed through the images and consumer goods we 'choose', a process perhaps given new impetus by the interactive and reproductive power of digital software;

- identity can be 'constructed' in cyberspace or virtual worlds;

- as individuals within virtual communities;

- virtual reality and cyberspace are undermining (our understanding of) the real, within which we have constructed our identities;

- an ever more intimate relationship with technologies and media from the Internet to genetic engineering, raising questions of the boundaries between the human body and consciousness, machines and networks;

- that new media are only a part, however significant, of the impact of broader historical, economic and/or cultural change on identity.

4.3.2 Key positions

Discussion of these factors, as we have said, takes place across a range of discourses. However, critical approaches to identity and technology are generally informed by various postmodernist theories of identity and subjectivity:

POSTMODERNIST CYBERCULTURE
An optimistic, positive reading of cultural change, in which new technologies free from the repressive 'master narratives' and hierarchies of the modern era: reified identities and regimented social structures. In media terms this position assumes the overthrow of passive consumption by interactive communication and creativity. Perhaps ironically, however, a modernist faith in technological progress seems to be revived, not least through the influence of Marshall McLuhan. See Poster (1995a), Stone (1995), Featherstone and Burrows (1995), Turkle (1996b), Bukatman (1993).

THE POSTMODERNIST POLITICS OF IDENTITY
Postmodernism here offers a discourse of progressive cultural change in which identity is something constructed (both fixing individuals and groups into subject positions based on gender and race), but also contested (providing sites and resources from which to develop political action). Here, media may be part of the means by which groups express themselves, but they constitute only one of many historical and cultural forces (diasporic migration, multicultural societies, the women's movement) influencing changes in subjectivity. This set of positions tends to be more or less critical of the class-based political subject of pre-1968 Marxism. See, for example, Hall (1987) and McRobbie (1986).

A READING OF POSTMODERNITY AS CRISIS
A key figure here is Jean Baudrillard, whose theories of simulation, while not exclusively located in digital media, have proved highly influential to cyberculture. Baudrillard diagnoses the postmodern world as hyperreal – a world where information and images

circulate to the extent that any sense of the real world is no longer tenable. Seen by some as apocalyptic, these ideas may be adopted by the postmodernist cyberculture position, with certain qualifications, to celebrate aspects of virtualisation. Fredric Jameson has drawn on Baudrillard's theories in his analysis of postmodernist culture. For Jameson, however, the real world (in Jameson's Marxist sense constituted by the world system of late capitalism) still exists, but we have no direct access to it, no critical or political position free from mediation from which we can analyse and transform it. Electronic and digital media and communications are complicit in this 'crisis of representation', but are seen as symptoms rather than causal. Thus the postmodernist subject may be dazzled and disoriented by new media culture, but this bedazzlement is the cultural logic of economic changes in the capitalist infrastructure. See Baudrillard (1983) and Jameson (1991).

THEORIES OF POSTMODERN MEDIA SUBJECT

Case study 4.1   The 'open' PC

Already touched on in **Case study 4.1**, here identity is shaped or constructed through the dominance of consumer and media culture:

> the mass media have become integrated into everyday life to the extent of being in some respects constitutive of social reality. Increasingly, the audience–public can be said to live inside 'the machine' of mass media, in a qualitatively new form of media environment.

(Jensen 1999: 189)

The influence of postmodernist theorists like Baudrillard and Jameson is evident, but the 'media environment' is here generally viewed as less then catastrophic. The theories may be used to examine specific, grounded examples of media use and identity construction. See Green *et al.* (1998) and Kinder (1991).

POST-STRUCTURALIST THEORIES OF THE SELF OR SUBJECT AS CONSTRUCTED THROUGH DISCOURSE (SEE 3.3).

3.3   Networks and identity

'The self is viewed largely as a product or construct of the symbolic systems which precede it' (Thompson 1995: 210). Whilst theorists such as Louis Althusser and Michel Foucault conceptualised the ideological or disciplinary fixing of identity in individuals, postmodernist cyberculture often reworks post-structuralism in a more optimistic light, seeing in new media the potential for challenging and escaping these subject positions. See, for example, Althusser (1984) and Foucault (1989).

CYBERPUNK

The science fiction genre of cyberpunk has had a remarkable influence on theoretical discussions of cyberculture and identity – not least as the origin of the term (and to a large extent the concept) 'cyberspace' from William Gibson's novel *Neuromancer*. Fictional cyberspace is read as evidence of the emergence of individuals' disembodied interaction, or even fusion, with digital technology and networks. Popular films such as *Bladerunner*, *Robocop* and *Terminator* are also frequently cited, suggesting new relationships between the body and technology, relationships heralding the possibility of cyborg subjectivities. See McAffrey (1991).

BOX 4.6: The subject

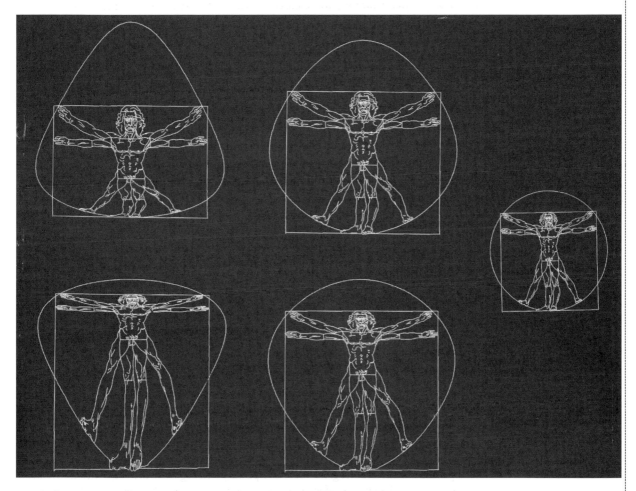

4.7 Charles Csuri, Leonardo Two (1966). Renaissance man, distorted by computer algorithms.

To make sense of the varying claims of these theories of changing identities in relation to media technologies, it is important to be clear what we mean by identity. 'Identity' as a concept is often used interchangeably with 'subjectivity', though they have distinct connotations. Whereas, for example, an individual designing a home page may choose aspects of their interests and personal life to present as their *identity*, their *subjectivity* may be seen as more fundamental to their sense of self and their place in the world. Subjectivity, then, is established through broader historical and cultural contexts, and positions individuals within the power structures of gender, class and race. The *subject* is a historical category of existence, emerging in the Renaissance, the beginning of the modern world. It can be seen as marking the end of the medieval world-view of a static, God-ordained

Descartes' famous dictum 'Cogito ergo sum' (I think therefore I am) is emblematic of the Enlightenment subject's ideal existence in the higher realms of thought and reason. As we will see, this philosophical separation of mind and body, or Cartesian dualism, has proved immensely popular in thinking through the status of thought and communication in cyberspace

universe of fixed hierarchies in which individuals and social classes, along with angels, animals and minerals, all had their immutable place:

> The Enlightenment subject was based on a conception of the human person as a fully centred, unified individual, endowed with the capacities of reason, consciousness and action, whose 'centre' consisted of an inner core [identity] which first emerged when the subject was born, and unfolded with it, while remaining essentially the same — continuous or 'identical' with itself — throughout the individual's existence.
>
> (Hall 1992: 275)

With the Reformation, the emerging social and economic forces of mercantile capitalism increased the mobility of individual traders, and with the beginnings of urbanisation established social relationships were shaken, requiring new relationships between individuals and society. The category of an autonomous individual helped to make sense of this new, non-natural order. Ideas of the freedom of the rational individual informed both the French Revolution and the development of liberalism in economics and politics.

Though central to modern notions of individuality and liberty, it should also be noted that the word 'subject' also carries connotations of *subjection*, of being an individual constituted within or by power structures, 'a subject of the Crown' for example. So, on the one hand this is a concept which constitutes an internal, private sense of self in individuals, but on the other it refers to the positioning of the individual within society. Michel Foucault's work is particularly influential here, and is central to post-structuralist concepts of subjectivity. He argues that these two concepts of the subject are not contradictory but inseparable: the very rationality celebrated by the Enlightenment is not a universal principle, but a discourse which positions some individuals as rational but others as criminal or insane (Foucault 1989)

If the subject, then, is the figure of Man (Hall *et al.* [1992] point out that the Enlightenment subject was generally assumed to be male) in the modern world, and if subjectivity is changing in some fundamental way, the argument runs that we must be seeing the emergence of a postmodern subject. Hall describes how this putative new subject is conceptualised as 'having no fixed, essential or permanent identity. Identity becomes a "movable feast": formed and transformed continuously in relation to the ways we are represented or addressed in the cultural systems which surround us'. This is not always the liberating, pluralising of identity celebrated in postmodernist cyberculture or postmodernist identity politics however. It could be catastrophic hyperreality: 'as systems of meaning and cultural representation multiply, we are confronted by a bewildering, fleeting multiplicity of possible identities, any one of which we could identify with — at least temporarily' (Hall *et al.* 1992: 277).

These diverse histories and hierarchies of subjective change are important to bear in mind as they underlie any idea of what subjective change might be today. All of the key positions covered here reject any idea of historical or cultural change as smooth and evolutionary. All are based on an understanding of distinct periods in history. Foucault, for instance, in charting the history (or 'archaeology') of knowledge, sees a profound break in our ideas of self in the Enlightenment, which established the rational and ostensibly universal principles on which the modern Western world is based. Other arguments seem to imply a *modernist* subject (i.e. late nineteenth century to mid-twentieth) rather than this *modern* one (i.e. Enlightenment or post-Renaissance), seeing the coming of industrial society and mass urbanisation as an environment that necessitates subjective change. Some discourses see different qualitative levels of change, some more significant than others. Marxists, for example, might see the modern subject as emerging with capitalism at the end of the feudal era. Subsequent changes, corresponding to changes of the mode of production (e.g. the shift from mercantile to monopoly capitalism), whilst perhaps significant, would not then be seen as fundamental. Feminists, while charting similar shifts in the modern world, may see the far older power structures of patriarchy as being the most significant.

4.3.3 The subject of (new) media

Cutting across postmodernism and cyberculture thought we can see quite diverse assumptions about relationships between the individual or subject, media technology, and historical and cultural change. The question we must now ask is: what role might media technologies play in effecting or facilitating changes in identity or subjectivity?

The development of print through movable type in the mid-fifteenth century is generally seen as the first mass medium. It is often cited as a key factor in the development of modern rationality and subjectivity, and the undermining of the medieval religious world. Mark Poster sees the advent of electronic media as analogous in historical importance to that of movable type. New media mark the end of the modern era and usher in postmodern subjectivity:

> In the twentieth century electronic media are supporting an equally profound transformation of cultural identity. Telephone, radio, film, television, the computer and now their integration as 'multimedia' reconfigure words, sounds and images so as to cultivate new configurations of individuality. If modern society may be said to foster an individual who is rational, autonomous, centered, and stable . . . then perhaps a postmodern society is emerging which nurtures forms of identity different from, even opposite to those of modernity. And electronic communications technologies significantly enhance these postmodern possibilities.
>
> (Poster 1995a: 80)

Poster is confused as to whether these 'postmodern possibilities' are the product of new media in particular, or electronic media (including television and radio) in general. The above quote suggests the latter, but elsewhere he specifically identifies digital media as the point of rupture. Against the 'alienation' of 'one-way' broadcast media, he posits the many-to-many system of the Internet:

> the question of the mass media is seen not simply as that of sender/receiver, producer/consumer, ruler/ruled. The shift to a decentralized network of communications makes senders receivers, producers consumers, rulers ruled, upsetting the logic of understanding of the first media age.
>
> (Poster 1995a: 87–88)

We have already questioned in some detail the assumption of binary oppositions between the old and the new, the passive and the active in media audiences. John B. Thompson argues that the mass media is a crucial source of 'mediated symbolic materials' that nourish this process of identity construction, or 'self-formation'; this is not a uniquely postmodern phenomenon however, but characteristic of modern societies more generally (Thompson 1995: 207).

If we accept this argument we must recognise that 'old' media (books, soap operas, and so on) are sources of symbolic materials as much as new media. Thompson also questions the postmodernist tenet that all contemporary experience is in and through the 'machine' of mass media. The world may be 'increasingly permeated by mediated forms of information and communication [and] mediated experience has come to play a substantial and expanding role in the daily lives of individuals', but Thompson argues that, far from disappearing, an everyday world external to the media is central to individuals' experience of their lives and their self-formation (Thompson 1995: 232). He distinguishes

There are contradictions here: on the one hand online communications create or realise a fluid, decentred subject, whilst on the other, by stripping away 'superficial' corporeal markers of identity we approach something like a 'truthful' essential self constituted in ideal communication with other disembodied but authentic identities. N. Katherine Hayles notes connections between recent cybercultural notions of identity and the long-established Enlightenment subject. Both, she argues, are based on the notion that 'embodiment is not essential to human being . . . Indeed one could argue that the erasure of embodiment is a feature common to both the liberal human subject and the cybernetic posthuman. Identified with the rational mind, the liberal subject possessed a body but was not usually represented as being a body. Only because the body is not identified with the self is it possible to claim for the liberal subject its notorious universality, a claim that depends on erasing markers of bodily difference, including sex, race, and ethnicity' (Hayles 1999: 5 quoted in Kitzmann 1999)

McLuhan (1962). See also Birkerts (1994) and Provenzo (1986)

John B. Thompson, *The Media and Modernity: a social theory of the media*, Cambridge: Polity Press, 1995

between 'mediated experience' and 'lived experience', the latter including face-to-face communication and the practices and routines of our daily lives. This is not to argue that there exists some rigid distinction between these two modes of experience:

> they are inseparable, intermingled, in the modern world. Lived experience may form the 'connective tissue' of daily lives, but mediated experience is selectively, but thoroughly 'interlaced' with it, and often acquires 'a deep and enduring relevance'.
>
> (Thompson 1995: 230–231)

We must be careful, in questioning certain cyberculture assertions of digital media as revolutionary, not to lose sight of genuinely new modes of identity play in networked media. Indeed, in some ways cyberculture does not so much ignore 'lived experience' as argue that we are more and more 'living' in networks, a union of the immediate and the mediated suggested by the term 'virtual reality' itself. We will now explore these issues with a number of case studies of specific online media and modes of interaction with new technologies.

CASE STUDY 4.4   The post-human, cyborgs and cyberfeminism

5.1.5 Technology and nature: the cyborg
5.4.4 Cyberculture and the body

A cyborg is a rather slippery thing.

(Kember 1998: 109)

Within cyberculture and postmodernist discourses it is not always clear what these new decentred, fluid subjectivities of new media might be. Stuart Hall sees them already existing in the complex identities and affiliations of migrants and diasporic peoples, of which he is one:

> Now that, in the postmodern age, you all feel so dispersed, I become centred. What I've thought of as dispersed and fragmented comes, paradoxically, to be the representative modern experience! . . . Welcome to migranthood.
>
> (Hall 1987: 44)

Donna Haraway 'A manifesto for cyborgs: science, technology, and socialist feminism in the 1980s', in Linda J. Nicholson (ed.) *Feminism/Postmodernism*, London: Routledge, 1990

Some postmodernist theorists of new media leave the question open, preferring not to speculate on these putative emergent identities. Others cite 'cyberfeminist' concepts of emergent and future subjects as key examples of technological, postmodern, but political forms of identity. 'Cyberfeminism' is not a movement as such; the term covers a diverse, even contradictory range of feminist theories on technological change and gender. These theories have been influential on many studies of new media. This section will introduce the arguments and points of contention of two of the most influential writers in this field, and will explore the invocation of the cyborg (both real and fictional) as an emergent postmodern (even 'post-human') subject position.

Donna Haraway's influential essay, 'A manifesto for cyborgs: science, technology, and socialist feminism in the 1980s', is a thorough postmodernist interrogation of binary oppositions, identifying:

> self/other, mind/body, culture/nature, male/female, civilized/primitive, reality/appearance, whole/part, agent/resource, maker/made, active/passive, right/wrong, truth/illusion . . . [as dualisms] systemic to the domination of women, people of color, nature, workers, animals.
>
> (Haraway 1990: 218)

4.8 Machogirl: videogame character designed by 10-year-old girl, South London, 1995.

These categories are not only excluded from, and dominated by, the universalising myth of the Western subject, importantly they are positioned as 'others' to define this subject 'to mirror the self'. Monsters, such as those in classical myth, demonstrate the ambiguities of self-definition through the other: the centaur, half-human, half-animal, represents 'boundary pollution'. The cyborg, then, is a contemporary monster, but, from the standpoint of a postmodernist politics of difference, one to be celebrated.

This 'challenge to Western either/or epistemology' is conducted through an 'ironic political myth' of the cyborg. This creature is 'a cybernetic organism, a hybrid of machine and organism' (Haraway 1990: 191). It is deliberately ambiguous, encompassing fictional cyborgs (*Robocop* perhaps), the increasing material intimacy between human bodies and machines (in medicine, warfare, or in miniaturised consumer electronics), a conception of networks as complex systems in which categories of biology and machines blur, and a postmodernist, 'post-gender' subject position. This latter is facilitated precisely by the cyborg's ambiguity. It is not reducible to either the natural or the cultural, and therefore is neither entirely male nor female. Haraway cites *Bladerunner*'s heroine, the replicant Rachel, as an image of the fundamental confusion the cyborg generates around distinctions between the technical and the natural, and questions of origins, of mind and body (Haraway 1990: 219). The cyborg comes into being through 'replication' rather than organic reproduction, so it lends itself to the 'utopian tradition of imagining a world without gender' (Haraway 1990: 192). This, then, is an attempt to think beyond difference, beyond the dualisms that structure the modern subject, an attempt in which science and technology, and particularly information technology, are central.

See Plant (1993, 1995)

Though sometimes bracketed together in a number of important ways, the works of Donna Haraway and Sadie Plant put forward quite different analyses of the sexual politics of new technologies and subjectivities. Whereas Haraway posits the cyborg as a figure that transcends sexual difference, Plant sees gender as the determining, even apocalyptic, factor in new identities. Though like Haraway she draws on ideas of embodied cyborgs (also using popular science fiction films as evidence), Plant's model of a blurring of boundaries between the biological and the machinic is predominantly one of networks rather than bodies. She sees the history of the computer's development as one of ever-expanding complexity, to the point at which this complexity is indistinguishable from the complex systems of both nature and culture:

> Parallel distributed processing defies all attempts to pin it down, and can only ever be contingently defined. It also turns the computer into a complex thinking machine which converges with the operations of the human brain . . . Neural nets are distributed systems which function as analogues of the brain and can learn, think, 'evolve' and 'live'. And the parallels proliferate. The complexity the computer becomes also emerges in economies, weather-systems, cities and cultures, all of which begin to function as complex systems with their own parallel processes, connectivities and immense tangles of mutual interlinkings.
>
> (Plant 2000: 329)

Plant isn't speaking metaphorically here, she is asserting that machines not only appear to take on the characteristics of biological systems, including the human brain, but that to all intents and purposes no meaningful distinction between the natural and the machinic can now be made.

For Plant the Internet, or matrix, is inherently feminine and manifests

> lines of communication between women, long repressed, . . . returning in a technological form . . . The immediacy of women's communion with each other, the flashes of intuitive exchange, and the non-hierarchical system which women have established in the networking practices of grass roots feminist organisations: all these become the instant access of telecommunication, the decentred circuits and dispersed networks of information.
>
> (Plant 1993: 13–14)

Plant's project is, like that of Haraway, to question and 'think beyond' the structuring binaries of Western thought, and again in particular the masculine subject as agent of history. Both draw on post-structuralist theories. Plant develops the ideas of French theorist Luce Irigaray who argued that, apparently paradoxically, machines and women are bracketed together in binary opposition to men. For though not 'natural' as such, machines are, like women, things existing to benefit man, 'mere things on which men worked', or objects of exchange (Plant 1993: 13). In opposition to men, they too have been seen as having no agency or self-awareness. Following this logic, then, Plant asserts that there is only one *homo sapiens* ('Man') and that 'Woman is a virtual reality'. The implication here is that women have always been positioned as some kind of biological-machinic hybrid, and that it is only with the emergence of information technology that this association ceases to be repressive. Instead it marks a revolution that doesn't so much undermine the male modern subject as sweep him away, in 'a fluid attack, an onslaught on human agency and the solidity of identity . . . It is the process by which the world becomes female, and so posthuman' (Plant 1993: 17).

See Kember (1998)

Sarah Kember is critical of Sadie Plant's analysis of the relationships between the human and the machine in the age of networked communication, arguing that collapsing any distinction between life and information – a concept she terms **'connectionism'** – runs the risk of conflating the complex systems of nature with social systems such as economies. While connectionism 'offers a rhetoric of resistance to control and authority which is based on the destruction of boundaries', Kember sees it as fundamentally anti-political in that the assertion of such systems as 'self-organizing, self-arousing' (Plant 1995: 58) denies any social or historical context. For Kember, Haraway, by contrast, seeks to 'trouble and revise the restricted rationality of conventional Western forms of knowledge' without recourse to connectionism (Kember 1998: 107; see also Squires 1996).

The term 'post-human' as used within cyberculture is, then, an articulation of a number of interlinked concepts:

- the cyborgian notion of the post-human as marked by material, corporeal change (whether through prosthetics or genetic manipulation);

- the challenge cybernetics makes to the established sense of the human body's boundaries – for example, 'the idea of the feedback loop implies that the boundaries of the autonomous subject are up for grabs, since feedback loops can flow not only within the subject, but also between the subject and the environment' (Hayles 1999: 2);

- the cyberfeminist critique of the Enlightenment subject, as founded on a Western epistemology of binary divisions (not least that of male–female), and the (more or less) ironic proposition that fictional cyborgs and actual technologies offer alternative ways of thinking about identity;

- post-structuralist critiques of post-Enlightenment humanism. Poster argues that 'We are moving beyond the "humanist" phase of history into a new level of combination of human and machines, an extremely suggestive assemblage in which the figures of the cyborg and cyberspace open vast unexplored territories' (Poster 1995b).

This is perhaps an echo of Foucault's prediction of the end of 'Man', not because of immersion in new technology but because his subjectivity is historically situated. Man is a chimerical figure within Classical thought, whose demise will be within knowledge, not cybernetics: 'It is comforting . . . and a source of profound relief to think that man is only a recent invention, a figure not yet two centuries old, a new wrinkle in our knowledge, and that he will disappear again as soon as that knowledge has discovered a new form' (Foucault 1970: xxiii)

Case Study 4.5   MUD ethnography

See Bassett (1997)

To bring the discussion back to the everyday, we will now look at an ethnographic study questioning identity play in online media. This in itself is a novel approach, ethnographic research having generally been rooted in the specific space of the culture under scrutiny.

See also Bromberg (1996) for an ethnographic study of MUDs

Caroline Bassett's study of MUDs questions any sense of firm boundaries between virtual and everyday social interaction, and addresses some of the implications for online identity play. She studies the online 'world' of Xerox's PARC research centre, LambdaMOO. As with other MUDs, LambdaMOO has a text-based interface, and citizens present themselves through three basic attributes: name, gender and appearance, all represented to other users as textual description. They can also 'build' themselves a textual home, its design reflecting their new identity. For example, exploring ambiguity and androgyny:

Neuterworld.

A bland, white room. Clean air is sucked into your nostrils and unclean exhalation is sucked out of the room through the huge roof mounted extractor fan. A sense of peace pervades the whole room. Bara is here.

   Bara.

   A tall, dark individual of slight build. This person is curious in that it is impossible for you to tell whether it is male or female!

   It is sleeping.

(Bassett 1997: 541)

Whilst sympathetic to the possibilities of MUDs and related online communication forms, Bassett questions uncritical notions of new free-floating identities in cyberspace, observing that whilst some participants do experiment with very different characteristics, or multiple 'identities', this is by no means practised by all. Thus while some take advantage of the transgressive genders allowed by the MUD:

E looks content, and eir eyes beam at you with a kind of amusement . . . the black suede mini hugs Peri's hips and barely covers eir crotch, black suede glistening in the light or lack there of. Carrying bodysuit, nipple clamps ...

   E carries a [hash] note on Eir gender in Real Life . . .

(Bassett 1997: 545)

Most adhere to stereotyped constructions of masculinity or femininity:

Beige Guest

One luscious babe, with a flowing mane of brilliant red hair, with crystal emerald eyes, and the most enchanting smile on earth.

(Bassett 1997: 546)

Bassett notes that it is probable that such hyperfeminine presentation is almost certainly that of a male participant. Even shifting identity to an inanimate object or animal does not automatically mean an escape from the gendered structures of Real Life:

Cyberferret is a ferret . . . with several cybernetic implants. One leg is bionic, and his entire skeletal system is made of titanium. He is looking for something to KILL!

(Bassett 1997: 549)

   Cyberferret aside, most online identities are, regardless of their play with gender, overwhelmingly presented as being white, attractive and young. This counters any straightforward assumption identity construction free from Real Life constraints and distinctions. Bassett draws on Judith Butler's concept of identity formation as 'performative'; that is to say, that identity (and gender in particular) is not so much constructed as constantly materialised through acts in language. 'This is . . . to understand the subject her/himself as contingent, formed and reformed in the act of performance' (Bassett 1997: 549). These performed identities, whilst ostensibly fitting a more unstable sense of identity as an ongoing process, are not by any means 'free-floating'. The

See also Don Slater's participant observation of the trading of sexpics (pornography) on Internet Relay Chat (IRC) (Slater 1998). In this particular new Internet medium, Slater found that the separation of mind and body is often perceived by participants to be a problem not a liberation. Indeed, there was a direct relationship between the degree to which 'real life' markers of identity (name, age, sex, location and so on) were known by IRC participants in communication and the degree to which genuine relationships developed and communities were established. Trust and communication were developed as 'authentic' evidence of the participants' identities was divulged

conventional gendered identities in MUDs are as performative as the apparently liberated ones. 'Even in cyberspace gender is . . . compelled' (Bassett 1997: 549).

Despite this, Bassett argues for two progressive readings of 'the small world' of Lambda. The first is that it highlights gender as constructed and 'unnatural', and secondly she implies that Real Life discourses are not entirely dominant in cyberspace, that Lambda does provide 'spaces for disruption, for the possibility of gender-play, and for the emergence of new forms of multiple subjectivity' (Bassett 1997: 550).

4.3.4 Consuming cybersubjectivities

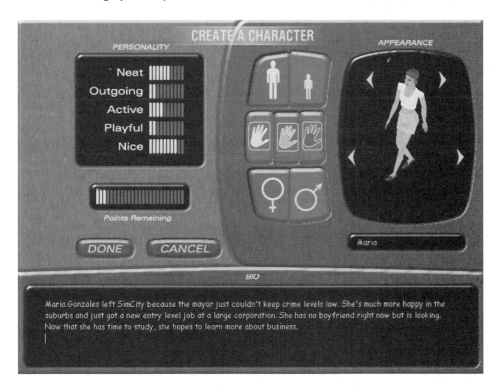

4.9 The Sims: Create a Character. © 2002 Electronic Arts Inc. All rights reserved.

We have seen then:

3.11 The post-web Internet

- profound claims for transformation of the underpinnings of everyday life, its politics and possibilities: sense of self, body and identity in new media world;

- demands to see the self in everyday life not as an autonomous subject but as, to varying degrees and with diverse conclusions, embroiled in networks, in intimate relationships with machines and media. Whilst this dependency on machines and media did not appear with digital technology (originating perhaps in the Industrial Revolution or with movable type), digital media do recast, perhaps accelerate, these relationships;

- enquiries into how real life and life online are related. Do new media bring separation and disembodiment or new manifestations of real life and communication?

There is, however, a key aspect of media subjectivity not fully acknowledged by cyberculture theories. Optimistic accounts of new media tend to ignore commercial forces in the shaping and use of computer networks and environments. Indeed, cyberculture tends to take the more 'public' types of new media as its object of study: communication media, the Internet as chat, MUDs, and so on.

Postmodernist media studies on the other hand tends to take commercial mass media as its object, and downplay any technological agency in identity construction. Thus, to put it crudely, the cyberculture subject enters cyberspace to engage in identity play, whereas the postmodernist media subject is always already enfolded in, and constructed by the mediasphere.

A recent advertising campaign in Britain for the Internet search site Excite featured photographs of individuals jumping exuberantly with arms and legs spread (to echo the company's 'X' logo). Text, listing the individual's interests and hobbies, was arranged around his or her head like a halo. Stuart Hall has pointed out that contemporary notions of 'free floating' identity are bound up with a consumerist logic of individual subject as choice-exercising shopper (Hall *et all.* 1992: 303). This leads us to ask what the role of commercial popular culture might be in the transformations brought by new media (and everyday understanding of these transformations). For cyberculture discourses (again we are generalising) new media either break free from or operate in a different sphere from the popular and commodified (indeed this is often the predication of cyberculture celebration). Yet these discourses, as should be apparent, are shot through with imagery and ideas drawn from cyberpunk science fiction, most notably of course William Gibson's *Neuromancer* and the film *Bladerunner*. Sadie Plant uses the blurb from the back cover of Pat Cadigan's novel *Synners* as evidence of emergent socio-technological forms (Plant 1993: 14). Donna Haraway is at pains to point out that her cyborgs are 'ironic', but does not explore what their status is in this context. These popular texts occupy an ambiguous position within theoretical discourses of new media. Indeed, discourses such as cyberculture and, to some extent, computer-mediated communication implicitly establish themselves as distinct from the commodified cultural forms, consumerist subjectivities and economic relations of late capitalism, but at the same time legitimate and romanticise themselves through popular commercial culture.

This is not to argue that popular genres such as cyberpunk should not be addressed, or that popular texts are any less significant parts of any emergent cyberculture: 'the literary texts often reveal . . . the complex cultural, social, and representational issues tied up with conceptual shifts and technological innovations' (Hayles 1999: 24). Indeed it is to argue that the study of cyberpunk is crucial, but that its ideas and predictions cannot be separated from consumerist popular culture any more than popular new media technologies can. With this point in mind we will now examine in detail the most well-established and widely consumed new medium: the videogame.

Cyberpunk's status as gendered popular culture has certainly been noticed; see Squires (1996), Kember (1998: 113)

4.4 GAMEPLAY

Videogames are the first popular computer-based medium. Predating the home computer, games devices such as the 'tennis' game Pong were first plugged into television sets in 1972. They brought with them fears and fascination — a sense that everyday life was meeting the future: new ways of relating to machines, new images and worlds, frightening narratives of symbolic violence and addiction.

This section aims to do two main things. To look at videogames as an extremely successful new medium in its own right, with arguably the greatest significance for the everyday consumption of new media, and to serve as an extended case study applying the key concerns of this part of the book to the consumption of this particular medium. Videogames will be studied as:

- consumer media technology, shaped by and shaping everyday activities and dynamics;

- commodified new media devices and texts, offering interactive pleasures and possibilities;

- games, inviting the analysis of play as a particular mode of use or consumption;

- computer media, whose consumption and meanings in everyday life are inseparable from their status as digital technologies.

4.4.1 New media's 'other'

'OK, you're haunted. You're seeing Cyber-Demon Lords in your dreams. You can't get to that Soul Sphere in the Military Base, and it's driving you nuts. You're a hopeless Doom addict. A Doomie. Yeah, it hurts. And yet . . . who would have thought going to Hell could be so much fun?'

(Barba 1994: v)

These are the opening sentences from *Doom Battlebook*, a manual and **cheats** guide for the popular computer and video game released in 1993. *Doom* is a first-person shoot-em up, a game in which the player's point of view is apparently through the eyes of the character he or she controls in the game. The premiss of the game is simple: the player must guide the character through maze-like corridors of a science fiction environment, shooting any creature he meets. Weapons and 'power-ups' (ammunition, first-aid kits, armour) are collected along the way to prolong the slaughter, and the whole experience is one of horror, panic, and the temporary satisfaction of annihilating a room full of enemies, satisfaction soon forgotten as the next level is explored. *Doom* is a grimy post-industrial universe of bubbling toxic waste and slimy metal walls. Perhaps now regarded by gameplayers as quaint in its simplicity, despite (by today's standards) low-resolution graphics and pixellated monsters, the game still generates controversy.

Doom is only one of the more notorious of an often-vilified new medium, which, since its introduction, has been the focus of fears of cultural and social change, particularly around childhood and youth. Seen as encouraging antisocial play in violent and morally dubious computer environments and narratives, videogames become everything that threatens an idealised children's culture. Against 'spontaneous play' on beaches and in woods, a 'play world of the natural child [that is] open and friendly', is set the play world of 'the "electronic child" . . . hemmed in by conflict and fear' (Stutz 1995).

Many of these anxieties and moral outrages follow the well-established patterns of the 'media scares' – video-nasties, comics, pinball and penny-dreadfuls have all in their time epitomised the new and dangerous (Barker 1984). Videogames add to this panic the threat of the computer's increasing influence in everyday life. These anxieties are evident in academic and theoretical discourses as well. Videogames are generally presented as a problem to be solved, threatening a future of hyper-gendered identities or a techno-consumerist 'Nintendo generation'. Julian Stallabrass articulates a nightmare of a cybernetic capitalism and the implosion of the public and private:

> There is a shadowy ambition behind the concept of the virtual world – to have everyone sagely confined in their homes, hooked up to sensory feedback devices in an enclosing, interactive environment which will be a far more powerful tool of social control than television.
>
> (Stallabrass 1993: 104)

Throughout this part of the book we have noted how the constitution of fields of study in new media (CMC, cyberculture, media educationalism, etc.) tends to marginalise or exclude popular, commercial and commodified versions of digital media and information technologies. Within education they are a dangerously seductive distraction from learning, or at best offer themselves as Trojan Horses or sweeteners for the real business of computer use. Within cybercultural discourses they haunt the fringes of MUDs and hypertext as gendered, commodified toys, as other to the online heterotopias of identity play. It is evident that discourses celebrating new media may do so in denial of certain key contexts for the development of new media as popular cultural forms.

For example, in an essay on the game Myst, David Miles identifies interesting precedents for the game's interactive narrative structure and atmosphere. The list is impressive: the gothic novel, Parsifal, Verne, modernist literature (Gide, Robbe-Grillet, Borges), Homer, early cinema. The essay is a perceptive and imaginative attempt to take the computer game seriously, and to think of what its future might be. However, in doing so it elides the very 'low' cultural pleasures that have popularised and developed the form. For Miles Myst is not a 'videogame' but an 'interactive multimedia novel on CD-ROM' (Miles 1999: 307). Non-violent, sedate and intellectually challenging, Myst, though published in the same year as Doom, seems to belong to a different world. Whilst the computer or videogame may well, as Miles hopes, offer art and literature new forms and aesthetics, to forget that Myst is still a computer game, and as such the hybrid offspring of less prestigious cultural forms (pinball machines, science fiction, fantasy and horror literature, toys, television), is to miss the central significance of the videogame to new media.

In both popular and academic discourses, videogames are often explicitly posited as emblematic of the troubled status of our understanding of the real world in media culture. The principal example is the 1991 Gulf War. The thorough control of news media by the coalition states, and the spectacle of 'smart' weapons and video footage from missiles at their point of impact epitomised a popular notion of 'simulation' as a conflation of digital and video imaging technology and a sense of a remote, mediated experience (by both domestic audiences and Western military). This 'simulation' was explicitly figured in terms of video games, as the 'Nintendo war'. Doom is often implicated in this blurring of the real and the mediated in violent events. Frequently cited in media scares around youth culture, particularly in the United States, the game has been blamed (along with other commercial youth-oriented media, particularly popular music) in the shooting of school students by classmates in Littleton, Colorado in 1999.

Widely quoted in press and television reports on the killings, the military psychologist Lt.-Col. David Grossman argues that, just as Doom is used by the US Marines as a training

See Norris (1992)

For a fascinating account of an attempt to challenge this scare around youth culture in the US, see Jenkins (2001) on his testimony to the Senate Commerce Committee

simulator, so it 'trained' these disturbed adolescents to kill. Moreover, the videogame's immersive mode of consumption encouraged a disastrous breaking down of the distinction between fantasies and reality. In a *New York Times* article reprinted in the *Guardian*, Paul Keegan discussed Grossman's views, concluding:

> And that's what makes shooters [first person shoot-em ups] unlike any other form of media violence we've seen before. You're not just watching a movie, you're in the movie. You're not just empathising with Arnold Schwarzenegger as he blasts the bad guy to smithereens, you're actually pulling the trigger.
>
> (Keegan 2000: 3)

This, then, is an extreme form of realism — the interactive manipulation of pixellated icons of hyperbolic violence mapped directly, unmediated, onto real-world behaviour. Such claims do not stand up to serious scrutiny, but they do highlight, through their resonances with certain discourses of VR and cyberspace, the underlying sense in the technological imaginary of interactive media of an idealist (whether utopian or dystopian) notion of the end of media. The shoot-em up genre can be seen then as the 'repressed' of the cybercultural enthusiasm for interactivity — losing oneself in the medium can be creative and liberating, but is haunted by the possibility that this immersion can be hypnotic, seductive, 'mindless' as well as bodiless.

Thus the positive aspects of new media such as CD-ROMs or the Internet are defined in opposition to the negative, the latter embodied in videogames:

New media/cyberspace/CMC	Videogames
creative communication	mindless entertainment
public space	private/commodified space
adult users	child/youth consumers
fluidity of identity	hypermasculinity
immersive	addictive
interactivity	reflex, 'twitch'
new realities	new delusions
popular culture as social theory	popular culture as commodification
art and literature	trash culture
'objects to think with'	toys

In this section we will challenge this marginalisation and argue that the study of videogames offers us analytical and critical purchase on the forms and consumption of new media technologies in general.

4.4.2 Videogames as new technology

Rather than being a marginal form of new media, videogames (as media texts and as new modes of play and consumption) are indivisible from the dissemination and popularisation, and even the development, of personal computing, its software and interfaces, its practices and meanings. The relationship between the emergence of home/personal computers and videogames is tangled and complex; in what follows we suggest some key strands.

VR may be figured precisely in terms of games and play. For example, Mark Poster approvingly quotes N. Kathryn Hales's definition of the 'revolutionary potential' of virtual reality as exposing 'the presuppositions underlying the social formations of late capitalism and to open new fields of play where the dynamics have not yet rigidified and new kinds of moves are possible' (Poster 1995a: 138)

Case study 4.1   The 'open' PC

This said, computer games did very quickly become an extremely popular cultural form in their own right. As Leslie Haddon puts it, home computer users' preference for games playing appropriated the 'micro' and transformed its meanings (Haddon 1992: 84)

4.2.5   Edutainment edutainment edutainment

3.4   Learning to live in the interface

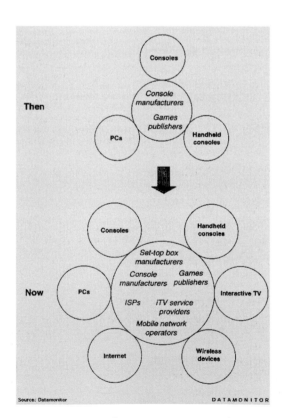

Source: Datamonitor   DATAMONITOR

4.10 Consumption and convergence. Courtesy of Datamonitor.

INSTRUMENTAL PLAY

Games software was central to the practices of early home computing, not only as entertainment but also as demonstrative of the power and possibilities of the new machines. As we have seen (**Case study 4.1**), home computers were distinctly 'open' devices. Games would be bought, copied, or written by users as much to see what the computer could do, exploring graphics, sound and interactivity, as for the pleasures of gameplay itself.

In a broader sense, home computer use has continued to be characterised by a kind of exploratory play with computer or software systems, whether or not game software itself was being used. Indeed, play in this general sense is a significant strategy for learning the computer's system. The governmental, educational and commercial discourses of the promotion of computer use since the 1980s have, sometimes anxiously, emphasised this 'instrumental play' – promising the purchasers of home computers that the information age can be fun. The experience of interacting with and controlling a computer, primarily through play, would link user and machine in the spare bedroom with the historic forces of the information revolution (**4.2.5**).

It could be argued that the relationship between computer games and personal computing is even more significant. The origins of personal computing lie in the philosophy and innovations of the first 'hackers', students at MIT in the late 1950s. These students challenged official uses of the institution's mainframe computers (statistical analyses, scientific simulations, and so on); instead they would develop non-instrumental ways of exploring the computers' potential. This exploration ranged from using the mainframe to play single-track classical music to programming the lights on the front of the machine to allow a game of computer ping-pong. Such play was not always wilfully trivial however – they also experimented with the possibilities of artificial intelligence in chess programs.

On one level these hackers were, like the home computer hobbyists to follow, 'just seeing what the machine would do'. However, in experimenting with realtime computer interaction and animation, through the design of games, they established a new mode of computer use which ultimately resulted in PC graphical user interfaces (see also **3.4**). The implications of one of the first computer games, *Space War*, were recognised early on: 'Ready or not, computers are coming to the people. That's good news, maybe the best since psychedelics', MIT researcher Stewart Brand, after watching the early computer game *Space War* at the Stanford AI lab in the early 1970s (quoted in Ceruzzi, 1999: 64).

HACKING AS CONSUMPTION

Not only have computer and video games played a significant role in turning computer technology into domestic computer media, they have, through their generation of new modes of interaction with screen-based information and communication, leaked out into many other everyday technologies and media – from the PC *Minesweeper* games and 'desktop' puzzles to the games-derived interfaces and 'help' screens on photocopiers, digital photo booths, and mobile phone text-messaging. From this observation, a number of questions can be posed:

1 If computer and video games have popularised computer technology and made it accessible, have they, in so doing, effectively commodified computer technology, turning the radical hacker ethic into a consumerist entertainment?

2 What are the implications of the study of media technology as games and its consumption or use as play?

3 Could the recognition of videogames as central to the information revolution ask us to look again at the long-established discursive oppositions between work/education and play, instrumental use and consumption, games and everyday life?

Programming as play

To address question 1 above, the focus must be shifted from the technologies themselves, to the practices of their use. Hacking as play has been seen as inseparable from the demands (in terms of expertise and time) of programming. For the producers and users of early home computers it was assumed that computer use meant programming. To run the most elementary game or application required a grasp of programming languages such as BASIC, and a grasp of coding was seen as central to the realisation of the potential of computers. Leslie Haddon has differentiated between 'computer games' and 'videogames' (arcade machines, or early dedicated consoles) on just such grounds. The keen player/programmer could intervene into the code of the home computer game, using 'pokes' or cheats to explore the game environment or change parameters (Haddon 1992: 89).

By the late 1980s however, as the micro gave way to IBM-compatible or Apple Macintosh personal computers with DOS (later Windows) and the Apple GUI, programming ceased to be needed in everyday computer use, and, partly as a consequence, the distinction between computer and video games became less clear. Today, the PC is regarded by videogame manufacturers as one platform alongside the various competing dedicated videogame consoles. The most popular games are adapted across these platforms. They are predominantly played as 'closed' texts, loaded from disk or cartridge, too complex now for amateur intervention.

Levy (1994) identifies a 'hacker ethic', a kind of politics of computer programming, as serious play. Many of the elements of this unwritten hacker manifesto (free exchange of information, mistrust of authority, meritocracy) are evident in contemporary Internet culture. Even the origin of the term 'hacker' is ludic. Deriving from MIT jargon for prank, a hack is: 'a project undertaken or a product built not solely to fulfil some constructive goal, but with some wild pleasure taken in mere involvement . . ., to qualify as a hack, the feat must be imbued with innovation, style, and technical virtuosity' (Levy 1994: 23)

Another example of an early computer game with far-reaching implications for the development of personal computing, and the Internet, is *Adventure* (1967). An interactive story, set in a Tolkeinesque fantasy world, with forking paths followed according to the user's choice, luck or ability to solve puzzles. As well as remaining popular in its own right for decades, it has been influential on a number of contemporary videogame genres, and is an early example of interactive narrative

Though largely overlapping, there are still games which seem to suit (or are at least designed and marketed for) PCs. They are generally adult-oriented, such as the more realistic flight and tank simulations, or *Myst* for example. However, as we will see, the archetypal violent videogame *Doom* is in important ways still a 'computer' game

---

BOX 4.7:   *Doom* as media, technology and new cultural economy

To draw together commercial entertainment, key hacker tenets (free access to code, the hands-on programming imperative), new consumption practices and new Internet-based production and marketing models, we will again enter the fun hell that is *Doom*.

As mentioned above, the US Marine Corps adapted this game as training simulator software. However they also then marketed their customised version as a game. Whilst this circularity may seem a useful example of the thesis that the boundaries between war, power, media and entertainment are now thoroughly blurred, it also allows us to make

See Manovich (1998)

more specific observations. The job of converting the game into training software (and back again) was facilitated by the innovative way in which *Doom* was distributed. Firstly, the initial levels of the game were given away, made available for download from the Internet (Manovich 1998). Secondly, in hacker tradition, the publishers made the code and file formats for the game's design freely available, allowing players (as had always been the case with early, simpler, computer games) to modify levels, add new enemies or construct new levels themselves.

Comparing *Doom* to *Myst* (both published in 1993), Lev Manovich argues that there is a fundamental difference between them that is not to do with violent content or cultural pedigree, but rather cultural economy. Whereas *Myst* invited its players to 'behold and admire' its images and narratives, *Doom* asked its players to take them apart and modify them. In this sense *Doom*, then, is a good example of the cyber-enthusiast view of computer media as enabling and creative. As Manovich puts it, the game 'transcended the usual relationships between producers and consumers' (Manovich 1998).

3.18 The development of the new economy

For an account of *Doom* as a popular cultural phenomenon and model for the 'new economy', see Herz (1997: 83–90)

Not only did this shareware marketing strategy continue and extend the long-established gaming culture of cheats and patches, it was also the inspiration for Netscape's early conquest of Internet browsing through free availability of its software (Herz 1997: 90). The free availability of the *Doom* and *Quake* (*Doom*'s successor) code has also led to them becoming the engines for other new media applications. For example, online virtual conferencing, and low bandwidth 3D digital animated film-making for Internet distribution. See www.plugincinema.com

Online gaming has developed from office-based, multi-player networks of *Doom* to *Quake* tournaments on the Internet. However, not all computer-mediated play and games fall within the videogame mode. Traditional games such as chess, bridge, quizzes are also being adapted, with more people playing through interactive television than PC-based Internet. It is estimated that 49 per cent of adult online gamers are female (Datamonitor 2000), and the online games market for consoles and PCs is predicted to be worth $4.9 billion by 2004. Here, the producers' dream of the videogame console as domestic entertainment 'black box' is challenged both by the open-ended technology of networks and competing popular forms of play.

Case Study 4.6   Pokémon: video games as new (mass) media

4.11 Pikachu – I choose you!

To explore the issues arising from popular new media's implication within commercial entertainment culture we will take the various incarnations of *Pokémon* as a case study.

An entertainment supersystem

Beginning life in 1996 as a game for the Nintendo Gameboy hand-held videogame console, *Pokémon* went on to achieve dramatic success as a card collecting and trading game, and is now a merchandising franchise worth $5 billion a year. The 'Pocket Monsters' feature in a television series, animated feature films, Nintendo 64 games, and all the other licensed products of children's media culture. It is estimated that, at the phenomenon's height, half of all Japanese seven- to twelve-year-olds were regular players. Even before it had been released in the UK, *Pokémon: the First Movie* had overtaken *Lion King* as the most successful animated film (*Guardian*, 20 April 2000). After pornography, *Pokémon* was the most searched for subject on the web in 1999 (*Guardian Editor*, 21 April 2000).

Pokémon is an example of an 'entertainment supersystem' (Kinder 1991: 1). Marsha Kinder defines a supersystem as a 'network of intertextuality constructed around a figure or group of figures from pop culture' (Kinder 1991: 122). These figures can be fictional or real celebrities:

> In order to be a supersystem, the network must cut across several modes of image production; must appeal to diverse generations, classes, and ethnic subcultures, who in turn are targeted with diverse strategies; must foster 'collectability' through a proliferation of related products; and

must undergo a sudden increase in commodification, the success of which reflexively becomes a 'media event' that dramatically accelerates the growth curve of the system's commercial success.

(Kinder 1991: 123)

Kinder takes the children's media craze of the late 1980s *Teenage Mutant Ninja Turtles* as a case study. Like the Turtles, *Pokémon* is based around ritualised conflict (and, like the Turtles a decade earlier, has had its products banned from schools for apparently provoking real fights). However, *Pokémon* has exceeded even the Turtles in its saturation of children's media and everyday lives:

> The real reason for the game's astounding success probably has more to do with the breathtakingly clever way in which Nintendo and its franchisees have created a self-referential world in which every product – every trading card, computer game, movie, cartoon and hamburger box – serves as propaganda for all the others.

(Burkeman 2000: 2)

Global culture

The idea that we are seeing the emergence of a global commercial popular culture is a familiar one. This global culture is, however, commonly viewed as evidence of US cultural dominance, with talk of Disnification or McDonaldisation as the analogue in the cultural sphere to globalisation in the economic sphere. *Pokémon* and *Teenage Mutant Ninja Turtles*, however (along with other supersystems such as *Power Rangers*), are evidence of a meeting and hybridisation of Eastern and Western popular cultural forms. Even before *Pokémon*, the videogame was perhaps the most thoroughly transnational form of popular culture, both as an industry (with Sony, Sega and Nintendo as the key players) but also at the level of content – the characters and narratives of many videogames are evidence of relays of influence between America and Japan.

Nintendo, in its pre-video game incarnation as playing card manufacturer, introduced the first Disney licensing into Japan soon after the Second World War, and a tremendous boom in (the already established) Japanese animation industry followed. As Disney took European folktales, stripped them of their original religious motivations, and animated them with the anxieties and morals of a Western bourgeoisie, so Japanese *anime* (animated films) and *manga* (comics) took Disney images, with their graphic resonances with traditional Japanese art, and charged them with very different philosophies.

Gotta catch 'em all!: acquisition as play

MacKenzie Wark asserts that videogames are 'primers in junk consumerism' (Wark 1994). If we accept this analysis, then the *Pokémon* card game could also be seen as an education in market economics as well. There are over 150 characters in the game, each with their own card, and the manufacturers ensure competition and trade between players (and sales) by restricting the supply of certain cards. This exploitation of the established children's culture of collecting has been widely criticised: 'the result is a particularly pure form of kiddie capitalism, in which acquisition is no longer just a means to further play, but the very essence of play itself' (Burkeman 2000: 2).

However, this trading aspect also makes it a sociable game, with its own improvised playground-level practices and the emergence of local cultural economies such as collectors' fairs. To determine whether *Pokémon* can in any way be seen to exceed 'kiddie capitalism' we would need to study in more detail the ways in which the games are played and articulated in children's everyday lives.

See Wark (1994); also available at http://www.mcs.mq.edu.au/Staff /mwark/warchive/Mia/mia-video-games.html This is a useful essay on videogames as media, and addresses this relationship between Japanese and Western popular culture in particular

A precedent for the kind of research needed is Leslie Haddon's study of 'computer talk' – the social activity around **microcomputer** use by young boys in the 1980s. The topics and modes of conversation demonstrate everyday computer game culture as constituted by discourses of technological innovation, practical playing tips, cheats and boasting, as well as the kinds of detailed knowledge of the release of new games, conversions and features. This talk indicated, according to Haddon, the computer game's shifting status from a sub-practice of home computer use to a cultural industry in its own right, as significant in young people's lives as the music industry (Haddon 1992: 89)

4.4.3 Play

Videogames ask us to look at the consumption of new media from the perspective of play, and raise the question: what is the cultural significance of play? The word 'play' appears repeatedly, though in quite different ways, across all the diverse discourses around new media. It is viewed suspiciously in some educational discourses, for example, but in others it is seen as fundamental to progressive theories of education. It underpins both cybercultural shifting subjectivities and the notion of identity construction through bricolage. We have also seen its ambiguous status in the analysis of new media consumption, from Baudrillard's notion of the ludic as symptomatic of contemporary technologies' fundamental uselessness, to the productive play of the hacker ethic.

Theories of time, space and games

Johan Huizinga, writing in the 1930s, suggested that play is not an ephemeral, See Huizinga (1986) inconsequential activity, but an essential, perhaps central, factor in civilisation. Religious rituals, sport and drama, to name but three near-universal cultural realms, are all characterised by types of play (play and games can of course be very serious activities). Huizinga's book is called *Homo Ludens* – the human, then, is not characterised primarily by rational thought and self-awareness (*homo sapiens*) or creativity and the use of technology (*homo faber*) but by play.

Though central to culture, play is always, according to Huizinga, separate from ordinary or real life: it is 'a stepping out of "real" life into a temporary sphere of activity with a disposition all of its own' (Huizinga 1986: 8). Separated from the materially necessary activities of work and the satisfaction of bodily needs, it occurs in interludes in daily life. Play is only superficially ephemeral however; through its often regular repetitions and rituals (football matches on Sunday, crossword puzzles in coffee breaks) it is integral to everyday life.

Play is distinct from other areas of everyday life both temporally and spatially:

> It is 'played out' within certain limits of time and place . . . the arena, the card-table, the magic circle, the temple, the stage, the screen, the tennis court, the court of justice, etc. are all in form and function play-grounds, i.e. forbidden spots, isolated, hedged around, hallowed, within which special rules obtain. All are temporary worlds within the ordinary world, dedicated to the performance of an act apart.
>
> (Huizinga 1986: 10)

Roger Caillois developed Huizinga's ideas. He categorised what he saw as the fundamental See Caillois (1962) elements of play:

- *Agon* – competitive play, as found in many sports (football for example), or games such as chess.

- *Alea* – taken from the Latin for the game of dice, this term refers to games decided not, as with *agon*, by skill or training, but by the workings of chance. Most evident in gambling, from roulette to lotteries.

- Mimicry, or 'simulation'. This term covers those aspects of children's play which involve role-play or make-believe, and extends to the adult actor playing Hamlet. Caillois also includes the identification of the film or sport audiences for the star performers they watch. This identification with stars is, in Caillois's terms, mimicry.

- Ilinx, or 'vertigo'. Ilinx refers to the willing inducement in oneself of dizziness and disorder, the surrender to shock, the temporary 'destruction' of reality. It is evident in children rolling down hills or screaming, but can also manifest itself as a 'moral' vertigo in which adults succumb to desire for destruction and disorder. This 'pleasurable torture' is now evident in theme parks: 'In order to give this kind of sensation the intensity and brutality capable of shocking adults, powerful machines have to be invented' (Caillois 1962: 25).

Though videogames are sometimes seen as culturally linked with theme park white knuckle rides, *ilinx* is the only one of Caillois's categories not present in conventional videogames. Videogames depict vertigo and disorder, but do not actually instil it in players

These categories are not mutually exclusive and are often evident as pairs within particular games. For example, though *agon* and *alea* are opposites, one relying on skill and dedication, the other on luck, they are both present in many card games.

Cutting across these categories is an axis that measures the underlying qualities of particular games or types of play. One pole on this axis is *ludus*, and the other *paidia*. *Ludus* denotes modes of play characterised by adherence to strict rules: 'calculation, contrivance, subordination to rules'. *Paidia* is the opposite: 'true' creative play – 'active, tumultuous, exuberant, spontaneous' (Caillois 1962: 53). Thus chess can be placed near the *ludus* end of this axis, whereas the imaginative and improvised make-believe of young children would sit at the opposite pole of *paidia*.

It is the values given to positions on this *ludus–paidia* axis, rather than the categories of *agon*, *alea*, mimicry and ilinx, which often underlie criticism of videogame play. Videogames are generally, in this sense, *ludic*: rule-bound and apparently not offering much space for spontaneity or innovation. As Eugene Provenzo, the influential critic of videogames put it, '[c]ompared with the worlds of imagination provided by play with dolls and blocks, [video] games . . . ultimately represent impoverished cultural and sensory environments for the child' (Provenzo 1991: 97).

Caillois, however, does not privilege *paidia* over *ludus*. For him, *ludus* is fundamentally linked with the development of civilisation. Rules, he asserts, transform play 'into an instrument of fecund and decisive culture' (Caillois 1962: 27). On a more everyday level, the ludic is also evident in more respectable activities such as crossword puzzles, chess problems and detective stories. Many videogames share this intellectual play – the solving of puzzles for no apparent reason other than the pleasure of doing so. Moreover, even ludic games need room for improvisation: 'the game consists of the need to find or continue at once a response which is free within the limits set by the rules. This latitude of the player, this margin accorded to his action is essential to the game and partly explains the pleasure which it excites' (Caillois 1962: 8). Sherry Turkle identifies a relationship between the *paidia* of fantasy, and the rule-bound ludic in videogames. Science fiction and fantasy fiction are extremely influential on the development of video and computer games, not only at the level of symbolic content (spaceships and monsters) but also because they operate through an analogous tension between the fantastical or imaginative, and the logical and rule-governed. 'A planet can have any atmosphere, but its inhabitants must be adapted to it . . . You can postulate anything, but once the rules of the system have been defined they must be adhered to scrupulously' (Turkle 1984: 77). Similarly, the logic of the videogame world is that events may well be surprising, but they shouldn't be arbitrary. Ultimately, then, Turkle argues that computer games are rule-governed (*ludus*) rather than open-ended (*paidia*) (Turkle 1984: 78; see also Provenzo 1991: 88ff.).

What do games mean?

Both Huizinga and Caillois link play and games with the production and reproduction of 'civilised' social forms in a very general sense. If so, it could follow that far from being one of the lowest, most despicable cultural forms, videogames could instead be seen as central to the understanding of any emergent social and cultural order, particularly one characterised by information networks, databases and a highly developed commodified entertainment cultural economy. To see if there is any mileage in such a suggestion, we will need to address questions of how games as cultural forms and play as a mode of cultural engagement or consumption, can be seen as constitutive of culture more generally.

The place of games and play in culture is profoundly ambiguous. For Caillois, whilst games are fundamental to civilisation, 'play and ordinary life are constantly and universally antagonistic to each other' (Caillois 1962: 63). For Marshall McLuhan games are at once communication media, a popular art form, and a collective modelling of society:

> Games, like institutions, are extensions of social man and of the body politic, as technologies are extensions of the animal organism . . . As extensions of the popular response to the workaday stress, games become faithful models of a culture. They incorporate both the action and the reaction of whole populations in a single dynamic image.
>
> (McLuhan 1967: 235)

They are not simple representations of a culture though. McLuhan's games share with those of Caillois an ambiguous relationship with the social world; they exist within it but distinct from it:

> Games are a sort of artificial paradise like Disneyland, or some Utopian vision by which we interpret and complete the meaning of our daily lives. In games we devise means of nonspecialized participation in the larger drama of our time.
>
> (McLuhan 1967: 238)

Games, then, are separate from the world in time and space, played within boundaries and bound by rules. However, in important ways they are part of the world: they may figure or model their larger social context, and of course they are part of the world in that people play games every day – they are no less real for being distinct from other cultural activities.

Media play

We have already seen (4.2.3) how media consumption can be discussed in terms of reference to the ludic. Roger Silverstone regards the mass media and play as inseparable:

> We are all players now in games, some or many of which the media make. They distract but they also provide a focus. They blur boundaries but still somehow preserve them. For, arguably we know, even as children, when we are playing and when we are not. The thresholds between the mundane and the heightened spaces of the everyday are still there to be crossed, and they are crossed each time we switch on the radio or television, or log on to the World Wide Web. Playing is both escape and engagement. It occupies protected spaces and times on the screen, surrounding it and, at some further remove. While we can enter media spaces in other ways and for other purposes,

In fact, for Caillois the separation of play from other areas of everyday life is essential. The danger in games comes not from restrictive rules but rather from their 'corruption' if their autonomy from the real world is undermined. For example, the horoscope's blurring of reality and *alea* (chance), or drug and alcohol abuse as the corruption of *ilinx*. It is precisely the sharp delineation between fantasy and reality that protects the player from alienation from the real world (Caillois 1962: 49). Like McLuhan, Caillois's games are inherently conservative, reflecting or modelling but not challenging cultural values. See Friedman (1999) for an enquiry into computer games as ideological

4.2.3 Consuming new media

for work or for information, for example, while they exist to persuade as well as to educate, the media are a principal site in and through which, in the securities and stimulation that they offer the viewers of the world, we play: subjunctively, freely, for pleasure.

(Silverstone 1999: 66)

'Play' and 'pleasure' are key terms in the postmodernist positions on consumption discussed in **4.2.3**. For John Fiske, the pleasure of engagement with the texts and images of the media is the 'active' consumer's articulation of relationship of the real world and media representations, the creative engagement of the reader with the text. However, the exploration of the boundary between the real and the representation in media consumption can also be an anxious activity. Fiske cites arguments that children's control of television sets, changing channels and switching on and off, is a kind of electronic fort/da game. Children will explore distinction between the symbolic and the real in the content of programmes – satirising representations they do not approve of (Fiske 1987: 231).

The fort/da game refers to Freud's observations of his eighteen-month-old grandson throwing a wooden reel on a string out of his cot and pulling it back in, making sounds Freud took to be 'fort' (gone), 'da' (there). Freud interpreted this as the infant playing out his anxieties over his mother's absence and return

Both of these elements of play – the anxious and the performative – are also evident in videogame play. They raise the question of the political dynamic of play in general and videogame play in particular: what is the relationship between the activity, performance and pleasure of the player, the specific rules of the game and broader social rules and ideologies? For John B. Thompson, the everyday politics of individual identities in the dominant symbolic systems (ideologies or discourses) can be discussed in ludic terms, 'Like a game of chess, the dominant system will define which moves are open to individuals and which are not' (Thompson 1995: 210). Whilst for Fiske, playing with the rules is an emancipatory activity:

> The pleasures of play derive directly from the players' ability to exert control over rules, roles, and representations – those agencies that in the social are the agencies of subjection, but in play can be agents of liberation and empowerment. Play, for the subordinate, is an active, creative, resistive response to the conditions of their subordination: it maintains their sense of subcultural difference in the face of the incorporating forces of the dominant ideology.

(Fiske 1987: 236)

However, if play as cultural practice so thoroughly suffuses contemporary media consumption and identity construction we are in danger of losing any sense of it as a critical or analytical term in understanding new media. We will, therefore, shift the focus to the more specific notion of games, and videogames in particular.

4.4.4 Playing with a computer

> Video games are a window onto a new kind of intimacy with machines that is characteristic of the nascent computer culture. The special relationship that players form with video games has elements that are common to interactions with other kinds of computers. The holding power of video games, their almost hypnotic fascination, is computer holding power.

(Turkle 1984: 60)

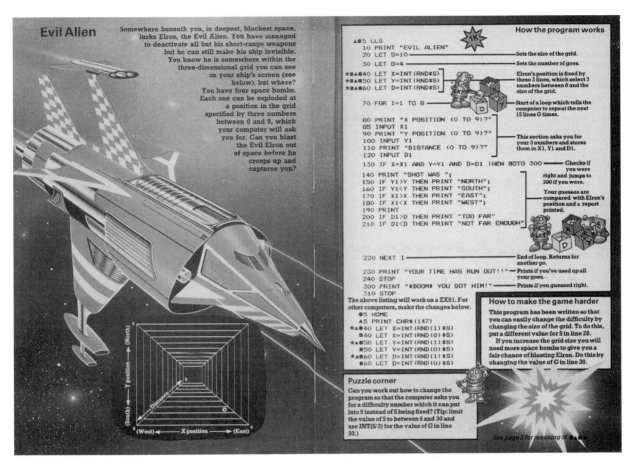

4.12 Evil Alien. Reproduced from COMPUTER SPACEGAMES by permission of Usborne Publishing Ltd © 1982.

'In TV, if you want to make someone die, you can't'
[nine-year old girl on the superiority of videogames].
(Marks Greenfield 1984: 91)

What does it mean to play with a computer? There is as yet no 'videogame theory' as a distinct discipline, so in what follows we will address aspects of videogames and gameplay that appear, often for very different reasons and with very different implications, in a range of debates around this new medium.

However, the term 'ludology' has been mooted to denote recent developments in the study of computer games *as games*. See *Game Studies* no. 1, July 2001 http://www.gamestudies.org/0101/

Videogames as media

If, on the one hand, videogames spring from mass media, and on the other, media consumption in general can be seen as playful, can the videogame be analysed as a specific new medium, and do its ludic practices have any distinct critical purchase? In shifting the emphasis to games as a specific set of cultural forms, rather than play as a general mode of consumption, we can see that videogames do mark a significant new medium: mass media as games. That is to say, though boardgames may draw on entertainment themes and images, they are not as thoroughly imbricated in, or formally similar to, the images and action of moving image media: film, animation and television. There is in the content of videogames a semiotic complexity at the level of content not evident in chess or golf or Cluedo.

However, despite evident continuities and connections between videogames and other popular media, we might ask whether established methods of media theory are fully adequate to the study of videogames. Where distinctions are made between videogames and earlier electronic media, they tend to be drawn along questions of the mode of consumption or spectatorship of these interactive, 'immersive' forms. The videogame as computer-based medium, and its interactive consumption, requires specific critical attention.

Virtual realities?

A jaundiced figure floats across the screen. He is constantly searching for things to eat. We are looking at a neo-Marxist parable of late capitalism. He is the pure consumer. With his obsessively gaping maw, he clearly wants only one thing: to feel whole, at peace with himself. He perhaps surmises that if he eats enough – in other words, buys enough industrially produced goods – he will attain this state of perfect selfhood, perfect roundness. But it can never happen. He is doomed forever to metaphysical emptiness. It is a tragic fable in primary colours.

(Poole 2000: 189)

As Steven Poole demonstrates in his tongue-in-cheek (though telling) interpretation of the symbolic content of *Pac-Man*, videogames may not be 'representational' in the same way as other popular visual media. Visually *Gran Turismo* represents a car race (or more accurately it remediates television's representations of motor racing), but playing the game is little like watching a race on television. The pleasures of controlling and responding to the screen representations follow the logic of the game itself, a logic of variables within a system. Videogames are, in the strict sense of the word, simulations.

Games, then, the media scares around shoot-em-ups and real world violence notwithstanding, cannot be analysed only in terms of methodologies of film or television textual analysis. They exist within the real world, but they also model it (and others). Neither Monopoly nor SimCity are accurate models of the complex systems of property markets or urban development. Each is a game, with its own structure and economy set up to defer and grant pleasure, to facilitate the solitary passing of time, or social interaction.

This said, the pleasures of many games cannot be entirely separated from the material dynamics and processes they simulate. Part of the pleasure of a videogame like *Doom* is the sense of more directly engaging with or intervening in (even 'controlling') popular media images and action. The ambiguities of the computer game's position between popular media and computer media is articulated in theoretical debates. Henry Jenkins sees the potential of videogames to develop as a new narrative medium (Fuller and Jenkins 1995), whereas Jesper Juul asserts what he sees as the computer-based and ludic essence of computer games (Juul 2001).

Whatever the narrative potential for the videogame, its conventions and modes of play are inseparable from its status as computer media. Playing a videogame requires an understanding of, even a decoding of, its structure or system. This system (of levels, of architectural organisation, of points, timing of events, of non-player characters' AI, etc.) is itself, of course, a highly complex semiotic system, which could feasibly be thought of as radically independent from the particular set of images or scenarios textured-mapped

See 2.6.3 Spheres collide: from imitation to simulation – VR's operational history

Perhaps due to the mathematical basis of computer code a number of commentators have seen computer games and videogames as powerful models of economic relationships. See Poole (2000) and Stallabrass (1993)

over it. For example, the *Doom* 'engine', as we have seen, has been used as the basis for a number of quite different interactive environments:

> underneath the flashy graphics, cinematic cut-scenes, real-time physics, mythological back-stories and everything else, a videogame at bottom is still a highly artificial, purposely designed semiotic engine.
>
> (Poole 2000: 214)

We will now shift our attention from the analysis of videogames as primarily visual media to their underlying structures and modes of consumption: gameplay and interactivity.

Interactivity as gameplay

Whilst action games are perceived as crude and one-dimensional, it must be remembered that game events unfold, through play, in real time. Key aspects of established narrative visual media (cinema and television drama), such as timing, plot, character development and depth, the controlled revelation of narrative information to the viewer, etc. are all extremely limited by interactivity.

The player is not only immersed in but is also 'responsible' for the onscreen events. If the game ends it is because of the player's failure, not the deeply established reassurance of narrative closure. It could be added that, contrary to the prevalent critical view of games such as *Doom* as an uncomplicated desire for control and mastery, gameplay is characterised as much by anxiety, even fear, as by triumphant machismo. Players lose constantly, replay and are 'killed' again.

There is a contradiction, or at least a tension, here between the player's awareness of the conventions and thorough artificiality of this experience, and the real, often visceral fear this experience can provoke. We know this from horror films – we are quite conscious, from the music and other signs, that something is about to jump out, but this knowledge only seems to heighten the experience rather than defuse it.

The videogame compensates with other features, depending on the genre: Tetris (reflexes and panic), Silent Hill (atmosphere), Tomb Raider (a mixture of reflexes, lateral thinking and spatial awareness)

Learning

Whilst all media consumption requires a knowledge of particular codes, and is always an active process, 'decoding' or learning is foregrounded in the interactive playing of videogames. The process of learning the codes and conventions, the ways of understanding and playing the game must take place with each genre of game. Each genre has its own mode of interaction – and each game within the genre invents its own variations, different combinations of buttons to press or peripherals to add.

Mastering the controls of each game is essential, and a fundamental pleasure in its own right. Videogames are, as Provenzo says, 'literally teaching machines that instruct the player . . . in the rules . . . as it is being played' (Provenzo 1991: 34).

It is not just the controls and rules that the player must learn. Each videogame is a semiotic universe – every element from backgrounds to characters, walls, trees, etc. is coded and its place within the meaning of the world and its playing decided. Nothing is incidental or random. Again we return to the peculiarly non-immersive quality of video game play – to some degree, the more sophisticated the representation of an immersive world, the more aware the player must be of its artifice. The graphic and conceptual simplicity of *Tetris* may leave the player, hours later, with a feeling of having been in a trance, but to play *Tomb Raider*, for example, is to learn the semiotics of virtual world construction. The environments are like stage sets: painted backdrops, with some elements

The peculiar constitution of genres in videogames reflects the ambiguous status of the symbolic content of this medium. Film genres denote content (Westerns, science fiction, and so on), whereas videogames are generally categorised according to their spatial structure and mode of interaction. Thus, the orientalist fantasy of Prince of Persia and the science fiction scenarios of Sonic the Hedgehog both fall within the genre of the platform game

See 4.2.5 Edutainment edutainment edutainment

that appear to function as we would expect their referents in the real world to (doors that open, stairs that can be climbed, etc.). Some elements do not – windows and doors can serve only a decorative function. Move Lara Croft up close to a foliage-covered wall or architectural ornament and they are revealed as pixellated graphics mapped onto the regular polygonal units that structure these artificial realms.

Identification

> it is often assumed in popular descriptions of game-playing that a facile process of identification occurs . . . given that one appears to play many games in the first person and that one is 'rewarded' by maintaining the 'life' of this character, it is all too easy to assume an identification between player and role, but characters in computer games are rarely complicated personae.
>
> (Sefton-Green, quoted in Green *et al.* 1998: 27)

This active engagement with the very structure of the videogame in its playing suggests that established critical frameworks for understanding the relationship of the media spectator to media text may not be fully adequate. Theories of cinema spectatorship, premissed on the assumption that viewers identify with the film's main protagonist, may initially appear useful to studying gameplay, given the videogame player's interactive control of the game's characters. However, as the shift from second to third person in this instruction book indicates, this is not a straightforward connection:

> Infiltrate without being seen by your enemies. You're Solid Snake and you've got to single-handedly infiltrate the nuclear weapons disposal facility, which is being occupied by a group of terrorists. If the enemy spots Snake, they will call in reinforcements and go after him. You can't win a firefight against superior numbers, so try to avoid unnecessary battles whenever you can.
>
> (Konami's *Metal Gear Solid* instruction book, 1999)

In section **5.4.4** we suggest that the relationship between player and computer game is a significant example of a cybernetic system

5.4.4 Cyberculture and the body

The consumption of this new medium can only be understood if the videogame is theorised as software as well as media text – as computer-based media. As Poole argues, the player of *Pac-Man* is 'having a conversation with the system on its own terms' (Poole 2000: 197).

We will now use two case studies to explore the complexities of the specific, perhaps cybernetic, relationship between players and the symbolic and abstract systems of the videogame.

Key text: Ted Friedman (1999) 'Civilisation and its Discontents: simulation, subjectivity, and space', in Greg Smith (ed.) *On a Silver Platter: CD-ROMs and the promises of a new technology*, New York: New York University Press, pp. 132–150. Available online: http://www.duke.edu/~tlove/civ.htm (accessed 6/11/00). See also Friedman (1995)

CASE STUDY 4.7   Identifying with the computer in simulation games

Ted Friedman has explored this question of the videogame player's identification with the texts, images and worlds of this new medium. He focuses on the successful genre of simulation games, games in which complex social, historical, geographical, or fantastical interactions are modelled by the computer (for example, *Populous, SimCity, Theme Park, SimAnt, Civilisation*, etc.). Sometimes known as 'God games', the player is usually 'omniscient', the interface is a bird's-eye view or isometric map-like representation of the game's world over which the player can scroll. The player is not, however, omnipotent. The object is not to control the simulation fully, but instead to intervene within the unfolding complex developments (geo-politics, city development or fantastical evolutionary processes, etc.), to shape these dynamic forces according to each game's algorithms. The game may be extremely open-ended – the *SimCity* player chooses the kind of urban environment they wish to encourage, and there is often no obvious end, solution or victory.

The player, therefore, does not 'identify' with any individual protagonist, as they might if watching a film. Instead, Friedman argues, in the game *Civilisation II*, the player has to juggle numerous different roles at the same time, 'king, general, mayor, city planner, settler, warrior, and priest to name but a few' (Friedman 1995). We cannot here talk, as film theory might, about occupying subject positions in our identification with this game. For Friedman, rather, the player must identify 'with the computer itself' . . . the pleasures of a simulation game come from inhabiting an unfamiliar, alien mental state: from learning to think like a computer' (Friedman 1999).

As we have seen, the interactive playing of a game does not allow the player free rein: computers 'teach structures of thought', 'reorganize perception'. Simulation games in particular

> aestheticize our cybernetic connection to technology. They turn it into a source of enjoyment and an object for contemplation . . . Through the language of play, they teach you what it feels like to be a cyborg.
>
> (Friedman 1999)

Here, then, we see videogames not as ephemeral digital toys but as offering distinct, perhaps unique, opportunities for engaging with and making sense of the complex and intimate relationships – networks even – between people and computer media and technology.

See Green *et al.*, 1998

CASE STUDY 4.8   Identifying with codes and demons

The complex shifting of focus and identification necessary to play videogames is clearly indicated in an Australian study of the implications of children's videogame culture for education. Two twelve-year-old boys were asked to play a favourite Nintendo game (*Super Ghouls and Ghosts*). One of the friends played the game and the other observed and offered commentary. Their dialogue is revealing of the complexities of their engagement with the game:

Louis: What is the game play about? What are you actually doing here?
Jack: Well, you're . . . what you do is you go around shooting zombies, with weapons like
          daggers, arrows . . .
Louis: Like medieval-time weapons?
Jack: Yes.
Louis: Yeah, OK – What is your favourite level that you have encountered?
Jack: My favourite level has to be the first level . . .
Louis: The first level . . . Easy?
Jack: Yes, it's fairly easy.
Louis: Now, do you like playing the game normally, or do you like having it with the codes
          inputted?
Jack: I like playing it with . . . both.

Louis: Oh, OK . . . What kind of codes would you put in for the action replay, which we have at this moment, Da Dah!!!!

Jack: I would, I would put . . . 'continuous jumping', which means you can just jump, and jump, and just keep jumping . . .

Louis: . . . and jump, and jump, and jump, and jump . . . What else? Infinite energy, is that a code?

Jack: I'd make it immune, I'd make myself immune to my enemies. That means no enemies could rip me.

Louis: Oh, that's alright. I like how that goes.

(Green *et al.* 1998: 27)

A little later:

Jack: Like, how about . . . I wish I was Knight Arthur. Could you please explain who Knight Arthur is?

Louis: He is the character you play in this story. I wish I could be Knight Arthur with my little pro-action replay plugged in . . . and then I would turn on, I'd turn on the action again. I'd put in, let's see, 70027602 in the code importer, and you would get, you'd be immune to enemy attacks if . . . I can walk around it going through flames and lava and big demons like hydras and things.

(Green *et al.* 1998: 28)

The researchers are particularly concerned with questions of the kinds of 'literacy' demonstrated here – as the children switch between text and images on screen and on printed pages. They point out that these children have a clear sense that they are playing a game, that they see themselves separately from the game's characters. 'Identification', then, is with the game as program, the boys are engaging with its semiotic structure, simultaneously articulating the iconography (medieval weapons etc.), its conventions (levels, bosses), and knowledge external to the game (codes and cheats). Playing such games involves the simultaneous mapping of the game as software, as simulated space, and as narrative, and within social circuits and resources.

Cybernetic play?

However, to understand the relationship of player to videogame we must also trace other circuits: the meanings and politics of the time and space of play, the texts and images of the game, the new subject-positions it has been argued are brought into play. The hand–eye reflexes of the cybernetic circuit need to be understood themselves as nodes in the larger circuits of the embodied new media subject:

It is, of course, a particular form of embodied subjectivity that is at issue here, a matter of game-players being and becoming abstracted body-subjects, congruent with new practices, formations and intersections of culture and economy, in a social world increasingly realised in and through images and information vectors.

(Green *et al.* 1998: 24)

4.4.5 Conclusion: cyberspace in everyday life

By exploring the everyday use of, and play with, popular new media, it quickly becomes clear that these new technologies do not mark the end of everyday life and relationships; the 'real world' is not left behind for the blinking lights, geometries and disembodiment of a fictional cyberspace. Instead we see a much more complex – and interesting – picture. The communication vectors of the Internet, the dynamic spaces of videogames, the 'technological imaginary' of all of these are interwoven, fitting into the architecture of the home, established rhythms of family and social life, and dramatised by the instrumental fantasies of hardware and software producers and retailers and the action-filled narratives of popular culture. Fitting in and transforming these everyday realities, flickering between technology and media, cyberspace and everyday space are enmeshed and interpenetrating, 'continuous with and embedded in other social spaces' (Miller and Slater 2000: 4).

Moreover, the everyday consumption of new media circulates through popular culture and computer culture. Its meanings cannot be separated from the fantasies and dramas woven around it. Sonia Livingstone recounts a story from her research, an account illustrative of the fundamentally enmeshed relationships between technology, media, imaginative play, 'real' and 'virtual' space:

> Two eight year old boys play their favourite multimedia adventure game on the family PC. When they discover an Internet site where the same game could be played interactively with unknown others, this occasions great excitement in the household. The boys choose their fantasy personae, and try diverse strategies to play the game, both co-operative and competitive, simultaneously 'talking' online (i.e. writing) to the other participants. But when restricted in their access to the Internet, for reasons of cost, the game spins off into 'real life'. Now the boys, together with their younger sisters, choose a character, dress up in battle dress, and play 'the game' all over the house, going downstairs to Hell, The Volcanoes and The Labyrinth, and upstairs to The Town, 'improving' the game in the process. This new game is called, confusingly for adult observers, 'playing the Internet'.
>
> (Livingstone 1998: 436)

These children have not left the real world for cyberspace, they have at once invented new games with new media, and demonstrated a powerful sense of continuity with play and games predating digital culture, playing with and performing in space that is both actual and imaginary. Technology, media, performance, play, consumption, family and gender relationships are all intertwined.

In this part of the book we have argued that established conceptual frameworks for studying media and culture in everyday life, whilst productive, do not fully address the specific questions raised by digital media technologies and the particular practices of use, play or consumption they facilitate. The final part will address in detail questions of the significance of science and technology to the critical understanding of new media.

BIBLIOGRAPHY

Aarseth, Espen *Cybertext: perspectives on ergodic literature*, Baltimore, Md: Johns Hopkins University Press, 1997.

Aarseth, Espen 'Computer game studies: year one', *Game Studies* 1.1 (July) http://www.gamestudies.org (accessed July 2001), 2001.

Abbott, Chris 'Making connections: young people and the internet', in *Digital Diversions: youth culture in the age of multimedia*, ed. Julian Sefton-Green. London: UCL Press, 1998, pp. 84–105.

Adorno, Theodor *The Culture Industry: selected essays on mass culture*, London: Routledge, 1991.

Alloway, Nola and Gilbert, Pam 'Video game culture: playing with masculinity, violence and pleasure', in *Wired Up: young people and the electronic media*, ed. Sue Howard. London: UCL, 1998, pp. 95–114.

Althusser, Louis *Essays on Ideology*, London: Verso, 1984.

Anderson, Benedict *Imagined Communities: reflections on the origin and spread of nationalism*, London: Verso, 1991.

Barba, Rick *Doom Battlebook*, Rocklin, Calif.: Prima Publishing, 1994.

Barbrook, Richard 'The digital artisans manifesto', http://www.hrc.wmin.ac.uk/hrc/theory/digitalArtisans/t.1.1 (accessed July 2002), 1997.

Barglow, Raymond *The Crisis of Self in the Age of Information*, London: Routledge 1994.

Barker, Martin *Video Nasties*, London: Pluto Press, 1984.

Barker, Martin and Brooks, Kate *Knowing Audiences: Judge Dredd, its friends, fans and foes*, Luton: University of Luton Press, 1998.

Bassett, Caroline 'Virtually gendered: life in an online world', in *The Subcultures Reader*, eds Ken Gelder and Sarah Thornton. London: Routledge, 1997, pp. 537–550.

Battelle, John and Johnstone, Bob 'Seizing the next level: Sega's plans for world domination', *Wired* (US) 6, December (1993): 73–76, 128–131.

Baudrillard, Jean *Simulations*, New York: Semiotext(e), 1983.

Baudrillard, Jean '*The Revenge of the Crystal*, London: Pluto Press, 1990.

Bazalgette, Cary and Buckingham, David *In Front of the Children: screen entertainment and young audiences*, London: BFI, 1995.

Benedikt, M. ed. *Cyberspace: first steps*, Cambridge, Mass.: MIT Press, 1991.

Berg, Anne-Jorunn 'A gendered socio-technical construction: the smart house', in *Bringing Technology Home: gender and technology in a changing Europe*, eds Cynthia Cockburn and Ruza Furst Dilic. Milton Keynes: Open University Press, 1994, pp. 165–180.

Bernstein, Charles 'Play it again, Pac-Man', *Postmodern Culture* 2.1 (September) http://www.iath.virginia.edu/pmc/text-only/issue.991/pop-cult.991 (accessed July 2002), 1991.

Bingham, Nick, Valentine, Gill and Holloway, Sarah L. 'Where do you want to go tomorrow? Connecting children and the Internet', *Environment and Planning D – Society and Space* 17.6 December (1999): 655–672.

Birkerts, Sven *The Gutenberg Elegies: the fate of reading in an electronic age*, London: Faber and Faber, 1994.

Boddy, William 'Redefining the home screen: technological convergence as trauma and business plan' at the Media in Transition conference, MIT, 8 October 1999. http://media-in-transition.mit.edu/articles/boddy.html (accessed May 2001).

Bolter, Jay David and Grusin, Richard *Remediation: understanding new media*, Cambridge, Mass. and London: MIT, 1999.

Booz, Allen *Achieving Universal Access*, 7 March 2000. http://www.pm.gov.uk/default.asp?PageID=1203 (accessed June 2000).

Bromberg, Helen 'Are MUDs communities? Identity, belonging and consciousness in virtual worlds', in *Cultures of Internet: virtual spaces, real histories, living bodies*, ed. Rob Shields. London: Sage, 1996.

Brown, Peter 'Toddlers take the initiative', in 'The Future of Learning' supplement, *The Times*, 8 January 1999, p. 2.

Buckingham, David *After the Death of Childhood: growing up in the age of electronic media*, Oxford: Polity Press, 2000.

Buick, Joanna and Jevtic, Zoran *Cyberspace for Beginners*, Cambridge: Icon Books, 1995.

Bukatman, Scott *Terminal Identity*, Durham, N.C.: Duke University Press, 1993.

Burgin, Victor, Kaplan, Cora and James, Donald *Formations of Fantasy*, London: Methuen, 1986.

Burkeman, Oliver 'Pokemon power', *Guardian G2*, 20 April 2000, pp. 1–3.

Caillois, Roger *Man, Play and Games*, London: Thames and Hudson, 1962.

Cameron, Andy 'Dissimulations; illusions of interactivity', http://www.hrc.wmin.ac.uk/hrc/theory/dissimulations/t.3.2 (accessed Jannuary 2002).

Cartmell, Deborah *Trash Aesthetics: popular culture and its audiences*, London: Pluto, 1997.

Cassell, Justine and Jenkins, Henry *From Barbie to Mortal Kombat: gender and computer games*, Cambridge, Mass.: MIT Press, 1999.

Castells, Manuel *The Informational City: information technology, economic restructuring and the urban–regional process*, Oxford: Blackwell, 1989.

Castells, Manuel *The Information Age: economy, society and culture. Vol. I: The Rise of the Network Society*, Oxford: Blackwell, 1996.

Central Office of Information *Our Information Age: the Government's vision*, London: HM Government, 1998. http://www.number-10.gov.uk

Ceruzzi, Paul 'Inventing personal computing', in *The Social Shaping of Technology: how the refrigerator got its hum*, eds Donald MacKenzie and Judy Wajcman. Milton Keynes: Open University Press, 1999, pp. 64–86.

Chandler, Daniel 'Video games and young players', http://www.aber.ac.uk/media/Documents/short/vidgame.html (accessed May 2000), 1994.

Chandler, Daniel 'Personal home pages and the construction of identities on the web', http://www.aber.ac.uk/media/Documents/short/webident.html (accessed May 2000), 1998.

Chandler, Daniel and Roberts-Young, Dilwyn 'The construction of identity in the personal homepages of adolescents', http://www.aber.ac.uk/Documents/short/strasbourg.html (accessed May 2000), 1998.

Cockburn, Cynthia 'The circuit of technology: gender, identity and power', in *Consuming Technologies: media and information in domestic spaces*, eds Roger Silverstone and Eric Hirsch. London: Routledge, 1992.

Cockburn, Cynthia and Furst Dilic, Ruza *Bringing Technology Home: gender and technology in a changing Europe*, Milton Keynes: Open University Press, 1994.

Collins, Jim *Architectures of Excess: cultural life in the information age*, London: Routledge, 1995.

Cooper, Hilary 'Fleecing kids', *Guardian*, 10 June 2000.

Cotton, Bob and Oliver, Richard *Understanding Hypermedia from Multimedia to Virtual Reality*, Oxford: Phaidon, 1993.

Cotton, Bob *The Cyberspace Lexicon: an illustrated dictionary of terms from multimedia to virtual reality*, Oxford: Phaidon, 1994.

Cunningham, Helen 'Mortal Kombat and computer game girls', in Cary Bazalgette and David Buckingham. *In Front of the Children: screen entertainment and young audiences*, London: BFI, 1995.

Datamonitor 'Digital Gaming White Paper: the future of gaming, *Information and Communication Technology: The National Curriculum for England*, London: Datamonitor, 2000. 20 June 2000 www.nc.uk.net

De Certeau, Michel *The Practice of Everyday Life*, London: University of California Press, 1988.

De Certeau, Michel 'Walking in the city', in *The Cultural Studies Reader*, ed. Simon During. London: Routledge, 1993, pp. 151–160.

Dery, Mark ed. *Flame Wars – the discourse of cyberculture*, London: Duke University Press, 1994.

Dewdney, Andrew and Boyd, Frank 'Computers, technology and cultural form', in Martin Lister, *The Photographic Image in Digital Culture*, London: Routledge, 1995.

Dibbell, Julian 'Covering cyberspace', Paper delivered at the Media in Transition conference at MIT, Cambridge, Mass., http://media-in-transition.mit.edu/articles/dibbell.html (accessed June 2000), 1999.

Digiplay Initiative http://www.digiplay.org.uk

Dovey, Jon ed. *Fractal Dreams: new media in social context*, London: Lawrence & Wishart, 1996.

du Gay, Paul, Hall, Stuart, Janes, Linda, Mackay, Hugh and Negus, Keith *Doing Cultural Studies: the story of the Sony Walkman*, London: Sage, 1997.

Dyson, Esther *Release 2.0: A design for living in the digital age*, London: Viking, 1997.

Economic and Social Research Council. *Virtual Society? The social science of electronic technologies* Profile 2000, Swindon: Economic and Social Research Council, 2000.

Edge, Future Publishing. '*X-Box from concept to console*', September 2000.

Edge, Future Publishing. February 2001.

Facer, K., Furlong, J., Furlong, R. and Sutherland, R. 'Constructing the child computer user: from public policy to private practices', *British Journal of Sociology of Education* 22.1 (2001a): 91–108.

Facer, K., Furlong, J. Furlong, R. and Sutherland, R. 'Home is where the hardware is: young people, the domestic environment and "access" to new technologies', in *Children, Technology and Culture*, eds Ian Hutchby and Jo Moran-Ellis. London: Falmer, 2001b, pp. 13–27.

Featherstone, Mike *Consumer Culture and Postmodernism*, London: Sage, 1990.

Featherstone, Mike and Burrows, Roger *Cyberspace, Cyberbodies, Cyberpunk: cultures of technological embodiment*, London: Sage, 1995.

Feldman, Tony *An Introduction to Digital Media*, London: Routledge, 1997.

Fidler, Roger *Mediamorphosis: understanding new media*, London: Sage, 1997.

Finnemann, Niels Ole 'Modernity modernised', in *Computer Media and Communication: a reader*, ed. Paul A. Mayer. Oxford: Oxford University Press, 1999.

Fiske, John *Television Culture*, London: Methuen, 1987.

Fiske, John 'Cultural studies and the culture of everyday life', in *Cultural Studies*, eds L. Grossberg *et al.* London: Chapman and Hall, 1992.

Foucault, Michel *The Order of Things*, London: Tavistock, 1970.

Foucault, Michel *Madness and Civilisation: a history of insanity in the age of reason*, London: Routledge, 1989.

Friedman, Ted. 'Making sense of software', in *Cybersociety: computer-mediated communication and community*, ed. Steven G. Jones. Thousand Oaks, Calif.: Sage, 1995.

Friedman, Ted. 'Civilisation and its discontents: simulation, subjectivity and space', http://www.gsu.edu/~jouejf/civ.htm (accessed July 2002), 1999. Also published in *On a Silver Platter: CD-ROMs and the promises of a new technology*, ed. Greg Smith. New York: New York University Press 1999, 132–150.

Fuller, Mary and Jenkins, Henry 'Nintendo and New World travel writing: a dialogue', in *Cybersociety: computer-mediated communication and community*, ed. Steven G. Jones. London: Sage, 1995, pp. 57–72.

Furlong, Ruth 'There's no place like home' in *The Photographic Image in Digital Culture*, ed. Martin Lister. London: Routledge, 1995, pp. 170–187.

Gelder, Ken and Thornton, Sarah *The Subcultures Reader*, London: Routledge, 1997.

Gray, Ann *Video Playtime: the gendering of a leisure technology*, London: Routledge, 1992.

Gray, Peggy and Hartmann, Paul 'Contextualizing home computing – resources and practices', in *Consuming Technologies – media and information in domestic spaces*, eds Roger Silverstone & Eric Hirsch. London: Routledge, 1992, pp. 146–160.

Green, Bill, Reid, Jo-Anne and Bigum, Chris 'Teaching the Nintendo generation? Children, computer culture and popular technologies', in *Wired up: young people and the electronic media*, ed. Sue Howard. London: UCL Press, 1998, pp. 19–42.

Green, Eileen and Adam, Alison *Virtual Gender: technology, consumption and identity*, London: Routledge, 2001.

Hables Gray, Chris *The Cyborg Handbook*, London: Routledge, 1995.

Haddon, Leslie 'Electronic and computer games – the history of an interactive medium', *Screen* 29.2 Spring (1988a): 52–73.

Haddon, Leslie 'The home computer: the making of a consumer electronic', *Science as Culture* 2 (19988b): 7–51.

Haddon, Leslie 'Explaining ICT consumption: the case of the home computer', *Consuming Technologies – media and information in domestic spaces*. ed. Roger Silverstone and Eric Hirsch London: Routledge, 1992, pp. 82–96.

Hakken, David *Cyborgs@Cyberspace: an ethnographer looks to the future*, London: Routledge, 1999.

Hall, Stuart 'Minimal selves', *ICA Documents 6: Identity*, London: ICA, 1987, pp. 44–46.

Hall, Stuart, Held, David and McGrew, Tony *Modernity and its Futures*, Cambridge: Polity Press, 1992.

Haraway, Donna 'A manifesto for cyborgs: science, technology, and socialist feminism in the 1980s', in *Feminism / Postmodernism*, ed. Linda J. Nicholson. London: Routledge, 1990.

Hayles, N. Katherine *How We Became Posthuman: virtual bodies in cybernetics, literature and informatics*, London: University of Chicago Press, 1999.

Hebdige, Dick *Subculture: the meaning of style*, London: Methuen, 1979.

Herz, J.C. *Joystick Nation: how video games gobbled our money, won our hearts and rewired our minds*, London: Abacus, 1997.

Highmore, Ben *Everyday Life and Cultural Theory*, London: Routledge, 2001.

Howard, Sue *Wired-Up: young people and the electronic media*, London: UCL, 1998.

Huhtamo, Erkki 'From kaleidoscomaniac to cybernerd: notes toward an archaeology of media', *Electronic Culture: technology and visual representation*, ed. Timothy Druckrey. New York: Aperture, 1996.

Huizinga, Johan *Homo Ludens: a study of the play element in culture*, Boston: Beacon Press, 1986.

Hutchby, Ian and Moran-Ellis, Jo. *Children, Technology and Culture*, London: Falmer, 2001.

Jameson, Fredric *Postmodernism, or the Cultural Logic of Late Capitalism*, London: Verso, 1991.

Jenkins, Henry 'X logic: repositioning Nintendo in children's lives', *Quarterly Review of Film and Video* 14 (August 1993): 55–70.

Jenkins, Henry 'From Home(r) to the holodeck: new media and the humanities', Paper delivered at the Media in Transition conference at MIT, Cambridge, Mass., http://media-in-transition.mit.edu/articles/australia.html

Jenkins, Henry 'Professor Jenkins goes to Washington', 11 June 2001 http://web.mit.edu/21fms/www/faculty/henry3/profjenkins.html

Jensen, Klaus Bruhn 'One person, one computer: the social construction of the personal computer', in *Computer Media and Communication: a reader*, ed. Paul A. Mayer. Oxford: Oxford University Press, 1999, pp. 188–206.

Jones, Steven G. *Cybersociety: computer-mediated communication and community*, London: Sage, 1995.

Juul, Jesper, 'Games telling stories? A brief note on games and narratives', *Game Studies* 1.1 (July) http://www.gamestudies.org (accessed July 2001), 2001.

Keegan, Paul 'In the line of fire', *Guardian G2*, 1 June 2000, pp. 2–3.

Kelly, Kevin *Out of Control: the new biology of machines*, London: Fourth Estate, 1995.

Kember, Sarah *Virtual Anxiety: photography, new technologies and subjectivity*, Manchester: Manchester University Press, 1998.

Kinder, Marsha *Playing with Power in Movies, Television and Video Games: from Muppet Babies to Teenage Mutant Ninja Turtles*, Berkeley: University of California Press, 1991.

Kitzman, Andreas 'Watching the web watch me: explorations of the domestic webcam', Paper delivered at the Media in Transition conference at MIT, Cambridge, Mass., http://media-in-transition.mit.edu/articles/kitzmann.html (accessed June 2000), 1999.

Kroker, Arthur *The Possessed Individual – technology and postmodernity*, London: Macmillan, 1992.

Landow, George P. *Hypertext – the convergence of contemporary critical theory and technology*, Baltimore, Md.: Johns Hopkins University Press, 1992.

Landow, George P. *Hyper/Text/Theory*, Baltimore, Md.: Johns Hopkins University Press, 1994.

Lea, Marin *The Social Contexts of Computer Mediated Communication*, London: Harvester-Wheatsheaf, 1992.

Levy, Steven *Hackers – heroes of the computer revolution*, Harmondsworth: Penguin, 1994.

Lister, Martin. *The Photographic Image in Digital Culture*, London: Routledge, 1995.

Livingstone, Sonia 'The meaning of domestic technologies', in *Consuming Technologies – media and information in domestic spaces*, eds R. Silverstone and E. Hirsch. London: Routledge, 1992: 113–130.

Livingstone, Sonia 'Mediated childhoods: a comparative approach to young people's media environments in Europe', *European Journal of Communication* 13.4 (1998): 435–456.

Lohr, Paul and Meyer, Manfred eds *Children, TV and the New Media: a research reader*, Luton: University of Luton Press, 1999.

Lunenfeld, Peter *The Digital Dialectic: new essays on new media*, Cambridge, Mass.: MIT, 1999.

MacCabe, Colin *High Theory/Low Culture – analysing popular television and film*, Manchester: Manchester University Press, 1986.

Mackay, Hugh *Consumption and Everyday Life: culture, media and identities*, London: Open University Press/Sage, 1997.

MacKenzie, Donald and Wajcman, Judy eds *The Social Shaping of Technology: how the refrigerator got its hum*, Buckingham: Open University Press, 1999.

Manovich, Lev 'Navigable space', http://www.manovich.net (accessed January 2001), 1998.

Marks Greenfield, Patricia *Mind and Media – the effects of television, computers and video games*, London: Fontana, 1984.

Marshall, David and Morris, Sue 'Game', *M/C: a journal of media and culture* 3.5 (2000), http://www.api-network.com/mc/0010/edit.txt (accessed March 2001).

Mayer, Paul 'Representation and action in the reception of Myst: a social semiotic approach to computer media', *Nordicon Review of Nordic Popular Culture* 1.1 (1996): 237–254.

Mayer, Paul A. *Computer Media and Communication: a reader*, Oxford: Oxford University Press, 1999.

McAffrey, Larry *Storming the Reality Studio – a casebook of cyberpunk and postmodern fiction*, Durham, N.C.: Duke University Press, 1991.

McLuhan, Marshall. *The Gutenberg Galaxy: the making of typographic man*, London: Routledge, 1962.

McLuhan, Marshall *Understanding Media: the extensions of man*, London: Routledge, 1967.

McNamee, Sara 'Youth, gender and video games: power and control in the home', in *Cool Places: geographies of youth cultures*, eds Tracey Skelton and Gill Valentine. London: Routledge, 1998.

McRobbie, Angela 'Postmodernism and popular culture', in *Postmodernism*, ed. Lisa Appignansesi. London: ICA, 1986.

Miles, David 'The CD-ROM novel Myst and McLuhan's Fourth Law of Media: Myst and its "retrievals"', in *Computer Media and Communication: a reader*, ed. Paul Mayer. Oxford: Oxford University Press, 1999, 307–319.

Miles, Ian, Cawson, Alan and Haddon, Leslie 'The shape of things to consume', in R. Silverstone and E. Hirsch. *Consuming Technologies – media and information in domestic spaces*, London: Routledge, 1992, pp. 67–81.

Miller, Daniel and Slater, Don *The Internet: an ethnographic approach*, Oxford: Berg, 2000.

Miller, Toby *Popular Culture and Everyday Life*, London: Sage, 1998.

Moores, Shaun 'Satellite TV as cultural sign: consumption, embedding and articulation', *Media, Culture and Society* 15 (1993a): 621–639.

Moores, Shaun *Interpreting Audiences: the ethnography of media consumption*, London: Sage, 1993b.

Morley, David 'Where the global meets the local: notes from the sitting room', *Screen* 32.1 (1991): 1–15.

Morley, David and Robins, Kevin *Spaces of Identity – global media, electronic landscapes and cultural boundaries*, London: Routledge, 1995.

Motorola. *Motorola Children and Technology Report*, 2000. http://www.motorola.com/General/Reports/British-Tech/children.htm

Myers, David 'Chris Crawford and computer game aesthetics', *Journal of Popular Culture* 24.2 (1990a): 17–28.

Myers, David 'Computer game genres', *Play and Culture* 3 (1990b): 286–301.

Myers, David 'Time, symbol transformations, and computer games', *Play and Culture* 5 (1990c): 441–457.

Myers, David 'Computer game semiotics', *Play and Culture* 4 (1991): 334–346.

Nava, Mica (with Orson Nava) 'Discriminating or duped? Young people as consumers of advertising/art', *Magazine of Cultural Studies* 1(1990): 15–21.

Negroponte, Nicholas *Being Digital*, London: Hodder & Stoughton, 1995.

Negroponte, Nicholas 'Beyond digital', *Wired*, 6.12 (December), http://www.wired.com/wired/archive/6.12/negroponte.html (accessed June 2001), 1998.

Nixon, Helen 'Fun and games are serious business', in *Digital Diversions: youth culture in the age of multimedia*, ed. Julian Sefton-Green. London: UCL Press, 1998.

Norris, Christopher *Uncritical Theory: postmodernism, intellectuals and the Gulf War*, London: Lawrence and Wishart, 1992.

Papert, Seymour *Mindstorms: computers, children and powerful ideas*, London: Harvester Press, 1980.

Papert, Seymour *The Children's Machine: rethinking school in the age of the computer*, London: Harvester-Wheatsheaf, 1994.

Peters, Michael 'Lyotard and philosophy of education', in *Encyclopedia of Philosophy of Education*, eds Michael A. Peters and Paulo Ghiraldelli Jr. http://www.educacao.pro.br/lyotard.htm (accessed August 2000), 1999.

Plant, Sadie 'Beyond the screens: film, cyberpunk and cyberfeminism', *Variant* 14, Summer (1993): 12–17.

Plant, Sadie 'The future looms: weaving women and cybernetics', in *Cyberspace Cyberbodies Cyberpunk: cultures of technological embodiment*, eds Mike Featherstone and Roger Burrows. London: Sage, 1995.

Plant, Sadie 'On the matrix: cyberfeminist simulations', in *The Cybercultures Reader* eds David Bell and Barbara M. Kennedy. London: Routledge, 2000, pp. 325–336.

Poole, Steven *Trigger Happy: the secret life of video games*, London: Fourth Estate, 2000.

Popper, Frank *Art of the Electronic Age*, London: Thames & Hudson, 1993.

Poster, Mark *The Mode of Information: poststructuralism and social context*, Cambridge: Polity Press, 1990.

Poster, Mark 'Postmodern virtualities', in *Cyberspace Cyberbodies Cyberpunk: cultures of technological embodiment*, eds Mike Featherstone and Roger Burrows. London: Sage, 1995a.

Poster, Mark 'Community, new media, post-humanism', *Undercurrent* 2 (Winter) http://darkwing.uoregon.edu/~ucurrent/2-Poster.html (accessed July 2000), 1995b.

Poster, Mark 'Community, new media, post-humanism', Interview conducted through e-mail, October 1994, by Erick Heroux, *Undercurrent: An online journal for the analysis of the present*, no. 2 (Winter) 24 July 2000 http://darkwing.uoregon.edu/~ucurrent/2-Poster.html

Potter, David 'Wealth creation in the knowledge economy of the next millennium' in *10 Downing Street Magazine*, 27 May 1999. 20 June 2000: http://www.number-10.gov.uk/

Provenzo, Eugene F. Jr. *Beyond the Gutenberg Galaxy: microcomputers and the emergence of post-typographic culture*, New York: Teachers College Press, 1986.

Provenzo, Eugene F. Jr. *Video Kids – making sense of Nintendo*, Cambridge, Mass.: Harvard University Press, 1991.

Pryor, Sally 'Thinking of oneself as a computer', *Leonardo* 24.5 (1991): 585–590.

Rheingold, Howard *Virtual Reality*, London: Mandarin, 1991.

Rheingold, Howard *The Virtual Community – finding connection in a computerised world*, London: Secker & Warburg, 1994.

Robins, Kevin and Webster, Frank 'Cybernetic capitalism: information, technology, everyday life', http://www.rochester.edu/College/FS/Publications/RobinsCybernetic.html (accessed July 2000). The print version appears in *The Political Economy of Information*, eds Vincent Mosco and Janet Wasko. Madison: The University of Wisconsin Press, 1988, 45–75.

Robins, Kevin and Webster, Frank *Times of the Technoculture: from the information society to the virtual life*, London: Routledge, 1999.

Ross, Andrew 'Hacking away at the counterculture', in *Technoculture*, eds Constance Penley and Andrew Ross, Minneapolis: University of Minnesota Press, 1991.

Sanger, Jack (*et al.*) *Young Children, Videos and Computer Games: issues for teachers and parents*, London: Falmer Press, 1997.

Sefton-Green, Julian *Young People, Creativity and New Technologies: the challenge of digital art*, London: Routledge, 1999.

Sefton-Green, Julian *Digital Diversions: youth culture in the age of multimedia*, London: UCL Press, 1998.

Sefton-Green, Julian and Parker, David *Edit-Play: how children use edutainment software to tell stories*, BFI Education Research Report, London: BFI, 2000.

Sheff, David *Game Over – Nintendo's battle to dominate an industry*, London: Hodder & Stoughton, 1993.

Silverstone, Roger *Why Study the Media?*, London: Sage, 1999a.

Silverstone, Roger 'What's new about new media?, *New Media and Society* 1.1 (1999b): 10–82.

Silverstone, Roger and Hirsch, Eric 'Listening to a long conversation: an ethnographic approach to the study of information and communication technologies in the home', *Cultural Studies* 5.2 (1991): 204–227.

Silverstone, Roger and Hirsch, Eric *Consuming Technologies – media and information in domestic spaces*, London: Routledge, 1992.

Skirrow, Gillian 'Hellivision: an analysis of video games', in *High Theory/Low Culture – analysing popular television and film*, ed. Colin MacCabe. Manchester: Manchester University Press, 1986, pp. 115–142.

Slater, Don 'Trading sexpics on IRC: embodiment and authenticity on the internet', *Body and Society* 4.4 (1998): 91–117.

Springer, Claudia 'The pleasure of the interface', *Screen* 32.3 Autumn (1991): 303–323.

Springer, Claudia *Electronic Eros: bodies and desire in the postindustrial age*, London: Athlone, 1996.

Squires, Judith 'Fabulous feminist futures and the lure of cyberspace', in *Fractal Dreams: new media in social context*, ed. Jon Dovey. London: Lawrence & Wishart, 1996.

Stallabrass, Julian 'Just gaming: allegory and economy in computer games', *New Left Review* March/April (1993): 83–106.

Sterling, Bruce *Mirrorshades – the cyberpunk anthology*, London: HarperCollins, 1994.

Stern, Susannah R. 'Adolescent girls' expression on web home pages: spirited, sombre and self-conscious sites', *Convergence: the journal of research into new media technologies* 5.4 Winter (1999): 22–41.

Stone, Allucquere Rosanne *The War of Technology and Desire at the Close of the Mechanical Age*, Cambridge, Mass.: MIT, 1995.

Strathern, Marilyn 'Foreword: the mirror of technology', in *Consuming Technologies – media and information in domestic spaces*, eds Roger Silverstone and Eric Hirsch. London: Routledge, 1992, pp. vii–xiii.

Stutz, Elizabeth 'What electronic games cannot give', *Guardian*, 13 March 1995.

Sudnow, David *Pilgrim in the Microworld: eye, mind and the essence of video skill*, London: Heinemann, 1983.

Sykes, Lisa 'Power to the people: if you thought the TV changer was an inspiration, the "smart house" is really going to impress', *Independent on Sunday*, 18 October 1998.

Terry, Jennifer *Processed Lives: gender & technology in everyday life*, London: Routledge, 1997.

Thompson, John B. *The Media and Modernity: a social theory of the media*, Cambridge: Polity Press, 1995.

Tobin, Joseph 'An American Otaku (or, a boy's virtual life on the net)', in *Digital Diversions: youth culture in the age of multimedia*, ed. J. Sefton-Green. London: UCL Press, 1998, pp. 106–127.

Turkle, Sherry. *The Second Self-Computers & the Human Spirit*, London: Granada, 1984.

Turkle, Sherry 'Constructions and reconstructions of the self in virtual reality', in *Electronic Culture: technology and representation*, ed. Timothy Druckrey. New York: Aperture, 1996a, pp. 354–365.

Turkle, Sherry *Life on the Screen: identity in the age of the internet*, London: Weidenfeld & Nicolson, 1996b.

Walkerdine, Valerie. 'Video replay: families, film and fantasy', in *Formations of Fantasy*, eds Victor Burgin, Cora Kaplan and Donald James. London: Methuen, 1986.

Wark, McKenzie 'The video game as emergent media form', *Media Information Australia*, no. 71, 1 February 1994. 28 August 2000: http://www.mcs.mq.edu.au/Staff/mwark/warchive/Mia/mia-video-games.html

Wheelock, Jane 'Personal computers, gender and an institutional model of the household', in *Consuming Technologies – media and information in domestic spaces*, eds Roger Silverstone and Eric Hirsch. London: Routledge, 1992, pp. 97–111.

Williams, Raymond *Television: technology and cultural form*, London: Routledge, 1975.

Williams, Raymond *Keywords: a vocabulary of culture and society*, London: Fontana, 1976.

Williams, Raymond *Problems in Materialism and Culture*, London: Verso, 1990.

Willis, Paul *Common Culture: symbolic work at play in the everyday cultures of the young*, Milton Keynes: Open University Press, 1990.

Wolf, Mark J.P. 'Inventing space: toward a taxonomy of on and off screen space in video games', *Film Quarterly* 51.1 Fall (1997): 11–23.

Woolley, Benjamin *Virtual Worlds – a journey in hype and hyperreality*, Oxford: Blackwell, 1992.

Yates, Simeon J. and Littleton, Karen 'Understanding computer game cultures: a situated approach', in *Virtual Gender: technology, consumption and identity*, eds Eileen Green and Alison Adam. London: Routledge, 2001, pp. 103–123.

5 CYBERCULTURE: TECHNOLOGY, NATURE AND CULTURE

CYBERCULTURE AND CYBERNETICS/PHYSICALISM, HUMANISM AND
TECHNOLOGY/BIOLOGICAL TECHNOLOGIES/THEORIES OF CYBERCULTURE

Introduction

New media form part of cyberculture, but they are not all there is to it. 'Cyberculture', a frequently used term, suggests something about the sort of culture we are dealing with: it is a culture in which machines play a particularly important role. Nobody who has heard the term is unaware of the other constituents of that culture: other than communications networks, programming, and software there are also the issues of artificial intelligence, virtual reality, **artificial life**, and the human-computer interface. The works of fiction that gave a cultural context to the computers, such as William Gibson's *Neuromancer* (1986), Richard Kadrey's *Metrophage* (1989), Pat Cadigan's *Synners* (1991), and Bruce Sterling's *Schismatrix* (1985), or the films that provided its characteristic images, from Ridley Scott's *Bladerunner* (1982, 1992) to the Wachowski brothers' *The Matrix* (1999), routinely not only play out plots concerning computers and computer media but also explore the construction and politics of artificial life (*Bladerunner*), the complexity and technological resources of organic bodies (*Neuromancer, Matrix*), and even, with Cadigan's (1991) famous online stroke, the indissociability of biological and technological systems: hence the 'syn-' part of her title.

For more on the fictions
surrounding cyberculture, see
McCaffery (1992)

As such fictions make often shockingly clear, cyberculture thus marks a threshold at which concepts, theories and practices stemming from cultural and media studies confront concepts, theories and practices stemming from the sciences — notably from **biotechnology**, robotics and AI research, genetics and genomics. Driving through this heady mix of concepts and traditions is, of course, the extraordinary pace of contemporary technological change. Our newspapers now routinely announce some new marriage of biology and technology in the form of intelligent prosthetics, implant technologies, cloning, and so on, while we are suffering new physical (repetitive strain injury) and psychological disorders (in-tray anxiety, information sickness) as a consequence of the ubiquity of computation.

Cyberculture, then, consists in a mass of new technological things, a wide range of imaginative fictions that have, as it were, seeped through the screens so that they may seem like realistic descriptions of our bewildering everyday lives. Moreover, it brings the theories and practices of the sciences into direct contact with those of cultural and media studies. Accordingly, it has given rise to questions concerning which of these traditions is better suited to characterise the emergent culture: popular science books vie with works in media studies, philosophy, cultural theory, and so on, over how precisely to characterise the seemingly unprecedented mix of culture and technology that is cyberculture. All involved in this contest seem beset with a certain theoretical anxiety, so that the flow of ideas, fictions, concepts and technologies has become seemingly inexhaustible.

Such anxieties, and the sudden confluence of culture and technology that fuel them, are not, however, new. The fictions, sciences and philosophies, alongside the sweeping changes in everyday life during the Industrial Revolution, were beset by a similar range of problems, and suffered a similar sense of cultural disorientation. So too, the rise of clockwork mechanisms, and the aggressively materialistic theories that accompanied them, upset the sense of humanity's place in the natural and divine order, changing medicine and psychology into branches of mechanics. Indeed, as far back as the first century AD cultures were awash with hypotheses and experiments concerning bringing machines to life.

In many other parts of the book we have sought to understand new media as subject to control and direction by human institutions, skill, creativity and intention in broadly the same terms as we have always assumed traditional media to be. But, in turning to the phenomenon of cyberculture, and the histories that feed it, we will be meeting other traditions of thought, some of surprising longevity, and their contemporary manifestations which do not always sit comfortably alongside this humanist emphasis. This being the case, no full account of the culture of new media can be given without exploring the flow of ideas from the other fields that inform cyberculture.

The proximity and traffic between the discourses about new media and cyberculture are reason enough to pay them full attention in this book, but there is another reason which may be more important. This is that many of the questions that the emergence of new media have given rise to are actually versions of larger and more fundamental questions about the relationship of culture to technology and technology to nature. These are not questions that media studies, in general, concerns itself with.

However, a number of studies and bodies of thought that attempt to address the nature of everyday life and experience in advanced technological societies under the name of 'cyberculture' or 'cybercultural studies' do have some things to say about culture, technology and nature. Indeed, these three categories and the shifting relations between them can be said to lie at the very heart of cyberculture. We may be used to dividing 'nature' from 'culture', and we routinely base our academic investigations on attending to one or the other realm, but the advent of technology troubles this simple distribution of academic labour, and compels us to ask the question of how to approach 'the question of technology' at all.

It is to these ideas, histories and theories that we now turn. While the ideas at the centre of cyberculture can all too easily seem to be either enjoyable or trite and naive, near-delirious imaginings of science fiction authors and screenwriters, it has also been recognised that 'cyberpunk' science fiction offers an address to many current developments in science, technology and culture that the divided academic world often fails to catch. As one media theorist has put it, 'cyberpunk can . . . be read as a new form of social theory that maps the consequences of a rapidly developing information and media society in the era of techno-capitalism' (Kellner 1995: 8). Thus, cyberpunk fiction is accorded the status of a sociology of new media cultures. Conversely, Kellner goes on to recommend that we read actual sociologies of media-saturated society, such as those by the notorious theorist Jean Baudrillard, as actually being a form of 'dystopic science fiction'. Kellner's view stands like a warning: we are about to enter a sphere in which distinctions between science fiction, sociology and philosophy can become hard to maintain.

We will not, however, merely be spinning bizarre riddles or presenting cyberculture as the realm of delirium some critics (including one of this book's authors!) have energetically insisted it is. Our attempt here is to take the reader behind the scenes of cyberculture by tracing the conceptual roots and histories of some theories and ideas concerning nature, culture and technology, automata and living machines, the actual and the virtual, and so on. It will then explore some core developments in the contemporary studies of science, technology and culture that place developments in new media in a very different light to that which we, by and large, shed upon it in other parts of the book.

5.1 CYBERCULTURE AND CYBERNETICS

> Gibson's fictions show, with exaggerated clarity, the iceberg of social change sliding across the surface of the late twentieth century, but its proportions are vast and dark.
> (Bruce Sterling, 'Preface' to Gibson [1988])

As Bruce Sterling reminds us, for cyberculture, computers as media and technologies of communication are just the tip of these arch-cyberpunks' iceberg of social change. It is cybernetics, the scientific source of the 'cyber' prefix, that points to the less visible, 'vast and dark proportions' of this iceberg. For cybernetics is interested in both 'animals and machines', in technology and biology. The biology that has, for centuries, been culturally intertwined with its technologies is now spliced with them, and has even itself become a source of technologies, as cybernetic digitality has spread like a cancer from telephones to genomes, faxes to foods. Cyberculture therefore combines cybernetics' interest in technology and biology, in physical and living things, with, as Kellner has it, an interest in mapping the consequences of this conjunction of technology, nature and culture.

Accordingly, section **5.2** will address technology as physical, **5.3** will focus on technology and biology, and **5.4** will offer a critical account of theories of cyberculture, paying particular attention to which theoretical perspectives provide a map that encompasses technology, nature and culture, the three points on our compass. The first section, meanwhile, explores some of the problems attendant upon finding a framework in which to address these three points, and will ask some orienting questions to help us navigate across these terrains.

5.1.1 Technology as real and material: media studies' blindspot?

However we think about it, technology is something real. Real in the obvious, material sense: we can touch it, it does things, it performs certain actions, it makes yet other actions possible, we rearrange our work and leisure around it, and so on. New technologies do produce highly tangible changes in the way everyday life is conducted (**4.1.1–4.1.3**): they affect the way in which labour power is deployed, how money is invested and circulates, how business is done (**3.17, 3.18**), how and where identities are formed (**4.3.1–4.3.3**) and so on. In such ways, technology, both in its forms and its capacities, profoundly affects human culture.

However, as we have seen (**1.6**), most media theorists are highly sceptical of such a claim. The very question 'how does technology affect us?' is traditionally criticised within media studies as being based upon a naive idea; the idea that technology itself determines anything is dismissed as faulty thinking, and then receives little attention. This has led both to a general blindness concerning the history and philosophy of technology in general, and a relative absence of studies that seek to understand technology's role within cultural and media studies.

At times of significant change in media technologies such as we are now witnessing, this very 'taboo' leads, in turn, to sudden outbursts of techno-enthusiasm and the making of vastly overinflated claims. Concentrating on what happens only at the very moment of new media technology's 'newness' means that questions of technology slip into the background once they are no longer new. When this happens, cultural and media studies can revert to its default state in which technology is a marginal issue and it again slips off the agenda. It then becomes too easy to regard technology as something that in itself, requires no further attention. The recurring moment of inflated claims has been criticised and passed. The 'silly season' is over again. In short, not asking questions, seriously and consistently, about technology produces a cycle of boom and bust in cultural and media studies.

The current advent of a 'new' set of media technologies therefore brings with it an unsettled problematic – that of how physically real technologies are understood within cultural and media studies – and affords an opportunity to develop a means of viewing technology and its cultural effects within a realist framework.

5.1.2 Studying technology

A consequence of sidelining questions of technology within media studies, except to roll back undisciplined euphoria and ideological overstatement by techno-enthusiasts, means that the field of media studies has largely failed to develop a means of addressing technology as a real and material phenomenon.

The current emergence of new media technologies highlights this lack. The major focus on technology within cultural and media studies is in the manner that discourses surround and construct its cultural meaning (this is dealt with in **1.5**). While such studies tell us a great deal about what technology means to particular cultural groups, they tell us much less about technology itself, and do not therefore provide an adequate means of studying it in itself. Indeed, such studies are often underpinned by the conviction that 'in itself' technology is nothing; it is just a collection of dumb stuff without purpose or meaning until a culture provides them. In this part of the book we recognise that technology is not only culturally constructed as a unit of meaning, it is also physically constructed and physically constructive of a vast array of cultural phenomena. Therefore, to be a realist about technology entails asking what technology really is.

5.1.3 What is technology?

So, the fundamental aim of this section is to answer a deceptively simple and frequently dismissed question: what is technology? Of course, we all take it for granted that we have a serviceable knowledge of what technology is, since we are surrounded by it. Technology itself is therefore no stranger to us, as we are more or less familiar with individual technological things. Consider, however, the topic of this book. The occasion for writing it at all is the relatively sudden appearance of what are generally referred to as new media technologies. Section **1.3** has critically discussed the sense of newness regarding 'new media', and **1.5** analyses the discursive construction of 'new media', but we now need to build on these discussions and address the sense in which the technologies themselves are 'new'; that is, what precursors they have in the history of technology.

For the moment, a realist view is one that includes the cultural consequences of non-human things on the basis of the physical being that machines and humans share. The concept of 'realism' is further discussed in section **2.8** in the context of filmic realism

2.8   Digital cinema

This 'rolling back' of techno-hype is normally achieved by stressing issues of how social power, investment, use and reception of technologies limits and directs their application, not by seeking to understand the material nature of technology in history

1.5   Who was dissatisfied with old media?

1.3   Change and continuity
1.5   Who was dissatisfied with old media?

In the attempt to provide an answer to this question it is important to consider how we may go about it. For example, we may answer straightforwardly, 'technology is another word for machinery'. But such an answer tells us nothing other than that the two terms are substitutable; any sentence containing the word 'technology' can substitute 'machinery' for it without loss of meaning. But this tells us nothing more about technology, but only how the word functions in the English language. Such an approach answers a semantic question, a question about the meaning and use of a word. If we want to know something about technology that is not simply semantic, then, we need to use other approaches than ones that involve us getting lost in a dictionary! We can immediately see, then, that answering this question involves attention to the means we employ to answer it (and that the substitution of terms does not get us very far). We can, for example, ask those around us to contribute elements to a definition of technology. Such contributions are likely to include:

1   constructed for some specific purpose;

2   mechanical, thermal, electrical or digital;

3   artificial rather than natural;

4   automates human labour;

5   a natural human capacity;

. . . and so on. Such contributions to a definition may be more or less complex, but when we bring them together as we have above we find that some elements of these possible answers contradict each other. For example, is technology a natural thing (5), because it is in the nature of human beings to produce it (even primitive humans used sticks to dig with)? Or is it a wholly artificial thing (3), since it must be constructed by humans, and is not to be found in nature? Such an approach does not solve the problem of knowing what technology is, but it can help sharpen up how we ask the question.

5.1.4 How to proceed?

If then, in asking 'what is technology?' we also have to ask how we should ask this question (in other words, how can we go about getting a meaningful answer), the following sections will advance slowly, making each stage of the process as clear as possible. We should also be clear that in moving from stage to stage, from observation to observation, we will inevitably be making an argument.

We will try to be clear about the stages in the argument we make or how we arrive at any specific point. However, it is important to see that the answers we arrive at need not be regarded as final and absolute, since they are bound to be the consequences of the argument we adopt. We recognise that other arguments will arrive at different answers. However, whatever the answers given, the important thing is that this section maps out the co-ordinates within which an answer to the question 'what is technology?' needs to be given.

We are bound to meet a number of problems in what follows. Our aim will not be to solve such problems straightaway, but rather to grasp them, to feel our way around them, as though they were three-dimensional things. In this way, we hope to make something that appears to be so abstract and slippery (the meaning of technology) quite concrete. But, it will take a little time! We start this journey by considering a big idea about what technology is not – nature.

5.1.5 Technology and nature: the cyborg

5.1a Terminator hand from T2. (1992). Ronald Grant Archive.

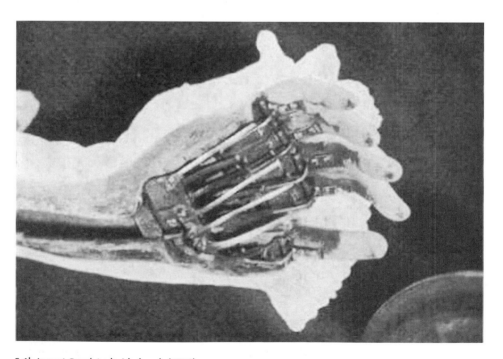

5.1b Jaquet-Droz' Androide hand. (1769)

5.1.5 Technology and nature: the cyborg

We are now familiar with the idea of the living machine: the cyborg. The sight of Arnold Schwarzenegger stripping away his skin to reveal the machinery beneath its surface is becoming as familiar to us as the revelation of skin beneath clothing. We may be less familiar with the fact that the cyborg has a history stretching back to the first century AD. What this history tells us is that technology has always been intimately involved with a fascination for the possibility of creating life. A very old idea, in which Terminator-style cyborgs, together with current projects in the biological sciences and in the field known as artificial life or Alife, are the latest manifestations. On the face of it, nothing could be further apart than technological and biological things. Technology is by definition artificial, and biology, by definition, investigates the natural. What then is it about technology that relates it to the creation of living things?

As cyborgs, clones, and prosthetics call into question the settled edge between the biological and the technological in the contemporary world, so too in the seventeenth century the entire natural universe, and all the things in it, were thought of in accordance with the technology that was then predominant: clockwork. The question of whether humans are little more than natural machines was initially posed, in an explicit form, in the seventeenth and eighteenth centuries (**5.3.2**). The same question now echoes in the problems explored through figures such as the 'replicants' in the film *Bladerunner*. Others have argued that, in much the same way that human beings (nature) evolved from apes, technology too has evolved (**5.3.5, 5.4.3**).

It seems then, that while drawing a line between technology and nature may seem like a good place to start if we wish to define technology, under examination even this line turns out to be questionable. There is a long history of doubting the distinction. It is less an answer to our question than a source of problems. From the question of what technology is, then, we derive further questions about the relationships between technology and nature, between physical machines, artifice, and physical things in general.

5.1.6 Technology and culture

If defining technology by opposing it to nature is not as straightforward as it may at first seem, how far do we get by opposing technology to another big idea or category of things: culture? In looking at the question this way we are immediately returned to the problem that we mentioned above: the tendency for cultural and media studies to dismiss the role that technology plays in shaping culture. (The question of whether technology is an agent which causes social and cultural change (technological determinism) formed the crux of the debate between McLuhan and Williams (**1.6**).) We are going to view this debate as unsettled. We now find, much to the scorn of some media theorists, that a magazine such as *Wired* (which adopted McLuhan as its patron saint), insists that the new technologies are literally changing the world. Such a view is not only touted by the 'digerati' who contibute to *Wired*, but is also argued by academic cyberneticians such as Kevin Warwick.

Warwick's scenario of a future dominated by machine life (Warwick 1998: 21ff.) forms the basis of the nightmare presented in films such as *Matrix*. Similarly, cyberpunk fictions such as William Gibson's *Neuromancer* (1986) present technologically driven futures whose outlines are just visible in the contemporary world. The possibility of the technological determination of culture appears to be far from exhausted in some quarters.

5.3.2 Clockwork: technology and nature, combined
5.3.5 Life and intelligence in the digital age
5.4.3 Cybernetics and culture

1.6 New media: determining or determined?

Kevin Warwick, Professor of Cybernetics at the University of Reading, UK, has not only argued that, within the next half century, machines will be at least as intelligent as humans, he has also, as he puts it, 'upgraded' his body with cybernetic implants. The first, in 1998, consisted of a one-way communications chip surgically inserted into his arm. This enabled him to 'communicate' with the computers in his home and workplace, causing doors to spring open, his computer to boot itself up and greet him, the lights and television to come on, and so forth. The second, in 2001, is a two-way chip, not only sending, but also receiving signals. This is also one of a pair, the other being inserted into his wife's arm, enabling signals to be sent directly from nervous system to nervous system. The experiment is designed to show whether or not sensations such as pain are physically communicable

Marx distinguishes the instrument or tool, 'which the worker animates', from large-scale machinery, in which 'it is the machine that possesses skill and strength in place of the worker . . . The worker's activity . . . is determined and regulated on all sides by the movement of the machinery' (1993: 693). See **5.2.1**.

5.2.1 Physicalism and technological dereminism

1.6   New media: determining or determined?

Let us then consider that while it may seem self-evidently true that humans put machines together, does it automatically follow that humans and their cultures remain in control of them? The view that human beings (or human cultures and societies) are in control of their machines works well as long as we consider simple machines or tools, but it works less well when we consider complex machines or systems of machinery. On an industrial assembly line, the human operator may have remained in limited control of a region of that machinery laying under their hands (riveting, panel-beating, etc.), but what was the relation between the entire system of machinery and the humans working on it?

Now, at the beginning of the twenty-first century, we also need to consider the extent to which digital technologies swiftly become invisible components that facilitate many of our actions and transactions in everyday life – a situation that makes new technologies less like discrete machines that we use and more like a technological environment, in which questions of control may pass from the hands of their users to the systems themselves (as in automated defensive missile-deployment systems or the automated stock market).

While we can, and need to, criticise and resist the deployment of technologies in the service of interests which are damaging to societies and to people (e.g. maximising profit by replacing human labour that an economic system deems too 'expensive' with cheaper machine labour or the escalation of deadly states of conflict), this does nothing to undermine the fact that technologies have profound effects on both the form and the functions of human cultures. Indeed, once technology becomes environmental (the phrase is McLuhan's – see **1.6**), as has been increasingly apparent since the Industrial Revolution in the nineteenth century, it makes increasingly less sense to distinguish technology from culture as cultures become increasingly technologised. Thus, while we might have become used to defining technology against culture, we can see that this is also problematic. Culture has become inextricably bound up with complex technological systems and environments. The very term 'cyberculture' stands for something like this: not a culture that is separate from technology but one in which these spheres fuse.

To sum up: as with the distinction between technology and nature, we again find ourselves faced with a problem when we consider the relations between technology and culture. In trying to define technology against nature and against culture, we end up with a series of problems. In order to begin examining these problems it will be helpful to reconsider the relations between all three terms that we are dealing with: nature, technology and culture.

5.1.7 Nature and culture

The now commonplace division of things into the realms of 'nature' and 'culture' has been a fundamental intellectual habit since the nineteenth-century German philosopher, Wilhelm Dilthey, carved up knowledge into the natural or physical sciences (*Naturwissenschaften*) and the cultural or human sciences (*Geisteswissenschaften*). Following this division, we are likely to agree with another seminal thinker of the nineteenth century, Karl Marx, when he states that, 'nature builds no machines' (1993: 692). It is still largely the case that, if we were asked if technology belongs to the realm of nature, we would almost certainly answer 'no'. We are, in fact, apt to experience difficulty with the very question. The question seems not to make sense. Can we therefore conclude that if technology is definitely not nature, it is solely a cultural phenomenon?

5.1.8 A problem with binary definitions

The question: 'does technology belong to the realm of nature or to that of culture?' is a troubling one because it suggests that the nature–culture divide, which has become 'second nature' in the humanities, is assumed to be a binary relation. A binary relation is an opposition of two terms where the difference between the terms is thought to tell us something about each of them. So, what it is to be 'feminine' gains some meaning by not being 'masculine', and what it is to be 'strong' gains meaning if we know what being 'weak' means. However, there is more to binary oppositions than that. Such oppositions also exhaust the field of possibilities that we can think of. Thus, 1 and 0 exhaust the elements (although not the combinations) of any binary system, just as 'guilty' and 'innocent' exhaust the system of legal verdicts under English law. However, our examination so far must lead us to consider whether a simple opposition of 'nature' to 'culture' can exhaust the field of possibilities regarding how one relates to the other? Just as black and white, while an opposition, does not exhaust the field of all possible colours that, in fact, lie between them and out of which each is constituted. Failure to pay attention to this simple point has resulted, in recent years, in a fundamental confusion with regard to what a binary relation is, so that we feel we have already explained something when we say 'it's a binary opposition'.

Many theorists in the human sciences, including media studies, have sought to retain such a binary relation between 'nature' and 'culture'. For example, in his *The Elementary Structures of Kinship* ([1949] 1969) the structural anthropologist Claude Lévi-Strauss declares that rather than 'confidently repudiating' the distinction between nature and culture, as many sociologists and anthropologists have done, he wishes to offer a 'more valid interpretation' of it and thus to save it ([1949] 1969: 9).

Through his new interpretation, Lévi-Strauss reinforced the binary opposition between nature and culture. His argument is exemplified by his treatment of the way that the practice of incest is prohibited in all human societies. He observes that the prohibition of incest has both 'the universality of . . . instinct, and the coercive character of law and institution . . . Inevitably extending beyond the historical and geographical limits of culture, [it is] coextensive with the biological species' ([1949] 1969; 10). In this way, the question then arises, is incest prohibition natural or cultural, inborn or invented, given or constructed?

If the prohibition is universal, it is tempting to regard this as evidence that it is a natural phenomenon, an attribute we humans are born with. Yet, at the same time, is not a prohibition, by definition, something cultural; a law or institution the observation of which is enforced? If an aversion to incest were natural, there would be no need of coercion or enforcement in its prohibition. As incest is actively prohibited must it therefore be cultural and not, after all, natural? One answer to this conundrum is that 'incest prohibition' demonstrates that the sphere of culture has its own universal laws, much as the sphere of nature does (as in the universal laws of physics, for example). So, here again we meet the idea that nature and culture are not governed by the same laws. While this may lie at the root of our present problem, it also offers scope and validity to the human or cultural sciences as independent of the physical sciences. Human societies are not, the argument goes, governed by the same forces that shape the natural world and are therefore a quite separate field of enquiry and explanation.

We have seen how the binary nature–culture distinction helps to make sense of a phenomenon such as a prohibition, and why, if this is established as a universal law (like the law of gravity in earth-bound physics), it provides the study of culture and society with solid ground, with its own puzzles, problematics and processes to explain. However, if we substitute the object that interests us, 'technology', for 'incest prohibition' in Lévi-Strauss's account, then the question becomes cloudy again.

Unlike a prohibition, a technology cannot be reduced to an outcome of a society's coercive and enforcing arrangements for behaviour, or the universal laws of the cultural anthropologist. While a society might control and legislate about the uses of technologies, these also necessarily function in accordance with certain physical laws (there needs, for example, to be contact or communication between parts of a machine if it is to function). Thus, even if we accept (with Marx) that it is only in human cultures that we find the construction and invention of machines, does this mean that technology is nothing more than a fact of culture? Is it solely an extension of the capacities of culture, or is it solely an exploitation of given physical phenomena (as steam-power exploits the combustibility of minerals, or nuclear power the fissionability of atoms)? A little thought will show that technology is both. It is physical (like nature) and invented (like culture). Technology 'belongs' exclusively to neither sphere. For this reason, we begin to see why it would be useful to accept that nature and culture, where technology is concerned, do not exhaust the field of things.

5.1.9 We have never been binary: Latour and 'actor-network theory'

Bruno Latour, an anthropologist of science, has sought to address precisely this problem. In his 1993 book, *We Have Never Been Modern*, he offers a diagnosis of modernity as a condition in which the humanities have become so embroiled in questions of the social, linguistic and discursive construction of meanings that we have forgotten how to ask questions about what things are.

At the root of this situation there lies a prejudice. The prejudice is that of humanism, which Latour argues is reductive 'because [it] seek[s] to attribute action to a small number of powers' – human powers – 'leaving the rest of the world with nothing but simple mute forces' (1993: 138). All that exists, meanwhile, exists only in 'the linguistic play of speaking subjects' at the expense of the material and technological world (1993: 61). In other words, we humans talk about talk, while things maintain their onward march beneath the level of our scrutiny.

We routinely discuss signs apart from what they are signs of, representations apart from what they represent, meanings apart from matter, and ideologies that mask realities, so that the world we inhabit now seems to be composed exclusively of linguistic, textual or interpretative acts. At the same time, a glance at a newspaper reveals how complex interrelations between this human world and non-human things (the environment, the life-span of the sun, the actions of viruses and, crucially, the actions of technology) have become. Is the HIV virus a textual construct? It involves certain constructions of meaning, certainly ('God's plague visited upon sexual deviants'; 'originating from human–animal intercourse in Africa', and so on); but is there not also a thing there, the virus itself? Latour's point is not that we should dismiss the discourses and address ourselves only to things; he is not suggesting that the virus's meaning is a pointless distraction from its biochemical properties and that we should therefore run from our libraries to laboratories. Rather, his point is that texts, meanings and intentions cover only a limited proportion of the surfaces of things. A full account of a thing must therefore situate it in the network of other things, texts, discourses and institutions of which it is part. Studying the HIV virus

The irony of this is that the very reduction that humanism wishes to achieve – that the sum total of actions in the world are achieved solely by the speaking animal – was always conceived as a critical gesture; in Williams, for example, it was intended to demonstrate the falsity of the idea that machines act without human intervention, so that when we are tempted to describe machines as active, as determinant – mere descriptions, these – we look instead for the human behind them, and the will to profit that guides their manipulations of objects. In Marx, the struggle against the 'self-acting mules' with which industrialisation threatened to render human makers redundant, is intended to bring about the conscious realisation on the part of labouring humanity that we alone are capable of making, since 'nature builds no machines' (Marx 1993: 706) therefore entails attention being paid to the literature, science, journalism, politics, hospital organisation, medical research, funding arrangements, the sociology of scientific breakthroughs, the aetiology of infection, the genetic structure of the virus, and so on. Instead of thinking about things in isolation from meanings, or of meanings in isolation from things, reality is composed of networks in which human things (meanings, texts, discourses, institutions, signs) interact constantly with non-human things (viruses, biochemistry, immune systems). Crucially, for Latour, what knits all these things together are the various technologies that facilitate these interactions: the technologies of medical research and intervention, communication and transportation systems, genomic technologies, and so on. Since networks are not stimulated into action exclusively by human actions, but also by non-human things, including the technological forms available to us, Latour sets out the concept of non-human agency against the humanist understanding of agency we find in contemporary social theory.

5.1.10 Media as technology

Having seen how and why a distinction is drawn between nature and culture, as the basis of the natural and cultural sciences, it may be that rather than ask what 'realm' technology belongs to we should ask what field(s) of study technology as such falls under. The question 'what is technology?' can then be answered in a number of different ways, depending on what field one is answering it from.

When looked at as a physical object, technology is the concern of the natural and applied sciences, since no technology can work unless it successfully exploits a set of physical laws. Thus a steam engine works by creating pressure from the combustion of a mineral fuel in a boiler, which drives a system of wheels and gears by way of a condenser and a system of valves. Each of these processes exploits combustible materials, the differentials between heat and cold sources, and so on, without which the engine would not work. But technologies do also have a high degree of cultural 'presence'; they are invested with meaning (see 1.1 and 1.5). This is what is foregrounded when technologies are looked at as cultural phenomena and is one reason why they are not thought of as only physical machines. A prime example of this is the sense the cultural or human sciences give to the term 'media'.

A medium is seldom treated as something 'in itself'. Even if the apparatus or the material nature of a technology is paid attention, as part of an analysis of what a medium is (Williams [1977] does so in 'From Medium to Social Practice'; in film theory, the 'apparatus' also supplies such attention [see 2.8]), cultural and media studies mainly looks at a medium as an instantiation of certain economic, communicational, political, commercial, or artistic interests. On the other hand, the physical sciences, even of the applied variety, do not address such technologies as 'media' but only ever as an arrangement of electrical circuits, functions, transmitters, pattern and noise. It is as if what is foregrounded in the physical or natural sciences becomes background in the cultural or human sciences, and vice versa, thus maintaining a blind spot between nature and culture.

Many cultural and media theorists seek strenuously to police the divide between nature and culture. This is done by wholly removing technology from the sphere of nature and subsuming it under the category of culture. The substantial argument, for example, behind Raymond Williams's idea of what he calls 'cultural science' (1974: 119ff.) is that, since cause and effect explanations cannot be transferred from the effect of cues hitting billiard balls to matters of social change, or from science to history, the idea of 'technological

This is one way to characterise a strong version of social construction: the world as we know it is the world that we know only in so far as we talk about it, and are aware of how we talk about it. Accordingly, from our present perspective, social constructionism is a form of humanism. Ian Hacking, in *The Social Construction of What?* (Cambridge, Mass.: Harvard University Press, 1999), pp. 1–34, carefully and clearly unpicks the varieties and uses of social construction. He argues that theorists seldom if ever put forward a positive account of constructionism, but only provide constructionist accounts of things – for example, gender – when their contingent and historical character, and the ideological motives they serve, have been forgotten

In this way, although we are in pursuit of a more realist view of technology, we need again to consider what the study of culture (or 'cultural studies') takes as so important; the way that discourses (in this context whole sets of historical disciplines) frame, select, and make sense of reality in different ways (see 1.5)

1.1   What are new media?
1.5   Who was dissatisfied with old media?

2.8   Digital cinema

effect' must be dropped altogether in favour of an account of social change that concentrates on the intentions and purposes of the groups who use technologies in the act of changing things.

This is humanism. The argument is that, instead of asking questions of cause and effect, that belong wholly to the physical sciences, the business of cultural science is to ask questions of agency. Agency replaces cause as an explanatory principle since the concept of agency involves not only the causing of an action but the desires, purposes and intentions behind it. Agency, on such a view, is exclusively therefore the property of socially interacting humans, restricting cultural science to the study of human actions, and ruling out of court the actions of anything else. Williams's cultural science, as Latour says of the modern humanities, is cut off from the physical world. Strictly speaking, there can be no cultural study of technology, only of its human uses. Conversely, the media as technology cannot be said to have any direct 'effects' on culture at all, since it is made up of the actions, purposes, desires and intentions of human agents.

This is why cultural and media studies in general feels confident about rejecting the notion that watching, say, a graphically violent movie, video or TV broadcast can be said to have an effect on the watcher, such that s/he then goes out and guns down the neighbourhood or murders a child. In this argument, however, the reluctance to transfer the language of 'cause and effect' from merely physical phenomena to human actions betrays, on both sides, a fundamental and necessary blindness to the role of technology. Implicit in the idea of causation is not just that event x causes event y, but rather that between them there is a sequence of physical events, a causal chain. However, the idea that human beings, who are after all equally physical as mental animals, are subject to no physical effects from phenomena they experience by way of the interaction between their senses and technologies, is as ludicrous and unsustainable as the idea that they are 'caused' to murder, maim and torture by viewing 'video-nasties'. Moreover, since Williams's arguments are held by traditional media and cultural studies to have won the day over McLuhan's technological determinism, they continue to frame the media and cultural studies approach to technology today. If we want, therefore, to ask questions of the technological elements of cyberculture, we need to remain critically aware of the humanism Williams bequeathed to media studies' approach to them (see 1.6).

1.6 New media: determining or determined?

Here we see two approaches to the question of 'what is technology' enter into an apparently unresolvable conflict: on the one hand, the apparent 'scientism' of the regular statistics and surveys that demonstrate that, for example, 'video game violence causes real violence'; on the other, the humanism of 'there are no causes in culture, only agents and their purposes'. These certainly provide two answers to the question 'what is technology?' – on the one hand, it is a set of machines that cause certain predictable effects; on the other, it is a means by which socially embodied purposes are achieved – but they bring us no closer to a satisfactory answer. What they do tell us, however, is that neither the insistence on pure, physical causality, of the sort modelled on the collisions of billiard balls, nor the equal and opposite insistence on no causality, only human agency, provides the frameworks necessary to answer it. We shall therefore explore other theoretical frameworks in what follows. To begin this process we shall revisit the issues at the heart of the Williams–McLuhan problematic: causality and technological determinism. If Williams's arguments bequeathed media studies a problematic humanism, has something been overlooked in the account of technological and cultural change McLuhan offered that might help us to answer the question, 'what is technology?'

5.2 REVISITING DETERMINISM: PHYSICALISM, HUMANISM AND TECHNOLOGY

Introduction

In 1.6.4, we noted that by tracing the influence of central theses in McLuhan's work we arrive at the idea of a physicalist understanding of new media and cultural studies. It is the physical aspects – especially as regards the new technologies and the physical relations of humans to them – that 'mainstream' cultural and media studies has proved to be unable to address. Yet this is an aspect of cyberculture that science fiction has been able to address. In his introduction to a seminal collection of cyberpunk fiction, author and manifestoist Bruce Sterling notes the following:

1.6.4 The many virtues of Saint McLuhan

> Traditionally there has been a yawning gulf between the sciences and the humanities: a gulf between literary culture, the formal world of art and politics, and the culture of science, the world of engineering and industry. But the gap is crumbling in an unexpected fashion. Technical culture has gotten out of hand. The advances of the sciences are so deeply radical, so disturbing, upsetting and revolutionary, that they can no longer be contained. They are surging into culture at large; they are invasive; they are everywhere.
>
> (Sterling, in Gibson 1988: xii)

This is our starting point for the considerations of technology that follow. Its purpose is to re-establish the physical continuity between bodies, technologies and images – between nature, technology and culture – that is necessary to examining the effects of the new technologies. Nor can such an account avoid attending to the role of the sciences in cyberculture, as Sterling alerts us. In this light, it is clear that the physicalist basis of McLuhan's theses, if not the specific theses themselves, offers the prospect of a framework within which cyberculture, in the inclusive sense Sterling gives it, may be examined. Moreover, from the example of Sterling we can see that such a basis is not merely a product of theorising about electronic technologies in the 1960s but is actually a core element of contemporary cyberculture. The contemporary centrality of such theorising is further demonstrated, in the popular realm, by the magazine *Wired* canonising McLuhan as its 'patron saint', and in the increasing amount of 'new media' research being done around McLuhan (Levinson 1997; De Kerckhove 1997; Genosko 1998).

If McLuhan retains a powerful presence in cyberculture, Williams's ideas on technology have, as we have argued (see **1.6.3**), effectively defined the theoretical stance of mainstream cultural and media studies and the humanities in general. The core of the problem remains that of technological determinism, which continues to haunt the humanities' treatment of the question of technology. Thus cultural historians of technology (Smith and Marx 1996), anthropologists (Dobres 2000), as well as culturalists (MacKenzie and Wajcman [1985] 2000), continue to devote books to arguing that physical devices do not have determining effects on culture. This alone demonstrates that technological determinism remains an important issue.

1.6.3 Williams and the social shaping of technology

One reason why this is so is that the new media are not simply new media but also new technologies. For that reason the question of the place of technology in culture has again become central. Cyberculture, as Sterling testifies, has reintroduced into culture at large an array of concerns that have become alien to cultural and media studies, but which are important elements of attending to technology in general, and to the inalienably technological component of that culture. Amongst such concerns are the histories and philosophies of science, as well as those sciences that rely on technology to investigate the physical world.

In the next section, therefore, we suggest ways in which a physicalist basis for cyberculture can provide important links between the histories of science, technology and culture, and thus address the question of technological determinism – whether technology causes, or human agents intend, the social changes that accompany technological change – from the point of view of cyberculture.

5.2.1 Physicalism and technological determinism.

We have argued (**1.6.3**, **1.6.4**) that the encounter between the cultural approaches to technology exemplified by Williams and McLuhan in the 1960s constitutes an enduring core of intellectual resources for contemporary addresses to cyberculture. In this section, therefore, we will revisit this problematic one final time in order to examine what is at stake in the concept of technological determinism. However, we should not be under the impression that the two approaches are only to be found in Williams and McLuhan. On the contrary, as we have seen, they continue to underwrite much contemporary debate around the issue of technological determinism (see Dobres 2000; MacKenzie and Wajcman [1985] 1999; Smith and Marx 1996). The virtue of addressing the problematic as it arises in Williams and McLuhan is that Williams in particular is concerned to argue the case against determinism through from first principles, while McLuhan offers a clearly deterministic counterposition. Finally, this latter is one that has been resumed in recent years in order precisely to address issues arising from cyberculture and digital media that mainstream cultural and media studies is ill-equipped to confront.

5.1.10   Media as technology

We have seen in **5.1.10** that the basis of the humanities' challenge to technological determinism is humanism. We saw that this challenge consists in the critique of the concept of *cause* applying to the cultural realm, and its replacement with the concept of 'agency'. Causes obtain only in the physical world, not in the cultural. If, however, there is merit to a physicalist approach to technology in culture outlined in **1.6**, then it is that it places culture within rather than outside the realm of physical causation. The consequences of this move are far reaching indeed, in so far as, just as Sterling insists, mapping cyberculture entails making ourselves passingly familiar not just with cultural accounts but with scientific and philosophical ones as well. Moreover, it will help us to see that 'cyberculture' is not a wholly new cultural phenomenon in its catholic inclusiveness, but rather just the latest in a long line of historical technocultures.

1.6   New media: determining or determined?

Yet the histories of philosophy and the sciences tell us there is not only one kind of cause. Aristotle distinguished four causes; the early moderns attempted to replace these four with just one; the contemporary sciences recognise at least two kinds of causation. Thus, when we say 'technology causes social change' we might be using one of any number of concepts of cause. Our first task will therefore be to map out some of the salient historical and contemporary concepts of cause, and then to ascertain which sense of causality Williams ascribes to what he takes to be McLuhan's determinism. Following this, we will attempt to characterise what senses of causality are involved in a range of theories of technology.

Nor is 'determinism' a simple, monolithic concept. Again, there are varieties of determinism. Mathematical determinism is not the same as historical determinism, for example. Even within the relatively restricted range of technological determinism, at least three versions of this theory have been distinguished (Bimber, in Smith and Marx 1996), while chaos theory is based not on randomness but on physical systems that are deterministic yet unpredictable (see **5.4**).

5.4   Theories of cyberculture

Finally, we will ask what varieties of agency are there, and can they be restricted to humans alone? Under what concept of agency can machines be accounted agents?

Each of these concepts is like a set of co-ordinates on the map of cyberculture that this section is concerned to draw. Knowing what these co-ordinates are will help us orient our way through that fraught terrain, but it will also help us to distinguish the routes other theorists take through it. Finally, it will enable us to locate the core questions of any technoculture, from the hydraulic age to the mechanical, and from the industrial age to the cybernetic.

5.2.2 Causalities

In this section we will meet three different types of cause. The concept of cause is important in examining technological determinism, in so far as the latter thesis attempts to explain *what causes cultural change* by way of technological change. However, what kind of cause is this? Does technology cause cultural change in the same way as the impact of one billiard ball on a second causes the latter to move? Do we search for the cause of cultural change in the same way that investigators seek the cause of an accident? Or is the cause of technological change itself deeply embedded in the natural blueprint of humanity, as Bergson, for example, argues?

Already it is clear that the question of causality is complex. The concepts of causality we will be looking at are:

• teleological

• mechanical

• non-linear

Each of these stems from a period in the history of the natural sciences. The point of examining them here is that it opens up two questions, which we will answer below:

1   What kind of causality does Williams impute to McLuhan's technological determinism?

2   What alternative concepts of causality are there?

Ultimately, what is at stake is whether technology can be examined on a physicalist basis, or whether, by dint of its cultural presence, we must, as traditional media studies does, give up this basis. Accordingly, we will carefully note in the following accounts the difficulties in transposing them from the realm of nature, where scientists and philosophers have deployed them, to that of culture.

Teleological causality

After Aristotle identified teleology as a form of causality in the fifth century BC, it became the dominant mode for explaining the natural world until the sixteenth and seventeenth centuries. Even in the contemporary natural sciences, particularly in biology, teleology continues to cause controversy amongst scientists. In the context of new media, however, we come across teleology whenever a history is concocted to explain that the modern computer, for example, is really the perfected form of an older technology. The story is then told of how the abacus is, in fact, the computer in germ, and that it took several thousand years for the abacus to unfold its potential and become the computer (see **1.4.1** for a critical discussion of teleological modes of explaining new media).

1.4.1   Teleological accounts of new media

Using the above example, we can see that teleology argues that the computer exists in some form in the abacus and that the abacus was destined or determined to become the computer over time. While this sounds improbable when applied to inanimate things like the abacus and the computer, it sounds much more plausible when applied to living things. Consider, for example, the acorn. As it grows, the acorn becomes an oak tree, and cannot become anything else. Thus we can see that the *telos* – the 'end' or 'goal' – of the acorn is the oak tree. If we accept this, we are arguing that the oak is the cause of the acorn, which is the argument that Aristotle put forward, calling such a cause a *final cause* (the oak is what the acorn finally becomes), and explanations of final causes, teleological explanations.

Consider the differences between these two examples: firstly, applied to the acorn and the oak, the teleology in question is internal to the acorn. However, applied to the abacus and the computer, the teleology is external to the abacus. In other words, there is nothing in an abacus *per se* that determines it to become a computer, as an acorn is determined to become an oak. Applied to the acorn, then, we are dealing with a kind of cause; applied to the abacus, merely with an explanation. That is why teleological arguments feature more regularly in contemporary biology than they do in the history of technology. This does not mean that there cannot be a teleology of technology; it may simply be that the processes by which technologies develop are insufficiently understood.

Mechanical causality

Teleological explanations of natural phenomena fell into disrepute in the sixteenth and seventeenth centuries – the dawn of the modern period. This period witnessed such a great increase in clockwork technologies that it sought to explain the world as a clockwork phenomenon:

> It is my goal to show that the celestial machine is not some kind of divine being, but rather like a clock . . . In this machine nearly all the various movements are caused by a single, very simple magnetic force, just as in a clock all movements are caused by a single weight.
>
> (Kepler 1605, cited in Mayr 1986: 61)

This conception of the world made philosophers sceptical of such 'occult causes' as teleology, requiring instead that there be evidence of causation. The basis of mechanical causation is that in order for anything to be called a cause there must be contact between it and the thing it causes to move. For example, winding a watch causes the hands to move, since the action of winding coils a spring, the subsequent unwinding of which turns cogs that in turn move the hands on the watch's face. But the watch cannot be said to cause a reorganisation of the social observance of time ('clocking on', timetabling, and so on), since there is no contact between the mechanical parts of the watch and the institutions that adopt it as an organising principle.

However, many philosophers, well into the eighteenth century, sought to explain the workings of human beings in terms of clockwork mechanisms as well, thus eradicating the distance between the material world of physics and the human world. Amongst the consequences of this view was that life itself began to be seen as something that could be created in technological form. We will explore the mechanical age's attitudes to 'artificial life' in section **5.3**.

5.3 Biological technologies: the history of automata

Non-linear causality

Mechanical causality works in what is called a linear fashion. This means two things:

- all actions are reversible: watches are wound from an inert state to which they return as they unwind, at which point they are ready to be rewound;

- there is always a chain of causes, leading from event X to event Y to event Z, and so on.

However, certain physical phenomena are not reversible: living things, for example, unlike watches, cannot be revivified once they die; life is a one-way street, as it were. If humans are to all intents and purposes walking, talking clockworks, then how is it we cannot be rewound? Living things proved such a problem to the mechanical world-view that philosophers despaired of finding 'a Newton of the blade of grass'.

Related to this point, if life is a one-way street, then how does it start? What causes life? If we are dealing with an individual creature, then we can say 'its parents', but if we are dealing with life in general then there is no obvious explanation. In the eighteenth century, philosophers thus sought the 'vital force' that caused life in the same way that all physical events on the earth could be explained by the actions of the gravitational force. Towards the end of that century, the philosopher Immanuel Kant concluded that we cannot avoid viewing living things as if they were 'natural purposes' (Kant [1790] 1986, §5), thus reintroducing teleology at the end of mechanism's long reign.

Secondly, how can we explain phenomena that appear to be effected not by causal chains but by cyclical behaviours? For example, what causes an amoeba to exist? Amoebas reproduce by dividing themselves into two new amoebas. Thus one amoeba is the cause of two more, each of which in turn is the cause of two further amoebas. The process has no beginning or end, but continues indefinitely. This is not so much a chain as a cycle, in which the effect (two amoebas) of reproduction is also its cause (two more amoebas).

BOX 5.1: Cybernetics and non-linearity

For cybernetics, non-linearity comes in two sorts: negative and positive feedback. Since cybernetics is concerned, like the thermodynamics on which it is based, with minimising loss (of energy, for thermodynamics; of information, for cybernetics), negative feedback is viewed as the source of maintaining order against the corrosive forces that threaten to destabilise it. These forces are always present since, just as energy always tends to dissipate according to thermodynamics, so too for cybernetics information always tends to become noise, or order, disorder. Some noise, disorder or energy loss is therefore inevitable, but order is maintained by negative feedback. Such feedback always 'tends to oppose what the system is already doing, and is thus negative' (Wiener [1948] 1962: 97). What the system is already doing, however, is losing information or increasing disorder, since this is in the nature of systems. This process can however become self-amplifying, multiplying geometrically the quantity of noise or disorder in the system, and leading to the system grinding to a halt or going out of control. This latter process is called positive feedback. (See **5.4.**)

The problem, then, with mechanical causation is that it did not explain all events in the physical world, and left biology almost entirely out of account. At best, therefore, mechanical causality accounts only for a region of physical events.

Both the origin of life and the amoeba's reproductive cycle are examples therefore not of linear but of non-linear causality. Somehow, life emerges, and amoebas keep dividing. These one-way processes are irreversible (life cannot be restarted; amoebas cannot divide less). While late nineteenth-century scientists conceded life was a non-linear phenomenon, the study of such phenomena has only really emerged in the last quarter of the twentieth century. The contemporary sciences that study non-linear phenomena concern themselves with what is called emergence: how order arises out of chaos (Prigogine and Stengers 1985), how organised life emerges from a chemical soup (Kauffman 1995); how mountains form (Gould 1987), and so on. Non-linear accounts have also been given of overtly social phenomena, such as how crowds develop, economic behaviour (Eve *et al.* 1997), and so on. In all cases, something coherent and organised arises not from a single cause but from any number of factors that converge to form a 'looping' or feedback structure, giving rise to what is called a 'self-organising' phenomenon.

BOX 5.2:   Chaos, complexity and non-linearity

Cybernetics, concerned as it is with communication and control, tended to be concerned to eliminate positive feedback as system-disruption, noise, and the eventual collapse of the system, and to construct devices that maintained an equilibrium between positive feedback (change) and negative feedback (control). Beyond a certain threshold of positive feedback, this equilibrium was fatally disrupted, leading only to systems failure and breakdown. The recent study of chaotic phenomena, however, is interested not in phenomena in equilibrium but in those that are far from equilibrium. The study of non-linear phenomena in chemistry, for example, led Ilya Prigogine to discover processes that took place apparently spontaneously in far from equilibrium conditions. Prigogine called such phenomena dissipative structures: 'dissipative' because they take place not when a system is in an equilibrium state but once positive feedback has dissipated that system; and 'structures' since these same dissipative processes give rise to spontaneous order. A frequently used example of such a process is the so-called 'chemical clock':

> Suppose we have two kinds of molecules, 'red' and 'blue'. Because of the chaotic motion of the molecules, we would expect that at a given moment we would have more red molecules, say, in the left part of a vessel. Then a bit later more blue molecules would appear, and so on. The vessel would appear to us as 'violet', with occasional

irregular flashes of red or blue. However, this is not what happens with a chemical clock; here the system is all blue, then it abruptly changes its colour to red, then again to blue. Because all these changes occur at regular time intervals, we have a coherent process.

(Prigogine and Stengers 1985: 147–148)

The example of the chemical clock thus demonstrates that there are such spontaneously arising pockets of order; that once systems go into chaotic positive feedback they do not merely collapse but rather give rise to new and different orders. Prigogine and Stengers therefore call this process 'self-organisation'. They go on to locate such processes in biology, such as in the growth and reproduction of unicellular organisms (amoebas).

We can see, then, that from the apparent limitation of mechanical explanation to a small region of physical phenomena, and the apparent limitation of teleology to living things alone, non-linear causality seems to work across the supposed boundary between the natural and cultural worlds. This is not, of course, an uncontroversial point, since many people would be reluctant to see what seemed to them to be utterly chance occurrences (finding oneself part of a crowd; going on a shopping spree) turn out to be functions of underlying organisations. But it is no more difficult to accept than that our beliefs and opinions, our desires and identities, are the fruits neither of nature nor choice, but of the effects of the economic, political and ideological structures of our culture.

Nor is this cross-border traffic between the sciences and the humanities one-way. Friedrich Engels, for example, noted that Marx considered that Darwin's work on evolution provided the naturalistic basis for 'dialectical history' (Engels 1964: 7). Engels went on to extend this principle, and to write Dialectics of Nature, providing a dialectical account of the natural world

Conclusion: Williams and McLuhan on causality

What concept of causality does Williams therefore impute to McLuhan's technological determinism? Although he does discuss the need for 'a very different model of cause and effect' (1974: 125) – which will turn out to be the replacement of the concept of causality with that of agency – Williams does not make explicit what model of causality he is ascribing to McLuhan's technological determinism. We can, however, infer what kind of 'model' he is using if we examine what he sees as the consequences of such a determinism:

If the medium – whether print or television – is the cause, all other causes, all that men ordinarily see as history, are at once reduced to effects. Similarly, what are elsewhere seen as effects, and as such subject to social, cultural, psychological and moral questioning, are excluded as irrelevant by comparison with the direct physiological and therefore 'psychic' effects of the media as such.

(Williams 1974: 127)

If X is a cause, then it cannot be at the same time an effect: we can thus see that Williams is using a linear conception of causality, ruling out teleology and non-linearity (of the sort, for example, found in cybernetics). From our discussion of concepts of causality, this leaves mechanical causality. Is this the conception of cause Williams is working with? Two points he makes support this view:

1   He calls the effects McLuhan describes 'physiological'.

2   He qualifies these physiological effects as 'direct'.

It is really (2) that makes it clear that the causality Williams has in mind is indeed mechanical, since 'direct physiological' effects means that these effects are produced by a physically proximate cause. Non-linear causality is indirect: causal, but unpredictable. If we add this to the idea that a cause cannot simultaneously be an effect, then we get the image of the causal chain that is the preferred explanatory mode of modern science between the sixteenth and eighteenth centuries. The argument has nothing to say, therefore, about other forms of causality, and *deals only with one view of determinism*.

Moreover, by tying 'physiology' to the version of causality he criticises as inadequate for understanding social practices, Williams effectively rules out the physical in any form having any influence whatever upon culture. Yet this is surely not true: one clear reason for the emergence of factories during the late eighteenth and early nineteenth centuries must be that the large machines they housed required their parts to be physically proximate to one another – an engine will not drive a conveyor belt unless they are connected by cogs. The physical form of a technology therefore constrains and determines how it can be used.

Through this analysis, therefore, we have opened up a route for studying technology in a physicalist manner that is not vulnerable to the sophisticated criticisms Williams levelled at McLuhan. We have not yet asked, however, what model of causality McLuhan is dealing with. While McLuhan is notoriously oblique (although not without reason), we can find repeated references to technologies creating new environments, to technologies as extensions, having physical effects on their users, and so on. However, in the first essay of *Understanding Media*, McLuhan writes:

> [A]s David Hume showed in the eighteenth century, there is no principle of causality in mere sequence. That one thing follows from another accounts for nothing . . . So the greatest of all reversals occurred with electricity, that ended sequence by making things instant. With instant speed the causes of things began to emerge to awareness again . . . Instead of asking which came first, the chicken or the egg, it suddenly seemed that a chicken was an egg's idea for getting more eggs.
>
> (McLuhan 1967: 20)

In other words, McLuhan disavows 'sequence', and is not therefore dealing with the causal chain beloved of mechanism. Further, the instantaneity of, for example, electronic communications, brings causality to the fore again, since it makes us ask, if two events happen instantaneously, can we say that one causes the other? Just as the idea of the sequence of causes and effects recedes from attention, therefore, the idea of causes being effects of effects, and of effects being causes of causes, arises. Thus McLuhan's conception of the causality employed in electronic technologies is non-linear. Given electronic technologies, then, our environment becomes non-linear. Similarly, however, given mechanical technologies, our environment becomes mechanical. In other words, the technology in question causes events in accordance with its physical principles: there are mechanical causes at work in cultures that are predominantly structured by mechanical machines, and electronic causes at work in those primarily structured by electronic machines.

While McLuhan does not spell this out, the crux of the point is this: that it is the physical principles of a given technology that cause it to be used in certain ways. These uses then amplify the impact of the technology on the culture, so that mechanical technologies will produce mechanised cultures, electronic technologies, cultures based on instantaneity, and so on. Moreover, since the use of particular technologies extends our bodies and senses, human beings tend necessarily to be unaware of the impact the technologies are having: they become our nature. Importantly, then, the conception of causality at work here is not direct, but it is physical. To clarify:

1   the physical method of working of a technology determines its possible uses, so that

2   that determination of possible uses becomes amplified through its use, so that

3   the governing technology of an age will shape the society that uses it accordingly.

This is a cybernetic understanding of the relations between humans and machines, which we will explore further in **5.4**.

5.4   Theories of cyberculture

To summarise: the version of causality Williams accuses McLuhan of working with is not the same version of causality that McLuhan is actually working with. Williams holds that determinism implies a mechanical causality, whereas McLuhan is actually working with a non-linear causality based on cybernetics (**5.4**).

5.2.3 Agencies

When Williams argues that McLuhan is a technological determinist, he bases this accusation on a certain type of cause, one that he identifies as stemming from the realm of 'physical facts' (1974: 129), that is, from the field of study proper to the natural sciences. Williams's own answer to the question of what causes cultural change does not therefore dispense with the concept of causality, but invokes an alternative concept – agency.

5.2.2   Causalities

As we have seen in **5.2.2**, however, there is no settled view regarding one kind of causality operative within the physical realm. Similarly, there is more than one account of agency. This section will discuss two basic kinds of agency: (1) humanist and (2) non-human.

The humanist concept of agency

At the root of the determinism problem is the question of what it is to ascribe agency to something. Williams, coming from a Marxist-humanist background, considers agency to be the ultimately reducible preserve of human beings as cultural actors. Contemporary cultural theory agrees almost entirely with this, viewing all other conceptions of agency as mystifications and distortions of our actual relations to things and to societal or cultural forms. If, accordingly, we were to accept the view that agency may indeed be ascribed to non-human phenomena, then we would be obscuring the reality of the situation, where in fact things are never innocently what they are, but serve some social purpose, follow an agenda of one or other interest group, or what have you. Let us call this the 'crime boss' theory of culture, in which we must be ever alert for the distortions of real cultural forms by mere ideological trappings, lest we find ourselves unwittingly serving a purpose contrary to our interests. In the loosest terms, this is what lies behind Marx's description of the factory system as inaugurating the dominance of dead over living labour, or machines over labouring humanity: such an arrangement serves the production process of capital, and has no other purpose than to line the pockets of the increasingly wealthy at the expense of the mass of labouring humanity.

At the root of this lies the view that it is indeed possible to reacquire one's total agency, to remove the shackles that bond us to the false gods of work, money, pain and misery, and to assume the mantle of free agents with which nature has endowed us but industrial culture steals. Such a view may justly be called humanism, since it jealously restricts agency to human beings as a matter of principle, despite any and all evidence to the contrary.

Non-human agency

What grounds, however, could there be to extend the concept of agency to non-human things? Before answering this, it is worth noting the following concerning humanism:

1   that since at least the eighteenth century human agency or 'free will' has been behind an attempt to isolate mere natural causality (that storms arise, that volcanoes erupt, that the earth circles the sun, that all earthbound phenomena are governed by the laws of gravity, and so on) and to add to it a form of causality specific to our freedom, to the fact that our choices and actions matter;

2   that this project survives in any attempt to isolate concepts of agency, and in consequence to argue against the view that machines themselves do anything of note to humans, without humans having already done something fundamental to machines;

3   that it takes no account of the extent to which human agency, even thus isolated, could be said to be independent of factors entirely beyond (restricted) human control.

It is by virtue of this last characteristic that Marx set such store by human consciousness, by the tricks that it plays on us, by things that appear to us and what we therefore think: not all our acts demonstrate agency, and those that do it takes hard work – becoming conscious of our real situation – to realise. We must labour to become conscious of our lost or alienated agency in order that we may resume it in resolute acts of will.

Thus the determinist ascription of agency to technology (it is technology that acts, and we who are acted upon) is perceived by the Marxist not as an evocation of real processes but as their distortion through reproducing the ideology of technology that causes events to occur, cultures to form and so on, over which we humans have little or no say. In truth, says the Marxist, this is simply a renunciation of our own agency, made palatable by the suggestion of inevitability. If, however, it were to turn out, as determinism suggests, that technology simply does drive history, then the suggestion that human consciousness and action are not the stage in which history is played out suffers irreparable damage, and Marx's 'historical materialism' becomes humanist idealism.

BOX 5.3:   Marx and materialism

Marx is concerned to defend his brand of 'historical materialism' from what he calls 'crude' materialism. Crude materialism 'regards as the natural properties of things what [historical materialism regards as] social relations of production amongst people' (Marx 1993: 687). The proponents of such 'crude materialism' include Dr Price and his 'notion of capital as a self-reproducing being' (ibid.: 842), and Andrew Ure's definition of the factory as conveying the idea of 'a vast automaton, composed of numerous mechanical and intellectual organs' (ibid.: 690). Marx himself, on the other hand, is not such a 'crude materialist' when he writes of 'living machinery' (ibid.: 693) or that 'capital employs machinery' to promote its 'metabolism' (ibid.: 701), since he is only describing how such machinery 'confronts the individual', and how 'machinery appears . . . as alien, external' to living labour. This is because the latter lacks an understanding of 'the science that compels the inanimate limbs of the machinery . . . to act purposefully' (ibid.: 693–695). In other words, Marx compels humanity to recognise these illusions as illusions (machines are not really alive) and to become conscious of the power we possess as a human being to dominate the machines, and equally to understand our power to imagine they dominate us. Thus, according to Marx, living machines, self-acting mules, automata comprising intellectual and mechanical organs, occur only in the minds of labouring humanity, and can therefore be controlled merely by how we think about them (of course, Marx says that such changes have as a consequence an action that seizes control of human destiny).

The three points listed on p. 308, however, serve to demonstrate the culturalist separatism that humanism has established between the worlds of culture and nature. The former is made up of institutions, beliefs, intentions and purposes, and the latter of blind causes. The sociologist of science Bruno Latour, however, has recently argued that to analyse the contemporary world, it is necessary to break down culturalist separatism and to establish in its stead a theory of how it is that technological and natural artefacts become agents. Thus Latour draws together the natural and the human sciences, and generalises the concept of agency to attach to 'non-humans'. Latour's '**actor-network theory**' disputes the notion that anything has agency on its own. Rather, agency is acquired by a thing being a component of a larger system (a network). Such systems dominate, he argues, the contemporary landscape: wherever we look, we see social action taking place not as a result of individually or collectively willed human actions but rather due to the relations between humans and the increasing quantity of non-human things that populate the cultural landscape. The consequence, however, of accepting Latour's account of how non-humans acquire agency is to abolish any sense in which the cultural field in general remains an exclusively human concern. Can we really therefore accept an account of agency that grants it to things?

To update this question, it lay behind philosopher Hubert Dreyfus's mistakenly arrogant challenge to a computer that it could never beat him at chess, since it necessarily lacked intelligence. Upon losing, Dreyfus then redefined what counted as intelligence to what could not be algorithmically coded, or turned into a program. L'affaire Dreyfus, as it has subsequently become known, demonstrated that humanists will do anything to safeguard their specialness, even when there is nothing special left, other than to invent games without rules to frustrate Deep Blue. However, does the computer in question possess agency of any sort, or are its actions entirely dependent on its makers? Black-and-white answers to this question are insufficient to answer it, since at the very least the actions of machine (Deep Blue), human (Kasparov, Dreyfus) and game are importantly interdependent: none acts without the others. And this is precisely Latour's point: it is as false to argue that a machine on its own has agency as it is to suggest that only humans do; rather it is the network as a whole that acts, effects and determines. Thus, he writes of large-scale social (legal, educational, medical), commercial (corporations, markets), political (governments) or military institutions that they are 'actors [or 'agents'] of great size . . . macro-actors . . . made up of a series of local interactions' (Latour 1993: 120–121). Humans are not therefore agents that create the networks, rather we are only involved in 'local interactions' that make up these macro-actors: IBM, the Red Army, and so on.

The cost and benefit of this extension of agency from humans to things is to give up on the humanist view that there are machines on one side, humans on the other, and that the machines are taking over! This is precisely the anxiety that lies behind the presentation of intelligent and independent machines in popular culture, from *Terminator* to *Tetsuo*; but it also, perhaps surprisingly, underwrites serious-minded speculations such as Kevin Warwick (1998) offers, concerning a future governed entirely by machines. But this humanism is also the source of almost all the critical approaches cultural and media studies has at its disposal to address cultural phenomena: Marxist humanism, as we have seen, rests on precisely this bedrock (see Feenberg [1991] and Mitcham [1994] for accounts of the critical and the humanist approaches to technology, respectively). The stakes involved in the issue of agency are therefore considerable.

Note, however, that Latour leaves the question of whether agency exists at all, intact. In other words, he renegotiates the source of social action from humans alone to humans and non-humans, but allows thereby that purposeful social action does take place. That is, Latour stops short of outright determinism. We will now consider the varieties of determinism, before drawing **5.2** to a close.

5.2.4 Determinisms

Some theorists cast serious doubt on even the validity of the concept of agency, suggesting that it is ludicrous to imagine that 'there exists at all, in the whole of reality, the sort of agency that can begin or purposively redirect causal chains, not merely serve as one more link inside them' (Ferré, 1995: 129). Such a view is an example of a very straightforward determinism that suggests that every event has a cause, and that ultimately the very idea of voluntary action or choice is therefore illusory: there is no agency, that is, only causality.

This is the starkest form of determinism, but not the only form. As Williams understands it, technological determinism answers a question as to the causes of social change. He then interprets this to mean either human agency causes social change, or, since technology is simply another physical thing, social change is just another instance of physically caused changes. We have, moreover, seen that Williams is operating with only one view of causality here, that of linear or mechanical causality. We have suggested already that this is not what McLuhan is getting at, but the point that remains to be considered is whether, without retreating wholly to a point where the only causes of social effects are mechanical, technology can be seen as determining. This is why we examined other concepts of causality. In this section, therefore, we will examine the kinds of determinism left out of the account by Williams's critique of McLuhan. These are:

- soft determinism;

- from soft to hard determinism.

We will see that soft determinisms tend to emphasise the formative role played in technologically determinist societies by non-technological factors, and do not therefore rule out the role of agency in principle. But we will also see that such accounts pave the way for a kind of historicised hard determinism modelled on non-linear causation.

Soft determinism

In *Does Technology Drive History?* (Smith and Marx 1996), a collection of essays taken from a 1994 symposium between historians, sociologists and theorists held on the topic of technological determinism, the editors arrange versions of determinism, following the philosopher William James, according to 'hard' and 'soft' poles. 'At the hard end of the spectrum', they write, 'agency (the power to effect change) is imputed to technology itself' (ibid.: xii), whereas 'soft determinists begin by reminding us that the history of technology is a history of human actions' (ibid.: xiii). Neither version, however, disputes the deterministic outcome of technology, since in both cases what may begin as an aid to human life ends up dictating what form it must take (consider how the car has changed the form and function of the city). What they dispute is the kind of agency or the kind of causality involved in technological determinism. Hard determinists, that is, insist that the cause of technological deterministic effects is itself technological. Soft determinists insist conversely that while determinism is the outcome, the agency that produces that outcome is not itself technological but consists additionally in a variety of factors: economic, political and social.

There are many soft-deterministic accounts of the role of technology in culture. The social theorist Jürgen Habermas (1970), for example, argues that what he calls 'capitalist **technoscience**' becomes deterministic due to the fact that its goals are strictly compatible with capitalism's, in so far as both triumph the validity of 'instrumentalist' – whatever gets the job done – behaviour over all other claimants to validity. Thus social justice, judgements and beliefs, since they do not simply aim to get something done, lose cultural authority due to the successes of capitalist technoscience. We can see what Habermas means by the instrumental form of reasoning embodied in technoscience if we consider why it is that social services such as schools are required to deliver 'results' for their pupils, and have their own value assessed by these results; or why 'efficiency gains' must be made in hospitals, etc. The purpose of schools is not to educate but to gain high grades for their pupils; the purpose of hospitals is not to cure the sick but to become efficient treatment centres for clients who want a job done.

Therefore **technoscience** is deterministic not in its origins (it required the collaboration of capitalism to become the dominant form of social organisation) but in its effects, since once established, it defines its own goals – to get the job done – and expands its influence into all forms of social activity. While the situation, as far as Habermas is concerned, is therefore deterministic (everything is defined in terms of technoscientific instrumentalism), it is not irrevocable, since behind this deterministic situation lies the capitalist will. Habermas therefore takes a classically humanist path, rejecting the idea that technology (or science) is determining on its own, and arguing instead for the human capacity for self-determination through instituting rational deliberation regarding the proper ends of society.

Similarly, the philosopher Jean-François Lyotard (1984), who accepts Habermas's view that technoscience has become determinant, argues that he offers a solution that no longer holds for the information economy. What the information economy consists in, argues Lyotard, is precisely the subjection of language – the medium in which Habermas's 'rational deliberation' is to take place – to technoscientific imperatives. In other words, once capitalism has got into our sentences, there is no longer any point in communicating unless we are going to get something done thereby. Moreover, these imperatives have been irrevocably settled into the social structure due to computerisation, since computers are precisely information processing devices. Since the computer has become a dominant technology for commercial and communicational purposes, this in turn alters the goals of communication from rational exchange to gaining information. Both Lyotard and Habermas therefore offer deterministic accounts of the social role and function of technology, given the social deployment of those technologies. In other words, their determinisms suggest that 'there's no going back', although Habermas argues that, if we cut through the ideology that promotes instrumentalism – getting the job done – as an imperative, the technoscientific tide can be turned, whereas Lyotard insists that it cannot.

From soft to hard determinism

Soft determinists are therefore concerned to highlight technological determinism as an effect of social forces, rather than as their cause. But the key issue they raise, regardless of identifying the causes of a deterministic situation, is that technological determinism now need not imply that it was always so. Such accounts therefore make room for those who argue that while societies have not always been technologically determined, they become so at specific historical junctures.

Precisely such a process was ascribed to technological change by Jacques Ellul in his book *The Technological Society*, published in France in 1954. Ellul calls this process the 'self-augmentation of technique'. He writes:

Note the echo of this self-augmentation in the concept of self-organization

> At the present time, technique has arrived at such a point in its evolution that it is being transformed and is progressing almost without decisive intervention from man . . . [T]his is a self-generating process; technique engenders technique.
>
> (Ellul [1954] 1964: 85, 87)

This is a version of determinism in which, given the interaction of technique by technique (for Ellul, '*la technique*' includes not only hard technologies such as machines, but soft technologies like statistical census methods, bureaucracies, political, medical, carceral and educational institutions and so on), technology simply 'reacts upon' technology, exponentially increasing its forms beyond the control of designers, policy-makers and so on. As he puts it, 'when a new technical form appears, it makes possible and conditions a number of others' ([1954] 1964: 87). As an example of such a process, consider what the replacement of valves with microchips has made possible and conditions: instead of room-filling immobile computing devices we have laptops and mobile Internet access devices, which makes possible (albeit not actual) a universally accessible global communications network, which in turns makes possible the extension of monitoring and surveillance techniques, the replacement of physical travel to work with remote access points, deregulating the culture of the office, global finance crashing, new cultural and political potentials for action, new non-terrestrial forms of corporate expansionism, and so on.

1.6.4 The many virtues of Saint McLuhan

On this reading, technology not only becomes its own governor, but begins to establish the physical framework for technological and cultural activity in general, making possible and necessitating not only further new technological forms but also new cultural ones. When, that is, a new technological form is introduced (the steam engine, the factory, the telegraph, the computer), the extent to which it spreads throughout a culture will determine in turn the extent to which subsequent technologies must conform with its principles of operation: there could be no place for a steam computer in a digital environment, for example; digital environments require digital augmentation. Similarly, manufacturing economies in information-rich environments tend to die out, whereas computer manufacture generally takes place in information-poor economies (see Castells [1996] 2000; Plant 1997).

Technical self-augmentation then, acts not merely to increase the quantity of technics but reacts on itself, creating a positive feedback that carries everything else along with it, causing therefore qualitative change. Ellul's account thus suggests that technological determinism is not an historical constant, but that it arises at a certain stage of technological development, where technology saturates the environment. At such a point, humans cease to create technologies as an extension of their own capacities and start instead to respond to the imperatives of the technologies they have created. Technology now 'engenders', as Ellul puts it, itself.

There is not a huge distance here between the prompting of human intervention by technological demand and machines becoming self-aware, a constant of science fiction from the intelligent computer Hal, in 2001: A Space Odyssey, to Skynet, the self-aware computer intelligence in Terminator 2. However, in the former example the computer is engineered to be intelligent; in the latter it becomes so of its own accord as a result of surpassing a critical mass: it self-organises, to use Prigogine and Stengers's term.

Finally, therefore, we must ask in what sense this is a hard determinism. Firstly, in the sense that Smith and Marx give to the term, technology, on Ellul's account, does become the cause of technological determinism, although this was not always the case. In other words, to demonstrate the technological determinist position we no longer need to construct a history in which all technologies have caused all social changes, but only identify those historical junctures at which technology, as it were, becomes self-organising.

Secondly, Ellul's is a hard determinism in the sense that it uses a model of causality that obtains in the physical as well as in the social world: that of self-organisation, or non-linear causality. In **Box 5.2**, we saw how non-linear processes are involved in cybernetics and in chaos and complexity theories, and noted that these non-linear processes have been described as 'self-organising'. Self-organising processes in the natural world arise not from a single cause, but from the emergence of order in a chaotic environment. One school of thought in artificial intelligence research, for example, looks not to programme intelligence into a computer, but to prompt it to learn, in the same manner as does a human infant. By connecting several processors together, and having them fire information at each other in a more or less random manner, the idea is that intelligence will 'emerge' or 'self-organise' (see **5.3.5**).

Consider the following account of the emergence of robotic intelligence:

[We] may without much difficulty imagine a future generation of killer robots dedicated to understanding their historical origins. We may even imagine specialized 'robot historians' committed to tracing the various technological lineages that gave rise to their species. And we could further imagine that such a robot historian would write a different kind of history than would its human counterpart. While a human historian might try to understand the way people assembled clockworks, motors and other physical contraptions, a robot historian would likely place a stronger emphasis on the way these machines effected human evolution . . . The robot historian of course would hardly be bothered by the fact that it was a human who put the first motor together: for the role of humans would be seen as little more than that of industrious insects pollinating an independent species of machine-flowers that simply did not possess its own reproductive organs during a segment of its evolution.

(De Landa 1991: 2–3)

Such an account of 'local' determinism also figures largely in the mathematics of **chaos** and complexity theory. In these accounts, determinism is not a global condition, but pertains only within the confines of a given region of phenomena. Lyotard, who coined the term 'local determinism' (1984: xxiv), borrows its formulation from the catastrophe mathematician René Thom, who writes: 'The more or less determined character of a process is determined by the local state of the process' (Thom 1975: 126; cited by Lyotard 1984: 56)

Box 5.2 Chaos, complexity and non-linearity

5.3.5 Life and intelligence in the digital age

This form of artificial intelligence is not the only technology that has been described as self-organising. Marx, for example, scolds Dr Price for his 'crude materialism' when the latter suggests that capital becomes a 'self-reproducing being' (Marx 1993: 842), yet he simultaneously describes the factory as a 'self-moving automaton, a moving power that moves itself' (ibid.: 692); Ellul's self-augmentation thesis, and Bergson's idea that technology 'reacts upon' itself, basically describe the same phenomenon

Here we can see how actions that are themselves effects (machines assembled by humans) can become in turn the causes of further effects (the evolutionary direction of biological and technological 'species'). We need not, however, resort to robo-history in order to find similar processes. This is precisely the order of effects found in any complex biological system (plants, animals, humans) in which effects become causes in turn. If we consider the growth of any organism, for example, it is clear that in no sense is this the consequence of a single cause. Again, it is worth noting that such processes are found equally in the natural world (storms, chemical clocks, the formation of mountains) as in the cultural (riots, market behaviours, settlement patterns). Thus self-organisation and technological self-augmentation provide a physicalist account of 'hard' technological determinism that yet remains sensitive to historical contingencies. At the same time, rather than restricting agency to humans, this account notes that the formation of purposes is itself a self-organising process, and that there is no reason therefore not to ascribe agency to non-humans.

5.3 BIOLOGICAL TECHNOLOGIES: THE HISTORY OF AUTOMATA

> In the game of life and evolution, there are three players at the table: human beings, nature and machines. I am firmly on the side of nature, but nature, I suspect, is on the side of the machines.
>
> (Dyson 1998: 3)

Introduction

5.2 Revisiting determinism: physicialism, humanism and technology

Having looked at the physicality of technology in **5.2**, this section will focus on the relations between biology and technology. While the popular figure of the cyborg suggests that the cybernetic age is the first time in history that biology and technology could (potentially) be combined, and while a lot of criticism in fact supports precisely this view, as we shall see there is a long history to the idea of living machines. As cyberneticist Norbert Wiener writes:

> At every stage of technique, the ability of the artificer to produce a working simulacrum of a living organism has always intrigued. This desire to produce and to study automata has always been expressed in terms of the living technique of the age.
>
> (Wiener [1948] 1962: 40)

5.3.3 Self-augmenting engines: steampower against nature

Following Wiener's lead, this section will primarily be concerned to outline the history of automata – of 'self-moving things' (**5.3.3**) – in order to display the relations between technology and biology at each stage of technological development. It will also, however, be posing questions concerning the biological and the technological in general.

Since the seventeenth century, mechanical monsters, demonic machines and living instruments have populated not only fictions, fairground spectacles of often dubious authenticity, magic lantern shows and cinema, but also engineering projects, physiological researches, and computing projects. From Julian de La Mettrie's *Man-Machine*, to Frankenstein's monster, to 'cellular automata' and De Landa's Terminator-type 'robot historian', living technology preoccupies the furthest reaches of each epoch's technological capacities and imaginary. In keeping with the lesson of the previous section (**5.2**), that we must pay attention to the physical underpinnings of culture if we are to understand the interaction between humans, machines and material nature, then it

5.2 Revisiting determinism: physicalism, humanism and technology

becomes necessary that we focus on a given technological culture's means for realising artificial life. Therefore, the rest of this section will chart the forms of autonomous or 'animate' machines – automata – whose spectres haunted, or whose matter constructed, life in Europe throughout various epochs of technological development.

Cyberculture may not, therefore, be the first time in history that a living machine stands on the horizon of a culture's technological capacities, but it perhaps encompasses a larger range of technological interventions in biology than previous ages. As we shall see, amongst the consequences of the influence of cybernetics has been a conception of life as information (DNA and genomics – **5.3.5**), and a conception of biology as technology, or of 'biotechnology'. At the same time, both in fiction and reality, there has been a renewed push to create living technologies, whether in the form of the cyborg, or of the field of scientific research known as 'artificial life' or 'Alife'.

5.3.5 Life and intelligence in the digital age

5.3.1 Automata: the basics

Throughout the history of automata certain concepts recur, forming a core of what sorts of things automata are. Particularly crucial here are two sets of differences: between *tools* and *machines*, on the one hand, and between *simulacra* and *automata* on the other.

Tools and machines

The former differentiation places the technological object along a scale of dependency relative to its user, with the hand-tool almost entirely dependent and the industrial machine almost entirely independent. The hand-tool needs to be *moved* by an external source, whereas the machine *moves itself*. In this sense, only machines can be automata. But there are also machines that use tools, or that automate functions hitherto requiring an external, human user. For example, the robots used in car manufacture use tools formerly wielded by humans, such as riveters, paint guns, and so on. A technology's dependency need not therefore always be on human users; nor is a human always the user of a technology – Marx, for example, argued that with industrialisation machines position humans as the dependent ones, reversing the situation between user and used, with humans possessing a low degree of independence in relation to the machines. Potentially, then, humans can become tools of machines, as Aristotle pointed out:

> Now instruments are of various sorts; some are living, others lifeless; in the rudder, the pilot of the ship [the *kybernetes*] has a lifeless, in the look-out man, a living instrument; for in the arts [*techne*] the servant is a kind of instrument. Thus too, a possession is an instrument for maintaining life. And so . . . the slave is a living possession, and property a number of such instruments; and the servant is himself an instrument for instruments.
> (Aristotle, *Politics* book 1, 1253b; in Everson 1996: 15)

Simulacra and automata

Thus, some twenty-five centuries ago, we find Aristotle taking the idea of 'living instruments' seriously. He continues:

> For if every instrument could accomplish its own work, obeying or anticipating the will of others, like the statues of Daedalus, or the tripods of Hephaestus, which, says the poet, 'of their own accord entered the assembly of the gods'; if, in like manner, the

shuttle would weave and the plectrum touch the lyre, chief workmen would not want servants, nor masters slaves.

(Aristotle, *Politics* book 1, 1253b; in Everson 1996: 15)

Homer's account of 'tripods', from which Aristotle quotes, contains further mentions of Hephaestus's mechanical wonders. A lame smith, Hephaestus, has undertaken to extend his thus limited capacities by mechanical means, extending himself, as it were, through these 'twenty tripods . . . fitted with golden wheels . . . so he could have them moving of their own accord'. He also sees to some of his more immediate needs with mechanical maids:

They are made of gold, looking like living girls; they have intelligent minds, and have learnt their handiwork from the immortal gods. So they busied themselves in support of their master.

(Homer, *Iliad* 18, in Hammond 1987: 304–305)

Here we have two sets of classical distinctions in the history of automata. In Aristotle, we have the distinction between living and lifeless instruments; in Homer, that between the tripods that *move of their own accord* and the maids who look like 'living girls'. In many ways, these distinctions are interconnected: what *moves of its own accord*, the 'self-moving thing', is a precise translation of the word *automaton*. Living things are therefore 'natural automata' or 'natural machines', as the philosopher, mathematician and calculator-maker G.W. Leibniz was still calling them in the early eighteenth century (*Monadology* ([1714] 1989) §64), and as early computer theorists called them in the middle of the twentieth (von Neumann [1958] 1999). Thus, although he elsewhere differentiates 'natural' from 'unnatural' things in that the former, unlike the latter, 'contain within themselves' their own 'source of movement and rest' – that is, *move of their own accord* (*Physics* bk. II.1, 192b, in Waterfield 1996: 33), automata are differentiated by Aristotle not according to whether they are biological or technological, but simply according to whether they have the power of autonomous motion. Thus, a slave may be biological, but the power of autonomous motion he possesses as a natural being may be inactive in him *because he is a slave*, an 'instrument' or extension of the master. Similarly, as his consideration of Hephaestus' devices shows, Aristotle sees nothing inherently impossible in the idea of self-moving technological things. Of the latter, there are therefore two types – the automaton or self-moving thing pure and simple (the tripod), and the automaton that *looks like something living* (the maid).

This same distinction was made in 1964 by the historian of science and technology Derek J. de Solla Price in the following terms: *simulacra* are 'devices that simulate' other things (spiders, humans, ducks) and *automata* are 'devices that move by themselves' (1964: 9). Arguably the only new distinction in the history of automata is that introduced by artificial life (Alife) researchers between *simulation* on the one hand and *instantiation* or *realisation* on the other. The distinction is neatly summed up in this comment by one of the major figures in Alife research, Christopher G. Langton:

We would like to build models of life that are so lifelike that they would cease to be models of life and become examples of life themselves.

(Langton citing Pattee, in Boden 1996: 379)

In section **2.8.2** of this book, the term 'simulation' is distinguished from 'imitation'. 'Simulacrum' as used here should not be understood as being related to the above sense of 'simulation'; strictly speaking, in terms of automata, the simulacrum is the imitation, whereas the automaton proper 'simulates' in the sense of section 2. We shall therefore only use 'simulacrum' and its cognate 'simulation' in this section to refer explicitly to the history of automata, since the distinction features throughout the literature (see Glossary)

2.8.2   Virtual realism

While digital simulacra of living systems (Alife is less concerned with biological individuals than with the systems they compose) become increasingly accurate, Alife's strong claim to instantiate or realise life poses questions to the very foundations of biology: to what extent is biology in principle limited to the study of 'life as we know it'?

BOX 5.4:   History of automata

AD1	Pneumatic and hydraulic automata, pneumatic theatre
9th–11th cent.	Water-clocks
14th cent.	Early mechanical clocks
17th cent.	Mechanism and the clockwork universe: natural and artificial automata, calculators, 'machine man'
18th cent.	Clockwork automata; mechanical pictures; chess-playing, writing, and speaking automata; physiological automata
19th cent.	Life as electricity, manufactures as automata; fairground automata, intelligent engines
20th cent.	Intelligent machines, cellular automata, cyborgs, robotics

5.2 Major stages in the history of automata.

Early automata

The history of automata is generally dated as having begun with the construction of hydraulic and pneumatic automata, worked by the pressure of water and air in pumps and pipes. Such automata were constructed in Ancient Greece, Byzantium, Old Iran and Islam, where they adorned temples, courts and monuments.

The best known of these ancient automata are two works by Hero of Alexandria in the first century AD. The first was his fountain or *pneumatikon*. A device now so commonplace as to escape our attention, the fountain worked by building air pressure in a container part-filled with water. When the pressure was released, it drove the water up and out of a vertical pipe, forming the crown of a fountain (Ferré 1995: 47). To consider the shock and entertainment this gave rise to, consider that in nature water never moves *upwards*. The second of Hero's automata was the mechanical theatre, as narrated in his book on automata, in which pneumatic and hydraulic forces propelled figures into movement, performing small scenes. Hero's automaton theatre was reconstructed, following its author's instructions, in the fifteenth century, and contained a mechanism sufficiently complex to narrate five scenes of the actions of the Gods Nautilus and Athene on Greek shipping. The construction of such technologised spectacles creates grounds for reconsidering the history of moving or *kinematic* pictures as stretching back to the first century AD, as Deleuze (1989) notes. Hero's automaton theatre, that is, connects automata not only to the history of puppet shows but also and more directly to the technologies of mechanical paintings of the eighteenth and nineteenth centuries, the first examples of moving *images*.

Pneumatic, non-simulacral automata went on to become objects of intense scientific and popular scrutiny, extending as far as the great Arabic water-clocks of the ninth century. The next major work on automata after Hero's, however, was

5.3 Hero of Alexandria's Automata: the mobile theatre, 1st century AD. Chapuis and Droz (1958): 34–5.

5.4 The first moving images: an eighteenth-century mechanical picture: front and rear views (Chapuis and Droz 1958: 142–3). Conservatoire des Arts et Metiers.

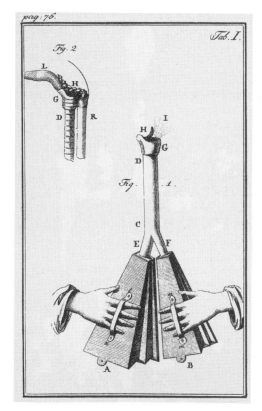

5.5 Lungs and bellows. Understanding the human body as composed of machines was an important aspect of mechanistic thought in the seventeenth and eighteenth centuries. (Hankins and Silverman 1995:194). Courtesy of the University of Washington Libraries.

Al-Jazari's *Treatise on Automata*, dating from the twelfth century. During that same century, it is said that Thomas Aquinas, shocked at the spectacle of a moving, speaking head made of baked clay by Albertus Magnus, smashed it, thinking it a great evil (White 1964: 124–125). But it was not until the rise of the mechanical clock in the fourteenth century that automata suddenly increased in the complexity of their operations. Enormous clocks were built, such as Giovanni di' Dondi's great 16 year project completed in 1364. This measured not only the passage of time, but also the movements of the sun and the planets (White 1964: 126). Already the suspicion was dawning that clockwork was more than a means to describe or model natural phenomena, but instead, the very mechanism of nature itself.

5.3.2 Clockwork: technology and nature, combined

Mechanism

Clockwork is the technology proper to the period of mechanism and the mechanical philosophy from the seventeenth century to the mid-eighteenth. This was the period in which philosophers and scientists devised the ambition of explaining all nature in terms of clockwork. The same period of history saw Newton's mechanism become the truly dominant world-view, which was to remain dominant, albeit with some major modifications, until Einstein's Relativity Theory in the early twentieth-century.

Mechanism constituted a triumph over the mere theorising, on the basis of Aristotle's texts, by means of which the medieval period had attempted to explain natural phenomena. Medieval natural philosophy utilised Aristotle's concept of 'final causes' or *teleology* (**5.2.2**). Final causes were extremely useful in explaining the 'what' of things (why a thing is what it is), but not for examining the detail of the *how* it became what it is; that is, it was exactly not what the moderns understood as science. In place of recognisably modern scientific explanations it offered definitions of things as *potentials* inhering in the essences of things that are *actualised* in the growth and development of that thing.

5.2.2   Causalities

To dispose of the concept of final causes in explaining nature, the mechanists of the seventeenth and eighteenth centuries insisted that *all things must be explained in terms of motion and the interrelations of parts*, thus replacing 'final' with 'efficient' (or 'effecting') causes. As to the cause of motion, however, there was considerable debate. The most extreme of mechanists left no room in the natural world for any other than mechanical, efficient causes. This was a giant clockwork universe, and God's role was merely to have created it, after which it ran its own course. Although mechanism typically resulted in making the concept of a divine being redundant, it is worth noting that even Newton considered that the forces by which motion was caused in the first place were ultimately the domain of theology rather than natural science. However, in a godless universe of mechanical motion and parts, all things within it must be explained in similar terms. For the mechanists, then, as Thomas L. Hankins puts it, 'there was no basic difference between one's watch and one's pet dog' (Hankins 1985: 114).

It was in consequence only a matter of time before philosophers began to explain even the most complex of physiological functions in mechanical terms, and, thereafter, to attempt the construction of artificial life forms based on clockwork principles. While at first these were strictly physiological demonstration models (cf. Hankins and Silverman 1995) showing the heart as a pump, the lungs as bellows, each linked by pipes and valves, the resultant 'automata' acquired great fame and value beyond their scientific and medical relevance to philosophers.

Man-machines: de la Mettrie and Descartes

During the reign of the mechanical philosophy, since the alternative to animals and man being clockwork creatures was that they were infused with divine sparks of life, the construction of automata became a profession of the secular triumph of the natural sciences. Accordingly, many physiologists and philosophers regarded living mechanical automata as an inevitable consequence of their philosophies: if science has shown that nature is mechanical, and has enabled us to make mechanical things, then science can construct artificial automata after the pattern of nature's own. Thus, the military field-surgeon, physiologist and philosopher Julian Offray de La Mettrie's 1747 manifesto-like treatise *Machine Man* considered and rejected all those views that did not accept that animate nature and machine-life were one and the same substance. He wrote:

> Let us conclude boldly that man is a machine and that there is in the whole universe only one diversely modified substance . . . Here is my system, or rather the truth, unless I am very much mistaken. It is short and simple. Now if anyone wants to argue, let them!
>
> (la Mettrie [1747] 1996: 39)

It was in precisely this vein that the French *philosophes* of the eighteenth century were to triumph scientific materialism over the mystifications of theology, leading, for example, Denis Diderot to advance the hypothesis that between rock and spider, spider and man, there were no essential differences in kind, but only in the degree of their organisation and complexity. Life, accordingly, was to be explained by an increase in the complexity of the organization of matter, and intelligence by a still higher increase (Diderot 1985: 149ff.).

Disputes such as this were nothing new, however. Debates between physicalists and theists regarding the natural or divine causes of life were a constant feature of the philosophical and scientific lanscape of the seventeenth century. What was new was that physicalist theories were being demonstrated by the construction of automata that replicated or simulated the functions of the various organs in the human body. Thus, as the philosopher René Descartes wrote in his 1662 *Treatise on Man*:

> I suppose the body to be just a statue or a machine made of earth . . . We see clocks, artificial fountains, mills, and other similar machines which, even though they are only made by men, have the power to move of their own accord in various ways.
>
> (Descartes [1662] 1998: 99)

Note that here Descartes specifically speaks of machines that 'move of their own accord', thus taking up the implication in Aristotle that there is nothing in principle impossible in the idea of self-moving, and thus effectively biological, technologies (5.4.1). Descartes now extends this supposition to understanding all the bodily machine's functions: the nerves are like the pipes in the mechanical parts of fountains; the muscles, engines and the tendons are springs; the blood, or 'animal spirit', to water and the heart to its source, a pump; respiration is like the movement of a clock or mill; perception, the passage of a visual impulse to the brain, is the impact of moving parts on one another, and so on (Descartes [1662] 1998: 106). Taking up the challenge of Descartes's hypotheses, Athanasius Kircher began construction of a mechanical speaking head for the entertainment of Queen Christina of Sweden (in whose service Descartes died), but never completed it. Announcing it in his *Phonurgia nova* ('New Voice-Magic') of 1673, he affirmed that the head would move its 'eyes, lips and tongue, and, by means of the sounds which it emitted, [would] appear to be alive' (Bedini 1964: 38). Such machines involved solving the problem of how to reproduce the functions of several different organs mechanically: the larynx, tongue, lips and palate, and the lungs, so their successful construction was neither physiologically nor technologically as trivial as the prospect of such machines might now seem. That said, of course, the technology we ritually implant in our bodies to replace failing organs, such as the heart, follows the same precepts as its eighteenth-century precursors, as do the clumsier yet functionally identical dialysis machines that stand in for the failed functions of human kidneys. The absolute lack of change in our thinking about such technologies has only recently been highlighted by the attempt to *grow* replacement organs in, as it were, organic factories, such as pigs' bodies. With a little genetic engineering, pig hearts can be made compatible with human bodies, thus enabling the transfer of organic rather than mechanical hearts. The apparent newness of these 'xenotransplantation' biotechnologies demonstrates instead a 300-year-old historical continuity, rooted in the attempt to construct mechanical organs which has held sway over medical and physiological thinking since Descartes and La Mettrie first promoted the idea of the human body as a machine. Even by the late eighteenth century, however, speaking heads with moving parts were finally built by, amongst others, the architect of the famous chess-playing automaton, Baron von Kempelen (Bedini 1964: 38; Hankins and Silverman 1995: 186ff.).

Before this time, however, a French surgeon and anatomist named Claude-Nicolas le Cat constructed an automaton 'in which one can see the execution of the principal

Consider also in this light the newer voice-magic displayed by Stephen Hawking's artificial speaking machine

functions of the animal economy, circulation, respiration, secretions' (Hankins and Silverman 1995: 183). This was constructed in order to settle a scientific question of the effects of the common therapeutic practice of 'bleeding' a patient in order to relieve the patient of her symptoms. If the automaton were to settle the question (as both Le Cat and François Quesnay, his adversary, agreed it would), then it must have been held to be not simply a visually accurate model of the human digestive and circulatory system but rather a physiologically accurate one. Thus even from the proposal for such a model, we can see the extent to which Descartes's physicalist and mechanistic physiological principles were by this time not being treated as wild hypotheses but as the basis of a scientific physiology. The seventeenth and eighteenth centuries thus witnessed a plethora of similar models of respiration, blood circulation and the like.

Vaucanson's duck

Sustaining the same goal of realising biological physiological systems in mechanical devices, Jacques de Vaucanson attempted in the 1730s to construct 'a moving anatomy' to reproduce all the major organic functions. This attempt reached an initial completion in the 'artificial duck of gilt brass' of 1738, 'which drinks, eats, quacks, flounders in water, digests and excretes like a live duck' (Vaucanson, cited in Bedini 1964: 37). In this mechanical bird, according to Diderot's *Dictionary of the Sciences* of 1777,

> the food is digested as in real animals . . .; the matter digested in the stomach is led off by pipes to the anus, where there is a sphincter allowing it to pass out. The inventor does not set this up as a perfect digestive system capable of manufacturing blood . . . to support the animal . . . [but] only to imitate the mechanics of the digestive process in three things, firstly, the swallowing of the food, secondly the maceration, cooking or dissolving of it, and thirdly the action causing it to leave the body in a markedly changed form.
>
> (Diderot, cited in Chapuis and Droz 1958: 241)

 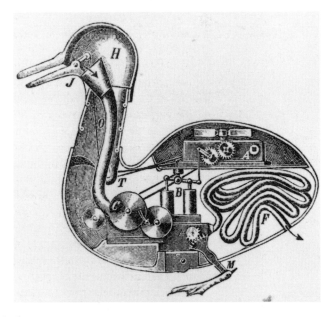

5.6 Vaucanson's mechanical duck (1738). Courtesy of the British Library.

The duck made its author instantly famous and wealthy, and brought about his election to the French Académie, where he was in charge of patenting new inventions in industry. Amongst these was Jacquard's automatic pattern-weaving loom, which was to play its role in Ada Lovelace's first attempts at understanding and creating what is now called programming. By 1805, however, Goethe reported having seen the duck, now 'completely paralysed' and incapable of digestion, like a dying animal condemned never finally to die, at the home of the new owner (cited in Chapuis and Droz 1958: 234).

Between the development of physiological automata and the early nineteenth century, when Goethe's comments on the gilt brass duck were written, automata gradually fell from scientific and philosophical grace, due to shifts amongst the community of scholars away from the Newtonian philosophy that gave mechanism its principal grounding. If mechanism gave a false view of biological phenomena, then the important questions about life could no longer be solved by mechanical means. It was during the late eighteenth and early nineteenth centuries that researches in galvanism (named after the Italian discover of 'animal electricity' or galvanism, Luigi Galvani) and electricity began to displace mechanical devices as the principal technologies of life, as we can see if we consider the role played by electricity as the 'life force' that 'galvanises' Frankenstein's monster into life. During this same period, however, mechanical automata began to acquire a significance far removed from the rarefied environments of scholarly dispute. While Vaucanson's brass duck convinced the editors of the 1777 edition of the *Encyclopédie* of the physiological validity of mechanism, the duck won more fame from public exhibition than from the scientific community. Thus Vaucanson became rich by it, and von Kempelen financed his serious-minded attempts to automate voice production with deliberately scientifically fraudulent devices for public entertainment, such as his famous chess-player of 1769.

The Jaquet-Droz Androïdes

The popularity of such devices returned attention from the scientific to the spectacular uses of automata. As early as 1610, mechanical automata were being produced that simulated spiders, birds, caterpillars and so on. Even before this, however, mechanical automata were produced as ornaments of the true automaton, the clock. These were automata that, rather than automating organic functions, simulated living things in clockwork. Thus, in 1773, thirty years after Vaucanson sold his automata and moved on, Pierre and Henri-Louis Jaquet-Droz produced what the *Encyclopédie* distinguished from physiological automata by calling them 'androids' – human-like things. Amongst the Jaquet-Droz androids or *simulacra*, are a writer (Chapuis and Droz 1958: 293–4; 396), an artist (ibid.: 299–300) and a musician (ibid.: 280–282). Of these life-size simulacra or androids, the writer writes messages of up to forty characters in length, the artist draws four sketches (a dog, a cupid, the head of Louis XIV and profiles of Louis XVI and Marie Antoinette [Bedini 1964: 39]), and the musician plays five tunes, composed by Henri-Louis Jaquet-Droz, on an organ (Chapuis and Droz: 283).

Further such simulated artists, along with magicians and acrobats, were commissioned and constructed (by the firm of Jaquet-Droz and the automaton maker Henri Maillardet) for specific purposes of public and popular exhibition, and commanded high prices (Jaquet-Droz's second musician of 1782 was sold to the London office of Jaquet-Droz's own firm for 420 pounds sterling [Chapuis and Droz 1958: 284]). While then simulacra towards the end of the eighteenth century were principally

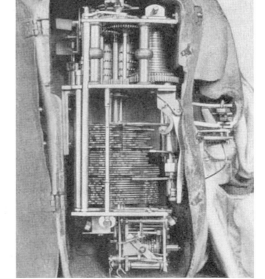

5.7a–f: Writer, draughtsman and musician (Chapuis and Droz 293–4; 299–300; 280–2)

e

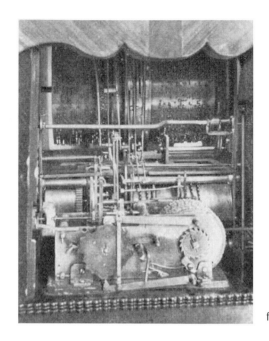

f

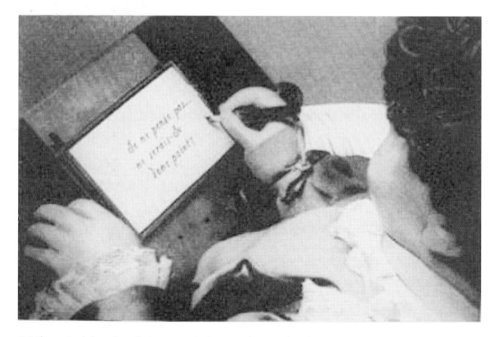

5.8 The writer's board reads 'I am not thinking . . . do I not therefore exist?' Chapuis and Droz: 396.

regarded as entertainments, these entertainments themselves contained both the source of and the fuel for further debate and often reflected on the automaton's status as a mechanical artefact. If automata appeared to be and to act as living things, then to what extent are they not what they appear? Of particular note here is one of the messages that Jaquet-Droz's writing android composed, seizing provocatively on a passage from Descartes's *Meditations*. In it, the author, looking down from his window onto people crossing the square, notes that all he is then observing is hats and coats, which as well as dressing men could equally well 'conceal automata' ([1641] 1986: 21). What differentiates those automata from me is simply that 'I am a thing which thinks'. Since I am thinking, I must exist. Jaquet-Droz's automaton writer writes: 'I am not thinking . . . do I not therefore exist?'

Popular mechanics: the ends of automata

Thus, if physiological automata were used for the scientific scrutiny of the mechanisms of living bodies, simulacral automata, or androids, result in queries being levelled regarding the nature of intelligence or the workings of the mind. While this shift from automata to androids occurs in the context of a shift away from mechanism and towards a more dynamic and vitalist world-view in the sciences of the period, it also sees mechanical simulacra acquiring an unprecedented popularity in fairgrounds and popular theatres.

Even as late as the mid-nineteenth-century, automata were constantly exciting audiences, although the nature of these audiences had begun to change: in place of the courts and aristocrats who initially delighted in these marvels, or the laboratories and scientists attempting to create life, automata became the preserve of fairgrounds and mass spectacles, touring not through the courts and palaces of Europe, but through its fairs and theatres. As early as 1805, we note the poet Wordsworth reeling disgustedly from the 'parliament of monsters' to be observed at fairs.

> All moveables of wonder, from all parts
> Are here – Albinos, painted Indians, Dwarfs,
> The Horse of knowledge, and the learned Pig,
> The stone-eater, the man that swallows fire,
> Giants, Ventriloquists, the Invisible Girl,
> The Bust that speaks and moves its goggling eyes,
> The Wax-work, Clock-work, all the marvellous craft
> Of modern Merlins, Wild Beasts, Puppet shows,
> All out-o'the-way, far-fetched, perverted things,
> All freaks of nature, all Promethean thoughts
> Of man, his dullness, madness, and their feats
> All jumbled up together, to compose
> A Parliament of Monsters.
> (Wordsworth, *Prelude*, 1805)

Wordsworth's repugnance notwithstanding, interest in mechanical automata had not waned by the mid-nineteenth-century, when Charles Babbage used to visit John Merlin's London Mechanical Museum to watch the mechanical silver lady who danced there (Shaffer, in Spufford and Uglow 1996). Between the heyday of mechanism and Babbage's time, however, clockwork or mechanical automata had fallen from scientific grace to

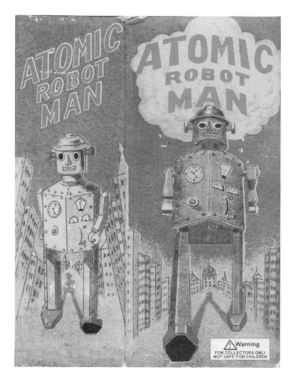

5.9 Atomic Robot man: a 1990s reproduction of a 1950s mechanical toy. Courtesy of Schilling Inc.

become fairground attractions on a par with stone-eaters, fire-swallowers, invisible girls, and puppet shows. The 'parliament of monsters' thus found at fairground spectacles degenerates further still, so that the marvels that had once replaced cathedral building as a statement of a culture's glory, pride and ability, became by the late nineteenth century, as Norbert Wiener notes, little more than adornments 'pirouetting stiffly on top of music boxes' ([1948] 1962: 40), and by the twentieth, as wind-up toys such as Atomic Robot Man.

Even such toys as pirouetting dancers and wind-up robots betray their lineage in the extraordinary mechanical creatures of the eighteenth century, and provide an ironic image of our perspective on that era's apparent naivety: imagine thinking that humans and other animals were mere mechanical creatures!

Following a period in which the popularity of such mechanical simulacra has reduced them to the status of playthings and ornaments, in the contemporary world the distinction between *simulating* intelligence and *automating* biological systems in technological form has resurfaced (**5.3.5**).

5.3.5   Life and intelligence in the digital age

5.3.3 Self-augmenting engines: steampower against nature

Continuities and breaks in the history of automata

Recounting the devolution of mechanical automata from being royally commissioned miracles in the eighteenth century to becoming fairground spectacles by the nineteenth and decorations or toys by the mid-twentieth, it is easy to imagine that there is a great historical rupture between their demise as serious objects of study and the rise of the cybernetic automata of John von Neumann and Norbert Wiener in the mid-twentieth-century. For example, as Silvio Bedini put it:

> A study of the history of automata clearly reveals that several of the basic inventions produced for these attempts to imitate life by mechanical means led to significant developments culminating in modern automation and cybernetics.
>
> (Bedini 1964: 41)

In other words, from the 1352 Strasbourg clock and the complex automata of the eighteenth century, 'to electronic and cybernetic brains, the road of evolution runs straight and steady' (Price 1964: 23). But such easy assumptions, especially in an age which automatically accepts the idea of historical discontinuities or ruptures, should not be made without examination.

The terms 'normal' and 'crisis' are here taken from Kuhn (1962). They will be discussed further at **5.4.3**.

5.4.3   Cybernetics and culture

We shall adopt two principles in offering this history of automata. First, that this history is discontinuous, marked by 'normal' and 'crisis technologies'; and second, carrying over from our discussion of Ellul's conception of the history of technology (**5.2.4**), we will note the broadening cultural impact of technology as it enters phases of 'self-augmentation'. Notably, we will see this in the discussion below of the steam technologies driving the Industrial Revolution.

5.2.4 Determinisms

Continuing to tack close to the line of life, however, we shall see that during the age of steam power and industrialisation, the conception and construction of automata change unrecognisably. If a Vaucanson or a von Kempelen were to be transported from the eighteenth to the nineteenth century they would not recognise the later century's machines as automata at all, for these latter no longer look like us.

Androides and intelligence

As has already been noted, d'Alembert's and Diderot's famous *Encyclopédie* (1751–65) contains entries on both '*automates*' and '*androïdes*'. Some seventy years later, David Brewster repeated the same classifications in the 1830 *Edinburgh Encylopaedia*, 'automata' and 'androides' (Poe 1966: 381; Chapuis and Droz 1958: 284). The same distinction is effectively made by Price during the second half of the twentieth century, although this time between 'simulacra (i.e., devices that simulate) and automata (i.e., devices that move by themselves)' (Price 1964: 9). The self-moving and the man-like, however, do not exhaust the field of the automaton. As can be seen from the fictions and automata of the late eighteenth century and the early nineteenth, attention had shifted somewhat from the earlier century's concern with *physiology* to the nineteenth century's fascination with *intelligence*. So, while Price suggests that 'the very existence' of automata 'offered tangible proof . . . that the natural universe of physics and biology was susceptible to mechanistic explanation' (1964: 9–10), the distinctions between automata on the one hand and androides and simulacra on the other seems to leave the question of *intelligence* outside the realm of what could be explained mechanically. What these distinctions therefore overlook in the history of technology is such experimental devices as calculators, many of which were invented and produced by Pascal and Leibniz in the seventeenth century, and Johannes Müller in the eighteenth. In this, Price adheres to a version of mechanistic explanation offered by René Descartes ([1641] 1986), who argued that the only thing not reducible to mechanism was the human mind. It is precisely this contention, however, that the history and development of technologies even prior to the mid-seventeenth century when Descartes was writing, undoes. Thus from Pascal to Charles Babbage's Difference and Analytical Engines of the mid-nineteenth century there extends a line of development in the technological embodiment of intelligence. Not only does this line of development tie the clockwork age to the computer age – thus perhaps providing a missing link between those periods – it also prepares the way for one of the chief themes of the 'philosophy of manufactures' during the industrial age: the question of intelligence as governance. Moreover, Babbage's proto-computers seem less of a historical surprise, less an act of lone genius than the development of potentials inherent in already existing mechanical devices. We will return to the technological embodiment of intelligence as a component of steam technologies.

Why there are no steam simulacra

However, a version of the same distinction offered by Diderot, the *Edinburgh Encyclopaedia*, and finally by Price (1964), between those automata that do and those that do not resemble human form, was offered closer to our own time by Jean Baudrillard. In 1976, he distinguished automata from robots, on the grounds that where the former looks like

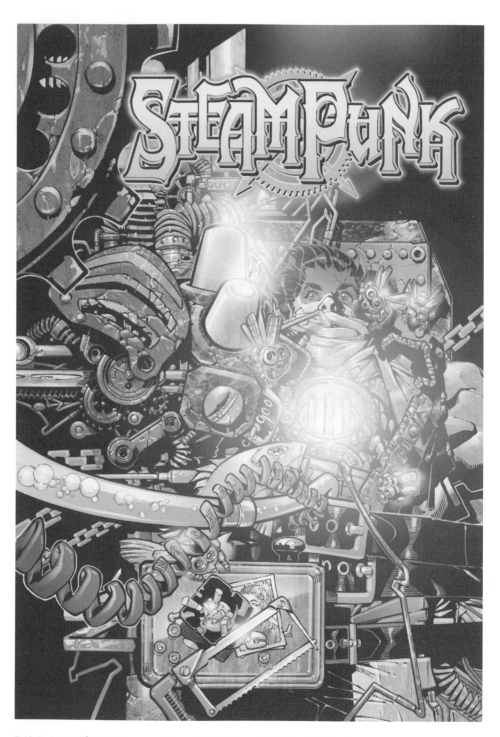

5.10 A steam cyborg? *Steampunk* issue 1, Cliffhanger/DC Comics 1999.

a human the latter need not, so long as it works like one ([1976] 1993: 53–55). Baudrillard offers this as proof of a shift in the ideals of simulation, of artifice. In the age of automata, immediately prior to the French Revolution, machines resembled human form; by the Industrial Revolution, Baudrillard argues, machines no longer resemble their makers' bodies but rather their functions. With functionalism, he writes, 'the machine has the upper hand' ([1976] 1993: 53) since the very idea of the machine is functional perfection. Such functionalism in the construction of automata is not new, however, but stretches back to the nineteenth century. In 1847, the physicist Herman von Helmholtz wrote:

> nowadays we no longer attempt to construct beings able to perform a thousand human actions, but rather machines able to execute a single action which will replace that of thousands of humans.
>
> (cited in Bedini, 1964: 41)

In this passage we can already see the passage to the 'self-acting mules', the great mechanical triumph of dead over living labour, that Marx witnessed in the practical, developmental logic of industrialism. The replacement of thousands of units of living, human labour with dead, machine labour, brings an end to the technologies of automation being applied to the charming ornamental devices adorning the clocks and snuff-boxes of the eighteenth century, and gave rise to the productivist rule of the physics of steam and connecting-rods over questions of will, intelligence and physiology.

'Man' remains the focus of eighteenth-century science; by the nineteenth century, however, that role has been rescinded, and granted instead to the machine. It is precisely this shift from simulacra to functional automata that differentiates the age of clockwork from that of steam. That is why, although we can trace, as it were, precursor-forms of the cyborg of contemporary fictions back to the mechanistic experiments and contrivances of the eighteenth century, with the rise of steam machines there are no longer any steam *simulacra*, but only steam *automata*.

Indeed, the development of technology during the nineteenth century completely disregarded the humanist conceit of the mechanical simulacrum or android, following a trajectory which takes technology further away from the anthropomorphism of the android and from simulacra of any sort, the nearer it comes to becoming a true automaton.

Reversing nature

The abandonment of the android notwithstanding, in whatever terms the distinction is made, it is intended to divide those automata or machines that resemble human beings from those that do not, *but are automata nevertheless*. To understand why this is so, consider the inscription on Figure 5.11: Athanasius Kircher designed this 'clock driven by a sunflower seed' (Hankins and Silverman 1995: 14) in 1633. But it is less the details of this (fraudulent) invention that matters than what it tells us concerning the proximity of technology to nature during that period when the mechanical philosophy dominated. Technology such as that deployed in the construction of automata being the *artificial realisation of nature's own mechanism* made it possible to conceive not only of naturally harmonious devices, it also, as already noted by a surgeon such as La Mettrie, led to an understanding of living bodies in terms of mechanism. After the mid-eighteenth century, however, there emerged a new understanding of life, one that emphasised a distance between life and clockwork, where the mechanists saw only an increasing proximity. Thus, at the turn of the nineteenth century, the name 'biology' was given to the field of study that had opened up, dividing living from non-living bodies.

'Biology' as the 'science of life' emerged simultaneously in works by Gottfried Rheinhold Treviranus and by Jean Baptiste de Lamarck published in 1802. Prior to 1750, Foucault asserts, 'life did not exist' (1970: 127–128). That is, there could be no biology because there was no understanding of living things separate from the understanding of non-living things

With the introduction of a distinct science called biology, and the consequent division of living from non-living things, life was no longer conceived as produced through mechanism alone. There had to be something else, a vital force or a major difference between organic and inorganic matter. The scientific grounds for the construction of mechanical simulacra of living, even human bodies had disappeared, leaving no further motive for their production than entertainment. Thus, instead of constructing machine life in human form, nineteenth-century physiologists began to measure living bodies as heat engines, and engines that functioned poorly when compared with other machines. Key to this shift was a new evaluation of respiration, the 'paramount function . . . providing the energy that powers the living being . . ., liberat[ing] heat and energy in a form useful to the organism' (Coleman 1977: 119). Marx makes this understanding of the organism clear: the machine, he writes, 'consumes coal, oil etc. . . . just as the worker consumes food' (1993: 693). If the intake of calories (literally, units of heat) provides machinery and organism with energy, then the use of this energy could be comparatively measured as units of work. Understood in accordance with this function, the organism becomes 'an energy-conversion device, a machine' (Coleman 1977: 123), one whose efficiency could be measured against others.

As a mode of analysis, many biologists argued, this was fine; but it told us nothing about life itself, how it arises, how it differs from lifeless things. Such analyses provide mere evidence of the energy-efficiency of biological heat engines. As biology was therefore turning away from technology for purposes of understanding life, engineers and industrialists simultaneously began to see the relative inefficiency of biological as opposed to technological heat engines. If, in working, functions currently allotted to humans could be given to machines, then a net increase in functional efficiency could be gained. The steam age no longer modelled machines on man, but measured humans against machines.

However, we should not conclude that the mechanists' aim of producing artificial yet living things becomes a quaint relic of an age ignorant of biology, just as the alchemists had been ignorant of chemistry. On the contrary, freed from the constraints of the simulation of life as it is, all life was redefined in accordance with the functioning of machines that, in Baudrillard's words, now 'had the upper hand' ([1976]1993: 54). Life was now imagined *as it could be* by 'philosophers of manufacture', engineers, politicians, and industrialists, spawning enormous social engineering projects. The steam-driven, mechanical pandemonium unleashed by large-scale industrial engines renounced the uncanny or distasteful status of man's double to achieve real dominion over human life and social organisation, producing, in Thomas Carlyle's words, 'a mighty change in our whole manner of existence' (in Harvie et al., 1970: 24). Where under mechanism art and nature were conjoint, as Kircher's print of the sunflower clock makes so abundantly clear, steam power predominantly offered a means to *reverse* nature.

New automata: engines and factories

Consider, for example, the first practically applied steam engine, assembled by Thomas Newcomen in the eighteenth century. It was used to reverse the flow of water into mines, a task that had hitherto been performed by slaves. Similarly, the steam engine enabled boats to navigate upstream in freshwater, rather than struggling against it with oars (Wiener [1958] 1987: 140). Effectively an autonomous power source, the steam engine made possible enormous gains against nature, improving hugely on inefficient human functioning. Moreover, it was in this sense that the 'philosophers of manufacture' in the

5.11 Sunflower clock; 'art and nature conjoined'. Courtesy of the University of Washington Libraries.

early nineteenth century — Andrew Ure, Charles Babbage and Dr Price, for example — were led to speak of factories as automata, as 'moving powers that moved themselves'. In the factory, the automaton no longer resembles living bodies as did mechanical simulacra, but, as Baudrillard notes, *duplicates* their functions in order, as Helmholtz confirms, to *replace* them. Not only did the great steam engines that powered the range of machines incorporated into a factory supply them with motive force, *cause* the movements of these machines, they also exerted their iron will over the hitherto independent will of machines' human users; indeed, 'the worker's activity . . . is determined and regulated on all sides by the movement of the machinery, and not the opposite' (Marx 1993: 693). As engines reversed nature, factories became autonomous entities. By giving up being simulacra of humans, automata become relatively automous, acquiring social and physical agency, their movements, as Marx noted, 'determining' the worker, 'and not the opposite' (1993: 693).

Automata and social engineering

The reasons for this acquisition of power over human labour stem ultimately from a division in the kinds of machines that Charles Babbage noted in his 1832 *On the Economy of Machinery and Manufactures*, between '(1) machines employed to produce power; (2) machines whose purpose is simply to transmit power and to perform the work' (1832: 10–11). While other forces — social, political, economic, and so on — undoubtedly drove the factory into realisation, it was simply a physical necessity that machines of the first type be physically connected to machines of the second type: *mechanised labour, in other words, necessitated centralisation*. As Norbert Wiener notes concerning the technological form of early factories, 'the only available means of transmission of power were mechanical. The first among these was the line of shafting, supplemented by the belt and the pulley' ([1958] 1987: 142). Indeed, he further notes that factories had barely changed even by the time of his own childhood at the turn of the twentieth century.

It is this technological necessity that made the rise of the factory as a relatively isolated, closed system of machinery necessary in turn, and that therefore gave rise to factories physically isolated in new, industrial spaces. In other words, a steam engine, no matter how powerful, can only drive those other machines to which its power is physically transmitted. It is this, in turn, that meant that human workers had to be situated in relation to the machine, rather than the other way around as was the prevailing situation in the hand- or foot-powered machines of earlier, mutually remote, cottage industries. Hence there arose the issue of the role of the human will and the human agent in these 'manufactories'. Rather than being the agents employing machinery to their own purposes, living workers were 'pushed to the side of the production process' (Marx 1993: 705), and merely 'watched attentively and assiduously over a system of productive mechanisms' (Ure 1835: 18). In consequence, rather than users external to the machine, they became the machine's 'intellectual organs', subject eventually to the 'will' of the engine that drove their actions. Thus Ure:

> In its most rigorous sense, the term [factory] conveys the idea of a vast automaton, composed of numerous mechanical and intellectual organs operating in concert and without interruption, towards one and the same aim, all these organs being subordinated to a motive force which moves itself.

> (Ure 1835: 18–19)

The steam automaton no longer *looks* like us at all, it no longer excites uncanny fears of our doubles; rather, it uses humans as subsidiary power sources devoted to an aim dictated to them by the mechanical arrangement of the automaton's parts. Humans for the first time become components of systems of machinery. It is worth noting, at this point, that the subordinate position of living with respect to non-living automata echoes Aristotle's definition of a slave as *not a self-moving thing* by virtue of being a tool of the master (**1.6.4**). This definition makes the 'master' interchangeably human or technological, the only condition being that the master *is that which moves itself*, and the slave that which is moved accordingly. With industrial machines, then, mastery is usurped by technology.

1.6.4 The many virtues of Saint McLuhan

Real and imaginary systems

While the worker is a part of the machine, a component-circuit designed by an alien will, the owner is not; rather, the factory is a realisation of his designs. It thus becomes possible to dismiss the idea of the technological system as a 'fancy' or a merely 'imaginary machine', as Adam Smith argued. Thus, although Marx's and Ure's great, steam automata subjugated the worker's body to the machines, even as its 'intellectual organs' or 'conscious linkages', the intellectual labour of the design and implementation of such automated systems of machinery still lay very firmly in the human domain. In accordance with this humanist view, Adam Smith further distinguishes *actual* machines from *imaginary* systems of machinery in the following terms:

> a machine is a little system created to perform as well as to connect together in reality those different movements and effects which the artist has occasion for. *A system is an imaginary machine invented to connect together in fancy those different movements and effects which are already in reality performed.*
>
> (Smith [1795] 1980: 66; emphasis added)

But whose 'fancy' is this? Not, of course, that of the worker, but of what Simon Shaffer calls the 'enlightened mechanics' (Clark et al. 1999: 145) that governed Diderot's and Smith's philosophy of manufactures. Just as the Enlightenment prized the exercise of reason above all else, such enlightened mechanics likewise prized *intellectual* over *manual* production, 'imagining' evermore mechanised forms of labour, as enlightened social order required. Thus Adam Ferguson, on the Enlightenment's ideal worker:

> Many mechanical arts require no [intellectual] capacity. They succeed best under a total suppression of sentiment and reason, and ignorance is the mother of industry as well as of superstition. Reflection and fancy are subject to err, but a habit of moving the hand or the foot is independent of either. Manufactures, accordingly, prosper most where the mind is least consulted, and where the workshop may, without any great effort of the imagination, be considered as an engine, the parts of which are men.
>
> (Ferguson [1767] 1966: 182–183)

Enlightened mechanists such as Ferguson, Smith and Diderot, then, were social engineers who commanded the division of labour between manual workers and machines as a single, rationally governed system. The question remains, however, whether such systems of machinery as *turn humans into simulacra of machines* in the mechanical repetition of their labour, remain *imaginary* creatures of fancy, as Smith and Ferguson argue, or whether the factory constitutes, as Ure, Babbage and Marx argue, *a real automaton that contains conscious linkages*, in so far as the whole factory is a self-moving machine. Following the idea of functional automata, we are no longer dealing with the mechanical simulation of human form or intelligence, but rather with their incorporation into a real, rather than an imaginary, system of machinery.

Real technologies of governance

There are, however, other, more specifically technological developments that solve the problem, posed by Adam Smith, of the merely imaginary or the actually technological status of the 'system'. Both have to do with the role of the 'conscious linkages' in systems of machinery. In the late eighteenth century, as the 'enlightened mechanists' were writing, the problem of the *control* of machines was always solved by a human supervisory presence. Intelligence was needed to keep a watch over the machines, since they could not be self-correcting. Machines could overheat, run out of coal, or simply fall apart if there were no human supervisor to ensure their correct functioning. Indeed, this regularly happened to early steam engines. Consider, however, this account of an 'automatic furnace' constructed in the seventeenth century:

> It is reasonably safe to state that cybernetics was already in a stage of potential realisation in the creations of the seventeenth century. Probably the first major step in this direction was taken with the design of thermostatic controls for chemical furnaces . . ., credited to Cornelius Drebbel (1573–1633) of Holland. A sketch in a manuscript dated 1666 shows an automatic furnace . . .; this used a thermostat filled with alcohol joined to a U-tube containing mercury. With the increase of heat, the alcohol expanded, forcing the mercury upward to raise a rod and by means of levers to close a damper. When the heat fell too low, the action was reversed by the contraction of the alcohol . . . This is unquestionably the first known example of a feedback mechanism which led to the self-control of mechanical devices.
>
> (Bedini 1964: 41)

The technological problem of self-control was equally a problem for the industrial application of steam technology. The engineer James Watt introduced what he called a 'governor' into his engines to enable control of their speed. Norbert Wiener writes:

> [Watt's] governor keeps the engine from running wild when its load is removed. If it starts to run wild, the balls of the governor fly upward from centrifugal action, and in their upward flight they move a lever which partly cuts off the admission of steam. Thus the tendency to speed up produces a partly compensatory tendency to slow down.
>
> (Wiener [1954] 1989: 152)

Such devices, evincing what cybernetics calls 'negative feedback' (Wiener [1948] 1962: 97), certainly enable the production of self-controlling machines, but they do not seem to supply a direct answer to the question of the imaginary rather than the technological status of *systems* of machinery. What they do indicate is that functions hitherto thought to be the sole province of living intelligence, such as monitoring and control, can be automated and thus ceded to machines. Wiener even suggests that machines able to respond correctively to their own functioning, or to environmental changes, effectively possess sense-organs.

However, the systemic automation of the intelligence needed to run a series of interrelated machines cannot be achieved with the same technologies as Drebbel's thermostat or Watt's governor.

It is Babbage in particular whose writings and inventions point up a solution to our problem: human agency remains the 'prime mover' of 'automatic' systems of machinery *only in so far as intelligence remains itself non-mechanical*. In this light, inventions that embodied intelligence in technological artefacts, such as Pascal's, Leibniz's and Müller's calculators, supply the missing link between the history of automata to cybernetics. And it was left to Ada Lovelace, 'the Queen of Engines', and the daughter of the poet Byron, to rejoin the history of automated intelligence to the factory system and early industrialisation in textiles. At this point, then, we must revert from the non-simulacral automata that characterise the rise of industrial machines to the last wholly simulational project regarding automata to date. That is, the automation of intelligence.

5.3.4 The construction of inanimate reason

The history of artificial intelligence begins with mechanical calculators. But calculators can simulate only one function of human intelligence, while human intelligence is capable of a high number of functions. Artificial intelligence comes one step closer to realisation, therefore, with the idea of the programmable; that is, a multifunctional machine. Here the efforts of Ada Lovelace to establish the language and capacities of programming from her own mathematical researches, her mentor Babbage's Difference and Analytical Engines, and Jacquard's pattern-generating automatic looms, form a crucial historical juncture between *calculating* and *programming* in the history of artificial intelligence.

The first attempts to automate intelligence, as opposed to physiological functions, take the form of *calculating* devices. Although devices such as the abacus or 'Napier's Bones' – sticks of different lengths with correspondingly different numerical values – considerably predate the mechanical calculators of the seventeenth and eighteenth centuries, it is only by this date that questions arise concerning the possibility of automating intelligence. Intelligence had been overtly acknowledged as the distinguishing feature of human beings since Aristotle, so the prospect of automated intelligence or 'inanimate reason' was a high-stakes venture.

The Pascaline and Leibniz's mechanical reasoner

The earliest mechanical calculators, however, were intended merely as labour-saving devices. The philosopher and mathematician Blaise Pascal began to design calculators, known as Pascalines, in 1642. Rather than automating intelligence, Pascal's intent was to free the mind from the burden of laborious calculation, specifically that of his government official father. The Pascalines were simple devices to facilitate error-free addition. While some have called them 'the first true digital computer' (Price 1964: 20), given their limited range of functions, this may be true only in so far as these were devices for computing digits, for they were primarily manually operated like the abacus. The Pascaline did, however, contain one feature that distinguished it from earlier 'arithmetical instruments' and made it into what can justly be described as a 'calculating machine', as one Dionysius Lardner wrote in an essay on 'Babbage's Calculating Engine' printed in the *Edinburgh Review* in 1843. Once again, we note the classical distinction between an 'instrument' or tool and a 'machine', based on the quantity of actions the latter can perform independently of its user. Thus, what distinguished Pascal's machine from a

5.12 The 'Pascaline' (1642), a semi-automatic calculator by Blaise Pascal. Science Museum/Science and Society Picture Library.

mere tool was that it contained a mechanical means to solve the problem of 'carrying' a number from, say, the column of single units to the column of tens. According to Lardner's account, Pascal's machine

> consisted of a series of wheels, carrying cylindrical barrels, on which were engraved the ten arithmetical characters . . . The wheel which expressed each order of units was so connected with the wheel which expressed the superior order [i.e., 10s rather than 1s], that when the former passed from 9 to 0, the latter was necessarily advanced one figure; and thus the process of carrying was executed by mechanism.
>
> (Lardner [1843], in Hyman 1989: 106)

While Pascal's machine automated addition, in 1673 the philosopher, scientist and mathematician G.W. Leibniz showed a prototype of his mechanical calculator, the *calculus rationator*, to the Royal Society of London. As well as addition and subtraction, this calculator could multiply and divide automatically, by way of Leibniz's 'stepped reckoner', containing cogs of different lengths which mechanically realised those functions (MacDonald Ross 1984: 12–13). Noting that Leibniz himself never published a detailed account of his calculator's mechanism (although one of his calculators remains extant in the Hannover State Library), Lardner concludes that, unlike the Pascaline, 'it does not appear that this contrivance . . . was ever applied to any useful purpose' ([1843], in Hyman 1989: 108). However, Leibniz's calculator was not, like Pascal's, a utilitarian device constructed to save time and reduce error; its real significance was that it demonstrated that reasoning could be mechanised. The calculator itself, therefore, was a by-product of this larger project, a project which led Norbert Wiener, amongst others, to herald Leibniz as 'the patron saint of cybernetics' ([1948]1962: 12).

Leibniz had noted that there was a similarity between all kinds of reasoning – moral, legal, commercial, scientific and philosophical – and calculation: like the latter, all reasoning followed rules. Unlike arithmetic, however, the terms in which broader forms of reasoning were conducted were unsuitably vague and general. In other words, while 1 + 1 could easily be automated, problems that involved concepts could not. This is because concepts were not simple like numbers, but had content. What Leibniz therefore sought to do was to break down this content into its basic elements and thus to discover the formal logic by which reasoning worked – the 'language of thought' as artificial intelligence researchers now call it – and to define the major concepts employed in terms of numerical or alphabetic values. When, for example, contemporary logicians say 'X is P' (bananas are yellow; men are mortal, etc.), they are using precisely the kind of 'universal characteristic' comprising 'all the characters that express our thoughts' that was Leibniz's lifetime project. Once such a universal characteristic was completed it would form the 'grammar and the dictionary' of 'a new language which could be written or spoken' (Leibniz [1677] 1951: 16). Once all our thoughts were given numerical expression, and given the rules of calculation in general (i.e., reasoning), it would, Leibniz reasoned, be possible to mechanise reasoning in its entirety, and thus to produce a reasoning machine. Thus, amongst Leibniz's experiments in constructing such languages is his invention of binary notation, in which all numbers are expressed as combinations of zeros and ones, such as all digital computers operate on. Although Leibniz drew up a plan for a calculator that used this binary arithmetic, he never produced such a machine. It is not simply the machines he produced, however, but the convergence between the idea of a formal, universal language and the construction of reasoning machines that is represented by Leibniz's calculator. As far as Leibniz was concerned, the mechanical calculator thus becomes the mechanical reasoner, the forerunner of artificial intelligence. As Wiener has it,

> It is therefore not in the least surprising that the same intellectual impulse which has led to the development of mathematical logic has at the same time led to the ideal or actual mechanization of processes of thought.
>
> (Wiener [1948] 1962: 12)

Thus, while Leibniz states that the universal characteristic is a tool to 'increase the power of the human mind' ([1677] 1951: 16), increasing the clarity, certainty, and communicability of our ideas, glimpsing the prospect of a larger calculator to mechanise all reasoning, he thought of engraving it with the legend 'Superior to man', and that in comparison with this, previous calculators 'are in fact mere games' (Leibniz [1678] 1989: 236). Leibniz is not a constructor of calculators for their own sake, therefore, but rather a forerunner of programming, computer construction and, as the logical conclusion of these latter, artificial intelligence.

Ada and Babbage: programmable engines

Leibniz, however, never constructed his mechanical reasoner. All that remains of it is his tentative draft (MacDonald Ross 1984: 30). To some extent, this was also the fate of Charles Babbage's Difference and Analytical Engines. Although he, with the help of engineer Joseph Clement, constructed a demonstration model of about one-seventh of the size of the completed Difference Engine in 1832, none was satisfactorily completed during his lifetime. However, the problem which Babbage faced was not the theoretical one of whether such mechanical reasoners were possible, but rather the state of the mechanical arts of the mid-nineteenth century. Babbage could not find engineers capable of cutting the brass components of his engines with sufficient accuracy, all but disabling the project's realisation. Of course, other factors – financial, lack of obvious applications, and political resistance – contributed to the lack of a working Analytical Engine, as has been suggested (see Woolley 1999: 273ff.); however, as Ada Lovelace's far-reaching analyses of that Engine show, what it causes us to imagine is precisely the interconnections between these new technologies and extant ones. Had they been fully realised, however, these machines, and especially the Analytical Engine, had the potential to turn the period of the Industrial Revolution into the first computer age, as William Gibson and Bruce Sterling's novel *The Difference Engine* (1990) hypothesises.

5.13 Charles Babbage's difference engine no. 1 built by Joseph Clement in 1832. Difference Engine No.2 was only assembled in 1991 by the London Science Museum. Science and Society Picture Library.

While the two engines have been celebrated as the precursors of modern computing, their significance might, as with that of Leibniz's calculator, lie elsewhere. Firstly, it is important to distinguish between the functional repertoire of the two machines. The Difference Engine, the first such calculating engine on which Babbage worked from the 1820s on, was so called because it worked on the method of *iterating finite differences*. In other words, it calculated according to a formula that, as it were, was hardwired – or more accurately, perhaps, 'hardcogged' (Spufford, in Spufford and Uglow 1996: 169) – into its mechanical structure. If the differences between terms could be specified as a formula, then it could be added or subtracted to produce numbers bearing the same relation to each other as to all the other numbers it could derive. The derivation of each number, or of each number thus similarly related, involved repeating or 'iterating' the 'programme' as a whole. The embodiment of such calculative possibilities in mechanical form was already a considerable advance on previous calculators – of which Babbage might well have said, as did Leibniz of the calculators preceding his own, that they were 'in fact mere games' (Leibniz [1678] 1989: 236). Although it was manually operated by means of a hand-crank, the engine's subsequent operation was entirely automatic, yielding its results without further human intervention. If it could be driven by a steam engine, then even this minimal intervention could easily have been removed.

Despite the gravity of its achievements, however, the Difference Engine had a profoundly practical intent: it was designed to calculate and print the mathematical tables on which human 'computers' had to rely for such tasks as calculating navigation, annuities, and so on, without the frequent errors of calculation or transcription that occurred in the production of tables. Babbage himself not only wrote such a table, but amassed a collection of some 300 volumes of them, through which he regularly trawled for such errors as he wished to eliminate through the 'unerring certainty of mechanism' (cited in Swade 1991: 2). However, as he notes in a letter announcing the project of the Difference Engine to the President of the Royal Society, Sir Humphry Davy, a M. Prony of France had established a means for producing such tables through the method of the division of labour (Hyman 1989: 47; see also Daston 1994: 182–202). Prony's method was to have mathematicians draw up a simplified formula, which was then applied by a mass of non-specialist workers – known at the time as 'computers' – to calculate the results of the arithmetical operations the formula specified. Upon witnessing Prony's 'arithmetical factories' in operation, Babbage remarked, in a tellingly prescient vision of the steam automata that Marx and others would argue factories became, 'I wish to God these calculations had been accomplished by steam' (cited in Woolley 1999: 151).

However, while the Difference Engine could realise the long-held dream of automated calculation by 'hardcogged' machines, as with Leibniz's mechanical reasoner, Babbage's Engines were not to be mere calculators but incidental by-products of larger-scale projects. That project was the automation not simply of calculation but of analysis. Thus the Analytical Engine, the Difference Engine's successor, was a machine that not only calculated, but also 'decided' what formula to use in order to do those calculations. It was in effect a programmable computer, whose programmes could include instructions for the utilisation of subsequent programmes without human intervention. Because this was such a difficult idea to grasp, even for those versed in mathematics and mechanics, Babbage encouraged Luigi Menabrea, an Italian military engineer whom he had encountered while presenting his Engine work in Italy, to publish his 'Sketch of the Analytical Engine' in 1842. A year later, Ada Lovelace translated them into English and published them with notes that far outweighed the slim essay they accompanied.

Although controversy arises surrounding both the extent to which the Analytical Engine can be compared to a computer (Hyman 1989: 242–3), and the real contribution made by Ada Lovelace to the development of programming (Woolley 1999: 276ff.; Plant 1997; Hyman 1989: 243), it is Ada's analysis of the machine's functioning and possibilities that make most apparent what advances in inanimate reason Babbage's second engine had made. She writes of the Anlaytical Engine as

> the material expression of any indefinite function of any degree of generality and complexity . . . ready to receive at any moment, by means of cards constituting a portion of its mechanism (and applied on the principle of those used in the Jacquard-loom), the impress of whatever *special* function we may desire to develop or tabulate.
>
> (Lovelace 1843, in Hyman 1989: 267)

In other words, the Analytical engine has no particular set function, as the Difference Engine does (the latter is, essentially, an 'Adding machine', according to Ada Lovelace), but can be programmed to perform any computable function. In this, it resembles the 'universal machine' described by Alan Turing in 1936, and thus forms the true (if inactual) forerunner of contemporary computing. The means by which it is 'programmed' are those Jacquard 'devised for regulating . . . the most complicated patterns in the fabrication of brocaded stuffs' (1843, in Hyman 1989: 272): punched cards. 'We may say', Ada wrote accordingly, 'that the Analytical Engine *weaves algebraical patterns* just as the Jacquard-loom weaves flowers and leaves' (1843, in Hyman 1989: 273).

In one sense, the relation of the Analytical to the Difference Engine is the same as that between Leibniz's calculator and the project of which it formed a part. Ada even echoes Leibniz's language: the Analytical Engine, she writes,

> does not occupy common ground with mere 'calculating machines'. It holds a position wholly its own . . . In enabling mechanism to combine together *general* symbols . . . , a uniting link is established between the operations of matter [i.e., the Engine itself] and the abstract mental processes of the *most abstract* branch of mathematical science. A new, a vast, and a powerful language is developed for the future use of analysis . . .
>
> (Lovelace 1843, in Hyman 1989: 273)

As regards what can be called its functional indeterminacy – the fact that it is equally well-suited to carrying out several operations – the Analytical Engine thus most closely approximates the modern computer, as we have already remarked. Indeed, as also noted, Alan Turing's first computers were just such 'universal machines' (Turing 1936; Hodges 1992, 1997), capable of enacting many processes and 'hardcogged' for none. Programmability, the distinction between a 'storehouse' and a 'mill', the terms Ada gave to those functions now called *memory* and *processor* (1843, in Hyman 1989: 278–281), where everything seems set up in advance so that *all* the Analytical Engine is is the precursor of the modern computer, just as all Leibniz's machine was, was an expensive labour-saving calculator. Lovelace, however, saw it as something infinitely more: the Analytical Engine was as improbable and yet as realisable as the idea of a 'thinking or of a reasoning machine' (1843, in Hyman 1989: 273). Following Leibniz and Lovelace, however, we must note that, as it were, the circuit of history that Babbage began but never completed, is not closed by the construction of a working Difference Engine in 1991 (Swade 1991, 2000). The Analytical Engine has never yet been built – although a partial model was under construction at the time of Babbage's death in 1871. Neither does the functional similarity of Babbage's designs and those of Turing, for example, who oversaw the construction of the earliest computers (Colossus in 1942 and ENIAC in 1946; Hodges 1997: 24–31), and who cited the Analytical Engine as precisely such a 'universal machine', imply that Babbage's second Engine has been superseded by subsequent developments. Viewing the 1991 Difference Engine as the *completion* of its 1832 counterpart, and the Turing machine or the modern computer as the *completion* of Babbage's designs of the mid- to late nineteenth century, locks these machines, along with those of Pascal and Leibniz, into the prehistory of *current* technologies, which therefore become those same designs, perfected.

Spufford views the Difference Engine in precisely this way. Taking it as a 'collaboration between [the] times' when it was designed and built, he writes that it thus forms part of the history of computing only 'retrospectively' (Spufford and Uglow 1996: 267–268), and only therefore in so far as it was, as of 1991, completed

   Gibson and Sterling's fictional account of a mid-nineteenth-century computer age is sometimes read as precisely this kind of operation: take a machine that remained unrealised in its time, have it realised then, and see the age of information powered by steam! The past becomes nothing other than the prehistory of present, cybernetic perfection, a 'virtual history' that in reality remained inactual (Spufford and Uglow 1996: 266ff.). However, this is a virtual history constructed not to account for present perfections but for future imperfections: it is the prehistory of the world inhabited not by us, but by the cyberpunk futures these and other authors began to invent in the 1980s (Gibson 1986; Sterling 1986). What Spufford and others overlook in offering such an account is the otherwise bizarre conclusion to their virtual history. It ends not with computing, but with corporate bodies in the present age becoming self-aware. London, 1991:

> a thing grows, an autocatalytic tree, in almost-life, feeding through the roots of thought on the rich decay of its own shed images, and ramifying, through myriad lightning-branches, up, up, towards the hidden light of vision,
>> Dying to be born,
>> The light is strong,
>> The light is clear;
>> The Eye at last must see itself
>> Myself . . .
>> I see:
>> I see,
>> I see
>> I
>> !

> (Gibson and Sterling 1990: 383)

Of course, this is fiction; but it points up an important objection to the kind of virtual history that, for example, Spufford and Uglow (1996), Warwick (1998) and De Landa (1991) engage in. That is, firstly, that in doing retrospective histories the object from which the perspective is articulated is a *contingent* object: there is no absolute end-point of technological development reached in contemporary computing, nor any end-point of technological evolution reached in futural robotic histories. In a sense, this is to make the same point as Leibniz does about the true value of his calculator, and as Lovelace does about that of Babbage's Analytical Engine: both refuse a reductive explanation of their machines' functional capacities, and argue instead for other *virtualities* those machines possess. In both cases, as in Gibson and Sterling's novel, those virtualities have to do with *artificial intelligence*, as though this were a virtual property of *all* technology.

CASE STUDY 5.1   Chess and 'inanimate reason'

Baron von Kempelen's celebrated Chess-Playing Automaton was contrived in 1769 as an entertainment for the Royal Court of his native Hungary. A mechanistic physiologist, von Kempelen also constructed a speaking automaton, featuring mechanically reproduced lungs, voice-box, mouth, tongue and lips, to better understand the functions of its organic counterpart and to re-engineer these in mechanical form. Less renowned than the chess-player (to which its subsequent owner, Johann Maelzel, the inventor of the metronome, ironically added a voice-box), the speaking automaton was a genuinely mechanical device, reproducing speech without hidden human intervention (Hankins and Silverman 1995: 178–220).

However, it was the mystery surrounding the precise mode of *human* intervention in the chess-player's operations that excited the greatest curiosity when von Kempelen, and later Maelzel, took it on extended tours of the cities of Europe and the United States. 'It is quite certain', wrote Poe, 'that the operations of the Automaton are regulated by *mind*', but the most pressing problem was 'to fathom the mystery of its evolutions'; that is, 'the manner in which human agency is brought to bear' ('[1836] 1966: 382–383). While others had sought principally to expose the secret hiding place of the child or dwarf who inhabited the chest upon which the chess-player was mounted, Poe demonstrates 'mathematical[ly] . . ., *a priori*' that the Automaton could be no 'pure machine' from the fact that no mechanism could either predict its antagonist's moves, or allow an indeterminate time to elapse between the moves of its antagonist. In other words, unlike a mathematical calculation or the performance of a rhythmic piece of music, there is neither a determinate sequence of events (each move will depend upon the machine's antagonist) nor a set period of time (the antagonist's moves will each take a different length of time to consider and execute). It could not, in other words, be 'programmed' in advance to carry out specific moves at specific points. Baron von Kempelen himself admitted as much in his own account of the chess-player as 'a very ordinary piece of mechanism – a *bagatelle* whose effects appeared so marvellous from the boldness of the conception, and the fortunate choice of the methods adopted for promoting the illusion' (ibid.: 382). Poe's own assessment of the inventor's intelligence is given dubious recognition in a short story entitled 'Von Kempelen and his Discovery', in which the eponymous hero is presented as an alchemist fulfilling the dream of turning base metal into gold (ibid., 72–77). Like the alchemist then, according to Poe, von Kempelen possessed a genius for the false, which made him a false genius.

If the fate of the first chess-playing mechanism was to expose the necessity of human intervention in a game that has often been seen as synonymous with intelligence, this is not the same fate shared by its machine successors. The first of these, constructed in the 1920s by the then president of the Spanish Academy of Science, Torrès y Quevedo, was an electrical 'adaptation of the mechanical inventions which moved the earlier automata' (Chapuis and Droz 1958: 387). It worked by responding to changing electrical contacts between the chess pieces and the board and, as Chapuis and Droz note, 'there is nothing more exciting than to watch this struggle between the machine and the man,

5.14 Torres y Quevedo's 1920s chess-playing machine.

who inexorably will be defeated', referencing Chapuis's silent film, *Le Joueur d'échecs* ['The Chess-Player'] of 1930, in which one such contest is recorded (Chapuis and Droz 1958: 387). Moreover, by virtue of the contacts by which the machine receives information from its antagonist's actions, the machine has acquired what Chapuis and Droz call, following Norbert Wiener, 'artificial senses' (1958: 389).

Curiously, the same comparison as Poe made in 1836 between *artificial intelligence* and *alchemy* was made 130 years later in an essay that was to be the undoing of the reign of human over machine intelligence. Philosopher Hubert Dreyfus wrote 'Alchemy and artificial intelligence' as an attack on the entire artificial intelligence research programme, specifically in so far as such researchers were attempting to develop chess-playing computers. As he recounts in *What Computers Can't Do* (1979), Dreyfus challenged any machine to beat him at chess, and lost. A mere quarter of a century later, in 1996, an individual who can only now be described as having been the World's greatest *human* chess-player, Gary Kasparov, accepted a challenge from IBM's supercomputer, 'Deep Blue' – and was defeated. There is therefore an entire history of chess-playing automata. Every challenge has been a spectacle, as though we were testing fate to maintain us as the only intelligent species on the earth. But coextensive with these spectacles there have been real developments in artificial senses and intelligence. Although an appropriate description of von Kempelen's automaton, and despite post-dating Quevedo's machine, it now seems that Walter Benjamin was wrong when he noted, in the first of his 'Theses on the Philosophy of History' (written in 1940), that the materialism represented by the automaton could only win philosophically by virtue of the wizened theologian hidden in the mechanism (1973: 255): after *L'Affaire Dreyfus* and Kasparov, materialism is the only game in town.

Just as automata provide a history of *artificial life*, calculators provide a history of *artificial intelligence*. While both research programmes derive essentially from work done in the last quarter century or so, their respective histories stretch further back, as the foregoing sections show. The next section will therefore consider the current state of these 'sciences of the artificial' (Simon [1969] 1996) and draw out the questions artificial life and intelligence pose regarding the relations between nature and culture that technology brings into play.

5.3.5 Life and intelligence in the digital age

As noted in the introduction to **5.3**, the digital age demonstrates a vast range of crossovers between the biological and the technological. Apart from the 'sciences of the artificial' (Simon [1969] 1996) – artificial intelligence (AI) and artificial life (Alife) – there is also the rise of 'molecular cybernetics' (Monod 1971) or genetics, and the various biotechnologies, in which organic matter becomes a technology in its own right. We will briefly survey AI and Alife, therefore, before moving on to discuss genetics and biotechnology.

5.3 Biological technologies: the history of automata

AI

Can machines think? Scientists say 'yes', humanists 'no'. AI researchers confidently predict that genuinely intelligent machines will be created – it's just a matter of time. So if we rephrase the question from 'can machines think?' to 'can they think *now*?', we must surely – scientist and humanist alike – answer 'no'. However, remember what happened to Hubert Dreyfus when he argued thus: a computer beat him at chess. Consider what this computer does. It calculates the possible moves against the consequences of those moves every time its opponents make a move of their own. The machine then calculates the most logical move to make in order to win the game, and prompts its human helper to execute that move. Is the machine thereby thinking? 'Not really', we are likely to answer, 'it's just calculating, treating chess as a series of maths problems'. Yet isn't this precisely what a human chess-player does when s/he reflects on the game, weighing up the possible moves and selecting the one most likely to achieve a win? Even if we concede this, however, we are likely to assert, 'there's nothing like thinking going on in the computer, only electrical charges exchanging input and output signals'. But isn't this exactly as the brain works?

There are two main approaches to AI:

1　Classical AI or 'good-old-fashioned-AI' (GOFAI), which is concerned to imitate human intelligence in machines.

2　Connectionist AI or 'neural networks', concerned to bring about machine intelligence, regardless of whether or not it resembles human intelligence.

Classical AI

Classical AI seeks to translate what it calls 'the language of thought' into a computer program. In principle, any consistent reasoning can be turned into a program using the intermediary of logic. What logical analysis enables AI researchers to do is to construct Leibniz's 'universal characteristic' (**5.3.4**) as program code, thus enabling thought to be realised in machines. In consequence, much classical AI has concentrated on the development of 'expert systems' to replace or augment existing human experts. Such systems are produced by gathering as much information as possible from human experts in a given field (medical diagnosis, for example), and then boiling down the information into logical form.

5.3.4　The construction of inanimate reason

EXPERT SYSTEMS

The chess-playing computer, Deep Blue, that defeated Gary Kasparov in 1996, is one culmination of this kind of GOFAI research. The other culminating technology is the expert system, a 'software superspecialist consultant' (Dennett 1998: 15). Such AIs have already been produced, and with startling results, as Dennett reports:

> SRI in California announced in the mid-eighties that PROSPECTOR, an SRI-developed expert system in geology, had correctly predicted the existence of a large, important mineral deposit that had been entirely unanticipated by the human geologists who had fed it its data. MYCIN, perhaps the most famous of these expert systems, diagnoses infections of the blood . . . And many other expert systems are on the way.
>
> (Dennett 1998: 16)

Expert systems are computer programs formed from the sum total of available knowledge in a given field. The most extreme case is Douglas Lenat's CYC project, an attempt to build a 'walking encyclopaedia' containing *all* knowledge, a project whose expected completion Lenat measures not in person-hours but in person-*centuries*, since all the various bits and pieces of 'knowledge' must be individually encoded into CYC's program, the most enormous database ever imagined.

SIMULACRA OF INTELLIGENCE

In terms of the distinctions we made in **5.3.1**, classical AI seeks to produce a simulacrum of human intelligence, or of 'the language of thought'. For critics such as Hubert Dreyfus (1979), however, the idea that this amounts to thinking is simply false. He insists that any really intelligent machine (which he thinks is impossible in principle) must demonstrate more than just the *logical* elements of human thinking. A truly intelligent machine would have to be capable of actual conversation, with all the vagaries, hints, jokes, blind alleys and false starts that are features of human conversations. This would be evidence of intelligence idling, rather than working towards some particular intelligent function (calculating the number of atoms in a table, for example, or predicting sites of mineral deposits). Dreyfus's implicit criticism of classical AI, therefore, is that true intelligence is more than logical functions: it must be capable of 'non profit-making' behaviour. In other words, a truly intelligent machine would have to be capable of real stupidity.

However, Dreyfus and classical AI alike share the view that AI must be about replicating human intelligence in machines, by copying it into programs that are then downloaded into the computer. This is the approach rejected by Connectionist AI.

5.3.1   Automata: the basics

Connectionist AI

Neural networks or connectionist AI, however, follow the other line of simulation that runs through the mechanistic physiologies of the eighteenth century: the simulation not of functions (such as intelligence) but of organs (hearts, lungs, voice-boxes; **5.3.3**). Instead of modelling high-level cognitive functions like intelligence, connectionist AI asks: how do biological *brains* work? Dennett puts the issue starkly:

5.3.3   Self-augmenting engines: steampower against nature

> If . . . [classical] AI programs appear to be attempts to *model the mind*, Connectionist AI programs appear to be attempts to *model the brain*.
>
> (Dennett 1998: 225)

Neural nets therefore attempt to model the brain's physical apparatus. Brains consist of neurones (brain-cells) firing electrochemical signals to each other in what appears to be a rather scatter-gun manner. No neurone taken on its own is *intelligent*, however, although neurone activity is obviously essential to the realisation of intelligence in brains. Intelligence might not, connectionists reasoned, be intelligent *all the way down* to brain architecture, but might *emerge* at a higher level of complexity from the interactions of these 'stupid' bits and pieces called neurones. A better way, therefore, to create intelligent machines might be to simulate brain architecture using computers. Thus, instead of trying to program intelligence into a single computer working through a CPU, connectionists build what are called *neural nets*, in which several computers are linked together, each playing the role of a 'neurone', sending signals to many others at once.

In the jargon, classical AI is 'top-down', in that it imposes a program on the machine; connectionist AI is 'bottom-up', in that it wants the machine to 'grow' intelligence.

Like classical AI, neural net or connectionist AI has had its successes: although classical AI could easily turn chess-playing into a program, it could not do anything with face-recognition. Humans recognise faces in microseconds, but if you pause to consider how many actions a computer would have to perform in order to distinguish one face from amongst many – how many comparisons, examinations, analyses of nose-length, eye-colour and so on – and what mammoth database it would have to possess to facilitate these comparisons, facial recognition becomes, from the programmer's point of view, an awesomely vast task. This is because brains do not run through a series of instructions, one after the other, in order to execute 'face-recognising'. Memory (Reagan's face) and perception ('Reagan's face!') work simultaneously. Exploiting this idea, connectionist AI researchers have been able to build face-recognising neural networks. Instead of having the information programmed in, the neural net must *learn* to recognise a face. Neural nets, given only a basic operating code (much as humans are born with – the hardwired ability to suckle, make noise, breathe and excrete), are 'trained' to pick up relevant traits and to discard irrelevant ones, until the face is literally imprinted on its memory. This 'evolutionary' approach to learning in order eventually to realise intelligence differs strongly therefore from the 'program-in, intelligence-out' approach of classical AI. Connectionists hope that, given neural nets that are sufficiently parallel (that possess a quantity of 'neural' connections comparable to biological brains), intelligence may eventually *emerge*.

Since connectionism regards intelligence as an *emergent property*, it is based on an understanding of the brain as a complex, dynamical system. In such a system, highly complex things can and do emerge from very simple things, like a chemical clock from a mixture of two chemicals, or like intelligence from the interaction of stupid neurones. Neural networks are therefore not just simulations of biological brains, but *actual*, technological brains.

Alife

Alife's computer-based history can be traced back to Alan Turing and John von Neumann, the designers of Colossus and ENIAC, respectively. Turing was convinced that the development of organic forms (morphogenesis) must be computationally modellable and therefore really computational, writing a paper to that effect in 1952. Beginning in the 1940s, von Neumann designed what he called 'cellular automata', composed of 'cells' of information capable of self-replicating – much like living or 'natural automata' (Boden 1996: 5–6). Although John Horton Conway developed his *Game of Life* in the late 1960s, AI dominated the sciences of the artificial from the 1950s on, until Alife regained some prominence in the 1980s due to the work of Thomas Ray and Chris Langton, both of whom implemented Alife programs and began to theorise about the field. Ray proposed in 1989 that the 'virtual organisms' grown in his *Tierra* program ought to be 'set free' to roam and replicate wherever they might find a niche on the net (Robertson *et al.*, 1996: 146). Outside the computer, however, Alife has had a long career, based on whatever technology happens to be 'the living technique of the age' (Wiener [1948] 1962: 40). Such approaches, which assume their current form in robotics (Warwick 1998; Dennett 1998: 153–170), are therefore known as 'hard Alife', while computationally based work is called 'soft Alife'. A third area, exemplified by the developments in reproductive technologies and 'genetic engineering', is sometimes known as 'wet Alife'. Apart from simulating biological brains in technology, one field of wet Alife known as 'neuromorphic engineering' is concerned to build 'brainlike systems . . . using real neurones' (Boden 1990: 2). In this context, biology simply becomes another technology.

Alife and biology

There are two reasons why Alife in general and Dawkins's simulations in particular are viewed as relevant methods for studying genetic behaviour, one stemming from biology itself and the other from computer science. First, the biological reason. Ever since Crick

Poundstone (1985) gives instructions for how to program this game into an IBM PC. Similarly, Dawkins (1991) provides his own Alife evolutionary simulation in *Blind Watchmaker: the Program of the Book*. Dawkins developed his influential theory of 'the selfish gene' (Dawkins 1976) on the basis of observations of a computer model of evolutionary behaviour (see Dennett 1998: 233n). Later in that work, Dawkins went on to propound an influential but contested evolutionary model of cultural phenomena such as ideas, musics, behaviours and social codes (1976: 206) and Watson decrypted the structure and behaviour of DNA in 1966, evolutionary biologists have generally accepted that there is a strong parallel between information processing and the activity of DNA. DNA is a code that is translated and carried by 'messenger RNA' to form new strands of DNA, much as information is the product of messages translated into codes, transmitted, and retranslated into messages.

Crick and Watson laid out the chemical structure and behaviour of the genetic code in 1966. Within a few years, biologists were already avowing the informational basis of life. Some, such as Jacques Monod, went so far as to rename genetics as 'microscopic cybernetics' (1971). Clearly, such a cybernetics must differ significantly from the version of it made famous for media studies through Shannon and Weaver. Such cybernetics aims above all at the reduction of noise to zero, and therefore at maximal information content. If all noise were eliminated from the reproductive process, for example, then there could be no evolutionary change, and the appearance of any and all offspring could be predicted on the basis of the genetic information taken from its parents. If, on the other hand, there were nothing but noise, there would remain no basic structure that all members of a given species exemplified. Thus reproductive or molecular cybernetics must consist of a simultaneous maintenance of perfectly reproducible information (giving humans, for example, the correct number of limbs) *and* a certain amount of noise (accounting for change and the appearance of individuals).

Using a science fiction of a Martian exobiologist attempting to distinguish living things from machines on earth, Monod runs through many characteristics shared by all things, organic and technological. He shows how, to the Martian biologist, every

Deleuze and Guattari's theory of biology–technology relations is profoundly influenced by Monod's cybernetics, which they cite repeatedly throughout *Anti-Oedipus* ([1964] 1984)

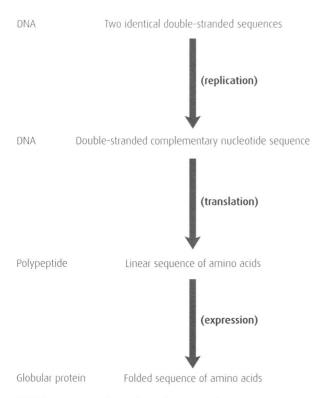

5.15 The structure of DNA (Monod 1971: 103)

apparently distinguishing characteristic fails. If we say, for example, that technological things will show their manufactured character in the fact that their structure is exactly identical in all instances, the same is manifestly true of crystals, bees and humans, all of which show exactly the same amount of structural *invariance* and complexity as do technological things. One part, therefore, of molecular cybernetics is devoted to the maintenance of order, repeating the structure of the species in all individuals. Monod's 'structural invariance' is therefore like cybernetic restraint, scrupulously maintaining order by the same processes of feedback inhibition and activation as a thermostatic device. Moreover, organisms, like crystals, are composed of 'self-replicating machines' such as von Neumann defined (**5.3.5**), whereas artefacts – human-made technologies, Monod says – are not so clearly so. This yields a degree of 'freedom' for the morphogenetically autonomous object – freedom, that is, from external causation: each organism applies its own restraints to itself as it develops. Finally, organic cybernetics achieve such autonomy through 'teleonomy', by which Monod understands 'being imbued with project' *by nature* – 'such as', he adds, 'the making of artefacts' (1971: 20), thus repeating Marx's formulation of *homo faber*. Neither of these latter are of themselves, however, absent from artefacts. Alife is composed entirely of self-replicating machines, while the problem of identifying the source of the project with which a thing is imbued is made manifest by the example of the camera. Is the project of capturing images inherent in the camera itself or in the eye? Since the functions of both are in the end identical, although the hardware is different in each case, there can be no quick solution to the problem. Monod's answer to this is not to decide once and for all which objects projects do or do not reside in, but rather to suggest that the differences between technological and biological things lies in a quantitative threshold, which he calls a thing's 'teleonomic level' which is set by the quantity of information that must be transferred in order to realise that object (1971: 24–25). Clearly, this is higher in a complex biological individual than in any technological thing (although this is not necessarily so – consider the complexity of information transfer in a fully functional neural net).

Monod's account of microscopic cybernetics therefore offers provisional means for identifying organisms as distinct from machines. But the rationale for his assertion that the organism is composed of many molecular cybernetic systems stems from the fact that he derives the two major functions – teleonomy and invariance – from actual constituents of biological systems:

> The distinction between teleonomy and invariance is more than a mere logical abstraction. It is warranted on grounds of chemistry. Of the two basic classes of biological macromolecules, one, that of proteins, is responsible for almost all teleonomic structures and performances; while genetic invariance is linked exclusively to the other class, that of nucleic acids.
>
> (Monod 1971: 27)

Once again, then, the distinction between the 'natural' construction of humanity and its construction of artefacts turns out, as we saw in our analysis of Marx's extensionalism, to be a mere quantitative threshold. Just as at a certain point technological extensions of human functions begin to alter those functions in turn, so too, at a certain point, the quantity of information transfer involved in the production of things is all Monod can assure us separates technological from biological systems. Nothing could make this issue clearer than the Human Genome Project.

The Human Genome Project is an attempt to map the entire gene sequence for a 'typical' human. It has been competitively pursued over the last decade by two groups: The Wellcome Institute, a UK-based charitable institution that wants full and immediate disclosure, via the net, of all their findings, and Celera Genomics, a US-based biotechnology company, which has been patenting in a piecemeal fashion those segments of the genome it has decoded. This battle between publicly funded academe and privately funded profit-making corporate culture has something of an epically cyberpunk quality about it. We are witnessing the genesis (almost literally) of genetic capitalism, the patenting of life. It is entirely imaginable that, for example, if Celera-patented genomic by-products were purchased for, say, infertility treatments, ownership of the resultant offspring could be legally contested. All that is needed now is a cultural sub-group of genome-hackers, disaffected biotechnology consultants, and a novel, perhaps entitled *Genomancer*, to spark – or perhaps catalyse – an entire new literary sub-genre. Moreover, given implants such as Kevin Warwick has been experimenting with since 1998, we can imagine patented genome-strings downloaded into implants to get past security systems, only to leak into the implantee's body.

From the current perspective, however, what is fascinating about the genome is the fact that it has been impossible to produce until such time as computing had reached what, after Monod, we might call a sufficiently high teleonomic level. The genome must, moreover, be housed in a computer memory, since human memory is insufficient for the job. This makes the genome a properly hybrid creature: it is a blueprint of human life that can only be realised as a blueprint in a technological medium. Here 'man' has been extended so far he has seeped into the machines. It is the role of these machines to set about reorganising the blueprint for manufacturing humanity, to eliminate imperfections and enhance existing capacities. Genomic propaganda regularly promises cures for cancer, longevity enhancement, an end to birth defects, and so on, although these remain for the moment of a science fictional order. There are already a variety of genetic anomalies available on the market: Dupont's Oncomouse™, a patented cancer experiment that is no longer a creature of nature but of commerce. GM foods, of course, are a well-known political horror story, prompting fearsome predictions of the rise of Franken-pharms to replace agriculture with pharmiculture. Each of these developments is contested, however, in official and unofficial manner, resulting in truly bizarre demographic combinations: bioethics committees composed of priests, politicians, scientists and lawyers deciding on the paths permissible for the re-engineering of the species, and modified grassroots political protest groups campaigning against such 'double helix hubris' (Harpignies 1997). In each case of biotechnology, be it the genome or Flavr Savr, the world's first commercially available GM vegetable (or is it a fruit?), however, the important thing to note is the extension of technology into nature. No longer content to sit idly by while culture and nature struggle over their two cultures, technology, and especially corporate biotechnology, has entered the fray, cyberneticising everything.

Perhaps when a new version of Monod's *Chance and Necessity* is written (it was reissued in 2000), the visitor trying to distinguish technology from biology will be itself technological, not just of another species, therefore, but another phylum.

See Haraway (1997) for an analysis of Oncomouse, and Myerson (2000) for a discussion of Haraway's work regarding actually existing hybrids. For a general, critical overview of 'Frankenpharming', see Harpignies (1997)

Alife and computation

Computer science did not have to wait long for intimations of artificial life. John von Neumann, who designed the computer ENIAC (along with Turing's Colossus, the first actual computer in history), was, like Vaucanson and von Kempelen (**5.3.2**), Diderot and Babbage (**5.3.3**), interested in constructing artificial automata that not only replicated various aspects of natural automata but, crucially, that reproduced. He thus asked:

> What kind of logical organisation is sufficient for an automaton to reproduce itself? Von Neumann had the familiar natural phenomenon of self-reproduction in mind when he posed [this question], but he was not trying to simulate the self-reproduction of a natural system at the level of genetics and biochemistry. He wished to abstract from the natural self-reproduction problem its logical form.
>
> (A.W. Burks on von Neumann, cited by Langton in Boden 1996: 47)

In other words, if Dawkins is concerned to *imitate* the actions of various evolutionary strategies, von Neumann was concerned to *construct automata* – which were called *cellular automata* – that had an appropriate reproductive strategy for their environment. This same distinction is core to artificial life. Chris Langton, author of what is widely regarded as the field's 'manifesto' (Langton, in Boden 1996: 39–94) writes that artificial life

> attempts to (1) synthesise the process of evolution (2) in computers, and (3) will be interested in *whatever emerges from the process, even if the results have no analogues in the natural world*.
>
> (Langton, in Boden 1996: 40; emphasis added)

If biology understands life *as it is* by taking living things apart (analysis), Alife wishes to understand life *as it could be* by putting it together (synthesis), in whatever way it happens. Alife is therefore referred to by Thomas Ray, for example, as 'synthetic biology' (in Boden 1996: 111–145). Both Langton and Ray, therefore, espouse what is called 'strong Alife', rather than its 'weak' variety, the concern of which is, as is Dawkins', merely to *simulate* 'life as it is'.

From 'self-moving things' to 'self-organisation'

The history of automata, from hydraulic or pneumatic, clockwork, galvanic or calorific, constantly runs close to the line of life that animates or drives these attempts to construct artificial life forms. Alife crosses this line, turning biological things into technologies (wet Alife) and technological things into biological ones (strong Alife). The very phrase 'synthetic biology' shows that the line dividing simulacra from automata, and technology from nature, has been crossed. Science is no longer exclusively concerned merely to understand the natural world; it actively desires to construct an artificial one. It is technology that has made it possible to cross this line; specifically, as point (2) of Langton's definition of Alife states, computing technology.

At the very beginnings of the digital computer in the 1940s and 1950s, Alan Turing began to work on computers and biology, and John von Neumann began to work on cellular automata. Cellular automata are pieces of code that are not only self-moving (automata), but self-replicating. Margaret Boden describes the cellular automaton as

> a computational 'space' made up of many cells. Each cell changes according to the same set of rules, taking into account the states of neighbouring cells. The system moves in time-steps [i.e., according to fixed periods], all the cells normally changing . . . together . . . After each global change, the rules are applied again . . .
>
> (Boden, in Boden 1996: 6)

Then the whole process begins again, ad infinitum. With the cellular automaton, von Neumann therefore succeeded in giving computational form to biological reproduction. Not only did the automaton change with each cycle of global changes, every time the cycle was repeated different changes resulted. Thus, from a simple set of initial instructions, cellular automata produced complex and unpredictable forms. What changed the forms the CA thus produced was the state of all the cells undergoing transformation, not an overall program with instructions that the CA change in some predetermined manner. Such phenomena are known as *self-organising*, in so far as it is the phenomena themselves, and not an overarching program, that organise themselves into a non-preprogrammed form.

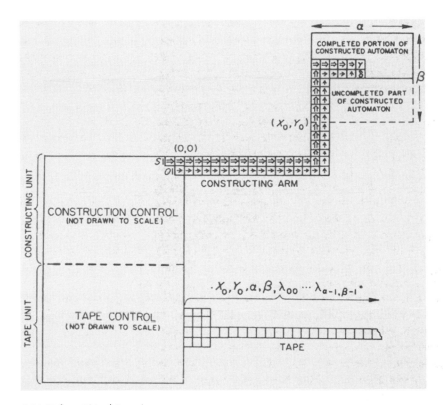

5.16 CA from Virtual Organisms.

5.3.6 Conclusion

Technology does not, as it were, veer away from the physical towards serving a purely human culture. On the contrary, by emphasising the difference between tools and machines, used and user, servant and master, we have seen that there is no historical constancy in the human user being the master, and the non-human technology, the servant. A machine, in other words, uses tools just as humans do; and, just as humans can be tools for human masters, so too they can be tools for non-human machines. This is not to say that there are never (or have never been) periods when control of machines did devolve to human users, merely that such periods tend to come under threat during times of large-scale technological expansion, or what Ellul (1964) calls technological self-augmentation.

Rather than veering from the physical to culture, technology veers towards the physics of living things, towards life. Always at the limit of a culture's technological imaginary, machines approximate life throughout history, whether in a form that *looks like us* (simulacra) or one that does not (automata). While the cyborg is the most widespread contemporary cultural manifestation of this tendency, it is not the only one, as we have seen. Rather, the devolution of automata from simulacra has meant that cyborgs, almost always given human form, pose the wrong questions about the prospects of 'artificial life'. By forsaking the prospect of the living simulacrum (like the figure of the 'double' that runs throughout a certain species of uncanny literature), the science of Alife is attempting to grow life-forms from the ground up, that do not resemble previously existing creatures but resemble their mechanisms. This has been made possible by the increasing proximity, during the age of information, of genetics and computation, the online marriage of which has given us the genome.

By placing the automaton centre-stage in histories of technology, we can see the constancy of this tendency towards life. However, it is not a continuous or cumulative tendency. Technological change forces new technologies to start again.

What we can learn therefore from the history of automata is the following:

• that the cyborgs of contemporary culture are importantly *not new*, but have precursors at every stage of technological development;

• that therefore *life* and *technology* have converged and diverged throughout history, forming an important constant throughout the history of technology;

• that every time the question '*what is technology?*' is answered, history is rewritten to suit, and the answers assume the status of a set of unbreakable assumptions ('normal' technology);

• that these assumptions – and that view of history – are disrupted and problematised with every change in the technological base of a given culture ('crisis' technology);

• finally, that during periods of normalised technology, the oppositions of human and machine, nature and artifice, nature and culture, the physical and the human, go unexamined.

To emphasise: these phenomena are historically cyclical, recurring at every technological age, as Wiener says. For the present, *digital machines represent for us a crisis technology, in so far as all the old stabilities regarding the relations between nature, culture and technology are once again disrupted.* This creates uncertainties for the cultural analysis of physical things, of course, but at the same time it provides us with opportunities to re-examine what has been taken for granted since the cultural approach to technology became normalised, and to reopen the questions that led it to become so. The histories of previous periods of crisis technologies provide us with glimpses into the form those problems have taken, and therefore provide guides as to how we might contemporarily pose those, and perhaps new, problems. Since history, however, is not theoretically innocent, but laden with often unacknowledged assumptions, it is also necessary to look at the theories those histories are made to subserve. In consequence, this is the task to which the following section now turns.

5.4 THEORIES OF CYBERCULTURE

Introduction

The science of cybernetics lies at the artificial heart of cyberculture. It is concerned with control and communication in animal *and* machine – in biology *and* technology. Although popularly associated only with digital technologies, cyberculture actually encompasses the relations between nature and technology, as we have seen. Since we have now looked at technology and biology, we will begin by taking a closer look at cybernetics. We will then move on to look at a number of theories of cyberculture itself; that is, the attempts to map it across the three domains that have structured **Part 5**: technology, nature and culture.

5 CYBERCULTURE: TECHNOLOGY, NATURE AND CULTURE

5.4.1 Cybernetics and human–machine relations

A short history of classical cybernetics

Cybernetics grew up, towards the end of the Second World War, around the work of a group of mathematicians, engineers and physicists investigating problems of communications systems and anti-aircraft targeting systems. The latter problems were the special preserve of Norbert Wiener, who wrote concerning them to Vannevar Bush, a computing pioneer, in 1940. Wiener was a mathematician and physicist working on problems of prediction, and therefore control: in order to target a moving object, that object's trajectory and speed need to be calculated quickly. Never attack the enemy where he is, but where he will be. Vannevar Bush and John von Neumann, another cyberneticist, were pioneers in computing machines, working on replacing mechanical calculating procedures (**5.3.5**) with electronic ones. Von Neumann, together with economic theorist Oscar Morgenstern, also developed an influential model of economic behaviour known as 'games theory', spreading cybernetics into the social world. Finally, in common with all cybernetics, Claude Shannon, working at the Bell Telephone Labs, was interested in the theoretical design and practical installation of maximally efficient communications systems. Shannon and Weaver's model of communications has since achieved infamy in media studies as less a theory of communication than of *propaganda* (Fiske 1990: 6–7), in that it is concerned only with the *successful* and *one-way* communication of information. Less pejoratively, however, this account of cybernetic theories of communications highlights the relation between communication and control. To understand this it is necessary not to think of all communication as verbal or symbolic. Communication takes place, argues cybernetics, when a signal produces a response, such as when a tongue of flame singes the flesh on your arm, and you withdraw it. This is not a message to be understood, but one inducing an action or reaction. It is this dimension which has drawn most fire from media studies commentators as it seems to reduce the idea of communication to one of mere 'response' or 'reaction'.

5.3.5 Life and intelligence in the digital age

However, in order to see the contribution that cybernetics makes to an understanding of human–machine relationships, we must take note of three main principles in its accounts of the processes of control and communication. These are:

1 Feedback, positive and negative.

2 Restriction produces action, not choice.

3 Information varies inversely as noise.

FEEDBACK

Feedback occurs in two ways: first, negatively. Negative feedback is what keeps a system operational within fixed parameters. For example, when a thermostat cuts power to a heat source it is doing so to prevent overheating. When it sends a signal to the heat source to bring it back online, it does so to prevent cold. As a consequence, a given temperature is maintained within a certain range of fluctuations: we could say that it is fundamentally conservative in that respect. Negative feedback is so-called because it 'negates' the tendency to continue heating, or to discontinue heating altogether.

Second, positive feedback is the type we are familiar with from live electronic music. The signal is too close to the source, reacting back on it to amplify the amount of noise (as opposed to information) produced by the system. If unchecked, positive feedback will continue to amplify until the speaker is destroyed. Similarly, if a steam engine without a governor were to keep building up pressure it would become an explosive rather than a motive force. Positive feedback leads to the eventual collapse of the system in which it is generated. But while the system survives it, positive feedback constantly changes the state of the system, and sometimes introduces surprising and unpredictable behaviours on the part of that system. In short, all change can be understood as the product of positive feedback.

RESTRICTION

When cyberneticists discuss control they are interested in preventing positive feedback and maximising negative feedback. The maximal state of negative feedback is total predictability in the system: it will never do anything remotely unexpected, and will continue indefinitely to serve its appointed purpose. For this reason, an action is never a consequence of an agent's choice but rather of the restriction of all possible actions bar one. This is interesting not only from the point of view of efficiently functioning machines but because it is based upon the realisation that the operation of a machine may lead to several possible outcomes; and the task of cybernetics is to see how only one of these, a preferred outcome, can be ensured. In this sense, cybernetics is 'realist' about producing an 'actual' outcome from a range of possible outcomes. This, as we will see, is important

5.4.2 Cybernetics and the virtual   when discussing what is meant by the 'virtual' (see 5.4.2).

For the moment, the important thing to grasp is this. We noted earlier that Wiener was interested in prediction systems, and with this sense of cybernetic restriction we get some sense of how it is that cybernetics sees things: any current state of affairs – what we might call the 'present actual' – is the consequence of eliminating alternative futures. If these alternatives need to be eliminated or negated it can only be because they in some sense exist in the present as potential outcomes, which would happen were they not checked. In other words, they exist as inherent tendencies. The important thing about such a view is that it incorporates the possible into the present, and produces the actual by splitting the present and discarding what remains. Control is not only conservative, then, it is also predictive, and *this sense of the future acting on the present* has become a core theme of cyberfictions.

INFORMATION AND NOISE

Classical cybernetics was principally concerned to eliminate noise from communications channels. One good way to understand what noise is, is to consider a telephone signal: when it is clear, and neither the apparatus nor environmental obstacles interfere (producing feedback in the first instance, and distorting or eliminating the phone signal in the second), the greatest amount of information is produced (both callers can hear each other perfectly). Simply put, the more interference in the signal, the less information is received. The clearest signal would therefore produce maximum information, and the least clear, the most noise. In any signal, however, there is always some noise, and the more information transmitted, therefore, the more the noise increases. For classical cybernetics, noise is a bad thing, and no information can result as noise increases.

Post-classical cybernetics

Cybernetics is not confined to the interests of geeks in Second World War military command, communication and control (otherwise known as C3; see De Landa 1991). Its proponents theorised about serial and parallel computing, and produced early valve computer systems. Symptomatic of the principal development, however, is cybernetics' concern with questions of learning. Gregory Bateson, in the late 1960s and 1970s, for example, was putting forward the notion that perfect replication of a message (i.e. perfect information retrieval) amounted to zero learning, echoing the adage that 'one repays one's teachers badly by imitation'. Learning always involves deviation, departure from a norm, and so on. While this may not sound startling, it opens important new questions.

First, it suggests that restriction, in the sense discussed above, not only destroys alternatives in order to arrive at perfect responses but also takes cues from information received and builds on them. Although cybernetics sees control as negative feedback, eliminating all but one response, learning involves positive feedback, producing new responses.

Second, taken alongside John von Neumann's theoretical account of the differences between parallel and serial computing, positive feedback devices became extremely interesting for artificial intelligence researchers (**5.3.4**). Rather than asking, in a cybernetically negative way, 'how can we ensure that the war machine – i.e., soldiers, tanks, planes, communications systems, strategies, and so on – obeys our commands to the letter?', they began to ask, in a cybernetically positive manner, 'how can we get machines to learn?' (**5.3.5**).

Third, the virtues of positive feedback began to be explored in other fields, notably chemistry and genetics. In chemistry, for example, questions began to be asked about spontaneously emerging 'order out of chaos', something many phenomena seemed to exhibit, but of which there was no available theoretical model. Hence there arose approaches such as non-linear, or 'far from equilibrium' dynamics (**5.2.2**). In genetics, perfect information transfer would mean no change from generation to generation, thus annihilating the genetic basis of evolution, which depends on change, and there could be no genetic means of accounting for mutation. Imperfect transcriptions therefore became a focus of research, explicitly premissed on positive feedback, and on change rather than control.

Fourth, rather than a principle of negation, therefore, selection became a positive principle. In answering the question 'why this outcome rather than another?', scientists' attention switched from a process of enforcing desired outcomes to seeking desirable ones. As Manuel de Landa puts it, every far-from-equilibrium phenomenon is formed as if it were in the wake of a kind of 'guiding head' or 'searching device' (de Landa 1993: 795) that eventually 'selects' a particular order. As opposed to the negative method of applying constraints to the system, this positive method cannot guarantee a particular outcome. Thus, storm-chasers learn to recognise the signs of impending storms, but there is no guarantee that a storm will occur, or that it will occur where it seems most likely. The storm has a life of its own.

PCs are serial computers, in so far as they have one central processing unit (CPU) through which all tasks must be processed, one after the other. A parallel computer involves several processors, and conducts several tasks at once. When von Neumann made this distinction, he considered computers to be inherently serial, but brains – 'natural automata' – to be inherently parallel. See von Neumann ([1958] 1999)

5.3.4 The construction of inanimate reason

5.3.5 Life and intelligence in the digital age

If this use of the phrase 'war machine' sounds metaphorical, evoking only the efficiently co-ordinated actions of bodies of soldiers, aircraft, tanks, etc. towards a single target, consider the US Gulf War pilots' complaints of 'information overload' from their cockpits. In the latter, the pilot no longer surveys a natural, but a simulated, vista, and receives more information from on-board computational devices than human neurophysiology proved capable of dealing with. The 'war machine' is no metaphor. See de Landa (1991)

5.2.2 Causalities

Storm-chasers feature not only as the heroes of Jan de Bont's film *Twister* (1998), but also in Bruce Sterling's novel *Heavy Weather* (1995). Sterling offers excellent illustrations of the above ideas throughout that work

Again, Sterling's *Distraction* (1999) provides a host of examples of such runaway processes. Set around the exploits of a political fixer in the US after its entire online economy has been wiped out by a Chinese electromagnetic pulse, the novel's hero expends all his energies trying to tap sources of disorder and to turn them into new forms of order, new political structures. These structures are not known in advance, but occur only within the specific process of which he makes himself part. As regards feedback in fiction, David Porush (1975) argued that cybernetic fictions (such as Thomas Pynchon's *Gravity's Rainbow* or *The Crying of Lot 49*) consist in a series of structures that contain their own momentum, and thus build like feedback rather than progressing like standard linear narratives (beginning, middle, end). More recently (in Broadhurst-Dixon and Cassidy 1997), Porush has made the same point in such a way as to involve the reader in the feedback: any text causes changes in the reader's brain, that in turn cause changes in the reader's normal cognitive behaviours. In this sense, it is always true to say 'that book changed my life'

Deleuze is often thought important *vis-à-vis* cyberculture for two reasons. One is the concept of the 'desiring machine' he and analyst Félix Guattari invented in their *Anti-Oedipus* ([1974] 1984); the other is Deleuze's own repeated engagements with the concept of the virtual, beginning with his 1966 book on Bergson (Deleuze 1988), and running through *Difference and Repetition* ([1968] 1994). We will address the latter concept in 5.4.2

5.4.2   Cybernetics and the virtual

5.2.4   Determinisms

Finally, since cybernetics never discriminated against a component of a system as to whether it was biological or technological, feedback ceased to be confined to the study of communications in general and instead began to find applications in chemistry, biology, economics, AI, Alife, sociology (Eve *et al.* 1997), politics and literary studies. It is arguably from the prevalence of runaway positive feedback that cyberculture, concerned as it is with rapid and unstoppable change, takes its cues.

The smallest circuit

Gilles Deleuze, a philosopher often associated with cyberculture (see for example Lévy 1998; Critical Art Ensemble 1995; Genosko 1998; Ansell-Pearson 1997), took the work of Bergson ([1911] 1920), who reduced cinema from an emergent art form to a producer of 'mechanical thinking', and sought to demolish its intellectual significance, as the philosophical basis of his own two-volume work on cinema (Deleuze 1986; 1989). In that work he put forward his thesis concerning the 'mental automaton' that is produced by the combination of cinematic spectacle and viewer. Deleuze takes this combination seriously, saying that this mental automaton consists of a body made of nerves, flesh and light. It is formed because the cinema is a device that creates a feedback circuit between organic bodies and sensory stimuli (sounds, images), that is so complete it forms a new system. It does this because the cinematic sign creates the shortest, most intense circuit between nerve signals and impulses. Once the circuit has formed, these impulses no longer come from the screen to the viewer, but form circuits with the brain that form in turn other circuits, mixing a multitude of cinematic signs with bodies. Crucial to this mental automaton is that it is a new system formed *in situ*, rather than a mere bringing together of separate organic and technological systems.

Deleuze's conception of the automaton demonstrates its allegiances to cybernetics in that it is not about bodies, but circuits. Moreover, rather than explaining its emergence as the effect of a cause, Deleuze presents the circuit as formed given simple contact between the brain and the cinema. The circuit, in other words, is self-organising (**5.2.4**). Further, the 'mental automaton' is physical, involving new circuits of neurones and light. From this, all the others devolve, in increasing degrees of complexity – sign and nerve, image and physical action. Being the shortest circuit, finally, it 'loops' more frequently than the others, thus forming a *subject* emerging from the circuit that experiences all the others. Deleuze thus develops a conception of a cybernetic subject that is neither reducibly technological nor biological, that self-organises, and that not only forms the basis for reconceiving debates about media effects and the causal force of images but also suggests that there is space neither for agency nor mechanical determinism (such as Deleuze finds, to an extent, in Bergson's critique of the cinema).

We can see then that Deleuze undertakes to develop Bergson's 'mechanical thinking': cinema is not the flat presentation of events unfolding mechanically in time, annulling our own sense of 'lived time', but rather a positive feedback circuit that forms a cybernetic subject specific to the physical environment that is the cinema: the 'mental automaton'.

Hybrids

Barring the mental automaton, all the cybernetic devices we have examined thus far – factory and worker, steam engine and governor, the telephone and the callers, pilot and aircraft, and any machine whatever – consist of combinations of parts that can be undone: the steersman (*kybernetes*) leaves his ship, workers leave factories, audiences leave cinemas, soldiers go on leave and detach themselves from the war machine, and so on. Although

Plant (1997), for instance, insists that all cybernetic systems constitute cyborgs simply by virtue of utilising technological and biological components, the cyborg itself, as figured in cyberculture more generally, is not so detachable.

Here we return to the distinction between automata that look like humans (simulacra), and those that do not (**5.3.2**). Factories, war machines, cinema circuits, and so on, do not look like humans but are automata in the strict sense, in that, once 'plugged in', they are *self-moving things*. Almost invariably, however (although there are notable exceptions, such as the cybernetic systems that run *The Matrix*), contemporary cyborgs do look like humans. Arnold Schwarzenegger's *Terminator* cyborgs vaguely resemble humans, as does *Robocop*, Stelarc, *Steampunk's* Cole Blacquesmith. *Star Trek: the Next Generation's* Lieutenant Data not only looks human, but notoriously wants to become more so – something the *Star Trek* franchise has demonstrated an alarmingly soapy determination to achieve, even humanising their unstoppably inhuman cybernetic nemesis the Borg through the figure of *Voyager's* Seven of Nine. Despite the questions of body boundaries posed by Allucquere Rosanne Stone (1995) concerning the precise limits of Stephen Hawking's body, the physicist remains manifestly human.

5.3.2 Clockwork: technology and nature, combined

It is not an objection to the 'self-moving' status of automata that they need a power source. As Marx says, the machine "consumes coal, oil etc . . . just as the worker consumes food" (1993: 693)

However, cyberpunk fiction focuses less on shiny metal cyborgs like the Terminator, or on the oily iron and muscle cyborgs known to Marx, than on the technology of the implant. Beginning with the contemporarily well-known artificial heart, *Neuromancer's* world contains artificially grown organs of all sorts, machine implants like eyes that record and playback the light stimuli they receive, undernail razors, flip-top nano-filament containing thumbs, and so on. Technology ceases to be big, but becomes instead invasive, sticky. Like the contact lens, it sinks quickly beneath the horizon of our attention as soon as it descends below the skin.

We are, of course, mixing fictional and factual sources of cyborgs here. But key to this discussion is not whether a fictional cyborg has less reality than a factual one; rather, it concerns identifying the *prevalent type* of the cyborg in contemporary culture, whether manifest in images, narrative, surgeries or laboratories.

Thus, rather than the simple, separable cyborg (pilot and aircraft, ear and hearing aid, etc.), Kevin Warwick, Professor of Cybernetics at the UK's Reading University, has been conducting experiments with invasive cybernetic technologies, with the express purpose of 'upgrading' himself to become a cyborg. He has already tried implanting a transmitter chip beneath the surface of his skin, as well as, more recently, a receptor chip. The purpose of these experiments is to interface the body and technology directly, through the medium of the electricity that nervous impulses and computer signals share. He hopes to create direct, person-to-person (or cyborg-to-cyborg) communications links, as well as ultimately, thought-operated computation. Such experiments concern direct neural interfaces linking technology and biology indissociably, changing what counts as a biological and a technological system. That this technological trajectory was first announced in cyberpunk fiction matters little. What does matter is that such fiction, and such experiments, bear witness to the indissociability of biology and technology that is cybernetics' core insight.

While Warwick explicitly calls the creature he is becoming a cyborg, others maintain the use of the alternative term *hybrid*. Donna Haraway, famous for her 'Manifesto for Cyborgs' (Haraway 1991), is one such theorist. By emphasising the hybrid, Haraway effectively re-biologises the militarily-tainted discourses of cybernetics. A hybrid is a biologically grafted organism (a new variety of rose, or a new breed of show dog), a mix of species. Of course, we are already familiar with the way that biotechnology has technologised the biological, making hybrids a bio-technological product. The Flavr-Savr tomato (Haraway 1997: 56), for example, the first GM foodstuff available on the US market, is raw (or should that be 'cooked'?) biotech, rather than 'nature's own' (Myerson 2000: 24).

Other hybridisers such as Bruno Latour (1993), whose work is a direct attempt to generate an anthropology of non-human things – that is, to frame the non-human social agents such as machines, viruses, mudslides, and so on, within a culture that does not reduce them to tools of humanity – insist that the hybrid is not necessarily an individual organism, but something much larger. His view is that human and non-human things form hybrid entities by virtue of the networks they share (**5.2.3**). Nothing is any longer purely human, not because of physical changes to the human being itself but because of changes to the environment in which humans live. We live in a bio-technological world where we are indissociably networked with other things, so that for every social action we engage in, there are agents that are human as well as agents that are not (machines, weather systems, viruses, institutions, and so on). Latour thus proposes a shift away from attention to a world which is somehow purely human to a world which is resolutely and increasingly hybrid.

What both the scientist and the cultural theorist, Warwick and Haraway, share with the world of cyberpunk fiction is an acknowledgement that the grafts between biological and technological parts and systems are becoming far more intimate. Cyborg components belong to a scale beneath that of the organism thus cyborganised: no longer is man spliced to machine by way of a steering wheel, a rudder, or a conveyor belt; instead, the machines have got you 'under their skin'. On this view, shared by novelists, scientists and cultural scientists, humanity faces the reconstruction of the species for the first time in its existence.

All the elements present in cyberculture's prehistory, then, which we encountered in **5.3**, remain present within its contemporary manifestation: automata that look like us (simulacra) and automata that don't; artificial life and natural technologies; debates on what lives and what causes, what determines and what acts. The distinction between the hand-held tool (the 'extension of man') and the environmental, 'self-augmenting' machine (**5.3.1**) reappears in contemporary cyberculture as that between micro and macro technologies: cyborgs as technologically enhanced biological units, and cyborgs as biologically powered technological units.

The Machinic Phylum

The above issues stem entirely from considering the interlacing of biology and technology that is at the centre of cybernetics. However, cybernetics is not the only theoretical approach premised on such a synthesis. For example, Deleuze and Guattari's concept of the machinic phylum places their thinking about machines on a firmly biological footing.

It is often assumed that their use of the term 'phylum' must be metaphorical; however, it is absolutely to be understood in the context of supplying a microbiology, a morphology, and an ecology of machines. Each of these three fields signals a scale in machine connections, beginning with the smallest (the permanently coupling desiring machines), up to the largest (the mechanosphere), with the phylum intermediate between them. By placing the machinic phylum on such a biological footing, however, machines become fundamental to the possibility of biology.

They take their concept of desiring machines from three sources: from Marx, they take the idea of material production; from Freud, the idea of desire; from Monod, the idea of microscopic cybernetics. Desiring machines are not to be understood as occupants of individual psyches but as the molecular assemblers of things, just as for Monod proteins and nucleic acids build bodies. Similarly, they are not metaphors, but real, producing not fantasies, as Freud would have us believe, but reality. 'The unconscious is not a theatre', they write, 'but a factory' (Deleuze and Guattari [1974] 1984: 311). Instead of identifying the machines with the already individuated psyche, so that 'we' human individuals simply *become* machines or machine-like, they identify them with the microscopic, pre-individual processes that form all chemical and biological bodies. These are the machine processes underlying all things. Thus the psychoanalytic focus on the subject is overturned in favour of the pre-personal material production of the realities of body and world. At the same time, Marx's grounding of material reality in the actions and productions of social human beings gives way to a microscopic material reality that is truly machinic: nature not only builds machines, it *is* machines. Monod, finally, is taken literally, but without his illegitimate attempts to maintain the superiority of complex bodies over molecular processes.

Just as they undercut the level of the individual, so they leap from these molecular assemblers to their next category in the biology of machines – the phylum. Where we hear and read a great deal about cyborgs as 'new species', they remain, on such views, members of the same phylum (a higher order of classification than species). In other words, with the concept of the machinic phylum, they are indicating that the real issue does not lie in the alterations wrought upon a single species – man – but on the phylum, a higher order of classification that is principally concerned with formal similarities and differences rather than with individuation. Species are defined as individuals by heredity: only members of the same species produce offspring. Phyla are not defined by heredity, but by shared form or characteristics. The machinic phylum therefore comprises all those things that share machinic form. We do not ask, under the rubric of the machinic phylum, what a machine *is*, but rather *what are the variations in its forms*. Cybernetics constitutes, in this sense, a characteristic morphology of self-regulating, self-producing assemblages, regardless of their material components, and is thus an attempt at a machinic phylum. Just as Wiener saw the remit of cybernetics extending from animal to machine, so too Deleuze and Guattari see 'a single machinic phylum . . . as much artificial as natural' (1988: 407). The phylum forms the basis on which all singular things are effected, cut from its flow, as it were. Because they are concerned only with one species (life) and with one phylum (the machinic), Deleuze and Guattari effectively ignore individual things in favour of constant variations of components. All organisms, in this sense, are cybernetic from the outset, and in consequence, cyborgs and artificial life forms do not constitute new species but merely constantly changing states of matter and organisation. And the machine is the very paradigm of this constant disassembly and reassembly: machines are not species of life, they *are* life in its purest state.

If everything belongs to the machinic phylum this seems to leave little room for the mechanosphere. However, Deleuze and Guattari use the latter concept to reject the idea of a purely biological evolution: 'There is no biosphere . . ., but everywhere the same Mechanosphere' (1988: 69). What this means is that everything that is organised matter – organic or otherwise – is a machine, differently realised. How a particular machine is put together, and what from, is always a question of technology and can never be reduced to biology. Their view of the relation between technology and biology, then, is one that usurps the role of biology as the science of life, and argues that the true science of life is technological in nature.

These are complex ideas, and perhaps the best way to sum up Deleuze and Guattari's work on the question of biology and machine relations is the following: life is nothing but machines.

In all this, Deleuze and Guattari are profoundly influenced by two 1950s works by Gilbert Simondon: *The Mode of Existence of Technical Objects* and *The Individual and its Physico-Biological Genesis*. Simultaneously biological and technological, Simondon's work in both contexts concentrates on the processes of concretisation that lead to the production of a biological or technological thing. In both cases, the thing becomes actual by restrictions placed on the matter from which they are formed by feedback processes that inhere in matter that is becoming organised. Thus a biological entity emerges because the materials it is made of are restricted in their pairings (i.e., molecule X cannot bind with molecule Z, but only with *A*), and turn these restrictions into a repeated pattern. A technological object comes into existence in exactly the same way. Core to both is the fact that they do not represent the total actualisation of all the potential inherent in the systems they constitute: the parts of a machine (for example, an internal combustion engine) or the functions of organic bodies (a beating heart, for example) can be reassembled to form a bomb, or be replaced by a mechanical device. More technically expressed, machines are functionally underdetermined. The sense in which these undeveloped potentials nevertheless exist *in a virtual state* will be core to our next section.

5.4.2 Cybernetics and the virtual

Perhaps no term has flourished more under cyberculture than the word *virtual*. Virtual reality machines, no matter how primitive they are, have become a central feature in the cybernetic landscape, since Jaron Lanier began using the term to denote the VR technology with which we are currently familiar: headset, data-gloves and treadmill. As a consequence, we tend simply to identify the 'virtual' with these, and indeed with practically any computer-based technologies, whether entertainment platforms or military training assemblages. It becomes hard to see just how the two terms 'virtual' and 'reality' add up to *more* than just 'simulation', and even harder to see that the two terms form an apparent oxymoron. It is the gap between VR machines and the concept of the virtual that this section is intended to open up for discussion.

In a strong sense, it is the *ontological* claim inherent in the concept of virtual reality that we wish to examine here. To explain: consider the everyday sense in which we say a task has *virtually* been completed, or that one thing is *virtually* the same as another. Such uses indicate that the task or the things in question are *almost but not really* complete, the same, and so on. If we attach this significance to the term virtual *reality*, then we see an immediate problem: almost real but not quite? In one sense, this seems a perfectly reasonable definition of virtual reality, something that *looks* and *behaves* like the real thing, but which isn't. On the other hand, if we take the 'reality' in virtual reality, this suggests something more than the everyday sense of the 'virtual' as *almost real but not*. It suggests that the virtual is *a kind of reality*, as distinct, perhaps, from 'real reality', which is the clumsy phrase Pat Cadigan has the characters in her novel *Synners* (1991) use in order to make a clumsy distinction between the world online and off. Now, how can something which *is almost real but not really real* be at the same time something that is *a kind of reality*? The everyday sense of the virtual is cast into doubt by the addition of 'reality'.

While this problem may seem to be of merely academic (in the pejorative sense) interest, in fact many things hinge on settling the issue regarding the reality of the virtual.

For more on Lanier, and the prehistory of the term VR, see Rheingold (1991), and Heim (1993: chs 8–9). Heim further discusses some of the issues regarding the virtual and the real which we address below

Firstly, and most obviously, what exactly are we doing when we enter a virtual reality environment and interact with objects within it? We assess the reality of an object in the real world in accordance with the evidence of our senses of sight and touch: if a desert traveller sees an oasis but upon reaching it notices that it has vanished, then the oasis is not real but a mirage. As in real reality, therefore, if we can touch a virtual object, albeit with the aid of a dataglove, is it not real? If it is not real, are we *not* interacting with anything at all, but merely *deluded* about what our senses are telling us, as though taking a dream for reality? In this sense, VR technologies would amount to *insanity engines*, propagating illusions that we mistake for the real. Clearly, then, virtual realities are more than mere illusions.

Moreover, forgetting for the moment the status of the environment we enter, what of the status of the real-world technologies we use to enter it, or the programs that *are* these virtual environments? Clearly, the illusions with which we interact are produced by complex and very real interactions between hardware (data-gloves, treadmill and headset), software (the actual program we are running) and our senses (how we experience these interactions). Even the simulated everyday world that Neo and his compatriots in *The Matrix* inhabit is produced by very real connections between machines, programs and nervous systems, and cannot therefore be discounted as illusory. Without these machines, there would be no simulation. Therefore, simulations are importantly real by virtue of the technologies necessary to producing them, and the effect they have upon us.

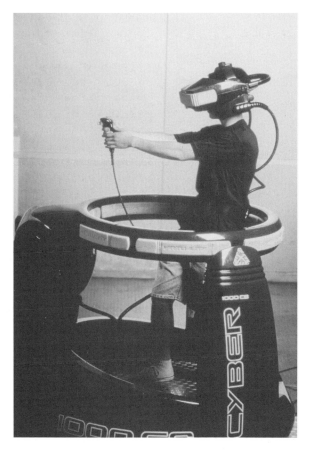

5.17 A VirtualReality machine and user, as seen from real life. Science Photo Library.

Deleuze and the virtual

What we learn from virtual reality *machines* is that we can no longer use the term 'real' as though it were the *opposite* of the virtual, or the illusory. By adding the terms together, we get differentiations *within* reality; different kinds of reality, rather than a contrast with it. On what are these different types of reality based? Firstly, consider the sense in which a task that is virtually completed is, in an everyday sense, *almost* completed. The reference to time is clear: the task's completion is *just about* upon us, but is not *yet*. In this sense, a reference to the virtual includes *future* states as a part of the real; the future has a kind of reality which is virtual, but not *actual*. This is the sense of the 'virtual' that Gilles Deleuze maintains: the virtual is real, but inactual. That is, it has real existence but not in the same way as the things that are *actually* around us.

Traditionally, however, the *actual* is the opposite of the *potential*. When, for example, we say that 'an acorn is a potential oak tree', we are saying that the acorn *will become* an oak tree, that the oak realises the potential of the acorn. Another way of putting this would be to say that the potential of the acorn ceases to exist as it becomes an oak; that is, that it no longer exists as potential. Thus Deleuze further distinguishes the virtual from the potential:

a thing potentially exists if it *might* or *could* exist; it is a *real possibility*, as we say. If we conceive of the virtual as *potential* existence, we implicitly suggest that this potential is realised in the thing that it becomes, and therefore that the virtual exists only in so far as it eventually ceases to be virtual as it becomes actual. But this is to suggest that the virtual has no existence of its own, that there is no sense in which the virtual is real. It also suggests that there is a predictable relation between virtual and actual things, so that, for example, a car is the actualisation of a particular virtual thing which can therefore become nothing but that car. It is as if the virtual car is the actual car in an imperfect or incomplete state. This would mean that there are a bunch of virtual cars queuing in the sky, as it were, waiting to take the exit to the earth. Such an image of the virtual merely doubles the actual world, and has to wait to become real rather than being real itself.

However, if we want to insist that the virtual is not just inactual (i.e. *not yet* real, but real as it is), then clearly the reality of the virtual must lie elsewhere than in the *potential* existence of a certain thing. What is the virtual if it is not an inferior copy of the actual? Ultimately, such a virtual reality stems from cybernetics. We can see precursors, however, to this idea in Gilbert Simondon's account of the 'mode of existence of technical objects', as the title of his (1958) book has it.

Simondon and the virtual-real

Simondon argues that in analysing any complex machine it must be broken down into its constituent parts, many of which are functionally independent of the actual (i.e., the current) function or use of the whole machine (see Dumouchel 1992). To define a machine by its function is to abstract that function from the range of functions of which it is capable. In other words, nothing in the machine itself predetermines it to functioning in the way it actually does. The inactualised capacities are *real virtualities* of the machine. In this way, complex technical objects provide a material basis for differentiating between the actual and the virtual, where it is the actual that is an abstraction from the virtual rather than the virtual being the abstract or potential existence of the machine.

Perhaps the best illustration of this idea is the status of computers as 'universal machines', which is how Alan Turing defined the computer in 1936. They are so called precisely because they do not have just one, but rather multiple functions. In other words, since it is a universal machine, a computer's possible functions can never be exhausted by any particular application or program. Simondon's point, however, extends to regard all complex technologies as essentially universal machines. That is, if we define a machine by its use, we mistake the complex interplay of its subsystems (for example, explosive chemical mixtures, electrical sparking, and cooling systems in a car's internal combustion engine) for a single system determined to certain functions, whereas each of these subsystems can of course form part of other machines (bombs, light bulbs and refrigerators). The history of any given machine is formed by the passage – or *evolution* – from the technical potentials to the concretisation of the various potentialities or virtualities the machine exploits. According to Simondon, therefore, in any given piece of technology there are complex relations between actual and virtual machines, all of which are, however, real.

If we consider simple machines in similar terms, by contrast, such as tools, we note that they have become, in Simondon's words, 'hypertelic'; that is, their purpose has become overdetermined to a single function. This means that they can no longer be used for anything other than a severely restricted range of tasks (consider how few functions a hammer has as compared to a computer). All the virtualities the tool exploits – the resistance and density of certain alloys, the conjunctions of wood and metal, the combination of hammer and claw, and so on – have been concretised, resulting in so rigid and inflexible a relation between the subsystems it exploits that these can no longer be dissociated (if just one part is damaged the whole is irremediably dysfunctional). A complex machine, then, is distinguished from a simple machine by the range of virtualities that it instantiates. This means in turn that the *use* of a technical object always seizes on an abstraction of the concrete machine from its virtualities, virtualities which, however, define and materially constitute the machine as such.

While this may seem improbably abstract, Simondon is essentially viewing complex machines from the standpoint of how cybernetic devices work. The point has often been made that cybernetics does not work through choice or purpose – that is, through positively selecting a purpose or object – but rather through restraint: we get a false picture of cybernetics if we consider it steering towards a single goal. In other words, a system does not produce what it does by virtue of opting for a single outcome, but by preventing or 'restraining' other possible outcomes (this is another way of saying that cybernetic systems work by minimising noise – see Bateson 1972: 399–400). It is as though a cybernetic device *deselects* virtualities in order to arrive at a realised function (e.g., amplifying a signal by acting on the noise). If this is the case, then a system is an actualised region of the virtual-real.

In both Simondon and cybernetics, then, the virtual is considered as a real space that remains both real and inactual. The actual is something that as it were is cut from this space by virtue of the actions of deselection performed upon it. Both Simondon and cybernetics, then, take the virtual to be real, but there are many who do not, and who in consequence dispute the ascription of 'reality' to the virtual.

Critiques of the virtual

One way to critique the virtual is to argue that it is not a real space at all, and certainly not one that we can inhabit. The idea of a 'virtual community' has, for instance, come in for considerable hammering. Critics argue that, instead of being a real community, a virtual community is a way of escaping the real-world decay of community. The virtual community therefore exists only in so far as it mystifies the community whose absence requires its replacement. Such critics consider 'virtual' to mean little more than 'illusory', 'mythical' or 'ideal': these terms all apply to the virtual, they argue, which is something that, because it *seems* real, is taken so to be, but which *really* is not. Virtual communitarians are therefore avoiding the real world, not interacting in a segment of it.

Of course, there is something going on when messages are exchanged across great distances, and responses from anonymous correspondents are elicited. That something, however, is akin to claiming that a telephone line constitutes an alternative reality, or that, for that matter, a book constitutes a world. In reality, books and telephones only do this *in the imagination*, since there are no real, offline differences produced in the real world. Thus critics do not go so far as to deny the existence of the virtual, but merely to say that such existence as it has it shares with phenomena like delusions, hallucinations, dreams or illusions that become public, much like Gibson's definition of cyberspace as a 'consensual hallucination' (1986: 12).

However, to argue that, whatever the appearance of community, for example, in the virtual world, there are no actual communities formed is a bit like arguing that changes in the social order of, for example, Mars, are not real because they do not affect what happens on earth. By extension, it is akin to arguing that changes in the social order of Burma are not real because they do not have any effect on the social order in Canada. What such critics are guilty of is mistaking the virtual-real as only real in so far as it forms a part of 'real reality' here and now. If the effects of the virtual remain virtual, then by definition they are not real. The virtual, however, cannot be regarded as a mere dreamscape, or an hallucination in itself; rather, by virtue of its *consensual* character (in Gibson's oft-quoted phrase), it must of necessity be real (something unreal cannot be shared). Instead of arguing that the virtual is *not* real, therefore, the topic for debate must be the limitations of the virtual, and the possible solutions to these limitations.

The theoretical grounds for arguing in this critical manner ultimately stem from the idea that the 'virtual' is just a *name*, that it therefore is nothing in itself but merely an unreal add-on that tells us something about its users' relation to what is really real. Such a theory is called *nominalist*, in that it insists that what is denoted by the term is reducible to an attitude towards reality, and has no physical or real embodiment. We shall see how such nominalist accounts fare when we consider the relations between cyberculture and the body (**5.4.4**).

5.4.4 Cyberculture and the body

What is virtual technology?

Let us return to the computer, and Alan Turing's definition of the computer as a 'universal machine'. What this means is that any programmable function can be implemented on a universal machine. It is the medium in which Leibniz's universal calculus is finally installed (**5.3.5**). Woolley suggests therefore that the computer itself is a 'virtual machine':

5.3.5 Life and intelligence in the digital age

> [the computer] is an abstract entity or process that has found physical expression. It is a simulation, only not necessarily a simulation of anything actual.
>
> (Woolley 1992: 68–69)

This is not to say that in some sense the computer does not exist, but rather that, like Simondon's complex machines, it exists primarily in a virtual state. Only component functions of the computer or the complex machine are ever actualised, rather than the whole machine. Of course, this does not mean that the computer as such is not actual, but only that it is never actual as the totality of functions of which it is capable. In this sense, the computer itself serves as a paradigm case of a virtual technology, but at the cost of alerting us to that fact that, as Simondon suggests, all complex machines – technologies that contain technological parts – are also themselves virtual machines in the same sense: technological parts can be separated and recombined endlessly, without exhausting their virtual functions in any given combination of them. Nevertheless, the actual machine does not contain these virtual functions as actual components of itself; the virtual components of a machine are real in so far as they are virtual, since the actual machine does have a specific function. Simondon's point is that in reality this is not all there is to it. The virtual, as Deleuze puts it, is like structure; it cannot be considered actual in itself but must be considered a real part of the machine, since if it were not the machine would have no structure.

Unlike nominalism, then, this view cannot reduce structure to a helpful name for an abstract account of a thing. For a nominalist, a machine does not have a structure like humans have skeletons, but has a structure in so far as it can be analysed in structural terms. The Deleuze–Simondon–cyberneticist view is therefore called *realist* in so far as it takes the virtual to be real in itself, and not to depend on what is actual for its reality. Everything virtual is real, in Deleuze's crystal-clear formulation of virtual realism: 'the virtual is not opposed to the real, but to the actual' ([1968] 1994: 208).

5.4.3 Cybernetics and culture

Crisis technology

In **5.1**, we discussed the view that cyberculture represents in some sense a revolutionary moment in the history of technology, and that cybernetic machines are therefore 'crisis technologies'. These terms, as stated in **5.3.3**, stem from historian and philosopher of science Thomas Kuhn's famous account of *The Structure of Scientific Revolutions* (1962). Kuhn's theory slices the history of scientific inquiry into two distinct periods: normal science, during which work goes on as usual, and crisis science, during which more questions than answers accumulate, and the basic theories and assumptions held by science – what Kuhn calls a scientific paradigm – come in for interrogation. Following a period of crisis science there occurs a scientific revolution or 'paradigm shift'. Crucially, Kuhn claims that the questions asked by scientists under the old paradigm can no longer be asked in the new one: the objects investigated under the old paradigm are simply no longer members of the new paradigm. Scientific paradigms are therefore **incommensurable** – literally, they lack all common standard of measure. A contemporary chemist, for example, has not acquired a better means to measure the ether; for the contemporary chemist, the ether *does not exist*, although it did until the early twentieth century.

The example of the ether makes clear the extent to which the objects of scientific scrutiny have a contested reality: such objects are deemed by Kuhnian accounts of science to have no independent reality, but rather to be theory-dependent. It is useless, say Kuhnians, to debate the extra-theoretical reality of theory-dependent entities (such as ether, or the thousands of species of subatomic particles physicists hypothesise about), since it is their usefulness to a dominant theory that establishes their status as real (useful). It is for this reason that Kuhnian accounts of science are antirealist (we would contemporarily say **constructionist**) concerning the objects of that science.

Although the question of technology differs from that of scientific objects in so far as technologies are uncontroversially real, there are important parallels with Kuhn's anti-realist story of science. It is only at points of crisis in the development of new technologies that they become subject to investigation as such. During periods of normal technology the machines are deselected as objects of theoretical scrutiny, prompting accounts of them that emphasise their social constructedness in accordance with broader contexts of their political and social usefulness to a particular project. This is precisely the account of technology that Williams, for example, offers. Such accounts of technology are importantly anti-realist in that they argue machines are themselves socially or politically dependent, since their reality is a matter of *how they are implemented or deployed*, rather than a question pertaining to technology itself. It is only during periods of rapid technological change, or 'crisis technology', that machines seem to rise up and confront us as 'an alien power, as the power of the machine itself' (Marx 1993: 693). Anti-realists would argue that to be realist about machines in such a manner amounts to abstracting them from all social context, or to being duped into thinking that the purposes given to the machines by their developers and deployers are somehow purposes that inhere in the machines themselves. Realists, meanwhile, would argue that the question of the determination of a given machine to a specific purpose (manufacture, militarism, etc.) is secondary to the capacities of the machine itself, as Simondon, for example, argues (**5.4.2**).

Whichever line of argument we take it is important to realise that the argument arises only in the context of crisis technology and almost never in that of normal technology. In other words, it is only because of technological change that such arguments are made.

5.1 CYBERCULTURE AND CYBERNETICS

5.3.3 Self-augmenting engines: steampower against nature

5.4.2 Cybernetics and the virtual

Figurative technology

The arguments that we are exploring in this section, that technologies have determinations beyond, or independently of, their social uses, can be called realist arguments. To grasp what is involved here it is important to understand the thinking behind 'anti-realist' or 'constructionist' viewpoints, in the sense these terms acquire from Kuhn's account of the history of science.

We can do this by considering the work of Claudia Springer. In her analysis of the concept and popular figure of the cyborg (1996), Springer argues that the most culturally representative cyborg in existence is Arnold Schwarzenegger. This is not just because he played the Terminator in the films of the same name, but also because his own, living, muscular body suggests the figure of the cyborg: it is a machined body, armoured against breakdown, whether by metal or muscle. The question is *how* has this body come to stand for the cyborg? Surprisingly, perhaps, Springer argues that the cyborg-status of Schwarzenegger's body is conferred upon it by commercial cinema's maintenance of conventional gender roles. The cinematic cyborg carries the cultural ideal of the masculine gender to its logical conclusion as a body armoured against intrusion and weakness, hard and unstoppable. Cyborgs are not really machines, therefore, but culturally forceful figures that reinstate a model of masculinity that can be traced back to the masculine ideal of the armoured, military body (see Theweleit 1986).

5.3.5 Life and intelligence in the digital age

For further constructionist, anti-realist accounts of technology, see Terranova (1996b), Ross (1991), Balsamo (1996), and, to a large extent, any work based on Haraway's famous account of the 'cyborg myth' (1991)

Springer's concern is not therefore to account for the cyborg as a technological possibility or actuality, but to locate it within the broader social and gendered relations that give rise to it. It is important to realise that constructionist and technologically anti-realist accounts such as Springer's are not confined to analysing *fictional* cyborgs. On the contrary, they emphasise the social constructedness of 'real' cyborgs. Springer also subjects scientific research into artificial intelligence (**5.3.5**) to the same analysis as she brings to bear upon filmic representations. Debates, for example, about the nature of human consciousness have a long history of separating 'mind' from 'body', which have in turn informed constructions of gender by associating the female with the body and the male with the mind, and have elevated cognitive above sexual activity. In this way the task for the anti-realist or constructionist cultural analyst is to see how the historical gendering of the mind and body is being manifested and continues in cyberculture – in the claim that interactive media are more active (male and intellectually alert) rather than passive (female and bodily), or in AI research, in which (certainly in its classical variant – **5.3.5**) scientists seek intelligence in software (mind, male) rather than wetware (body, female). As a consequence, such constructionist analysis is in danger of making it seem irrelevant whether AI is *actually* real, or whether it is a project, a dream, a fantasy or a fiction. For the cultural constructionist they all share and promote the same sexist ideology at work in society at large.

Ideological technology

Our third example of constructionist accounts of technology is accounts which seek to show that ideas about the progressive power, the inevitability or autonomy of technology, are driven and shaped by capitalism. Such ideas about technology are seen to be an expression of an economic and political system pursuing its own interests in extracting profit out of human labour. Such accounts argue that we are presented with a false picture of the inevitability of things, which prevents us from overthrowing the tyranny of machines over human beings, and that, therefore, the determinist view, or picture of how things stand, is ideological. There is a long tradition of such accounts of the effects of technology on society which stems from the economic and social theories of Marx.

Such accounts share with the 'figurative' kind the agenda of political criticism of technology: for both, technology has no independent reality outside of the social relations that form it. To political analysts of technology, history demonstrates that the horror and social pandemonium produced by the onslaught of new machinery are symptoms of the social agendas of those that deploy it. Thus, if we look at the rise of the factory during the Enlightenment period (**5.3.4**), we can see that technology serves both as a means and as an ideal for organising the production of goods. The distinction drawn between mechanical and intellectual labour not only separates humanity from machines but also separates control from productive activity. Workers become cogs in a machine whose design reflects the social and economic agenda of factory owners. To the owners, this is merely the establishment of an appropriate social order, reflecting the priority of mind over muscle. On the other hand, for the workers, the machine is a new and inhuman governor of their lives and their labour. However, accounts of technology as ideology will argue that both views, those of the capitalist and those of the labourer, are false. This is because the owners are wrong when they claim that technology embodies rationality and social order, and the worker has a false relation to the same machinery in so far as the new order s/he experiences is not an irrevocable force of governance but a potential means to reorganise human work and productive activity.

5.3.4 The construction of inanimate reason

So the primary aim of such accounts is to insist that technology can only be understood within the context of the organisation of human productive activity. Further, they will argue that accounts that fail to do this are ideological, not real. However, from the kind of 'realist' standpoint that we have been outlining in the previous sections, the purpose of such criticism of technology as ideology is not able to establish the true nature of technology itself; rather, it is concerned to reveal technology's uses and revolutionary potentials, and the forms of organisation it makes possible.

Such a view of technology stems ultimately from Marx's analyses of machinery as 'dead labour', and informs much cultural analysis of technology.

For such accounts, the distortions of human life introduced by technology can only be understood against the historical constant of human productive activity itself. It is thus only by 'revolutionising the mode of production' (Marx and Engels 1973: 104) that the interests of all human beings as workers will be put before those of the owners of technology and seekers of profit, allowing technology to be used for wider human ends.

THE FRANKFURT SCHOOL AND TECHNOLOGICAL RATIONALITY

The social theorists and philosophers of the Frankfurt School – chiefly, Adorno and Horkheimer (1996), along with Marcuse (1968) and their successor Habermas (1970) – extend the humanistic basis of the Marxist account of technology with their critique of what they call 'technological rationality' or 'instrumental reason'. They see such technological rationality or 'instrumental reason' exemplified in the military and in economic production. Importantly, they also see it in the 'culture industry', where the arts, humanities and critical thought ceased to be questioning or subversive of the established social order, and became instead so many commodities produced for a mass market.

They argue that instrumental reasoning has no other purpose than achieving goals, and that this leads to a radical impoverishment of the possibilities of thought, culture and social life. Everything becomes a machine, not merely metaphorically but in its fundamental modes of operation.

They see the roots of this situation in the eighteenth-century Enlightenment (Adorno and Horkheimer 1996), where the glorification of pure reason removed social constraints

Two members of the Frankfurt School, Marcuse (1968) and Habermas (1970), reject the idea that science and technology are necessarily symptoms or products of instrumental reason. Thus Marcuse calls for alternative sciences and technologies, while Habermas calls for a rethinking of how they are deployed, and the means by which their deployment is rationally constrained. Putting forward a view of rationality concerned with communication rather than with means–ends (instrumental) reasoning, therefore, Habermas advocates the creation of discursive institutions to humanise the applications of science and technology, leading, he proposes, towards a more generous conception of rationality than Horkheimer and Adorno allow for

Feenberg (1991) provides a recent version of this account of technology. It is worth noting that Habermas's own successor, Niklas Luhmann (1995), rejects the critical approach common to Habermas and the earlier Frankfurt School, and instead conceives of 'social systems' in a broadly cybernetic model

such as religion or objective morality from its use and at the same time therefore, with nothing else to aim for, ends up establishing reason as a means to achieve a subject's purposes, whatever they may be. In terms of reason alone, they argue, a situation is reached where there is no longer any difference between making a film, wooing a lover, or engineering the Final Solution.

In short, all are plans transformed into actions, and their rationality is measured merely in the appropriateness of the means to ends. Under the tyranny of instrumental reason, Adorno and Horkheimer (1996) argue, all culture becomes mechanical, and technological and scientific advance is merely symptomatic of this instrumentalisation.

All these accounts conceive of technology as a symptom of broader social issues. Adorno and Horkheimer see technology as, above all else, an expression of an increasingly instrumental culture in which goals have become separated from wider human and moral values. They urge that this situation can only be thwarted by a radical project of self-criticism on the part of that culture as a whole (a prospect of which Adorno was massively sceptical), while Habermas considers the uses of technology as potentially reflecting a broader and non-instrumental usage of human reasoning (1970). At the basis of each of these accounts of technology, therefore, there lies a conception of a properly human life laid waste by a technology under the sway of 'inhuman' capitalism or mechanised thought. Therefore accounts that focus on opposing humans and machines tend to be anti-realist about technology in order to emphasise the priority of their human users. The question we must ask, therefore, is whether these accounts constitute theories of technology at all, or whether instead they are theories of human nature (as in Marx) or human culture (as in Springer, in Adorno and Horkheimer, in Marcuse and in Habermas).

5.4.4 Cyberculture and the body

Disembodiment

It has been a commonplace anti-realist criticism of cyberculture in general and cyberpunk fiction in particular that it promotes a new form of disembodied, purely mental existence. By asking the vexing question 'What do cyborgs eat?', for example, Margaret Morse (1994) highlights the tendency to repudiate the body that can be found thoughout cybercultural phenomena, from the magazine *Mondo 2000* to William Gibson's *Neuromancer*. Other critics have been less cautious in their formulations, leading some to insist on the dangerous 'disembodied ditziness' (Sobchack 1993: 583) inherent in cyberpunk; or to follow Springer (1996: 306) in disparaging its 'willed obliteration of bodies'; or merely to entertain 'the possibility of a mind independent of the biology of bodies' (Bukatman 1993: 208) ambivalently proffered by cyberspace.

But what would such a thing as 'a mind released from the mortal limitations of the flesh' (Bukatman 1993: 208) be? Not only is a disembodied mental existence, Bukatman's version of cyberspace as a 'celebration of spirit', a facile misunderstanding of cybernetics, it is also inconceivable unless we acknowledge, with Descartes and popular Christian mythology, that mind, spirit or what have you *could* have independent, that is, non-biological existence. Bukatman seeks to get around this cartesianism by stating that in cyberspace, although 'consciousness becomes separated from the body . . ., it becomes a body *itself*' (1993: 210); but this does little more than reiterate Descartes's argument that mind, though immaterial, is nonetheless a *thing* (res cogitans), albeit in less clear terms.

Meanwhile, Gibson's fiction, the repeated target of critics of cyberpunk's supposed advocacy of 'the bodiless exultation of cyberspace' (Gibson 1986: 12), takes considerable care to position such views of the possibilities of cyberspace within the perspective of Case, the 'console cowboy', who, as a result of an assault on his nervous system by a nerve-toxin given him as a punishment, is now reduced to living as an exile from cyberspace, in the 'prison of his own flesh'. In other words, such positions are given as a character's mourning for a loss that was itself *physically* induced by way of the nerve-toxin. Possibilities for alternative or enhanced embodiment are presented throughout the novel as poor substitutes, despite their technological sophistication, for the sheer complexity, the 'infinite intricacy' of the body's biochemical structure (Gibson 1986: 285).

Bukatman's gestures towards the possible impact of complex technologies on the modes of survival of organic bodies, along with the criticisms of cyberpunk's 'disembodied ditziness', seem to fall between two chairs: the reflex criticism of received mind–body dualism, and maintaining an *ambivalence* as regards these possibilities. Gibson's own fictions may often seem to share this sophisticated blend of cultural criticism, the heady potentials of computing technology, and embodied, animal ambivalence; however, Case's realisation of the body's importance is based not on its animal confrontation with a technological world but instead on the degrees of complexity afforded by technological with regard to biological platforms. When, for example, Dixie, an artificial intelligence or uploaded personality ('ROM construct'), asks Case to do him a favour and 'erase this goddam thing' (1986: 130), it is because of the poor fit between the construct's memories and his actuality. His entire body has been removed, like his friend's frostbitten thumb, and the newly immobile program *feels* its absence, albeit artificially. This points to limitations in the technological platform that are not inherent in it, indicating instead a relative paucity of information as compared with the biological body. Conceiving of the issue of the relation between body and technology in this manner does not create essentialist divisions between the two, but rather places both on the properly cybernetic footing of informational complexity.

These instances create a context in which it makes sense to interrogate the place of the body in cyberculture. To be sure, there has been a great deal of such interrogation (**5.3**): questions regarding the nature of cyborg bodies, the role of physical activity in VR, and the sexuality of online avatars, have excited a great deal of comment in the last few years. However, perhaps by virtue of the critical component of cultural analysis, such accounts have in the main remained within the ambit of humanism, even if their principal agenda is to advocate 'posthumanism'. While this latter term is more often employed by the more evangelical wings of cyberculture (such as the Extropians, *Mondo* 2000, or Timothy Leary), it has also been subject to more critical scrutiny in, for example, N. Katherine Hayles's *How We Became Posthuman* (1999). As the pronoun in Hayles's title indicates, the concern of posthumanism, whether critical or evangelical, still orbits around the centre of human being, making such an approach extremely vulnerable to Marxist or Frankfurt School criticism. However, if we examine the manner in which Gibson's fiction relates biology and technology, we see that it does not centre around the question 'what is it to be human?', but rather, 'what is the relative complexity of information as encoded by biological and technological objects?' As discussed above (**5.4.2**), there has been a significant intertwining of biology and information technology since the late 1940s, which has taken the contemporary forms of genomics, on the one hand, and biotechnology, on the other. Apart from the fact that such questions are implicit in that text of Gibson's most often criticised for its anti-body, pro-technology, culturally and historically masculinist dualism, but have not received the same critical attention, there are two further reasons to pursue such an approach:

5.3 Biological technologies: the history of automata

5.4.2 Cybernetics and the virtual

1   It avoids the pitfalls of treating new technologies, and the changes that ramify from them, in terms of the critical models these technologies contest.

2   It attempts to integrate cyberculture as a purely cultural phenomenon with scientific and technological attempts to eradicate the boundary between biology and technology.

Finally, if (1) is a *theoretical* issue, (2) invests this theory with a practical significance: that is, whatever the theoretical adequacy of the models used by cultural and media studies, commercial biotechnology has already condemned humanism to history, and is challenging discursive with physical **constructionism**.

Cybernetic bodies 1: gaming, interactivity and feedback

Gibson has often been reported as remarking that the idea of cyberspace came by noticing the way that videogamers were involved with their machines. Given that this is the situation from which Gibson began to populate cyberspace with novel bio-technological entities, it makes sense to begin our examination of cybernetic bodies by revisiting that games arcade in Vancouver:

> I could see in the physical intensity of their postures how *rapt* the kids inside were. It was like one of those closed systems out of a Pynchon novel: a feedback loop with photons coming off the screens into the kids' eyes, neurones moving through their bodies, and electrons moving through the video game.
>
> (Gibson, in McCaffery 1992: 272)

Again, just as with the biological and the technological objects discussed immediately above, we do not see here two complete and sealed-off entities: the player on the one hand and the game on the other. Rather, there is an interchange of information and energy, forming a new circuit. Although this is merely a description of an impression, it poses a question concerning the much-hyped property of interactivity (**1.2.2**) in computer gaming: what if the relation between user, program and technology were closer to the cybernetic circuit Gibson describes than to the voluntarist narrative underpinning the options, choices and decisions on the part of the user such games are said to demand?

    In a cybernetic circuit there is no point of origin for any action that circuit performs. In other words, it would make little sense to talk of one component of a circuit initiating that circuit. By definition, a circuit consists in a constancy of action and reaction. In gaming, for example, not only is there the photon–neurone–electron circuit Gibson evokes, there are also macroscopically physical components of that circuit, such as the motions of finger, mouse or stick. Motions of a finger, prompted as much by changes in the display as by any 'free will' on the part of the player, also provoke series of neuroelectrical pulses resulting in hand–arm–shoulder–neck movement, even in whole-body motion, for which the individual whose body it is, is far from responsible. Through the tactile and visual interface with the machine, the entire body is determined to move by *being part of the circuit of the game*, being, as it were, *in the loop*. If games in general, as McLuhan suggests, are 'machine[s] that can get into action only if the players consent to become puppets for a time' (1967: 253), this is true above all of computer gaming, where users become, in Gibson's terms, 'meat puppets' by virtue of their dependency on the physical aspects of the circuit.

1.2.2   Interactivity

Noting that cybernetic control works by eliminating possible actions rather than prompting particular ones (**5.4.1**), we begin to gain a picture of what is physically going on in gaming: the circuit serves to reduce the possibilities of motion and action and to amplify the remaining actions through a delicate balance of feedback mechanisms: just enough positive feedback to produce local changes, and enough negative feedback to ensure global stability on the part of the game circuits. Cybernetically, then, interactivity is a false description of a process of the programmed elimination of possible actions, not of creating possibilities of actions.

See **5.4.1** for Deleuze's emphasis on the cybernetic idea of the shortest circuit.

5.4.1 Cybernetics and human–machine relations

The most important aspect of this account of gaming is that it shifts attention from the interactions between two discrete entities towards the cybernetic processes that, as it were, edit parts from each to create an indissociable circuit of informational-energetic exchange. Gaming, we could say, is here not an action, nor even an *inter-action*, but literally a *passion* – a 'being-acted-upon'. Consider the extent to which cultural and media studies argues for a conception of the viewer, user or spectator as *active*. Even interactivity (as we noted in **5.4.3**) contains a measure of activity that makes it a more desirable state than passivity. This is because, when one is *passive*, one is acted upon. This sense of 'passivity' draws on the root of the word – *pathe* – which it shares with 'pathology', 'sym-pathy', 'patient', and so on. In ancient Greek philosophy, if a person was 'pathic' they were precisely being acted upon. However, there is another sense of 'passion', involving an absorbing pleasure that blinds the 'patient' to everything else. It is in *both* senses that the term can be used here; as a passion in which the gamer surrenders to being acted upon by the game, its apparatus, its signs, its action-prompts and so on. The term thus preserves the 'inter' of 'interactivity', and yet instead of ascribing the hard duty of action to the gamer, ascribes to her a passion for letting the game take her over. It is surely this that Gibson saw in the Vancouver arcade.

5.4.3 Cybernetics and culture

Of course, even if we accept this reformulation of what happens in gaming as a cybernetic circuit, we also have to recognise that such circuits are temporary, coming into operation, if recurrently, for only a matter of minutes or hours, apparently far removed from the cyborgs we are said to become as we grow more intimate with our machines. However, we have such machine-passions in all our technological interactions; as McLuhan noted, for example, 'one of the benefits of motivation research has been the revelation of man's sex relation to the motorcar' (1967: 56). It is the passional conduct of gaming that explains the 'rapt' physical intensity of the players Gibson saw in the Vancouver arcade; but it also suggests something much broader concerning human–machine relations, on the one hand, and the dependent circuits formed by parts of each, on the other. That is, it suggests that cybernetic bodies are not whole organic bodies that have technological parts added to them, but bodies which have abstracted from them into passional circuits with parts of other bodies.

In many ways, arguments about interactivity replay those concerned with whether technology or human, social purposes form the principal historical actors: whichever way we argue these cases, we conclude that one, and only one, component of human–machine relations contributes action to history, while the other plays a merely supporting role, and is acted upon by the active one. Such concerns are explicit in Marx, for example, when he writes that with industrial machinery, man 'steps to the side of the production process, instead of being its chief actor' (1993: 705), and in the very idea of machinery as 'self-activating objectified labour' (1993: 695). Indeed, the entire history of technology amounts to a series of attempts to produce precisely this kind of self-acting machine (**5.3**). Thus, in its broadest terms, the ideal of interactivity is an attempt to resolve the confrontation of machine and human into a more collaborative view of history. In the

5.3 Biological technologies: the history of automata

same terms, the cybernetic view of gaming is also non-confrontational; but it is less collaborative than it is constructivist – that is, it is concerned with the formation of new circuits. In terms that Deleuze and Guattari borrow from Monod, cybernetics is **molecular** rather than **molar**: it concerns the small circuits of photons, neurones and electrons rather than relations between a ready-made and whole subject, on the one hand, and its incomplete, otherwise inert technological objects on the other.

Cybernetic bodies 2: prosthetics and **constructivism**

Accounts of actual cyborgs often begin by focusing on the prosthetic devices we regularly incorporate into our bodies, or that are formed by incorporating our bodies into larger technological devices. Effectively a version of the theory that technology constitutes a physiological or sensory extension of our bodies (**1.6.4, 5.4.2**), such an account will tend to highlight how it is humans have already become cyborgs through the use of pacemakers, contact lenses, hearing aids and prosthetic limbs, on the one hand, and of cars, factories and cities on the other. The general point being made in such accounts is that humans are no longer separable from the technologies that biologically and environmentally saturate our lives. In contrast with the 'molecular' account of gaming above, we can call this a 'molar' account of the cyborg, since it concentrates on whole machines that become part of us (pacemakers etc.), or that we form part of (cars etc.). In other words, it maintains that cyborg bodies are formed by the incorporation of whole bodies into whole machines, and vice-versa. Indeed, this is characteristic of the extension theory of technology in general: there must be something to be extended, and something to do the extending.

However, if we take the example of gameplaying used above, in what sense can the cybernetic body thus formed be accounted for within the extensionalist or prosthetic theory of the cyborg? Instead of looking at what physiological or sensory functions of the organic body are extended by the prosthetic of the machine, we focused on the loop of constant information and energy exchange formed between parts of the machine and parts of the user's body. An example will be useful to make the issues clear. Just as the gaming example was drawn from fiction, so this example will be drawn from the arts.

The artist Stelarc stages performances in which various mechanical and digitally controlled devices are attached to his body. On the surface, then, this looks like a classic, prosthetic case of extensionalism. One such device is called the Stimbod. The Stimbod is a 'touch screen muscle stimulation system' (Stelarc 2000: 568), a computer map of the performer's body, attached to it by electrodes and stimulators. By touching points on this map of the body, the performer's body is in turn stimulated to move (hence 'Stimbod') by an electrical current sent through the electrodes attached to that body. This turns the performer's body into an 'involuntary body'. In one sense, it is clear that the performer's body has its sensory field and muscular activation extended by the Stimbod, since by virtue of the machine it is subject to stimuli it would otherwise not receive. On the other hand, the Stimbod connects muscles, sensors, pixels and finger into an electrical-informational circuit that does not so much change the existing body as construct a new one. Further components, moreover, can be added: in 1995 Stelarc put the Stimbod on the web and attached the sensors and stimulators to the involuntary body, allowing remote access to that body's musculature. Similarly, by recording the motions thus produced, a muscular memory is effectively produced *in the computer* which can be deployed independently of the touch-screen interface. Stelarc calls this new body a 'collaborative physiology' (2000: 569), making it clear that, rather than simply extending an existing organic body with a

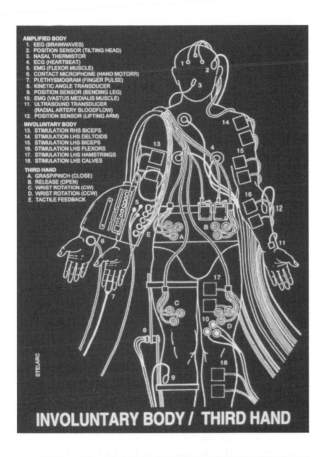

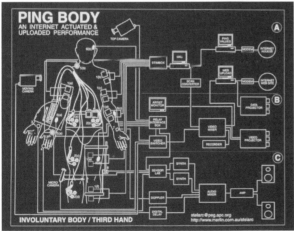

5.18 Stelarc's STIMBOD – a touch-screen interface for the remote manipulation of the body. Information from the touch-screen is sent to receptors attached to the body's muscles, and a signal from these stimulates the muscle to contract, forcing the body to move.

technological one, a *new physiological entity* is thus constructed from this network of organic and technological parts, combined into a circuit of information and energy exchange.

As with the gaming circuit, the Stimbod-Involuntary Body circuit remains impermanent; it is something from which the performer's body, like the gamer's, can be detached whole and unchanged. The technological components in this sense remain prosthetic. It is also important to note, however, the sense Stelarc's performances give to the idea of the *construction* of cybernetic bodies from physical parts of heterogeneous origin. Here the construction is not only molar, composed of whole entities, but also molecular, composing the body of the performance.

By dint of the separability of bodies, such phenomena as gaming and the Stimbod do not seem to back up claims made to the effect that the cyborg marks the 'end of humanity' in some sense. Stelarc himself, echoing claims made by cyberneticists such as Kevin Warwick, notes that technology potentially transforms the relationship between the evolution of the species and the physical alteration of its members. Technology, he writes, 'provides each person with the potential to progress individually'. Because one *can* technologically transform one's body, and since the limits of such transformations are marked only by technological thresholds and questions of surgical practice, the technological transformation of the human body will mean that 'it is no longer of advantage to either remain "human" or evolve as a species' (2000: 563).

See **5.4.2** for the role of cybernetics in biological theory in general, and biotechnology in particular

5.4.2 Cybernetics and the virtual

To some extent, such an approach to the cybernetic body underscores an agenda it shares with biotechnology. Just as for Stelarc the problems of the human body stem from its inefficiency with regard to the technological environment it has fashioned, so, as its name implies, for biotechnology, the difference between biological and technological objects has all but disappeared: biological components *carry out specific tasks*, and are therefore subject to replacement by technological parts (such as pacemakers) that perform those same functions, or can themselves be deployed in contexts other than those in which they naturally function. In this context, we may consider the stem cell. Stem cells are undifferentiated according to particular functions, but differentiate into the various tissues and muscles only later in the development of the organic body. Biotechnologists therefore reason that undeveloped stem cells may be used to 'regrow' damaged areas of the body, irrespective of what areas these are. Although this has recently been attempted as a cure for Parkinson's disease, and met with disastrous results (patients reported a marked improvement in their condition throughout the first year following treatment, but subsequently developed new disorders as the stem cells continued to grow, leaving the biotechnologists and surgeons with no clue as to what to do to halt this runaway process), what is important from the present perspective is the sense that biological entities have become, under biotechnology, components for the technological reconstruction of bodies.

Cloning presents a similar attitude to the technology of the body: cells whose nucleii have been removed can be turned into engines for the production of new creatures by means of refilling the empty cell with new nucleic material. The biotechnological procedure known as transgenics, for example, often fills thus enucleated cells with hybrid genetic matter, so that we can 'grow' pigs with human DNA, making inter-species organ transplants possible by diminishing the risk of the host body's rejection of foreign organic matter.

We can see then that all biotechnological phenomena emphasise the proximity between biological and technological function, just as the uses of technology in altering or complementing human biology can potentially be indefinitely extended. In both cases, we note a use of constructivism that, unlike its discursive or ideological variant, is profoundly physical. Both non-organic technology and biotechnology provide means for constructing or reconstructing bodies that go beyond the limits of the prosthetic devices that provide us with examples of actual cyborgs. This helps to clear up the reason we may feel that while *technically* a woman with a pacemaker *may* be defined as a cyborg, this is a kind of loose extension of the term, and is not really what we mean by it. A wholly constructed creature composed of biological and technological components, on the other hand, is *exactly* what we mean by the cyborg.

5.4.5 Conclusion: science, cyberculture and the humanities

To conclude this section, it is worth revisiting two issues arising from the examples selected:

1   the relation between individual and social biotechnological constructivism;

2   the question of cyberculture's often criticised quest for disembodiment.

The relation between individual and social biotechnological construction

Once we have absorbed the various ways in which cyborgs can be constructed, we begin to notice that even now there are issues affecting the likely paths such constructivism will follow. We noted above that Stelarc suggests that technology provides the individual with the potential to progress apart from the species' evolutionary processes. Stelarc thus raises a fundamental problem concerning the relation between constructivism and freedom. We can best approach this issue by way of the example of cosmetic surgery.

Most cosmetic surgeries fall into two types: firstly, reconstructive surgery, following a burn or some other accident, and secondly, elective surgery, which concerns the removal of undesired features, or the creation of desirable ones. The first is palliative, undoing damage done to a body; the second is aesthetic, remodelling the face and gross body parts in accordance with an ideal. The last of these is perhaps the second millennium's version of pre-photographic portraiture, in which the artist commissioned would abide by the wishes of his patron-sitter to 'iron out' or 'improve' aspects of the sitter's appearance for purposes of producing a better portrait. That cosmetic surgery does approach the condition of art is often noted, and a London reconstructive surgeon recently employed a portraitist to capture his work in various stages of completion, providing his patients or subjects with a non-clinical visual account of their progress.

Like portraiture in painting, elective surgery has also tended to correspond to certain ideals of 'beauty': how long will it be before we see a rise in the fortunes of Rubensesque elective surgical techniques? To highlight this fact, the French performance artist Orlan subjects her face to frequent surgical alterations that *do not* correspond to these ideals; instead, she implants horns, ridges, and other grotesque features into her face. Similarly, the surgeon who provided artist Mark Pauline, of the Survival Research Laboratories, with a prosthetic thumb to replace the one he lost during a performance, later became disenchanted with medicine for its lack of creativity, despite its plastic potential, and joined the artist's group.

Such examples of the proximity of art and surgery remind us of the body's *plasticity*, its malleability, and thus pose a question to elective surgery: why treat it as a means to impose an ideal upon one's face and body rather than using it to treat the body as a site of experiment, as both Orlan and Stelarc do? Of course, posing such a question, as Orlan explicitly does, has the effect of highlighting the gendered social pressures that result in the maintainance of the ideal female form by surgical means. As she puts it in the text of one of her performances, 'I Do Not Want to Look Like . . .':

> many damaged faces have been reconstructed and many people have had organ transplants; and how many more noses have been remade or shortened, not so much for physical problems as for psychological ones? Are we still convinced that we should bend to the determinations of nature? This lottery of arbitrarily distributed genes . . .
>
> (Orlan 1995: 10)

As does Stelarc, Orlan proposes her work as a plastic challenge to nature's provision; unlike Stelarc, her work also engages the social pressures on women's bodies, and so does not place as much weight on the category 'individual' as does the former. Nonetheless, Stelarc's work does confront and name a major social issue concerning the age of constructivism both he and Orlan usher in. 'In this age of information overload', he writes,

> what is significant is no longer freedom of ideas, but freedom of form . . . The question is not whether society will allow people freedom of expression, but whether the human species will allow individuals to construct alternate genetic coding.
>
> (Stelarc 2000: 561)

Stelarc effectively recasts the issue of human freedom in biotechnological terms. Biotechnology itself, however, has other ideas. The recent competition between the public sector, in the form of the Wellcome Institute, and the private sector, in the form of Celera Genomics, Inc., to decode the human genome has predictably resulted in victory for the latter. While the significance of this event itself is great as regards the future of state health-care provision and drug or treatment prices, it is of importance here in so far as it demonstrates that the pressure against the biotechnological individual freedom Stelarc champions is likely to come from the corporate environments that can afford to sponsor the research. If biotechnology in general is producing a more constructivist ethos as regards the human body, then one of the major components of this constructivism will be financial. Perhaps species-difference will replace class as the front line of constructivist social struggle.

Cyberculture's quest for disembodiment

5.4.4 Cyberculture and the body

Finally, we are now in a position to return to the issue raised at the beginning of **5.4.4** concerning cyberculture's quest for disembodiment. While there may be a *sense* of disembodiment attaching to the use of computers for accessing cyberspace, the gaming example that Gibson provides, and our exploration of it, shows that far from disembodiment it is a question of the constitution of other, cybernetic circuits. Indeed, cyberculture in general is a highly physicalist environment in which the lines dividing biology from technology are erased by biotechnology, art and surgery. If cyberculture has a bias, then, it is not towards disembodiment but towards physicality. As Bruce Sterling (in Gibson 1988: xii) says concerning cyberpunk fiction, the traditional 'yawning gulf between . . . literary culture, the formal world of art and politics, and the culture of science, the world of engineering and industry' is crumbling, and in its place looms the cybernetic culture that combines them.

The challenges posed by cyberculture, then, consist not only in providing theories that can articulate the products or texts of that culture, but in providing theories that can reintegrate the long-severed intellectual and practical relations between the worlds of science, engineering, technology and the humanities. It is for that reason that this final part of the book has taken a broad view of cyberculture, as Sterling asserts cyberpunk does, and has included the history and philosophy of science and technology, alongside theoretical questions arising from both the humanities and the scientific contexts concerning the cybernetic objects that are not only a part of popular culture but actually populate our world.

BIBLIOGRAPHY

Adorno, Theodor and Max Horkheimer *Dialectic of Enlightenment*, tr. John Cumming. London: Verso, 1996.

Ansell-Pearson, Keith *Viroid Life*, London: Routledge, 1997.

Aristotle, *The Politics and The Constitution of Athens*, ed. Stephen Everson. Cambridge: Cambridge University Press, 1996.

Aristotle. *The Physics*, ed. Robin Waterfield. Oxford: Oxford University Press, 1996.

Babbage, Charles *On the Economy of Machinery and Manufactures*, London: Charles Knight, 1832.

Balsamo, Anne *Technologies of the Gendered Body: reading cyborg women*, Durham N.C.: Duke University Press, 1996.

Barnes, Jonathan ed. 'Eudemian ethics', in *The Complete Works of Aristotle*, vol. 2. Princeton: Princeton University Press, 1984.

Basalla, George *The Evolution of Technology*, Cambridge: Cambridge University Press, 1989.

Bateson, Gregory *Steps to an Ecology of Mind*, New York: Ballantine, 1972.

Baudrillard, Jean *Symbolic Exchange and Death* [1976], London: Sage, 1993.

Baudrillard, Jean. *The System of Objects*, London: Verso, 1996.

Baudrillard, Jean *Simulacra and Simulation*, Ann Arbor: University of Michigan Press, 1997.

Bedini, Silvio 'The role of automata in the history of technology', *Technology and Culture* 5.1 (1964): 24–42.

Bell, David and Kennedy, Barbara M. *The Cybercultures Reader*, London: Routledge, 2000.

Benjamin, Walter *Illuminations*, London: Fontana, 1973.

Bergson, Henri *Creative Evolution* [1911], London: Macmillan, 1920.

Bergson, Henri. *The Two Sources of Morality and Religion* [1932], London: Macmillan, 1935.

Bertens, Hans *The Idea of the Postmodern: a history*. London: Routledge, 1995.

Biagioli, Mario ed. *The Science Studies Reader*, New York: Routledge, 1999.

Blackmore, Susan *The Meme Machine*, Oxford: Oxford University Press, 1999.

Boden, Margaret *The Philosophy of Artificial Intelligence*, Oxford: Oxford University Press, 1990.

Boden, Margaret *The Philosophy of Artificial Life*, Oxford: Oxford University Press, 1996.

Braudel, Fernand *Capitalism & Material Life 1400–1800*, New York: Harper and Row, 1973.

Broadhurst-Dixon, Joan and Cassidy, Eric, eds *Virtual Futures: cyberotics, technology and posthuman pragmatism*, London: Routledge, 1997.

Bukatman, Scott *Terminal Identity*, Durham, N.C.: Duke University Press, 1993.

Butler, Samuel. *Erewhon*, New York: Signet, 1960.

Cadigan, Pat *Synners*, London: Grafton, 1991.

Carter, Natalie *Interview with Kevin Warwick*, Videotape, 2001.

Castells, M. *The Rise of the Network Society*, London: Blackwell, [1996] 2000.

Chapuis, Alfred and Droz, Edmond *Automata: a historical and technological Study*, Neuchâtel: Editions du Griffon, 1958.

Clark, William, Golinski, Jan and Schaffer, Simon *The Sciences in Enlightened Europe*, Chicago: University of Chicago Press, 1999.

Coleman, William *Biology in the Nineteenth Century. Problems of form, function and transformation*, Cambridge: Cambridge University Press, 1977.

Critical Art Ensemble. *Electronic Civil Disobedience and Other Unpopular Essays*, New York: Semiotext(e), 1995.

D'Alembert, Jean and Diderot, Denis *Encyclopédie, ou Dictionnaire raisonné des arts, des sciences et des métiers*, Paris, 1777.

Darwin, Charles *Origin of Species*, Harmondsworth: Penguin, 1993.

Daston, Lorraine 'Enlightenment calculations', *Critical Inquiry* 21.1 (1994): 182–202.

Dawkins, Richard *The Selfish Gene*, London: Granada, 1976.

Dawkins, Richard *Blind Watchmaker: the Program of the Book*, PO Box 59, Leamington Spa, 1991.

De Kerckhove, Derrick *The Skin of Culture*, Toronto: Somerville House, 1997.

De Landa, Manuel *War in the Age of Intelligent Machines*, New York: Zone, 1991.

De Landa, Manuel 'Virtual environments and the emergence of synthetic reason', in *Flame Wars*, Special edition of *South Atlantic Quarterly* 92.4, ed. Mark Dery. Durham, N.C.: Duke University Press, 1993: 793–815.

De Landa, Manuel *A Thousand Years of Non-linear History*, New York: Zone, 1997.

Deleuze, Gilles *Cinema 1: the movement image*, trans. Hugh Tomlinson and Barbara Haberjam. London: Athlone, 1986.

Deleuze, Gilles *Bergsonism*, trans. Hugh Tomlinson. New York: Zone, 1988.

Deleuze, Gilles *Cinema 2: the time-image*, London: Athlone, 1989.

Deleuze, Gilles *Difference and Repetition* [1968], London: Athlone, 1994.

Deleuze, Gilles and Guattari, Félix *Anti-Oedipus*, London: Athlone, [1974] 1984.

Deleuze, Gilles and Guattari, Félix *A Thousand Plateaus*, London: Athlone, 1988.

Dennett, Daniel *Darwin's Dangerous Idea*, Harmondsworth: Penguin, 1995.

Dennett, Daniel *Brainchildren: essays on designing minds*, Cambridge, Mass.: MIT, 1998.

Dery, Mark ed. *Flame Wars*, Special edition of the *South Atlantic Quarterly* 92.4, Durham, N.C.: Duke University Press, 1993.

Descartes, René *Meditations* [1641], ed. John Cottingham. Cambridge: Cambridge University Press, 1986.

Descartes, René, 'Treatise on man', in *The World and Other Writings* [1662], ed. Stephen Gaukroger. Cambridge: Cambridge University Press, 1998.

Diderot, Denis *Rameau's Nephew and D'Alembert's Dream*, Harmondsworth: Penguin, 1985.

Dobres, Marcia-Anne *Technology and Social Agency*, Oxford: Blackwell, 2000.

Dreyfus, Hubert *What Computers Can't Do*, New York: Harper and Row, 1979.

Dumouchel, Paul 'Gilbert Simondon's plea for a philosophy of technology', *Inquiry* 35 (1992): 407–421.

Dyson, George *Darwin Among the Machines: the evolution of global intelligence*, Harmondsworth: Penguin, 1998.

Ellul, Jacques *The Technological Society* [1954], New York: Vintage, 1964.

Engels, Friedrich *Dialectics of Nature*, trans. Clemens Dutt. London: Lawrence and Wishart, 1964.

Eve, Raymond E., Horsfall, Sara and Lee, Mary E. eds. *Chaos, Complexity and Sociology: myths, models and theories*, London: Sage, 1997.

Feenberg, Andrew *Critical Theory of Technology*, London: Routledge, 1991.

Ferguson, Adam *An Essay on the History of Civil Society* [1767], ed. Duncan Forbes. Edinburgh: Edinburgh University Press, 1966.

Ferré, Frederic *Philosophy of Technology*, Athens, Ga: University of Georgia Press, 1995.

Fiske, John *Introduction to Communication Studies* (3rd edn), London: Routledge, 1990.

Foucault, Michel *The Order of Things*, London: Tavistock, 1970.

Foucault, Michel *Discipline and Punish*, tr. Anthony Sheridan, Harmondsworth: Penguin, 1979.

Foucault, Michel *Birth of the Clinic*, London: Routledge, 1986.

Foucault, Michel *Technologies of the Self*, ed. Luther H. Martin, Huck Gutman and Patrick H. Hutton. London: Tavistock, 1988.

Galison, Peter 'The ontology of the enemy: Norbert Wiener and the cybernetic vision', *Critical Inquiry* 5.1 (1994): 228–266.

Genosko, Gary McLuhan and Baudrillard, London: Routledge, 1998.

Gibson, William Neuromancer, London: Grafton, 1986.

Gibson, William Burning Chrome, London: Grafton, 1988.

Gibson, William and Silverman, Robert Instruments of the Imagination, Cambridge, Mass.: Harvard University Press, 1995.

Gibson, William 'An interview with William Gibson', in Storming the Reality Studio: a casebook of cyberpunk and postmodern fiction, ed. Larry McCaffery. Durham, N.C.: Duke University Press, 1991, pp. 263–385.

Gibson, William and Sterling, Bruce The Difference Engine, London: Gollancz, 1990.

Gillespie, Charles Coulston. Genesis and Geology, Cambridge Mass.: Harvard University Press, 1992.

Gleick, James Chaos, London: Cardinal, 1987.

Gould, Stephen Jay Time's Arrow, Time's Cycle, Harmondsworth: Penguin, 1987.

Habermas, Jürgen Towards a Rational Society, London: Heinemann, 1970.

Hankins, Thomas L. Science and the Enlightenment, Cambridge: Cambridge University Press, 1985.

Hankins, Thomas L. and Silverman, Robert J. Instruments and the Imagination, Princeton, N.J.: Princeton University Press, 1995.

Haraway, Donna Primate Visions: gender, race and nature in the world of modern science, London: Verso, 1989.

Haraway, Donna Simians, Cyborgs and Women: the reinvention of nature, London: Free Association, 1991.

Haraway, Donna Modest Witness @ Second Millennium: FemaleMan meets OncoMouse, London: Routledge, 1997.

Harpignies, J.P. Double Helix Hubris: against designer genes, New York: Cool Grove Press, 1994.

Harvie, Christopher, Martin, Graham and Scharf, Aaron eds Industrialization and Culture 1830–1914, London: Macmillan, 1970.

Haugeland, John Mind Design: philosophy, psychology and artificial intelligence, Cambridge, Mass.: MIT, 1981.

Hayles, N. Katherine 'Narratives of artificial life', in Futurenatural. Nature, Science, Culture, ed. George Robertson et al. London: Routledge, 1996, pp. 146–164.

Hayles, N. Katherine How We Became Posthuman: virtual bodies in cybernetics, literature, and informatics, Chicago: University of Chicago Press, 1999.

Heim, Michael The Metaphysics of Virtual Reality, Oxford: Oxford University Press, 1993.

Hodges, Andrew Turing: the Enigma, London: Vintage, 1992.

Hodges, Andrew Turing. A natural philosopher, London: Phoenix, 1997.

Hoffman, E.T.A. 'Automata', in The Best Tales of Hoffmann, ed. E.F. Bleiler. New York: Dover, 1966.

Homer The Iliad, ed. Martin Hammond. Harmondsworth: Penguin, 1987.

Hughes, Thomas P. 'Technological momentum', in Does Technology Drive History? eds Merritt Roe Smith and Leo Marx. Cambridge, Mass.: MIT, 1996, pp. 101–113.

Hyman, Anthony Science and Reform: selected works of Charles Babbage, Cambridge: Cambridge University Press, 1989.

Kadrey, Richard Metrophage, London: Gollancz, 1989.

Kant, Immanuel Critique of Judgement, trans. Werner S. Pluhar. Indianapolis: Hackett, [1790] 1986.

Kauffman, Stuart At Home in the Universe, Harmondsworth: Penguin, 1995.

Kay, Lily E. Who Wrote the Book of Life?, Stanford, Calif.: Stanford University Press, 2000.

Kellner, Douglas Baudrillard: a critical reader, Oxford: Blackwell, 1994.

Kellner, Douglas Media Cultures, London: Routledge, 1995.

Kelly, Kevin Out of Control, New York: Addison-Wesley, 1994.

Kleist, Heinrich von 'On the marionette theatre' [1810], in Essays on Dolls, ed. Idris Parry. Harmondsworth: Penguin, 1994.

Kuhn, Thomas The Structure of Scientific Revolutions, Chicago: University of Chicago Press, 1962.

La Mettrie, Julian de Machine Man and Other Writings [1747], ed. Ann Thompson. Cambridge: Cambridge University Press, 1996.

Langton, Christopher G. 'Artificial life', in The Philosophy of Artificial Life, ed. Margaret Boden. Oxford: Oxford University Press, 1996, pp. 39–94.

Lardner, Dionysius 'Babbage's Calculating Engine', Edinburgh Review CXX [1843], ed. Anthony Hyman, Cambridge: Cambridge University Press, 1989, pp. 51–109.

Latour, Bruno *We Have Never Been Modern*, tr. Catherine Porter. Hemel Hempstead: Harvester-Wheatsheaf, 1993.

Latour, Bruno 'Stengers's shibboleth', Introduction to Isabelle Stengers *Power and Invention: situating science*, Minneapolis: University of Minnesota Press, 1997, pp. vii–xx.

Latour, Bruno 'One more turn after the social turn', in *The Science Studies Reader*, ed. Mario Biagioli. New York: Routledge, 1999, pp. 276–289.

Leibniz, G.W. 'Towards a universal characteristic' [1677], in *Leibniz: Selections*, ed. Philip P. Wiener. New York: Scribner's, 1951.

Leibniz, G.W. 'Letter to Countess Elizabeth' [1678], in *Leibniz: Philosophical Essays*, eds Robin Ariew and Daniel Garber. Indianapolis: Hackett, 1989.

Leibniz, G.W. *Monadology* [1714], eds Robin Ariew and Daniel Garber. Indianapolis: Hackett, 1989.

Lenoir, Timothy '*Was the last turn the right turn? The semiotic turn and A.J. Greimas*', in *The Science Studies Reader*, ed. Mario Biagioli. New York: Routledge, 1999, pp. 290–301.

Levinson, Paul *Digital McLuhan*, London: Routledge, 1997.

Lévi-Strauss, Claude *The Elementary Structures of Kinship* [1949], Boston: Beacon Press, 1969.

Lévy, Pierre *Becoming Virtual: reality and the digital age*, New York: Plenum, 1998.

Levy, Steven *Artificial Life*, London: Jonathan Cape, 1992.

Lovelace, Ada 'Sketch of the Analytical Engine invented by Charles Babbage, Esq. by L.F. Menabrea of Turin, with notes upon the memoir by the translator', *Scientific Memoirs* (1843), in *Science and Reform: selected works of Charles Babbage*, ed. Anthony Hyman, Cambridge: Cambridge University Press, 1989, pp. 243–311.

Luhmann, Niklas *Social Systems*, tr. William Whobrey. Stanford: Stanford University Press, 1995.

Lyotard, Jean-François *The Postmodern Condition: a report on knowledge*, tr. Geoff Bennington and Brian Massumi. Manchester: Manchester University Press, 1984.

MacDonald Ross, George *Leibniz*, Oxford: Oxford University Press, 1984.

MacKenzie, Donald A. and Wajcman, Judy *Social Shaping of Technology*, London: Open University Press, [1985] 1999.

Mandelbrot, Benoit *The Fractal Geometry of Nature*, New York: Freeman, 1977.

Marcuse, Herbert *One Dimensional Man*, London: Sphere, 1968.

Marx, Karl *Capital*, Volume 1, London: Lawrence and Wishart, 1974.

Marx, Karl *Grundrisse*, tr. and ed. Martin Nicolaus. Harmondsworth: Penguin, 1993.

Marx, Karl and Engels, Friedrich *The Communist Manifesto*, Harmondsworth: Penguin, 1973.

Mauss, Marcel *General Theory of Magic*, London: Routledge and Kegan Paul, 1974.

Otto Mayr, *Authority, Liberty and Automatic Machinery in Early Modern Europe*, Baltimore, Md.: Johns Hopkins University Press, 1986.

McCaffery, Larry ed. *Storming the Reality Studio: a casebook of cyberpunk and postmodern fiction*, Durham, N.C.: Duke University Press, 1992.

McLuhan, Marshall *The Gutenberg Galaxy*, London: Routledge and Kegan Paul, 1962.

McLuhan, Marshall *Understanding Media: the Extensions of Man*, London: Sphere, 1967.

McLuhan, Marshall *Counterblast*, London: Rapp and Whiting, 1969.

Mitcham, Carl *Thinking Through Technology*, Chicago: University of Chicago Press, 1994.

Monod, Jacques *Chance and Necessity*, London: Fontana, 1971.

Morse, Margaret 'What do cyborgs eat? Oral logic in an information society', *Discourse* 16.3 (1994): 87–121.

Myerson, George *Donna Haraway and GM Foods*, London: Icon, 2000.

O'Brien, Stephen 'Blade Runner: if only you could see what I have seen with your eyes!', *SFX* 71 (December 2000): 7–9.

Orlan. '"I do not want to look like . . .": Orlan on becoming-Orlan', tr. Carolyn Ducker. *Women's Art* 64 (1995): 5–10.

Plant, Sadie *Zeros and Ones: digital women and the new technoculture*, London: Fourth Estate, 1997.

Poe, Edgar Allan 'Maelzel's chess-player' [1836], in *The Complete Tales and Poems of Edgar Allan Poe*, ed. Mladinska Knijga. New York: Vintage, 1966.

Poundstone, William *The Recursive Universe: cosmic complexity and the limits of scientific knowledge*, New York: William Morrow, 1985.

Price, Derek J. de Solla 'Automata and the origins of mechanism and mechanistic philosophy', *Technology and Culture* 5.1 (1964): 9–23.

Prigogine, Ilya and Stengers, Isabelle *Order out of Chaos*, London: Flamingo, 1985.

Ray, Thomas S. 'An approach to the synthesis of life', in *The Philosophy of Artificial Life*, ed. Margaret Boden. Oxford: Oxford University Press, 1996, pp. 111–145.

Rheingold, Howard *Virtual Reality*, London: Secker and Warburg, 1991.

Robertson, George, Mash, Melinda, Tickner, Lisa, Bird, Jon, Curtis, Barry and Putnam, Tim, eds *Futurenatural. Nature, science, culture*, London: Routledge, 1996.

Ross, Andrew *Strange Weather: culture, science and technology in the age of Limits*. London: Verso, 1991.

Schaffer, Simon 'Babbage's intelligence: calculating engines and the factory system', *Critical Inquiry* 5.1 (1994): 203–227.

Schaffer, Simon 'Babbage's dancer and the impressarios of mechanism', ed. in *Cultural Babbage: time, technology and invention*, eds Francis Spufford and Jenny Uglow. London: Faber, 1996, pp. 53–80.

Schaffer, Simon 'Enlightened automata', in *The Sciences in Enlightened Europe*, eds William Clark, Jan Golinski and Simon Schaffer. Chicago: University of Chicago Press, 1999, pp. 126–165.

Simon, Herbert *The Sciences of the Artificial*, Cambridge, Mass.: MIT, [1969] 1996.

Simondon, Gilbert *Le Mode d'existence des objets techniques*, Paris: Aubier, 1958.

Smith, Adam *Essays on Philosophical Subjects* [1795], Oxford: Clarendon Press, 1980.

Smith, Anthony *Goodbye Gutenberg: the newspaper revolution of the 1980s*, Oxford: Oxford University Press, 1981.

Smith, Merritt Roe and Marx, Leo eds *Does Technology Drive History*, Cambridge, Mass.: MIT, 1996.

Sobchack, Vivian 'New age mutant ninja hackers: reading Mondo 2000', in *Flame Wars*, Special edition of the *South Atlantic Quarterly*, 92.4, ed. Mark Dery. Durham, N.C.: Duke University Press, 1993, pp. 569–584.

Springer, Claudia *Electronic Eros: bodies and desire in the postindustrial age*, London: Athlone, 1996.

Spufford, Francis and Uglow, Jenny eds *Cultural Babbage: time, technology and invention*, London: Faber, 1996.

Stelarc 'From psycho-body to cyber-systems: images as post-human entities', in *The Cybercultures Reader*, eds David Bell and Barbara M. Kennedy. London: Routledge, 2000.

Stengers, Isabelle *Power and Invention: situating science*, Minneapolis: University of Minnesota Press, 1997.

Sterling, Bruce *Schismatrix*, Harmondsworth: Penguin, 1985.

Sterling, Bruce ed. *Mirrorshades*, New York: Ace, 1986.

Sterling, Bruce *Heavy Weather*, London: Phoenix, 1995.

Sterling, Bruce *Distraction*, New York: Ace, 1999.

Stone, Allucquere Rosanne *The War of Desire and Technology at the Close of the Mechanical Age*, Cambridge, Mass.: MIT, 1995.

Swade, Doron *Charles Babbage and his Calculating Engines*, London: Science Museum, 1991.

Swade, Doron *The Cogwheel Brain*, New York: Little, Brown, 2000.

Terranova, Tiziana 'Digital Darwin: nature, evolution and control in the rhetoric of electronic communication', *Techoscience: New Formations* 29, eds Judy Berland and Sarah Kember (1996a): 69–83.

Terranova, Tiziana 'Posthuman unbounded: artificial evolution and high-tech subcultures', in *Futurenatural. Nature, science, culture*, eds George Robertson et al. London: Routledge, 1996b, pp. 165–180.

Theweleit, Klaus *Male Fantasies*, vol. 2, Minneapolis: Minnesota University Press, 1986.

Thom, René *Structural Stability and Morphogenesis*, New York: W.A. Benjamin, 1975.

Turing, Alan 'On computable numbers', *Proceedings of the London Mathematical Society*, series 2.42 (1936): 230–265.

Turing, Alan. 'Computing machinery and intelligence', *Mind* 51 (1950): 433–460, in *The Philosophy of Artificial Intelligence*, ed. Margaret Boden. Oxford: Oxford University Press, 1990.

Turing, Alan 'The chemical basis of morphogenesis', *Philosophical Transactions of the Royal Society of London* B 237 (1952): 37–72.

Ure, Andrew *The Philosophy of Manufactures*, London, 1835.

von Neumann, John. *The Computer and the Brain* [1958], New Haven and London: Yale University Press, 1999.

Ward, Mark *Virtual Organisms: the startling world of artificial life*, London: Macmillan, 2000.

Warwick, Kevin *In the Mind of the Machine*, London: Arrow, 1998.

White, Lynn *Medieval Technology and Social Change*, Oxford: Oxford University Press, 1964.

Wiener, Norbert. *Cybernetics: control and communication in animal and machine* [1948], Cambridge, Mass.: MIT, 1962.

Wiener, Norbert *The Human Use of Human Beings*, London: Free Association, [1954] 1989.

Williams, Raymond *Television, Technology and Cultural Form*, London: Fontana, 1974.

Williams, Raymond *Marxism and Literature*, Oxford: Oxford University Press, 1977.

Woolley, Benjamin *Virtual Worlds: a Journey in hype and hyperreality*, Oxford: Blackwell, 1992.

Woolley, Benjamin *The Bride of Science: romance, reason and Byron's daughter*, London: Macmillan, 1999.

Wordsworth, William 'Prelude', in *The Poetical Works of William Wordsworth*, vol. V, eds E. de Selincourt and Helen Derbyshire. Oxford: Oxford University Press, 1949.

Ziman, John M. ed. *Technological Innovation as an Evolutionary Process*, Cambridge: Cambridge University Press, 2000.

GLOSSARY

Actor-network theory

Actor-network theory derives from the work of Bruno Latour (see especially Latour [1993] for an excellent account of it). It has been highly influential in the field of 'science studies', but has also, through Donna Haraway (1989, 1991, 1998), become an important component of cybercultural studies. Actor-network theory offers a means to treat not merely of cultural things, but also of physical things. Thus it presents an alternative to (a) transforming technology into a discursive entity in order to discuss it in terms of cultural and media studies; and (b) treating cultural phenomena as irrelevant from the point of view of engineering and the sciences. It gives, therefore, ideally equal treatment to human and non-human agents in the analysis of highly technologised socio-cultural phenomena. In Carl Mitcham's (1994) terms, it bridges the gulf that exists between 'humanities philosophy of technology' and 'engineering philosophy of technology'. The goal of the theory is to provide a symmetrical account of the relations between human and non-human actors, although changes in these relations become difficult to model in accordance with this demand for symmetry, since they are often precisely not symmetrical.

Algorithm

A series of instructions - a recipe or formula - used by a computer, or a program, to carry out a specific task or solve a problem. The term is generally used in the context of software to describe the program logic for a specific function. The two important factors in determining how to design an algorithm are the accuracy of the result and the efficiency of the processing.

Analogue

A form of representation, such as a chemical photograph, a film, or a vinyl disc, in which a material surface carries continuous variations of tone, light, or some other signal. Analogue representation is based upon an unsegmented code while a digital medium is based upon a segmented one in which information is divided into discrete elements. The hands of a traditional (analogue) clock which continuously sweep its face, in contrast to a digital clock which announces each second in isolation, is a common example.

Artificial intelligence (AI)

One of the two main 'sciences of the artificial' (Simon 1996) artificial intelligence is an ongoing research programme aiming to produce intelligent programmes (soft AI), or artificially intelligent things (robotics, hard AI). The two main branches of the first are Good Old Fashioned AI (GOFAI; see Haugeland 1981), and connectionism.

Artificial life (Alife)

Otherwise called 'synthetic biology', artificial life does not seek to understand life as it is but to create life as it could be. This can be in any one of three forms: hard Alife, or robotics; soft Alife or online 'creatures'; and wet Alife or engineering life from the ground up. The most extreme form of soft Alife argues that virtual 'creatures' are already alive, albeit in a silicon, rather than a carbon, environment. See Langton in Boden (1996), Ward (1999), Terranova and Hayles in Bird et al. (1996).

ASCII (American Standard Code for Information Interchange)

ASCII is a standard developed by the American National Standards Institute (ANSI) to define how computers write and read characters. The ASCII set of 128 characters includes letters, numbers, punctuation, and control codes (such as a character that marks the end of a line). Each letter or other character is represented by a number: an uppercase A, for example, is the number 65, and a lowercase z is the number 122.

Authorship

The idea that the meaning and quality of a text or other product is explained by name, identity and inherent abilities of the individual person who made it rather than seeing a text as the outcome of wider cultural forces or its meanings arising in the act of its being read.

Avatar

Originally the incarnation of a God in Hinduism. A visual representation of a participant in a shared digital environment (e.g. in online chat). It can look like a person, an object, or an animal. An interface for the self.

Bandwidth

Capacity to carry information. It can apply to telephone or network wiring as well as system buses, radio frequency signals, and monitors. Bandwidth is most accurately measured in cycles per second, or hertz (Hz), also as bits or bytes per second. So, for example, we might describe certain kinds of transmission capabilities as a narrow bandwidth carrying small amounts of data slowly, and others as wide bandwidth, carrying large amounts of data fast.

Biotechnology

Biotechnology, at once a scientific, a corporate and an artistic concern, consists in various approaches to re-engineering organisms for new purposes. Cloning, crop re-engineering, xenotransplantation, genomics and transgenics derive their principal impetus from the informational nature of genetic transfer, whose greatest artefact thus far is the human genome. It features heavily in cyberpunk fiction, as well as in the work of performance artists such as Orlan and Stelarc.

Browser

Viewing software that interprets HTML. A variety of extensions allow the display of other formats for audio, video and animation.

Bulletin board system

A computer that many users can connect to through phone lines and associated telecommunications networks. Usually has email and message conferences, as well as files and chat. A BBS may or may not have connections to other computers. A common communication 'space' for people with similar interests or goals.

Canon, canonical
A cultural product or collection of products (books, works of art, theories, buildings), which has come to be a defining product in the orthodox history of a discipline or practice.

Cartesian grid
A schema or conception of space defined by the co-ordinates of height, width, and depth, a cubic, gridded, measurable space: the classical, mathematical representation of three-dimensional space.

CGI
Computer-generated imagery. The term is commonly used to describe computer animation and special effects in film and television production.

Chaos
Chaos theory stems from mathematical researches into unpredictable phenomena arising in otherwise determinist systems. A determinist system is one in which, given a knowledge of the initial state of the system, its future may be accurately predicted or modelled. The famous 'butterfly effect', which occurs when tiny changes in a system (a butterfly in Florida flaps its wings) give rise to large-scale effects (there is a storm in China), is therefore both deterministic (it arises from given causes) and unpredictable (these causes cannot be modelled). Chaos theories are important here because they enable us to model technological determinism without forsaking the complexity of social and technological relations, on the one hand, and, on the other, emergent determinisms, such as Ellul (1964) and de Landa (1991) argue for.

Cheats
In computer and video games, to 'cheat' is to use a code or password to either gain access to another section or level of the game, or to change certain of the game's parameters. For example, a cheat may give the player more 'lives'. Originally included in games by programmers to facilitate testing of games before publication, they quickly became part of game culture as shared knowledge between players, and also support the production of published guides and magazine supplements. More recently 'patches' have added to the possibilities of manipulating the computer game. Available from the Internet for example, patches change a game's parameters more significantly, adding new levels or different characters.

Commodities, commodification
A commodity is a product or service that is bought or sold. In the Marxist sense used within this book, the commodity form underpins the capitalist market and, to a greater or lesser extent, modern society. For Marx, commodities were not simple objects, but, once they were exchanged in markets they took on values and a 'life of their own'. Commodification is, on one level,

the process described above, but it is often applied to questions of the commercialisation of culture – for example, it might be argued that with the arrival of advertising, online shopping, etc. the World Wide Web has been 'commodified'.

Community
Our sense of belonging to social groups which often extend beyond the boundaries of specific place to include taste, consumption, shared interests and shared discursive codes. Used here to describe groups of Internet users sharing a common interest connected via networked digital media.

Computer-mediated communication (CMC)
Simply the activity of communicating with other individuals or groups using digitised information transmitted through telephone and other telecommunications links such as cable, and satellite. This covers everything from email, to participation in shared communication forums such as newsgroups or bulletin boards, chat rooms and avatar-based communication spaces online. A major site of study in the development of new media studies.

Connectionism
Connectionism is one of the major branches of AI research. As opposed to 'Good Old Fashioned AI', which is effectively concerned to model intelligent functions in software, it understands intelligence as a function of the structural complexity of brains, and seeks to reproduce that complexity in artificial forms. In connectionist computation, instead of pushing all tasks through a single central processing unit (CPU), it 'connects' several, on the understanding that each CPU represents not a whole brain, but rather a brain cell or neurone (see the papers by Clark and Cussins in Boden (1990). Like many of the sciences of the artificial, cyberculture has provided an occasion for it to migrate from the sciences into culture at large (see Plant 1997).

Constructionism
An important theoretical approach to social and cultural phenomena, constructionism consists in the rejection of the idea of firm foundations for concepts such as 'identity', 'gender', and so on, in favour of trying to understand them as emerging from social and cultural interaction, usually (but not always), of a linguistic or discursive character. It is therefore highly opposed to any and all forms of physicalism or essentialism, which it regards as making unwarrantable claims to authority on the grounds of a presumed 'prelinguistic' or 'prediscursive' access to an unconstructed real. Not to be confused with *constructivism*.

Constructivism
This concept, derived from the philosophical work of Gilles Deleuze and Félix Guattari (1988) and Isabelle Stengers (1997), arises on the back of the inroads into physical re-engineering that have been made by the sciences of the artificial – AI and Alife – and by biotechnology. These sciences show us that things

themselves are constructed, and can therefore be reconstructed. Unlike constructionism, however, it emphasises that the construction in question is physical, not merely discursive or social.

Convergence

Term used to describe the ways in which previously discreet media forms and processes are drawn together and combined though digital technologies. This occurs both at the levels of production and distribution. At the level of production, for example, newspapers, music, and television once had very different physical production bases but could all now be substantively produced using the same networked multimedia computer. Secondly, at the level of distribution previously discrete networks are absorbed into the single process of online networks – news, music, entertainment can all be accessed through the Internet. Third, convergence also refers to the ways in which media ownership is increasingly concentrated through mergers of corporations that would previously have operated in different sectors (e.g. Time-Warner and AOL).

Cyberculture

We use this term in two related, but distinct, ways in this book. In the first it is taken to refer to the complex of 'culture + technology' derived from the history of cybernetics. This is because cybernetics is concerned with information systems not only in machines but also, as Norbert Wiener (1948) has it, in animals and in social structures. Accordingly, the term does not only refer to a culture with digital machines, but applies equally to industrial and mechanical cultures.

Secondly, cyberculture is used to refer to the theoretical study of cyberculture as already defined; that is, it denotes a particular approach to the study of the 'culture + technology' complex. This loose sense of cyberculture as a discursive category groups together a wide range of (on many levels contradictory) approaches, from theoretical analyses of the implications of digital culture to the popular discourses of science and technology journalism.

What unites these approaches is the assertion that technology, particularly computer technology, and culture are profoundly interrelated in the contemporary world.

Cybernetics

Cybernetics, according to Norbert Wiener (1948), who coined the term, is the science of 'control and communication in the animal and the machine'. Already, then, heralding the rise of the concept of the 'cybernetic organism', or cyborg, cybernetics views the states of any system – biological, informational, economic, political – in terms of the regulation of information. This occurs in two ways. Most systems are governed by negative feedback, whereby systems reinforce their stability by reference to an optimal state of the system that negates other states (i.e. resists change). For example, a thermostat responds to both heat and cold in order to ensure an optimal temperature. On the other hand, processes governed by positive feedback are said to be in a runaway state,

where minute changes become self-amplifying and change the overall state of the system. An example of this latter would be any process of historical change. Although cybernetics fell into disrepute in media studies due to the rejection of Shannon and Weaver's essentially one-way theory of communication, cyberculture has predictably seen a rise in its fortunes. See Plant (1997).

Cyberpunk

A genre of science fiction that has had a marked influence on the theoretical study of digital technologies and networks. William Gibson's novel *Neuromancer* is particularly influential, as is the film *Bladerunner*; both are characterised by gritty, noir-influenced narratives and a fascination with new, intimate relationships between the human body or mind and technologies. Gibson's cyberspace is a key example, as is the figure of the cyborg. A similar genre is evident in Japanese popular culture. Examples familiar to Western audiences include the animated film *Akira*, and the comics *Bubblegum Crisis*. The influence of cyberpunk themes is evident in a wide range of popular fantasy texts, from *Pokemon* to *Robot Wars*. The term has also been taken to refer to an actual youth subculture in the 1980s – of postpunk streetwise hackers. Other cyberpunk writers include Pat Cadigan, Bruce Sterling and Neal Stephenson.

Cyberspace

A term coined by science-fiction writer William Gibson to describe his fictional computer-generated virtual reality in which the information wealth of a future corporate society is represented as an abstract space. Predating the Internet as a popular phenomenon, Gibson's cyberspace has been widely interpreted as prophetic (though he says he got the idea from watching children playing video games).
The word is also used in very general terms to cover any sense of digitally generated 'space', from the World Wide Web to virtual reality.

Cyborg

Cybernetic organism. Refers to a wide range of actual and fictional hybrids of the human and the machine, from the use of medical implants such as pacemakers to the technologically enhanced individuals of science fiction. The figure of the cyborg has become one of the defining moments of recent cinematic culture, as well as a central figure in theorising 'post-human' relationships with technologies. Arnold Schwarzenegger stripping living flesh from his titanium-alloy frame is as familiar an image in cyberculture as the gamer in the arcade that set Gibson's fictions off towards cyberspace. The concept originates from work done by Manfred Clynes in 1960, who was seeking a solution to the problems posed by the sheer volume of information an astronaut must process, along with the environmental difficulties of space flight. A machine-mediated human, Clynes reasoned, would be better placed than an unaided human, to cope with these problems. As the examples show, key to the cyborg is the conjunction of biological and technological elements. Notions of the implications of these hybrid entities are similarly various: they may offer new ideas for thinking about the individual in the technologised postmodern world (e.g. Haraway 1990), or offer solutions to a perceived redundancy of the unenhanced human body in the near future (e.g. the work and ideas of the artist Stelarc).

Desktop

Another term for the PC or Apple Mac Graphical User Interface. These GUIs use the desktop and stationery as a metaphor – hence files are stored in folders, unwanted files are placed in a wastebin, and so on.

Diegesis

All of the narrative elements in a film that appear to emanate from the fictional world of the film itself – the words the actors speak, the music whose source we can see in a scene. A non-diegetic element, for example, would be a voice-over.

Digital

New media are also often referred to as digital media by virtue of the fact that media which previously existed in discrete analogue forms (e.g. the newspaper, the film, the radio transmission) now converge into the unifying form of digital data. They can now all be either converted to or generated as a series of numbers which are handled by computers in a binary system. Media processes are brought into the symbolic realm of mathematics rather than those of physics or chemistry. Once coded numerically, the input data in a digital media production can immediately be subject to the mathematical processes of addition, subtraction, multiplication and division through algorithms contained within software.

Discourse, discursive

Discourses are elaborated systems of language (conversations, theories, arguments, descriptions) which are built up or evolved as part of particular social behaviours (e.g. expressing emotion, writing legal contracts, practising medicine). The suggestion is therefore that ideas do not circulate in a vacuum but are bound up with forms of social practice and institutional power. Discourses, like the words and concepts they employ, can then be said to construct their objects because they lead us to think about them and know them in particular ways. 'Discursive', as used in this book, refers to the way members of a culture invest meaning in and think, talk, and write about new image and communication technologies.

Dispersal

Used in this book to characterise some aspects of new media which, by contrast with traditional mass media, exist in a more diffuse and fragmented way within the culture at large. Networked-based communications are more dispersed than centralised means of distribution. New media production resources are more widely dispersed than centralised mass media production resources.

Dotcoms

Businesses attempting to use the Internet as their primary marketplace. The term comes from the widespread use of URLs as company brands, for example Boo.com (when spoken aloud: 'boo dot com'). Dotcoms generated a great deal of excitement and speculation in the late 1990s, excitement that soon proved misplaced.

Dystopian

Usually used in discussions about new media that see developments in technology as primarily malign. The opposite of utopian.

Email

A system of servers and software that allows messages to be sent to a particular individual in accord with agreed standards.

Embodiment

Referring to the assertion that human knowledge and experience is inseparable from the biological and socially constituted human body, this term is generally used to counter assumptions or claims, in the study of new technologies, that the body is becoming less important – for example, that we 'leave our bodies behind' when we enter Virtual Reality.

Enlightenment

An intellectual and historical period in Europe dating from the early eighteenth century. Enlightenment thought challenged the intellectual dominance of the Church and a religious world-view in the name of reason and science. The Enlightenment attitude to technology – that it was inherently progressive and a force for reason and moral good – has been challenged recently in postmodernist thought. Postmodernism is sometimes seen, then, as, amongst other things, the end of the 'Enlightenment project'.

Ethnography

The empirical study of ways of life of particular groups or cultures through participant observation. In the study of new media this may involve established media audiences methodologies (interviews, observations of media use, etc.) or the development of new methodologies to study on-line communities.

Flaming

The practice of sending abusive messages to one with whom one disagrees. An aggressive use of email, bulletin boards or chat rooms.

Frankfurt School

A group of scholars and critics associated with the Institute for Social Research founded in Frankfurt in 1923, before dispersing during the Nazi period and returning to Frankfurt in 1953. Leading authors include Theodor Adorno, Herbert Marcuse, Max Horkheimer, Walter Benjamin and Jurgen Habermas. These writers all engage in a critical theory using the Marxist idea of 'critical theory'; that is, to change as well as to describe the world. Of particular historical significance in so far as they were the first scholars to write about the culture industry, seeing it as part of a system which produced passive consumers rather than active citizens.

Genre

Used in media studies to describe particular groups or categories of text that are recognisable to producers and to audiences (typically, for example, 'the western', 'the soap opera', 'the romance'). The identity of the genre resides in shared textual characteristics, common signs that the reader would expect to be able to identify within similar kinds of texts. Characterised in the contemporary period as much by the breakdown of specific genre boundaries in the circulation of 'hybrid' texts produced in the search for innovative media products – for example, reality TV documentary programmes of emergency service activities that combine highly fictionalised action techniques with factual actuality footage.

Hackers

Popularly understood to mean destructive and antisocial computer experts (usually youthful) breaking into computer networks and designing computer viruses, and the subject of media scares in the 1980s. However, the term originates in the computer research facilities of US universities in the late 1950s. These hackers, though often given to pranks, were not so much antisocial as instrumental in the development of personal computing and, with their 'ethic' of open-source coding and anti-authoritarianism, influential on later discourses of computer media, especially around the Internet.

Home computer

Or microcomputer. Predating the personal computer and its move from office to home in the mid- to late 1980s, home computers were first produced at the end of the 1970s. Whereas PCs are either IBM or Apple Mac compatible, home computers were based on a wide range of platforms. In the UK, Clive Sinclair's ZX80 and ZX81 were among the first popular models.

HTML (HyperText Markup Language)

HTML is a collection of formatting commands that create hypertext documents or web pages. A web browser interprets the HTML commands embedded in the page and uses them to format the page's text and graphic elements. HTML commands cover many types of text formatting (bold and italic text, lists, headline fonts in various sizes, and so on), and also have the ability to include graphics and other non-text elements.

Humanism

Everything is by man and for man: this is perhaps the most straightforward characterisation of humanism. In more detail, humanism is the theoretical (and political) prioritisation of the subject over the physical and/or social forces that act upon it. This is a problem for cyberculture, since it is concerned with precisely the technologies with which subjects interact, or which, many argue, act on humans in culture. Some theorists, such as Bruno Latour (1993), therefore argue that it is necessary to grant the status of agency to

non-human entities, such as machines, animals, institutions, diseases, and so on (see *actor-network theory*).

Hyperreality, hyperrealism

As used by postmodernist thinkers Umberto Eco and Jean Baudrillard, hyperreality as a concept is a response to the problematic theoretical status of the 'real world' in contemporary media culture. For Eco it refers to an emerging culture of 'fakes' in the US in particular (waxwork museums, theme parks, animatronics), whereas for Baudrillard it is synonymous with simulacra – hyperreality is not a distortion of reality, rather it has superseded reality. Hyperrealism is also a term for a dominant aesthetic in animation in which realist cinematic codes (of narrative and visual imagery) are adopted, but exaggerated, in animation.

These two terms, though distinct, come together in critical studies of the products of the Walt Disney Corporation. Eco and Baudrillard both use Disneyland as a case study of hyperreality, and it is Disney's animated films which are the prime exemplars of hyperrealism.

Hypertext

A kind of writing facilitated by computer technology in which documents and parts of documents are linked together to allow the reader to follow his or her own 'path' through a body of information or a narrative. Developed by Ted Nelson in the 1960s (though often regarded as originating in the ideas of Vannevar Bush, Roosevelt's science adviser, at the end of the Second World War), the hypertext model forms the basis of the organisation of the World Wide Web.

ICT (Information and communications technologies)

Used to denote that range of technology associated with the distribution of information in both *analogue* and *digital* formats.

Idealism

See *Materialism*.

Immersion

While normally referring to being under the surface of, or 'in' a body of liquid, in the present context it refers to the experience of being inside the world of a constructed image. The image is not before the viewer on a surface from whose distance they can measure their own position in physical space. Rather, it appears to surround them. By extension the term is used to describe the experience of the user of certain new media technologies (particularly VR, but also videogames) in which the subject loses any sense of themselves as separate from the medium or its simulated world.

Incommensurability

The concept of incommensurability stems from Thomas Kuhn's famous work, *The Structure of Scientific Revolutions* (1962). In it, Kuhn argues that during periods of large-scale change in scientific theories, the new theory does not explain the same phenomena as the old theory did. The two theories – or paradigms – are therefore said to be incommensurable in that they do not measure the same phenomena, nor can they be subsumed under a common measurement (this is what the word 'incommensurable' literally means). Implicit in this is the further idea that the entities to which theories refer do not really exist, but are only functional terms within a given theory (that is, they are said to be theory-dependent). Thus Kuhn's argument is often used in support of constructionist positions.

Information revolution
See *Knowledge economy*.

Instrumental, instrumentalism
As used in this book, the instrumental refers to the use of media technologies for practical, educational or productive ends, rather than for pleasure or entertainment. In general terms, instrumentalism concerns the 'editing out' of social, political and economic phenomena that have no clear output. Under technoscience, for example, such outputs are measured by efficiency gains alone. Recently, educational policies in a number of countries have emphasised the instrumental uses of learning for the knowledge economy at the expense of more abstract notions of knowledge as an end in itself.

Interactive
Technically the ability for the user to intervene in computing processes and see the effects of the intervention in real time. Also used in communications theory to describe human communication based on dialogue and exchange.

Interface
Usually used to denote the symbolic software that enables humans to use computers, and to access the many layers of underlying code that causes a software to function (e.g. the *desktop*).

Internet
The collection of networks that link computers and servers together.

IRC
Internet Relay Chat – chat room technologies that allow many users to type text into a common 'conversation' in more or less real time.

Knowledge economy
The widely expressed thesis that, at the end of the twentieth century, the industrialised world is undergoing some kind of economic restructuring. The depth and significance of this 'revolution' is argued over, depending on the theoretical or political position of the commentators, but there is a widespread sense that information, knowledge, intellectual property, etc. are increasingly important factors in late capitalist political economy. ICTs are usually seen as instrumental in these changes, precisely because of the significance of information processing and communication.

Materialism
Two concepts of materialism are relevant in this book:
1 the doctrine that we are dealing always with physical things, whether we are looking at machines, meanings, or effects. Further, materialism is the doctrine that all is matter, such that automata could be constructed from metal, or that machines need no 'soul', 'mind' or 'personality' in order to be intelligent;
2 derived from Marxist thought, a materialist approach within cultural and media studies is one that foregrounds the economic and social contexts and determinants of cultural and media forms. These forms then are understood as historically situated and the product of conflicting power relationships. They may well function ideologically, distorting our understanding of the real, material relations that govern our work, leisure and lives. This sense of materialism sets itself against idealism – an approach which assumes an inherent logic or teleology to particular cultural phenomena. To an idealist, technocultural change (for example, developments in cinematic realism) is the gradual, but inevitable, realisation of a true essence, independent of historical or social contingencies (for example, the assumption that CGI will one day exactly replicate the look of conventional cinematography).

McLuhanite
Associated with the claims and ideas of Marshall McLuhan – in particular the idea that media systems have transformative effects on human subjectivity and society.

Microcomputer
See *Home computer*.

Modernism
Modernism takes shape definitively as a series of artistic (e.g. impressionism, cubism, futurism) and philosophical (i.e. Marxism) movements that were themselves responses to the problems and crises of social life brought about by the mass industrialisation and urbanisation of nineteenth-century Western countries. In this book the term is more often used to refer to the kinds of centralised methods of state and economic organisation and their associated mass media systems developed in the first half of the twentieth century.

Modernity
The condition of being modern – derived originally from the upheavals in Western thought that date from the eighteenth-century Enlightenment, i.e. a sense that to be 'modern' is to be *against* traditional hierarchies of state, monarch and religion and to be *for* the novel, the innovative and the progressive.

Molar, molecular
This pair of contrasting (not opposing) terms was borrowed, by Deleuze and Guattari (1984, 1988), from Jaques Monod's use of them in his (1971) account of 'molecular cybernetics'. Firstly, molar phenomena (subjects, bodies, objects) are composed of molecular ones. If we concentrate our theories of things on molar

phenomena, as for example humanism must, being essentially based on human actions, we therefore start from a position of several autonomous things, each disconnected from the other. If we start, however, from the molecular level, we do not merely start with smaller items, we start with connective phenomena, from which larger-scale entities may arise. While the contrast may appear to be between large and small entities, it really lies between isolated entities and connectivity. The example of gaming is used to discuss this contrast in **5.4.4**.

MOO

See MUD.

MP3 (Motion Picture Export Group Layer 3)

A popular format for encoding sound, widely used for the digitisation of music

MUD

Multi-User Dungeon (sometimes also 'domain' or 'dimension') Dating from the early 1980s, an online role-playing environment originally derived from Dungeons and Dragons type games. Normally text-based, Multi-User Dungeons allow numerous people to play and interact in the same game scenario at the same time. Also MOO, Multi-User Object-Oriented spaces in which users built an environment in 'object-oriented' language which allowed pre-coded navigation through text-constructed 'spaces'. Increasingly replaced by shared spaces in which users speak to each other and interact through 'avatars' in, for example, online gaming.

Neo-liberalism

Used to describe the economic theory that argues for a return to completely free and open markets as the best way of ordering society. Originating in the US in the late 1970s as a response to crises in the post-war economic consensus, neo-liberalism aggressively seeks to turn as many goods and services as possible into commodities and to find as many markets as possible for trading those commodities. Characterised by a critique of state regulation of both the economy and social questions, neo-liberalism attacks the post-war consensus on welfare, as well as media regulation, for example. Neo-liberal attitudes were evident in the promotion and celebration of the 'new economy' of the **dotcom** phenomenon of the late 1990s.

Networked

Denotes a collection of computers connected to each other. May be as few as two PCs

Newsgroups

Name given to the topic-specific information and opinion exchange sites on the Internet that are collectively known as 'Usenet News'. The newsgroup has the quality of an unending text conversation in which the messages respond to and comment on previous messages. Some newsgroups have an editorial control policy run by a discussion 'moderator'; others are simply open to anyone to say anything.

Nominalism

Nominalism is opposed to the philosophical sense of realism. Kuhn's *incommensurability* thesis, for example, could be said to be nominalist in so far as it makes the entities referred to by theories into mere names (hence nom-inalism) of things, rather than names of real entities. Similarly, then, all constructionist accounts of things are philosophically nominalist, diverting attention from what really exists to the ways they are named or constructed through discourse.

Online

To be logged on to a server.

Paradigm

The term 'paradigm', like incommensurability, stems in its contemporary usage from Thomas Kuhn (1962). In its loosest sense, it refers to the set of beliefs and opinions about particular knowledges that are regarded as 'established'. In this sense, the paradigm operates as a kind of 'horizon of askable questions' at a certain cultural–historical juncture. More specifically, it refers to the explicitly formulated governing ideas of the time; eighteenth-century physics, for example, had mechanism as its paradigm. In this instance, the paradigm identifies the genuine problems that arise within it. A paradigm shift occurs when the problems begin to outnumber the solutions, thus turning critical attention on the paradigm itself. Kuhn calls this situation one of 'crisis'. A new paradigm will then arise that solves these new problems at the expense of the old paradigm. MacKenzie and Wacjman (1999) make use of Kuhn's language in this context.

PC (personal computer)

Originating in the early 1980s on the one hand as computer enthusiasts such as Steve Jobs and Steve Wozniak moved out of the *home computer* culture and founded the Apple Corporation and on the other as companies such as IBM moved from the institutionalised mainframe market towards producing smaller individualised computers.

Physicalism

Physicalism, in the present context, can be taken to be a theory of technology that prioritises its physical aspects, and the conjunction of these aspects with the physical aspects of humans. Physicalist theories therefore emphasise the technological artefacts themselves, along with the body, the senses, and the physical environment in which they are located. Accordingly, it is philosophically realist, rather than nominalist. Such a view, we argue in **1.6.4**, is held by McLuhan, and by many of those who exploit his work in the context of cyberculture. The interaction between humans and machines is therefore a physical moment as well as whatever symbolic dimensions it may have.

Post-structuralism

'**Structuralism**' is the name given to a dominant strand of French literary and cultural investigation from the 1950s through to the 1970s. In media studies it is associated with semiotics as a method for reading texts as sign systems. In general it is a method that sees all phenomena as determined and made meaningful through the operation of underlying structures and systems which have their own grammar. Post-structuralists have tended towards the rejection of such 'totalising' theoretical approaches, through, for example, deconstruction, feminism and postmodernism. In particular in this book the term is used to denote the idea that the human subject is not a fixed identity but is in a permanent process of becoming through language and text. The post-structuralist method challenges the idea that there is a permanent fixed or stable subject.

Postmodernism
The term 'postmodernism' is used in a tremendously wide range of discourses to account for an equally wide range of phenomena. It can mean a particular change in the aesthetics of certain cultural forms from the late 1970s and early 1980s (postmodern architecture for example), or postmodern culture as symptomatic of fundamental economic or cultural change. This change might be the end of the Enlightenment project for example, or the product of a restructuring of global capitalism in the latter half of the twentieth century. Many accounts of postmodernist culture are predicated on a notion of the significance (or dominance) of a commodified media culture. In all of these concepts, moreover, there is a sense of a blurring of boundaries between previously distinct or opposite phenomena: between high culture and popular culture, the local and the global, the public and the private.

Prosumerism
The term 'prosumer' is originally from the video industries referring to technologies aimed between the consumer domestic market and the professional production market. By extension used here to refer to technologies of media production that are economically within the range of the domestic consumer but technically capable of producing work for large-scale distribution.

Public sphere
The model of disinterested open public conversation based in rational critical debate identified by Jurgen Habermas as evolving in eighteenth-century Europe (1989). More recently interpreted as the communicative space which is open and accessible to the maximum numbers of a society and which therefore provides the foundation for democratic governance and culture.

Realism
Realism is used here with two distinct but overlapping meanings. The first, derived from literary theory, film and media studies, refers to the idea that representations either conform to realism as a generic form (believability, 'realistic' scenes and characters), or that they are coherent references to a reality beyond the representation itself, thus transcending or denying their status as representations by appearing as a 'window on the world'. Secondly, realism is also the philosophical view opposed to constructionism. Whereas, for example, a constructionist viewpoint would take the phenomena under consideration to be products of the discourses used in their consideration, to be theory-dependent, the contrary realist view would be that things exist whether or not they are objects within a discourse or theory. The realist is therefore committed to the view that things are not reducible to ways of speaking or representing them.

Referentiality
The manner in which representations refer to things in the real world. How a representation depicts or denotes an object or event existing in the physical world.

Remediation
A central idea for thinking about 'new' media since the concept of remediation suggests that all new media, in their novel period, always 'remediate'; that is, incorporate or adapt previously existing media. Thus early cinema was based on existing theatrical conventions, computer games remediate cinema, the World Wide Web remediates the magazine, etc. Originally from Marshall McLuhan (1964: 23–24), but more recently usefully applied by Bolter and Grusin (2000).

Server
A computer that provides the information, files, web pages, and other services to the client that logs on to it.

Simulacrum, simulation
There are two main uses of these terms in this book. The first derives from the history of technology. In the history of technology, automata are divided into two classes: automata and simulacra. Simulacra are self-moving things that look like something they imitate (Vaucanson's duck, for example, or anthropomorphic robots like Star Wars' C-3PO – see 5.3.2), and self-moving things that do not resemble anything in particular (factories, cellular automata, fountains, clocks, and so on). This use of simulacrum gives it a realist slant: it names one kind of automaton, or self-moving thing, but the simulacrum is itself as real as the thing it imitates.

The second and more common use of the term here derives from the work of French postmodern theorist Jean Baudrillard (1983) who argued that the sign and what it refers to had collapsed into one another in such a way that it had become impossible to distinguish between the real and the sign. According to Baudrillard, simulacra are signs that can no longer be exchanged with 'real' elements, but only with other signs within the system. For Baudrillard reality under the conditions of postmodernism has become *hyperreality*, disappearing into a network of simulation. This has been conceptualised as a shift from the practice of 'imitation' (or 'mimesis', the attempt at an accurate imitation or representation of some real thing that lies outside of the image or picture) to that of 'simulation' (where a 'reality' is experienced that does not correspond to any actually existing thing). A simulation can be experienced as if it were real, even when no corresponding thing exists outside of the simulation itself.

Spam
The email equivalent of junk mail. Usually offering commercial services and opportunities.

Spectacle, the spectacular
As well as its commonly understood reference to visually striking (though perhaps superficial) cultural forms and texts (blockbuster films, firework displays), the 'spectacular' has a specific intellectual pedigree in cultural theory. The French theorist Guy Debord developed the Marxist concept of the commodity to explain the persistence of post-war capitalism. If commodities are products alienated from their producers through the operations of markets and money, the spectacle is the commodification of (consumer) society as a whole – a profound alienation: 'capital accumulated until it becomes an image'. Advertising, cinema, publicity and the media are just aspects of the general form of the spectacle.

Structuralism
Structuralism is a mode of thinking and a method of analysis practised in twentieth-century social sciences and humanities. Methodologically, it analyses large-scale systems by examining the relations and functions of the smallest constituent elements of such systems, which range from human languages and cultural practices to folktales and literary texts.

Technoculture
A characterisation of contemporary cultures in which technology (especially but not only information and communication technology) has so deeply saturated into cultural practices that the two previously distinct spheres (of technology and culture) are seen to be inseparable.

Technological determinism
Technological determinism remains, as MacKenzie and Wajcman ([1985] 1999) argue, the 'dominant account' of technology in everyday or 'common sense' culture. In its bluntest form, it argues that technology drives history – that is, that social arrangements are determined by technological ones. However, there are other accounts of technological determinism, such as that offered by Ellul (1964). He argues that technology does not directly drive history, in a billiard-ball manner, but rather that given a certain degree of complex interrelatedness, technology becomes determinant at a certain stage in history. This is also the view of Thomas Hughes (see Smith and Marx, 1996), who argues that it is not individual technologies or technology in general that are determinant, but rather technological systems in which there is a high degree of interrelatedness. See **5.2** for a variety of accounts of determinism.

Technological imaginary
The concept of a technological imaginary draws attention to the way that (frequently gendered) dissatisfactions with social reality and desires for a better society are projected onto technologies as capable of delivering a potential realm of completeness. It is used here, therefore, as a characteristic of many of those arguments for new media that see them as a solution to social and cultural ills.

Technology
Commonly used to describe socially or economically useful artefacts and associated processes – therefore as 'tools' or machines which extend the capabilities of the human body. Usually perceived as derived from applied scientific development. However, also used here in a wider sense to imply technology not only as object but also as a process that includes the socially constructed knowledges and discourses that enable the technology to function.

Technoscience
Technoscience refers to the conjunction of technological success with general social effectiveness: what works in technology becomes the model of how we ought to think about what works socially, economically, educationally, and so on. Because its efficiency becomes its own criterion of success, technoscience tends to become the dominant ideological position, as argued by Jurgen Habermas (1970). This view of technoscience is further amplified and explored by Jean-François Lyotard (1984), where it is given the status of one of the chief determinants of the 'postmodern condition' in matters of science, politics, philosophy, and so on.

Teleology
Arguments, theories or histories that explain the nature of something not by their original cause but by ideas about the purpose or 'end' that something appears to have. In this context an example would be that virtual reality is the 'end' to which cinema was striving as a stage in a long historical drive to achieve perfect illusions of reality.

Text, textual
In media studies a 'text' means more than a written text. It is used to refer to any artefact or product (a TV programme, a video game), even an activity or performance (a dance), which has structure, specific qualities, meaning and which can be analysed and 'read'. 'Textuality' – the properties of texts.

Ubiquitous computing
Term used to describe the diffusion of computing technologies throughout our environment through increasing miniaturisation and the development of 'smart' (i.e. predictive) computing applications. Therefore the idea that computers will soon be an embedded function of our physical environments.

Usenet
See *Newsgroups*.

Utopian

Usually used in discussions about new media that see developments in technology as primarily beneficial. The opposite of *dystopian*.

Virtual

The concept of the virtual is in widespread, but varying use. Firstly, it is the name of a branch of technologies, most specifically of virtual reality. Here, the sense of virtual is almost synonymous with 'simulation', if we understand this as meaning something that is 'not really real'. Accordingly, virtual reality becomes a simulated reality, more or less a fantasy world we can step in and out of by virtue of the technologies that allow humans to access it. However, the idea of a 'not really real reality' seems confusing (see Heim [1993] for an analysis of this sense of the virtual), not least because we enter VR by way of real machines, and experience it through our bodies. In what sense then can we say that virtual reality is not real? Such accounts of the virtual leave this physical aspect out of the picture. In contrast to this sense of the virtual, a growing field of theory, much of it informed by Gilles Deleuze's (1994) philosophical analyses of the concept, argues that the virtual is that part of the real that is not actual. 'Actuality' here means both real and current; that is, if we identify the real only with what is current, then future and past states cannot be real. Yet whatever future events will actually befall us, the future itself remains a permanently real and inactual presence. We can therefore say that the future has a kind of reality that is not actual but virtual. This sense of the virtual is in turn given physical form by the processes of feedback that are key to cybernetics.

Visuality

The culturally and historically specific way in which vision is practised. The manner in which vision (and the various modes of attention that we commonly identify: seeing, looking, gazing, spectating and observing) is historically variable. It reminds us that 'vision is an active, interpretative process strongly governed by communities and institutions, rather than an innocent openness to natural stimuli' (Wood 1996: 68).

Windows

A Graphical User Interface combined with an operating system. It provides both the software to make the various parts of the hardware to interact with each other and allows the input of commands and the output of results in forms accessible to non-specialists. The windows metaphor, of multilayered frames offering data access, has become the standardised interface for PCs. Originally developed by Apple Mac and later imitated by Microsoft.

INDEX

Page references for glossary entries are in **bold**;
those for marginal notes are followed by (m)